Harnessing Tangible and Intangible Assets in the context of European Integration and Globalization. Challenges ahead

Luminita Chivu / Valeriu Ioan-Franc /
George Georgescu / Jean-Vasile Andrei (eds.)

Harnessing Tangible and Intangible Assets in the context of European Integration and Globalization. Challenges ahead

Proceedings of ESPERA 2019

Volume 1

PETER LANG

Bibliographic Information published by the Deutsche Nationalbibliothek
The Deutsche Nationalbibliothek lists this publication in the Deutsche Nationalbibliografie; detailed bibliographic data is available online at http://dnb.d-nb.de.

Library of Congress Cataloging-in-Publication Data
A CIP catalog record for this book has been applied for at the Library of Congress.

ISBN 978-3-631-83825-9 (Print)
E-ISBN 978-3-653-06574-9 (E-PDF)
E-ISBN 978-3-631-70801-9 (EPUB)
E-ISBN 978-3-631-70802-6 (MOBI)
DOI 10.3726/ 978-3-653-06574-9

Peter Lang – Berlin · Bern · Bruxelles · New York · Oxford · Warszawa · Wien

This publication has been peer reviewed.

www.peterlang.com

Contents

List of contributors

Roxana Adam
National Institute of Statistics, email: roxana_adam2004@yahoo.com

Matei-Alexandru Apăvăloaei
The Bucharest University of Economic Studies, email: matei.apavaloaei@rei.ase.ro

Daniela Antonescu
Institute of National Economy, Romanian Academy, email: daniela.antonescu25@gmail.com

Jean-Jacques Askenasy
University of Tel Aviv, Israel; Romanian Academy, email: ajean@post.tau.ac.il

Irina Băncescu
"Costin C. Kiriţescu" National Institute for Economic Research; The School of Advanced Studies of the Romanian Academy (SCOSAAR), Bucharest, Romania, email: irina_adrianna@yahoo.com

Valentin Bilyanski
University of National and World Economy, Bulgaria, email: v.bilyanski@unwe.bg

Cristian Bîrdac
Department of Urban Mobility, City Hall Sector 4, email: cristian.birdac@mobilitateurbana4.ro

Cristina Boboc
Department of Statistics and Econometrics, Bucharest University of Economic Studies and Institute of National Economy, Romanian Academy, email: cristina.boboc@csie.ase.ro

Constanţa-Nicoleta Bodea
Informatics and Economic Cybernetics Department, Bucharest University of Economic Studies; Centre for Industry and Services Economics, Romanian Academy, email: bodea@ase.ro

Alina Bratiloveanu
"Valahia" University of Târgovişte, Doctoral School of Economic and Humanistic Sciences, email: alina.bratiloveanu@yahoo.com

Gheorghe Horia Chivu
Department of Urban Mobility, City Hall Sector 4, email: gheorghe.chivu@mobilitateurbana4.ro

Luminiţa Chivu
"Costin C. Kiriţescu" National Institute for Economic Research, Romanian Academy, Bucharest, Romania, email: chivu@ince.ro

Daniel Ciuiu
Technical University of Civil Engineering Bucharest, Center for Macroeconomic Modelling, Romanian Academy, email: dciuiu@yahoo.com

Viorel Cornescu
"Nicolae Titulescu" University, email:cornescuviorel@yahoo.com

Laurenţiu David
Centennial College of Applied Arts and Technology, Toronto, Canada, email: laurentiu.r.david@gmail.com

Andrei-Marius Diamescu
"Costin C. Kiriţescu" National Institute of Economic Research, Romanian Academy, email: dandreimarius@yahoo.com

Emil Dinga
Center for Financial and Monetary Studies, Romanian Academy, email: emildinga2004@email.com

Nenad Djokic
University of Novi Sad, Faculty of Economics in Subotica, Serbia, email: djokicn@ef.uns.ac.rs

Vasile Dogaru
West University of Timişoara, email: vasile.dogaru@e-uvt.ro

Gabriela Drăgan
Department of International Economic Relations, The Bucharest University of Economic Studies, email: gabriela.dragan@rei.ase.ro

Marija Drobnjaković
Geographical Institute "Jovan Cvijić", Serbian Academy of Sciences and Arts, Serbia, email: m.drobnjakovic@gi.sanu.ac.rs

Vasilii Erokhin
Harbin Engineering University, China, email: basilic@list.ru

Frantz Daniel Fistung
Centre for Industry and Services Economics, Romanian Academy, email: dfistung@yahoo.com

Simona Frone
Institute of National Economy, Romanian Academy, email: frone.simona@gmail.com

Ioan I. Gâf-Deac
"Costin C. Kiritescu" National Institute for Economic Research, Romanian Academy, email: gafdeac@ince.ro

Simona Ghiță
Department of Statistics and Econometrics, Bucharest University of Economic Studies and Institute of National Economy, Romanian Academy, email: simona.ghita@csie.ase.ro

Anda Ghizdavu
Department of Statistics and Econometrics, Bucharest University of Economic Studies, email: anda.ghizdavu12@gmail.com

Jaime Gil Aluja
President, Royal Academy of Economic and Financial Sciences, Barcelona, Spain, email: secretaria@racef.es

Bogdana Glovațchi
PhD student, Marketing specialization, email: bogdana.glovatchi68@e-uvt.ro

Zizi Goschin
The Bucharest University of Economic Studies, Institute of National Economy, Bucharest, email: zizi.goschin@csie.ase.ro

Adriana Grigorescu
National University of Political Studies and Public Administration, Bucharest, Romania; Correspondent Member Academy of Romanian Scientists; email: adriana.grigorescu@snspa.ro

Aleksandar Grubor
University of Novi Sad, Faculty of Economics in Subotica, Serbia, email: agrubor@ef.uns.ac.rs

Erna Hennicot-Schoepges
Institute for Cultural Diplomacy, email: hennicotschoepges@gmail.com

Mihaela Iacob
The Bucharest University of Economic Studies, email: mihaela.iacob@fabbv.ase.ro

Valeriu Ioan-Franc
Corresponding member of Romanian Academy, "Costin C. Kiriţescu" National Institute for Economic Research, Romanian Academy, Bucharest, Romania, email: cide90@gmail.com

Amalia-Elena Ion
Doctoral School of Management, Valahia University from Targoviste, Romania, email: amalia.ion@live.com

Alexandru Isaic-Maniu
Centre for Industry and Services Economics, Romanian Academy, e-mail: alex.maniu@gmail.com

Laura Istudor
The Bucharest University of Economic Studies, Faculty of Theoretical and Applied Economics, email: laura.istudor@gmail.com

Octavian-Dragomir Jora
The Bucharest University of Economic Studies, email: octavian.jora@rei.ase.ro

Dorin Jula
Institute for Economic Forecasting, NIER, Romanian Academy, Ecological University of Bucharest, Faculty of Financial Management, email: dorinjula@yahoo.fr

Nicolae-Marius Jula
University of Bucharest, Faculty of Business Administration, email: mariusjula@yahoo.com

Alexandra-Ioana Lazăr
Ph.D. Student, School of Advanced Studies of the Romanian Academy, "Costin C. Kiriţescu" National Institute for Economic Research, email: alexandra.lazar@ince.ro

Beatrice Leuştean
Politehnica University of Bucharest, email: leusteanbeatrice@yahoo.com

Elena Otilia Manta
"Victor Slăvescu" Center of Financial and Monetary Research, Romanian Academy, email: otilia.manta@icfm.ro

Andra Mărculescu
Romanian Academy, email: andra@acad.ro

Stanciu Mariana
Research Institute for Quality of Life, Bucharest, Romania, email: mariana3stanciu@gmail.com

Gheorghe Meghişan
University of Pitesti, Faculty of Economic Science and Law, Romania, email: gheorghemeghisan@yahoo.fr

Georgeta-Mădălina Meghişan-Toma
The Bucharest University of Economic Studies, Faculty of Business Administration in foreign languages; Romanian Academy, National Institute of Economic Research "Costin C. Kiritescu", Bucharest, email: madalina_meghisan@yahoo.com,

Nikola Milicevic
University of Novi Sad, Faculty of Economics in Subotica, Serbia, email: milicevic.nikola@ef.uns.ac.rs

Mircea Mitiucă
The Bucharest University of Economic Studies, Faculty of Theoretical and Applied Economics, email: mircea.mituca@gmail.com

Firicel Mone
Department of Engineering, Mechanics, Computer, School of Advanced Studies of the Romanian Academy (SCOSAAR), Research Institute for Artificial Intelligence "Mihai Drăgănescu", Romanian Academy, Bucharest, email: mone@acad.ro

Mihai Sabin Muscalu
Centre for Industry and Services Economics, Romanian Academy, email: msmuscalu@yahoo.com

Biljana Petrevska
Faculty of Tourism and Business Logistics, University "Goce Delcev" Stip, North Macedonia, email: biljana.petrevska@ugd.edu.mk

Napoleon Pop
"Costin C. Kiriţescu" National Institute for Economic Research, Romanian Academy, Bucharest, email: iemnapoleon@gmail.com

Dan Popescu
"Lucian Blaga" University of Sibiu, email: dan.popescu@ulbsibiu.ro

Sorin Mihai Radu
University of Petrosani, Romania, email: upet@yahoo.ro

Otilia Teodora Rachieru
RNP Romsilva, Bucharest, Romania, email: otilia.ciutacu@yahoo.com

Rossitsa Rangelova
Economic Research Institute – BAS, Bulgaria, email: r.rangelova@iki.bas.bg

Corneliu Russu
Centre for Industry and Services Economics, Romanian Academy, email: corneliu_russu2007@yahoo.com

Ioan Petru Scutelnicu
University of Petroşani, IGR, Bucharest, Romania, email: pinklloyd73@yahoo.com

Adrian Simion
The Bucharest University of Economic Studies, Faculty of Theoretical and Applied Economics, email: adriansimiont@yahoo.com

Stelian Stancu
Informatics and Economic Cybernetics Department, Bucharest University of Economic Studies; Centre for Industry and Services Economics, Romanian Academy, email: stelian_stancu@yahoo.com

Gheorghe-Alexandru Stativa
The Bucharest University of Economic Studies, Faculty of Theoretical and Applied Economics, email: alexstativa95@gmail.com

Maria Livia Ștefănescu
Research Institute for Quality of Life, Romanian Academy, livia.stefanescu@gmail.com

Ştefan Ştefănescu
Research Institute for Quality of Life, Romanian Academy, stefanst@fmi.unibuc.ro

Ivona Stoica
Institute of National Economy, Romanian Academy, Bucharest, email: stradivonas@gmail.com

Viorel Streza
University of Petroşani, Romania, email: upet@yahoo.ro

Marta-Christina Suciu
The Bucharest University of Economic Studies, Faculty of Theoretical and Applied Economics, Economics and Economic Policies Department, Romania, email: christina.suciu@economie.ase.ro

Aleksandra Terzić
Geographical Institute "Jovan Cvijić", Serbian Academy of Sciences and Arts, Serbia, email: a.terzic@gi.sanu.ac.rs

Iuliana Ţoropoc
Bucharest University of Economic Studies, Actuarial Techniques Master's Program, Romania, email: iulia_toropoc@yahoo.co.uk

Alina Roşca Ţurcanu
University of Petroşani, Romania, EM Chisinau, Republic of Moldova, email: upet@yahoo.ro

Anna Maria Vasile
Ph.D. Student, School of Advanced Studies of the Romanian Academy, "Costin C. Kiriţescu" National Institute for Economic Research, email: anna.vasile@mail.com

Valentina Vasile
Institute of National Economy, Romanian Academy, email: valentinavasile2009@gmail.com

Maria Vişan
Department of Engineering, Mechanics, Computer, School of Advanced Studies of the Romanian Academy (SCOSAAR), Research Institute for Artificial Intelligence "Mihai Drăgănescu", Romanian Academy, Bucharest, email: mone@acad.ro, maria.visan@ingr.ro

Gheorghe Zaman
Corresponding member of Romanian Academy, Institute of National Economy, Romanian Academy, Bucharest, gheorghezaman@ien.ro

Plenary papers

Luminiţa Chivu

Harnessing tangible and intangible assets in the context of European integration and globalization: challenges ahead

Abstract The presentation, from the beginning of the 2019 edition of the ESPERA international scientific conference, with the theme "Harnessing Tangible and Intangible Assets in the context of European Integration and Globalization. Challenges ahead" makes in the first part a review of the main activities carried out between the two editions of ESPERA, by the "Costin C. Kiritescu" National Institute for Economic Research and the institutes and centers in its network. In the second part, arguments are brought for the choice of the theme for ESPERA 2019 and landmarks are presented regarding Romania's positioning in terms of tangible and intangible assets among the member states of the European Union through an approach from the perspective of national wealth. The presentation ends with thanks to all those involved in the organization of the conference, national and international partners at the event and best wishes for the success of the conference.

Keywords: Romanian Academy, economic research, ESPERA 2019

Most Distinguished Audience,

We are now in the Aula Magna of the Romanian Academy, and the first words of my presentation today are to express our gratitude that, in keeping with tradition, you have joined us here for this important event in the life of the "Costin C. Kiriţescu" National Institute for Economic Research (INCE) – The International Scientific Conference ESPERA 2019.

Thanks to the resonant effect at home and abroad of the publication by Elsevier (first two editions) and Peter Lang Academic Publishing Group (starting with 2015 until present), and of the entry to ISI – Clarivate, of the works put out on the occasion of its previous editions, ESPERA, now featuring its 6th edition, has prompted a quality leap forward of the results of the Romanian academic economic research, rendering it more visible and making it broadly known.

Allow me to congratulate you for this success!

ESPERA is also an opportunity to test the relevance and topicality of the subjects approached, and we invite our Romanian and foreign partners to join our debate and develop new joint projects.

The Scientific Committee, the scientific coordinators and reviewers working in the 14 workshops have made substantive effort to have this annual test happen, and I cannot thank them enough for this.

This event is drawing its roots from the academic propensity of our research institutes and centers, and we must express our gratitude for the scientific fervor and freedom inspired to us by the Romanian Academy, the highest national forum of sciences, under the wing of which we have conducted our activities for more than 30 years now.

Most Esteemed Audience,

ESPERA is also an opportunity for us to cast a retrospective glance at the fruits yielded by the economic research work in the institutes and centers of our Academy in the time between the past two editions.

At the previous edition of ESPERA, at the plenary session held on 24 May 2018, Professor Aurel Iancu, Member of the Romanian Academy (MRA), in his capacity as main coordinator, introduced to us the structure of the two volumes of "Romania's Economy after the Great Union of 1918" (Vol. I – Macroeconomy, and Vol. II – Sectoral Economy), which forms part of the "Romanian Civilization," a collection of works among which some of the books were, at that date, still being written by a large number of contributors: academy members, science researchers, professors, and authors that have gained an undeniable prestige in their fields of research.

At the end of 2018, as a result of the remarkable perseverance and joint effort of both authors and coordinators, the two volumes saw print (Slide I).

Volume I, "Macroeconomy," coordinated by Professor Aurel Iancu, Member of Romanian Academy, and Professor Nicolae Păun, is comprised of 26 chapters spanning over 500 pages that treat the macroeconomic evolution of this country in the hundred years since the Great Union of 1918. The century's economy has been studied in its three specific time segments: 1918–1947 (the economy in the inter-war period, the economic policy during WW II, the post-war recovery period, and the Soviet occupation period); 1948–1989 (the socialist experiment); 1990–2018 (the transition to a functional market economy by way of institutional and structural transformations, and the accession to the European Union).

Research Programmes of National Coverage – GREATER ROMANIA CENTENNIAL 1918-2018

❑Romanian Civilisation, coord. by Victor Spinei, Member of the Romanian Academy

- **Romania's Demography**, Vasile Ghețău (coord.);
- **Romania's Social History**, Cătălin Zamfir, Member of the Romanian Academy (coord.)
- **Romania's Economy after the Great Union of 1918, Vol. I, Macroeconomy**, coordinated by Professor Aurel Iancu, Member of the Romanian Academy, scientific consultants, Victor Axenciuc, Honorary Member of the Romanian Academy, George Georgescu, Florin-Marius Pavelescu, authors of book chapters from National Institute for Economic Research network, Lucian-Liviu Albu, Member of the Romanian Academy, Corneliu Russu, Napoleon Pop and Dan Constantin Olteanu;
- **Romania's Economy after the Great Union of 1918, Vol. II, Sectoral Economy**, has been put together by Professor Aurel Iancu, Member of Romanian Academy (head coord.), George Georgescu, National Institute for Economic Research (INCE), Victor Axenciuc, Honorary Member of the Romanian Academy, Florin Marius Pavelescu, Institute of National Economy, Constantin Ciutacu, National Institute for Economic Research, coordinators. The volume consists of 34 chapters, spanning over more than 1,000 pages, authored by over **64 contributors, most of them being researchers in the Romanian Academy's economic, social, and juridical sciences institutes, joined by members of the Academy, academics, and other experts of an established repute in their fields of expertise.** The volume hosts retrospective studies based on the diachronic approach of specific areas (demographics, natural resources, urbanization, progress of production factors, scientific research and development), inter-stage sectoral studies (agriculture, manufacturing, energy, etc.), as well as other aspects of the administrative and land management policies, industrial architecture, environmental protection, and the role of the Romanian Academy in strengthening the Romanian people's awareness of their national unity;

Slide 1: INCE research programs of national coverage

Volume II, Sectoral Economy, has been put together by Professor Aurel Iancu, MRA (head coordinator), George Georgescu, INCE, Victor Axenciuc, HMRA, Florin Marius Pavelescu, IEN, and the late Professor Constantin Ciutacu, INCE, as coordinators. The volume consists of 34 chapters, spanning over more than 1,000 pages, authored by over 64 contributors, most of them being researchers in the Romanian Academy's institutes of economic, social, and juridical sciences (Slide 2).

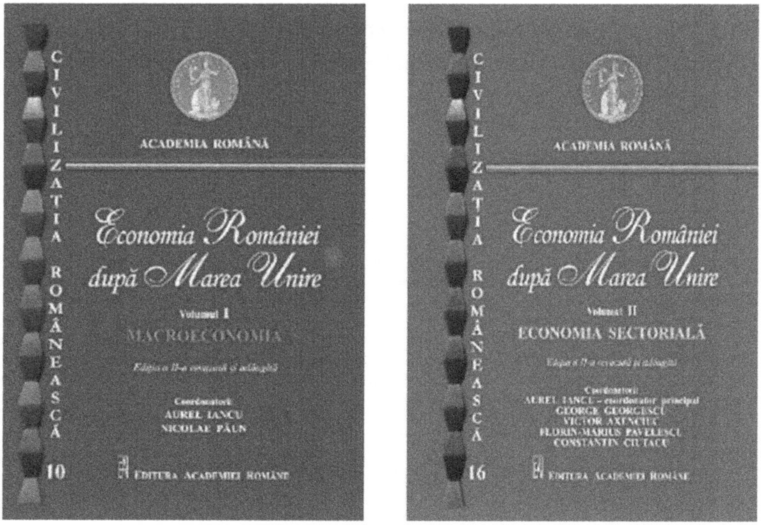

Slide 2: Covers of the volumes "Romania`s economy after the Great Union"

This volume contains retrospective studies based on the diachronic approach of specific areas (demographics, natural resources, urbanization, progress of production factors, scientific research and development), inter-stage sectoral studies (agriculture, manufacturing, energy, etc.), as well as other aspects of the administrative and land management policies, industrial architecture, environmental protection, and the role of the Romanian Academy in strengthening the people's awareness of their national unity.

As part of the same collection, in addition to the books devoted to the country's economy, other two volumes, authored with the major contribution of INCE researchers, have been published. Both of them being of tremendous value through the sensitive issues of the past 100 years they address: Romania's Demography, coordinated by Professor Vasile Ghețău, of the Centre for Demographic Research, and Romania's Social History, coordinated by Professor Cătălin Zamfir, MRA, of the Research Institute for the Quality of Life (Slide 3).

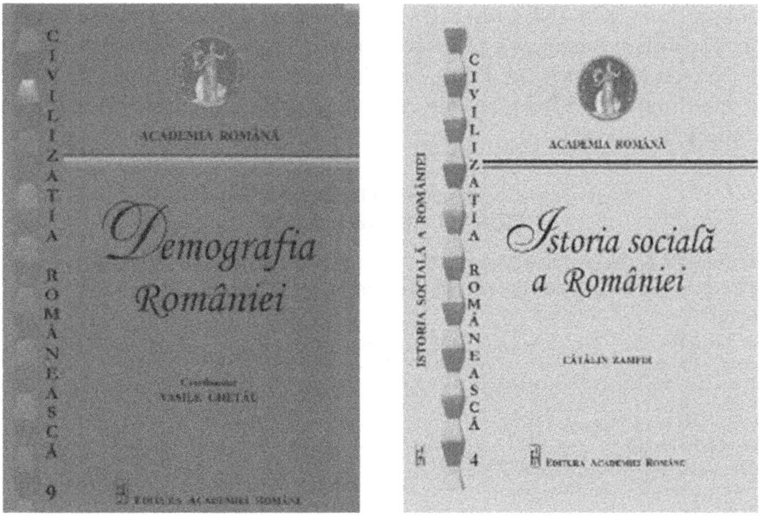

Slide 3: Covers of the books "Romania`s Demography" and "Romania's Social History"

In sign of homage to the same Centennial of the Great Union, the proceedings of the 2018 edition of the ESPERA International Conference were published. Their main topic was Romania's Economy. A Century of Evolution (1918–2018), and they were posted on the site of Peter Lang Academic Publisher Group, on 30 September 2019 (Slide 4). And we want to present our thanks to the professional team of Peter Lang, with special thanks to Ute Winkelkoetter, Senior Commissioning Editor, that made it possible.

Slide 4: Covers of "Romania's Economy. A Century of Evolution (1918–2018)" and Peter Lang website

Starting from 2018, INCE researchers have brought a substantive contribution to the Romanian Academy's priority project: "Romania's Economic and Monetary Convergence with the European Union. A Necessary Step." The study is being coordinated by Professor Ioan Aurel Pop, MRA and president of the Romanian Academy (Slide 5).

Research Programmes of National Coverage — CONVERGENCE to EURO

❑ **Romania's Economic and Monetary Convergence to the European Union – a Step to Be Taken, as a priority project of the Romanian Academy,** coordinated by its President, Ioan Aurel Pop

Under the coordination of the National Institute for Economic Research 'Costin C. Kiriţescu' / Institute of World Economy, the studies were carried out by an impressive number of researchers from:

- National Institute for Economic Research 'Costin C. Kiriţescu' (INCE);
- Institute of World Economy (IEM);
- Institute of Economic Forecast (IPE);
- Institute of National Economy (IEN);
- Research Institute for the Quality of Life (ICCV);
- Institute of Agrarian Economy (IEA);
- Centre of Research in Industrial and Services Economics (CEIS) "Victor Slăvescu";
- Centre of Demographic Research (CCD).

The studies that resulted from debates have been published, with the support of the *Patrimonium* Foundation, in two volumes (abstracts and *in extenso*), under the patronage of the Centre for Economic Information and Documentation.

Slide 5: Research program – Convergence to euro

INCE, through its Institute for World Economy (Institutul de Economie Mondială – IEM), acted as a coordinator of the convergence studies. The first stage of these studies had as a purpose the evaluation of the Romanian economy's preparedness to convert to the euro currency. A large number of INCE researchers have contributed to it, through INCE's Institute for World Economy, Economic Forecast Institute, National Economy Institute, Research Institute for the Quality of Life (ICCV), Institute of Agrarian Economy (IEA), Centre for Research in the Economics of Industry and Services (CEIS), the Centre of Financial and Monetary Research "Victor Slăvescu" (CCFM), and the Centre of Demographic Research (CCD).

The results of these studies, as they emerged from the debates held all along the year 2018, were published, with the aid of the Patrimoniu (National Heritage) Foundation, in two printed volumes (abstracts, and in extenso), under the aegis of the Centre for Economic Information and Documentation (Centrul de Informare şi Documentare Economică), and under the editorial supervision of Professor Valeriu Ioan Franc, Corresponding Member of the Romanian Academy (CMRA) (Slide 6)

Slide 6: Cover of the book "Romania's Economic and Monetary Convergence with the European Union. A Necessary Step"

INCE researchers have had significant contributions to the drafting of national strategies.

Among these were their participation in:

- the proceedings of the National Committee for the conversion to the euro currency, and in the writing of the Explanatory Memorandum for the National Plan regarding the adoption of the euro as legal tender, and of the related Plan of Action;
- the National Strategy for the Sustainable Development of Romania 2030;
- Romania's Energy Strategy for the period 2018–2030, with further projections to 2050;
- Romania's Multiannual Strategy for the Protection and Sustainable Development of Its Mountain Regions (Slide 7).

CONTRIBUTIONS TO AND CONSULTANCE ON NATIONAL STRATEGIES

- **Explanatory Memorandum to the National Plan for the Transition to Euro Currency,** and the **National Plan for the Transition to Euro Currency**;
- **Strategy for Romania's Sustainable Development until 2030;**
- **Romania's Energy Strategy for the period 2018-2030,** with projections until **2050**;
- **Mountain Act No. 197 / 2018,** and secondary legislation for its implementation, as well as the proposed **Multi-annual Strategy for the Protection and Sustainable Development of Romania's Mountain Areas, The Governance Programme 2017-2020 for the Mountain Areas,** made available to the Ministry of Public Works, Development and Administration (MDRAP), Ministry of Agriculture and Rural Development (MADR), and to the UN/FAO Mountain Partnership;
- **Council for Economic Planning**;
- **National Statistic Council**;
- **Labour Committee, Parliament of Romania**;
- **Working Group for the Business Environment, Competitiveness, and Research-Development-Innovation,** set up by the Ministry of Foreign Affairs to draw up the **Plan of Action for the implementation of the National Reform Programme 2018 (PNR) and of the Specific Country Recommendations 2018 (RST)**;
- **Committee for Environment, Climatic Change, and Energy** in the **European Committee of Regions,** Brussels;

Slide 7: Contributions to and consultancy on national strategies

As a complement to these, comes our researchers' contribution as coordinators or members of the Council for Economic Planning, the National Statistic Council, The Labor Committee of the Romanian Parliament, the Working Group for the Business Environment, Competitiveness, and Research-Development-Innovation set up by the Ministry of Foreign Affairs to carry out the Plan of Action of the 2018 National Reform Program (NRP), and the 2018 Specific Country Recommendations (SCR), and in the Committee for Environment, Climatic Change, and Energy of the European Committee of the Regions, Brussels.

Prompted by the willingness to meet the real needs of the Romanian society, our scientific researchers have offered consultancy services, either through an institutional framework or as independent experts, in matters involving the development of the administrative capacity of the Ministry of Labor and Social Justice, Ministry of Environment, Ministry of Regional Development and Public Administration, Ministry for the Business Environment, Trade and Entrepreneurship, Ministry of National Education, Ministry of Health (Slide 8).

PROJECTS FOR THE DEVELOPMENT OF ADMINISTRATIVE CAPACITY

INSTITUTIONAL PARTNERS:

❑Beneficiary: **Ministry of Labour and Social Justice, SIPOCA 4,"Analysis and assessment of vulnerable groups, in order to determine the need for social services in Romania"**;

❑Beneficiary: **Ministry of Environment**, Project **SIPOCA 22**, "Development of the Ministry of Environment's administrative capacity to carry out biodiversity policies";

INDEPENDENT EXPERTS:

❑Beneficiary: **Ministry for the Business Environment, Trade and Entrepreneurship, SIPOCA 5**, "Development of the Ministry for the Business Environment, Trade and Entrepreneurship's capacity to put in place and further the system of evidence-based public policies";

❑Beneficiary: **Ministry of Regional Development and Public Administration, SIPOCA 9**, Reinforcing the framework for increasing the quality of public services and supporting local development **(SPC)**;

❑Beneficiary: **Ministry of National Education, SIPOCA 3**, Project for the Development of the Ministry of National Education's capacity to monitor and forecast the progress of higher education in relation to the labour market;

❑Beneficiary: **Government's General Secretariat, SIPOCA 28**, Enhancing the relevant ministries'capacity for strategic planning.

Slide 8: Project for the development of administrative capacity

It was also 2019 that saw the launch of the series of scientific debates under the umbrella of the Academy's Section for Economic, Juridical, and Sociological Sciences, in cooperation with INCE's network of research institutes and centers.

Scientific debates bring to the fore topics of utmost interest for the Romanian economy: the impact of foreign direct investments (FDI) on Romania's foreign trade (IEN), the quality of life in Romania from a European perspective, and the related social policies (ICCV), the future Common Agricultural Policy (CAP) and its effects on Romanian Agriculture (IEA), the assessment of Romanian economy's sustainability (CCFM), Romania's Industry: Present and Future (CEIS), the consequences of the 4th industrial revolution on the economic model and economic modelling (Institute of Economic Forecasting– IPE), and the mountain regions of Romania (CEMONT), the status of the economic convergence of the EU member states (IEM), the demographic crisis of the EU countries, and Romania's place in the context (CCD), the energy strategy for 2019–2030, with projections until 2050 (CPEREE), new prospects for the food production (CSCBAS), the financial and monetary economy (CCFM) (Slide 9 and Slide 10).

The calendar of the scientific debates held under the aegis of the Romanian Academy's Department for Economic, Juridical, and Sociological Sciences, in cooperation with the institutes / centres in INCE's network (I)

7 March 2019, ***ISD's IMPACT ON ROMANIA'S FOREIGN TRADE DURING THE TRANSITION PERIOD***, InstitutE OF National Economy (IEN);

8 April 2019, ***QUALITY OF LIFE IN ROMANIA FROM A EUROPEAN PERSPECTIVE. THE CRISIS AND ITS LESSONS***, Research Institute for the Quality of Life (ICCV);

18 April 2019, **HOW CAN WE TAILOR CAP INTERVENTIONS TO THE NEEDS OF ROMANIAN AGRICULTURE?**, Institutul de Economie Agrară (IEA);

17 May 2019, ***ROMANIAN ECONOMY'S LEVEL OF SUSTAINABILITY. A STOCK-TAKING ENTERPRISE***, Centre for Financial and Monetary Research "Victor Slăvescu" (CCFM);

20 June 2019, ***ROMANIA'S MANUFACTURING INDUSTRY NOW AND IN A GLOBALISED FUTURE***, Centre for Research in the Economics of Industry and Services (CEIS);

24 June 2019, ***SOCIAL POLICIES IN ROMANIA***, Research Institute for the Quality of Life (ICCV);

27 June 2019, ***IMPACT OF THE FOURTH INDUSTRIAL REVOLUTION ON THE ECONOMIC ENVIRONMENT AND MODELLING***, Economic Forecast Institute (IPE);

4 July 2019, ***ROMANIAN MOUNTAIN AREAS – A NATIONAL PRIORITY***, Centre for Mountain Economics (CE-MONT).

Slide 9: Calendar of debates under the aegis of Romanian Academy`s Department for Economic, Juridical and Sociological Sciences – 2019 (I)

The calendar of the scientific debates held under the aegis of the Romanian Academy's Department for Economic, Juridical, and Sociological Sciences, in cooperation with the institutes / centres in INCE's network (II)

- ***THE PROGRESS MADE IN THE ECONOMIC CONVERGENCE OF THE EU MEMBER STATES***, Institute of World Economy (IEM);
- ***ROMANIA'S PLACE IN THE DEMOGRAPHIC CRISIS OF THE EUROPEAN UNION***, Centre for Demographic Research (CCD);
- ***ROMANIA'S ENERGY STRATEGY 2019-2030, WITH PROJECTIONS UNTIL 2050 – APPLIED RESEARCH REGARDING THE IMPLEMENTATION PLAN IN EUROPEAN CONTEXT***, Centre for the Promotion of Renewable Energies and Energy Efficiency (CPEREE);
- ***WORLD FOOD DAY. NEW FOOD PROSPECTS FOR MANKIND AND FOR ROMANIA***, Centre for Studies and Research in Farm and Forest Biodiversity "Acad. David Davidescu" (CSCBAS);
- ***INTERNAŢIONAL CONFERENCE ON FINANCIAL AND MONETARY ECONOMY***, Centre for Financial and Monetary Research (CCFM).

Slide 10: Calendar of debates under the aegis of Romanian Academy`s Department for Economic, Juridical and Sociological Sciences – 2019 (II)

In 2019, the INCE researchers brought substantive contributions to the series of debates held under the care of the Academy's Section for Economic, Juridical and Sociological Studies, on the subject: The Romanian Economic Model in the European Union – Romania 2040, at the initiative of the Association for Economic and Social Studies and Forecasting (ASPES) in partnership with AGER, AFER, ASE, INCE – AR, ASAS, ROMÂNIA DURABILĂ, SAMRO, ACPR, ANOSR (Slide 11).

Under the aegis of the Romanian Academy's Departement for Economic, Juridical, and Sociological Sciences

Substantive contributions by INCE researchers to the:

Round of debates on

"Romanian Economic Model in the European Union – Romania 2040"

Organised by the Association for Economic and Social Studies and Forecasting (ASPES) in partenership with

AGER, AFER, ASE, **INCE - AR**, ASAS, ROMÂNIA DURABILĂ, SAMRO, ACPR,ANOSR

The final document reflecting the conclusions of the debates will be presented in the Aula Magna of the Romanian Academy of Sciences, in 2020.

Slide 11: Romanian economic model in the European Union – Romania 2040

The final document resulting from these debates will be presented in the Romanian Academy's Aula Magna, next year.

Another remarkable achievement of INCE and CIDE in 2019 was the publication of an outstanding book: Principles of Economics for a Post-Meltdown World, by John Komlos, Emeritus Professor of the Ludwig-Maximilian University in Munich. The Romanian version is a special edition for Romania, which includes segments from books published by the same author in 2016 at Springer's, and in 2018 at Routledge's. As the author of a new concept about economy, Professor Komlos reveals the weaknesses of the standard economic theory, and supports, with arguments, the need to change the paradigm, and to understand the real-life post-crisis economy with the aid of an alternative approach of traditional models (Slide 12).

Slide 12: Cover of "Principles of Economics for a Post-Meltdown World"

The book, which I strongly recommend, was written for academics and students of economic schools, but also for Academy researchers and business people, for decision makers in any society, for all researchers that choose to follow the difficult road towards rethinking the fundamentals of economic science.

The publication in Romania of this book is a remarkable event that has been coordinated, with his well-known punctiliousness and scientific rigor, by Professor George Georgescu, and thanks to the contribution and keenness of Professor Valeriu Ioan Franc, who, in cooperation with Mr. Mircea Fâţă, the translator, and Ms. Paula Neacşu, the editor, have produced an exemplary version of Professor John Komlos' book in the Romanian language.

In response to the imperatives of the Romanian economy, since 2019, INCE, in its capacity as coordinator of a consortium formed of 7 Romanian and foreign partners, has been conducting 3 projects financed by the World Bank, for the benefit of the Ministry of Waters and Forests.

The term of the 3 projects is three years, during which, in an integrated system bringing together champion farmers and facilitators, a number of 6,000 farmers, 980 representatives of the Agency for Finance to Rural Investment (AFIR) and the Agency for Disbursements and Intervention in Agriculture (APIA), as well as representatives of local administrative bodies, will be trained in the regulations of the Code of Good Agricultural Practice (COGAP), to prevent and reduce the risk of soil pollution with nitrogen fertilizers.

Among other benefits, the three projects will create a network for the transfer and exchange of agricultural knowledge in the entire country, will enable the collection of data on the farmers' feedback, thereby providing decision makers an instrument to identify the problems encountered by farmers, and prepare Romanian agriculture for the new CAP.

Until 30 September 2019, approximately 3,000 farmers and representatives of the public entities involved had been trained.

INCE's international visibility, as measured in August 2019, brought our Institute to the echelon of the top 3 % in the world classification of the RePEc international data base, which is the most prestigious central index of papers in economic sciences. INCE was assigned position No. 240, in a total of 7,900 institutes/universities/departments dealing with economics in the whole world (Slide 13)

ROMANIAN ACADEMY
"COSTIN C. KIRIŢESCU" NATIONAL INSTITUTE FOR ECONOMIC RESEARCH

INCE

INCE in the world hierarchy of the institutions of economic research

Top 7898 institutions enclosed in RePEc – August 2019:

1. Department of Economics, Harvard University (SUA)
2. National Bureau of Economic Research (SUA)
3. World Bank Group
4. Economics Department MIT (SUA)
5. London School of Economics (UK)

....

240. National Institute for Economic Research – Romanian Academy (Top 3%)

Slide 13: INCE in the world RePEc hierarchy of the institutions of economic research

While in January 2015 INCE held the 380th position in the same classification, by mid-2019 INCE had leaped up 140 notches in only four years, which is a remarkable achievement of the entire research network, in the face of the sharp international competition in the field. First in this hierarchy are the Department of Economics, Harvard University; National Bureau of Economic Research; World Bank Group; Economics Department, MIT; London School of Economics.

In the classification of economic research entities in Europe, INCE placed 96, in a total of 2,890 institutes/universities/departments pursuing economic research (Slide 14).

Slide 14: INCE in the Europe RePEc hierarchy of the institutions of economic research

In the national RePEc classification, INCE (with 141 registered authors) comes second after The Bucharest-based Academy of Economic Studies (291 registered authors). A number of 21 INCE researchers are among the top 5 % of the 1,097 Romanian authors with citations in RePEc (Slide 15).

Slide 15: INCE in the national RePEc hierarchy of the institutions of economic research

Dear Audience,

In the time between its editions, the ESPERA Conference has increasingly acted as a platform of scientific dialogue and exchange of opinions, and we plan to further establish connections between researchers, academics, experts with hands-on experience in the real economy, and members of the civil society, all of whom can contribute to identify the sensitive issues that claim intensive research work for the benefit of the Romanian economy and the society at large.

Since the May 2018 ESPERA edition to date, the exchange of ideas and the debates between scientists have led to the conclusion that this year's edition should focus on the topic of How to make the best of [Romania's] tangible and intangible assets in the context of its European membership, with an eye to globalization, all while preparing for future challenges (Slide 16).

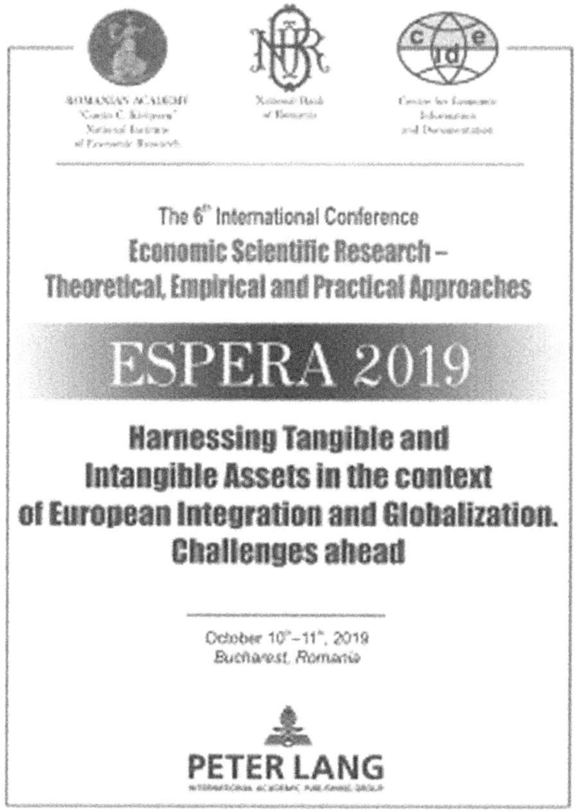

Slide 16: ESPERA 2019 program cover

While, at the beginnings of economic science, the economic perspective of intangible assets was that they "had no price," and therefore they were not duly quantified as production factors capable to generate richness, now they seem to have become "priceless" in the balance of a country's national wealth, and are quoted in economic writings as the fourth production factor.

Although there are numerous analyses of this concept in the dedicated literature, the incomplete statistic information, and the delay with which such information becomes available are an impairment precluding us to issue opinions regarding the current value of Romania's tangible and intangible assets, and the contribution of each such asset to the creation of national wealth in Romania.

In the Romanian dedicated literature, a prominent place is held by the book written by Professor Victor Axenciuc, OMRA: "The National Wealth of Romania, 1860–1939: A Comparative Historical Research," that saw print at the Expert Publishing House, in 2000.

The most recent information about Romania is featured in a World Bank Report published in 2018, based on data valid for the year 2014, which placed Romania 16th among the 26 EU member states, with a national wealth estimated at 2,131 bn. US dollars. The 16th place came as an average between place 15 for tangible assets, and place 16 for intangible assets (Slide 17).

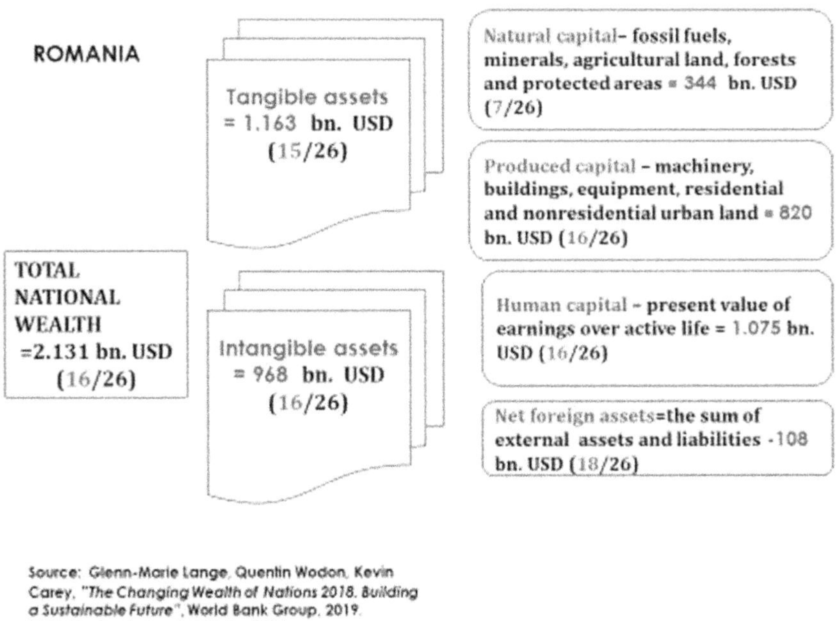

Slide 17: The national wealth of Romania and its main components in 2014

In the same Report, Romania came 7th for its natural capital, but held positions nos. 16 and 18 in respect of produced capital, human capital, and net foreign assets.

The average national wealth per capita of 107 thou' US dollars placed Romania 25th among the 26 EU member states (Slide 18).

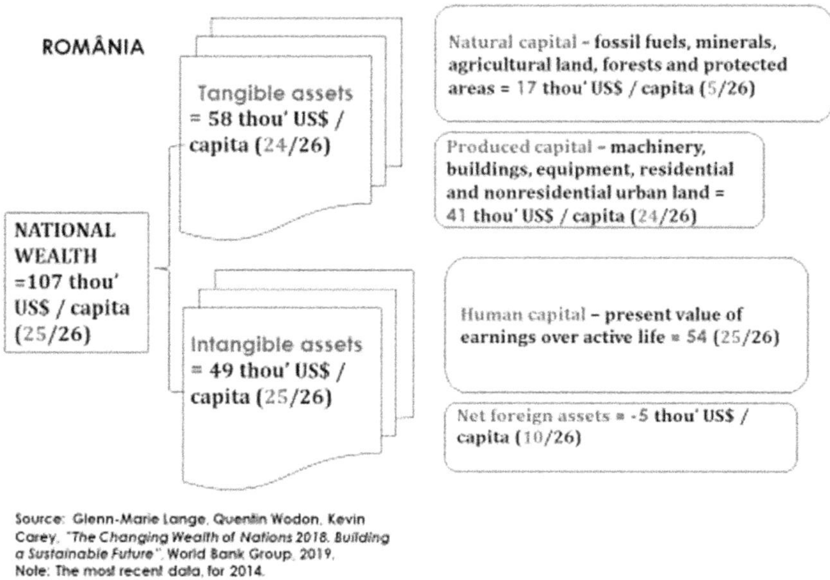

Slide 18: The national wealth of Romania and its main components, per capita, in 2014

Even though the price of farm land is still among the lowest in the EU, Romania positioned 5th in respect of its average natural capital per capita, 10th in respect of the net foreign assets, but 24th for the produced capital, and 25th for the average human capital per capita.

The produced capital has undergone deep changes in point of structure and incorporated technology, bearing the strong mark of the industrial revolutions, deindustrialization, digitalization, and robotisation of the past three decades.

Romania has lost, in the past 20 years, numerous industrial structures, manufacturing shops, facilities, equipment, that were pulled down and turned into scrap iron, after they had previously served for scale production processes. Other industrial facilities were created, in line with the new technologies.

An example that aptly illustrates the magnitude and speed of these changes is the comparison between the production of crude steel and the export of scrap iron (Slide 19).

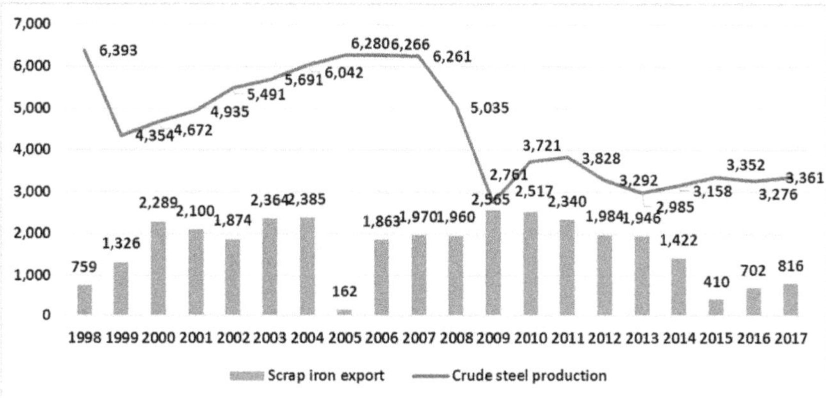

Slide 19: The crude steel production and scrap iron export in Romania, 1998–2017 (mil. tones)

Over the double decade 1998–2017, Romania manufactured 91.2 mil. tones of plain steel, and exported 33.8 mil. tones of scrap iron. In the year when the world economic and financial crisis made its debut, the two indicators were very close.

With regard to its human capital, Romania has reached the 30th year of demographic decline.

Professor Vasile Gheţău's estimation is that, in the time frame 1990–2018, the natural loss of population exceeded 1 mil. inhabitants. The net migration balance during the same period is estimated by official statistics to stand at 2.6 mil. persons.

The labor market, therefore, suffers from imbalances caused by labor deficits, both in quantity and quality. INCE and KPMG researchers, commissioned by the Concordia Employers Confederation, conducted a study, published in March 2019, on the quantitative side of the shortage of labor. Their estimations indicated that the labor deficit stood at over 550 thou' persons, and was likely to grow to approximately 950 thou' persons in the next 4 years. All while there is a significant segment of unused labor.

Based on Eurostat data regarding the average annual spending per student, and the number of NEETs and their last graduated school, we estimated that, in Romania, for the training of the approximately 1 million NEETs, the government invested some 11.1 bn. euro, and their families spent around 13.6 bn. euro, which, summed up, gives a total of 24.7 bn. euro wasted on unused human capital (Slide 20).

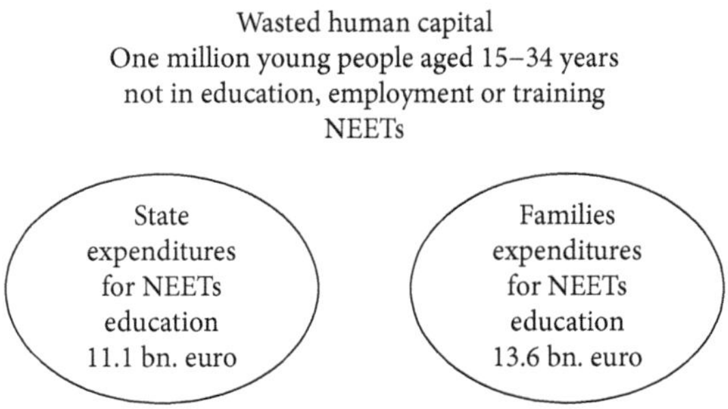

Slide 20: Expenditures with wasted human capital in Romania – NEETs, 2016

The above estimations did not take into account the contribution to the growth of the added value that the NEETs could bring if they were in employment.

One possible explanation of the low share held by intangible assets in Romania's national wealth may derive from the fact that one of the World Bank's methods of evaluation of human capital is based on the current value of the revenues estimated to be earned during an individual's active life (45 years, on the average) (Slide 21).

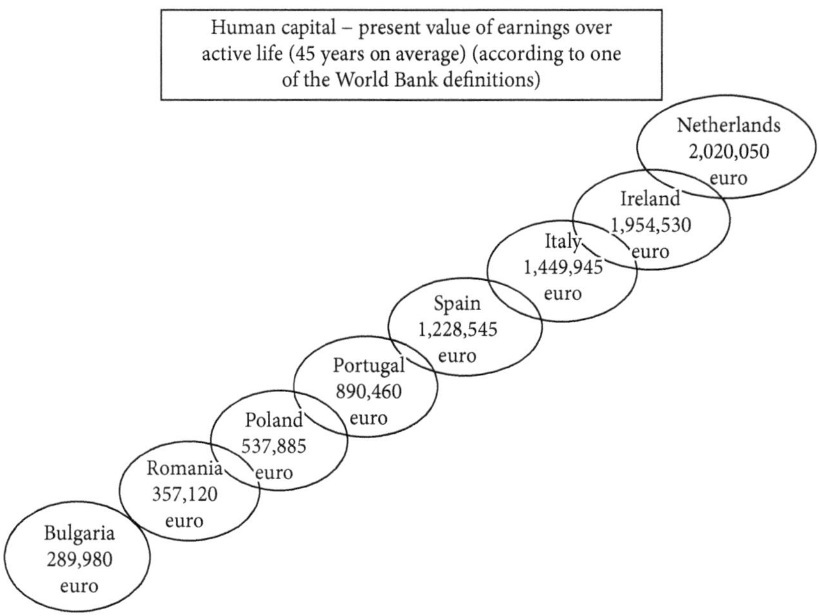

Slide 21: Estimation of the present value of earnings over active life in some EU member states, in 2016

We have chosen only a few criteria to illustrate the important role the tangible and intangible assets of a country can play in the creation of national wealth, if they are wisely harnessed to do so.

Distinguished Audience,

We are glad to see that this sixth edition of the ESPERA Conference is attended by many more scientific researchers and academics, and this is an encouragement for us to broaden our cooperation with the universities.

Present at this edition, for the second consecutive year, is the Association of Economic Faculties of Romania (Asociaţia Facultăţilor Economice din România – AFER), and we wish to express our gratitude to Rector Nicolae Istudor, who is honoring us with his presence today, and who has been supportive in our endeavor to forge closer ties and open new windows of cooperation with the researchers in universities.

This is an opportunity for me to thank our guests from Romania and abroad for the interest shown in our Conference. I must confess that we are impressed by the scholarly and complex level of the papers contributed to the Conference.

We also wish to welcome the presence here of the Chairman of the Romanian Academy's Department of Economic, Juridical, and Sociological Sciences, Mr. Mugur Constantin Isărescu, MRA, to whom we take this opportunity to thank for the poise and tactfulness with which he has always guided and coordinated the scientific activity of the Romanian Academy's Institutes and Centers involved in economic and social studies.

This is the second edition in which the European Academy for Business Management and Economics (Academia Europea de Direccion y Economia de Empresa – AEDEM), Spain, has joined us as our partner. We wish to express our special thanks to the Honorable Gil Jaime Aluja, Member and President of the Spanish Royal Academy of Economic and Financial Sciences (Real Academia de Ciencias Economicas e Financieras – RACEF), and the Spanish Institute. Professor Gil Jaime Aluja will kindly share with us today his personal contribution to the new theory of self-induced incidence.

We greatly thank the distinguished Ms. Erna Hennicot Schoepges for her participation, a champion of cultural diplomacy, a warm friend of our Institute, of the Romanian Academy, and of Romania.

We also owe our gratitude to the eminent neurologist Honorable Jean Jacques Askenasy, of the University of Tel Aviv, Israel, for his presence here today, and I am looking forward with tremendous expectation to hear his presentation on the economic triangle of the brain.

Side by side with our traditional partners, the National Bank of Romania, the Centre for Economic Information and Documentation, and our brotherly Moldovan Academy of Economic Studies (and our thanks go to Professor Cornel Guţu, its Pro-rector, who is honoring us in person, bringing us a beautiful message from Chişinău), we also have the pleasure to welcome to this year's edition of ESPERA the Romanian National Committee –the World Energy Council and The West University, Timişoara (represented by Professor Dogaru)

Our international partners are still with us at this 6th edition: Research Network on Resources Economics and Bioeconomy Association, Gestion y Planificacion Research Group (GESPLAN, Spain), Institute of Agricultural Economics (Belgrade, Serbia), Institute of Economic Sciences (Belgrade, Serbia), Faculty of Social and Cultural Service and Tourism, Stavropol State Agrarian University (Russia), Faculty of Economics and Business Administration, "St. Kliment Ohridski" University (Sofia, Bulgaria) and Faculty of Hotel Management and Tourism, University of Kragujevac (Serbia). Special thanks for their support and our fruitful collaboration.

All the papers to be presented here will be as many contributions to the growth of the value of Romania's intangible assets.

Our special thanks go to the two deputy directors general of INCE, Professor Valeriu Ioan Franc, and Professor George Georgescu.

I wish to thank to a small but enthusiastic team of people who made this event possible: Carmen Gheorghe, Laura Anghel, Alina Rădoi, Nicolae and Luminiţa Login, Ovidiu Sârbu, and Mircea Fâţă.

Allow me to express our gratitude to all the today's participants in the ESPERA session, and to all those who contributed scientific papers to the Conference, because, without you all, our effort would be pointless and our enterprise would not reach its purpose.

The number of papers proposed for presentation at the Conference has grown every year. For this edition, we have received over 250 papers, authored by more than 500 contributors, 50 of them being colleagues from abroad.

We are glad that ESPERA, and the publication by Peter Lang Academic Publishing Group, give prominence to our ideas, help us make them known and acknowledged in the international arena for debates, and enhance the visibility of the Romanian scientific research under the aegis of the Romanian Academy. All the contributions become pages in the Thesaurus Book of INCE, of which Professor Valeriu Ioan Franc speaks so proudly, and of which he has been taking care of, unabatedly, since the foundation ofINCE.

And, in this context, I would like to congratulate Professor Valeriu Ioan Franc for his admission this year as Corresponding Member of the Romanian Academy, and to wish him, as well as Professor Cătălin Zamfir, a full Member of the Romanian Academy, and Professor Radu Rey, an Honorary Member of the Romanian Academy, the success and accomplishment they deserve – because they are among the most prominent intangible assets of our Institute.

Last, but not least, heartfelt thanks to the other persons invited to our Conference, who could not participate, but who have sent messages of encouragement and support, and demonstrated, once more, that a scientific event of this amplitude was necessary and worth having.

My opening speech ends with our best wishes of success to our Conference.

Valeriu Ioan-Franc, Napoleon Pop

Reconfiguration of globalization: relevant issues to Romania

Abstract The answer can be a handy one – globalization can't be stopped, but it can't continue with the faults that brought its negation, either. The relationship between the winners and the losers of globalization to be found globally both inside nation-states as well as smaller communities, can't be changed but through a dynamic mechanism and not one that is interrupted or going in the opposite direction.

Unfortunately, we are only left with questions regarding the good or less good effects of globalization, which, in order to be answered to, necessitate lots of cycles of in-depth studies. The management of these effects remains the crucial problem to all actors of the world that, it is our opinion, should take a global responsibility – to use an appropriate term. The transition to a new order, in which globalization with new rules is considered, means to reconstruct it all over again from bottom to top, the historical societal revolutions did.

The remaining question is whether the restart of globalization can be made from top to bottom as the results were felt from bottom to top. The lessons of popular revolutions in world history showed us that there isn't enough to get revenge on any status quo and overthrow a ruling elite, without knowing where to head to afterwards. And this is something that can't be planned from top to bottom, but starting with the choice, behaviors and decisions of million people who believe that the future should secure a dignified existence before everything else.

Keywords: general equilibrium and disequilibrium; business economics; government, general economic systems; sociology of economics; globalization

1. Preliminaries

In spite of biased analysis regarding it as beneficial for all, globalization has been, obviously, following the path of economic, commercial and financial interests, maintained by certain factors. It is noticeable, from the very beginning, the fact that the origin of these interests – to seize the opportunities of globalization – can't be strictly located with one group of states or another depending on the degree of development and economic strength, but by applying criteria that to us seem the most significant.

The first criterion is the nature of the economic model's efficacy. The profitability of the open economy determined the investors, the capital holders to continue service externalization and industry delocalization, aiming to optimize production, supply and distribution costs etc. A manufactured product, an industrial and/or financial service have become the result of global elaboration, with technological inputs, know-how, workforce preparation targeting specific goals: workforce costs to be as low as possible with the highest possible return on capital; detailed transfer prices methods, avoidance of high tax rates.

The second criterion, the political one, is exclusively linked, in our view, to the way the political class capitalized, up to Brexit and the presidential elections in the U.S.A., the advantages of globalization strictly in its own interests, that is, in order to perpetuate power through strengthening the liberal and neoliberal establishment. Maintaining the super bureaucratic institutional system needed more and more financial resources. Making available such resources could only be done by pushing globalization towards ever growing advantages for the investors in the good graces of the political class. The simultaneous manifestation of the two operating ways intersecting the technological progress bearing the traits of the fourth industrial revolution (see the debates of the Economic Forum, Davos, 2015), both linked to massive liberalization brought about by globalization have determined social effects less noticed at the right time.

Judging from the current situation, the initial image of globalization should be "reversed" if one wants to see an already concerning reality. The benefits "for all" announced in the beginning meant actually the filtering of the globalization losers, with the political class reacting too late. Political opponents took advantage of this kind of treatment, appealing to nationalist and populist feelings of the society, seeking in its turn a relief of its own situation. The negative effects of globalization have eased the appeal to economic nationalism, a possible illiberal politics meant to soothe society on a short term.

One may say that, due to the problems it created and the delayed solutions, in a world more rapidly moving than in the moment of the writing and enforcing the regulations of the currently disappearing international order, globalization has reached "a moment of cataclysm" when everything is possible. The awareness of this moment is shown in the many discourses of high officials and politicians, be they of EU member states or EU management boards. Is it, however, a delayed awareness, especially regarding the social and societal problematic set in movement by globalization, the very consideration of this "benefiting" from the placidity of the politicians attached to their offices and the bureaucracy themselves had created in the faith it would last forever. To invoke the real-politic now is late and dangerous, on the way to break certain values of the democracy that some of us are still innocently venerating.

The answer can be a handy one – globalization can't be stopped, but it can't continue with the faults that brought its negation, either. The relationship between the winners and the losers of globalization to be found globally both inside nation-states as well as smaller communities, can't be changed but through a dynamic mechanism and not one that is interrupted or going in the opposite direction.

Unfortunately, we are only left with questions regarding the good or less good effects of globalization, which, in order to be answered to, necessitate lots of cycles of in-depth studies. The management of these effects remains the crucial problem to all actors of the world that, it is our opinion, should take a global responsibility – to use an appropriate term. The transition to a new order, in which globalization with new rules is considered, means to reconstruct it all over again from bottom to top, the historical societal revolutions did.

The remaining question is whether the restart of globalization can be made from top to bottom as the results were felt from bottom to top. The lessons of popular revolutions in world history showed us that there isn't enough to get revenge on any status quo and overthrow a ruling elite, without knowing where to head to afterwards. And this is something that can't be planned from top to bottom, but starting with the choice, behaviors and decisions of million people who believe that the future should secure a dignified existence before everything else.

Nick Pearce[1] (Pearce, 2016) (professor at the University of Bath) states that the last decades were deprived of the will and power to interpret the deep changes that we are all, worriedly, going through. Research for more solid theories regarding social justice and liberal political philosophy were abandoned in favor of sustaining, maybe daily, a fight to better human condition which is exactly what the faults of globalization finally attacked. Liberalism lost its own roots, even the rebellion against everything that is enforced by order, institutions and rigid norms. Through the new liberalism, the politics built a similarly rigid societal structure, but in institutions and a bureaucracy contrary to the mainstream harming the individual it was supposed to defend: to offer jobs, security and identity to, says Pearce.

2. Romania and the reset of the New Economic Order

Romania, as an EU member state is compelled to only choose between: (a) to be an active contributor to the process of European integration from the inside; (b) to be a follower or a neutral observant; (c) spectator waiting for the benefits, believing that the losses will be suffered only by those who get involved. It is annoying that the current lack of political vision carelessly simplifies the conceptualizations and the approach of these options, oriented only towards the same old benefit-cost ratio, a ratio that is mainly, obviously, expressed as money. Where is, then, our political track record through which Romania decided to join the EU?

The road to European integration as it had been taking shape since the Treaties of Rome (signed in 1957 and entered into force on the 1st of January, 1958) up to the Treaty of Lisbon (signed in 2007 and entered into force on the 1st of December, 2009) proved to be difficult and it stays this way, not necessarily due to external circumstances but mostly due to certain European Council leaders' subjectivity. We are prisoners of economics, overwhelmed, captured by and obsessed with the

1 See article "Liberalism can survive but it has to renew its social traditions", Financial Times, Dec. 2016.

economic dimension of the European integration which, eventually, proved not to be the highlight of the European political project, but, according to society's expectations, a basis for a multinational construction, on many layers, having a healthy economy as foundation and time resistant social peace as an effect.

Unfortunately, it was forgotten, that the simple message of mobilizing the European citizens for a better living standard (offered to everybody as a promise in exchange of European integration in the 6th decade, but impossible to make it happen without their economic and political input in the spirit of an authentic home of democratic values) had in its subsidiary the subliminal message, less sensitive and less explicit to begin with, for well-known reasons (the division of Europe was one of consciousness and historical stubbornness, not of artificial borders freshly discovered and transposed into political texts and textbooks), but subtle and firm enough – achieving political union.

Were we allowed to remember the "perversity" of the European integration project, we should start with a first evaluation concerning the placing next to each other of the terms economic and monetary inside the rhetoric concept of union. From the point of view of authors' concerns and their belonging to significant research institutes[2] (Pop; Ioan-Franc, 2018), we think that resorting to an actual plan of achieving the Economic and Monetary Union of the European Economic Community (EEC) member states, initially during a ten years period (1971–1980, the Werner Plan) was not accidental, even though it suffered due to oil shocks, to stick to only one example.

Regarding the actual, extremely complicated situation, and referring to the European political project – the Political Union – it is important to reflect on a moment of revival of the European integration, connected to the establishment of the Economic and Monetary Union, in an almost similar period from the point of view of political will and the European social and economic situation. It is about the effects of the Delors Report (1989), a great endeavor aiming to reach the European monetary integration under the lead of an important politician who took on the gathering together within the European Communities. He managed this not merely by statements made in Brussels and forgotten when in the national capital cities, but by initiating complete phasing, starting on July 1st 1999, of the achievement of the Economic and Monetary Union (EMU) and by engaging political commitment by irrevocable consensus for the entire process as well as for each one of its phases. Introducing the euro as a single currency on the 1st of January 1999 is the result of this approach, maybe unparalleled in the entire history of Europe. It marks the beginning of an unique historical experiment, this time not left to historical hazard in the hands of certain important figures of the moment, but pushed through by a vivid intelligence and a strong political will.

2 The Institute of World Economy and, respectively, the "Costin C. Kiriţescu" National Institute for Economic Research of the Romanian Academy.

2.1. Where is European governance heading?

Here's the greatest challenge for Romania and not only, if we consider that its option for European integration was the only one possible and the best in the context of the end of the Cold War and the dismantle of the ideological blocks (or "the only movie to see in town," according to an American saying). Moreover, one should take into account analyses of Nobel winners and other notables in geopolitical and geostrategic fields, even though their predictions turned 180 degrees around.

Joseph Stiglitz (2002) warns about the possibility for the single currency to disappear, while Mark Blyth (Blyth, 2011), in the paper "Austerity – The History of a Dangerous Idea" and George Soros (Soros, 2014), in the book *The Tragedy of the European Union*, both state that lacking major reforms in areas such as finance-banking and economic governance, the European construction, built with sustained efforts over so many decades, runs the risk to crash.

In our view and for its own national interest, Romania needs to stick to the irreversible European political integration, from inside the process of integration. We believe it is time for Romania to persuade its European partners that the EU needs a speedy reset of its strategic vision, not on alternatives to weaken it, but on strengthening the EU position in the global concert, where our country is still expected as an economically viable partner, but, more importantly, as a strong and politically determined one.

2.2. Romania in the European community concern

We are compelled to design the steps of our evolution inside the EU through the objective of an authentic and lasting European social peace that will give new perspectives to future generations, keeping in mind that the project of the founding fathers of the European Union aimed exactly that. Unfortunately, generations of politicians who came after the founding fathers, forgetting the saying "contracts are to be respected" are about to give up, in order to perpetuate their power, project ends exactly when there are enough accumulations. Adding to this the danger of a drifting community institutional scaffolding, with a more and more bureaucratic technocrat but biased, educated and selected by – some outdated – textbooks technical body, and looking towards realities that are passing us by in great speed due to the very fact that current reaction procedures are outdated etc., than we have a challenge to face, one that needs to be taken seriously. For Romania, which stays firmly on the road of adopting euro (thus the political project of the Union) and that holds the presidency of the EU Council for the second part of 2019, it is important to arm itself starting now with its share of contribution and initiative regarding the relevance of the reset of EU's strategic vision in the current global and European context while including its own national interests.

At the same time, while we accept the free and unrestricted studies pursued by some foreign as well as Romanian analysts, dedicated to other options, to be and to stay in the EU or to leave the EU (many considerations being inspired primarily by what happens in the European governance), we don't believe that Romania, as a "young" member state of the EU, with a rather short and debatable career regarding the promotion of self interests should follow scenarios that won't be of any use to it after choosing the European integration. In this context, we shouldn't forget for a minute the great consensual effort Snagov 1,[3] that allowed the reaching of an irreversible acceptance of a nation's geographical compass and progress vector changing.

We thus benefit from additional elements, the study of which could provide answers to many of the questions about the future structuring of the likely-to-be European political union that should become the compass of the EU governance.

3. The third modernization of Romania

Romania's future, seen from the lenses of an uncertain present, should be a challenge impossible to face only by admitting the defeats up to now and contemplating those as being fate. The internal and international situations are complicated enough to grasp a new historical opportunity. This is worth the effort, as for the opportunity, there is a professional elite to seize it, but it can show itself due to increasing ignorance.

Romania's fundamental issue, when it comes to catching the train of an authentic modernization, for the third time throughout its modern history, is the lack of a permanent institutional framework (which is actually avoided) to draw the perspective seriously and continuously. There is utterly necessary that a permanent strategic planning organism is created. Romania doesn't have an authentic medium and long term development strategy[4] although efforts are being made for sectoral strategies. Any attempt to integrate those is bound to fail due to the impossibility of making them coherent and to estimate a creditworthy value of employee resources.

---

3 The works of the Snagov Commission from March-June 1995, coordinated by the late acad. Tudor Postolache, made history with the first national political consensus after December 1989, by adopting "The Snagov Statement" (Ioan-Franc, 2000), respectively assuming the "National Strategy for Romania's EU Accession Preparation", documents on which the head of the state based, at Cannes, in June 1995, Romania's EU Accession Request.

4 Praiseworthy will be, in this context, the recent long-term strategic planning exercise (up to 2038) completed by the Romanian Academy which, on the 150th celebration of its foundation and the high occasion of the Centenary (1918–2018) presents the nation with its own vision regarding Romania's future (Pop; Ioan-Franc, 2018). The full text of the four volumes is available at www.acad.ro.

The existence of a national scalar strategy, always linked to real life's challenges would give substance and continuity to governmental programs, but also to electoral debates through the relatively binding anchors established beyond electoral cycles. We could thus, avoid, the ossification of populism and irrational ideas regarding what the Romanian economic system can deliver. Everything that's opposite to stability, predictability, ordinary transparency, non partisan consultations is characteristic to the beginnings of new governance.

Reformation of political class can only be achieved through higher professional competence which means education, training, acquiring good practices; it also means engaging in dialogue with strong arguments. And, while talking about competences and results, it seems that reality places us in the trap of a paradigm we should exit (the Legend of Master Manole[5]) in order to accomplished the third modernization of Romania. The political class doesn't seem to have acquired a historical cultural, and this fact shows in the content of textbooks getting poorer and the missing of the logical axis from past to future.

More than a quarter of a century later, after the acquisition of authentic European democracy values, we need to turn our attention again to the systemic functioning of our society, in order to make it perform better and to give up the simple palliatives presented as performance. There is a lot to (re)adjust in the structure of the rule of law for social stability to help, through everybody's contribution, the modernization of Romania. When the rule of law was established, between 1990–1993, the political elite of the time focused strongly on their role in the modernization of Romania. Unfortunately, the new generations of politicians respond less and less to the normal requests of systemic evolution, their professional inconsistencies attacking the foundation Romania's macroeconomic and financial stability, especially on the background of the increasing "contamination with evil" intrinsic to globalization. But, the challenges of globalization are mainly risks while opportunities can only be capitalized in an increasingly competitive environment.

It was expected that, more than a quarter of a century since the events in December 1989, Romania had approached the third phase of its modernization, in all respects, through its simple reacceptance in the democrat European family. By becoming an Euro-Atlantic partner, Romania was granted, politically speaking, the status of a rule of law with a market economy resilient to competition, in the sense of the Western democratic values. Technically, the efforts to strengthen the

---

5 Famous piece of Romanian folk literature, a fundamental popular ballad of the national culture, according to which the master builder Manole, in order to defeat the curse due to which everything he would build in daytime crashed at night, put his own wife in the wall of the building that finally was to become an unique construction through its haughtiness and beauty. Curtea de Arges Monastery, a real construction in Romania, became in time a universal asset, inscribed in the UNESCO Patrimony.

two dimensions of the Romanian society not only have a long way to go, but they were also subject to numerous contestations and internal as well as international criticism.

The "extract" of this conclusion is that the force delaying modernization points to Romania's entering a new plan of geopolitical interests, stronger than its own will. To this an inclination towards original experiments, as if pushed or imposed both from the inside and the outside is added, while the weak political capacity of negotiation as in granting a chance to the country's future, lead to a high and inefficient consumption of public resources (privatization, restitutions, investments) hard to be regenerated by economy. Also it is worth noticing the increase of the time lag of a so-called catching up process to European standards and the best practices in almost all fields of activity. The GDP per inhabitant, as an indicator of socioeconomic performance, is relevant of Romania's delay in entering the third phase of modernization in comparison to other former socialist states, members of the Union. We can't speak about the third phase of Romania's modernization without bringing up the first two, recalling mainly what the Romanian elites did in the specific national and European context. The first phase of Romania's modernization, between 1848–1916 started with the Revolution of 1848 and the Union of the Principalities (1859), the second one, initiated by the Great Union and the establishment of Greater Romania (1918) up to The People's Republic of Romania (1947). Through the new "republic" a historical break from the European path of Romania occurred, the path being recovered after 1989.

It is to be kept in mind, either as an asset or a downside, the fact that the modernization of Romania, in all its phases marks the European becoming of the country with the following characteristics:

- Romania's modernization was always influenced by the European mainstream trends while the recovery of national interests took place in an ever complicated context;
- The modernization process *per se* was marked by the political decisions inclining towards imperialism of the Great Powers which suggests that the dream of a unitary state since Michael the Brave (1601) was a "political creation" relevant for the continental interests;
- The evolution of Romania has always been monitored by its external "founding fathers" suffering the consequences (the War of Independence, 1877; the Treaty of Trianon, 1916; the Vienna Dictate; the break of Bessarabia from Romania; Romania after the Second World War are only a few examples)
- There have always existed, but unfortunately, only for certain periods of time and randomly, an interest on the part of the external partners – i.e. the Great Powers – for Romania's geostrategic position thus affecting positively or negatively its stability as a state;
- There have always been a European, and, more recently, an international expectance (directly or via the EU state membership) regarding the takeover

of Romania's responsibilities concerning its own evolution and external involvement.

All of these raise the problem of the options made by the Governs of each period, regarding alliances and consequences.

From this point of view, in this historical moment when new reforms are needed, the most relevant lessons are:

- Independence and national sovereignty are subordinated to the European/international partnership, chosen or imposed due to multiple reasons, dependent on the meeting point of national and partners' interests;
- Accepting Romania in a partnership was, as a rule, an initiative of the other party, thus involving expectations and engagements to fulfill;
- Being in a partnership such as the Euro-Atlantic one means rights and obligations, both assumed through responsibilities, controllable formally and reciprocally. It should be noted that our obligations keep a partnership alive, strengthen it, so that it has rights as a dividend and this means allocating resources;
- Preeminence of obligations assumed in any partnership means accepting certain "interferences" of the strongest ones and following them in a participatory manner, possibly capturing the national interests provided they are clearly defined and followed steadily.
- The participatory, proactive manner only can open the way for an authentic advance of national interests and their validation in a partnership.
- The speed of events requires that partners know Romania's interests in advance, but the delays in their decline also forces us to identify and formulated these in the sense of the partners' actions.

There are consistent minuses in the third part (25 years!) of the third phase of Romania's modernization, with a general tendency of lacking authentic strengthening of democratic values:

- The confuse regulation of the property right, the fundament of all individual rights;
- Failure to complete the separation of powers, balance and mutual control;
- The problem of competences, in the sense of the democratic values, greatly alters the functioning of the institutions of the rule oflaw;
- Political culture develops in an opposite direction to the formation of a trustworthy ruling elite;
- The state-market relationship is unstable, confused, being an impediment to modernization and progress, leading to formation of criminal interest groups;
- The principle of normality is destructured by excess in exceptions as well as positive and negative discrimination, which makes every kind of exception endanger all the time the unitary, uniform and equal applicability of juridical norms.

These faults are the strongest argument for the necessity of an authentic radical mental and action reform doubled by a strong political will. The process dedicated to carrying out reforms needs to be institutionalized in a credible manner, opposing to our partners and attracting an elite from outside the government.

Coming back to the idea of formally instituting a permanent strategic planning structure for Romania, in order to avoid being perceived as a country always lacking a comprehensive and coherent strategy, we believe that the respective structure must be animated by a an elite uninvolved in the daily governance, mainly of academic nature and with competences covering the entire range of public policies, to create a medium and long term strategy. A strategy proposed by the actual government must be approved by law, by the Parliament, enforcing all the following government to manage it. Any temptation to discontinuity in ongoing projects considered crucial for Romania and adopted by law as well as any tendency to deprive a strategy of the planned resources to translate ii into reality must be definitively rejected. This is the only guarantee to manage Romania's convergence to the European standards, emphasizing that any kind of representation must be accompanied by authentic competences.

4. Identifying and addressing national interests

In the logic of the integration process, Romania's interest as an EU member state must be connected to the areas that grounded the national political decision to join the Union. The exploratory negotiations that allowed the association and then the consensus of Snagov (1995) after which the accession application was sent were keen on "repatriation" of Romania to the democratic Europe provided the commitment regarding systemic transformation on a path that secured the progress and development of Romania in the direction of the European developed countries' standards, the consolidation of the European security within which Romania would strengthen its own national security. The commitment meant to benefit from the advantages of the integration processes while covering the costs involved.

Considering the multiple dimensions of the integration process at Union and member state level, we believe that selecting certain national priorities facilitates concentration of political efforts and resources in certain areas that can trigger benefic action to other domains too, the established priorities following also the options made in the decisional board of the EU. In the context of EU rotating presidency there should also be launched and promoted priorities conveying national interests on medium and long term. They can be better formulated now, ten years since the accession. Beyond certain failures (Romania not being admitted into Schengen, the continuation sine die of MCV monitoring, difficulty of access to some of the community resources etc.) we have accumulated our own experience in the community decision-making process regarding the European construction imposed by treaties, we've been sounding out alliances with other member states already experienced in pursuing their own national interests.

Currently, there is better knowledge regarding the resources that can be attracted from the EU and the mechanisms to use them in order to support national interests inside the community as well as the impact of bringing together national priorities and community resources at national level. We believe that the fact that national priorities need to take into account the geopolitical dynamics in Europe, Ukraine crisis being an example of imperialistic behavior (Russia's), alteration of political and social stability as well as regional security.

It's in Romania's best interest to maintain that, by enlarging the space of European integration, the Union must support and vitalize this stature of Romania both by its own efforts and the EU resources, such as strengthening this stature it's in the advantage of the Union. The processes of strengthening democracy, the competitive market economy, social progress by the standards of the Union inside Romania will maintain a territory of community force and stability, especially from the center to the margins of the EU, the shock of the differences being more visible by the EU's Eastern border. Not solving certain regional economic offsets with the focus on the Eastern side and, implicitly, exposing itself to the risk of being vulnerable beyond its Eastern border, is a failure of the EU's policies. This failure constitutes one of the reasons of acknowledging the fact the Union works on several speeds and not only because of certain new acceding member states.

The fundamental criteria of identifying Romania's national interests as an EU member state must keep on being its geostrategic positioning, considering that the current European integration process is obviously exceeded by the remnants of the Old Empires ways of relating to one another, even in a modern Europe. At the same time and for this particular reason, there must be identified the potential leader positions, even temporary ones, of Romania's European projects, taking into account, of course, the context in which European history showed that Romania needed alliances of the "follower" kind and that, by and large, the Romanian modern state and its territorial integrity depended on the European Great Powers' decisions.

There is, however, a great problem to identifying Romania's medium term interests: that of accommodating the other member state's interests while considering some delimitations as well. The first one is the quality of an old member state versus a new member state, after the resuming of the enlarging the European integration process after the Cold War, through the Copenhagen criteria. One also needs to understand the power play between the founding countries of the European Communities (to become the EU) and the ones who joined the Union later.

The second delimitation, a fundamental and unavoidable one, is that all countries, current member states of the Union, have a historical course of self interests that are still exceeding the platform of community interests, the latter ones being thus conceived even though the vote power has changed with the increase of the number of member states. But, actually this strengthens the perception of Romania as a "follower" state with respect to the Union's decisions, a perception that has to be changed, as we previously stated, through Romania's own initiatives to stimulate the interest of the Union. These initiatives can grant Romania a leader's position on certain projects, provided that the political will determined the "delivery" according to the partners' expectations.

Romania is going through a period of modernization, facilitated not only by the social- political orientation that stimulates the private initiative of the citizens as a result of guaranteeing democratic rights, but also due to the advantages of technological progress. In addition to these, Romania's "return" to Europe took place in a certain framework of its evolution, characterized by the existence of a collective security alliance and a wide economic integration process, on the background of the longest time of peace since the Second World War.

All these considered, and without prejudicing certain political and governance efforts that shaped Romania's new political orientation and made it possible for it to become a contracting party both of the security alliance and the economic integration process, over a quarter of century later, we are facing a worrying result. Yet, these currently worrying aspects are not the problem of Romania's modernization, but the constant failure of citizen's expectations as a result of a low-performance governance called to capitalize to the highest degree the new positioning in the Euro-Atlantic relationship.

As a member state of NATO and EU, Romania made commitments to keep up (and also "deliver") with the pace of the two club's internal developments. This pace takes into account both Romania's own targets and external challenges, the final result showing, more than once, delays, steps back and complications in accomplishing its own targets. Although Romania is part of a combined process measuring its performances through indicators, we need to ask ourselves where the fault is. Twelve years after the de jure integration in the EU, noticing net benefits coming out of its own contribution and EU's offer to support development, Romania hasn't progressed maintain the lowest position within the performances' hierarchy.

Internal analyses, biased or not, showing mostly the glass half full, interpreted from bottom to top or from top to bottom point to the attitude of temporary leaders in approaching solutions to fulfill the citizens' expectations. This very attitude is revealed by a synthesis of the ways of capitalization of the country's socioeconomic potential in the last quarter of a century, showing that we seem to have missed that potential: 3–4 million of Romanians are using their professional abilities abroad leaving in an almost state of emergency public utility domains important for the rest of the population in the country; Romania's own natural resources are exploited through decisions that no longer belong to us, aside from maintaining royalties insufficient to provide forms of recovery; national governance ensured the economic development through vertical financing, between public budget and privileged economic actors, the optimal allocation of resources being thus lost (to rigged auctions finalized with expensive contracts without qualitative accomplishment of their objectives, timely or not; investment objectives financed through public money without self-support, recovery or ensuring high quality, structured public goods; tax evasion and corruption); the horizontal development of economy is exclusively stimulated by multinational corporations with the effect of production oriented towards their countries of origin; too little is being done for increasing jobs in the private sector. Instead, the burden of budgeters of all kinds and bureaucracy to the detriment of the citizens increase etc.

The necessity of changing attitude became acute in order for us to get out of a vicious circle that finds us with the worst infrastructure in education, health, public order, transportation, tax collection with a probable effect in the bankruptcy of Romania (a scenario that doesn't belong to us but that we warn about). Maybe from the good current macroeconomic situation one should draw the path to follow provided a serious understanding of qualitative economic development instead of a simple economic growth carrying the germs of unsustainability.

5. The opportunities of globalization: why is there necessary a change of attitude?

Now more than ever, at the moment when the successful globalization is about to end in order to take a different orientation, the continuous identification of its impact on Romania becomes urgent. Regarding the capitalization of the globalization's opportunities up to now, a necessary change of attitude becomes obvious as globalization per se will continue and not sink back in history (O'Neil, 2017). At this time, globalization brings about multiple uncertainties, which should stimulate the study if its effects not only through the lenses of its 3–4 decades short history but also of the "disruption" the process of globalization itself is suffering. This moment allows a clearer observation of the balance of the effects in a fluid context of changes. From this point of view at least four preliminary comments regarding Romania's attitude towards the effects of globalization are required – even with the risk of repeating some ideas formulated or left to mature previously.

The first comment refers to the dynamics of the changes throughout the world, entering a new stage of searches/options, understood in the sense of the impatience of certain global powers to seize the new opportunities opened by the losers of globalization. This is actually an invitation for the winners of globalization to fill new positions in the hierarchy of the economic powers and their geopolitical projection worldwide.

The second comment refers to the fact that the effects of globalization, as felt in Romania, are less direct and more indirect, by sensing the EU's necessity to become a global actor acknowledged as such. From this point of view and regarding the EU's decisional system, Romania seems to have been more of a "victim" of EU's governance with respect to globalization and the results in development, ten years from the accession, speak for themselves. The towing effect of Romania's EU membership can be noticed on a whole scale, from the legislative and institutional harmonization to economic constraints and the high share of trade with the countries of the Union. In this regard, Romania remains a "follower" concerning the capitalization of some of the globalization's benefits, lots of its claims falling to the vote.

The third comment, connected to the things mentioned in the second comment, is that Romania, through the accession treaty, became de jure a full member of the EU with the same rights and obligations as all the other member states – founding and newer members – with a voice that has to be heard. There are no privileges for one member of the Union or another in the treaty. Slipping by the treaties, there can be noticed the discrimination attempts on the part of certain contracting parties, including legal attempts to legitimize them.

The most recent reports regarding the improvement of the EU governance refer to the fact that there is differentiation between member states, a pernicious example being the dichotomy between the center and the periphery of the EU, let alone North-South, Euro Zone and ex-Euro Zone etc. Solidarity and cohesion, EU values mainly accentuated these differences instead of reducing them. The fundamental error, in our opinion, was determined by the expectation that the new member states would immediately reach the highest standards, that the founding states or the ones that joined in 1986 needed decades to reach. The waiver from the accession treaties of the new member states, including Romania, were few, hardly accepted by the EU and their validity has already expired!

The fourth comment is inspired by the "street movement" that spread on many regions and continents, EU included. It is the social movement, violent in many cases also expressing the new relationship between generations, determined by the contradiction between individual expectations – of the ones affected by the last crisis, especially the young ones – and the political offer which is disappointing in many ways. The beginning of 2017 (ten years after the accession) showed for Romania a kind of confrontation that followed the general European pattern with very weak communication and lack of sound arguments on both sides. Thus, the feeling of social instability, with possible political effects, was and stays fluid, with periods of calm that prevent absolutely necessary governance corrections through legislation.

The conclusions regarding attitude of the four comments are pertinent with respect to a way of action and they are of concern to us as a sovereign country. As a consequence, there seem to be necessary: (a) real time impact studies related to the speed of events, the year 2017 being one of confirmations by clarifying uncertainties. Romania must be deeply interested by the regional geopolitics (of one EU region actually); (b) a future-oriented choice, for a more direct confrontation with the effects of an orientation-changing globalization, for a louder voice inside de EU in defending our own interests, a Union open to functioning at more than one speed; (c) use of force granted by EU membership structured not necessarily and exclusively by GDP, but also by geographical size, population, geographical and geostrategic localization (including from the point of view of EU and NATO interests). All these are relevant to the potential of economic growth and EU's obligations to the particular situation of some members in these times of change; (d) metaphorically it's time that Romania presents a "to do list" to the Union too and not only the other way around, that is, to assume political commitment for a future vision of the Union which also has to include Romania's aspirations regarding national interests as a sovereign state and full member of the EU.

The need for the change of attitude starts from the premise of Romania's trust in the European political project, in the necessity for it to continue with the expected benefits for Romania too, in the joint engagement to the quality economic development of the region considered the "EU periphery" where Romania is placed. Its mission is to defend its own interests and those of the EU's assembly with solid, credible and engaging arguments. All these involve not only stating political will but also concrete, continuous, insistent action according to consensual will.

Once such a conclusion is drawn, one must ask oneself what academic research is supposed to do. Our project[6] (Pop; Ioan-Franc, 2018–2019), the source of the points of view expressed in this research-essay, represents the biggest challenge on the topic we propose. This lies in the necessity to pay as much objective attention as possible to the areas in which the effects and/or the impact of globalization attract stimulation, amendment, inhibition or harmonization of the (mix of) policies which give meaning to the societal development towards higher standards. To the benefit of such treatment there comes the argument that we, the authors of the study, were involved academically, in a direct and indirect way, along with many other researchers at the Romanian Academy's National Institute for Economic Research "Costin C. Kiritescu," in the conception and evaluation of so many aspects of Romania's development with certain societal connotation for Romania's present and future.

Also, we are continuously concerned with theoretical study, but mostly with the applied one – as required by the reality of systemic evolutions – being also highly reputed scientifically together with numerous other colleagues who expressed opinions, analysis results and complex evaluations in papers[7] published between 1990–2017: Victor Axenciuc, Ilie Bădescu, Nicolae Belli, Gheorghe Leonard Cazan, Luminița Chivu, Mircea Ciumara, Constantin Ciutacu, Emilian Dobrescu, Gheorghe Dolgu, Florin Georgescu, Vasile Ghețău, Aurel Iancu, Constantin

6 The factors of configuration of the New Global Order and the reconfiguration of post crisis globalization concept, the "Costin C. Kiritescu" National Institute for Economic Research and The Institute of World Economy, Romanian Academy, 2018–2019.

7 The link "Tezaur INCE" (Ioan-Franc, 2019), created by The Center for Economic Information and Documentation on the page www.ince.ro, presents *in extenso* (more than 60 volumes, approx. 48,000 pages) the studies conducted by the "Costin C. Kiritescu" National Institute for Economic Research of Romanian Academy between 1990–2005, the time of ripening of ideas regarding Romania's track to the European Union.

Ionete, Mugur Isărescu, Paul Cosmovici, Ion Păun Otiman, Tudorel Postolache, Hildegard Puwak, Stefan Răgălie, Corneliu Russu, Vasile Stănescu, Mihai Ştefan, Vladimir Trebici, Iulian Văcărel, Gheorghe Zaman, Cătălin Zamfir.

The financial crisis was the trigger for integrated academic research of globalization as slipping on the tracks of narrow specializations or ideas based on allegedly flawless theories raised more questions that received no answer, rather than credible clarifications.

The unanswered questions faced us with the highest challenging/risky sphere, that of prevailing uncertainties over certainties. Doubt arises even over certainties, though, which are most of the times the result of the malfunctioning of the widely accepted theories, analytic/rational econometric models. It is should be no longer current practice, we believe, to place the current state of facts with a limit of knowledge sui generis, but it is rather recommended to talk about the moral limits of knowledge which create, at least for researches approaching a certain age, serious problems in contemplating or analyzing the reality in which we live.

As academically educated researches we walk away considerably from the biased tendencies and we observe, through the diversity of the research models, the fundamental skeleton of a societal construction in connection to which the individuals made a system political choice. In this approach, cleared of alleged "ideological orientations," we should see inclinations or behavioral propensities with an extremely complex substrate that doesn't lack mission or one's own belief.

From this point of view, we can but express our satisfaction regarding the opening to academic opinions, rationally argued debates and compromises and especially to mutual respect that invites new debates and constructive approach in hard times. The Romanian society still has to walk a long way to exclude irreconcilable antagonism or radicalism that tears apart through obsessions, doubts and paralyzing fears the coherent action towards a better future. If we were to fall prey to those, that would mean surrender to damaging politics.

Therefore, we, the authors, took it to approach Romania's actions to the new challenges through the perspective of the interactions among the most important fields, without which the European integration and globalization with their good and bad sides wouldn't exist in our tumultuous contemporary life.

6. The chances of a national project

We state from the beginning that the project in question is only apparently a traditional one although, under its generic name, it left its mark on Romania's stages of progress and development and, cyclically, it needs to come back as an adagio better written and better interpreted by the citizens of this country. It is the modernization of Romania project, upgraded to the opportunities and challenges of the 21st century.

There is the risk of repeating terminology, but the background to express was always connected to modernization times and main European main who had become examples for Romanian Principalities, United Principalities, The Greater Romania, the postwar Romania etc. (1884, 1859, 1866, 1918, 1930, 1947 etc.). Now we are talking about Romania that has come back to the family of European democracies, a member of two elite-clubs that mark the course of economic development (integration-globalization) under collective security circumstances (NATO, PSE) in the framework of the most advanced forms of partnerships known in history. The latter is by no means synonymous with perfection of international relations.

What makes a new modernization project different than others more or less followed to their end is the context, already described, in which it is to be born, promoted and accomplished, to reach certain standards and, mostly, consensual political will regarding its validation above election cycles and political commitments. In the complex fabric of the global system in which so many national interests need to fit, the first chance a country can grant itself is the credibility and predictability of a strategic national project.

Knowing what a certain political class wants for its own nation and the way in which it is going to act, orderly and fluidly, on a medium and long term, is currently, for all partners sharing the same values (mind this requirement!), the guarantee for a stronger partnership, equivalent with taking on responsibilities accordingly, in the spirit of „burden sharing" increasingly present in globalization. This concept, in the framework of the new international order in progress, applies as well to countries that do not, for the time being, commit completely to being loyal to the same shared values creating antagonisms on multiple levels (economic, military, security etc.).

6.1. The arguments

Romania needs to set its modernization in relation to the new realities, but this project became urgent after 25 years of fragmentary and fragmented searches. The arguments of the compulsory aspect of the strategic project of Romania's modernization are numerous and can be subject to many debates, but these shouldn't stand in the way of its accomplishment. We shall try to enumerate the arguments we find crucial to start this process.

1) The systemic transformation, started in 1990, remains an institutionally and legislatively unaccomplished process, and the end of the road has to lead to modernization as far as democracy and market economy are involved. The acknowledgement of Romania as a rule of law with a market economy is still "rough," if we are to consider MCV's supervision or the fluctuation of attractiveness for investments due to lack of consolidation of the factors that can stimulate it on a long term – the lack of predictability and stability of the rules of the business environment, the lack of commercial court of laws with fast procedures determined by the market's opportunities that come and go etc. – and that have a substantial impact on the real economy, not the speculative

one. The low number of significant investments, even large-scale ones (the automotive industry, cement, oil processing etc.), their concentration on certain branches, but mostly the unequal development of counties (an important aspect in adopting the euro currency) are aspects many times interpreted as an "invasion" of foreign capital and not necessarily as benefits for economy. This can hardly be considered an invitation for the increase of investments or jobs.

2) Romania's being part of EU and NATO still needs a much better structured and more proactive implication, but, apparently, the political will is more coherent and reactive in the "command" obeying area only, the way in which, in other areas, applying community's decisions smells of foreign interventions. We are the witnesses of the lack of continuity in the great politics of integration, which means, thus, that the possible recipients of the new rules of international cooperation, at institutional level, are too often changed on political grounds leading to the incapacity of accumulating knowledge in the area. In crucial moments, there is forgotten that the principle of transferring competences from the national level to the one of the community, from treaties to regulations, directives and decisions was accepted. Not following them, in letter and spirit deprives everyone of the advantages of the integration, among which there is the use of structural funds as a lever for national developments that would bring us closer to the performances of real convergence.
3) The real convergence, as a permanent support, absolutely necessary to the stability and sustainability of the nominal convergence criteria, needs a continuous, disciplined, political action dedicated to a long term national development program that is to use the (too much criticized) experience of economic policies imposed by the international financial partners – IMF, World Bank, IFC –, in the sense of mastering the macrostability through the firm control of budget and external deficits (of the sovereign debt). Instead of understanding the taking on "schooling" that is not imposed on us, we ended up asking for it each and every time lacking the steadiness we should prove by our membership to NATO and EU. The constraints on our course had the bright side of preparing us for the perspective of development less exposed to the risks of external contamination.
4) The international experience with the international financial partners that led to the reduction of Romania's financing costs from private resources on the capital markets is the best guarantee of a partner ready to take on new responsibilities – such as the one of increasing the defense budget which was imposed by Romania's accession to NATO, now accelerated due to the geostrategic situation in Eastern Europe – of long term economic responsibility, provided the macroeconomic gain is perpetuated.
5) The new macroprudential stability structures, under Romania's favorable macroeconomic circumstances, constitutes the very tool of the necessary continuity of political-professional training that shouldn't be lost. Instead

of speaking with unjustified anger about the constant amazement regarding the bureaucratic multiplication (yesterday's news after the lessons of the last financial crises) we should better accept the fact that global economy is changing paradigms and that one should let go of the old bureaucratic institution in economy making place for the new ones. Maybe this way the structural reforms of some highly and uselessly financial resources consuming state entities would be better understood. According to the requirements of the new economic paradigm, bureaucratic apparatus would be reduced for: anticipating adverse shocks, generated by globalization and the orderly absorption, without shaking the social order in a world of uncontrollably developing inequalities (the disappearance of the middle class, the unbalance of income distribution, globalization of inequality etc.).

6.2. Reconstruction

1) The Romanian societal system is the biggest challenge of our times, because the current situation determines Romania's own future. The concern is not about the lasting of the people in this geographical space, the tradition, the culture or the psychology of the people, but about the interferences of imperial nature that reflects the importance of the geographical space occupied by the respective population. The enduring traits showed, even with some delays, the great capacity of a nation to align with the great changes of social progress in Europe. The modern history of Romania makes it obvious to notice this alignment, starting with the European Revolution of 1848. The "accidents" in this alignment depended on the extent to which "we were us" and "how much others forced us not to be us." There were moments when we managed to sail through such accidents (for example the achievement of Greater Romania) even when we were snubbed and almost silenced (The Vienna Dictate, the ultimatum for the surrender of Bessarabia, the Stalinist communism). The ones who "interfered so that we wouldn't be us, didn't manage to prevent us from being us." The preservation of the Latin language, of the European ideals, hospitality instead of aggression etc., all these aspects came back to the present.

Regarding the stability of the foundation of the Romanian societal system, after the choice made a quarter of a century ago, that is the return to the pattern of Western democracy, after the detour to totalitarianism (imposed on us by the way the Great Powers decided to end the Second World War), few questions arise: Have we strengthen the pillars of the Western model of democracy? Is this model in our geographical space credible for our partners, especially the European ones, that we share the same values with? Is it "politically correct" that our attempt to return to the fundamental pillars of the political-social model of our choice to be considered a slip in the foreigner and partially internal view, although it was validated by the very same external partners before being deviated? Which is the real meaning of a stream of criticism in almost all areas and especially in that of corruption, coming from our current alleged partners of strategic relationships? What is desired from Romania in this complex regional geopolitical stage? Would it be possible that the underdevelopment Romania stayed in, compared to other former socialist states, is the very stake of our European partners' expectation? Which is the mark of normality for the rule of law in the case of Romania, when even our partners are confused regarding the realities and the expectations of the Romanian electorate?

At the same time, it is desirable that, in addition to academic concerns, reports by officials involved in the management of the respective challenges start to be prepared (at least as an inventory considering that many concrete aspects are missed or not known by researchers) including the arguments of the approach, the results and future intentions. This approach is strategic programming, predictability and transparency, being useful not only to officials, but also to everyone interested in the normal functioning of economy – investors, manufacturers, private and public traders –, respectively everybody in charge with the performance of a benefit shared with the state.

2) The rule of law. After the Constitution in 2003 with the amendments to the initial version in 1991, there appeared an increasing tendency of interpretation and voluntary application of it, in the very substance of the fundamental law. Subsequent secondary laws, modified from one regime to another, but which should be inspired by the Constitution only, eventually led to the contestation of the rule of law both form the inside as well as outside. We are inclined to state that there is a slip beyond the level of perceptions, generated by intended interpretations, with a certain purpose, as long as neither the Constitution nor the law of the Constitutional Court have changed.

Challenging the rule of law happens on a daily basis and ignoring it has major consequences on the citizens and the image of Romania in Europe. The pros and cons have lost sight of the normality of the rule of law and, consequently, the natural question is whether Romania of this current quarter of a century is truly a rule of law. The question is inspired by the current debates at the meeting point of two celebrations: 100 years from the achievement of The Greater Romania and 60 years from the initiation of the European project which is today the European Union. These moments are far from being celebratory only, faced with the subtle questioning of Versailles Treaties and the irredentist tendencies around us (a new Valev plan?), respectively the launching of a "multi-speed Europe" (again a divided Europe?).

The nation-states are facing challenges too while being revitalized by the step back in globalization and the way it defends statehood, respectively the quality of the democratic rule of law. In our view, maybe theoretically and practically (through our own involvement) limited, Romania is a rule of law in the very form it conceived its institutional structure after the 1991 Constitution, while explaining our intentions and perspectives to our Western partners in the first years of the 9th decade were persuasive enough. To our knowledge, the 1991

Romanian Constitution, as amended and supplemented in 2003, is an elaboration based on constitutional law comparisons, supported by specialized international fora (mainly the Venice Commission) and many twinning activities done with some of our Western partners.

3) Market economy. We hope there are not many of those who believe that Romania "begged for" the accession to the EU while the EU had no interest in this, at least regarding the essence of the European project and its intentions of geographical inclusion. The game of integration was a "game" of two, each of the partners seizing the opportunities in projecting their own interests in a geographical space (seen as a market) as wide as possible. Currently, we are witnessing many critical analyses regarding the preeminence of our European partners' interests in Romania, the conclusion being always the lack of appropriate response. At the moment, one can put together a long enough list of patterns of unbalanced interactions between Romania and its European partners resulting in the perception of the difficult road towards the modernization of the country through the European integration[8] (Pop; Ioan-Franc, 2016; Pop; Ioan-Franc, 2012–2014).

All these are happening on the background of the functionality of a still emerging market economy, acknowledged by our Western partners, that must accept the rules of fair competition, transparency, equal and even treatment etc. Surely, a national market must also be competitive and resilient to competition, which means a productive structure adequate to the available resources, stimulate and/or protected by the state to serve the interest of its own citizens: jobs, decent wages, specialization in professions required by the labor market, integration capacities etc.

There is a talk about the relationship between the market and the state, considering the bitter reality that, after 25 years of market economy, there still hasn't been established the formula of the optimal involvement of the state in the regulation of economy so that the private sector is not only prevalent (as it is now!) but also as efficient and lasting as possible, through healthy companies with ongoing activity, in development etc. But everything that is being discussed in the specialists' circles – that the state interferes where it shouldn't and it doesn't do it where it should – doesn't surprise anyone any longer. Moreover, the findings regarding the increasing regional social and economic imbalances, the emigration of the qualified work labor, the poor management of corporate insolvencies, the perception of colonization of the national economy, the drainage of natural resources through low royalties, the perception of foreign companies being favored to the detriment of the national ones, the ongoing undercapitalization of Romanian companies etc. are visible certainties. There are obvious gaps in the regulation of the functioning of the market economy, and time shows that these

8 Napoleon Pop, Valeriu Ioan-Franc, 2016, "L'europenisation de la Roumanie. Un acte de recherche academique", in "Review of general management", no. 1(23), p. 16–25.

aren't the result of lack of competence but of the way in which the state manages private interests in politics.

As economists, we pointed out that the take on a public acquisition law according to European standards, without considering the national interests expressed in a credible vision, will bring the blocking of the structural development of Romania's economy. After flawed privatizations reputed national executants and designer engineers for large-scale public projects in all infrastructures were lost. Due to the manner the state manages/protects private interests we saw the birth and growth of the economy on a vertical axis, between the state budget and a (political) selection of private favorites (companies established over night, without proven and professionally acknowledged performances in their areas) as a means of drainage, through rigged public auctions, of public funds, with minimum practical results. Instead, we notice an unprecedented increase over night of the millionaires in euro, which makes us wonder: how is that possible when 40 % of the population is on the brink of poverty and social exclusion?

The general image of market regulation in Romania, from the point of view of material resources, development factors and economic liberties in a world as integrated as possible, is good and attractive. Unfortunately, many of the national and foreign investments in all counties are based on agreements with the local administrations in what is probably a local vision framework not integrated in a national vision where there is a balance between production and consumption structure. The culture of consumption in Romania has reached the highest standards with substantial import supply. The lack of diversity in the national supply determines that each wage increase, creating a propensity towards consumption, results in an immediate increase of the disproportion between the balance of trade and the balance of payments.

In almost all famous crises of the developed market economies the state was called to take action. We recall here the memorable statement of acad. Tudorel Postolache during the agitated times when the Draft of transition to market economy in Romania was being elaborated: "in times of crisis, the economy is the main realm of national consensus" (quote from memory). Romania answered in the same way to the first recurrent economic crisis triggered by the financial crisis in 2008, in the period of the new democratic rule of law and the market economy after 1990. The state got indebted by 20 billion euro without knowing precisely what it was to be saved, but it is a sure fact that the debt was paid by the budget taxpayers (the reduction of wages by 25 % and then taxes and fees) on the expenses of their life standard.

Beyond the few public debates, somewhat harsh, regarding the size of the state and the part it plays in the market economy, the prevailing message in the end is that the politicians (the elites), their partisans and many of the citizens (the public sector at large) got used to the fact they are to benefit from the public funds forgetting where these come from: the private sector. Moreover, there is an interest for the salaries, allowances, subsidies, scholarships, aids to grow even with the risk of paralyzing the private sector with supervision, tax changes etc.

But, it is these very elites that took on a type of liberalism (the obligations of the community acquis) behind which, by using the tools that could bring them continuous prosperity (the free market, the competition, the financial stability etc.) also stimulated a quick transfer of fortunes (through privatization, corruption etc.). Unfortunately, we catch a glimpse of the same specificity but also superficiality (!) of the way in which the role of the state in the Romanian economy is understood which increases the risks we have already referred to.

6.3. Instead of conclusions: about democracy and sovereignty

The spreading of the antiglobalization feeling, including in the form of anti-EU protests, is about to attack democracy in the member states, a potential danger for Romania, too. The parliamentary democracy, in the sense of acknowledging the results of elections and their effects during the term of office, seems to have no relevance from the point of view of traditional mechanisms (the laws are issued by the Parliament only, the minority obeys the majority etc.). The minority questions democracy and its values in the name of fundamental liberties, only if these can belong to them alone. The intention of using the tools of democracy to express opposition in public squares, without these being approved by law, is about to create a major break within the legal-illegal balance. Trying to emphasize legality in this context becomes a challenge that can cause even greater excitement to those who don't obey the law, claiming their own rights.

Reconstructing democracy (Ioan-Franc, 2019) takes a flexible form between legal and illegal, which can lead to chaos, ruining the essence of the rule of law that is ruled only by law. The immediate effect of the destruction of a state's internal democracy is the emergence of the intentions not to follow or to break the rules governing the state, but also the relationships between the states. Brexit is the example of the first breach of the community law and it inspired similar intentions during the pre-electoral periods in Holland, France, Germany, Italy etc., generating great emotion in the European space.

The democratic system, especially the European Council decision making rules, starts to be challenged by the possible future representatives of the member states in this organization. Breaking the community democracy is motivated by sovereignty, by the need that the nations-states come back to the strict rules of independence and sovereignty. The pressure for this return is determined and it is growing due to the centralization of the community power in the hands of bureaucrats lacking legitimacy.

This fact actually shows the divergence of the project from its political stake, respectively the strengthening of the democratic principles at the level of states union.

In globalization, and especially in European integration, there is a permanent transfer of sovereignty in exchange of certain benefits considered to be effects of the leveling of mutual advantages for all: reduction of custom duties, free movement, free trade areas, single market etc. Romania, as an EU member state, renounced sovereignty in trade policy by acceding to the single market, renounced parts of sovereignty by embracing discipline towards PSC. It will transfer sovereignty in monetary politics if it adopts euro, it already has shared sovereignty in EU's external policy and of common security and other sovereignty transfer occasion are to occur.

The immediate sovereignty transfer areas are the criminal and military matters as new government functions are agreed at Union level: EU Attorney General, respectively the position of Commissioner for Military Procurement for common security etc. It is not the transfer of sovereignty parts that represents a risk for Romania, but the manner in which it manifests, supports and imposes independence of opinion and the position as a EU member with equal rights. The "being proactive" Brussel's euphemism encloses a multitude of past frustrations accumulated in the 10 years since the accession of Romania to the EU. As it was shown, mending "the impositions of others" is difficult. Rules that aren't applied to other states (the MCV) became a stain on Romania's image. Some compatriots also contributed to this being worried about any return to the normality required by Romanian Constitution.

Claiming our sovereignty could have a serious reason, considering the fact that, almost constantly, the attempts to make the genuine corrections required by the Constitution (not by amending it as it happened in other EU member states) are seen as offenses to certain principles that are not lived by those who claim to be their guarantors.

The problem of the sovereign nation-state for Romania, starting from the hypothesis that the EU membership must be strengthen, regards the EU restructuring through its own contribution too. We have to admit that EU is facing a crisis, and leaving things as they are means, according to the opinions of many, the collapse of this form of integration. What it could be useful though, even from the perspective of EU becoming a global actor, is an agreed diminishing in the European Council decision making power over the other member states paralleled by the strengthening of the legitimacy of the ones who propose decisions applicable to all member states. We believe that Romania remains interested to be part of a powerful Union. This interest, however, involves also our own effort to restructure it, even if some of the fundamental objectives are postponed (fiscal and political union).

The major achievements stage, such as the initiation of integration through the Treaty of Rome, the establishment of the Economic and Monetary Union, getting the EU out of the 1980s crisis etc., was marked by political will and action, before getting to ways of sharing power. Stages of such kind claim, consequently, highly performing politicians that we miss now, in a moment when it is necessary to shape the near future European policies that are to strengthen the European project. This is confirmed by the very alternatives of the Juncker Report speaking about a multi-speed Europe of the future. But this Europe already exists as a result of inconsistent policies, little related to the very political nature of the European project.

The great challenge consists of the fact that the political line of the integration was shaded by a bureaucratic institutional architecture which delegitimized the trust in the project, determining also the withdrawing of the member states and their inclination towards the sovereign nation-state rather than the community. For the ordinary citizen, the interpretation is simple and it is also food for thought: the Union can do less for the ordinary citizen than can the state he/she is a partof.

References

Blyth, Mark, Austerity – The History of a Dangerous Idea, Oxford University Press, 2011.

Ioan-Franc, Valeriu, Din lucrările Comisiei de la Snagov, CIDE – Academia Română, 2000.

Ioan-Franc, Valeriu, Tezaur INCE, created by the Center for Economic Information and Documentation on the page http://www.ince.ro/Publicatii/Tezaur/tezaur.html.

Ioan-Franc, Valeriu, Un seule Europe unie pour les prochaines gènèrations d'Europèens. Quelques questions que nous inquetent, Conferinţa internaţională "Economic Complexity: A More United Iberian Peninsula for Stronger Europe", RACEF, Portugalia, 18–22 June 2019.

O'Neil, Jim, In Defense of Globalization, Project Syndicate, January 2017, https://www.project-syndicate.org/commentary/defense-of-globalization-by-jim-o-neill-2017-01?barrier=accesspaylog

Pearce, Nick, Liberalism can survive but it has to renew its social traditions, Financial Times, dec. 2016.

Pop, Napoleon; Ioan-Franc, Valeriu, L'europenisation de la Roumanie. Un acte de recherche academique, in Review of general management, no. 1(23), p. 16–25, 2016.

Pop, Napoleon; Ioan-Franc, Valeriu, New Global Order and the reconfiguration of post crisis globalization concept, the "Costin C. Kiritescu" National Institute for Economic Research and The Institute of World Economy, Romanian Academy, 2018–2019.

Pop, Napoleon; Ioan-Franc, Valeriu; România în globalizare, Editura Centrului de Informare si Documentare Economica, 2018.

Pop, Napoleon; Ioan-Franc, Valeriu, Spre o Monedă Globală – vol. 1 Preliminarii, vol. 2 Calea posibilă, vol. 3 Realităţi şi constrângeri, Editura Expert, Bucureşti, 2012–2014.

Soros, George, The Tragedy of the European Union, Public Affairs, 2014.

Stiglitz, Joseph E., Globalization and Its Discontents, W. W. Norton & Company, 2002.

Jaime Gil Aluja

Personal contributions for a new theory: the theory of self-induced incidences

1. A theory stated in artificial intelligence

It doesn't matter if you are a scientist or not, the brain is the human organ that most fascinates everyone who tries to know it. And, at the same time, it is the most complex and mysterious. It is still the great unknown for science.

It is also true that they have explained to us more and more precisely how it works, that is, the mechanisms that control the reticular activity that connects it to other human organs.

This fascination has also reached the area of the social sciences and especially economics.

For the person presenting this article, the aforementioned curiosity was a constant, which, in a way, was renewed in an irregular way when we tried to formally reproduce the circuits that follow thoughts, dreams, ideas and, ultimately, economic decisions.

In this sense, we try to imitate nature, appealing to the notion of a network, which we call, perhaps excessively daring, "a neural network."[1]

This paid off: the nature of the networks, their characteristics, their characteristics, and the operators they accept provided, as in the past, a good "playground."

From the beginning, we assumed that, by integrating elements of network theory in the treatment of social phenomena, the use of neural networks would facilitate expanding the possibilities of using it in the specific field of economics.

And, despite this fact, we were often aware that immediate and simple incorporation into successful economic phenomenology was not possible. The history provides quite a few examples: to fly, man did not imitate the bird, to walk faster, man did not copy the horse, the computer has nothing to do with the nervous system ... but let us introduce you some nuances, like nature It can be a guide, reasoning can be a support, but without imagination, the creative activity of science and technology is almost impossible. This fact makes us place this proposal in the field of Artificial Intelligence.

---

1 Kaufmann, A., Gil Aluja, J.: "Grafos neuronales para la economía y gestión de empresas", 2ª edition, Ed. Pyramide, Madrid, 1995 (ISBN: 84-368-0917-3).

2. The concept and content of the notion of incidence

In a first approximation, the concept of incidence relation can be associated with the idea of causality of elements of a set on the elements of another set, of a different nature or on its own elements. In a way, it is a notion associated with the well-known concept of function.

And we use the associated term because, very often, one concept is used instead of the other interchangeably. Although we do not want to cause a radical confrontation with those who do, we want to clarify our point of view on this problem.

Let's start by emphasizing that the incidence relationship is part of life in society and occurs in an infinite number of situations in our coexistence. It is so common that it became one of our automatisms of thought in many cases.

As far as we are concerned, we support the idea that the notion of incidence is a generalization of the notion of causality because, although this relationship is only mechanical, in addition to relationships structured by reason, unstructured relationships resulting from the imagination are admitted in the incidence.

This implies the need to use operators carefully to use them in one case or another: causal measures, measures and incidence evaluations.

Generally, incidences are represented through the arcs of an oriented network that is linked in a succession of phases or stages.

But the propagation of the incidence through the network (from now on we will talk about the flow) encounters obstacles in the nodes that we formally represent by means of thresholds that prevent its passage, cut the flow for the direct route or, in the same way, it deviate to other arcs in the network.

In other words, the flow can be cut off or can continue on other paths. But, in all cases, the flow level may not be the same or it may not pass through the same network arcs as originally planned.

The flow cutoff or its deviation actually takes the form of "omissions" (oublis) or other circumstances that are not necessarily negative. When there is no cut, but one or more new incidence ratios (one or more new arcs are used in the network), second-generation effects sometimes occur, in the terminology of Jean Fourastié (1907–1990). The "omissions" generally appear to be deviations or even deviations from the initially planned route for the incidence to achieve its purpose.

To graphically represent the appropriate functions of the reticular incidence, we incorporate the new concepts of the supply networks of liquid or gaseous goods. These are as follows:

1. Channels of incidence: arcs of the networks and subnets through which the incidence flows.
2. Incidence flow: the level of flow through the channels. It is evaluated in the interval [0, 1]

3. Incidence deposits: arc peaks in a network where the incidence flow can reach or leave
4. Channel confluence: the peaks of a network can be deposited where the incidences that arrive from two or more channels flow.
5. Incidence distribution center: peaks of a network where two or more channels exit.
6. Dilution of incidence flows: a phenomenon that occurs in an incidence deposit when the arrival flow is less or greater than that generated by the deposit itself. The deposited flow is reduced to the lower of the two.
7. Incidence Flow Evaporation Threshold: The degree or level below which the incidence flow stops in a reservoir and stops passing through the next channel or channels.

By establishing these concepts, we can present the most important aspects that we propose to achieve the following two objectives:

I. Obtain the total number of incidences from the incident entities to the affected entities, as well as detect the incidents that act as the most important intermediaries.
II. Establish the level or degree of incidence flows that reach the final deposits.

The chosen image of a network formed by channels through which an incidence potential flows that may or may not converge in some peaks of the network, allows, in our opinion, a deepening of certain aspects that open the doors to a further course. throughout our research.

In fact, in the studies we know, it is common to use Boolean algebra to determine the existence or absence of incidence: 1 for yes, 0 for no. It is the sacralization of the binary.

But, as we said more than once, the binary does not fit well in the social sciences. Therefore, our proposal to use fuzzy or multivalent incidence relationships. In these, the incidence can take a value between zero and one, so that the higher the incidence, the closer the unit value is.

In our article we usually use the endecadarian system to assign values (eleven values in the interval [0; 1], including zero and one). In this study, the assessment of incidence is not limited to the existence or non-existence of the incidence, but the degree or level of it is assessed. This is a crucial aspect for the unfolding of the theory we try to develop.

3. The basic principles for a theory of incidences

The objective of establishing a high generality degree theory involves accepting, from the very beginning, of the following principles:

a. The natural quality of the human being doesn't allow the use of just the two positions of the binary system: the incidence exists or it doesn't exist. Let's introduce nuance by appealing to multivalent logic and, mathematically, to fuzzy sets.[2]

b. Incidences propagate with a chain of relations through a network. To formalize it, we use the image of a flow of incidences with a degree or level of intensity that flow through the connected channels with a capacity degree or level.
c. Incidence is a notion with a highly subjective content, which, consequently, can't be generally treated through the operators proper to determinism, certainty and hazard, as it is not the object of quantification (objective numerical assignment) but of an assessment (subjective numerical assignment). Determinism is not a good bet for human adventure. Everything evolves, and adaptability has become essential.
d. If in Boolean algebra values are taken from the set [0, 1], in multivalence we establish that these are included in the interval [0, 1]. In this sense, we propose an endecadarian numerical-semantical correspondence as an indication (we can use another one too.) Here is the correspondence we suggest:
0: no incidence
0.1: virtually no incidence
0.2: almost no incidence
0.3: very low incidence
0.4: low incidence
0.5: average incidence
0.6: enough incidence
0.7: sensitive incidence
0.8: strong incidence
0.9: very strong incidence
1: total incidence

Alternatively, there can be used other words in the correspondence too, directly linked to the specific study the degree or the level refers to.

In case that the nuancing by the eleven values is considered insufficient it is possible to use another scale in [0; 1], with an odd number of values.

4. Direct or first generation incidences

We accepted these basic principles tant we intend to examine in relation with direct of first generation incidences. To do this, we shall use the symbols below:

$A = \{a_1, a_2, \ldots, a_n\}$ a set of incidence elements.

$B = \{b_1, b_2, \ldots, b_m\}$ a set of affected elements.

2 Zadeh, Lofti A., Fuzzy Sets, Information and Control 8(3), 1965, p. 338–353.

We say that there is an incidence from $a_i / i = 1, 2, \ldots, n$ on $b_j / j = 1, 2, \ldots, m$, if the value of the couple (a_i, b_j) is included in $[0, 1]$. There is no incidence when the value of this couple is zero.

The set of evaluation $\vartheta(a_i, b_j) \,/\, i = 1, 2, \ldots, n; j = 1, 2, \ldots, m$, can be defined through a fuzzy incidence matrix $\begin{bmatrix} M \\ \sim \end{bmatrix}$:

$[\underset{\sim}{M}] =$

A \ B	b_1	b_2		b_m
a_1	$\vartheta(a_1, b_1)$	$\vartheta(a_1, b_2)$		$\vartheta(a_1, b_m)$
a_2	$\vartheta(a_2, b_1)$	$\vartheta(a_2, b_2)$		$\vartheta(a_2, b_m)$
a_n	$\vartheta(a_n, b_1)$	$\vartheta(a_n, b_2)$		$\vartheta(a_n, b_m)$

Sometimes we use (x_i, y_j) instead of $\vartheta(a_i, b_j)$, $i = 1, 2, \ldots, n$; $j = 1, 2, \ldots, m$. It is fine too.

In a fuzzy matrix or a fuzzy relation, the evaluation of each couple through (x_i, y_j) takes a value between zero and one:

$$\forall (x_i, y_j) \in \begin{bmatrix} M \\ \sim \end{bmatrix} :$$

$$\vartheta(a_i, b_j) \in [0, 1]$$

The fuzzy matrix thus formulated expresses the direct or first generation incidences of the set A on the elements of the set B, where both A and B are given referential sets.

5. Self-induction of incidence

We introduced the concept of self-induction to express the relations of incidence of each element in a set with itself and with all the elements of its own set.

We then write for the incidences from $a_i / i = 1, 2, \ldots, n$ on $a_h / h = 1, 2, \ldots, n$ if the value of the couple $(a_i, a_h) \in [0, 1]$:

$$\vartheta(a_i, a_h) = (x_i, x_h) \in [0, 1], \; i, h = 1, 2, \ldots, n$$

This set of evaluations $\vartheta(a_i, a_h) = (x_i, x_h)$ can be represented throught a fuzzy matrix $\begin{bmatrix} A \\ \sim \end{bmatrix}$ which will be square and reflexive: square because $i = h$; (x_i, x_h); and reflexive because $(x_i, x_i) = 1$

The same is true for the referential set B whose set of evaluations $\vartheta(b_j, b_k) = (x_j, x_k) \in [0,1] \quad j, k = 1, 2, \ldots, m$ can be represented by fuzzy matrix $\left[\underset{\sim}{B}\right]$, which is also square and reflexive, because $j = k; (x_j, x_k); (x_j, x_j) = 1$.

The self-induced incidence matrix $\left[\underset{\sim}{A}\right]$ and $\left[\underset{\sim}{B}\right]$ can be represented as follow:

$[\underset{\sim}{A}] =$

A \ A	a_1	a_2		a_n
a_1	$\vartheta(a_1, a_1)$	$\vartheta(a_1, a_2)$		$\vartheta(a_1, a_n)$
a_2	$\vartheta(a_2, a_1)$	$\vartheta(a_2, a_2)$		$\vartheta(a_2, a_n)$
a_n	$\vartheta(a_n, a_1)$	$\vartheta(a_n, a_2)$		$\vartheta(a_n, a_n)$

$[\underset{\sim}{B}] =$

B \ B	b_1	b_2		b_m
b_1	$\vartheta(b_1, b_1)$	$\vartheta(b_1, b_2)$		$\vartheta(b_1, b_m)$
b_2	$\vartheta(b_2, b_1)$	$\vartheta(b_2, b_2)$		$\vartheta(b_2, b_m)$
b_m	$\vartheta(b_m, b_1)$	$\vartheta(b_m, b_2)$		$\vartheta(b_m, b_m)$

These two fuzzy matrices $\left[\underset{\sim}{A}\right]$ and $\left[\underset{\sim}{B}\right]$ show that, beside the direct or first generation flows of incidences, expressed in the fuzzy matrix $\left[\underset{\sim}{M}\right]$, there are also other channels belonging to the general network that the flow can move through, the ones corresponding to the elements of self-induction of set A on themselves and of set B, also on themselves.

Now we need to correctly reunite these three incidence networks in one unique general network, so that the flow can move through all channels.

We need to observe that both the elements of set A and those of set B act as emitters and receivers of an incidence flow.

We repeat, it is a question of establishing, correctly, the composition of the three fuzzy matrices: $\left[\underset{\sim}{M}\right], \left[\underset{\sim}{A}\right], \left[\underset{\sim}{B}\right]$

6. Composition of fuzzy incidence matrices

Knowing the three fuzzy incidence matrices is valuable information. This allow, in our opinión, to get a very well focused idea of the flows, meaning: direct incidence relations, the matrix $\left[\underset{\sim}{M}\right]$, and the relations, also of direct incidence, of incidence elements with themselves at departure, which, through the matrix

$\begin{bmatrix} A \\ \sim \end{bmatrix}$ are also affected elements, as well as the incidence relations of the initially affected elements with themselves, which, through the matrix $\begin{bmatrix} B \\ \sim \end{bmatrix}$ are also incidence elements.

These being said, considering that there is a global relations between the three matrices, the question is to establish the nature and the content of this global relation, in other words, we have information that needs to be structured. To make this possible, we need to choose one or several operators.

Indeed, any manager that acts in his/her interest or representing a company or an institution, does it in a certain "spirit": radical conservative, cautions to a certain extent, talking a low risk,... in the manner of an adventurer. And he be aware of this, little aware or not at all. The operator to be used in each of the rods of this fan must or it may be different. Luckily, every human being is different.

Certain or some of these "features" accompany the human beings for their entire lives, although their duration may be transient or lasting, but always changing. In our paper, as well as in the preceding ones, we choose an operator that formalizes the actions considered very ordinary and that we could describe as being moderately: "we choose the best out of the worst solutions."

We refer to the convolution operator or the max-min composition. It is usually represented by a small circle at the bottom between the elements of the compound: $\circ$.

As we have already emphasized, the fuzzy matrices $\begin{bmatrix} A \\ \sim \end{bmatrix}$ y $\begin{bmatrix} B \\ \sim \end{bmatrix}$ are reflexive because the incidence of each element of these matrices on themselves is total. The value assign in this case is one to all the element of the main diagonal.

Reflexivity allows us to use a property, i.e. associativity:

$$\begin{bmatrix} M \\ \sim \end{bmatrix} \circ \left(\begin{bmatrix} A \\ \sim \end{bmatrix} \circ \begin{bmatrix} B \\ \sim \end{bmatrix} \right) = \left(\begin{bmatrix} M \\ \sim \end{bmatrix} \circ \begin{bmatrix} A \\ \sim \end{bmatrix} \right) \circ \begin{bmatrix} B \\ \sim \end{bmatrix}$$

But commutativity must be evolved: $\begin{bmatrix} M \\ \sim \end{bmatrix} \circ \begin{bmatrix} A \\ \sim \end{bmatrix} \neq \begin{bmatrix} A \\ \sim \end{bmatrix} \circ \begin{bmatrix} M \\ \sim \end{bmatrix}$

Let's notice, finally another important property. We call $[u]$ the unit matrix (with one on the main diagonal and zeros in the rest of the boxes).

Given the fuzzy matrix $\begin{bmatrix} M \\ \sim \end{bmatrix}$ we have: $\begin{bmatrix} M \\ \sim \end{bmatrix} \circ [u] = \begin{bmatrix} M \\ \sim \end{bmatrix}$

and also:

$$[u] \circ \begin{bmatrix} M \\ \sim \end{bmatrix} = \begin{bmatrix} M \\ \sim \end{bmatrix}$$

Given a reflexive fuzzy matrix such as $\begin{bmatrix} A \\ \sim \end{bmatrix}$, when we compose $\begin{bmatrix} A \\ \sim \end{bmatrix} \circ \begin{bmatrix} M \\ \sim \end{bmatrix}$ we always have: $\begin{bmatrix} M \\ \sim \end{bmatrix} \subset \begin{bmatrix} A \\ \sim \end{bmatrix} \circ \begin{bmatrix} M \\ \sim \end{bmatrix}$

because: $\left[\underset{\sim}{A}\right] \supset [u]$

The same is true if $\left[\underset{\sim}{B}\right]$ is a reflexive fuzzy matrix.

If we compose $\left[\underset{\sim}{M}\right] \circ \left[\underset{\sim}{B}\right]$ then we have: $\left[\underset{\sim}{M}\right] \subset \left[\underset{\sim}{M}\right] \circ \left[\underset{\sim}{B}\right]$

Eventually, associating the two inequalities, we can write:

$$\left[\underset{\sim}{M}\right] \subset \left[\underset{\sim}{A}\right] \circ \left[\underset{\sim}{M}\right] \circ \left[\underset{\sim}{B}\right]$$

Here is a very interesting expression for our approach, as it shows that, considering the matrices that express the incidence of the matrix $\left[\underset{\sim}{A}\right]$ elements on themselves and the ones of the matrix $\left[\underset{\sim}{B}\right]$ also on themselves, the levels of incidence resulting from the composition made, $\left[\underset{\sim}{M^*}\right]$, are greater than or equal to the ones of the direct incidence matrix $\left[\underset{\sim}{M}\right]$ So, there occurred "omissions."

If we call $\left[\underset{\sim}{M^*}\right]$ the matrix that provides, the first and second generation cumulative effects, we write: $\left[\underset{\sim}{M^*}\right] = \left[\underset{\sim}{A}\right] \circ \left[\underset{\sim}{M}\right] \circ \left[\underset{\sim}{B}\right]$

obviously: $\left[\underset{\sim}{M}\right] \subset \left[\underset{\sim}{M^*}\right]$

The matrix $\left[\underset{\sim}{M^*}\right]$ allows an excellent solution for the problem of researching incidence elements of set A that effects directly and indirectly, with a higher intensity, on itself or on the affected elements of set B.

7. Obtaining cumulative incidences

We presented below a calculation sample chose to obtain the cumulative incidences.

We find semicumulative incidences $\left[\underset{\sim}{A}\right] \circ \left[\underset{\sim}{M}\right]$ for each element (a_i, b_j) by doing:

$$\vartheta'(a_i, b_j) = \bigvee_j (\vartheta(a_i, a_h) \wedge \vartheta(a_h, b_j))$$

meaning:

$$\vartheta(a_1, b_1) = (\vartheta(a_1, a_1) \wedge \vartheta(a_1, b_1)) \vee (\vartheta(a_1, a_2) \wedge \vartheta(a_2, b_1)) \vee \ldots \vee (\vartheta(a_1, a_n) \wedge \vartheta(a_n, b_1))$$

And we do this for all $\vartheta'(a_i, b_j), i = 1, 2, \ldots, n; j = 1, 2, \ldots, m$

It is continued this way for all incidence elements represented in the rows 2, 3, ... n of the matrices and we will obtain the semiconvoluted matrix (partial calculus)

$$\underset{\sim}{[A]} \circ \underset{\sim}{[M]}$$

We emphasize that, in this first part of the convolution, the incidences (evaluations existent in every box) must be equal or greater than those of the primary incidences matrix as these need to satisfy: $\underset{\sim}{[M]} \subset \underset{\sim}{[A]} \circ \underset{\sim}{[M]}$

It can't be otherwise, because in $\underset{\sim}{[A]} \circ \underset{\sim}{[M]}$ we include beside the direct incidences, $\underset{\sim}{[M]}$, the ones that correspond to matrix $\underset{\sim}{[A]}$.

Now, we are able to calculate the max-min convolution that collects as well the incidence of each element of matrix $\underset{\sim}{[B]}$ on all the others in this matrix.

Thus, the matrix $\underset{\sim}{[A]} \circ \underset{\sim}{[M]}$ being known the convolution $\left(\underset{\sim}{[A]} \circ \underset{\sim}{[M]}\right) \circ \underset{\sim}{[B]}$ i.e. $\underset{\sim}{[A]} \circ \underset{\sim}{[M]} \circ \underset{\sim}{[B]} = \underset{\sim}{[M^*]}$ is immediate.

The result obtained in the form of a rectangular matrix $\underset{\sim}{[M^*]}$, emphasizes the total incidences of the set A on the ones of set B, not only talking into account the direct incidences of each element of A on all the elements of B, but also those that may result from the incidences of the elements in A on themselves as well as those in B, also on themselves. All these, without any error or omission.

8. An algorithm of self-induced incidences

An algorithm of self-induced incidences We won't hide the fact that our paper has a debt to pay. We are indebted to a paper first published by the professors Arnold Kaufmann and Jaime Gil-Aluja in 1988. It was translated in several languages, it served as a guide in providing solutions in macro and microeconomics and it was the foundation of several PhD theses in a number of countries. We refer to: "The theory of forgotten effects"[3].

It is a collection of technical elements starting for which there have been built, in the last 30 years, management methods, models and algorithms created to solve a variety of complex problems in which there are usually "omissions" in the causality relations, omissions that can lead to incorrect decisions. The algorithms

3 Kaufmann, A.; Gil Aluja, J., Modelos para la investigación de efectos olvidados, Ed. Milladoiro, Vigo, 1998 (ISBN: 84-404-3657-2).

created to recover these omissions are a significant example of the interest for the cited paper.

The modest contribution of the author of this paper only seeks to answer to the new challenges that have arisen in the last three decades and to enlarge the validity range of everything I did working with our late Arnold Kaufmann.

And we do it the way he taught us: "The theories must be as general and broad as possible to save as many computation procedures as come from our imagination."

Before making this contribution known in Bucharest, at ESPERA Seminar 2019, I tested this study developing some algorithms. These algorithms worked. This is why we can't help to show the structure of one of them.

I synthesized accordingly the computation procedure as to fit a session of such a rigorous and important Seminar as the one we celebrate today.

The human mind has still its own limits. It is able to create a logical and imaginative concatenation, linking the connections that stretch along and across increasingly complex networks.

This reflection may seem limited to words only. But a short example is enough to show how quickly highly complex processes and phenomena appear from a few relations between two sets of different nature.

Let's have as a reference model the study of a set of only 8 elements which have incidence on 12 elements that are affected. The direct incidence matrix is thus 8 × 12.

If we take into consideration the incidences of one incident on one affected, the necessary mental connections to consider all "mental paths" possible without forgetting any incidence would be as numerous as the arcs of the arrows graph below:

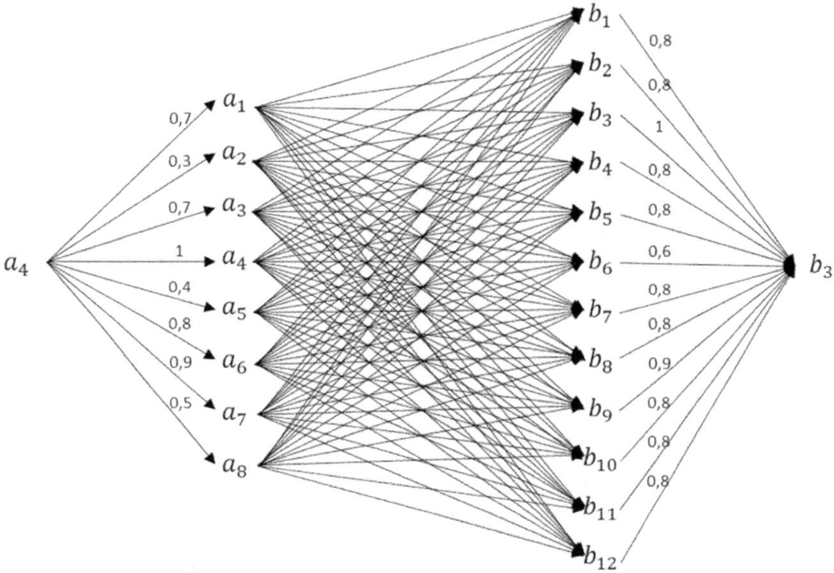

To take into account all the connections incident-affected necessary in order to know the entire network, i.e., all the incidences of the 8 incidents on the 12 affected elements we should multiply the number of the precedent graph's arcs by 8 × 12 or by 96.

For this presentation, we chose to describe the phases of the algorithm accompanied, as per case, by the values, measures and operators used in the initial paper.[4]

The algorithm we present consists of the following phases:

1.- Formation of the set elements acting as incidents:

$$A = \{a_1, a_2, \ldots, a_8\}$$

2.- Formation of the set of affected elements:

$$B = \{b_1, b_2, \ldots, b_{12}\}$$

3.- Determining the set of values $\vartheta\,(a_i, b_j)$, $i = 1, 2, \ldots, 8$; $j = 1, 2, \ldots, 12$, represented in a fuzzy incidence matrix $\left[\underset{\sim}{M}\right]$

4 Gil Aluja, J.: "La escisión de territorios. Y después ¿qué?". Conference given on the occasion of the granting of the Doctor Honoris Causa title from the University of Extremadura. Cáceres, December 4, 2017.

$[\underset{\sim}{M}] =$

$\underset{\sim}{M}$	b_1	b_2	b_3	b_4	b_5	b_6	b_7	b_8	b_9	b_{10}	b_{11}	b_{12}
a_1	0.9	0.7	0.3	0.5	0.8	0.3	0.6	0.8	0.5	0.7	0.4	0.5
a_2	0.9	0.9	0.8	0.6	0.6	0.8	0.7	0.5	0.9	0.2	0.5	0.7
a_3	1	0.8	0.7	0.8	0.8	0.7	0.8	0.5	0.4	0.3	0.5	0.3
a_4	0.8	0.5	0	0.1	0.9	0.6	0.6	0.5	0.6	0.2	0.6	0.1
a_5	0.8	1	0.3	0.6	0.6	0.2	0.8	0.9	0.7	0.9	1	0.7
a_6	0.9	0.7	0.7	0.6	0.7	0.7	0.8	0.8	0.7	0.5	0.7	0.3
a_7	0.6	0.7	0.8	0.6	0.8	0.6	0.8	0.7	0.9	0.8	0.7	0.5
a_8	0.2	0.8	0.8	0.7	0.9	0.1	0.4	0.8	0.5	0.3	0.9	0.6

This table expresses the "direct incidences" of each element in the set A of incidences on each element of set B of affectations, with values in [0,1] in the endecadial system.

4.- Determining the set of values $\vartheta\,(a_i, a_h)/i$, $h = 1, 2, \ldots, 8$ presented in a fuzzy matrix of self-induced incidences $\left[\underset{\sim}{A}\right]$

$[\underset{\sim}{A}] =$

$\underset{\sim}{A}$	a_1	a_2	a_3	a_4	a_5	a_6	a_7	a_8
a_1	1	0.2	0.8	0.9	0.5	0.7	0.6	0.3
a_2	0	1	0.6	0.6	0.3	0.4	0.6	0.2
a_3	0.5	0.6	1	1	0.7	0.9	0.8	0.4
a_4	0.7	0.3	0.7	1	0.4	0.8	0.9	0.5
a_5	0.1	0	0.5	0.1	1	0.6	0.8	0.4
a_6	0.8	0.4	0.7	0.8	0.7	1	0.8	0.7
a_7	0.3	0.4	0.8	0.9	0.5	1	1	0.4
a_8	0	0.6	0.5	0.5	0.7	0.7	0.2	1

This matrix presents the self-induced incidences of all the incidents on themselves and on other incidences of set A, thus evaluated in [0,1] through the endecadial system.

If we take one row out of the self-induced incidence matrix $\begin{bmatrix} A \\ \sim \end{bmatrix}$, for example, a_4, we can represent though the subnetwork below the incidence flux that moves through all the channels that leave from a deposit, in this case a_4.

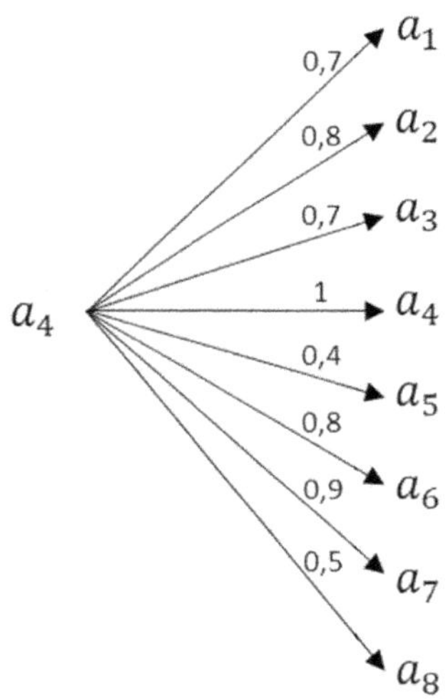

In this subnet of self-induced incidents, heavily schematized, it is noticeable that, considering only matrix $\begin{bmatrix} A \\ \sim \end{bmatrix}$ that relates the elements $a_i \ / \ i = 1, 2, \ldots, 8$ with the elements $a_h \ / \ h = 1, 2, \ldots, 8$, there are two incidences equal o greater than 0,9:

- Incidence of a_4 on itself, with value 1, obviously total incidence.
- Incidence of a_4 on a_7, with value 0.9, very strong incidence.

5.- Obtaining the set of evaluations $\vartheta\,(b_j, b_k)$/j, $k = 1, 2, \ldots, 12$ presented in a fuzzy matrix of self-induced incidences $\begin{bmatrix} B \\ \sim \end{bmatrix}$. The result of direct self-induced incidences in this phase is as follow:

$[\underset{\sim}{B}] =$

$\underset{\sim}{B}$	b_1	b_2	b_3	b_4	b_5	b_6	b_7	b_8	b_9	b_{10}	b_{11}	b_{12}
b_1	1	0.9	0.8	0.8	0.8	0.6	0.9	0.4	0.7	0	0.7	0
b_2	0.2	1	0.8	0.7	0.3	0.9	0	0.1	0.8	0.7	0.1	0.8
b_3	0.9	1	1	0.8	0.4	0.9	0.8	1	1	0.7	0.6	0.8
b_4	0.7	0.8	0.4	1	0.9	0.3	0.8	0.7	0	0.3	0.9	0.4
b_5	0.8	0.3	0.2	0.6	1	0.4	0.7	0.7	0.2	0.1	0.8	0.5
b_6	0.7	0.7	0.6	0.7	0.2	1	0.8	0.9	0.5	0.6	0.1	0
b_7	1	0.4	0.2	0.1	0.2	0.1	1	0.3	0.8	0.2	0.6	0.7
b_8	0	0.9	0.8	0.6	0.8	0.9	0.1	1	0.9	0.7	0.2	0.1
b_9	1	0.7	0.9	0.1	0.3	0.6	0.8	0.6	1	0.2	0.8	0.9
b_{10}	0.8	0.4	0.7	0.2	0.5	0.2	0.1	0.1	0.7	1	0.8	0.8
b_{11}	0.5	0.9	0.7	0.6	0	0.1	0.9	0.5	0.8	0.6	1	0
b_{12}	0.9	0	0.6	0.2	0.3	0.2	0.7	0	0.8	0.1	0.9	1

Once this phase of the algorithm completed, we have three direct incidence matrices. Starting from the operations the contain, we will do the necessary operations to find the accumulation of the flow up to the final deposit.

6.- Obtaining the semicumulated incidences of the matrix $\left[\underset{\sim}{A}\right] \circ \left[\underset{\sim}{M}\right]$, using the max-min convolution operator.

We use the expression already described:

$$\vartheta\left(a_i, b_j\right) = \underset{j}{\vee} \left(\vartheta\left(a_i, a_h\right) \wedge \vartheta\left(a_h, b_j\right)\right),$$

$$i,\ h = 1, 2, \ldots, n$$

$$j = 1, 2, \ldots, m$$

As an example, we detail this operation for a value such a $\vartheta\left(a_4, b_3\right)$
It will be:

$$\begin{aligned}
&\vartheta\left(a_4, b_3\right)\\
&= (0.7 \wedge 0.3) \vee (0.3 \wedge 0.8) \vee (0.7 \wedge 0.7) \vee (1 \wedge 0)\\
&\quad \vee (0.4 \wedge 0.3) \vee (0.8 \wedge 0.7) \vee (0.9 \wedge 0.8) \vee (0.5 \wedge 0.8)\\
&= 0.3 \vee 0.3 \vee 0.7 \vee 0 \vee 0.3 \vee 0.7 \vee 0.8 \vee 0.5 = 0.8
\end{aligned}$$

And this will be done for all $i = 1, 2, \ldots, n;\ j = 1, 2, \ldots, m$

7.- Obtaining the semiconvoluted matrix $\left[\underset{\sim}{A}\right] \circ \left[\underset{\sim}{M}\right]$

It is enough to sum up all the values found in this way to obtain the matrix $\left[\underset{\sim}{A}\right] \circ \left[\underset{\sim}{M}\right]$.

Thus, we have:

$[\underset{\sim}{A}] \circ [\underset{\sim}{M}] =$

$\underset{\sim}{A} \circ \underset{\sim}{M}$	b_1	b_2	b_3	b_4	b_5	b_6	b_7	b_8	b_9	b_{10}	b_{11}	b_{12}
a_1	0.9	0.8	0.7	0.8	0.9	0.7	0.8	0.8	0.7	0.7	0.7	0.5
a_2	0.9	0.9	0.8	0.6	0.6	0.8	0.7	0.6	0.9	0.6	0.6	0.7
a_3	1	0.8	0.8	0.8	0.9	0.7	0.8	0.8	0.8	0.8	0.7	0.7
a_4	0.8	0.7	0.8	0.7	0.9	0.7	0.8	0.8	0.9	0.8	0.7	0.5
a_5	0.8	1	0.8	0.6	0.8	0.6	0.8	0.9	0.8	0.9	1	0.7
a_6	0.9	0.7	0.8	0.7	0.8	0.7	0.8	0.8	0.8	0.8	0.7	0.7
a_7	0.9	0.8	0.8	0.8	0.9	0.7	0.8	0.8	0.9	0.8	0.7	0.5
a_8	0.7	0.8	0.8	0.7	0.9	0.7	0.7	0.8	0.7	0.7	0.9	0.7

In next subnet, we will present as incidence elements of set A, only those whose evaluations are equal or greater than 0.9 (a_4 y a_7) as well as the degree or the flow of their incidence on the 12 **affected elements**.

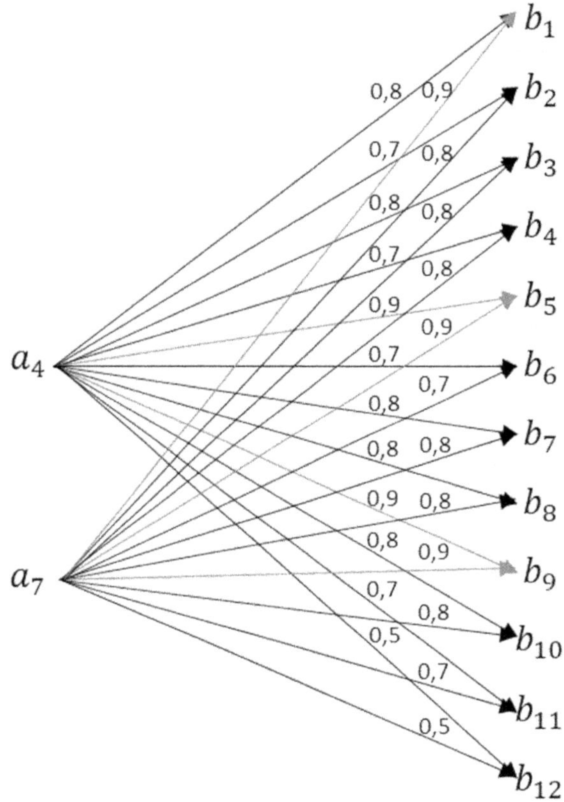

8.- Obtaining total incidences

We use the expression:

$$\vartheta^* (a_i, b_j) = \bigwedge_j (\vartheta (a_i, b_j) \wedge \vartheta (b_j, b_k)),$$

$$i = 1, 2, \ldots, n$$

$$b_j, b_k = 1, 2, \ldots, m$$

As a sample, we continue to perform the operation to find $\vartheta^* (a_4, b_3)$. It is the following:

$$\begin{aligned}\vartheta^* (a_4, b_3) &= (0.8 \wedge 0.8) \vee (0.7 \wedge 0.8) \vee (0.8 \wedge 1) \vee (0.7 \wedge 0.4)\\ &\quad \vee (0.9 \wedge 0.2) \vee (0.7 \wedge 0.6) \vee (0.8 \wedge 0.2) \vee (0.8 \wedge 0.8)\\ &\quad \vee (0.9 \wedge 0.9) \vee (0.8 \wedge 0.7) \vee (0.7 \wedge 0.7) \vee (0.5 \wedge 0.6)\\ &= 0.8 \vee 0.7 \vee 0.8 \vee 0.4 \vee 0.2 \vee 0.6 \vee 0.2 \vee 0.8 \vee 0.9\\ &\quad \vee 0.7 \vee 0.7 \vee 0.5 = 0.9\end{aligned}$$

This computation sample to obtain the overall incidence relation must, obviously, be repeated for all the relations that connect the semiconvolution $\left[\underset{\sim}{A}\right] \circ \left[\underset{\sim}{M}\right]$ with the self-induced elements of set B, i.e. $\left[\underset{\sim}{B}\right]$.

In next subnet, also very simplified, we show the incidences of the affected elements b_1, b_5, b_{19} which now act as incidents on all the elements of set B.It is the second self-induction.

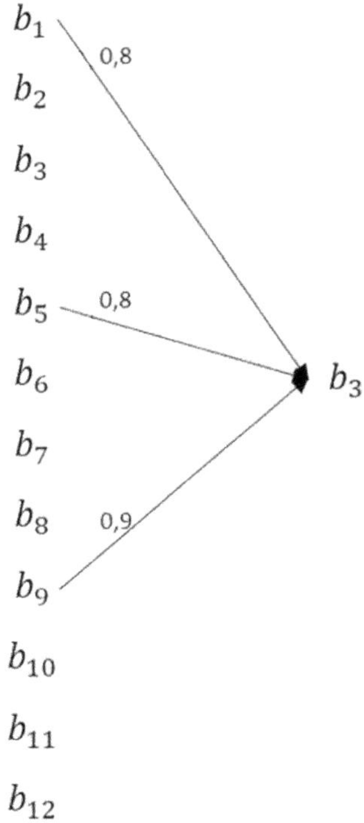

9.- Obtaining the convoluted matrix $\left[\underset{\sim}{M^*}\right]$

The results obtained in the previous phase are reunited in a matrix $\left[\underset{\sim}{M^*}\right]$ using the max-min convolution operator. We find:

$\underset{\sim}{A} \circ \underset{\sim}{M}$	b_1	b_2	b_3	b_4	b_5	b_6	b_7	b_8	b_9	b_{10}	b_{11}	b_{12}
a_1	0.9	0.8	0.7	0.8	0.9	0.7	0.8	0.8	0.7	0.7	0.7	0.5
a_2	0.9	0.9	0.8	0.6	0.6	0.8	0.7	0.6	0.9	0.6	0.6	0.7
a_3	1	0.8	0.8	0.8	0.9	0.7	0.8	0.8	0.8	0.8	0.7	0.7
a_4	0.8	0.7	0.8	0.7	0.9	0.7	0.8	0.8	0.9	0.8	0.7	0.5
a_5	0.8	1	0.8	0.6	0.8	0.6	0.8	0.9	0.8	0.9	1	0.7
a_6	0.9	0.7	0.8	0.7	0.8	0.7	0.8	0.8	0.8	0.8	0.7	0.7
a_7	0.9	0.8	0.8	0.8	0.9	0.7	0.8	0.8	0.9	0.8	0.7	0.5
a_8	0.7	0.8	0.8	0.7	0.9	0.7	0.7	0.8	0.7	0.7	0.9	0.7

$\circ$

$\underset{\sim}{B}$	b_1	b_2	b_3	b_4	b_5	b_6	b_7	b_8	b_9	b_{10}	b_{11}	b_{12}
b_1	1	0.9	0.8	0.8	0.8	0.6	0.9	0.4	0.7	0	0.7	0
b_2	0.2	1	0.8	0.7	0.3	0.9	0	0.1	0.8	0.7	0.1	0.8
b_3	0.9	1	1	0.8	0.4	0.9	0.8	1	1	0.7	0.6	0.8
b_4	0.7	0.8	0.4	1	0.9	0.3	0.8	0.7	0	0.3	0.9	0.4
b_5	0.8	0.3	0.2	0.6	1	0.4	0.7	0.7	0.2	0.1	0.8	0.5
b_6	0.7	0.7	0.6	0.7	0.2	1	0.8	0.9	0.5	0.6	0.1	0
b_7	1	0.4	0.2	0.1	0.2	0.1	1	0.3	0.8	0.2	0.6	0.7
b_8	0	0.9	0.8	0.6	0.8	0.9	0.1	1	0.9	0.7	0.2	0.1
b_9	1	0.7	0.9	0.1	0.3	0.6	0.8	0.6	1	0.2	0.8	0.9
b_{10}	0.8	0.4	0.7	0.2	0.5	0.2	0.1	0.1	0.7	1	0.8	0.8
b_{11}	0.5	0.9	0.7	0.6	0	0.1	0.9	0.5	0.8	0.6	1	0
b_{12}	0.9	0	0.6	0.2	0.3	0.2	0.7	0	0.8	0.1	0.9	1

$[\underset{\sim}{A}] \circ [\underset{\sim}{M}] \circ [\underset{\sim}{B}] =$

$\underset{\sim}{A} \circ \underset{\sim}{M} \circ \underset{\sim}{B}$	b_1	b_2	b_3	b_4	b_5	b_6	b_7	b_8	b_9	b_{10}	b_{11}	b_{12}
a_1	0.9	0.9	0.8	0.8	0.9	0.8	0.9	0.8	0.8	0.7	0.8	0.8
a_2	0.9	0.9	0.9	0.8	0.8	0.9	0.9	0.8	0.9	0.7	0.8	0.9
a_3	1	0.9	0.8	0.8	0.9	0.9	0.9	0.8	0.8	0.8	0.8	0.8
a_4	0.9	0.8	0.9	0.8	0.9	0.8	0.8	0.8	0.9	0.8	0.8	0.9
a_5	0.8	1	0.8	0.8	0.8	0.9	0.9	0.9	0.9	0.9	1	0.8
a_6	0.9	0.9	0.8	0.8	0.8	0.8	0.9	0.8	0.8	0.8	0.8	0.8
a_7	0.9	0.9	0.9	0.8	0.9	0.8	0.9	0.8	0.9	0.8	0.8	0.9
a_8	0.8	0.9	0.8	0.8	0.9	0.8	0.9	0.8	0.8	0.7	0.9	0.8

Next arrows subnet, which reunites the previous three, shows some paths, as well as the best of all:

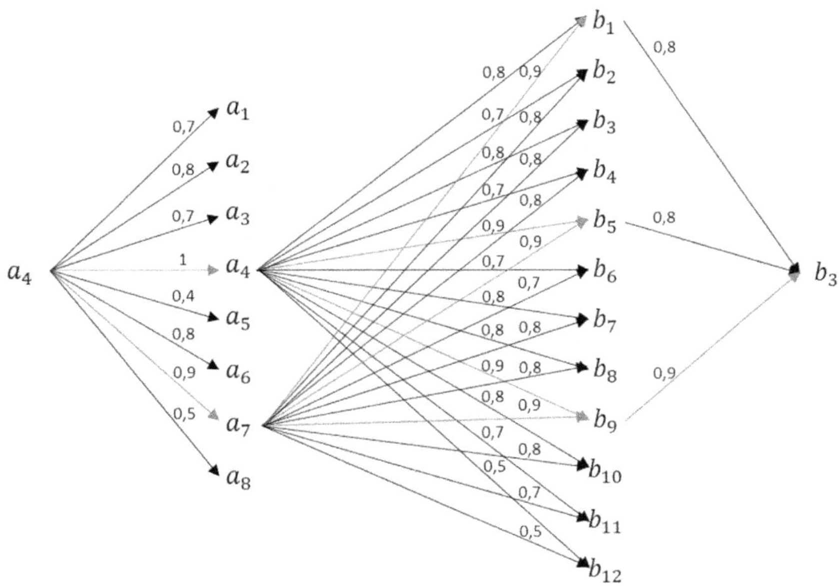

As our readers may have noticed, the above arrows net contains only the arcs that we considered the most interesting for a decision.

They also may have noticed that in the origin of the network we highlighted in red the incidence arcs of $\underset{\sim}{[A]}$ which start from a_4 and have an incidence degree o level equal or greater than 0.9, $\alpha \geq 0.9$.

A quick look at the matrix $\underset{\sim}{[A]} \circ \underset{\sim}{[M]} \circ \underset{\sim}{[B]}$ is enough to confirm the high level of overall incidence of each element of the set incidents ***A*** on each element of the affected set ***B***. All of them are included in the confidence interval $[0.7, 1]$ and mostly in $[0.8, 0.9]$. This suggest, among other reasons of satisfaction, the good choice of set A and set B.

There can be notice, as well, in some incidences an important difference between the initial value contained in the fuzzy matrix $\underset{\sim}{[M]}$ and the one in the cumulated incidences matrix $\underset{\sim}{[A]} \circ \underset{\sim}{[M]} \circ \underset{\sim}{[B]}$ that we designated in $\underset{\sim}{[M^*]}$.

There were some significant omissions.

Acknowledging these omissions and the degree or level of each "omissions" can be important information for management.[5] Thus, for the incidence of a_4 on b_3 the incidence that the experts had directly given that it was zero, "without incidence," but, on the contrary, the incidence flow through other channels of the network became 0.9 "very strong incidence."

9. Looking to the future with hope

In the area of social science research and especially in economics, we inherited from previous generations the use of mechanistic approaches to find solutions to our problems. "The law of excluded middle" and its binary overflows the documents that could have been of extraordinary value if they had been treated differently.

All reality, whether physical or mental, manifests itself through a grade or level. Everyone, even the most radical or populist, has it, even if they are located at the extremes of the interval within which the degree or level moves. Multivalent logics also take into account these particular cases.

This transition from binarity to multivalence, of great scope, forces far-reaching methodological changes that go from the definition of new concepts and operators to the elaboration of the techniques that will be, we are sure of this, more and more adjustable to the New World that awaits us.

5 This was the objective of the work contained in the aforementioned work by Kaufmann, A. and Gil Aluja, J.: "Modelos para la investigación de efectos olvidados" Ed. Milladoiro. Vigo, 1998. (ISBN: 84-404-3657-2)

We increasingly use new theories in our documents such as "Fuzzy set theory," "Theory of forgotten effects" and, as concepts, those already known as incidence and evaluation, among others. The use of algorithms is once again in force as a result of the digital revolution, of "big data" and "transhumanism."

As far as we are concerned, with the previous definition, the enumeration and the description of the operators that are likely to be used, we try to present the phases of an algorithm in which, given a set of incident elements, we search for the degree or level that it must be assigned to each of the elements of the affected set. And we did this using non-numerical mathematics to address uncertainty.[6]

This is an abridged presentation, adapted, at least in our opinion, for a contribution to a collective volume.

However, we do not give up one of the instructions of our late teacher Arnold Kaufmann: "In a changing world, research must be flexible and adjustable." We try to keep it that way.

For many years, the problems caused by the transhumanist movement have infiltrated the cracks in our research. At first it seemed that the imagination was overflowing, exceeding the limits of our possible future realities, only to enter the realm of fiction.

But, as the media was facilitating information about the process of digitization on the one hand, and about the greater data storing and reproducing possibilities on the other hand, our interest grew in the direction of recovering the old algorithms we had learned from Kaufmann and of getting to back to life our illusions to build others, far from the traditional mechanical line, suited to be placed on our desired humanist path.

In this respect, we can cite, among the most recent ones, the "Algorithm of Portugal"[7] which aims to obtain a better cohesion of the countries and regions of the Iberian Peninsula and the "Algorithm for distribution of migrants,"[8] which, in its general version, tries to make compatible the possibilities and aspirations of the migrants with the wishes and needs of the enterprises and institutions that receive them. A version of this paper was the solving of the huge problem of MENAS (unaccompanied under aged) for the best distribution of the migrant under aged in the receiving families.

---

6 Gil Aluja, J.: "Elements for a Theory of Decision in Uncertainty" Kluwer Academic Publishers. Dordrecht, Boston, London 1999. (ISBN: 0-7923-5987-9)

7 Gil Aluja, J.: "Papel de la memoria en la armonía entre territorios: el Algoritmo de Portugal" in the book "Complejidad económica: una península Ibérica más unida para una Europa más fuerte" Ed. RACEF, Barcelona 2019, pages 365–398. (ISBN: 978-84-09-12599-9)

8 Gil Aluja, J.: "Un ensayo para solución al problema migratorio a través de la Inteligencia Artificial" in the book "Migraciones". Ed. RACEF Barcelona 2020, pages 67–97. (ISBN: 978-84-09-18254-1)

In all these papers there weren't missing the interest and reference, voiced or silent, to guess how the future life of people in society will be like, thus the Spanish Royal Academic of Economic and Financial Sciences, which I chair, organized an international event on November 15 and 16, 2018, with the theme: "The challenges of the new super-complex society: humanism, transhumanism, dataism and other isms."

At this meeting,[9] the scientists reunited presented their opinions regarding the questions that were raised, although a sense of longevity could be felt in the air as if the answers targeted the next generations only. The same thing happened in the conference held on the conclusion of this important event, the last words of which I can't help myself not to hereby reproduce:[10]

> "Let us in the end come back to the possible common action of transhumanism and dataism, to the unwanted use of implants and other cybernetic changes in the human brain on the one hand, and to the accumulation of personal information in the central computer on the other hand."

Will we be able to affect the cyberbiologic people by following the commands of a central computer?

What will be left of what we are if we erase the differences between the organic life and the mechanical one?

Allow me to subject to your reflection a possible answer: we are going to be our memories.

They are what makes a person unique, as our memory is unique… for now.

But what is memory if not the set of stored information, i.e., the set of data which give us identity?

And, what seemed to be the dream of a visionary or a science fiction movie, is already in our lives, even if we want it or not, one year later.

There is no doubt that we are knocking at the doors of the deepest and the quickest changes that we have ever had in the history of our societies.

The position of our country in the concert of the future world depends now on the decisions made. An appropriate algorithm could be a gateway to a shortcut. But this is only the tip of an immense iceberg.

And, to conclude, let us remember that the European Union was built in its time as a space of freedom and solidarity. And it was more or less faithful to these principles, when events tested it.

9 Gil Aluja, J.: "Las revoluciones tecnológicas frente al mandato biológico" in the book "Desafíos de la nueva sociedad sobrecompleja: humanismo, transhumanismo, dataismo y otros ismos", Ed. RACEF. Barcelona 2019, pages 20–21. (ISBN: 978-84-09-08674-0)

10 Gil Aluja, J.: "En el horizonte del poshumanismo" in the book "Desafíos de la nueva sociedad sobrecompleja: humanismo, transhumanismo, dataismo y otros ismos", Ed, RACEF. Barcelona 2019, pages 238–239. (ISBN: 978-84-09-08674-0)

It is the only way we can understand that such a heterogeneous economic conglomerate, with its natural frictions and imperfections, allowed the general progress, shared in a certain sense.

The different nations that constitute it got specialized in creating goods and services that best suit their personal structures and natural resources.

Yet, this specialization necessitated an indispensable condition: a great freedom of trade within the Union. In other words, the goods, and services of one country are transferred to one or many other countries, that, in exchange, provide what they produce. "The game" worked due to solidarity and shared progress.

Where is the weak link able to destroy the structure of the European Union, so strong until now?

In our opinion, the danger comes from the weakening of solidarity. And there is no greater danger than solidarity turned into selfishness.

We are convinced that the solidarity we claim at a general level is to the same extent indispensable to our field of economic research; the increasing complexity of the social systems always require the deepening of knowledge which go beyond the field of individual specialization.

Therefore, the increasing interest for meetings such as ESPERA. The unity of solidarity is one reason among many, because it takes real effort to maintain knowledge exchange. And this is what the Royal Academy of Economic and Financial Sciences will do in the future as well.

References

Gil Aluja, J.: "Elements for a Theory of Decision in Uncertainty" Kluwer Academic Publishers. Dordrecht, Boston, Londres, 1999. (ISBN: 0-7923-5987-9).

Gil Aluja, J.: "En el horizonte del poshumanismo" in the book "Desafíos de la nueva sociedad sobrecompleja: humanismo, transhumanismo, dataismo y otros ismos", Ed., RACEF. Barcelona 2019, pages 238–239 (ISBN: 978-84-09-08674-0).

Gil Aluja, J.: "La escisión de territorios. Y después ¿qué?" Conference given on the occasion of the granting of the Doctor Honoris Causa title from the University of Extremadura. Cáceres, December 4, 2017.

Gil Aluja, J.: "Las revoluciones tecnológicas frente al mandato biológico" in the book "Desafíos de la nueva sociedad sobrecompleja: humanismo, transhumanismo, dataismo y otros ismos", Ed, RACEF. Barcelona 2019, pages 20–21 (ISBN: 978-84-09-08674-0).

Gil Aluja, J.: "Papel de la memoria en la armonía entre territorios: el Algoritmo de Portugal" in the book "Complejidad económica: una península Ibérica más unida para una Europa más fuerte " Ed. RACEF, Barcelona 2019, pages 365–398 (ISBN: 978-84-09-12599-9).

Gil Aluja, J.: "Un ensayo para solución al problema migratorio a través de la Inteligencia Artificial" in the book "Migraciones". Ed. RACEF Barcelona 2020, pages 67–97 (ISBN: 978-84-09-18254-1).

Kaufmann, A. y Gil Aluja, J.: "Grafos neuronales para la economía y la gestión de empresas". Ed. Pirámide. Madrid 1995, 2ª Ed. (ISBN: 84-368-0917-3).

Kaufmann, A. y Gil Aluja, J.: "Modelos para la investigación de efectos olvidados". Ed. Milladoiro, Vigo 1998. (ISBN: 84-404-3657-2).

Zadeh, Lofti A.: "Fuzzy Sets" Information and Control 8, (3), 1965, pages 338–353.

Erna Hennicot-Schoepges

Europe and culture, our promise for the future

Distinguished Audience,

In 1936 Pierre Werner (then aged 22 a student in Paris at the Faculty of Law and Political Science) asked R. Schuman, who was then Member of Parliament for the Moselle in the French Parliament, to make a speech to the association of Luxembourgish students. In this speech Schuman denounces two major dangers. "The first is the tendency of each country to fall back on itself, the second being the hesitations of weak governments, not having the strength to avoid the interference of powerful interest groups in the affairs of the State." (Pierre Werner, 1986)

Sometimes reminding what has been said helps us identifying weaknesses in current situations. Schuman's answer has to be looked at in the French historical context before the Second World War. Schuman, who was born in Luxembourg and had studied there before going to university in Germany, was "a border man" he lived in Scy-Chazelles, near Metz, not far from Germany and the Grand Duchy.

Visionary before the Second World War, he has later on indicated the road to take. He agreed with Jean Monnet that it was better to start after the Second World War by the common market for coal and steel, preventing unilateral rearmament in Germany.

The integration of Germany into the new construction, was announced by Schuman in his famous speech of the 9th of May 1950. The concern for a common defense policy, a preoccupation addressed in a first initiative in 1952, the Treaty of Paris, signed by the governments of the six founding members. After the rejection by the French National Assembly of the European Defense Community, the London Conference decided in 1954 the creation of the Western European Union with a Parliamentary Consultative Assembly, an Arms Control Agency and a Standing Armaments Committee. This Union, which initially also had to control the production of weapons in its member countries, was dissolved in 2011 (CVCE.eu).

With the signature of the Treaty of Rome in 1957 by the six founding member countries, and the CECA treaty, signed in 1951, the vision of Robert Schuman and Jean Monnet has still not been realized. Schuman had declared: "Europe will be born of this, a Europe solidly united and constructed around a strong framework" as drafted in his own preliminary remarks, but not in the final declaration of the Monnet team. In addition to the Community of Coal and Steel, the Common Market and Euratom had been added. But above all beyond the institutions and responding to a deep desire of the people, the European idea, the spirit of common solidarity took root. "This idea of Europe will reveal to all the common bases of our civilization and will gradually create a bond similar to that of which the homeland was forged. It will be the force against which all obstacles will be broken." (Robert Schuman Foundation, 1957)

Today we are far from this vision. Europe in the midst of globalization is dominated by so many challenges that have resulted from the market. "The strength of our common civilization" invoked by Robert Schuman, should give new energy for the future. And the fact that he spoke of civilization is revealing: Schuman had foreseen that the vision should be broad and encompass all aspects of human activity. This has been defined by UNESCO in 1982 under the term "Culture." The definition says: "Culture, in its broadest sense, is considered as the set of distinctive, spiritual, material, intellectual and emotional features of society or a social group and that it encompasses, in addition to arts and literature, lifestyles, the fundamental rights of the human being, value systems, traditions and beliefs."

This definition has been described as "impracticable" or even as "the product of romantic dreamers." However, the broader concept has been taken up in international codes, such as "normative instruments on cultural diversity." (Traugott Schoefthaler, 2008)

Jean Monnet, the architect of the construction of the future European Union, is supposed to have said: "if it were to start again I would start with culture." But this was indeed not pronounced by Monnet himself, but by Helen Ahrweiler, rector of the Academy of Paris. She testified in her letter, sent to the Journal Le Monde in June 1998, that she had pronounced it in her speech on the occasion of the meeting of the General Assembly of European students by putting it into the mouth of Jean Monnet as following: "if I had to do it again I would start with culture, could have exclaimed Jean Monnet." The report in the newspaper failed to mention the correct pronunciation and attributed to Jean Monnet the expression, that has since kept its place in European history. (Robert Grégoire, 2000)

This for the small talk. As for the difficulty of transgressing the sensitive borders of cultural diversity, it is quite impossible to deal with the mechanisms of European jurisdiction, so neither directives, nor binding rules or regulations, only financial support and common initiatives, recommendations and a multitude of organizations that are fruitful, but reserved to an elite are dealing with culture. By naming Lighthouse Years, such as the Year of Intercultural Dialogue 2008, which could not be extended to interreligious dialogue, given the texts of the treaties, the aim is to attract the attention of a larger public. The European Heritage Year, the Cultural Capital are some examples of success, as well as the mobility of students, thanks to the Erasmus project. However, the results from all the resolutions adopted during especially the Year of Intercultural Dialogue remained a dead letter.

The era of globalization that we are living today shows us that cultural and religious diversity is often at the root of conflicts, also in Europe.

Many publications have deepened the subject on "A Europe of Culture, its History and its issues" which is the title of the book by Anne-Marie Autissier. The author of the preface, of Syrian origin, Chérif Khaznadar summarizes so well the problem that arises when he writes: "Europe and culture are they condemned to remain an antagonistic couple, bound by misunderstandings and expectations, disappointed on both sides?" (Anne-Marie Autissier, 2005)

A petition has just been launched with a call to the new President of the Commission: Bring Culture back Ms. President. The European Commission has somehow drowned the child in the bath, when in 2010 education, culture, multilingualism sports and youth were merged. The "systems of values, traditions and beliefs" are not addressed. Moreover, from the beginning, in the first treaties especially beliefs seemed to be problematic.

Thus, already in the drafting of the preamble to the 1957 Treaty of Rome, the controversy was launched, between secularism and spirituality, in other words between the defenders of the different religious communities and the followers of secularism.

I do not want to mix culture with religion, and Robert Schuman, a practicing and convinced Catholic, avoided the trap when he spoke of civilization.

The Charter of Fundamental Rights, adopted on 7 December 2000 in Nice, revives the debate of values. A statement by the Bishops' Commission asks to mention God in the Charter, but France refuses to recognize the religious heritage of Europe in the preamble and the compromise was to mention "the spiritual heritage." In 2004, during the debate on the adoption of the draft Constitution, the new Speaker of Parliament Josef Borrel declares on this subject: "Let God be apart from all that." The ratification of this text had to be approved by all member states and was finally rejected by France and the Netherlands. (Gérard Bossuat, 2019) Finally, the reform of the institutions and more flexible decision-making was taken up in the Lisbon Treaty in 2007.[1] (All of Europe, 2018)

Sometimes reality exceeds the academic debates concerning cultural policy. While the principle of freedom of expression seemed to have been achieved, a Danish newspaper reopens the debate in February 2006: a caricature of the Prophet provoked a crisis in public opinion, opposing freedom of expression to the violation of religious sensibilities. In the European Parliament a deputy noted during the debate, that it is also the responsibility of governments not to ignore religious sensitivities. The European Commission sent the following message to the public and the Arab world: "Freedom of opinion and expression and freedom of the press are among the top priorities of our European values." (Traugott Schoefthaler, 2008)

Since these facts more than a decade has changed the game with digitalization and the space of freedom of online communication. The European Union

---

1 All of Europe: The legal personality, the simplification of the decision-making process, the permanent presidency of the Council, the representation of the common foreign policy, the strengthening of national parliaments, the Central Bank becomes an institution, the citizens' initiative, finally the Charter of Fundamental Rights, the fight against climate change. In addition, the Lisbon Treaty of the Union provides for an exit clause.

has framed this space by the Data Protection Directive, which does not facilitate communication, but should protect us from suspicious intruders.

The battle of ideas has certainly also been a power struggle. Our democratic systems have transferred it to the field of expression and assertion of the right to be different. Among the 27 member countries, no dictatorship, the democratic election of the governors is compulsory Is there a calm future ahead? The worry of what is happening elsewhere, in the globalized world, outside the muffled backgrounds of political forums is concerning the EU as well. The challenge of the future will be to find ways to unite people by cultivating minds. The lack of cultural education, of language learning, religious illiteracy in the service of secularism, (Traugott Schoefthaler, 2008) are provoking intellectual impoverishment. Let`s take a look at the evolution of culture at Member State level: the means available for culture are around 1 to 1.5 % of GDP. Hungary and Estonia spend more than 2 % 5 countries (Bulgaria Croatia Latvia Finland and Denmark) between 1.5 and 2 %. But the figures are sometimes misleading as spending for culture in the broad sense as defined above, are not expenditures, but "investments" in future generations.

The digital revolution is ahead. Some countries have already adopted the computer in the classroom, learning to write is done on the tablet. It will be necessary to organize a better understanding between generations and between nations. If the computer offers simultaneous translation, is there no need to learn foreign languages? But it is scientifically proven that early multilingualism is beneficial for the brain development and comprehensiveness. The European Schools innovated by accepting multilingualism in their system and they also kept religious education of all faiths in school. But the system has remained elitist, admitting only the children of EU officials or ambassadors. A resolution of the European Parliament following the Year of Intercultural Dialogue, to generalize this education system in the member countries has had low effect.

The European Commission`s White Paper on Education in 1997 set out among other objectives the learning of 3 Community languages in each country. (at the time 12 member countries) Learning the language of the neighbor was another goal, but considering the sensitivities of linguistic regions in some countries, this may not happen so easily.

In conclusion, the decisions taken at the level of the Member Countries reflect national and regional sensitivities, and send criticisms back to Brussels.

The history of culture is universal. The mobility of artists was, and still is, remarkable.

Mozart in Prague, Handel in London, Ionesco in Paris, and so on, their experience was a reciprocal enrichment, reflected in their works. Supported by Kings and Aristocracy, the arts were synonymous with nobility and wealth, but without commercial interests, sometimes back thinking of today's financiers. The budget of the European Commission was unable to finance the Youth Orchestra, founded in 1976, and recruiting musicians in the member countries. The best ambassador of the European Union, as said the President of the Commission Jean Claude

Juncker, finally convinced the Council in 2018 to grant funding through the Creative Europe Program. The budget adopted for the period 2021 to 2027 provides for 1.85 billion euros for the financing of this Program. (EC) This commendable effort gives hope that culture, as defined by UNESCO, will be our guarantee of the future.

References

Anne-Marie Autissier, Europe of Culture International of the Imaginary no. 19, Babel House of Cultures of the World publication, 2005.

Gérard Bossuat, History of a Controversy: The Reference to Spiritual Legacies in the European Constitution Persee, Portal Digital Library: Materials for the History of Our Time, accesed 2019.

Pierre Werner, Robert Schuman`s Political Thought and the May 9, 1950 Statement, Preface by Pierre Werner in the catalog of the exhibition The roots and the work of a great European Robert Schuman, Court Printer Victor Buck Luxembourg, 1986.

Political Writings, Robert Schuman Foundation Editions Nagel SA 24, avenue de l'Aurore Ch-1225 Chêne-Bourg, 1957.

Robert Grégoire, Towards a Europe of Culture, L` Harmattan, Paris, edition 5–7, 2000.

Traugott Schoefthaler, The European Cultural Space: Secularism and Religious Cultures, Editions Saint-Paul, 2008.

Further Reading

All of Europe, reference site on European issues, 02/14/2018.

European Commission (EC) website.

The creation of the Western European Union Resources (92), https://www.cvce.eu/en/education/unit-content/-/unit/803b2430-7d1c-4e7b-9101-47415702fc8e/6d9db05c-1e8c-487a-a6bc-ff25cf1681e0.

Jean-Jacques Askenasy

Homo economicus: the economic system of the brain

Abstract All the acts performed by a human being have received the approval of the brain decision-making prefrontal center, except those diagnosed by specialists as automatic acts or nonintentional acts. Among the systems involved in the decision-making process the economic system has an important role. All the acts elaborated by the decision-making prefrontal area are motivated and include the reward expectation. The infrastructure of the economic system consists in a triangle of three nuclei, (1) the ventral tegmentum area (VTA), (2) nucleus accumbens (NAcc) and (3) Hippocampus. This economic triangle evaluates permanently the need and the risk to achieve something as well as the reward to be expected. The economic evaluation of the act is continuously transmitted to the decision-making prefrontal center, offering impulses in favor or against the decision to act. The economic triangle elaborates feelings of pleasure, amusement, joy, aversion or suffering as well as retrieval from long-term memory of previous experiences.

Keywords: human brain; economic system; biodiversity; social reasons; biochemical examinations of involved neurotransmitters

Most Distinguished Audience,

Human life has a clear-cut economic dimension equal in importance to its social dimension. This economic dimension ensures the availability of resources for living and their administration. In this dimension, humans have developed a science to study the best methods of producing, obtaining and administering wealth.

From the beginning of the 3rd millennium, humanity is facing a new historical period in which the economy is increasingly becoming a major health problem. The causes of this problem can be divided in two types:

Type 1 – Environmental reasons including reductions in the biodiversity of animal and vegetable species, deforestation, pollution, disappearance of water resources, climate changes, and enlargement of ozone hole (Fig. 1)

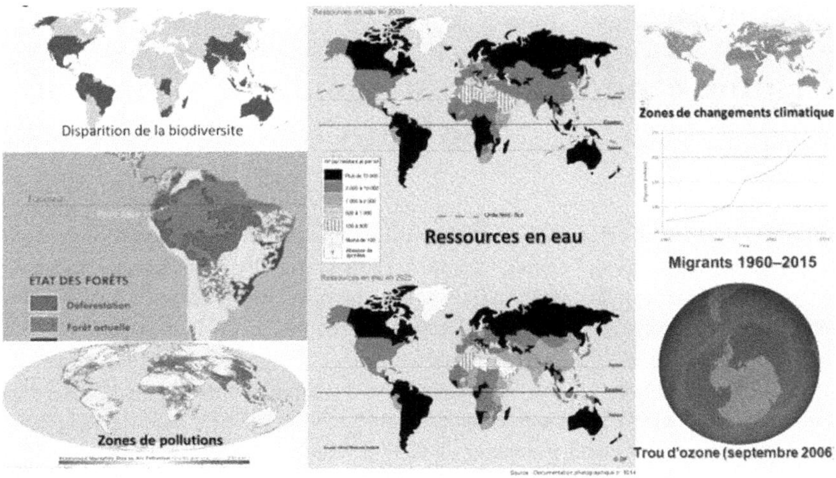

Fig. 1: Resource utilization in 2000 and 2025 (est.)
Source: Futura Planète.

Type 2 – Social reasons: Capitalist democracies in which 40 % of the world's wealth is controlled by 1 % of its population; economies divided into public and private segments; subsidized air, water, food and energy sources; and pandemics that restrict productivity. The last two generations display an obsession for making money. This social situation increases conflicts between states or group of states, such as conflicts with Iran, China, North Korea, and increases the danger of an atomic war (Fig. 2).

Fig. 2: Nuclear Weapons controlled by Russia and USA
Source: http://www.businessinsider.com/category/nuclear-weapons.rss.

To summarize the history of neuro-economic science, we must mention these 3 steps.

(1) Daniel Bernoulli's essay appeared in 1738. Mathematicians, physicists, and economists consider it to be the source of understanding the role economic risk. It described the relation between evolution and risk in the light of reproductive lifespan, dormancy and diapause, sexual versus asexual reproduction, and population dynamics (Stearns, Bernoulli, 2000).
(2) In 1944, the Theory of Games and Economic Behavior, by mathematician John von Neumann and economist Oskar Morgenstern, provided the classic work on which game theory is based (von Neumann, 1944).
(3) Around the year 2005, economists began examining the black box of the brain. Behavior studies, brain imaging, and neural activity invaded the interaction between supply and demand, risk, decision making, and game theory. This was the beginning of neuro-economics (Camerer, 2005).

Neuro-economics is a hegemonic paradigm of modern society. The brain has also to adapt itself to the economic environment in which it is involved.

The human brain is a monstrous mega-complex organ and nature's highest level of creativity. The brain has a large number of built-in systems that participate in decision making in the prefrontal cortex in order to achieve its needs. The brain's built-in economic system uses financial tools in its synthesis and analysis of the risks and rewards associated with its life resources.

Together with the economical system, decision making acts involve many other systems including the cognitive, rational-logic, affective, and retrieval of previous experience systems. The economic data and other data flow towards the decision-making center until the process ends by acting (or deciding to do nothing, which is also an action). Modern neuroscience research indicates that new data impacts the economic system in the decision-making process.

The omnipresent economic system activity of the brain is sometimes dominant, sometimes minimal. What makes a human being humane is the balance between the economic and moral domains. An overly economic brain can become immoral and an overly moral brain can become an economic failure.

The economic system of a human brain can be tested according to the degree of pleasure & joy or sadness & aversion associated with the test. There are two modes of investigation:

(1) Investigations such as: functional Magnetic Resonance Imaging (fMRI) and Positron Emission Tomography (PET) which measure changes in blood flow to reveal the activity of thousands of neurons over a period of seconds; and the registration of brain electrical waves by Magneto-ElectroEncephaloGraphy (MEEG); or
(2) qualitative and quantitative biochemical examinations of involved neurotransmitters.

The brain's economic system can be treated as a motivation reward system. The measurement of risk when gambling, implies evaluating also factors such as fear and greed, which are involved in the economic neural system.

In 1950, psychologists James Olds & Peter Milner implanted electrodes in the brains of rats and enabled them to press a lever to receive a mild burst of electrical stimulation. The rats would press the lever up to 2000 times per hour to receive a tiny jolt of current through electrodes implanted in areas around the nucleus accumbens. The pleasure center of the brain was discovered (Olds, Milner, 1954).

Brain-imaging experiments by Princeton University psychologist Samuel M. McClure and his colleagues in 2004 discovered that when there is emotional involvement, decisions about monetary rewards are heavily influenced by the length of time until the reward is received (immediate vs. delayed). In contrast, decisions that involve abstract reasoning without emotional involvement do not present this disassociation whether the rewards are immediate or delayed (McClure et al., 2004).

The young field of neuroeconomics converges around behavioral modifications between Homo sapiens and Homo economicus. In this historical moment characterized by economic crises, neuro-economics offers new answers to the question: Why do humans value the present at the expense of the future? Should the brain be conceptualized as a unified decision-making apparatus, with many built-in systems involved, and with an impetuous limbic system at perpetual odds deliberated to the prefrontal cortex? Daniel Kahneman, won the 2002 Nobel Prize in economics, for describing the economic infrastructure of the brain (Kahnemanet et al., 2011).

The economic infrastructure circuit starts at the Ventral Tegmentum Area (VTA). From there the medial forebrain bundle which is a dopaminergic pathway reach the other two vertices of the triangle (Goldman-Rakic, 2013). A large collection of nerve fibers travels between the VTA and the nucleus accumbens (NAcc) to ensure the determination of pleasure or aversion. Therefore, the NAcc is also called the "hedonic nuclei" (Ikemoto, 2007; Wise, 2004).

The last 2 decades brought arguments for the evoked feelings of satisfaction, pleasure, joy or aversion and sadness produced by the NAcc as a response to the process of risk calculation arriving from the VTA. These feelings can be recorded electrically or by imaging at the level of the NAcc.

The VTA belongs to the autonomic nervous system, localized at the frontier between the brainstem and the brain in the *mesencephalic* region that belongs to the limbic system. The limbic system is a complex set of structures that lies on both sides of the thalamus, containing the hypothalamus, hippocampus, amygdala and autonomic nervous system (sympathetic and parasympathetic chains), all representatives of our vegetative life (Figs. 3 and 4).

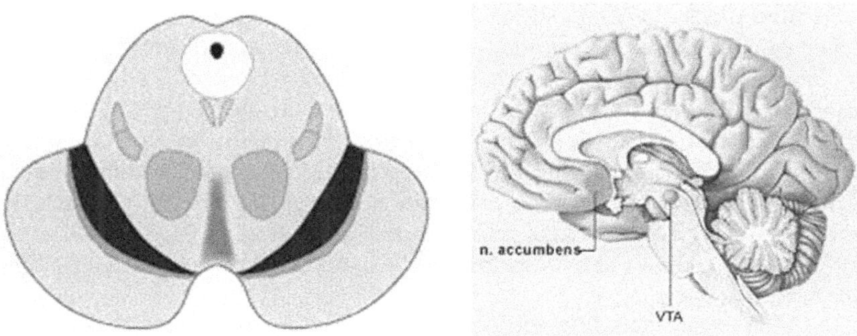

Fig. 3: Coronary section of VTA (left) as shown on the brain profile (right)
Source: Vytiacil et al., 2014.

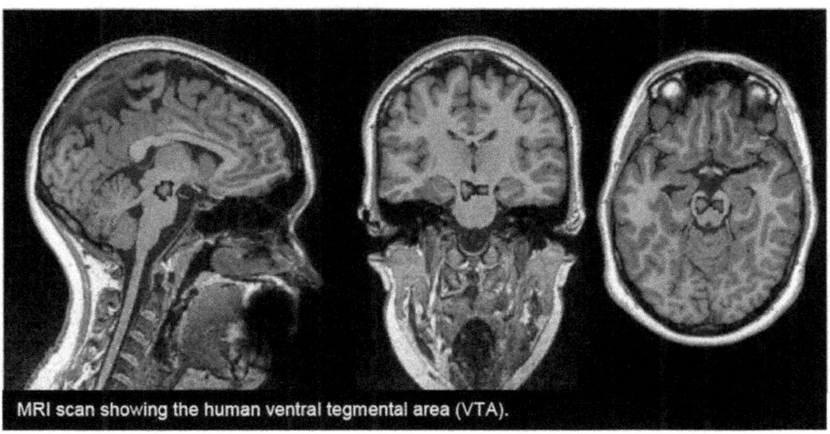

Fig. 4: Magnetic Resonance Imaging of the VTA
Source: Vytiacil et al., 2014.

People with VTA damage tend to have difficulty obtaining pleasure in life and often turn to alcohol, drugs, sweets, and gambling. The VTA also has glutamatergic, adrenergic, serotoninergic and GABAergic neurons that project to the NAcc. The VTA is involved in the cognitive and behavior data which are continuously flowing toward the decision-making center (Urman-Yotam, Ostacher, 2014). The VTA is notably active in circumstances of arousal, stress, motivation, or memory retrieval (Urman-Yotam, Ostacher, 2014).

Cocaine affects the VTA and the nerve fibers that extend from it to the *nucleus accumbens*. Cocaine enhances dopamine, norepinephrine, and serotonin activity by blocking their respective reuptake transporters, which results in increased neurotransmitters in the presynaptic cleft (Breiter et al., 1997).

The VTA also sends dopaminergic neural projections to the limbic and cortical areas. VTA activation has been positively correlated with feelings of euphoria reported by cocaine users (Kufahl et al., 2007). However, VTA activity decreases during acute cocaine intoxication (Schott et al., 2008; Kroemer et al., 2016). The VTA shows activation related to motivation reward activity (Wise, 2004) (Fig. 5).

The VTA is considered integral in reward behaviors and cognitive functions, and is activated in circumstances of arousal, stress, motivation and memory retrieval (Wise, 2004).

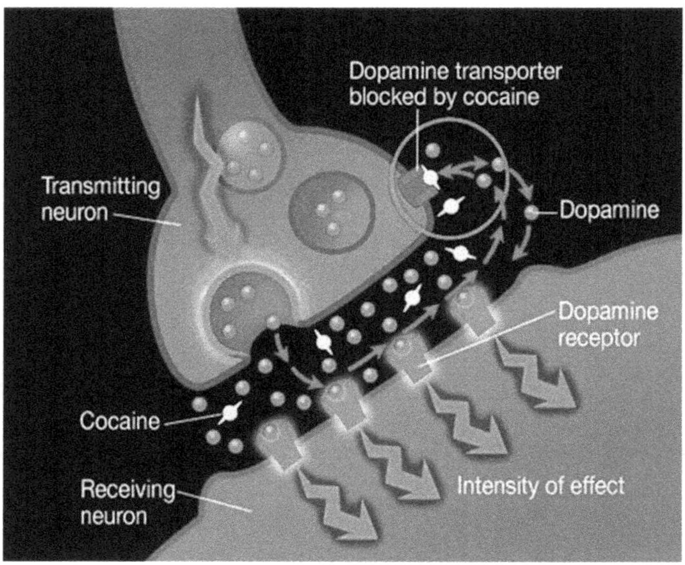

Fig. 5: Cocaine effect in Dopamine transporter system

Source: Fig. 4, Synthesis of Novel Azetidines, Amber Thaxton, from Cocaine Abuse & Addiction, National Institute on Drug Abuse, 2013

A brainstem group of dopaminergic, gabaergic and μ-opioid receptors on the VTA and *substantia nigra pars compacta* cells have a psycho-stimulant effect. The VTA has been shown to encode prediction errors, control freezing behavior and locomotor activity, influence motor coordination performance and motor skill learning, promote avoidance behaviors, participate in responses to aversive stimuli and drugs of abuse, and to be a key structure for opioid-induced disinhibition of dopamine neurons (Barrot et al., 2016).

Ghrelin, a hormone produced by the endocrine cells of the gastrointestinal tract, has receptors localized in the dopaminergic neurons of the VTA. Ghrelin signals hunger or satiety through the dopaminergic pathway. Direct injection of ghrelin into the VTA region increases food and alcohol intake doses dependently.

The *nucleus accumbens* (NAcc), the second corner of the triangle, is a neuronal conglomerate in each hemisphere of the frontal brain in the vicinity of the olfactory tuberculi. It represents the hedonic center of the brain in which pleasure or aversion is established and transmitted to the decision-making prefrontal center. It has a closed connection with the VTA and prefrontal cortex and participates to all of its decisions. Oxygen consumption in the NAcc rises with each emotional event of the human body (Figs. 6, 7 and 8).

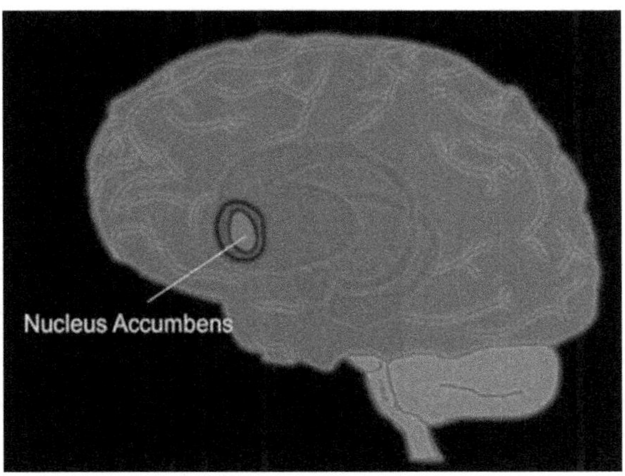

Fig. 6: NAcc with adjacent Putamen and Caudate
Source: Oscar Castillero Mimenza, Núcleo accumbens: anatomía y funciones.

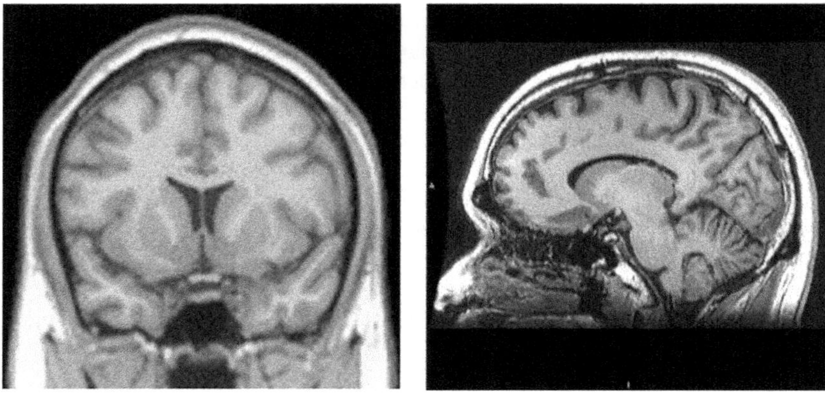

Fig. 7: Coronal MRI slice of NAcc (in the left side) and Sagital MRI slice of NAcc (in the right side)

Source: Genesis 12, public domain, 18 Dec 2009

Geoff B. Hall, CC0, 8 Sept 2011

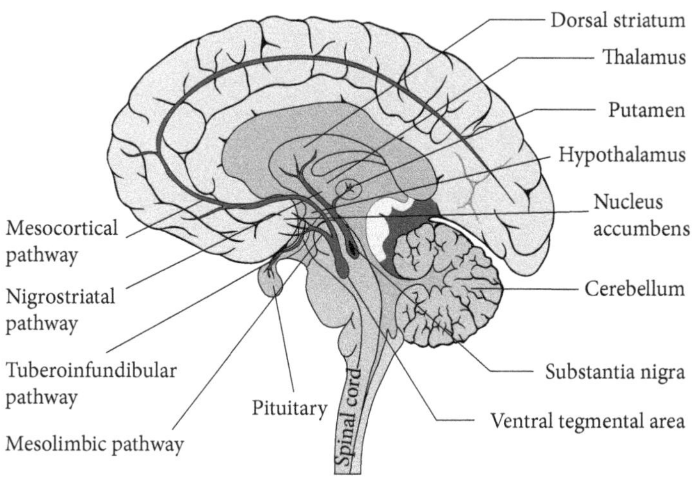

Fig. 8: Correlations of major dopaminergic pathways

Source: Patrick J. Lynch & Fvasconcellos, CC by-SA 4.0.

Robert Galbraith Heath, a psychiatrist at Tulane University, performed ethically questionable experiments involving electrical stimulation of the brain via surgically implanted electrodes in humans. He placed deep brain stimulation (DBS) electrodes in more than 54 mentally ill patients, obtaining pleasure and orgasm. These "reward areas" situated along the medial forebrain bundle of the human being can be manipulated (Heath, 1958; Bishop et al., 1963; Moan, Heath, 1972).

Roy Baumeister proposed the female erotic plasticity hypothesis, stating that women have higher erotic plasticity than men, and therefore their sex drives are more socially flexible and responsive than those of men. Factors such as religion, culture and education have a greater effect on women's sexual behaviors. Men, on the other hand, remain relatively rigid after puberty and rarely can be affected by these factors. He also predicted that acculturation (the process of adopting the behavior patterns and attitudes of the surrounding culture), should have a greater effect on the sexual behaviors and attitudes of female immigrants (Baumeister, 2000).

There are two nuclei in the hippocampus (Hp) zone (the third corner of the economic triangle), where in favor or against stimuli are retrieved from long-term memory experiences (Fig. 9).

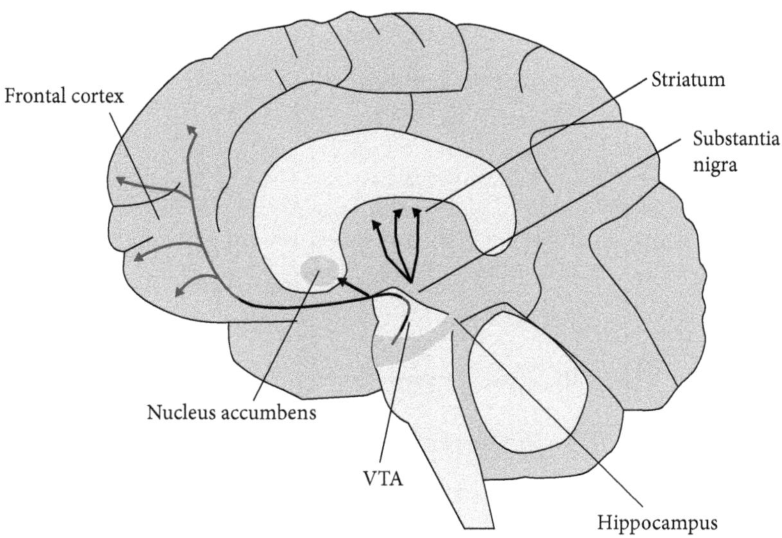

Fig. 9: Dopamine pathways.

Source: National Institute on Drug Abuse, 2012.

The activation of the economic triangle, including the VTA autonomic nuclei, the NAcc hedonic nuclei, and the long-term memory of the hippocampus inform the prefrontal cortex with the results of the economic triangle analysis – synthesis and the act is performed (Fig. 10).

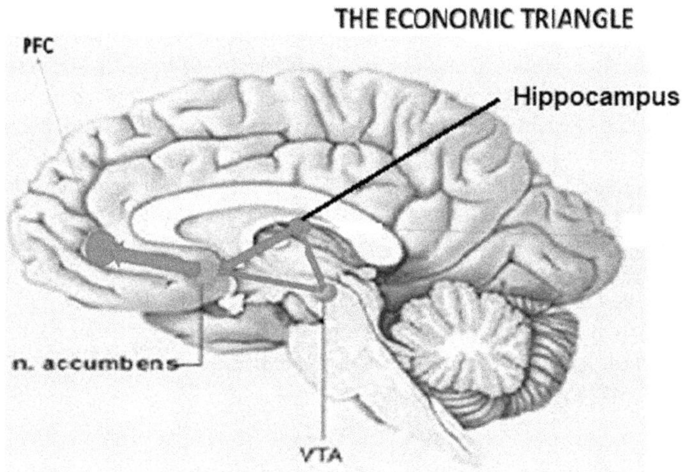

Fig. 10: The economic triangle
Source: McGill University, CC BY-SA 3.0, Jan 2008.

A huge number of other brain systems such as digestive, sexual, anxiety, or panic recommend either to block or to favor the decisions of the prefrontal cortex. The triangle activity and the motivation-reward system are interrelated and implicated in everyday life events (Figs. 11 and 12).

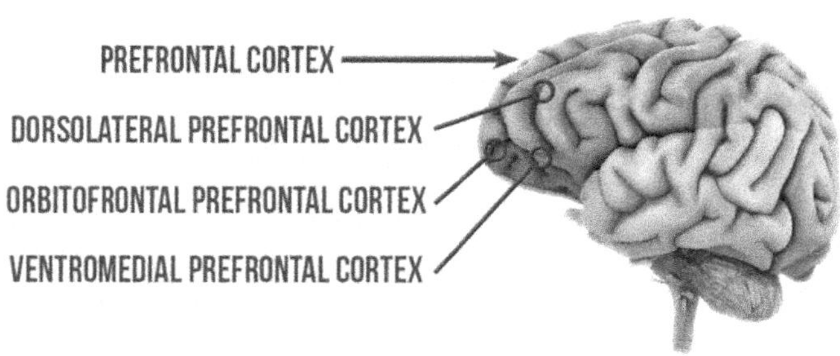

Fig. 11: Prefrontal Cortex
Source: Matthew Dahlitz, Neuroscience, January 2017.

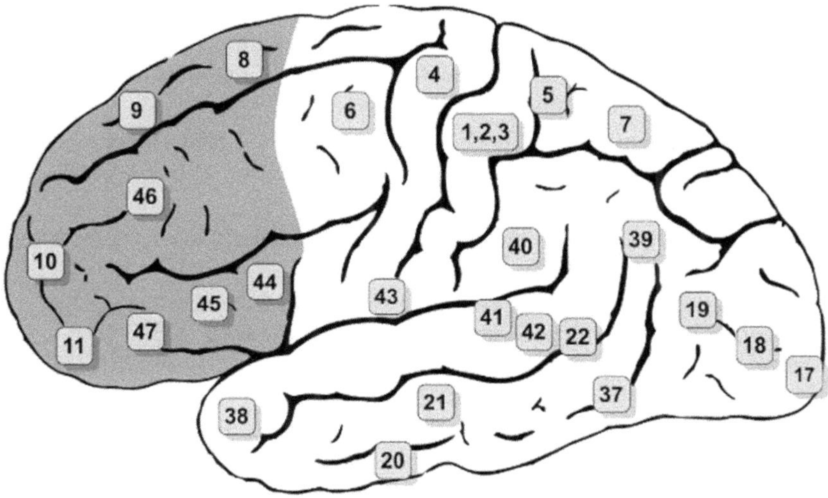

Fig. 12: Prefrontal Cortex (PFC) Decision-Making Center
Source: Gray's Anatomy, Plate 726, 1918, public domain.

The economic dimension of the brain is the expression of the economic dimension of human society. Its infrastructure, the economic triangle, provides motivation to find food, shelter and other survival needs through the interaction of 3 areas: the ventral tegmental area (VTA), *nucleus accumbens* (NAcc), and the hippocampus. This triangle enables us to seek primary rewards such as an attractive face, chocolate and money. During the coming decades, the neuro-economics will become an important field of every day interests. The human brain's economic system may transform sometimes Homo Sapiens into a Homo Economicus.

References

Barrot, M.; Georges, F.; Veinante, P., The Tail of the Ventral Tegmental Area/ Rostromedial Tegmental Nucleus: A Modulator of Midbrain Dopamine Systems, Handbook of Behavioral Neuroscience, 24: 495–511, 2016, https://doi.org/10.1016/B978-0-12-802206-1.00025-8.

Baumeister, R. F., Gender Differences in Erotic Plasticity: The Female Sex Drive as Socially Flexible and Responsive, Psychological Bulletin, 126(3): 347–374, 2000.

Bishop, M. P.; Elder, S. T.; Heath, R. G., Intracranial Self-Stimulation in Man, Science, 140(3565): 394–396, 1963, DOI: 10.1126/science.140.3565.394, PMID 13971228.

Breiter, H. C.; Gollub, R. L.; Weisskoff, R. M.; Kennedy, D. N.; Makris, N.; Berke, J. D.; Goodman, J. M.; Kantor, H. L.; Gastfriend, D. R.; Riorden, J. P.; Mathew, R. T.; Rosen, B. R.; Hyman, S. E., Acute Effects of Cocaine on Human Brain Activity and Emotion, Neuron, 19(3): 591–611, Sept 1997.

Camerer, C.; Loewenstein, G.; Prelec, D., Neuroeconomics: How Neuroscience Can Inform Economics, Journal of Economic Literature, 43(1): 9–64, 2005, DOI:10.1257/0022051053737843.

Goldman-Rakic, P., The Neurobiology of Thought, Cerebral Cortex, 23(10), 2013, DOI:10.1093/cercor/bht195.

Heath, Robert G., Correlation of Electrical Recordings from Cortical and Subcortical Regions of the Brain with Abnormal Behavior in Human Subjects, Stereotactic and Functional Neurosurgery, 18(2–4): 305–315, 1958, DOI: 10.1159/000105075, PMID 13597512.

Ikemoto, S., Dopamine Reward Circuitry: Two Projection Systems from the Ventral Midbrain to the Nucleus Accumbens-Olfactory Tubercle Complex, Brain Research Reviews, 56(1): 27–78, Nov 2007.

Kahneman, D.; Lovallo, D.; Sibony, O., Before You Make that Big Decision, Harvard Business Review, 89(6): 50–60, 2011.

Kroemer, N. B.; Burrasch, C.; Hellrung, L.; To Work or Not to Work: Neural Representation of Cost and Benefit of Instrumental Action, Progress in Brain Research, Elsevier, 229: 125–157, 2016.

Kufahl, P. R.; Rowe, D. B.; Li, S.-J., Processing the Acute Cocaine FMRI Response in Human Brain with Bayesian Source Separation, 17: 965–978, 2007. https://doi.org/10.1016/j.dsp.2007.03.001.

McClure, S. M.; Laibson, D. I.; Loewenstein, G.; Cohen, J. D., Separate Neural Systems Value Immediate and Delayed Monetary Rewards, Science, 306 (5695): 503–507, 2004.

Moan, C. E.; Heath, R. G., Septal Stimulation for the Initiation of Heterosexual Activity in a Homosexual Male, Journal of Behavior Therapy and Experimental Psychiatry, 3: 23–30, 1972, DOI:10.1016/0005-7916(72)90029-8.

Olds, J.; Milner, P., Positive Reinforcement Produced by Electrical Stimulation of Septal Area and Other Regions of Rat Brain, Journal of Comparative and Physiological Psychology, 47(6): 419–427, 1954, https://doi.org/10.1037/h0058775.

Schott, B. H.; Minuzzi, L.; Krebs, R. M.; Elmenhorst, D.; Lang, M.; Winz, O. H.; Seidenbecher, C. I.; Coenen, H. H.; Heinze, H. J.; Zilles, K.; Düzel, E.; Bauer, A., Mesolimbic Functional Magnetic Reasoning Imaging, The Journal of Neuroscience, 24, 28(52): 14311–14319, Dec 2008, DOI: 10.1523/JNEUROSCI.2058-08.2008.

Stearns, S. C., Bernoulli, Daniel, Evolution and Economics under Risk, Journal of Biosciences, 25: 221–228, 2000.

Urman-Yotam, M.; Ostacher, M. J., Stimulant, an Overview, Science Direct Topics in Reference Module in Biomedical Sciences, 2014.

von Neumann, J.; Morgenstern, O., The Theory of Games and Economic Behavior, Princeton University Press, Princeton, 1944.

Wise, R. A., Dopamine, Learning and Motivation, Nature Reviews Neuroscience, 5(6): 483–494, Jun 2004, DOI: 10.1038/nrn1406.

Articles

Dan Popescu

What will be after globalization?

"The man living a decayed life, having no revolutionary spirit in himself is the last cretin on Earth", *Emil Cioran*

Abstract What is globalization and what follows? In this case, what is post-globalization? What essential coordinates can be seen in today's world attesting to a true process of globalization? How do such mutations occur in post-globalization conditions? Are globalization and post-globalization processes of the present and the future, or are we now dealing with a setback, especially the first half of the 20th century, the next 2–3 decades? Here are the questions that I intend to answer in the current article.

Keywords: globalization, post-globalization, trade, development, integration, internet, citizens ofEarth

Introduction

Paul Valéry, an exceptional French cultural personality, poet, writer, essayist, interested as well in politics, stated, realistically, that "le mélange du vrai et du faux est plus faux que le faux" (a mixture of truth and lie is more fake than fake itself). Another Paul, also a Frenchman, Paul Géraldy this time, also a poet, making reference to the triviality of love in certain situations, wrote, pretty cynically the renown verses "...Mais l'amour c'est un besoin. M'aimerais-tu beaucoup moins si j'etais un autre?" (...but love is a need. Would you love me less if I was another?). These are two well-known quotes, realistic and cynical at the same time, that may describe matters of globalization (content, significations, stage, prior-stage, post-stage and so on) for reasons we are to show in the current analysis.

For many, many years, the many and most significant Nobel Prizes for Economy were awarded by the juries to American researchers, for valuable research, of course, highlighting, however, a relative narrowness also in the research area, though in-depth research work. There have been a few exceptions among which one is representative, namely that of the Indian Amartya Kumar Sen, yet a professor in America, at Harvard University, who was concerned with the social, poverty issues and possibilities to diminish it. However, the contribution of many Nobel Prizes for Economy did not prove, yet, to have practical and socially important effects, at least not for the United States of America (USA) economy, but not only: it was from the USA, at the time less attractive for the Nobel Prize in Economy, which was awarded later, that the devastating economic crisis to spread worldwide between 1929–1933 once started, with the famous "black Thursday." To some extent, it was in the USA as well, see IMF network, that the economic crisis in South East-Asia between 1997–1998 emerged. And it was again from the USA that the also devastating financial-economic crisis of 2007–2008 started. It was here that – along with Germany – protectionism started from 1850 and even earlier, only to spread afterwards. And it was here as well, following the British and French doctrines, that important steps ahead regarding free-trade were made, of course only after the American economy became strong enough in order to protect itself and strongly penetrate other economies (Popescu, 2019).

"The Thirty Glorious Years (Les Trente Glorieuses)" have shown themselves, however, mostly in the European West – with the Plan of the American General George Marshall, it needs to be said – and from here all over the world etc. These are only modest statements and not critical analyses. Actually, when I finished printing out this lines, the Nobel Prize for Economy 2019 had been awarded to three researchers: Abhijit Banerjee, born in India, but an MIT Professor (Massachusetts Institute of Technology – SUA), his wife, Esther Duflo, of French origin, an MIT Professor as well and the American Michael Kremer, also a Professor in USA, at Harvard University. The Academy Bulletin reads: "the winners this year have brought a new approach for obtaining trustworthy answers on the best ways to fight global poverty…". Certainly, fighting poverty, especially worldwide, involves workplaces, amplification of the economic, national and global potential, education, trading, financial policies, political decisions and so on, which complicates the problem granting it an obvious multidimensional character. Therefore, to some extent, it is a further development of what Kumar Sen not wrongly said. So we get to globalization.

1. Globalization – main features from various perspectives

1. Globalization – as I have been using this term during the last 15 years – is not a new process. Alone to begin with, the individual, in order to survive in time, started to live in clans, families, farms and local settlements, then in cities, regions, countries and national states which were formed afterwards. Later on, there came the groups of countries and empires set to rule the whole world etc. One needs to observe the direction of evolution: from the individual towards huge crowds of people, working together, living together; from the individual living locally towards the individual living globally. Certainly, the individual has continued to represent an essential nucleus of all activities, together with his/her horizon, with his/her hobbies amplified within above-mentioned structures. Therefore, in a certain sense, when thinking globalization, we only mean people and entities having common goals and interests, thinking in a convergent

manner and not in a divergent one, even though the great empires were constituted, many times, not by convergence but by force, blood and oppression.

As a first stage of globalization one can thus mention the Roman Empire (Popescu, 2018a), a superior civilization, well-structured, the same laws, customs, objectives, interests, hopes, many times spread on three continents. The trading would take place, sometimes, faster than activities, the borders of the empire were fragile, no documents were required, the capitals and the workforce were in an almost free circuit etc. and what mattered everywhere was "lucrum," profit – more specifically to gain profit beyond expenses. One can speak about a local and a central budget, public expenses, investments etc. In the year 476, the Roman Empire – Rome, actually (particularly a Roman emperor used to say that "Rome is where I am") – fell under the scathing blows of the barbarians of Odoacru, but it was also weakened, even destroyed, from the inside by an economy growing in debility, non-functionality, in the numerous unemployed, – "panem et circensis" – by a familial unity in harsh decay, by an even more embarrassing political life, by all kinds of decrepitude – the frontiers, for example, being guarded by the same barbarians who would make their own "politics" while perpetrating the borders. It would not, however, be the first time when a superior civilization and all that was essential to it, bowed under the blows of an inferior civilization. Certainly, Rome collapsed, but not the Roman civilization which went on to impress and influence society even nowadays.

Then, the second stage of globalization came: the great geographical discoveries beginning with the 15th century, which allowed for the expansion of the European civilization founded on Latinity, on knowledge, as well as its correspondent economic categories, over the two Americas, Australia etc. It is quite certain that rivers of blood were spilled, that oppression and exploitation were in place. But, this way colonialism had revealed its good parts too. In fact, everywhere in the world, production and activities would develop almost similarly, with profit-loss, expenses and revenues, import-export, budget, investment, payment and cashing balance sheets etc. It was the very system of developing activities during the mercantile times that stated, fundamentally, that the richness of one country is shown in the quantity of gold, silver, gems etc. that it accumulates. Of course, once here, one would need production as well.

Production and its efficiency as such, individually and socially, were literally reinstated with the industrial revolutions – the third stage of globalization – beginning in England and Europe in the middle of 18th century. Respectively, the Revolution of passage from wood to coal and metal and then machinery, the revolution of electricity – all on land, but also on water and by air –, continue nowadays with cybernetics, informatics, computers and the internet and so on (Popescu, 2018a). Everywhere in the world people seem to think alike in whatever they do, their hopes and ideals as individuals are similar etc. This is how, in a logical economic chain, humanity came to the nowadays globalization, understood, however, differently, firstly by the states and strong companies thinking of it as a system meant to preserve their power and the major interests. Secondly, the smaller countries, with delayed economies, a great part of their population under the limit of harsh poverty, states which, unwilling to make, internally, the necessary efforts, still want to get rid of poverty and thus to become equal with "the powerful" ones. Hence, as far as those units are concerned, particularly the nation-states, category which is sometimes understood superficially and from a biased point of view, through the lenses of de-bordering, disappearance and a total freedom etc., the matters are not at all simple, but very complicated, and even more so because of the fight for resources, at the surface but also, politically, among other aspects, in the underground, matters in which some lose and others win. Unfortunately, for the moment, this kind of problems is to a low extent solved through negotiations and satisfaction of mutual interests. This intensifies dissatisfaction and even revolt. Let us still hope. This is only an outline of the situation. It is obvious that, anyway, we are going towards globalization, we are within the process of globalization. And post-globalization will certainly mean the intensifying and deepening of the features of globalization, especially the positive ones, more functional global institutions with attributions and suitable responsibilities to solve global problems: poverty, ignorance, climate, entertainment, an individual conscience, a social conscience, a social conscience as such.

2. This is the "academic version" of globalization, the fruit of intense economic research, of the actions of some very productive intelligences. Lacking the understanding of this version, makes room for a "conspiracy version" (Taguieff, 2016). In this view, globalization is the fruit of some super-state, super-national schemes, conspiracies of the "rulers of the world." "Conspiracy" is not a new issue. Let us understand, analyse such problems in yet another key. There is negative symmetry: while there were made immense successes in informatics, in quantic physics, in sub-molecular chemistry etc., the great threats of poverty went along – over 5 million people living nowadays under the limit or by the limit of poverty. These people are hardly at peace with their fate. As negative symmetry there is also the endemics, the epidemics and pandemics of certain diseases that have become immune to known medicines and which put in peril the health of hundreds and hundreds of people. Similarly, there is the serious life threats of a blooded environment – with extremely dangerous, morbid and deadly bleeding –, to a great extent provoked by human activity seriously affecting health and existence etc. Similarly, one may speak about the terrorism generated, among other things, by breaches in civilization, by the contagious alienation of many individuals, by ignorance and misery, by people with an insufficient social education because of systems incompatible with the times we live in.

Therefore, one looks, many times, not with optimism, but skeptically at the present and future as well. "The recipes of political people," often weakly educated and dominated by personal interests are far from making this state of facts right. This happens in Romania but also in other states. What can there be changed? A lot of things can. We shall stick however to a few economic facts. Without adequate scientific knowledge, the judicious study of experiences so far, the economic history up to now, we are tempted to fall pray to the prophets of unhappiness, from time to time expressing noisily spectacular catastrophic ideas. We are tempted to fall prey to theories of "conspiracy," much easier to "digest" by sick stomachs in comparison to the truth, to economic realism as such, much harder to discern and understand. In economy, in economic doctrines, two groups are confronting each other. There is the "old school," the scientists who, ever-since 1980–1990, have submitted to mathematics and excessive shaping a more and more rebellious and disobedient economy, trying to make the so called "abstract rationality" prevail. The other one is the group of economists and specialists with a broad opening to the economic world and its evolution, the group of more or less young people who want to understand the facts, using, of course, mathematical instruments as well, in order to at least understand what it was in order to guess what it willbe.

Nevertheless, econometry, better said, economy based on mathematics, has acquired a fruitful ground. Is it, I wonder, enough to learn, to understand economy as such? Are the great businesses of the world being conducted by using mathematic models only or also by using political influence bought due to corruption and classified as theft? It is certain that these evolutions are important, if not vital. A whole world experience proves it. Economy must, therefore, be studied in its essential dimensions: in time, space, in the here and now, in perspective. Naturally, it is a wide subject submitted to debate (Popescu, 2018a). However, what is to be noticed, by and large, in this framework? In an economy more and more dominated by specific interests and which hardly, forcefully, may represent an abstract territory to be dominated by the laws of mathematics, the topics related to economic history, however essential, are, as we have mentioned before, practically removed from the university curricula. Not to mention that history as a subject matter became less significant in the high school curricula. What about international congresses of economic history and the national ones – almost non-existent? Ever more difficult from a professional point of view, but ever less minded by the ignorant and the non-initiated that have reached leading positions. In other words, green light to ignorance, to the confusing understanding of reality. Green light – which is extremely dangerous – to taking into consideration exclusively "the major conspiracies that have been ruling our world"! Here we are again, facing "conspiracies."

By "conspiracy theories," one may usually mean, those statements regarding the existence of one or more organized groups secretly conceiving or acting upon a project that has as a purpose to dominate, exploit, corrupt or exterminate. They are as old as forever. When Brutus staggered the body of his "beloved" Caesar he acted according to a plot set against the victim. However, the waves of conspiracy are rising these days to even a greater extent in the context of crises, of global crises or of profound confusion in the social order shaking the foundation of values and norms available for a while. The French Revolution of 1789, the Russian Revolution of October (November) 1917, the great world economic crisis of 1929–1933, the terrorist attacks of September 11, 2001, the financial crisis of

2007–2008 as well as other events are of the kind to challenge certainty. They are more like landmarks of delirious interpretations based on conspiracy theories seeking to make sense – a false one – of the world history and to give it a seeming coherence. This would not only be the expression of a sensitive evolution in time and space, but as previously shown, more of some conspiracies (Taguieff, 2016). What is harder to understand from history now becomes intelligible, to a great extent, through such falsities.

3. Such theses, even if they have one bone of truth, emerged in more shape due to the myth of the "illuminati." Their common mythology associates faith and firm action in a great revolutionary scheme; firm action, thus, on the one hand, and ideas and elements from the range of esoterism, on the other. In fact, it is stated, undefeatable international secret societies like these to set subversive conspiracies against the established order were and still are created. And this is done successfully. The order of "the illuminati" generating plots was founded in Bavaria by a certain Adam Weishaupt in May 1, 1776. In the same key, identifying the combination between true and false, so suggestively mentioned by Paul Valéry as being worse than false, one may look at masonry and masons –, an organization rather discrete than secret, with over 3000 years old traditions. The masons allegedly involved themselves in conspiracies, plotted political attacks, and are influent in the economic, political, social, culturally subjective areas seeking to change the world to their advantage. The world has been, thus, "threatened by a serious and great masonic danger." Very strong trends in masonry have appeared – Bildelberg, maybe Davos, however, all sorts of meetings in Switzerland, Italy, USA etc. – but it turned out to be difficult for the masons to change the world. Although, they seemingly have the means and keep trying. The truth is that masons are very few and the world "is large."

The "conspiracy theory," however, did not stop to masonry, it went further to "Judaic-masonry." This is, in the framework of Paul Valéry's reflections about true and false, more dangerous than false. What is true: the Jews are an old, civilized people, forced to scatter worldwide by unhappy circumstances. They joined trading, finances, banking, these being vacant places, especially that European religions kept their believers away from such jobs. Consequently, they acquired experience and huge fortunes. Moreover, Jews have been, as a rule, united in their ethnicity and religion, which has preserved their national being and the feeling of belonging everywhere they went. Certainly, there are also bits of truth, some negation as everywhere else, but, in our view, these are traditions worth following, not rejecting.

Using these circumstances, the followers of the "theory of conspiracies" have essentially integrated Jews in the theory of "world conspiracy." The so-called Judaic-masonry danger had become the major topic of anti-Jewish propaganda in the Europe of the 1880s and until after the First World War. Such Judaization of subversive revolutionary, worldwide conspiracies went to extreme in the apocalyptic context of the Bolshevik Revolution of 1917 Russia and further on. The revolution was faultily interpreted as a political take-over in Russia by

Judaic-Bolsheviks, who were a reincarnation of "the illuminati." Similar things happened to "Spartans" in the interwar Germany (Karl Liebnecht, Rosa Luxemburg) in reference to the first thus named, Adam Wieshaupt-Spartacus of Bavaria (Taguieff, 2016). Without such interpretations and lacking serious, solid analysis of economic history, events both terrifying and difficult to discern were in sight! Therefore, the solution was found: the Judaic-masonry.

Great people of the world fell in the trap of the Bolshevik Revolution "conspiracy," Here's Winston Churchill's statement made in February 1920 for a great audience magazine: "this movement among Jews is not knew. Ever-since the age of Spartacus Weishaupt, passing afterwards through that of Karl Marx in order to get now to Trotski (Russia), Bela Kuhn (Hungary), Rosa Luxemburg (Germany) and Ema Goldman (United States), such a world conspiracy aiming at killing civilization and reconstructing a society of wanted malice and improbable equality, did nothing but regularly growing. Between 1918 and 1920 'the illuminati' of Bavaria turned into 'The Wisemen of Sion', namely into 'Judeo-Masons' having a 'Judaic-Bolshevik' face" (Didier, 2017; Taguieff, 2016). In our opinion, this is a difficult statement to comment in any kind of reasonably positive terms. There is no way this can be done. On the contrary these are not the only horrible statements uttered by Churchill. Let us remember the cession of countries and economies in Eastern Europe to the Soviet Union in 1944–1945 etc.

Let us agree upon something! It is not conspiracy that changes the world but economy, the heart and soul of people. However, the "conspiracy theory" hasn't ceased for a moment. It is progressing. After September 11, 2001, it entered another stage, a more "developed," more refined one. It was when the "secret masters of the world" were accused that they had plotted, that they had organized the chaos and had manipulated the international public opinion with the purpose of pulling out a "world government" of an "American-Zionist" nature, in any case "giving power to Zionists." In this situation, allegedly the great conspiracy weren't generated by one or another of the active minorities, even though international, but by some states ruled by esoteric forces, beginning with USA and Israel. This is how participants become fantasy, de-historicized characters. They allegedly coagulate into invisible and horrid powers, governed by diabolic beings to whom an unbeatable esoteric force lost in the darkness of the past is attributed. Moreover, a new conspiracy rhetoric has been emerging during the last years. Along with denouncing "the new international order" and the "Government occupied by Zionists," in this new discourse, "anti-globalism" is found next to "radical Zionism" and "anti-Americanism" suggesting the demonization of bankers and international finances. This is how the world is interpreted risking a rebirth of faith in the devil. And it's been 2000 years after Christ.

4. This is an extremely faulty framework: the state of facts is not the one suggested by the academic theory, nor the one proposed by the "conspiracy" theories. As we said before, it seems to be somewhere in the middle: it's neither 100 % mathematic formulas, nor necessarily conspiracies everywhere. However, for example, IMF, the institution representing international finances has become

less credible than in the past, because it supports austerity most of the times regardless of the fact that there are billions of people who wouldn't be able to live on the proposed incomes and wages, reduced under IMF influence. Even more so, economies from South East Asia and South Korea, but also some from Latin America, grew after they gave up conciliation and solutions offered by IMF. Certainly, there were successes as well, but reality is as shown (Kerdelant, 2013). The interesting fact is that, in general, they propose cuts in wages and pensions for most people who had gained huge fortunes from making business with the state. At the same time, it is reality again that shows us the fact that rarely had the banks agreed for nations to live better.

Another topic is "the double standard": one for the West, superior, attractive and another one, more diminished, for the East. For example, at "Dacia" Pitești, in Romania, a factory technically equipped by the same standards as the factory in France and with a much similar productivity, wages are about 4 times smaller for similar positions. There are numerous examples of this kind, out of which France is the least significant. The situation regarding grocery products is really scandalous as the West seems to get products of an excellent quality for a small price, while the East buys the same products, of a lesser quality, for a higher price. Are there superior people and inferior people? It doesn't seem like that (Popescu, 2018b)

One needs, thus, to seek possible directions of action. If the States with developed economies continue to understand globalization and post-globalization – an intensified globalization, raised to higher dimensions – as an opportunity to preserve not the economic advantages – many times these belong to productivity – but their privileges, then, the expected positive results might not be reached. On the contrary, let us take into consideration that, out of a total of over 7 billion people on Earth, USA, the European Union and European Russia add to something more than 1 billion, given the fact that there are isles of poverty, some really important, on these territories too. Still, the rest of about 6 billion people belong to other countries and unions. Most of them poor, under the limit or with a risk of poverty under the limit, essentially different in faith, ideologies, civilization. And what happens then? Who guards who? Will we repeat the mistake of the Roman Empire? (Dumezil, 2013; Popescu, 2014) What about the fight for resources, for intelligences, the emigration-immigration, the threats and the battle of interests?

Conclusions

A few conclusions regarding globalization and especially post-globalization: "One world or no world at all," Einstein would write by the end of the 1930s; in a period when people weren't noticing – or they were merely noticing – the morbid, criminal malice of Nazism. They were merely noticing the imperial folds – those, too, bringing death and suffering – of dictatorial communism (totalitarianism). They were merely noticing, and in this sense the remarks of "the great scholar" were relevant, the emerging power of some terrible mass destruction weapons that, when used in wars, could lead to the destruction of the world. A single world, some peace and understanding, otherwise the world won't exist any longer, it will disappear. The dramatic call of Albert Einstein, through his terrible premonition, foresaw, even then, without the nowadays arguments, the perspective of a unique world. A world as much as possible based on agreement and not on extermination or extremism. A world based more on agreement and tolerance rather than wars. A world belonging to a greater extent to a free individual, whose humanitarian rights are respected, no matter of the skin color and other details of this kind. Not even by far a world belonging to economical and political masters who took great advantages from the setbacks caused to other people, even in the case of a united world and not of a split one, until a certain moment, strictly severe and implacable into nation-states.

Thus, a world where the individual is respected. A global world, in this respect, but even more so, a post-global one that should represent a real, let us say, human "cradle" for each individual. No hatred but agreement, no confrontations and rough military conflicts, but, to a great extent, understanding, reason, tolerance, cooperation. Generosity too, but, even more, essential economic foundations, mutual interest, interests of individuals to accomplish, one way or another, in a wide space of reference, general human collective interests. Are these utopia, dreams, fantasy, poetry, delusion? They can't be, or else, we shall no longer continue to exist.

Currently, globalization and even post-globalization are obvious, and not just from the perspective of international exchanges. The world economy is dominated not by small companies but by the great international economic trusts, these being partners, thus with small companies. In Germany, the "M.B.B" company who used to make, along with companies in France, England, Belgium etc. the "Air Bus" planes used to have about 80 % of their activity developed in cooperation with small companies, some even "home based," but all equipped with the entire modern necessary technique. At the same time, a certain levelling of production quality in highly important fields – aviation, certainly, but also auto, maritime transport, nuclear energy, mine exploitation, pluming, other machine assemblies, chemistry etc. – needs certification of that quality, and not by any means, but internationally, through institutions specialized in granting such recognition. Possibly, the range of products requiring certification will expand, including the following: food products, more medicine, building construction etc. Everywhere, the standard quality means an important feature of globalism.

Unfortunately, in general, one can't expect standardized wages or incomes; this can't be done, incomes being related to productivity, which generates numerous inadequacies, even dissatisfaction. Under such circumstances, many people living in countries where economies are without potential, offset, without a good yield, the many people from the furnace-like economies – with a few extremely rich people at the top and an immense mass of very poor, with no perspective people at the basis –, from dictatorial, non-democratic, immutable, no reform economies, from countries facing bloody attacks, ethnical discrimination massively migrate towards the civilized countries and economies. The mentioned reasons of such movements, most of them economic ones, make it so that immigrants won't be stopped "by walls," by restrictive measures, that certainly complicating the problem as the migration continuous, whether we like it or not. However, the immigrants, many of them, seek to integrate themselves as well as possible into the new world. Yet, they stay in touch with those "at home" and influence them too. Eventually, this is also a way to make steps ahead towards globalization. It is quite obvious that offset economies must make themselves important efforts – regarding capacities, productivity, wages, income – in order to progress.

There is yet another aspect: computerization, the internet, the rest of the systems in this framework allowed for companies, not necessarily multinational ones or with international capital, to hire remote, cross countries employees. Their residence is in Romania, India or Italy while they are being paid by the company they remotely work for with headquarters or one of their head-offices in US or Belgium. This is one example. Such situations – more and more numerous – define more and more our world, the world of the future, as a global world. And one may think post-globalization in the same terms.

Difficulties are shown more in case of economic crisis, structural or conjunctural crisis. In this respect, one is to consider the 2007–2008 crisis and the years that followed, with the crisis spreading from US to the entire world. A crisis that emerged in the international banking system, mostly generated by the "inadequacies" – so to say – in the real estate system that resulted in billions of underperforming credits. The crisis was resolved on the expenses of the public sector that generated the money spent to help many large banks that became bankrupt and to pay compensation "wages" of tens and hundreds of million dollars to bank leaders who were responsible for the crisis in the first place. There were broad, negative reactions from people in many states of the world, but in the end things calmed down. The recurrence of such situations – perfectly possible, even more so when having cyclical crises as background – and, even more so, applying repeatedly the same solutions to end the crisis could strongly shake the system – which is not good. In this regard, national authorities – with major competences in economy, even more so when conditions of financial balance in a country are community established while decisions regarding budget and development are national – play an important part, promoting anti-crisis and anti-cyclical investment policies. Regarding this last aspect, the measures taken few years ago to end the crisis, that is wages and pensions cuts, were difficult to understand as they were measures proposed by politicians and administrators with huge incomes, mostly resulted from businesses with the state. Most of the businesses haven't been investigated or solution reached or prejudice recovered to this very day. From this privileged position of wealth it is quite easy to propose cuts for others (Popescu, 2018b). Further on, the international institutions worldwide play no minor role in conceiving and developing anti-crisis policies.

However, whether we like it or not, we have to admit that we are heading towards globalization. Perhaps stumbling and maybe in stages not yet enough delineated and separated, but still going ahead.

We are in Europe. We are in the USA. We are right in the European Russia. Generally, with not too many exceptions, we understand events, processes as such, dynamics, evolutions from a European perspective. It is the one that in the modern age – "modern" by European criteria too – begins, after Cromwell's Revolution and especially after the French Revolution of 1789, with the industrial revolutions. It is to be stated that in the concept of "world," particularly in contemporary times, there were integrated more and more theories, states, economies, be they recognized, or independent, emancipated in one way or another, with populations currently amounting to over 6 billion people, numerous different cultures, so diverse religions, so different customs, diverse ways of thinking etc. In such circumstances, technical progress was dissipated everywhere, some stages were skipped etc., while Europe and the US with a population amounting to more than 800 million people have become "smaller and smaller," at least concerning the population number, the land areas, territorial waters, resources at the surface, in air and underground, no matter their current status. This has caused the European or American parameters to lose audience. We mentioned several times the French Revolution. But what did it represent for the hundreds of million inhabitants in a Chinese county or in India, respectively, where the population has its own essential landmarks? Less than for the Europeans. What did the two great world wars mean for the population in Patagonia? Certainly, as the world civilization got inspired from the European civilization, I may be contradicted with relative success. Still, not in absolute terms and certainly not for a long while. That is why the more profound understanding of multiculturality, of contacts and dialogues is essential. This understanding is a vital feature of globalism, of post-globalism without cataclysms of one way or another.

There is, at the same time, a re-dimensioning of religions, among others things, after the negative effects provoked to Protestantism by the revocation of the Nantes Edict by king Louis XIV in 1685. Then, there is Catholicism, at the beginning of 19th century, just on the background of defiance caused by the French Revolution of 1789 and by its lay ideas, more of these stated starting with the Enlightenment. Phenomena of one kind or another – with sensitive effects in the economic field – would not be limited however only to the European and Christian space, but they include the spiritually and philosophically emancipated Buddhist and Muslim worlds. Attracting "downwards" the fidelity of the Europeans, thus, even a little gap becomes relevant. Is this a reverse of the former colonial world with consequences as far as Central Asia or Western China? It is possible, nevertheless real. It is not by chance, that in Paris, right next to the Nôtre Dame Cathedral, one can hear now, daily, the calls of the muezzins. They will continue to be heard in the future as well. Moreover, if in 1893, accompanying the Universal Exhibition in Chicago, there took place a World Congress of European Religions, this made non-European religions to structure themselves, from a "technical" perspective as well, as world organizations that would adopt institutions of the kind existent in Western religions. That is, unless they did not have them before. Was it, is it right?... Yes, because this way there appeared and there will continue to appear many more convergence elements than before. Certainly, the economic fund was and still is essential. The dynamics will continue. Yet, we don't have in view either fundamentalism or criminal terrorism, both of which we firmly reject.

A pass is being made from a "Malthusian" world in which the relation between wages and rents was essentially influenced by the demographic evolution, to a "modern" world, where such a relation is weak and temporary. The economies have become fundamentally dependent of international trading, of the international world: resources, technologies, companies, costs, banks, stock exchange market, management, work force etc. The current world is more and more international heading towards "globalization" in a more firm fashion than the previous one. It is not only about the transatlantic dimension, but about all dimensions and all oceans. Romania is part of the European Union and, obviously, its behavior must be aligned as such, especially if the approach of our country at UE level is similar to other States. Yet, behind some of the proposed measures, not only the economic interests of the powerful ones are hidden. However, on the background of globalization, both EU's and each EU state's relationships with the global world acquire specific dynamics. More than one reason of "Brexit" originate in such a framework, Great Britain not being ready to lose positions it's been holding for centuries.

Here are some other aspects. We are more and more in a global world but more and more in an unequal world. As previously said, here one may find the inadequacies, and it is here that the setbacks may be "hidden." Before the beginning of the globalization in the 19th century, the difference between the average income per inhabitant in the poorest countries compared to the more developed, richer ones, was of 1 to 6. Currently, this difference is of 1 to about 60 and it continues to grow. Migration can't, thus, but grow. If around the First World War, only 2.5 % of the world population used to live in another country than the native one, today figures boom to greater percentages with a world population abruptly growing. Yet, beside the population and even more than that, what makes more our world to be global are the environmental problems. The migration of the population as well as environmental problems need to be addressed by global, "powerful" institutions, generally acknowledged. This a global defying that need a global response. Otherwise, we can undoubtedly head towards human catastrophes. But how many of "the powerful ones" acknowledge the competences of the really global institutions?

What about the globalization of the underworld or that of terrorism? We shall consider them one at a time. Regarding the underworld globalization matters unfolded as follows: after the USSR disintegration, Russia and the ex-soviet republics massively "exported" lowlifes in the US especially, but also in other occidental states where the stakes seemed very high as compared to the local ones.

And while accumulating stolen capital, as main "technologies," beside violence, corruption and tax evasion came along. In US, in time, and not only recently, there also came in great numbers the interlopes from Asia, from the area of "Trident" – China, Singapore and especially Hong Kong, then from Latin America etc., all of them often connected with the existent mafia. The USA, in turn, "exported" them to other countries. In this respect, among others, one could give an interesting lecture on the topic "Great crookeries and financial businesses that have been aggressing the destiny of the world" – showing how crookeries and onerous businesses follow a "pattern" currently found on a smaller or larger scale almost everywhere in the world. I have been writing about them for more than 30 years, I recommend them in bibliographies to my students, but I am pretty much alone in this one and this is hardly a "lecture."

The secret services? The ones in powerful states support their interests entirely. While in states with offset economies, influence can be bought, agents, politicians become corrupt etc., their interests far from the real interests of the state. To testify this, there are important works about the secret services in the world, written by their bosses, by remarkable publishers in USA, USSR, Russia, France, Italy, Israel etc. Do we need to discuss about the message in the movies, especially American, British, French, Italian etc.? Police, agencies, and certified departments as well as the financial ones, the "services" per se at their best fought heroically many times often with less means than those of the bandits and crooks and confrontations are at their peak. Then there is also "the Interpol," the well-known institution, with broad responsibilities, which exerts its tasks and authority almost on the entire globe, stands for a meaningful action-reaction feature of globalization and post-globalization as well.

The nowadays terrorism passed a long time ago from anarchism, from isolated criminal acts to mass attacks committed by some brainless people against innocent people. The attacks were disguised as religious fundamentalism, but, not a few times, they happened due to economic, political reasons etc. Yet, the terrorist acts take place in Western Europe – France, Germany, Italy, Spain, Belgium etc. –, in the USA, in Asia, in Africa, dwelling, especially in Asia and Africa, on ethnic conflicts. How can we fight against such criminals, who are recruited "by the book," being supported with important funds by fundamentalist groups seeking that their horrible crimes against innocent people, to unbalance life everywhere? Obviously, again globally, distinctly tracing their resources, destroying their training camps, their leaders, pursuing the strengthening of individual security, but also the national and international one. Thus, globalism again. Certainly, a meaningful tool in the fight against terrorism and banditry is to increase civic education, development, education, especially in the offset states but not only, as it is known that ignorance, poverty, misery, drugs amounting to the highest revenue numbers in the world constitute "hot places for recruiting agents" (Popescu, 2018b). Are all of these economic problems? Obviously, they are and they need to be approached in courses of macro and world economy etc.

I shall conclude in an optimistic manner: sports. This is a fundamental feature of globalization as sports can erase the differences between people everywhere. Televisions especially, but also the radio, the internet, the phones bring into the domestic comfort, at any time of the day or night, the toughest competitions in almost all sports worldwide: football, tennis, handball, volleyball, basketball, rugby, athletics etc. Thus, there are quite a few Romanians – and there is nothing wrong or bad in this –, who are more passionate about championships in England, Spain, Italy, Germany, about the great tennis contests from around the world, than the competitions in our country. What about players joining foreign teams in almost all sports? Within the same range, the above mentioned systems show films, events, shows from everywhere, on hundreds of channels, targeting an immense audience. It is in this way that we find out much more about each another, about our everyday life, we get hopes, while our differences diminish. At the recent "Penser l'Europe" event in Bucharest, there were two presentations from another interesting field of knowledge: globalization of literature… not only are we tempted but we can, thus, go through other segments. What the world has more valuable to itself starts to belong virtually to each of us. If nowadays things look like this, what will they be like in 10, 20 or 30 years? People, citizens of Earth, will have acquired new qualities, but also new responsibilities. With all the reflections written down here, we only lifted a small part of the great curtain covering the grand show of the world. There is much more to say…

References

Popescu D., 2019, Jurnal de cercetător (A Researcher's Journal), cap. Mondializarea: realități, dezamăgiri, speranțe – preliminarii ale unei dinamici complicate (chapter: Globalization: Realities, Disappointment, Hopes – Preliminaries of Complicated Dynamics), Continent, Sibiu-Bucharest.

Popescu D., 2018 a., Fascinația istoriei ignorate (The Fascination of Ignored History), cap. Popescu D., Economia: o învățăm și altfel? (chapter: Economy: Will We Learn It Differently?), Continent, Sibiu-Bucharest.

Popescu D., 2018b., Alerte: La paix pourrait vaincre, in Penser L'Europe, 2018, Academia Romana, Bucharest, pp. 81–88.

Didier R., 2017, Et si Karl Marx revenait? (What if Karl Marx Came Back?) L'Expansion no. 788.

Dumezil B., 2013, Les Barbares imposent leur loi (The Barbarians Impose Their Law), Historia, Le crepuscule de Rome, no. 802, Octomber.

Kerdellant C., 2013, La fin du monde? De la mondialisation plûtot, L'Expansion nr. 788.

Popescu D., 2014, The Fall of Rome and the Decay of Our Present Civilisation. The Decay of Goods, Economic and Finance, no. 8.

Taguieff P.A., 2016, Complotisme, mille ans des mensonges (Conspiracies, Millions of Years of Lies) Historia, no. 833, May.

Gabriela Drăgan

Towards a new international trading order: who is going to settle the bill?

Abstract Over the last few years, the foundations of the international trade order, built after World War II, are increasingly called in question. Although the role of developing countries in the international trade is more and more important, developed economies, which have established the rules of the game over the past decades, do not seem willing to give up this position or take into account decisions taken by a supranational institution such as the WTO (particularly the US). In this context, the gradual conflict between the Trump administration and the Chinese government is seriously threatening to disturb the global economic balance. The article aims to provide a realistic perspective on the current situation in international trade, starting from changes registered in its structure following the emergence of new global competitors – emerging economies. The article also focuses on certain sensitive issues related to the functioning of the WTO (in particular, related to the Dispute Settlement Body), with the aim of providing a broader perspective on where the international trade framework could evolve in the coming years.

Keywords: World Trade Organization, international trade, multilateralism, trade war

Introduction

The current international order reflects the existence of a framework of liberal political and economic rules, whose bases were established after World War II, with the creation of the Bretton Woods institutions (International Monetary Fund, World Bank, General Agreement on Tariffs and Trade – GATT). During the seven decades that followed, the network of international institutions and agencies greatly diversified, while facilitating and enhancing at the same time global cooperation in different areas. In the case of international trade, the GATT, a provisional agreement, was replaced by the World Trade Organization, an international institution which not only took over all of the duties of the GATT but also completed them. Thus, the mechanism aimed at resolving disputes between states is an example of supranational institutionalization of a highly sensitive area, in which the governments of the Member States agreed to cede prerogatives of national sovereignty to a supra-state body.

Although new players with an impressive rate of economic growth entered international trade, developing countries, which play an increasingly important role in determining how international rules apply and/or change, developed economies that established rules for decades do not seem willing to give up their stance, nor willing to take into account decisions taken by a supranational institution such as the WTO (distinctly the US). The ongoing trade war between the USA and China reflects a change in global power centers, with all the consequences deriving from it.

Starting from the relevant literature in the field and using conclusive statistical data from international organizations (IMF, WTO, OECD etc.), this article aims to provide a realistic radiography of the current situation in international trade. Changes in the structure of international trade are being analyzed through the emergence of new global competitors, developing countries (emerging economies), as well as the most important sensitive aspects recorded in the WTO's functioning. The latest section of the article develops a number of assumptions concerning the possible development of global trade relations over the next period of time.

1. Review of relevant literature

Amid continued deadlocks in the Doha Round, attacks coming from the Trump administration, as well as trade policy measures against China, interest in reforming WTO activity appears to have been increased in the recent years. The dynamics of the period that followed the global financial crisis after 2008, which led to increased inter-state rivalry and exacerbation of bilateral and regional trade agreements, is also not far from this new tendency. Marianne Scheider-Petsinger (Scheider-Petsinger, Chatham House, 2019) observes that all important WTO functions must be reformed: the way multilateral trade rules are administered, the way the deployment of global negotiations is ensured, and also the way in which trade disputes between Member States are regulated. Her conclusion is that it must be acted quickly because the global trading system is at a time when one has to "act or leave" (the so called "make or break"). Scheider-Petsinger believes that "despite this gloomy outlook, there is reason to be cautiously optimistic" because "a dead WTO would lead to more trade barriers as well as a less predictable, transparent and enforceable trading environment" and she counts on the rationale of the Member States in taking the right decisions. But the WTO's reform can run into what Phil Levy (Levy, Forbes, 2018) calls "the Trump problem," which derives from the US president's lack of appetite for multilateral solutions.

The significant return of protectionism and unilateralism, to the detriment of free trade and multilateralism, raises real concerns and many doubts. Why the negative effects of globalization have suddenly become much more visible in relation to favorable effects? Is this a last minute, transient tendency or is it the result of a process whose effects accumulated over time? In 1997, economist Dani Rodik, professor at Harvard University, published a relatively small book with a title considered at the time excessively alarming: Has Globalization gone too far (Rodik, 1997). He was then pointing out that a number of decisions taken over the past few years put into question the thesis that free trade was beneficial to everyone. More recently, Alan Blinder (2019), former economic consultant for President Clinton and current economics professor at Princeton, offered a number of arguments aimed at explaining the fall of the theory of comparative advantage. Blinder shows that free trade always produces winners and losers, with losers being those advocating free trade. As such, it is not surprising that, in times of crisis, politicians embrace protectionist measures and quickly put them into practice. For this reason, Blinder says, Donald Trump "was able to push so many Americans into sixteenth century thinking," turning himself into "the most prominent mercantilist of today" (Blinder, 2019).

Of course, resistance to globalization can be related not only to its negative social effects, where it can bring about both unemployment and increasing inequalities between high and low income earners, but also to its negative effects at macroeconomic level, where the dramatic increase in trade, both at the level of exports and imports, together with flows of capital and labor, is reflected in important (positive or negative) balances of the current account. A recent Bruegel report (2019) observes that "current account imbalances remain a source of tension, despite the narrowing of China's overall surplus and the United States overall deficit in recent years" (Dadush, Wolf, 2019). According to the World Economic Forum,[1] we are now on a new stage in the development of the global economy, where states and not the supranational institutions are those controlling the global policies (strongly state-centered politics): "Global risks are intensifying but the collective will to tackle them appears to be lacking. Instead, divisions are hardening. [...] The energy now expended on consolidating or recovering national control risks weakening collective responses to emerging global challenges" (World Economic Forum, 2019).

2. New competitors on the global stage: will E7 follow G7?

The past decades marked important changes in the balance of power in the global economy. While in 1995 the force of G7, the group of the seven most developed economies in the world, consisting of the United States, Great Britain, France, Germany, Japan, Canada and Italy, was twice as large as force of the group E7 (emerging countries), which includes seven of the most dynamic emerging economies (China, India, Indonesia, Brazil, Russia, Mexico and Turkey), in 2015 the gaps were already fading and the two groups were having a relatively equal value of cumulated GDP (in PPP). According to data from the International Monetary Fund (IMF), in 2019, the US, China, Japan, Germany and India ranked the

1 World Economic Forum is much better known due to its annual meetings with leading representatives of the business environment, political life, journalists, non-governmental organisations in the Swiss municipality ofDavos.

highest five places in the GDP-based ranking, in money terms.[2] The purchasing power parity (PPC) ranking includes the same states, placed in only slightly modified order: China, the US, India, Japan and Germany. We can easily observe that regardless of the method of calculation used, in the case of GDP value, the US and China are placed in the top two places. Estimates by Pricewaterhouse Coopers and the Organization for Economic Co-operation and Development (OECD, 2018) show that the much faster growth trend of emerging countries will continue and, in 2040, G7 is to be dethroned by E7, with the combined GDP of seven emerging countries double that of G7 developed countries. Consequently, according to a Pricewaterhouse Coopers Report (PwC, 2019), in 2050, the top two places in the global ranking will be taken by two emerging states, China and India, while the US will descend to the third place.

These estimates obviously take into account current tendencies and start from the assumption of a stable political environment. The modification of these assumptions, by the emergence of certain armed conflicts or unexpected changes to the political regime etc., can radically change these estimates (Tab.1).

Tab. 1: The share of the most important economies in global GDP (in PPP) between 2016 and 2050

Country	2016	2050
US	16 %	12 %
China	18 %	20 %
EU 27	15 %	9 %
India	7 %	15 %
Japan	4.9 %	6.8 %

Source: PwC (2019) projections.

Given these developments, the presence of a large number of developing states in the ranking of the leading ten exporters and importers in international merchandise trade is not surprising (five of the ten countries are emerging economies).

2 Statistics Times, Projected GDP ranking, 2019–2023, http://statisticstimes.com/economy/projected-world-gdp-ranking.php.

Tab. 2: Ten leading exporters and importers in international merchandise trade in 2017 ($ billion and %)

Exporters			**Importers**		
Country	US $ billion	%	Country	US $ billion	%
China	2263	16.2	US	2410	16.9
EU 28 (non-EU trade)	2122	15.2	EU 28 (non-EU trade)	2097	14.7
US	1547	11.1	China	1842	12.9
Japan	698	5.0	Japan	672	4.7
Korea	574	4.1	Hong Kong	590	4.1
Hong Kong	550	3.9	India	447	3.1
Canada	421	3.0	Canada	442	3.1
Mexico	409	2.9	Mexico	432	3.0
Singapore	373	2.7	Singapore	328	2.3
United Arab Emirates	188	1.3	Switzerland	142	1.0

Source: Created by the author, based on WTO, World Trade Statistical Review 2018, Table A 6 and A 7, p. 124–125, https://www.wto.org/english/res_e/statis_e/wts2018_e/wts2018_e.pdf

The data presented in Tab. 2 also reveal the high level of concentration of international trade, China, the US and the EU covering more than 40 % of world exports and imports.

3. WTO – an institution in deadlock?

For more than four decades after the end of World War II (1947) and until the creation of the WTO (in 1995), international trade was governed by the General Agreement for Tariffs and Trade (GATT), initially intended as a simple provisional agreement. The GATT, although it did not intend to take over the duties of an international organization, was gradually forced to take on this role as well and did so successfully. However, as the dynamism and complexity of international trade increased, the limits of this simple provisional agreement have become increasingly apparent. Therefore, in the 1980s, the GATT Member States ("Contracting Parties") decided to expand the multilateral system and establish a self-sustainable institution, the World Trade Organization (WTO), which happened during the Uruguay Round. Currently, the WTO brings together 164 countries, 117 of which are developing countries or separate customs territories. The organization covers more than 98 % of international trade and represents the current institutional framework for negotiating agreements liberalizing international trade.[3]

The WTO activity covers four large areas, common in scope with the previous GATT interventions, yet different in content: negotiating the reduction or elimination of different categories of barriers to international (tariff and non-tariff) trade, management and enforcement of rules agreed upon in the multilateral framework for merchandise trade, services, intellectual property rights, management of disputes between members through the interpretation and application of negotiated agreements (Dragan, 2004). Rapid reform is required for each of the four main areas of competence, with a lack of concrete action (especially in the area of dispute settlement between Member States) risking to paralyze the WTO's activity in short time. In the short term, the greatest danger comes from the area of regulating trade differences between countries.

Since its creation, through the specific structures created, the WTO has managed an impressive number of trade disputes. Only the European Union, represented in the WTO by the European Commission, was involved in 187 dispute resolution files, out of which 102 as the complainant and 85 as the defendant, and in 197 other cases the EU requested the right to intervene as a "third party."[4] The dispute settlement system between the WTO Member States was mainly conceived as a mechanism designed to encourage members to observe the WTO rules. There is also a possibility that when the parties do not agree and the decision is contested, a specially constituted structure may be used, the Standing Appellate Body (established in Geneva), whose members are appointed by the Dispute Settlement Body (DSB).

Even if any of the WTO members can resort to this mechanism (DSB) when they consider that the established rules have been infringed, we should mention that the mechanism is a very unwieldy one.[5] Moreover, in addition to the fact that the dispute settlement mechanism takes a long time, it currently functions faulty. In fact, the work of the Appellate Body is now quasi-paralyzed. This structure,

---

3 The WTO's work is carried out by a Secretariat of 700 people, led by a Director General. The WTO's head office is located in Geneva, Switzerland and the annual budget is around $ US 180 million (€130 million). The official working languages are English, French and Spanish. Data taken from the official WTO website, https://www.wto.org/english/thewto_e/whatis_e/wto_dg_stat_e.htm.

4 This allows the WTO Members to follow disputes involving other parties. For details, see European Parliament, Descriptive Resources, European Union and World Trade Organisation: data available on 19 September 2018, according to: https://www.wto.org/english/tratop_e/dispu_e/dispu_by_country_e.htm.

5 First, the parties receive a deadline for conciliation, which could reach up to 60 days; later, if no agreement is reached, a litigation committee (panel of experts) is called upon, and the duration of the conciliation is of approximately 18 months, but it may be slightly exceeded. When a decision is finally reached, it must be executed, otherwise sanctions may be imposed. In the case of the Airbus-Boeing dispute, for example, the decision was taken after about a decade.

which should have seven members, works today with only three of them to complete their mandate in December 2019.[6]

4. Instead of conclusions: lost in scenarios...

If, in the context of globalization, post-war commercial order appeared as an indisputable victory of free trade over protectionism, we are witnessing today a double offensive, both against globalization and free trade. Reforming the multilateral trading system (namely the WTO) will depend primarily on how the two superpowers, the US and China will position themselves on this topic and their availability to resume negotiations within a multilateral framework (provided by the WTO) (Rodik, 2018).

In the US case, the favorable scenario is that the US will not give up the legal framework represented by this organization and will only want to change it. What do these changes mean, however? In the case of the Appellate Body, the US demands either substantial procedural changes, or even its total abolition (under the current US administration, the second scenario is more likely to happen). In the case of the pessimistic scenario, we are considering the possibility that, within the framework of the Dispute Settlement Mechanism, the US could be condemned, which could prompt the US to leave the organization. However, such a situation would raise serious questions about the relevance and effectiveness of an international organization that the US would no longer be part of.

For China, the favorable and extremely realistic WTO reform scenario is that China will support maintaining the current organization and the system it represents. In support of such an assumption, it is worth to be mention that China has benefited from access as a WTO Member State (since 2001) to developed countries' markets under most favorable conditions granted to developing countries. Equally important were the different favorable resolutions that China benefited since its WTO' accession within the dispute settlement procedure.[7] The negative scenario is the one involving that the reform of the WTO rules could lead to China's resistance, especially in areas involving State intervention in the economy, protection of intellectual property rights or entry into the Chinese market. Another pessimistic scenario would be that tension between China and the US would continue to escalate and China would decide to set up its own international trade organization, which would further deepen global fractures.

Currently, uncertainties are extremely numerous and the direction of evolution is hard to predict. However, it is certain that there will be a period of resettlement and reconfiguration, during which the growing tensions between

---

6 WTO, Appellate Body Members, https://www.wto.org/english/tratop_e/dispu_e/ab_members_descrp_e.htm.

7 For instance, in 2003, China received a favorable resolution in a dispute against the US over the steel import restrictions imposed by President George W. Bush.

the slowdown in globalization of the world economy and rising nationalities in global politics will increase the imbalances in the world economy.

References

Blinder, Alan, The Free-Trade Paradox. The Bad Politics of a Good Idea, January/February 2019, https://www.foreignaffairs.com/articles/2018-12-11/free-trade-paradox, accesed 05.04.2019.

Dadush, Uri and Guntram, Wolf, The European Union's Response to the Trade Crisis, Bruegel Policy Contribution Issue n°5, March 2019, http://bruegel.org/wp-content/uploads/2019/03/PC-05_2019.pdf, accesed 06.05.2019.

Drăgan, Gabriela, Fundamentele comerțului internațional (Fundamentals of International Trade), AES Publishing House, Bucharest, 2004.

Levy, Phil, What's Next for the World Trade Organisation?, Forbes, 31 October 2018, available from https://www.forbes.com/sites/phillevy/2018/10/31/whats-next-for-the-world-trade-organization/#346cb0986ce8.

OECD, Long Term Baseline Projections, Economic Outlook, no. 103, July 2018.

PricewaterhouseCoopers (PwC), The World in 2050. The Long View: How Ill the Global Economic Outlook Change by 2050?, February, 2017, available from https://www.pwc.com/gx/en/issues/economy/the-world-in-2050.html; https://www.pwc.com/gx/en/world-2050/assets/pwc-the-world-in-2050-full-report-feb-2017.pdf, accesed 02.03.2019.

Rodik, Dani, Has Globalization gone too far?, Institute for International Economics, Washington, DC, March, 1997.

Rodik, Dani, How to Avoid a Trade War, July 10, 2018, www.project-syndicate.org/commentary/china-europe-reaction-trump-trade-tariffs-by-dani-rodrik-2018-07.

Scheider-Petsinger, Marianne, The Path Forward on WTO Reform, Volume Ideas for Modernizing. The Rules-Based International Order, Chatham House. Expert Perspectives, June 2019, https://www.chathamhouse.org/expert/comment/path-forward-wto-reform.

Statistics Times, Projected GDP Ranking, 2019–2023, http://statisticstimes.com/economy/projected-world-gdp-ranking.php.

World Economic Forum, Global Risks Report, 2019, http://reports.weforum.org/global-risks-2019/executive-summary/.

World Trade Organisation (WTO), Appellate Body Members, https://www.wto.org/english/tratop_e/dispu_e/ab_members_descrp_e.htm.

World Trade Organisation (WTO), China Initiates WTO Dispute Complaint against Additional US Tariffs on Chinese Imports, https://www.wto.org/english/news_e/news18_e/ds565rfc_27aug18_e.htm.

Gheorghe Zaman

Early warning gaps regarding difficulties of Romania's sustainable development

Abstract The paper examines in the EU-27 international context the "early warning gaps" for the case of Romanian economy taking into consideration the size and evolution of a series of relevant macro indicators such as population, GDP per capita, R&D expenditure public debt interest rate and resource productivities in the period 2010–2019.

The main objective pursued in our analysis consists in revealing the certain limits of alarm warning indicators in Romania in order to avoid the possible risks and vulnerabilities just in time and just in case. Our intuition was to submit to the attention of interested specialists aspects, problems and mechanism that should be taken into consideration by implementing strategies, action plans, economic and financial mechanisms aiming at alleviation and prevention of vulnerabilities and other economic and social losses in parallel with strengthening of Romania's resilient capacity against internal and external economic, social, environmental, technological and geopolitical risks on different horizon time.

Key words: early warning, demographic decline, R&D sub funding, external public debt threshold, resource productivity

Introduction

In our research we have examined several relevant macroeconomic indicators (population, R&D expenditure vis-à-vis GDP, R&D staff, 60 % public debt to GDP, GDP per capita absolute and relative gaps, resource productivity and the size of interest rate) in Romania in comparison with the size of these indicators in EU-27 member countries with different development level.

The main aim of this comparative analysis was to highlight the absolute and relative gaps between Romania and other EU member states and their evolution in 2010–2019 so that we can draw a series of conclusions which can be considered "early warning" signals for decision-makers and a challenge for further basic and applied research.

An important task for decision-makers at different level of hierarchical organization consists in the improvement of priorities setting under alternative conditions of financial, human and material resource scarcity (Briguglio,1997)..

The types, dimensions and evolution of gaps between Romania and EU member-countries reflects the degree of urgency and celerity with which it is necessary to try to solve, alleviate and combat the existing vulnerabilities by creating resilient mechanisms resistant to internal and external shocks.

In our opinion, these gaps under the alarm signal of early warning systems have the chance to be solved or ameliorate only by an efficient public-private, public-public and private-private partnership.

1. Literature review

Systems of indicators, coefficients. rates, thresholds and warning intervals regarding developments, trends, imbalances, crises, recessions are currently an increasingly complex concern due to the rapid rate of changes with which macroeconomic phenomena and processes occur most of them producing possible events with negative effects, consequences and results which, as a rule, presuppose the determination of their probability, impact and exposure degree (Beckmann, Menkhoff, & Sawischlewski, 2005; Berg, Borensztein, & Pattillo, 2005).

The logic of the development of these events in time, as it results from the special literature, reflects the cause-effect connections at between VULNERABILITIES – WARNING INDICATORS, SYSTEMS, RESILIENCE, according to Fig. 1.

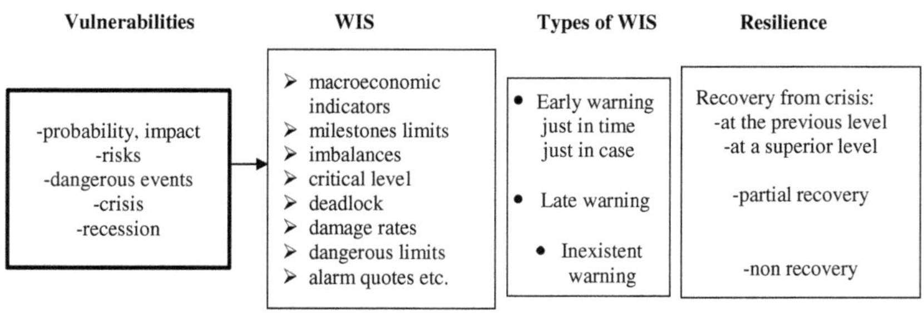

Fig. 1: Relationship between vulnerabilities warning indicators and systems (WIS) and resilience

Source: own contribution.

As an element of novelty, we considered it necessary to distinguish three categories of warnings, namely: early, late, inexistent warnings.

Assuming the well-known notion of resilience, I conventionally considered that early warning, just in time and just in case (just in time and just in case), represents a favorable situation in the sense that it allows recovery at the highest previous level or even at a superior level (Minsky, 1986).

The late warning allows only partial recoveries, and the lack of warning is characterized by modest recoveries, both situations proving the lack of interest or professionalism on the part of stakeholders and/or decision makers at large.

The development, updating, measurement and diversification of indicators on vulnerability and resilience is an important activity for the accuracy of predicting the time frame in which an undesirable macroeconomic event will occur (Well, 1997; Atkins et al., 1998; IMF, 1998; Kaminsky et al., 1998; Spratt, Bernini, 2010).

EWI is based on several methods and models including models based on signal extraction, logit probit models which indicate the occurrence of banking, financial, debt and currency crises taking into consideration a lot of factors influencing vulnerabilities and resilience (Herrera, Garcia, 1999; Krkoska, 2000; Briguglio, 2004; Barrito, 2008; Briguglio et al., 2009).

In Romania, there is a comprehensive system of early warning indicators applied in studies on financial stability and free currency crises regularly elaborated by National Bank of Romania (Codirlascu, 2002; Racaru, Copaciu, & Lapteacru I., 2006; National Bank of Romania, Financial Stability Report, June, 2020).

EWI is a factor contributing to the compilation of a general indices of vulnerability and resilience which can determine the predominance of one or another indicator (Fig. 2).

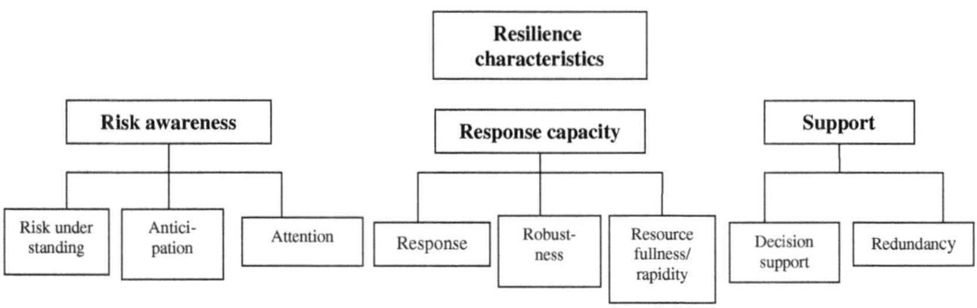

Fig. 2: Contributing Success Factors of Resilience

Source: K. Oien et al., 2010, Development of Early Warning Indicators based on Resilience Engineering, Institute for Energy Technology, Paper presented at PSAM 10, 7–10 June, Seattle, USA.

2. Main early warning indicators gap between Romania and EU-27 member country

2.1. Demographic decline

The analysis of the size and demographic dynamic of a country, in an international comparative context, highlights the interfering action of a multitude of economic, social, environmental, technological and geopolitical factors, knowing that population is the most important driving force of progress and level of development of that country.

In general, population growth is considered to be a relevant synthetic indicator of a country's human capital potential and its reduction a weakening.

Moreover, a situation of substantial demographic decline, over relatively long periods, in which the emigration of labor, especially the highly skilled (brain drain) registers alarming rates in tandem with the negative natural demographic increase can only indicate an unfavorable phenomenon for a country or region.

The opinions according to which the demographic decline of a country would be a positive factor for the increase of the GDP per capita represent a "seductive trap" only in the very short term, in the theoretically unlikely case of such an increase, because in the medium and long term the assumption is not valid.

For the reasons previously presented to which many others could be added (for example, pandemics, natural hazard, wars, terrorism, etc.) we believe that a quasi-permanent demographic decline, with greater or lesser variations from one year to another can be an early warning indicator, which decision makers and not only will have to take into account when developing strategies and measures for sustainable development.

Tab. 1: Population change in Romania and EU-27 in the period 2010–2019

-mill. Persons

Country	**2010**	**2015**	**2019**	**Difference ± 2019–2010**
EU-27	440.66	443.66	446.82	+6.16
Romania	20.29	19.87	19.41	-0.88

Source: EUROSTAT

Countries with demographic increase in 2019 versus 2010 in mill. persons: UK (+4.13), France (+2.36), Italy (+1.25), Germany (+1.21), Sweden (+0.89), Belgium (+0.61), Austria (+0.50), Spain (+0.45), Netherlands (+0.38), Denmark (0.27), Czech (+0.23), Finland (0.16), Luxembourg (+0.09), Slovakia (+0.06), Malta (+0.05), Slovenia (+0.04).

Countries with demographic decrease in 2019 versus 2010: Romania (-0.88), Bulgaria (-0.42), Greece (-0.39), Lithuania (-0.35), Croatia (0.23), Latvia (-0.21), Hungary (-0.09), Poland (-0.05), Portugal (0.03).

From the Tab. 1 it results that over the period 2010–2019 Romania has registered a demographic decline of −0.88 million persons while in the EU-27 the population increased by + 6.16 million persons.

Such a negative tendency in Romania has to be carefully analyzed and stopped as soon as possible.

In a number of more than 15 EU countries during the reference period a more or less increase of population was a clear cut trend which could be explained by the impact of several factors among the most important could be the size of immigration and to less extent the natural demographic increase. The major part of the countries in this category are relatively developed.

In a group of eight countries the population has decreased. These countries belong to the category of new country members, relatively less developed, except Greece where the impact of economic and financial crisis was one of the most important determinants of the demographic decline.

From our short analysis it resulted that Romania has recorded the highest demographic decline as compared with other country members and this situation is not at all good!

If we take into account the population forecasts for EU countries until 2050 it results that in Romania the population will decrease up to 16.5 million persons, what is a real warning for our country. Urgent strategies and measures initially to stop the demographic decline and after that to restart the increase of the population could be the first path of recovering the decline.

2.2. R & D expenditures

The role of science and technology in supporting the pillars of global competitiveness is unanimously recognized at least from a theoretical point of view. How this role can be put into practice is a problem as attractive as it is complex. In this context I will paraphrase what they mentioned:

J.M. Keynes – science does not give the practitioner ready-made recipes, but the practitioner who knows the theory does much better than the ignorant;
Albert Einstein – theory without practice is empty, and practice without theory is blind.

In order to successfully fulfil their role, science and technology are increasingly expensive as an investment, and require the allocation of a growing volume of financial and human resources. Millennial practical experience has shown that the application of scientific research has had the effects far superior, quantitative, qualitative and value (pecuniary) compared to expenditures. A margin of risk has always existed but this was not an obstacle to stop expenditures in this domain.

In order to minimize the risk, R&D decision makers must identify the "critical" mass (optimal) of the volume of costs. Exceeding up or down this mass will result in the consequences of non-optimality.

In a period of 10 years, the expenditures on research and development in Romania as a share in GDP were characterized by the following:

- in the period 2013–2018, Romania ranked on the last place with the lowest share of research and development expenditures, at a great distance from the EU average level;
- in the entire analyzed period, the indicator registered a decreasing trend in some years the decreases being important;

- on the contrary, in the vast majority of member countries and at the EU-27 average, there is a tendency to increase the respective share, except for Sweden, which had the highest weight in the whole period, with a decrease in 2013 followed by an increase in 2018.

This gap in the share of research and development expenditures in GDP in our country compared to other member countries, as well as its declining trend, it has to be considered as an alarm signal for decision makers who until now have always cried out in words and less in deeds about the vital role of scientific research and innovation for the sustainable development of Romania. Regarding the allocation of financial resources they did not act properly. The financial support of the R&D sector is a sine qua non condition that if we meet it as soon as possible it will be as good as possible (Tab. 2).

Tab. 2: Research and development expenditure all sectors of performance as % of GDP

Country	**2008**	**2013**	**2018**
Low Romania	0.55	0.39	0.50
Bulgaria	0.45	0.64	0.76
Average EU-27	1.87	2.08	2.19
High Germany	2.62	2.84	3.13
Denmark	2.77	2.97	3.03
Sweden	3.49	3.27	3.32

Source: EUROSTAT

In a period of 10 years (2008–2018) the expenditure on R&D in Romania were characterized by the following:

- in the period 2013–2018, Romania ranked on the last place with the lowest share of research and development expenditure at a great distance from the EU average level;
- in the entire analyzed period, this indicator registered a decreasing trend, in some years the decreases being important; on the contrary, in most EU member countries and at the EU-27 average there is a tendency to increase the respective share, except for Sweden which had the highest weight in the whole period, with a decrease in 2013 followed by an increase in 2018.

The role of science and technology in supporting the pillar of global competitiveness is unanimously recognized at least from a theoretical point of view. How this role can be put into practice is a problem as attractive as it is complex.

2.3. R&D staff

R&D personnel is an indicator which, as shown in Tab. 3, in the period 2007–2017, increased in most EU member states, except for Romania, where it decreased, especially since 2011. The trend of decreasing in Romania which is opposite to that in most countries can only be explained by the policies promoted in the field of science and technology largely induced by the fact that the subsidiaries of multinational corporations, based in Romania, receive the results of scientific research from parent companies and, consequently, they no longer need to conduct their own research. And as these subsidiaries hold a dominant position in almost all private sector of the Romanian economy, the domestic financing of the research activity is no longer predominantly provided by the private sector, as it happens in developed countries, where a proportion of about 50–80 % of the total research financing comes from private corporations.

Another aspect that should be taken into account is that, unlike Romania, during the international financial crisis 2008–2010, almost all member countries pursued a policy of promoting and supporting the R&D sector, including increasing the degree of employees considering that this sector is one of the important factors in overcoming the crisis and recovering the economic decline generated by it.

Another factor that contributed to the underfunding of the R&D activity in Romania was the relatively low degree of absorption by Romanian researchers of the European funds allocated to the research programs in the financial years 2007–2013 and 2014–2020.

As a final remark of this type of discrepancy, we emphasize the fact that in the period 2007–2017 the R&D staff in Romania decreased by 12.3 % points, while on the whole of EU-27 it increased by 44.03 % points.

Science and technology human resources as a percentage share of the total active population increased from 39.4 % to 46.9 % in EU-27, as compared to Romania respectively from 24.1 % to 28.2 %.

Tab. 3: Total researchers head count – All sectors

Geo/Time	2007	2008	2009	2010	2013	2017
European Union - 27 countries (from 2020)	1,792,809	:	1,945,535	:	2,246,947	2,582,202
Belgium	51,278	54,624	55,858	59,403	66,724	78,867
Bulgaria	13,090	13,416	14,699	14,138	16,095	20,971
Czech	42,538	44,240	43,092	43,418	51,455	59,789
Denmark	42,992	48,442	54,049	54,813	57,654	61,961
Germany (until 1990 former territory of the FRG)	437,780	:	487,242	:	549,283	623,125
Estonia	6,826	7,226	7,453	7,491	7,515	7,344
Ireland	19,407	21,040	20,901	20,801	32,084	34,721
Greece	:	:	:	:	53,744	61,616
Spain	206,190	217,716	221,314	224,000	208,767	225,995
France	278,480	289,041	296,093	324,551	366,299	416,217
Croatia	11,109	11,915	12,108	12,527	11,168	13,708
Italy	141,878	145,594	149,314	149,807	163,925	195,560
Cyprus	1,532	1,565	1,696	1,776	2,228	2,357
Latvia	7,823	7,447	6,324	6,517	7,448	7,504
Lithuania	13,393	13,518	13,882	14,056	18,083	18,767
Luxembourg	2,470	:	2,951	:	2,713	3,540
Hungary	33,059	33,739	35,267	35,700	37,803	42,729
Malta	996	1,087	945	1,062	1,383	1,546
Netherlands	60,106	60,969	54,505	64,829	110,536	115,185
Austria	53,590	:	59,341	:	71,448	83,648
Poland	97,289	97,474	98,165	100,934	109,611	187,905
Portugal	51,443	75,073	75,206	80,259	78,290	89,659
Romania	30,740	30,864	30,645	30,707	27,600	27,367
Slovenia	8,742	10,124	10,444	11,056	12,111	14,079
Slovakia	19,375	19,814	21,832	24,049	24,441	26,861
Finland	53,420	55,195	55,797	57,163	56,720	54,139
Sweden	71,244	:	73,025	:	101,820	107,042
United Kingdom	377,210	:	385,489	394,755	466,689	520,936
Norway	41,327	43,699	44,762	44,774	47,795	57,934
Switzerland	:	45,874	:	:	:	73,502

Tab. 3: Continued

Geo/Time	2007	2008	2009	2010	2013	2017
Serbia	:	11,534	12,006	12,637	14,643	16,182
Turkey	101,961	106,423	114,436	124,796	166,097	210,769
Bosnia and Herzegovina	:	:	:	:	1,245	:
Russia	392,849	375,804	369,237	368,915	369,015	359,793
Japan	883,386	890,669	889,341	894,138	892,406	930,720
South Korea	289,098	300,050	323,175	345,912	410,333	482,796

Source: EUROSTAT

2.4. The Maastricht convergence criterion of 60 percent public debt to GDP does not fit Romania

The current situation, semester 4 2019, of complying with the 60 % criterion is the following:

- over 60 % of GDP: EU-27(27.8), Eurozone 18(84.4), Belgium (48.6), Spain (95.5), Greece (176.6), France (98.4), Croatia (73.2), Italy (134.8), Cyprus (95.5), Austria (70.4), Portugal (117.7);
- under 60 % of GDP: Bulgaria (20.4), Czech (30.8), Denmark (33.2), Germany (59.8), Estonia (8.4), Ireland (87.8), Latvia (36.9), Lithuania (36.3), Malta (45.1), Netherlands (48.6), Poland (46.1), Romania (35.2), Slovakia (48.0), Sweden (35.1);
- about 60 % are registered in Finland (59.4). Germany (59.8), Slovenia (66.1), Hungary (66.3).

From the figures previously presented, it results that more countries in the euro area do not fall within the 60 % ceiling than they do. Therefore, the question arises whether this criterion, in the sense of "one size fits all" or a Procustian bed (?!), is rather established so as not to be respected as soon as a country becomes a member of the euro area.

Regarding Romania, the situation is somewhat special because, according to the specialists, but also to the law, 60 % would be an unsustainable target that is too burdensome if we take into account the country's repayment capacity. Several specialists are of the opinion that, for Romania, the most suitable ceiling would be 45 %.

According to the Law no. 69/2010 (the Law of fiscal-budgetary responsibility) Art.13 the limits for public debt calculated according to the European Union's methodology are:

1. If the public debt exceeds 45 % of the GDP, but it is below 50 % of the GDP, The Ministry of Public Finance presents the Government a report regarding the increase in debt and presents proposals to maintain this indicator at a sustainable level.

2. If the public debt exceeds 50 % of the GDP, but it is below 55 % of the GDP:
   a) the Government presents publicly and applies a program for the reduction of the public debt's weight to the GDP in the shortest time;
   b) the program at letter a) includes, but is not limited to, measures that cause the freezing of total expenditures on public sector wages;
   c) measures comprised in the program provided at letter a) are applied.
3. If the public debt exceeds 55 % of GDP, but it is below 60 % of the GDP:
   b) the Government initiates measures to determine the freezing of the total costs regarding social assistance from the public sector;
4. If the public debt exceeds 60 % of the GDP:
   b) The Government initiates and applies a program to reduce the public debt according to art.10.

In conclusion, if the public debt's level of 45 % would be the best for Romania, the 60 % Maastricht criterion would become unaffordable from the debt's burden viewpoint.

2.5. The trap of relative gap

The analysis of the economic and social gaps between the countries is made with the help of several methods and models, among which the most common are the absolute and relative gaps. There are situations in which there are opposite tendencies between the two types of gaps, most often the relative gaps decrease and the absolute gaps increase or remain almost constant. In such situations it is difficult to draw a single conclusion regarding the evaluation of the respective gaps (Tab. 4).

Tab. 4: GDP per capita in some member countries, absolute and relative gaps compared to the EU-27 average, in 2010 and 2019 (market prices)

UE-28=100.0						
Country	**GDP level**	**2010 GAPS**		**GDP level**	**2019 GAPS**	
		Absolute ±	**Relative**		**Absolute ±**	**Relative**
Belgium	33,330	+8,430	133,8	41,200	+10,100	132,5
Bulgaria	5,050	-19,850	20,3	8,680	-22,240	27,9
Czech	14,900	-10,000	59,8	20,640	-10,460	66,4
Germany	31,946	+7,046	128,3	41,350	+10,250	132,9
Greece	20,320	-4,580	81,6	17,500	-13,600	56,3
Spain	23,040	-1,860	92,5	26,440	-4,660	85,0
France	30,690	+5,790	123,3	35,960	+4,860	115,6
Italy	26,930	-2,030	108,2	29,610	-4,490	95,2
Hungary	9,900	-15,000	39,8	14,720	-16,410	47,3
Poland	9,390	-15,510	37,7	13,780	-16,380	44,3
Slovakia	12,540	-12,630	50,4	17,270	-13,830	44,5
Romania	6,190	-18,710	24,8	11,500	-19,600	36,9
UE-27	24,900	-	100,0	31,100	-	100,0

Source: own calculations based on EUROSTAT primary data.

The main conclusive results from the above table are the following:

- in the case of Romania GDP absolute gap increased from 18.710 euro in 2019 to 19.600 euro in 2010, the same trend taking place in Belgium, Bulgaria, Czech, Greece, Spain, Hungary, Poland, Slovakia;
- a decrease of GDP gap compared to the EU-27 average in relative terms registered by Romania, Poland, Bulgaria etc.;
- in 2019, below the EU-27 average level (=100) were Bulgaria (27.9 %), Romania (36.9 %), Poland (44.3 %), Greece (56.3 %), Czech (66.4 %), Spain (85.0 %), Italy (95.0 %).

In our opinion, the most relevant indicator for confirming a real convergence are the absolute gaps, expressed in monetary terms or in physical, natural quantities, as opposed to the relative gaps, expressed in percentages that lose their significance when in absolute terms the gaps increase. Only in cases the absolute gaps decrease, we can say that there is a real convergence. The deceptive trap of relative gaps must be avoided in decision making processes, because only absolute gaps can have a genuine real character of early warning indicator.

2.6. Romania is among the last countries in terms of resource productivity

From the data of the previous table presented, the following conclusions for Romania result:

- It has one of the lowest degrees of processing of material resources;
- The degree of diversification of production and competitiveness decreased with unfavorable effects for the economic efficiency of exports;
- Digitization, intelligent specialization and the circular economy are in incipient stages.

These unfavorable aspects for the country's economy, if they continue, will make a long-term mark on the external competitive capacity of the national economy (Tab. 5).

Tab. 5: Resources productivity (euro PPS per 1 kg DMC*) in Romania

Country	**2010**	**2015**	**2019**	**2019 Romania=1,00**
EU-27	1.72	2.22	2.27	5.04
Euro Zone	-	-	-	-
Romania	0.45	0.35	0.45	1.00
Bulgaria	0.32	0.29	0.39	0.86
Germany	2.03	2.34	2.57	5.71
Greece	1.27	1.34	1.54	3.42
Czech	0.93	1.01	1.22	2.71
Italy	2.35	3.43	3.60	8.80
France	2.54	2.97	2.99	6.64
Sweden	1.80	2.00	1.86	4.13

*) DMC = domestic material consumption.

Source: Eurostat.

The gap reduction of resource productivity indicators between Romania and other member country of EU-27 is possible first of all by improving technological level of national production of goods and services on the one hand and by saving natural capital and reducing, recycling and reusing the waste volume per capita which in Romania is much more higher than in other EU countries.

2.7. The costs of banking loans is rather higher in Romania

It seems to be a little strange that in Romania a developing emergent country loans are more costly than in a developed country. In Romania the bank with foreign capital participation have about 95 % of banking capital market where as in other countries the percentage share of foreign banks is more reduced, domestic banking public and private capital being active on the capital market.

From the Tab. 6 presented, the interest rate on bank loans, in 2019, in Romania was 4.1 % points higher than the EU-27 average level, with 4.79 respectively than in Germany, 4.4. higher than in France and Sweden. This early warning indicator persists for a long time in the national economy and until now, even if the interest rate in Romania has decreased, this has occurred with great delay compared to other countries, and the reductions have been relatively small so that the interest rate has remained relatively high in Romania, which is a factor in slowing down the investment advance on bankloans.

Tab. 6: Interest rate per annum for banking loans in Romania and other EU countries

-% per annum-

Country	**2010**	**2015**	**2019**	**Percentage points at Romania's interest rates compared to other countries**
EU-27	3.89	1.38	0.71	+3.83
Euro Zone	3.60	1.21	0.44	+4.10
Romania	7.34	3.47	4.54	0.00
Bulgaria	6.01	2.49	0.43	+4.11
Germany	2.74	0.50	-0.25	+4.79
Greece	9.09	9.67	2.59	+1.95
Czech	3.68	0.50	1.55	+2.99
Italy	4.04	1.71	1.95	+2.59
France	3.12	0.84	0.13	+4.41
Sweden	2.89	0.72	0.04	+4.40

Source: Eurostat

To diminish the predominance of foreign bank, we propose to help create and develop national banking capital private or state-owned which could reduce the imbalance in this domain.

Concluding remarks

Early warning indicators represent a valuable tool for improving decision-making if they are understood from the viewpoint of the necessity to reduce economic risks and vulnerabilities.

Each of the early warning indicator at macro level has revealed its systemic role in the framework of national economy, and its structural impact on the whole economy.

The risk and vulnerabilities generated so far or that could be generated in the future presuppose an in-depth analyses and accurate estimations, early warning indicators playing an active role for improved economic performances if it is well understood their meaning and capacity by stakeholders.

It is necessary to take into consideration their complex character which involves an integrated approach capable to analyse quantitative and qualitative aspects at national and international levels.

The analysis of improving predictive capacity of early warning systems and indicators needs to up-date them with new method and models of regarding probability, impact and degree of exposure to environmental, economic, social, technological and geopolitical risks.

References

Atkins, J., Mazzi, S., & Ramlogan, C. (1998). A Composite Index of Vulnerability. London, Commonwealth Secretariat.

Baritto, F. (2008). 'Disasters, Vulnerability and Resilience from a Macro-Economic Perspective: Lessons from the Empirical Evidence', Background paper for the 2009 ISDR Global Assessment Report on Disaster Risk Reduction. Geneva, International Strategy for Disaster Reduction.

Beckmann, D., Menkhoff, L., & Sawischlewski, K. (2005). Robust Lessons about Practical Early Warning Systems, Diskussionspapiere der Wirtschaftswissenschaftlichen Fakultät der Leibniz Universität Hannover dp-322, Leibniz Universität Hannover, Wirtschaftswissenschaftliche Fakultät accessed on November 2012 at http://econstor.eu/bitstream/10419/19796/1/Beckmann.pdf.

Berg, A., Borensztein, E., & Pattillo, C. (2005). Assessing Early Warning Systems: How Have They Worked in Practice?, IMF Staff Papers, Volume 52, Issue 3, pp. 462–502, accessed on January 2013 at http://www.imf.org/External/Pubs/FT/staffp/2005/04/pdf/berg.pdf.

Briguglio, L. (1997). Alternative Economic Vulnerability Indices for Developing Countries. New York, NY, United Nations Department of Economic and Social Affairs.

Briguglio, L. (2004). 'Economic Vulnerability and Resilience: Concepts and Measurements' in L. Briguglio & E. J. Kisanga (eds), Economic Vulnerability and Resilience of Small States. Valletta/London, Islands and Small States Institute of the University of Malta and the Commonwealth Secretariat.

Briguglio, L., Cordina, G., Farrugia, N., & Vella, S. (2009). 'Economic Vulnerability and Resilience: Concepts and Measurements', Oxford Development Studies, 37(3), 229–247.

Codirlascu, A. (2002). Sisteme de avertizare timpurie a crizelor financiare, BNR. Direcţia Studii şi Publicaţii, accessed on October 2012 at http://www.dofin.ase.ro/acodirlasu/wp/ince2002/ince2002.pdf.

Herrera, S. & Garcia, C. (1999). 'User's Guide to an Early Warning System for Macroeconomic Vulnerability in Latin American Countries', Policy Research Working Paper. No. 2233. Washington, DC, Economic Policy Sector Unit, Latin America and the Caribbean Region, World Bank.

IMF (1998). 'Financial Crises: Characteristics and Indicators of Vulnerability' in IMF (ed.), World Economic Outlook. Financial Crises: Causes and Indicators. Washington, DC, IMF.

Kaminsky, G. L., Lizondo, S., & Reinhart, C. M. (1998). 'Leading Indicators of Currency Crises', Staff Papers, 45(1). Washington, DC, IMF.

Krkoska, L. (2000). 'Assessing Macroeconomic Vulnerability in Central Europe', Working Paper, No. 52. London, European Bank for Reconstruction and Development, Office of the Chief Economist.

Minsky, H. (1986). Stabilizing an Unstable Economy. New Haven, CT, Yale University Press.

National Bank of Romania (2020). Financial Stability Report, National Bank of Romania, Bucharest, June, 2020.

Racaru, I., Copaciu, M., & Lapteacru, I. (2006) Sisteme de avertizare timpurie a crizelor valutare, BNR, Caiet de studii, accessed on February 2013 at http://www.bnro.ro/PublicationDocuments.aspx

Spratt, S. & Bernini, M. (2010). 'Measuring Economic Resilience and Vulnerability: Towards an International Index', paper presented at the 'Second Annual ESRC Development Economics Conference', Manchester, January 2010.

Wells, J. (1997). Composite Vulnerability Index: A preliminary report. London, Commonwealth Secretariat.

Octavian-Dragomir Jora, Matei-Alexandru Apăvăloaei, Mihaela Iacob

The tangible problems of an intangible objective: culturally sustainable development

Abstract The mainstream approach to the "economics of culture" assumes that "cultural value" and "cultural capital" comprise distinct epistemic categories that warrant different treatment from that given by mundane economic science to the concepts of value or capital. By adding the "cultural" qualifier, some authors affiliated with the field claim that particular objects and services possess special characteristics that set them apart from ordinary tangible and intangible goods. Therefore, market transactions are incapable of reflecting their true value and cannot ensure that the right amount of such goods is provided or preserved. Assuming that this is just another type of market failure, some authors call for the enactment of measures that will set humanity on a "culturally sustainable" path. This paper aims to provide a critique of the prevailing approach in cultural economics. We propose a fundamental analysis of the concepts of cultural value, cultural capital, and cultural sustainability and argue that this subfield of economics rests upon value-laden constructs. In the end, the main argument behind mainstream cultural economics boils down to an unscientific lamentation that the free market does not provide a sufficient amount of a specific type of good. Also, cultural sustainability may find itself at odds with the political objective of sustainable development, if we consider that the latter implies the abandonment of the current anthropocentric culture.

Keywords: economic value, cultural value, economic capital, cultural capital, economic sustainability, cultural sustainability

Introduction

The epistemic encounter between economics and culture domains is inevitable despite the fact that economists are advised to enter the "cultural" territory with "civilized" timidity, because the science of "prices" and "production" is rather weak in mapping the "priceless" and the "ineffable." This bias seems legitimate when the cold objectivity of the tools of the natural sciences is called in the subjective-value universe of human actions, but "humane-centered" kind of economics is in no case eccentric to culture. Despite the energies invested in fitting the economic life in the Procrustean bed of mechanics, economics does deal with a different kind of "animal." Human sense (even if far from being flawless) and sensibility (always larger than any straitjacket whatsoever) provide efficient and orderly responses to resources scarcity: through information, incentives, and institutions. Moreover, culture cannot escape such a dialectic: cultural life relies on the world of scarce means, critical for artefactually expressing different attitudes, beliefs, customs, habits, values, practices shared by individuals within a community.

The issue of means-ends adequacy, the meta-rationale of human action, closes the "electric arc" of (economic) value and (ethic/aesthetic) values. Satisfactions and significations are caught in the human universe of scarce resources (that have competing serviceability), transformed to meet, either physical or spiritual, needs (being in interpersonal competition). In other words, the cultural spaces eventually become economically intelligible through the genus proximum of the productive transformation of scarce resources in the framework of "cooperative division" of labor (a kind of "manufacture of societal fabric"), as well as through the differentia specifica of identity creation, manifested by any culture's foundational feature of "distinctive cohesion." Putting it otherwise, the production of culture is served by anonymous markets and hierarchies; while the consumption of almost every good or service involves, ultimately, a kind of cultural experience. Those endemic concepts within economic science are well-placed for analyzing culture: i.e., from value to welfare, from stage of production to capital, from efficiency to sustainability.

The present article is going to embrace a rather unusual route concerning problematizations pertaining to the field economics of culture. We begin by addressing and assessing two "classical" economic concepts which in the economics of culture received a rebranding by adding the "cultural" epithet – value and capital –, only to point to the analogous mutation of a star-concept in contemporary/mainstream/neoclassical economics – sustainability. Topical in defining and defending the (mainstream/neoclassical) concept of cultural sustainability are Thorsby's (1995; 1999; 2001) discussions, previously debated at length, on logical, epistemological and praxeological grounds by Jora (2015; 2016) and Jora et al. (2019). The line of reasoning warns against the temptation to consider culture (otherwise a spiritually enriching activity for human beings) as sufficient in itself to further enrich economic theory. Untrained economists could easily be distracted by the profession's use of specialized and hybridizing concepts. In summary, the line of criticism lying at the very root of the present analysis runs as follows:

- There is an illusion in emphasizing and decomposing "cultural value" on top or out of "economic value," while still giving it a monetary expression. Value is just ordinal (only prices are cardinal). Cultural value is neither "part" of nor "greater" than economic value (i.e., I sell cheaply one heritage asset I find invaluable to a new owner who has the means to conserve it).
- Instead of working hard to fabricate some original (accounting) setting for "cultural capital," it is much more relevant to note that capital, in both material and monetary expressions, requires keen evaluation of depreciation, exhaustion, maintenance or replenishment, which is best done in markets by "self-interested" owner-entrepreneurs (rather than by "selfless" public servants).

- Consequently, the crux of "cultural sustainability" (pair to the ecological concern), proper to human species as the only one conscious and capable of building an institutional infrastructure for its non-instinctual perpetuation, is best served not through central planning, but through the consolidation of the best institution equipped for cross-generation flourishing: private property.

1. Literature review: "neoclassical" sustainability under "classical" scrutiny

Sustainability became established as a scientific discipline with the advent of the new millennium. However, its exploratory roots stretch deeper, going back to the well-known "Brundtland Report," Our Common Future (WCED 1987). The message perpetuated since then is that the human species needs a new sense of mediation and moderation in its environmental dimension of existence. Following the symmetrical mapping of human existence laying at the crossroads of nature and culture, a parallel worldwide concern unfolded, devoted to the social and cultural dimension of human "ecology" and "ecosystem." This focus is present at both scholarly (Throsby 1999; Hawkes 2001; Littig and Grießler 2005; Saastamoinen 2005; Chan et al. 2012; Daniels et al. 2012) and policy designing and making levels (Council of Europe 2000; UNESCO 2001; Culture 21 2011; Forest Europe, UNECE and FAO 2011).

Noteworthy, the mainstream message of both natural and cultural sustainability advocates is this: while Western capitalist markets were found better equipped than Eastern socialist gulags in delivering prosperity, the same way-too-free markets look poorer in addressing sustainability issues compared to democratic-governmental public-political tools. These "market failure" warnings in acknowledging and managing the natural/cultural preservation-oriented processes – tackling the depletion/misuse of resources –, as well as the protection-oriented ones – tackling the (")pollution(") of third-party resources – gained preeminence in scientific literature and policy-making. However, despite its popularity, the mainstream vision on sustainability, and the economic stream of thought on which it relies seem, on several accounts, far from being fully sustainable theoretically and practically.

Economic neoclassicism (in theoretical premises) and state interventionism (in practical consequences), inspired by the former, still deserve scrutiny. Exploring and exploiting the best path towards the universal goal of sustainable development (SD), in both natural and cultural environments, remain legitimate worries.

From neoclassical theory...

The mainstream theory of SD is suspected of relying too much on "metaphors" of critical economic concepts: value, capital, income (Taylor 2002; Brätland 2006). These metaphors of economic reality (and science) are tributary to the positivistic, neoclassical paradigm, where economics is modelled and moulded to mimic the formal rigor of maths and experimental natural sciences; this is, however, a debatable epistemic view in the subjective field of human action (Huerta de Soto 1998; Hülsmann 1999).

- Regarding value and valuation, the so widespread, yet highly fictional, image is that, on the one hand, there is something "objective" and "measurable" in valuation, as well as in the utility functions thereof, and that, on the other hand, there is something like a "higher social standard of welfare," that transcends individual valuations. These are reckoned by some superior scientific and societal authority capable of inferring "true values" out of it and provide the public good "SD."
- Regarding capital, the picture is of a "broadly defined capital stock," that is no more than an agglomeration of heterogeneous physical things, defying coherent aggregation (including items like "atmosphere, oceans, and ecosystems"). Here, the micro-processes of private, calculated, entrepreneurial allocation and maintenance leave room to confiscatory taxation needed to fuel the investments that the current generations are required to make so that the future ones can secure dire assets.
- Regarding income (which in private undertakings is simply the return on a capitalized asset), this gets in the logic of public management of resources to become the flow of benefits that a "whole generation," acting "as one," succeeds to sustain. However, the "generation" is only a "quasi-owner" of the assets. Therefore, it faces insurmountable difficulty in calculating (as against a true owner) how much to "consume" without diminishing the value of the same capital as perceived by another future quasi-owner.

Back to classical thinking

Translating sustainability into a much more classical mind-set, sustainability cannot escape from being reduced, before anything else, to fundamental problems related to the scarcities of various resources and to the proper ways in which people discover and manage them. The main fallacies of the "engineering" approach on sustainability are: (1) it ignores the profound subjectivity of human evaluations and the teleological, non-determinable aspects of human action (Reisman 1996); (2) the essential role of social institutions in disciplining individual behavior and especially the crux of private property rights (Hoppe 1989); (3) the importance of the functional free-market setting, based on voluntary exchanges, money prices emerging out of them and economic calculation enabled thereupon (Mises 2008). Losing from sight these basic features of human action, emphasized in the Austrian School's refurbishing of the classical economic tradition, the current SD theory exposes itself to ineligible risks concerning the capacity to provide "round," rational, realistic and reliable assessments.

Evaluation, capital, and income make sense before anywhere else in the context of individual (rather than collectivized) actions, of private property and market contracts (Mises 1959). Only in such a landscape, real individuals can calculate and then coordinate within communities the rational use of resources (avoiding both abuse and misuse) and address real sustainability concerns (Apăvăloaei and Miron 2009). While this consideration seems theoretically-alien to the pragmatic issue of sustainability, they lay at the very core of any meaningful approach. Private property and monetary exchange facilitate entrepreneurial calculation (faintly mimicked by bureaucratic or technocratic analyses) with respect to capital formation, maintenance, or consumption. Shifting to sustainability requires the substitution of private stewardship for public one, seeing "environments" not as a bulk of things, but as capital assets. What we will try to point out is that such principled considerations are equally valid for both natural/environmental goods and for spiritual/cultural goods too.

2. Cultural sustainability: a "colossal" concept with "clay" pillars

Throsby (1995, pp. 203–205) argues that the idea of sustainability can be used to bring economic and cultural systems together, in the same manner as the concept originated by Brundtland has been used to link the economic and ecological systems in order to identify critical relationships between mankind's manufacturing acts and the natural environment items. Specifically, he proposes that this link be achieved by means of a concept which he named culturally sustainable development (CSD).

The quoted author notes that, given the complexity inherent in each constituent part of this concept (i.e., culture, sustainability, development), it is not surprising that a concise definition would be illusory. Therefore, he proposes to substitute a definition with a set of criteria (to be discussed below) through which programs, policies, and strategies can be evaluated. CSD could thus be seen as more of a conceptual framework through which things can be judged, rather than a piece of precise standard.

Throsby argues that CSD includes both traditional interpretations assigned to culture – functionalist ("anthropologic") and structuralist ("artefactual"). It includes both the idea of cultural development in the "hardware" sense (stocks of goods/assets, services/techniques), as well as the idea of culture in the "software" sense (attitudes and practices which fuel creativity). It is envisaged that CSD could be broadly and roughly defined/identified in terms of the following four principles/properties/pillars:

(1) "Advancement of material and non-material well-being." It is suggested that the features of cultural progress within a society should be considered as integrated into the notion of development. For this, it would be necessary to find the type of economic and social indicators appropriate to the perspective of "human development" in the broad sense (beyond "economic growth"), cumulated with a range of cultural indicators, chosen to reflect the cultural status of the community in accordance with any cultural definition that is preferred. Therefore, economic, social, and cultural aspirations are seen in equilibrium; this also implies a properly balanced articulation of national priorities between economic, social, and cultural goals. The processes that determine these priorities require the consideration and consensus of the community and, inevitably, a political decision.

(2) "Intergenerational equity and the maintenance of cultural capital." A basic component of sustainability, the concern for long-term issues is translated by the assumed responsibility of a generation to manage resources in a way that recognizes the needs and rights of future generations. Sustainability, therefore, invokes the desirability of intergenerational equity, which is the fairness of distribution of resources and opportunities between generations, particularly between the present and future ones. The principle of intergenerational equity in a cultural context requires the operationalization of the notion of "cultural capital." This principle affirms that if development is to be culturally sustainable, society, from the position of custodian of the inherited cultural capital that is then passed on to the future generations, needs to recognize a responsibility towards those future generations.
(3) "Equity within the present generation." There is a complaint that economists' concerns for "social justice" have diminished as the focus turned toward economic functionality and efficiency; equity and welfare should be addressed through a separate process with the help of various economic policies. It is considered that although proper functioning markets can be effective wealth generators, they are very poor wealth distributors, and in many capitalist countries the established redistribution mechanisms have been insufficient to maintain the existing patterns of income distribution throughout time, let alone to reduce inequality. The distribution of cultural resources, access to culture, provision of cultural services for disadvantaged groups are all aspects of fairness or justice in the conduct of cultural life, recognizable as ethical axioms, and basic rights.
(4) "Recognition of interdependence." This feature – paramount to the others – stems from the assertion that the proper conceptualization of economic activity and culture does not separate the two processes, but views them as part of a single process, which requires a "whole-systems" vision. It is compared with the analogous perspective in the environmental sphere, where crucial interconnections between ecological and social systems are noted; for example, it is now acknowledged that the continued degradation of soil, water or air quality will compromise the chances of future economic and social progress. In CSD, the basic principle that recognizes the interdependence between cultural and economic systems implies acceptance of the perspective that the maintenance of cultural processes is no less vital than the maintenance of bio-processes within the continuous development of humankind.

3. Cultural sustainability: towards a property-based reinforcement

When Mises launched "the debate on economic calculation in socialism" in the 1920s, very few economists understood it correctly in the context, and even fewer understood the complex and complete extension of the argument, valid for any kind of monetary-pricing-system process. This baseline of resource allocation is not addressed in the intergenerational sustainability economy as it is now conceptualized and approached by mainstream neoclassical economists. Such a finding is not at all surprising if we correctly grasp the epistemological premises of neoclassicism in economics. For instance, the alleged "objectivity" of value (utility) and the market-free imputability of "income defined in a broad sense" led sustainability economics toward severe analytical errors.

By default, sustainability mechanisms are treated as a "public good/service," eminently provided by the public authorities. However, without private property and monetary exchange, there can be no calculation regarding capital, nor rational means of maintaining capital or income for current and future generations. As obvious as this seems to scholars of the Austrian School of economics, as disregarded it is to neoclassic economists (such as R. Solow or G. Heal), who seem ignorant/neutral of/to the weight of monetary/economic calculation based on entrepreneurial pricing, not on values derived from fictive functions, in appraising the need to preserve resources. Speaking of "cultural" sustainability does not fade away the economic logic.

Properly defining property rights is as important as duly enforcing them. If property rights are to ensure social coordination, randomness cannot play any part in establishing them. There is no room left open for principled equivoque (yet this does not guarantee the practical effectiveness of their exercise). Arguably, in the history of social thought, despite sophisticated sophistry, the most coherent articulation of a private property-based order traces its roots back to Roman Law, refreshed by Scholastic (jus naturalis) and Lockean logical defence, brilliantly synthesized and restated by Rothbard (1982) and Hoppe (1989). Only non-aggressively acquired property (from self-ownership to homesteading, production and voluntary exchanges) passes the tests of genuine normativity.

In a proprietarian/calculational sense, economic and ethical sustainability may gain in realism, for we live in the territory of subjectivity, scarcity, sociality, so pervasive in the cultural realm. Culture is about subjective value, translatable from spiritual intimacy to scaled preferences demonstrated in action and then to scalar pricing. The prices spur from markets for scarce resources/factors of production/assets, crucial in edifying production capacities for cultural consumption-goods/services (tangibles/intangibles). Producing and consuming them becomes a social/sharable experience to be bequeathed/inherited across generations, as cultural products and their cultural production recipes need to be sustainably reproducible in an economic sense.

What can the proprietarian and calculational economics paradigm teach as in the field of culturally sustainable development?

Firstly, an owner (i.e., of cultural goods) is entitled to decide the desired uses and obtain a price from third parties for the services provided by his property. Having the right to exclude non-paying partners, he manages the "social scarcities," determining what resource will serve what use, depending on the price-signaled intensity of the need. The rationale is valid whether we are talking about "trivial" goods or services, whether we are talking about "the (re)productive consumption" of Hausmann's or Mincu's architecture, Rodin's or Brâncuşi's sculpture, Vermeer's or Baba's painting, Wagner's or Enescu's music, Dostoievsky's or Rebreanu's literature, Pliseţkaia's or Popescu's dance, Chaplin's or Caragiu's acting performance, or the directorial perspective of Fellini or Ciulei. By "valuing" such works, rather in the private system than in the public domain, we convey social signals about the relative scarcity of these goods through a valid "pricing" process that correlates offer with demand, limiting the problematic cohabitation between shortage and surpluses, thus (re)establishing the basis for sustainability.

Secondly, well-defined and defended property ownership imposes responsibilities on the owner (i.e., of cultural heritage/patrimony assets). In situations where the damage on private property can be proved as caused intentionally or negligently, the owner is entitled to claim compensation, thus rendering fully responsible the third parties. Liability becomes a mark of scarcity and displays generalized disciplinary effects on property use, indicating, for instance, which uses are sustainable and which are not. The reality of cultural heritage and its sensibly greater degradation in public "tragedies of the commons" rather than in private hands can be acknowledged pointing to "responsibilization." Sadly, inside the prevailing institutional reality, there are limits to defining and defending property, due to unnecessary public bureaucratic burdens and of politicized privileges. Rational agents, relievable from the consequences of their actions or inactions, tend to become and behave "morally hazardous" by depleting/destroying or leaving in dereliction and exposing to deterioration certain cultural-heritage (capital-) goods.

Given the above considerations on the relationship between property and sustainability, Throsby's incomplete analysis reveals its problematic foundations when attempting to apply the mainstream/neoclassical institutionally-neutral/property-rights-free theory of SD and its fundamental state-derived practical solutions in nurturing cultural value and cultural capital. He argues that cultural sustainability is a matter of both efficiency and equity, and identifies those previously mentioned principles considered important for the sustainability of cultural capital. However, if some of the principles he listed are less justifiable, others are outright confusing. For example, when he claims that intragenerational equity is important for sustainability. This principle "supports the right of the current generation to justice in terms of access to cultural resources and the benefits of cultural capital." However, the author does not spend time to expose the theoretical equity – sustainability ties. Historically, the very sustainability of Western Civilization itself invalidates such allegations: inegalitarian as it was, it flourished across ages.

Intergenerational equity refers to "justice in the distribution of welfare, public goods and resources between generations," Throsby often using the term "intertemporal distributive justice." This argument is that future generations have the right to their culture, and in order for this right to be respected, cultural development must become a sustainable one. However, the failure to clarify the "subjective vs. objective" debate on cultural value/valuation is fatal to his argument. If we talk about cultural value in terms of subjective preference, then all the distress is in vain – parts of any culture will be, anyway, sustained. Even if done objectively, the transformation of aesthetics into ethics becomes inconsistent because the support of cultural production through the sacrifice of non-cultural production can be reduced to the same intra-generational ethical arbitrariness, in which the principles are no longer universal, but contingent personalized following the whims of "some." This situation is even "more" absurd if we speak of violating actual, real rights (on property, of expression), to ensure some future, unborn ones.

Conclusions

Perhaps the most important point we tried to make with the foregoing discussion is that much value can be added to the field of cultural economics via a common-sense approach to the topic. Both the "anthropological" and the "artefactual" dimensions of culture are indeed important to living a fulfilling life and leaving things better than we found them for the next generations. Even this statement is a distilled product of our culture; it is a result of human thought that transcends any biological/materialist view of human beings. However, what we contend is that nothing meaningful can be added to the discussion by inventing new concepts or by ignoring the contributions of modern economics. Modern economic science is centered on the theory of subjective value, and it is only common-sense to hold the field of cultural economics to the same standard. In this vein, there is no way to identify some (objective) "cultural value." As long as cultural economics is seen as a subfield of economics, we cannot assume that certain goods and services have inherent value inter-personally observable outside market transactions.

Also, it defies common sense to talk about "cultural capital." By and large, there is some agreement that capital is an intellectual category that exists only in the minds of entrepreneurs. It is not a technologically determined bundle of objects, nor can its monetary expression exist independent of the subjective appraisement of each entrepreneur. There is no way of estimating the value of a capital good outside the market, i.e., outside the nexus of exchanges that take place between private property title holders. Only through an entrepreneurially driven market process can material objects become capital goods with an associated monetary value. Any talk of capital outside this specific institutional setting is only a fiction, a mere metaphor with no epistemic value whatsoever. From an economic point of view, there is no "cultural capital" in any other sense than what entrepreneurial judgment can imagine and employ in production or exchange on the market. There is no economic theory of "cultural capital" as there is no distinct theory of "beauty capital," which would apply to the study of the economics of beauty pageants.

Now, if common-sense tells us there is nothing special about "cultural value" and that any use of the concept of "cultural capital" is, at best, confusing, what can be said about a political goal like "culturally sustainable development"? For conducting a meaningful conservation policy, market prices are a (scientifically determined) prerequisite, which, in its turn, presupposes private property and free markets in "all" goods and services. Based on this view, we argued that the market is the best solution for achieving the goal of culturally sustainable development, from both a theoretically and historically informed perspective. It goes without saying that such argumentation in favor of private property and free markets for cultural artefacts is based on utilitarian reasoning, even if we alluded that an objective ethics argument can also be adduced. Finally, we would like to leave the reader with a rhetoric question: If the concept of sustainable development contests the currently prevailing anthropocentric culture that defines capitalism, how (environmentally) sustainable got to be the proposed objective of cultural sustainability?

References

Apăvăloaei, Matei-Alexandru; Miron, Dumitru, "Sustainable Development. An Old Concept in Search of the New Efficiency". "Quality – Access to Success" Journal 10(106), 2009, pp. 200–206.

Brätland, John: "Toward a Calculational Theory and Policy of International Sustainability". Quarterly Journal of Austrian Economics 9(2), 2006, pp. 13–45.

Chan, Kai Ming Adam; Guerry, Anne D.; Balvanera, Patricia; Klain, Sarah; Satterfield, Terre.; Basurto, Xavier; Bostrom, Ann; Chuenpagdee, Ratana; Gould, Rachelle ; Halpern, Benjamin S.; Hannahs, Neil; Levine, Jordan; Norton, Bryan; Ruckelshaus, Mary; Russell, Roly; Tam, Jordan; Woodside, Ulalia, "Where are «Cultural» and «Social» in Ecosystem Services? A Framework for Constructive Engagement". BioScience 62, 2012, pp. 744–756.Council of Europe: European Landscape Convention. Treaty Series no. 176. Council of Europe: Firenze. 2000.

Culture 21: Lobbying for Culture as the 4th Pillar of Sustainable Development in the Process of the Rio+20 Summit. Agenda 21 for Culture. United Cities and Local Governments – Committee on Culture. 2011.

Daniels, Terry C.; Muhar, Andreas; Arnberger, Arne; Aznar, Olivier; Boyd, James W.; Chan, Kai M.A.; Costanza, Robert.; Elmqvist, Thomas; Flint, Courtney G.; Gobster, Paul H.; Grêt-Regamey, Adrienne; Lave, Rebecca; Muhar Susanne; Penker, Marianne; Ribe, Robert G. ; Schauppenlehner, Thomas; Sikor, Thomas; Soloviy, Ihor; Spierenburg, Marja; Taczanowska, Karolina; Tam, Jordan; von der Dunk, Andreas, : "Contributions of Cultural Services to the Ecosystem Services Agenda". Proceedings of the National Academy of Sciences of the United States of

America 109, 2012, pp. 8812–8819.Forest Europe, UNECE and FAO: State of Europe's Forests 2011. Status and Trends in Sustainable Forest Management in Europe. Rome. 2011.

Hawkes, Jon: The Fourth Pillar of Sustainability: Culture's Essential Role in Public Planning. Common Ground Publishing Pty Ltd, Cultural Development Network (Vic): Melbourne. 2001.

Hoppe, Hans-Hermann: A Theory of Socialism and Capitalism. Kluwer Academic Publishers: Norwell, MA. 1989.

Huerta de Soto, Jesús: "The Ongoing Methodenstreit of the Austrian School". Journal des Economistes et des Etudes Humaines 8(1), 1998, pp. 75–113.

Hülsmann, Jörg Guido: "Economic Science and Neoclassicism". The Quarterly Journal of Austrian Economics 2(4), 1999, pp. 3–20.

Jora, Octavian-Dragomir: "Economic Freedom and Cultural Flourishing: A Praxeological Account on Value, Capital, Sustainability, and Identity". Romanian Economic Journal, 18(57), 2015, pp. 51–66.

Jora, Octavian-Dragomir: Spiritualitate, materialitate şi proprietate. Cultura mea, cultura ta, cultura noastră, cultura lor. Editura ASE: Bucureşti. 2016.

Jora, Octavian-Dragomir; Iacob, Mihaela; Apăvăloaei, Matei-Alexandru: "Public Cultural Heritage and Private Property Rights: Building Sustainable Community Through Individuality". In Vasile, Valentina (ed.), Caring and Sharing: The Cultural Heritage Environment as an Agent for Change. 2016 ALECTOR Conference, Istanbul, Turkey. Series: Springer Proceedings in Business and Economics, pp. 213–224, Springer Nature: Heidelberg, Germany. 2019.

Littig, Beate; Grießler, Erich: "Social Sustainability: A Catchword between Political Pragmatism and Social Theory". International Journal of Sustainable Development 8, 2005, pp. 65–79.

Mises, Ludwig von: Human Action: A Treatise on Economics. Ludwig von Mises Institute: Auburn, AL. 2008.

Mises, Ludwig von: Socialism: An Economic and Sociological Analysis. Yale University Press: New Haven, CT. 1959.

Reisman, George: Capitalism: A Treatise on Economics. Jameson Books: Ottawa, Illinois. 1996.

Rothbard, Murray Newton: Ethics of Liberty. Atlantic Highlands, Humanities Press: New Jersey. 1982.

Saastamoinen, Olli: "Multiple Ethics for Multidimensional Sustainability on Forestry?". Silva Carelica 49, 2005, pp. 37–53.

Taylor, Jerry: "Sustainable Development: A Dubious Solution in Search of a Problem". Cato Policy Analysis Series 449, 2002, pp. 1–49.

Throsby, David: “Cultural Capital”. Journal of Cultural Economics 23, 1999, pp. 3–12.

Throsby, David: “Culture, Economics and Sustainability”. Journal of Cultural Economics 19, 1995, pp. 199–206.

Throsby, David: Economics and Culture. Cambridge University Press: Cambridge, Illinois. 2001.

UNESCO: UNESCO Universal Declaration on Cultural Diversity. Records of the General Conference, 31st Session, 15 October–3 November 2001, Paris, France. Annex I, Volume 1 Resolutions. UNESCO: Paris. 2001.

World Commission on Environment and Development: Our Common Future (Brundtland Report). Oxford University Press: Oxford. 1987.

Zizi Goschin

How did regional specialization influence the post-crisis economic growth in Romania?

Abstract The role of economic specialization in regional development has been extensively research, with a renewed interest triggered by the recent economic crisis, as high specialization is believed to increase vulnerability to economic shocks. This paper tackles the neglected perspective of specialization's influence in the post-crisis economic growth of the regions. To this end, spatial regression models are used for estimating specialization's effects on the GDP growth of Romanian counties over 2011–2016. Specialization is measured using two specific indexes – Herfindahl and Krugman, as well as location quotients for the main economic sectors. Additional control variables, both in static and dynamic form, are included in the models to account for other factors of influence on economic growth, such as domestic and foreign investments, employment, R&D, etc. Among them, two custom made resilience indicators have been added to capture the differences in counties' response to the crisis. The findings support the empirical studies arguing that high specialization is not only detrimental to absorbing economic shocks, but can also impede economic recovery and growth.

Keywords: specialization; economic growth; economic resilience; spatial model; Romania

Introduction

The role of economic specialization in regional development has been extensively researched (Hallet, 2002; Aiginger and Davies, 2004; Ezcurra et al., 2006; Goschin et al., 2009; Boschma et al., 2012), with new interest triggered by the recent economic crisis, as high specialization (especially in low-tech activities) is believed to increase vulnerability to economic shocks (De Groot et al., 2011; Cuadrado-Roura and Maroto, 2016).

Aiming to fill a gap in the literature, this paper tackles the neglected perspective of specialization's influence in the post-crisis economic growth of the regions. We use spatial regression models for estimating specialization's effects on the GDP growth of Romanian counties over 2011–2016. Specialization is measured with two specific indexes –Herfindahl and Krugman–, as well as location quotients for the main economic sectors. Additional control variables, both in static and dynamic form, are included in the model to account for other factors of influence on economic growth, such as domestic and foreign investments, employment, R&D, etc. Among them are two custom made resilience indicators that capture the differences in counties' response to the crisis.

1. Literature review

High regional specialization means that one or a few economic activities dominate or hold large shares in the region's economy. The empirical findings related to the role of specialization in regional growth and in vulnerability to economic shocks are mixed. Based on the trade theories, researchers believe that specialization exploits local comparative advantages and can promote productivity and economic growth, while, on the other side, it might bring vulnerability and decline during economic crises (Hallet, 2002; Trăistaru and Păuna, 2003; Aiginger and Davies, 2004; Ezcurra et al., 2006; Marelli, 2006; De Groot et al., 2011; Boschma et al., 2012).

Although economic diversity seems to support economic growth in countries having lower income/capita, this relationship is less clear or doesn't hold altogether at a higher development level (Kaulich, 2012). In general, developed countries have lower degrees of specialization, since economic growth opportunities are more evenly distributed across regions, reducing investors' preferences for certain locations. Even if economic growth is territorially uneven, it radiates from the development poles to periphery, propagating economic chances that favor all regions (European Commission, 2010).

Regional specialization is commonly blamed for dampening resilience to the economic shocks hitting its dominant sectors, although more nuanced analyses showed many deviations from this rule. Investigating the regional resilience to crisis in Spain, Cuadrado-Roura and Maroto (2016) found that "regions with a faster and stronger recovery are those that previously specialized and reinforced more productive industries, such as some manufacturing, energy and some advanced services." The findings might heavily vary depending on the specificities of economic sectors, as well as regional particularities (Hallet, 2002). Moreover, the choice of the measure of specialization (given that the empirical literature promotes a wide range of simple and complex indicators) and also the specific dataset to be employed can largely affect the results (Kaulich, 2012).

Previous research targeting Romania indicated limited and declining regional specialization during the country's transition to market economy, as well as afterwards (Traistaru, Iara, and Pauna, 2002; Traistaru and Pauna, 2003; Andrei et al., 2007; Neagu and Neagu, 2016; Yaskal, Maha, and Petrashchak, 2018). Romania is mainly specialized in medium and low-tech activities.

2. Method, variables and data

There are both simple and synthetic indicators to measure regional specialization and to find the spatial specialization patterns. One of the commonly used indicators, the location quotient (Florence, 1939) indicates the share of each economic activity in the regional economy relative to the national economy. The location coefficient is determined using either the concentration rate g_{ij}^{C}, or the specialization rate g_{ij}^{S}, as follows:

$$LQ_{ij} = \frac{E_{ij}/E_j}{E_i/E} = \frac{E_{ij}/E_i}{E_j/E} \Leftrightarrow LQ_{ij} = \frac{g_{ij}^{C}}{E_i/E} = \frac{g_{ij}^{S}}{E_j/E}, \tag{1}$$

where: E_{ij} – employment in sector j and region i; E_j – total employment in sector j (at national level); E_i – total employment in region i; E – total employment in the country; g_{ij}^{C} – the share of region i in sector j; g_{ij}^{S} – the share of sector j in region i.

The Herfindahl-Hirschman index (Hirschman, 1964) is an absolute indicator of specialization calculated by summing the squares of the weights g_{ij} of all economic sectors j in the regional economy i, as follows:

$$H_i^S = \sum_{j=1}^{m} \left(g_{ij}^{S}\right)^2. \tag{2}$$

The bigger the index, the higher the specialization level.

The Krugman dissimilarity index (Krugman, 1991) is a relative indicator of specialization comparing the shares of economic activities in each region (g_{ij}) with the economic structure of the national economy as a whole (g_j):

$$K_i^S = \sum_{j=1}^{m} \left|g_{ij}^{S} - g_j\right|, \tag{3}$$

where $g_j = E_j/E$.

The bigger the index, the higher is the region's distance from the structure of national economy.

The relation between the specialization indicators and the regional growth, the latter proxied by GDP per capita dynamics, will be further explored in the framework of simple spatial regression models. The analysis must consider the possibility of spatial interactions among neighbors, which rises specification issues and is addressed by using specific regression techniques. We are going to test for potential spatial autocorrelation by employing a basic indicator in spatial statistics, namely Moran's I:

$$MI = \frac{n \sum_{i=1}^{n} \sum_{j=1}^{n} w_{ij}(x_i - \bar{x})(x_j - \bar{x})}{\left(\sum_{i=1}^{n} \sum_{j=1}^{n} w_{ij}\right) \sum_{i=1}^{n} (x_i - \bar{x})^2} \tag{4}$$

where x_i and x_j represent the values of the variable x under investigation in the regions i and j respectively, $\bar{x}$ stands for the average and w_{ij} are the spatial weights (more specifically w_{ij} = 1 if regions i and j are neighbors, and w_{ij} = 0 otherwise). Moran's I ranges from −1 (perfect dissimilarity among neighbors) to +1 (perfect similarity), while the null value corresponds to random spatial distribution of values.

From an econometric perspective, the presence of spatial dependence should be corrected by introducing a spatial variable in the model (Anselin et al., 2006), which is either a spatial lag of the dependent variable y (spatial autoregressive model):

$$\mathbf{y} = \rho \cdot \mathbf{W} \cdot \mathbf{y} + \mathbf{X} \cdot \beta + \varepsilon, \tag{5}$$

or spatial errors ε (spatial error model):

$$\boldsymbol{y} = \boldsymbol{X\beta} + \boldsymbol{\varepsilon}, \text{ where } \boldsymbol{\varepsilon} = \boldsymbol{\lambda W \varepsilon} + \boldsymbol{\nu} \tag{6}$$

where W stands for the spatial weight matrix nxn capturing the spatial structure (neighbors), Wy is the spatial lag of the dependent variable y and X is the matrix of regressors.

In order to choose the best model for our data, the Lagrange multiplier test for both spatial error and spatial lag is used. Failing to reject the null hypothesis of spatial randomness implies that classical OLS regression is more appropriate.

3. Variables included in the analysis and data sources

The analysis of economic specialization uses statistical data regarding the spatial and sectoral distributions of employment. Official data on civil employment at NUTS 2 level (county) is issued by the National Institute of Statistics. Employment was broken down in 16 major sectors of activity, namely Agriculture, forestry and fishing; Manufacturing; Mining and quarrying; Electricity, gas, steam and air conditioning; Construction; wholesale and retail trade; Transportation and storage services; Accommodation and food service activities; Information and communication services; Professional, scientific and technical activities; services; Public administration and defense; Social insurance from the public system, administrative and support service activities; Education; Health and social care; Water supply; Sewerage, waste management and remediation activities.

The dependent variable in the regression models is GDP growth after the crisis (2011–2016). The explanatory variables of interest are the specialization indices Herfindahl and Krugman, as well as the location quotients for the main economic sectors (agriculture, manufacturing and trade). Control variables, accounting for other factors of influence, have been selected based on the findings of previous empirical research addressing the topic of regional growth. Given that our control variable covers the post-crisis period (2011–2016), we used three types of controls. A first group includes indices that capture variables' growth over 2011–2016: gross investment growth, FDIs growth and employment growth. The second group captures the regional characteristics at the beginning of the recovery (2011) and are expressed in logarithms: GDP per capita, Average monthly wage, Gross investments per capita, Foreign Direct investments per capita, number of graduates from tertiary education per 1000 inhabitants. A third group of variables, also for 2011, represent various rates and are not logarithmic: GDP resilience, measured as regional relative to national % change in GDP during crisis and employment resilience, as regional relative to national % change in employment (both variables resulted from own computations, based on data from National Institute of Statistics), unemployment rate (%); urbanization rate (%of urban population in the county), industrialization rate of the county (%of employment in industry). All initial data come from the National Institute of Statistics (Institutul National de Statistica, 2019), except for Foreign Direct investments, downloaded from The National Trade Register Office site.

4. Results and discussion

Romanian counties displayed large territorial variation in their economic specialization (Appendix 1). There is also wide variation in their resistance to the recent financial and economic crisis, from the perspective of regional, relative to national, percentage change in employment and GDP (Appendix 2). When comparing GDP decline during crisis with the decrease in employment we find many outliers, meaning there are counties that have been much better or worse than average at absorbing GDP shocks.

The results from estimating the economic growth model show only a few significant variables, which are displayed in Tab. 1. Most variables from our initial list of potential factors of influence (see Section 2) are statistically insignificant and have been dropped from the final specification of the model. The results indicate that the rise in employment has been the most powerful factor behind the Romanian counties' growth over 2011–2016. It compensated for the loss in employment during the crisis (2009–2010) and it supported the subsequent economic recovery.

Tab. 1: The results

Variables	Classic (nonspatial) model*		Spatial lag model**		Spatial error model**	
	Coefficient	**Prob**	**Coefficient**	**Prob**	**Coefficient**	**Prob**
Spatial lag for GDP	-	-	0.0747288	0.64018	-	-
Constant	1.30615	0.00195	1.22684	0.00175	1.27381	0.00075
Employment Growth	1.13802	0.00401	1.14182	0.00086	1.32715	0.00005
Location Quotients for Manufacturing	-0.164994	0.00208	-0.166953	0.00029	-0.211964	0.00001
Resilience (employment)	-0.0703871	0.00229	-0.0685317	0.00058	-0.060929	0.00112
lnGDP/cap	-0.144712	0.03003	-0.146712	0.01319	-0.163594	0.01505
Herfindahl specialization index	-0.697998	0.08850	-0.698227	0.05786	-0.706371	0.04552
Lambda	-	-	-	-	0.458975	0.00845
Statistics	*Value*	*Prob*	*Value*	*Prob*	*Value*	*Prob*
Log likelihood	61.3382	-	61.4365		62.8856	
R-squared	0.51338	-	-	-	-	-
F-statistic	7.59601	0.0000	-	-	-	-
Akaike info criterion	-110.676	-	-108.873	-	-113.771	-
Schwarz criterion	-100.25	-	-96.7094		-103.345	-
Breusch-Pagan test	5.9776	0.3084	5.8538	0.32071	7.0101	0.21989
Moran's I (error	2.2703	0.0231	-	-	-	-
Likelihood Ratio Test	-	-	0.1966	0.65746	3.0949	0.07854

Note: *- Ordinary Least Squares Estimation; **- Maximum Likelihood Estimation.

The Herfindahl specialization index at the beginning of the recovery period (2011) is statistically significant and correlates negatively with the economic growth rate. As expected, based on previous findings in the empirical literature, a high degree of specialization hinders the economic growth rate, while the more economically diversified counties grow faster. From the three Location Quotients included in the model, only Manufacturing is statistically significant. Counties highly specialized in manufacturing seem to have lower economic growth rates. This suggests that manufacturing isn't the sector leading the regional growth, but it might be also a limit of the aggregated data used in this analysis. We had to use broad economic sectors (due to lack of more detailed data at county level) forcibly neglecting the high-tech, dynamic sub-sectors that might have propelled the economic growth during economic recovery.

The general level of development of a county, proxied by GDP/capita, is significant and correlates negatively with the economic growth rate. This is in line with the convergence theories stating that less developed regions tend to grow faster, thus moving towards reducing the inequalities. Although economic growth is territorially uneven, economic opportunities extend from the development poles to periphery, benefiting all regions and leading to a convergence process.

The indicator measuring counties' resilience to crisis based on employment loss is significant and has a negative impact on the dependent variable. Since low values of this indicator signify better resilience (less than average % decline in employment during crisis), the negative sign of the coefficient means that resilient counties, that managed to preserve more of their workforce, were able to reach higher growth rates in their GDP. This finding provides empirical support for the labor hoarding theory that recommends keeping as much and as long as possible the existing employees even during economic downturns, in order to have skilled and experienced workforce readily available for the subsequent recovery.

The Lagrange multiplier test rejected the null hypothesis of spatial randomness, implying that a spatial model is more appropriate than classical OLS regression. Consequently, both spatial error and spatial lag models have been estimated. All standard statistical information used for selecting the best model for our data (Log likelihood, Akaike info criterion and Schwarz criterion) indicated the spatial error model as the best specification. This means that economic growth in a county depends on and also influences economic growth in the surrounding regions. Economic opportunities can spread across county borders through capital, knowledge and workforce mobility.

Final remarks

The findings of this paper support the literature pointing to the disadvantages of high specialization not only in the context of economic shocks, but also during recovery and growth. The results from our analysis indicate that a high degree of specialization tends to hinder the economic growth rate. On the opposite, the more economically diversified counties tend to grow faster. Nevertheless, we are aware that a more nuanced analysis is needed, since specialization has some advantages and specializing in high-tech, fast growing industries is highly beneficial for the regional economy. For instance, implementation of smart specialization policies is considered a good strategy for boosting local development, even in the rural and peripheral regions (Camagni and Capello, 2013; Boschma, 2014; McCann and Ortega-Argilés, 2015; Naldi et al., 2015). Arguments for smart regional specialization aiming at higher economic growth and more balanced regional development have been stated in Romania as well (Sandu, 2010), although there are still important obstacles on this path (Ionescu, 2015).

References

Aiginger, K. and Davies, D. (November 2004). "Industrial Specialisation and Geographical Concentration: Two Sides of the Same Coin? Not for the EU", Journal of Applied Economics, Vol. VII, No. 2, p. 231–248.

Andrei, T., Iacob, A., and Vlad, L. (2007). "Tendencies in the Romania's Regional Economic Development during the Period 1991–2004", Economic Computation and Economic Cybernetics Studies and Research, Vol. 41, No. 1–2, p. 107–120.

Anselin, L., Syabri, I., and Kho, Y. (2006). „GeoDa: An introduction to spatial data analysis". *Geographical Analysis, 38*, pp. 5–22.

Boschma, R. (2014). "Constructing Regional Advantage and Smart Specialisation: Comparison of Two European Policy Concepts", Science Regionali, Vol. 13, No. 1, p. 51–68.

Boschma, R., Minondo, A., and Navarro, M. (2012). "Related Variety and Regional Growth in Spain", Papers in Regional Science, Vol. 91, No. 2, p. 241–256, https://doi.org/10.1111/j.1435-5957.2011.00387.x

Camagni, R. and Capello, R. (2013). "Regional Innovation Patterns and the EU Regional Policy Reform: Toward Smart Innovation Policies", Growth and Change, Vol. 44, No. 2, p. 355–389, DOI: 10.1111/grow.12012

Cuadrado-Roura, J. R. and Maroto, A. (2016). "Unbalanced Regional Resilience to the Economic Crisis in Spain: A Tale of Specialisation and Productivity", Cambridge Journal of Regions, Economy and Society, Vol. 9, p. 153–178, Doi:10.1093/cjres/rsv034

De Groot, S. P. T., Mohlmann, J. L., Garretsen, J. H., and De Groot, H. L. F. (2011). "The Crisis Sensitivity of European Countries and Regions: Stylized Facts and Spatial Heterogeneity", Cambridge Journal of Regions, Economy and Society, Vol. 4, p. 437–456.

European Commission. (2010). "Europe 2020: A European Strategy for Smart, Sustainable and Inclusive Growth", Publications Office of the European Union: Brussels.

Ezcurra, R., Pascual, P., and Rapun, M. (2006). "Regional Specialisation in the European Union", Regional Studies, Vol. 40, No. 6, p. 601–616.

Florence, P. S. (1939). Report of the Location of Industry, Political and Economic Planning, London.

Goschin, Z., Constantin, D. L., Roman, M., and Ileanu, B. (2009). "Regional Specialisation and Geographic Concentration of Industries in Romania", South-Eastern Europe Journal of Economics, Vol. 7, No. 1, p. 99–113.

Hallet, M. (2002). "Regional Specialisation and Concentrantion in the EU", in J.R. Cuadrado-Roura, M. Parellada (eds), Regional Convergence in the European Union. Facts, Prospects and Policies, Springer-Verlag, Berlin.

Hirschman, A. O. (1964). "The Paternity of an Index", The American Economic Review, Vol. 54, p. 761–762.

Institutul National de Statistica. (2019). TEMPO Database – Time Series, accessed on September 14, 2019 https://statistici.insse.ro/shop/.

Ionescu, C. (2015). Smart Specialization in Romania. Specific Objective of the National Strategy for Research, Development and Innovation 2014–2020, paper presented at The 3rd International Conference Economic Scientific Research – Theoretical, Empirical and Practical Approaches ESPERA 2015, Bucharest, Romania, December 2015.

Kaulich, F. "Diversification vs. Specialization as Alternative Strategies for Economic Development: Can We Settle a Debate by Looking at the Empirical Evidence?", Development Policy, Statistics and Research Branch UNIDO Working Paper 3/2012 (Vienna: UNIDO).

Krugman, P. (1991). Geography and Trade, MIT Press, Cambridge.

Marelli, E. (2006). "Specialisation and Convergence of European Regions", The European Journal of Comparative Economics, No. 2, p. 149–178.

McCann, P. and Ortega-Argilés, R. (2015). "Smart Specialization, Regional Growth and Applications to European Union Cohesion Policy," Regional Studies, Vol. 49, p. 1291–1302.

Naldi, L., Nilsson, P., Westlund, H., and Wixe, S. (2015). "What Is Smart Rural Development?, Journal of Rural Studies, Vol. 40, p. 90–101.

Neagu, O. and Neagu, M. I. (2016). "Regional Specialisation and Economic Concentration in Romania", Studia Universitas Economic Series, Vol. 26, No. 3, p. 1–17.

Sandu S. (2010). "Smart Specialization Concept and the Status of Its Implementation in Romania", Procedia Economics and Finance, 3, p. 236–242, DOI: 10.1016/S2212-5671(12)00146-3.

Traistaru, I., Iara, A., and Pauna, C., (2002). Regional Structural Change and Growth in Romania, paper presented at the 42nd congress of the European Regional Science Association, Dortmund, August 2002.

Traistaru, I. and Pauna, C. (2003). "The Emerging Geography in Romania", In: P. Nijkamp, I. Traistaru, L. Resmini (eds) The Economic Geography in EU Accession Countries, Aldershot, Ashgate, p. 242–282.

Yaskal, I., Maha, L. G., and Petrashchak, O. (2018). "Spatial Distribution of Economic Activities and Internal Economic Integration in Romania", Journal of Urban and Regional Analysis, Vol. X, No. 2, p. 217–240.

Appendix 1. Location quotients for the main economic sectors: agriculture (a), manufacturing (b) and trade (c)

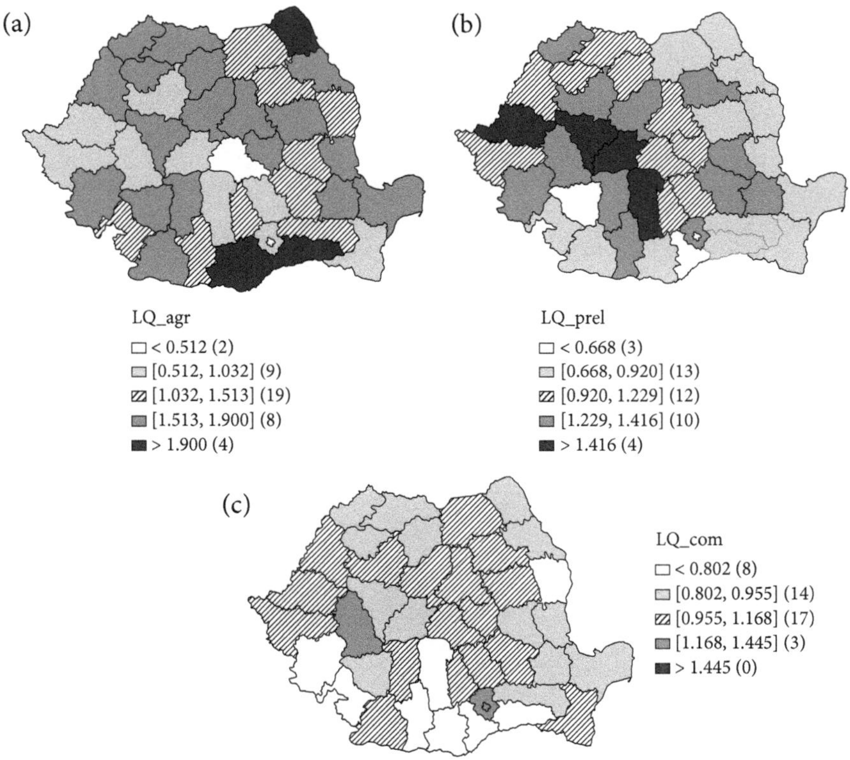

Source: own processing

Appendix 2. Employment (a) and GDP (b) resilience during the crisis (2008–2010)

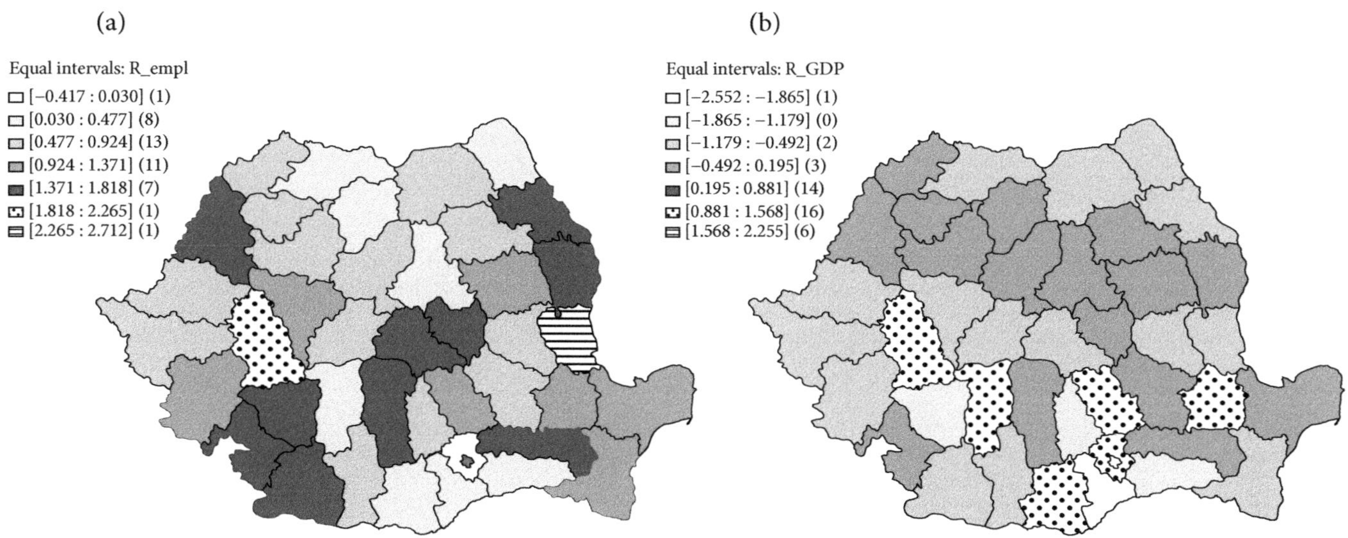

Note: low values signify better resilience. Source: own processing

Corneliu Russu, Daniel Ciuiu

Development gaps between NUTS2 regions in Romania: the convergence of their development with that of some euro area regions

Abstract The paper deals with the gaps in the economic development of NUTS2 regions in Romania, explained mostly by the "historical heritage" in their evolution. All regions made significant progress in their economic and social development over the 2000–2016 period, which allowed them to reduce the gaps separating them from NUTS2 regions selected from euro area countries, a reality confirmed by the results of a econometric modeling.

Keywords: regional development, competitiveness, convergence, disparities

Introduction

Regional development is a complex process that has many deeply interdependent dimensions of very different nature – institutional, legislative, economic, demographic, socio-cultural, ecological, etc. – whose state and interaction condition, to a decisive extent, the chances of achieving the goals and objectives of the regional progress.

For Romania, the problem of regional development is one of the most difficult, given the considerable disparities between the regions on the national territory, between the counties of these regions, and between the regions of Romania and those of the other EU member states. The disparities are of historical origin, being determined by many factors – geographic conditions, resource endowment, specific socio-cultural model, demographic dynamics, structure of economic activities, etc.

1. Literature review

The theories of regional development have the quasi-general characteristic of the unilateral approach, from a single perspective, which makes their practical usefulness to be diminished. In addition, some of the theories that initially had a great impact diminished it strongly afterwards since the economic realities that they determined were far from expectations (the case of the growth poles theory).

The series of theories regarding the regional development highlights the existence, as in other sciences and disciplines, of an evolution in their orientation and content. In this sense, the New Regionalism deals with the regional development in the context of current globalization and accelerated technological progress, which makes the development less dependent on extra-regional factors (government policies, infrastructures, etc.) and be assured in an overwhelming proportion by the regional government, strongly supported by the creation and consolidation of the regional networks focused on learning and innovation; this last theory marks a fundamental transition from the traditional hierarchical system of organizing the economic activities carried out at regional level to the network one, corresponding to the revolutionary architecture of the knowledge society.

2. Interregional disparities in Romania

The combined action of the main determinants of regional development finds its end in the GDP per capita indicator (Annoni and Dijkstra, 2013). The evolution of this indicator over a sufficiently long period clearly highlights the existing regional disparities and provides indications about the prospects for reducing them.

The figures in the following table show the progress achieved by Romanian development regions in the significant increase of the level of the above mentioned indicator, as well as the deepening of the gaps between them, but also the gradual approach of the country level to the EU average during the 2000–2016 period (Tab. 1).

Tab. 1: GDP per capita by development regions, Romania and the EU average, 2000–2016

(euro/inhabitant)

Development regions NUTS2, Romania and EU	**2000**	**2005**	**2010**	**2015**	**2016**	**2016/2000 (%)**
North-East	1300	2400	3900	4900	5300	407.7
South-East	1600	3200	5100	6900	7400	462.5
South Muntenia	1500	3100	5100	6400	6800	453.3
Bucharest-Ilfov	4000	8800	14600	19500	20500	512.5
South-West Oltenia	1500	2900	4800	5800	6300	420.0
Center	1900	3600	6000	7500	8000	421.1
West	1900	4100	7100	8400	8900	468.4
North-West	1600	3500	5600	7100	7600	475.0
Romania	1800	3800	6200	8100	8600	477.8
European Union	19800	23400	25500	29000	29200	147.5

Source: EUROSTAT. Gross domestic product (GDP) at current market prices by NUTS2 regions, Code [nama_10r_2gdp]

The progress made by the development regions is varied, the most developed regions – in decreasing order: Bucharest-Ilfov, West, Center, North-West and South-East – registered the highest increases of indicator level; the other less developed regions – in decreasing order: South Muntenia, South-West Oltenia and North-East – also recorded notable percentage progress, sometimes even at the level of more developed regions, but the low base from which they started in 2000 is the explanation for the still low level of the indicator registered in 2016. The least developed region – North-East – also had the lowest increase in the indicator level. The Bucharest-Ilfov Region is, by far, the one with most spectacular progress, its GDP per capita being, in 2016, 2.3 times higher than the one achieved by the next development region – West. Moreover, the performance of this region contributes substantially to raising the level of the indicator across the country, which, if it represented the average of the other regions, would be much lower.

The main explanation for the different progress made by the regions is the presence of more FDI in developed regions with more consistent and attractive location advantages. The substantial contribution of FDI to the economic development of more advanced regions, along with the ability of local authorities to combine in a synergistic way the action of the development determinants, ensured their progress and opened up broad prospects for their future development.

This is also the explanation for the growing dispersion of the most developed region and the least developed, considered in terms of GDP per capita; this analysis excludes the Bucharest-Ilfov Region from the above-mentioned considerations. The ratio between the levels of this indicator recorded by the two categories of mentioned regions had, in the years presented in the previous table, the following values: West/North-East. 2000: 1.46/1; 2005: 1.71/1; 2010: 1.82/1; 2015: 1.71/1; 2016: 1.68/1. Even though the value of the ratio fluctuated over the period under review, it is obvious that it increased significantly in 2016 as compared to 2000, indicating an amplification in the regional development dispersion.

The different progress made by the development regions and Romania is convincingly highlighted by comparing the ratio of the GDP per capita of the regions and the country to the European average in two reference years – 2000 and 2016 –, sufficiently remote in time to ensure the character of a lasting tendency evolution and, therefore, acceptable for sure (Fig. 1).

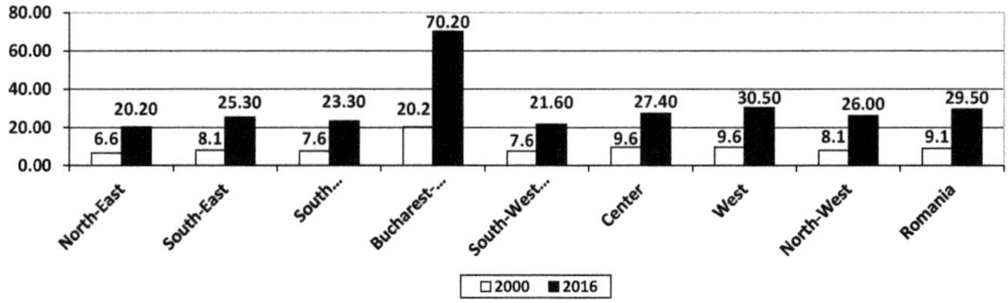

Fig. 1: Share of GDP per capita of development regions and of the country in the EU average, 2000 and 2016 (%)

Source: Own calculations based on EUROSTAT. Gross domestic product (GDP) at current market prices by NUTS2 regions, Code [nama_10r_2gdp].

Despite the significant progress made at national and regional levels, the level of the indicator under review continues to be modest compared to the European average: over 2/3 that of the most developed region, below 1/3 the national average, and about 1/5 that of the less developed region.

By deepening the analysis, the current state of the development regions in Romania and their position in the NUTS2 region hierarchy in the European Union can be realistically assessed by international comparisons, choosing sufficiently representative entities to ensure the judiciousness of the resulting conclusions.

The entities selected for analysis are two NUTS2 regions, the most developed and the least developed in the Euro Area countries, three developed in Western Europe – France, Italy and the Netherlands – and three in Central and Eastern Europe – The Czech Republic, Slovakia and Slovenia –, and the eight development regions in Romania. The NUTS2 regions of the Euro Area countries have been identified by GDP per capita in 2016, selecting the most developed and the least developed region in each country. The GDP per capita in the NUTS2 regions selected from the Euro Area countries in the years 2000, 2005, 2010, 2015,2016 is shown below (Tab. 2).

Tab. 2: GDP per capita by regions in the euro area member countries, 2000–2016 (euro)

Country	Region	Region position *	2000	2005	2010	2015	2016	2016/2000
France	Ile de France	md	38100	43300	51600	55100	56000	1.47
	Languedoc Roussillon	ld	18700	21900	23600	24200	24400	1.30
Italy	Provincia Autonoma di Bolzano	md	30000	34000	38000	41600	42600	1.42
	Calabria	ld	13000	15800	16700	16400	16800	1.29
The Netherlands	Noord-Holland	md	34700	41700	46600	51800	53000	1.53
	Friesland	ld	19900	23300	26800	28300	28800	1.45
Czech Republic	Praha	md	12800	22800	32200	33600	34700	2.71
	Severozápad	ld	5400	8600	11500	11800	12000	2.22
Slovakia	Bratislavský Kraj	md	9000	17800	30400	35400	35800	3.98
	Výhodna Slovensko	ld	3100	5200	8500	10200	10400	3.35
Slovenia	Zahodna Slovenija	md	13100	17800	21400	22400	23400	1.79
	Vzhodna Slovenija	ld	9300	12000	14500	15600	16200	1.74

Note: *md – the most developed region; ld – the less developed region

Source: Eurostat, Gross domestic product (GDP) at current market prices by NUTS2 regions, Code [nama_10r_2gdp]

The analysis of the figures in the table highlights the following:

- In all the analyzed countries, the most developed regions progressed faster than the least developed ones, which means an increasing gap between them, a natural consequence of the higher factor endowment of the first category of regions. The highest ratios between GDP per capita in the final year of the data series by the most developed region compared to the least developed region were registered in Slovakia, the Czech Republic and France, i.e. 3.44, 2.89 and 2.30, these Euro Area countries presenting the largest regional disparities in 2016;

- in all the countries shown in the table the mentioned ratios were significantly lower than in Romania in the same year 2016 (Bucharest-Ilfov Region/North-East Region: 3.87), that is the regional disparities in our country are higher compared to analyzed countries;
- in the countries where the NUTS2 regions selected for analysis include the Capital or are located in the metropolitan area, namely France, the Czech Republic, Slovakia and Slovenia, the progress of these regions was spectacular, much more consistent compared with those of the regions immediately following in rank determined by GDP per capita; is a situation similar to that of the Bucharest-Ilfov Region compared to the next region – West.

The tendencies of approaching or departing the levels of development of the NUTS2 regions in Romania from those of the selected regions of the Euro Area member countries can be highlighted by looking over the analyzed period at the share of GDP per capita registered by the Romanian regions in the one recorded by the respective regions from abroad. The logical comparison is between the most developed regions and, separately, between the least developed regions in Romania and in the Euro Area member countries.

The division into the two categories of Romania's regions was made according to the level of their GDP per capita, higher or lower than the national average; it is a conventionally chosen division in order to facilitate international comparisons, but which is unfair regarding some regions considered underdeveloped (Center, North-West), whose characteristics place however them in the national context among the developed ones.

The analysis of the figures obtained by the comparison the two categories of regions – developed and less developed – from Romania and from selected Euro Area countries, shows the following aspects:

- all development regions in Romania made significant progress in raising the GDP per capita, visibly reducing the gaps that separated them from the regions from abroad compared, in both the developed ones and the less developed;
- the progress made by Romania's NUTS2 regions in reducing the gaps with the selected regions of the Euro Area countries are, largely, directly proportional to the GDP per capita they recorded: higher for developed regions and more and more lower as the indicator level decreased, which means that for the latter regions, while the current pace of their economic growth remained, the period of filling the gap is considerably longer;
- the 2008–2010 global crisis seriously affected, of course both NUTS2 regions in Romania and those selected from the Euro Area countries, with all regions registering significant rebounds in GDP per capita in 2009. Romania's development regions managed to exceed the GDP per capita registered in 2008 after many years: North-East in 2013, South-East in 2012, South Muntenia in 2014, Bucharest-Ilfov in 2015, South-East Oltenia in 2013, Center in 2013, West in 2015, North-West in 2014.

The different but significant reduction in the gaps between, on the one hand, the development regions of Romania and the country as a whole and, on the other hand, the correspondent entities of the Euro Area, demonstrates that there are sufficient reasons for continuing this course and even for accelerating progress.

3. Convergence of the development of NUTS2 regions in Romania and NUTS2 regions of the Euro Area – econometric modeling

To assess the convergence of GDP per capita of the Romanian development regions and that of the NUTS2 regions selected from the Euro Area during the 2000–2016 period, as well as the moment when the level of the respective indicator will equalize, the following steps have been taken:

- the estimation of the time series stationarity (the evolution of the data over time), representing the differences between the log values of GDP per capita registered by the developed regions of Romania (those above the national average, i.e. Bucharest-Ilfov and West), and those achieved by the most developed regions of the compared Euro Area countries, as well as the analogous differences between the less developed regions in Romania (those below the national average, i.e. the other six regions) and the least developed regions in the other countries; the result of the assessment is that the data series are non-stationary for both categories of regions;
- on the basis of the result of the time series stationarity evaluation the order of their integration was determined, concluding that in both categories of regions the series are of the integration order 2 (ID2), and the average of the staged series is null, for this reason being determined a regression equation for each difference in the log values of GDP per capita depending on the moment of determination;
- the time coefficient in the regression equation is negative and the free term is positive, showing that there is a more or less accelerated convergence of the indicator levels analyzed in both categories of regions; at the same time, the moments at which the levels of that indicator recorded by the compared entities are equalized have been determined.

The results of the analysis carried out according to the above steps are as follows:

a) In the case of the Romanian developed regions and the most developed regions of the Euro Area countries, the convergence process is convincingly illustrated by the graph below, which shows that the differences between the compared regions in terms of GDP per capita diminishes continuously (Fig. 2).

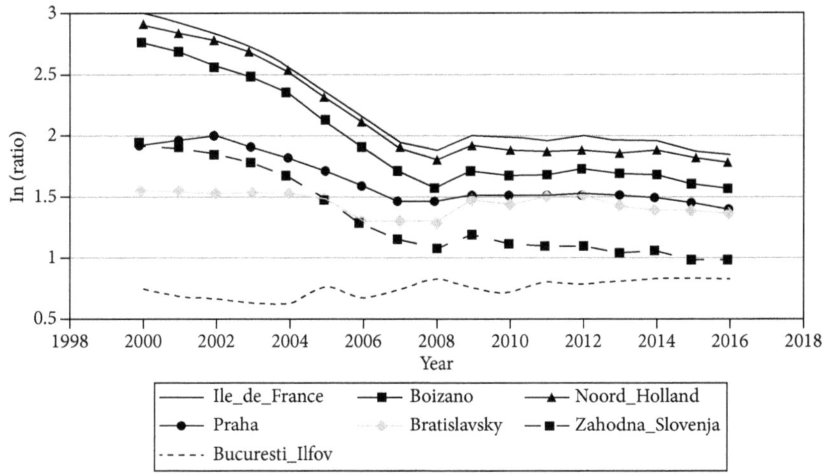

Fig. 2: The logarithms of ratio of GDP per capita in the six developed regions from the Euro Area and Bucharest-Ilfov to that of the West region in Romania, 2000–2016

Source: authors' calculations.

b) In the case of the Romania's less developed regions and the least developed regions of the Euro Area member countries, the same convergence process occurs, as illustrated by the graph in the Fig. 3.

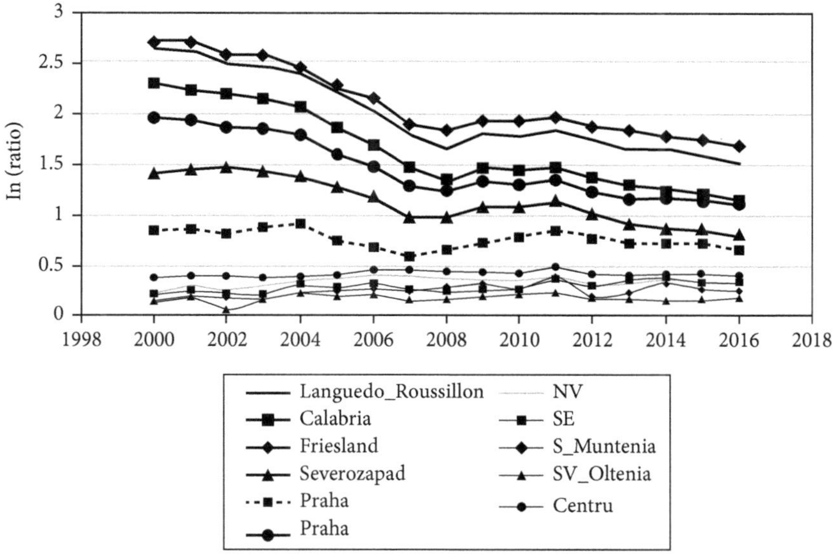

Fig. 3: The logarithms of ratio of GDP per capita in the six least developed regions from the Euro Area and five less developed regions in Romania to that of the North-East region in Romania, 2000–2016

Source: authors' calculations.

These conclusions, which refer to the development regions of Romania (West and North East respectively), are valid for the other regions of Romania, both developed (Bucharest-Ilfov) and less developed (the other five less developed regions);

c) The moment of equalization of the GDP per capita registered by the regions of Romania and that achieved by NUTS2 regions in the countries considered for comparison is deduced from the regression equation mentioned above. The moment differs by the growth rate of the respective indicator recorded by the different regions compared. The calculation showed that the years in which the GDP per capita of the compared regions will be equalized, given the continued growth rate of the 2000–2016 period, are presented in Tab. 3 and Tab. 4.

Tab. 3: Years in which the GDP per capita registered in the developed regions of Romania equals that recorded in the most developed regions of the compared countries

Region	Ile de France	Bolzano	Noord Holland	Praha	Bratislavsky	Zahodna Slovenja
Bucharest-Ilfov	2025	2022	2024	2024	2053	2015
West	2039	2034	2037	2048	2334	2028

In the case of the developed regions, the convergence with the Bratislavsky region is very slow, which can be explained by the fact that the R^2 minimum for the other developed regions is 0.7826 compared to the West region, and 0.8183 compared to Bucharest-Ilfov, respectively, and for the Bratislavsky region R^2 is 0.0656 against the West, and 0.3811 towards the Bucharest-Ilfov region.

Tab. 4: Years in which the GDP per capita registered in the less developed regions of Romania equals that recorded in the less developed regions of the compared countries

Region	Languedoc Roussillon	Calabria	Friesland	Severozapad	Vichodne Slovensko	Vshodna Slovenja
North-West	2029	2024	2032	2024	2035	2026
South-East	2028	2024	2032	2024	2033	2026
South Muntenia	2029	2024	2033	2026	2037	2027
South-West Oltenia	2032	2027	2036	2030	**2060**	2030
Center	2029	2023	2032	2024	2036	2025
North-East	2035	2030	2040	2035	**2085**	2033

In the case of less developed regions, the coefficient of determination for the Vichodne Slovensko region is small, ranging from 0.3151 to 0.6236, and for the other less developed regions, the R^2 minimum is 0.8431, which explains the time farther from equalizing the indicator level in comparison with the mentioned region.

Conclusions

Among the eight development regions of Romania there are significant gaps in terms of the level of economic and social indicators which reflect their status, noticeable both in the level statics (the one existing each year) and in its dynamics (growth indices during the analyzed period). The indicator of maximum relevance of the regional development – GDP per capita – is the one that synthesizes the performances achieved by the regions and highlights the dynamics of the discrepancies in the progress made by them.

The variations in the GDP per capita growth during the analyzed period, which are not always proportional to the level of development of the eight regions, highlight the varied paces at which they improve their performances as a result of their very different efforts made for development.

The growth rates of the GDP per capita indicator recorded by all the Romanian development regions and throughout the country are higher than those recorded by the EU, which reflects the existence of a convergence process of the compared entities' development. The approach of the level of development of the eight development regions to the average one in the EU is certain, although still slow, and with wide variations between the regions.

The comparison of the GDP per capita registered by the development regions in Romania and by some selected regions from countries of the Euro Area of the European Union leads to the same general conclusion that there is a process of gradual approach of the levels of the compared entities.

References

Annoni, Paola; Dijkstra, L. European Union Regional Competitiveness Index, European Commission, Brussels, 2013.

Antonescu, Daniela. Theoretical Approaches of Regional Development, Munich Personal RePEc Archive, MRPA Paper No. 60524, posted 11 December 2014.

Armstrong, Harvey; Taylor, Jim. Regional Economics and Policy (third edition), Blakwell Publishing Inc., Oxford, 2000.

Asheim, Bjørn; Gertler, Meric,The Geography of Innovation: Regional Innovation Systems, in: The Oxford Handbook of Innovation. J. Fagerberg, D.C. Mowery, R. Nelson (eds.), Oxford University Press, Oxford, 2005.

Aydalot, Philip, Dynamique spatiale et développement inégal, Economica, 1976.

Barca, Fabrizio; McCann, Philippe; Rodriguez-Pose, Andrés. The Case for Regional Development Intervention: Place-Based vs. Place-Neutral Approaches, in: Journal of Regional Science, 62(1), 2012, pp. 134–152.

Constantin, Daniela Luminița. Economie și politici regionale, Universitatea "Alexandru Ioan Cuza" Iași, Centrul de Studii Europene, 2010.

Dawkins, Casey. Regional Development Theory: Conceptual Foundations, Classic Works, and Recent Developments, in: Journal of Planning Literature, 18(2), November 2003, pp. 131–172.

European Commission. Key Achievements of Regional Policy. Commission staff working document. Ex-post evaluation of the ERDF and Cohesion Fund 2007–2013, SWD (2016) 318 final, Brussels, 2016.

European Commission. Regional Policy. Making Europe's Regions and Cities More Competitive, Fostering Growth and Creating Jobs, Online: http>//europa.eu/Iby34KD.

European Parliament. Resolution on Community Regional Policy and the Role of Regions and Annexed Community Charter for Regionalization, Minutes of the Sitting of 18 November 1988, Official Journal C 326, 19 December 1988.

Handbook of Regional Growth and Development Theories, Roberta Capello and Peter Nijkam editors, Published by Edward Elgar Publishing Ltd., 2009.

Higgins, Benjamin. Regional Development Theories and Their Application, Routledge, New York, eBook Published, 2017.

Iancu, Aurel; Pecican, Eugen; Olteanu, Dan. The Regression Calculus of the Economic Convergence and the Contribution of the Institutional Factor, in: Economic Convergence (Aurel Iancu Editor), Editura Academiei, Bucureşti, 2009, pp. 42–79.

McCann, Philippe. The Regional and Urban Policy of the European Union: Cohesion, Results-Orientation and Smart Specialisation, Edward Elgar, Cheltenham, 2015.

Mereuţă, Cezar. Some Microeconomic Landmarks of the Transition Process in Romania, Editura Economică, 2018.

Sachs, Jeffrey D.; McCord, Gordon M. Geography of Regional Development, The New Palgrave Dictionary of Economics Online (Edited by Steven N. Durlauf and Lawrence E. Blume), Second Edition, 2008.

Uniunea Europeană – FEDR, Guvernul României, Ministerul Dezvoltării Regionale şi Administraţiei Publice, Instrumente structurale 2007–2013. Strategia naţională de dezvoltare regională 2014–2020, 2013, Bucureşti, 2013.

Gheorghe Zaman, Ivona Stoica

Robotization – trends and impact in the framework of 4IR

Abstract The paper presents in an international comparative context, the robotization impact and trends as a factor of 4IR (the 4th industrial revolution). Within this framework, the peculiarities of robotization in Romania are emphasized, to pursue the objective of designing conclusions and recommendations in the sense of integrating Romania into the worldwide trends and positive structures.

Keywords: trends, 4IR, robotization

Literature review

This paper presents an overall image taking into consideration the trends in different countries, how 4IR (the industrial revolution 4.0) has been spread in different fields such as economic, healthcare, financial retail, energy, automotive. Within the 4IR we are going to analyze robotics, impact and trends, automation, Internet of Things (IoT), artificial intelligence (AI), digital transformation and digitalization. The concept of Industry 4.0 (4IR) has been developed starting with the industry of manufacturing and then was spreading in other industries like power, oil and gas, mining companies, construction, transportation, logistics. The interest is how much are willing the stakeholders to invest in business digital transformation and strategies to create their own direction in this trend of technological progress. "Organizations are largely still finding a path that balances improving current operations with the opportunities afforded by Industry 4.0 technologies for innovation and business model transformation." (https://www2.deloitte.com/, *The industry 4.0 paradox*) "Is an industrial revolution of networks, platforms, individuals and digital technology." (www.jademy.ro)

The development of technology has been developed since ancient history and each technology of today is a disruptor to a today device, robots have been for many researchers a challenge starting with rudimentary models from the automotive industry (Ford case study) and continuing today with Sophia and many other social robots that reproduce the human communication as so-called Human-Robot Interaction (HRI).

The most important and interesting observation of researchers is "in the human innate ability to recognize humans and prefer human interaction; the human brain does not react emotionally to artificial objects, such as computers and mobile phones. However, it has many associations with the human face and can react positively to resemblances to the human likeness" (Kanda & Ishiguro, 2013, 5).

> "The social consequences of robotics depends to a significant degree on how robots are employed by humans, and to another compelling degree on how robotics evolves from a technical point of view. As we can see, social robots are mainly humanoid or animaloid in form. Their shape is of fundamental importance, since their function is to interact with humans on an emotional level, and this type of interaction is grounded in visual and tactile perception no less than in verbal communication." (Campa, 2016)

In figure 1, there are presented the results of a survey developed by KPMG in 2018 on identifying the technologies that will have greater impact (Fig. 1) in the next three years on a sample of over 750 global tech industry leaders, has shown a top trends as regards the business transformation, consumer technology and benefits to life, society and environment.

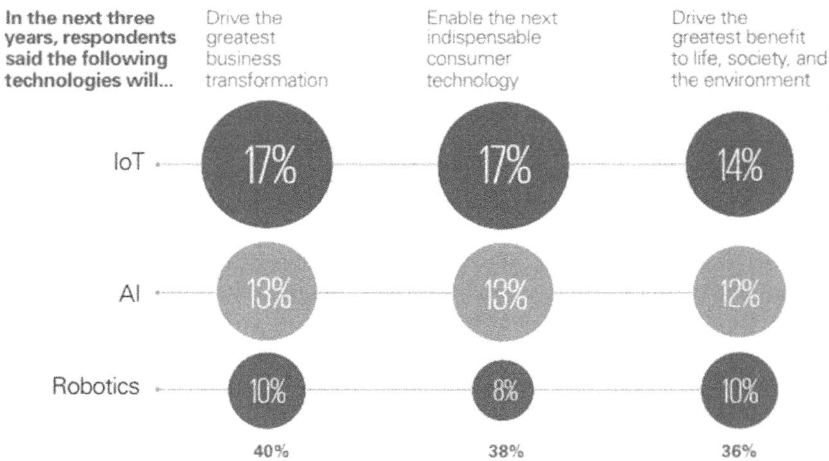

Fig. 1: Top trends impact technologies

Source: KPMG Technology Innovation Survey, January 2018, partial list – percentages do not sum to 100 %.

> "The technology industry continues to drive massive economic value as platform companies – the largest by market cap - make big investments in AI, IoT, robotics and other technologies that have great influence on the way business and consumer engage with the world. The convergence of these technologies is enabling profound changes that impact enterprises, consumers, societies, and the environment." (Zanni, 2018)

These technologies are more and more focusing on creating highly detailed Artificial Humans, with personality and character and bring them to life with

Embodied Cognition Platform as the Soul Machine enterprise is doing giving to customers a robot with human face, more natural and intuitive interactions for the new revolution of customer support. (www.ibm.com)

Robots, artificial intelligence (AI), automation, robot process automation (RPA) have evolved rapidly with high potential to bring benefits to the economy, by increasing productivity and creating new products and services on a competitive market. Another important aspect is the saving of the most important resource of the century of speed, namely the time, but also reducing errors to none. The clerical work, meaning the routine and boring activities, filling forms, creating schedules that each employee must be doing, starting with entry to top level, but the most are entry level, by using a RPA or a robot who can do things better, the business can grow fast and the employees can be creative for the benefit of the company. According to the statistical report from 2018 conducted by PwC, it was estimated that robotics could contribute up to 14 % to global GDP by 2030, the equivalent of about $ 15 trillion to current values.

The technological progress achieved by robots along the three waves (algorithm, augmentation and autonomous), in developed countries the impact is much faster and stronger and in the least developed it is weaker. “In order to gain a better understanding of the topic, OECD data were used to analyze the jobs comprising all the tasks of 200,000 workers from 29 countries (27 countries from OECD, plus Singapore and Russia), which they had based on previous research conducted by Frey and Osborne (Oxford University, 2013) and Arntz, Gregory and Zierahn (OECD, 2016), the proportion of existing jobs that could be at high risk of automation by the 2030s was estimated for each of the these 29 countries, different industrial sectors, occupations in industries, demographic variables of workers by gender, age and different levels of education. ” (https://www.weforum.org/)

PwC, in the Impact of automation on jobs report of 2018, appreciates the existence of three waves of evolution of the development of IT&C technologies that have been progressively developed and are expected to extend over a longer period, algorithmic, augmentation and autonomous wave.

Algorithmic wave – this wave is still present and is focusing on computational task automation and data analysis in different fields regarding information technology and communications (the period of development is until early 2020).

Augmentation wave – is centered on clerical work and decision making; clerical work is compound of routine tasks like filling forms, communication, email, information exchange, schedules, unstructured data analysis regarding semi-controlled objects by using devices such as moving products in warehouses and logistics; this wave is still present and will get to a hot point of maturity in late 2020s.

Autonomous wave – the centricity is on the automation of physical labor and rapidly manual handling in solving problems in case of dynamic situations which needs autonomy and full control from robots in transport (vehicles without drivers), logistics, production, construction, healthcare (surgery 5G technology, organ transplant, stomatology by creating teethes in 3D printing), these technologies are still in a development stage of preparation and tests and predicted to evolve in mid 2030s.

In Fig. 2, we can see which are the top industries that will have the greatest disruption/trasnformation in the next years.

	Global	U.S.	China	India	Japan	U.K.
Automotive/ transportation	13%	13%	**18%**	**14%**	13%	16%
Consumer markets/ retail	11%	13%	14%	9%	7%	8%
Education	8%	13%	8%	5%	13%	5%
Energy/ Utilities	8%	5%	6%	**14%**	0%	10%
Healthcare	12%	11%	11%	6%	17%	11%
Industrial manufacturing	10%	10%	4%	8%	13%	15%
Media	**14%**	**18%**	11%	6%	13%	**18%**
Telecommunications	10%	7%	16%	12%	23%	5%

Fig. 2: Top industries that will have the greatest disruption/transformation in the next years

Source: KPMG Technology Innovation Survey, January 2018, partial list – percentages do not sum to 100 %.

In the labor market, the financial services are going to be replaced by artificial intelligence and workers will lost their jobs or they are going to be forced to reorient their jobs by handling robots and robots process automation. Also the transportation jobs will be replaced, being less threatened by the robots age. Workers with less education could be directly affected by the introduction of robots in different fields and automation process and they will have to deal with career reorientation and long life learning process.

In the case of developed countries with strong economies, such as the US, some EU countries and Japan, robotics could negatively affect productivity growth, and the most affected will be the labor market. The conclusion of the specialists is that for the most part, the workers consider the danger of the wave of robotics due to layoffs as they will no longer have jobs, these being replaced by robots.

Opinions are divided as some specialists believe that the labor market is reshaping, new jobs will be created, workers will reorient in the field of robot use, and salaries will be awarded according to the degree of specialization. Experience has shown that there is a short-term shock in the workforce, but gradually, in the medium and long term, that surplus work is absorbed with the lack of workforce.

1. Automation versus robotization

Many terms have been promoted being very popular to everyone but not used in the correct form by meaning and content. So, here are a few conclusive definitions for dedicated terms for digital transformation, digitalization, automation and robots.

First of all, digitalization and digital transformation cannot be done without digitization.

Digitalization is referring to automation of a process using information digitization and technology administration in the purpose of automation. It is considered as a link to digital businesses and digital transformation in the road of creating new flows and digital revenues.

Digitization is referring to recording systems and digitalization are more used at the insight systems and understanding the digital data and processes, and the path from digitization to digitalization. Business digitalization is conducting to development of digital businesses starting with supply chain, store, shipping. In logistics, appears the term of 4PLP (fourth party logistics) meaning integrative supply chain that manage all the resources of a supply chain technology, both the enterprise and the network providers. More concrete, we could have the digitalization of an environment or a business and the digital job where the worker is reducing the use of paper, but is different to the digital labor force where each individual has dedicated digital tools and mobile devices, technologies, collaborative platforms, unified communications and digital systems.

In this era of changes, technology creates new employment opportunities. All these changes needs infrastructure, changes of the data store and information process, time for adapt to new forms of business, markets and jobs. Digital transformation comprise digital data, automation, connectivity and client's access to the digital environment.

"Digital transformation involves the deep and accelerated transformation of business activities, processes, competencies and models to fully capitalize on the changes and opportunities of digital technologies and their impact on society in a strategic and priority way." (Roy, 2015) Digital transformation has a direct impact on the social, economic and environmental pillars of the sustainability process.

Business process automation (BPA) is the use of technology to automate clerical work, routine tasks by helping workers to focus on decisional making process and strategies to grow company productivity, helps on "routing tasks to the right persons at the right time through user-defined rules and actions." (https://www.laserfiche.com)

Artificial Intelligence (AI) is the capacity of a software to learn and think. AI "is wide-ranging branch of computer science concerned with building smart machines capable of performing tasks the typically require human intelligence; it is also an interdisciplinary science with multiple approaches, but advancements in machine learning and deep learning are creating a paradigm shift in virtually every sector of the tech industry." (https://builtin.com)

Robot Process automation (RPA) means according to McKinsey white paper is the "new promising development in business automation" with a return of investment (ROI) of 30–200 % in the first year. (https://www.mckinsey.com) RPA is "the disruptive force for digital transformation," (https://rpa.sysinconsult.ro) contributing to the company to become more competitive in regard of digitalization, impersonated in a robot software that imitate the human behavior, helps companies to eliminate errors to 0 % – high accuracy and speed in solving tasks, reduce risks and time on a large scale, high control and supervising, high scalability – quick implementing no matter the distance, low costs. In Romania, UiPath is producing RPA for AnaPan pastry business with Pişcot – processing orders in retail, "Gloria is a software robot SPA automation expert trained to identify differences in inter-company invoicing process, between data sent from one subsystem to another and send them to IT for fixing" (https://www.aggranda.com), Rosy that weekly "is downloading performance reports from the Google Ads in excel, offers advice on how to optimize campaigns, download and creates invoices and emailing them to the clients" (https://www.aggranda.com), Jorah the RPA dedicated to the finance field, Arya the HR software robot and like these are many others used in the Romanian business environment.

Robots can replicate and substitute the human actions also reproducing emotions, using a humanoid interface, highly interactive. Robotics is the technology dealing with the use of robots, starting from design, conception, operation system, control and information system.

2. Analysis of robotics in Romania and worldwide based on a system of indicators

In every country and around world, the 4IR and especially robotics accelerates the next wave of disruptors creating new business models. It is interesting the penetration rate of the robotics in the manufacturing industry, healthcare, economy, education, transportation, logistics, construction and the speed of the future generation technology that continues to accelerate.

As a first indicator we will analyze the labor force of unemployed workers and the employment rate in USA, the changes that come once with introducing robots in different field of industry.

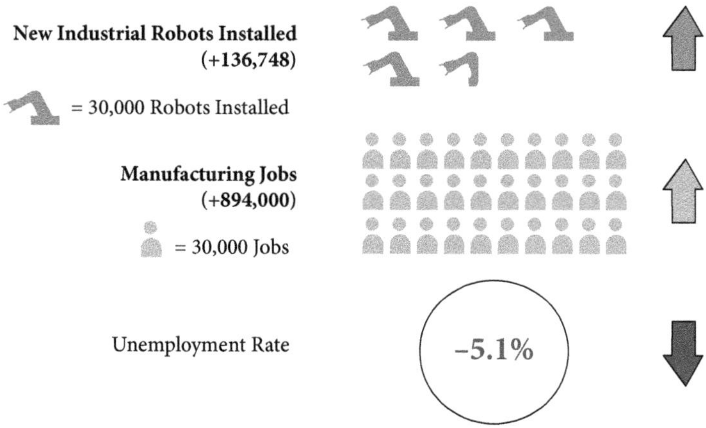

Fig. 3: The unemployment rate in USA and creating new jobs in the stage of robotization, period 2010–2016

Source: US Bureau of Labor Statistics and RIA data, https://www.designnews.com/automation-motion-control/2018-will-be-year-robot-roi/181817437457965.

As we can see in Fig. 3, according to the US Bureau of Labor Statistics and RIA data and the Association of Advancing Automation, implementing robots creates new jobs and reduce the unemployment rate with 5.1 %. Once the new industrial robots are installed, meaning a number of 136,748 in the period of 2010–2016 plus 30,000 of robots installed, the manufacturing jobs reached to 894,000 added to the 30,000 existed jobs. Thus the unemployment rate has been reduced with 5.1 %.

This conclusion is contrary to other opinions in which robots are raising the unemployment rate.

> "Robot sales for the first nine months of 2017 increased 32 % over last year, while automotive stayed about the same, because of faster ROI, those in nontraditional robot industries see that they can get their investment back, plus, gripper advances are making robots more available to other industries." (https://www.designnews.com)

The second indicator is the market share of robots industry. "The industrial robotics market was valued at USD 18.05 billion in 2018 and is expected to reach USD 37.75 billion by 2024, at a compound annual growth rate (CAGR) of 12.15 % as seen in Fig. 4 over the forecast period (2019–2024), industrial robots playing a crucial role in manufacturing industrial automation, with many core operations in industries being managed by robots, with economic growth across regions, the growth of e-commerce, electronics, and the automotive industry, among others has been on the rise." (https://www.mordorintelligence.com)

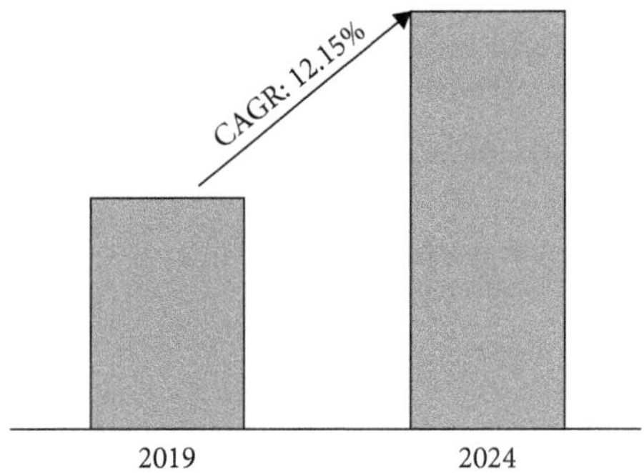

Fig. 4: The industrial robotic market

The third indicator is the worldwide annual shipments of industrial robots by regions in the period of 2007–2017. In the Fig. 5, it is presented the shipment of industrial robots in Asia/Australia, Europe and America.

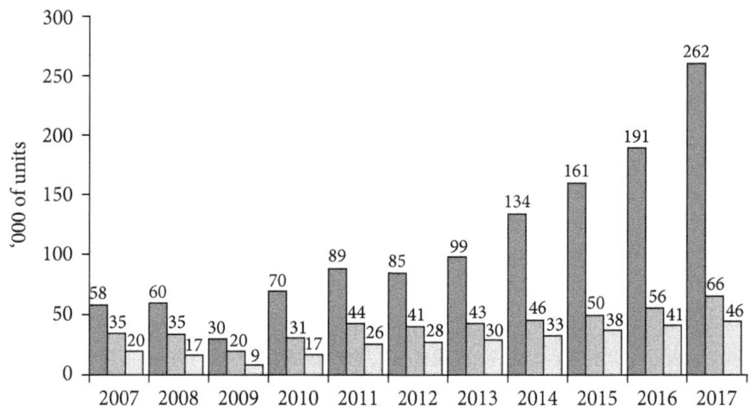

Fig. 5: Worldwide annual shipments of industrial robots by regions

Source: IFR World Robotics 2018.

Below, in Tab. 1, we are analyzing the trends for the annual growth rate worldwide shipments of industrial robots. In 2017, comparing to 2007, the annual worldwide shipments of industrial robots have raised 4 times.

Tab. 1: Annual growth rate worldwide shipments of industrial robots by regions (thousands units)

Year	Asia/Australia		Europe		America	
	thousands units	**%**	**thousands units**	**%**	**thousands units**	**%**
2007	58	100.0	35	100.0	20	100
2008	60	103.4	35	100.0	17	85
2009	30	51.7	20	57.1	9	45
2010	70	120.7	31	88.6	17	85
2011	89	153.4	44	125.7	26	130
2012	85	146.6	41	117.1	28	140
2013	99	170.7	43	122.9	30	150
2014	134	231.0	46	131.4	33	165
2015	161	277.6	50	142.9	38	190
2016	191	329.3	56	160.0	41	205
2017	262	451.7	66	188.6	46	230

Source: Formulas used by authors based data from IFR World Robotics 2018.

In Tab. 2, we can see that Asia/Australia is the most powerful regarding the share of total units by regions (thousands units). In 2009 after the economic crisis there has been a decrease of share and in 2010 the recovery of decline increased significantly until 2017. The recovery decline for Europe and America wasn't so high and decreased in 2017 face to 2007.

Tab. 2: Share of total units by regions (thousands units)

Year	Thousands units	100 %	Asia/Australia (%)	Europe (%)	America (%)
2007	113	100.0	51.3	30.9	17.6
2008	112	100.0	53.5	31.2	15.1
2009	59	100.0	50.8	33.8	15.2
2010	118	100.0	59.3	26.2	14.4
2011	159	100.0	55.9	27.6	16.3
2012	154	100.0	55.1	26.6	18.1
2013	172	100.0	57.5	25.0	17.4
2014	213	100.0	62.9	21.5	15.4
2015	249	100.0	64.6	20.0	15.2
2016	288	100.0	66.3	19.4	14.2
2017	374	100.0	70.0	17.6	12.2

Source: data processed by the authors based on the IFR World Robotics 2018 statistics.

The fourth indicator is the estimated worldwide annual shipments of industrial robots in the period of 2008–2019 in thousands of units. In Fig. 6, we can see that in 2019 is being estimated an annual growth of industrial robots shipments by 421 thousands ofunits.

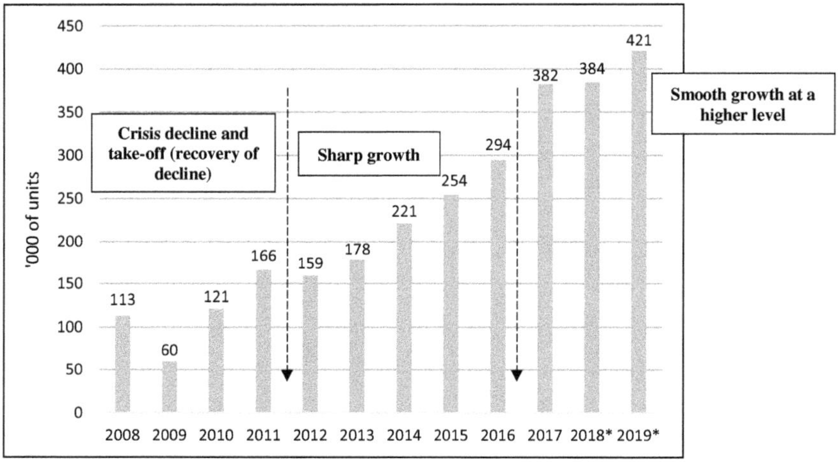

Fig. 6: Estimated worldwide annual shipments of industrialrobots
*Source: IFR Statistical Department 2019; Note: *: preliminary data.*

In this Fig. 7 is presented the annual installations of industrial robots in Asia/ Australia, Europe and America. We can observe that it has been registered a growth from year to year, but in the last years the growth is not so high comparing to the years of 2009 and 2010 which is after the economic crises and reached twice as much in 2010.

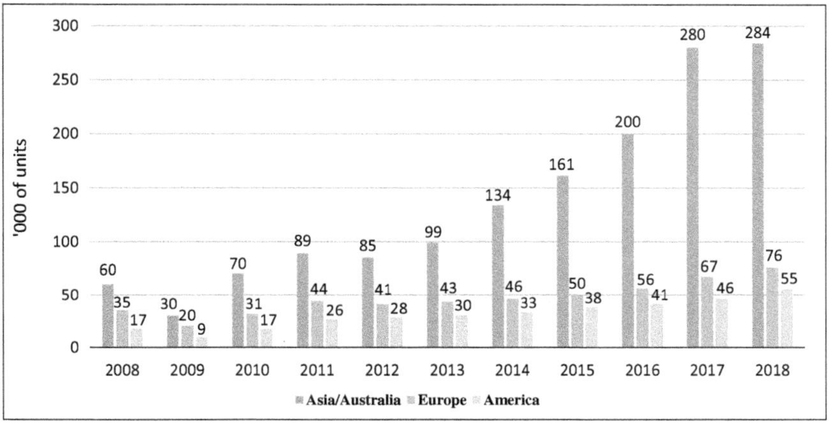

Fig. 7: Annual installations of industrial robots by region

Source: IFR Summary report 2019.

The fifth indicator used to this exploratory research is the estimated worldwide annual supply of industrial robots at end-year, 15 main markets were identified in the year of 2018. As we can see China is on the top regarding the supply of industrial robots with 133.2 thousands of units, followed by Japan with 52.4 thousands of units and United States with 38.1 thousands of units.

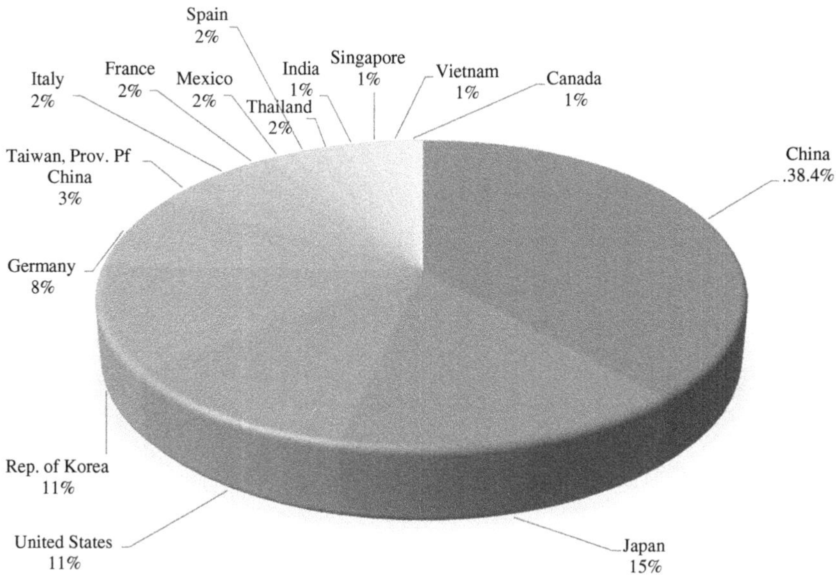

Fig. 8: Estimated worldwide annual supply of industrial robots at end-year, 15 main markets identified in the year of 2018 (thousands ofunits)

Source: data processed by the authors based on the IFR Statistical Department 2019.

In Fig. 8, there are five countries with large supply of robotics: China (38.4), Japan, United States, Republic of Korea and Germany. The market is fragmented in three category of countries: China occupies the first place being far away from the other four countries, countries with relatively significant share, Japan, United States, Republic of Korea and Germany and relatively low share which is compound of the other 10 countries (Taiwan, Italy, France, Mexico, Spain, Thailand, India, Singapore, Vietnam and Canada).

In the Fig. 9, regarding the number of installed industrial robots per 10 000 employees in the manufacturing industry 2017, appears also Romania with a modest number of 18 units installed at 10,000 employees which is a small value comparing to other countries. The data provided tells us that Romania is not a very well developed country and does not have a strong economy, there are low investments in technology and is present a lack of interest in digitization the business environment first of all because of the infrastructure.

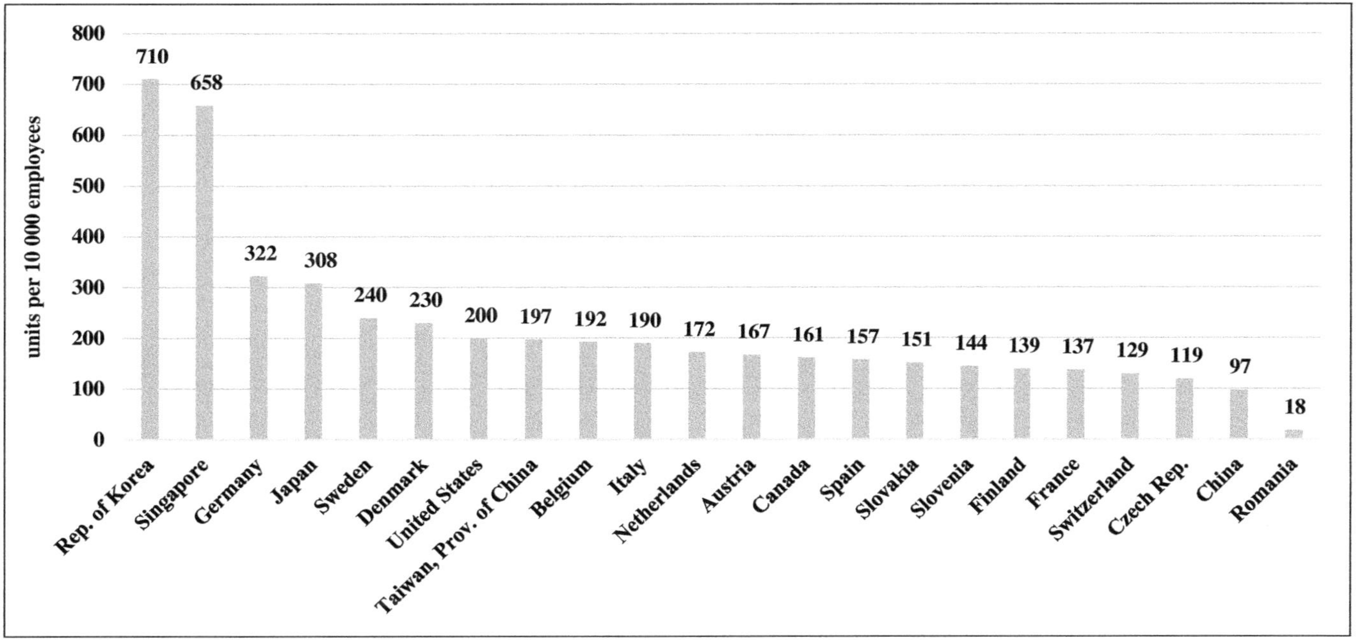

Fig. 9: Number of installed industrial robots per 10 000 employees in the manufacturing industry 2017

Source: IFR World Robotics 2018.

Conclusions

The robotics impact on labor market has been analyzed thoroughly and the conclusions are the future jobs loss generate by robotics will be replaced by new jobs with different tasks due to the 4IR.

On the other part, there are specialist which consider that this industrial revolution will conduct to a mass technological unemployment until 2030 and will register higher values than in the beginning of the industrial revolution.

There are several effects regarding the integration of robots in the business environment that have negative impact on the labor force.

A first disadvantage that came as a result of the clerical work mitigation and replacing employees with robots, is the unqualified and low qualified labor force dismissal.

The implementation of robots is conducting to an alarming rate of increase of the unemployment.

> "Employment in the buggy-whip industry is about 0 %, that's the example economists cite when they talk about technology and employment, as automobiles replaced horses, industries based on the old order shut down, the Industrial Revolution left millions unemployed, their jobs rendered obsolete by machines." (Oxford Economics, 2019)

There are some specialists in economics that appreciate a mass dismissal will take place in the near future. However, during the dismissal period, will be found new jobs for the unemployed, as it happened in the previous technological waves. "Job loss due to automation statistics from 2019 demonstrate that each industrial robot is on average replacing 1.6 human workers, meaning that the number of displaced workers could reach tens of millions in the coming decade and low-income regions of the world are going to feel the impact of automation in manufacturing much more than average and high-income areas." (Oxford Economics, 2019)

Another disadvantage is that "new technologies are contributing to increasing inequalities – both between different groups of workers and between labor and firm owners." (United Nations, 2017)

As a new strategically movement for the dismissal labor force is the diminishing of the working week to 4 days which will have a favorable effect for the low-qualified to work within the household or to participate at training courses in different qualifications. "Businesses do not need large numbers of employees, so individuals can devote most of their waking hours to hobbies, volunteering, and community service. In conjunction with periodic work stints, they have time to pursue new skills and personal identities that are independent of their jobs." (West, 2018) Another solution is to create new products and markets for those workers that have no longer a job.

Migration of unemployed towards those countries that have penury of labor force.

Robotization, as well as the other components of industry 4.0, have effect on long term over the behavior of children's. If they use the tablets or the smartphones at young ages they will become individuals with less focus capacity. Another behavior characteristic, beside the lack of attention is the reduced availability to dialogue because they have only robot friends (humanoid or animaloid). They will not know how to protect themselves in the real life of people with disorders, or malicious replies in an ordinary conversation, being unable to integrate in groups, teams or any kind of social activities.

In this continuous change, there is the possibility that the organizations will not be able to adapt, and the Romanian labor market will not be ready for the industrial revolution 4.0. It is necessary to find a way for the regulation of new technologies in order to take full advantage of the benefits offered. This transfer of technology from the traditional to the digital will generate new needs and concerns about safety, increasing inequity and disruption of society.

The evolution due to progress is spreading exponentially, bringing changes of impact in each sector of industry. In Romania, depending on the degree of Internet penetration, the changes that the new economy brings, are less relevant for the country as it is still considered poorly developed according to Eurostat statistics.

Depending on the development potential of the country, the 4.0 revolution can create phenomena of social inequity, disrupting the balance in the labor market, which the specialists consider that in the future, the more skills and competences will lead to a higher salary, this fact leading to social tensions.

References

Arntz, M., T. Gregory and U. Zierahn (2016), The risk of automation for jobs in OECD countries: a comparative analysis, OECD Social, Employment and Migration Working Papers No. 189.

Campa, R. (February 2016), The rise of social robots: A review of the recent, Journal of Evolution and Technology, 26(1), pp. 106–113.

Ford, M. (2015), The Rise of the Robots: Technology and the Threat of Mass Unemployment, London: Oneworld Publications.Frey, C.B. and M.A. Osborne (2013), The Future of Employment: How Susceptible Are Jobs to Computerisation?, University of Oxford, Oxford.

Kanda, T. and H. Ishiguro (2013), Human-Robot Interaction in Social Robotics. Boca Raton: CRC Press, p. 5.

Roy, A.K. (2015), Impact of Big Data Analytics on Business, Economy, Health Care and Society: Impact on Society (Big Data Analytics-Series-4), Editura CreateSpace Independent Publishing Platform, 2015.

West, M.D. (2018), TECHTANK, Will robots and AI take your job? The economic and political consequences of automation, https://www.brookings.edu/blog/

techtank/2018/04/18/will-robots-and-ai-take-your-job-the-economic-and-political-consequences-of-automation/, retrieved 03.10.2019.

Zanni, T., Global and US Technology Sector Loader, KPMG U.S., 2018. http://www.pwc.co.uk/assets/pdf/ukeo-regional-march-2015.pdf, retrieved 02.09.2019.

Further Reading

Artificial intelligence, https://builtin.com/artificial-intelligence, retrieved 02.09.2019.

Automation motion control, https://www.designnews.com/automation-motion-control/2018-will-be-year-robot-roi/181817437457965, retrieved 02.09.2019.

Ce este Robotic Process Automation, https://rpa.sysinconsult.ro/ro/ce-este-robotic-process-automation-rpa/, retrieved 04.09.2019.

Discussion papers and briefings, https://www.mckinsey.com/mgi/our-research/discussion-papers-and-briefings, retrieved 02.09.2019.

Gloria SAP Automation with UiPath, https://www.aggranda.com/rpa-case-study/gloria-sap-automation-with-uipath/, retrieved 02.09.2019.

IFR International Federation of Robotics, World Robotics 2018 Industrial Robots, https://ifr.org/downloads/press2018/Executive_Summary_WR_2018_Industrial_Robots.pdf, retrieved 01.10.2019.

Industrial Robotics Market, https://www.mordorintelligence.com/industry-reports/industrial-robotics-market, retrieved 02.09.2019.

Industrial Robotics Market, https://www.mordorintelligence.com/industry-reports/industrial-robotics-market, retrieved 02.09.2019.

Oxford Economics, (2019), Robots could displace 20 million manufacturing jobs by 2030, https://fortunly.com/statistics/automation-job-loss-statistics#gref, retrieved 03.10.2019.

PwC, Sizing the prize (2017): https://www.pwc.com/gx/en/issues/data-and-analytics/publications/artificial-intelligence-study.html, retrieved 01.10.2019.

PwC, Workforce of the future (2017): https://www.pwc.com/gx/en/services/people-organisation/publications/workforce-of-the- future.html, retrieved 01.10.2019.

Soul machines hybrid cloud AI chatbot, https://www.ibm.com/case-studies/soul-machines-hybrid-cloud-ai-chatbot, retrieved 05.09.2019.

The industry 4.0 paradox, https://www2.deloitte.com/content/dam/Deloitte/cn/Documents/energy-resources/deloitte-cn-er-industry-4.0-paradox-overcoming-disconnects-en-full-report-190225.pdf, retrieved 16.09.2019.

The robots are coming but take a breath, https://www.weforum.org/agenda/2019/08/the-robots-are-coming-but-take-a-breath, retrieved 12.09.2019.

What is the fourth industrial revolution, https://www.jademy.ro/blog/industry-4-0-ce-este-a-patra-revolutie-industriala-si-cum-ne-afecteaza/, retrieved 03.09.2019.

https://www.laserfiche.com/ecmblog/what-is-business-process-automation-bpa/#,retrieved 02.09.2019.

United Nations, (2017), Will robots and AI cause mass unemployment? Not necessarily, but they do bring other threats, accessed https://www.un.org/development/desa/en/news/policy/will-robots-and-ai-cause-mass-unemployment-not-necessarily-but-they-do-bring-other-threats.html, retrieved 03.10.2019.

Cristina Boboc, Simona Ghita, Valentina Vasile, Anda Ghizdavu

The impact of artificial intelligence on the labor market

Abstract The automation process as well as the artificial intelligence evolves at an amazing speed. The impact of automation on the regional and local labor market depends greatly on the characteristics of the local economy. In this context, the objectives of this paper are: the classification of EU countries by using the cluster analysis according to the development of artificial intelligence in each country; the visualization of the activity sectors with the highest influence on the stability of the labor market; the assessment of the impact of artificial intelligence on the employment rate.

With the automation of certain routine jobs, new jobs will emerge in the marketplace that will lead to the stability of the labor market over time. In order to protect the labor market from the shocks caused by automation, and to provide citizens with the necessary conditions to reintegrate into the labor market, specific policies are needed, especially in some activity sectors identified in this paper.

Keywords: Artificial intelligence, cluster analysis, industry, labor market, automation process

Introduction

The fast progress of technology is currently helping to rapidly change the way of working throughout the company, creating new job opportunities and improving the quality of life. How can workers adapt and take advantage of the technology? Which workers will be replaced by robots? The main challenge that analysts face in estimating the number of jobs that present a risk of automation is to define the work tasks exposed to automation. Many recent studies have tried to show how developing digital capabilities will affect employment. Frey and Osborne (2013) are the ones who have tried to find out which jobs are likely to be automated due to machine learning techniques. The two concluded that jobs that require creativity and social intelligence as main skills are safe in the struggle with automation.

According to the OECD study (Nedelkoska & Quintini, 2018), 14 % of all jobs present a high risk of automation, while for the other 32 % there is the possibility of being affected by significant changes. The percentage of jobs that present a high risk of automation varies widely from country to country (a job is considered to be at risk if the probability of being automated is at least 70 %). The percentage of jobs with high risk of automation varies between 5.7 % in Norway and 33.6 % in Slovakia. Unlike the east and south of Europe, where the highest risk of automation was registered, the northern part of Europe and North America

(Canada and the United States) present the lowest risk of automation. Differences between risk values were not registered due to differences between economies, but rather to organizing different jobs in each country.

According to the OECD's report on Job Creation and Local Economic Development (OECD, 2018), one-third of job vacancies requiring higher education will be replaced by a robot or software program that will be based on an algorithm developed using artificial intelligence. The geographical distribution of the jobs that present a high risk of automation varies according to the technological progress in the regions of the European countries. For example, the country with the highest percentage of jobs to be automated is Slovakia, where 40 % of jobs are exposed to automation in the coming years, and at the opposite end are some regions in Norway where the percentage of jobs with high risk of automation is of only 4 %. From 2011, most of the countries (60 %) have been able to create more jobs with low risk of automation than the loss of jobs suffered in the sectors with a high degree of automation. Countries with a small percentage of the jobs exposed to automation are the highly urbanized ones with highly marketable services and the ones where the workers have higher education. Regions with low productivity growth and high unemployment will be the most affected by automation in the future.

Since it is almost impossible to predict with high accuracy how many jobs will be automated in the coming years, the two main objectives of this paper are: to classify, using a cluster analysis, the countries of Europe according to the development of artificial intelligence in each country and to measure the impact of each artificial component on the employment rate.

1. Methodology

In order to analyze EU countries according to the level of development of artificial intelligence and the impact of automation on employment, we have used two multidimensional techniques: nonhierarchical cluster analysis techniques (K-means method) and multiple regression analysis. We used data on the employment rate and the percentage of robots in eight major industries of the labor market (transportation, manufacturing, trade, construction, telecommunications, research, logistic support and IT) in 2016 for 27 EU countries. The data source was Eurostat (Eurostat, 2019a, 2019b). The data processing was performed using the SAS Studio program.

2. Results

In the last decades, the development of new algorithms and the increase of computer performance, have led to the increasing use of robots in all activity sectors. In Transportation Sector, the robots are designed to transport both products and people, by minimizing the costs and streamlining the workflow. Manufacturing Sector is the industry with the highest risk of automatization because it includes all the elementary professions that are based on manual work. For example, several industries that will be automated soon are: the food industry, the agricultural industry, the chemical industry, the metal processing industry. In Trade Sector, automation involves the provision of enterprises with intelligent devices, such as automatic payment, weighing, price scanning systems. Construction Sector is the industry with the lowest degree of automation.

However, the dangerous activities were automated by using the latest generation devices. For example, many companies use drones to monitor or inspect the status of some projects. Also, the automation of this sector is closely linked to the Internet branch of things which involves the construction of smart homes, where all the devices will communicate with each other. Telecommunications Sector has been developed a lot in recent years by using new technologies for offering new, innovative, customer-oriented services to the clients. In Research Sector automation will help the development of other new industries for the digital society. For example, in medicine the research contributes a lot to the development of new branches and of new devices developed with the help of artificial intelligence. Administrative and Support Services Sector involves a lot the human interaction, meaning that the risk of automation is very low. Communication and Information Services Sector is the sector that created the foundations of artificial intelligence and could contribute even more to the automation process.

2.1. EU countries by the artificial intelligence development

In the first phase of our analysis we have clustered the EU countries by the percentages of robots used in eight major activity sectors, previously described. By applying the Elbow method for choosing the optimal number of groups and the nonhierarchical K-means clustering method, there are obtained 4 homogenous groups (Fig. 1).

First cluster contains the most developed countries in terms of work automation: Germany, Italy, Latvia, France, Hungary, Slovenia, Finland, England, Norway. Latvia and Hungary were characterized by very low levels of labor productivity between 1995 and 2018, providing the premises for an accelerated development of artificial intelligence. Germany, Norway, Finland, England, although they have a stable labor market with high productivity levels, high employment rates and low unemployment rates, invest intensively in technologies, helping the people to carry out their activities in the most efficient way.

The second cluster consists of six European countries with a medium development of artificial intelligence underlying automation jobs: Belgium, Lithuania, Greece, Croatia, Romania, Serbia. Companies from Belgium, Croatia and Romania are constantly investing in the development of artificial intelligence because these countries are facing a major shortage of manpower which threatens the stability of companies in the market. On the other hand, Lithuania and Greece had very low labor productivity over a long period of time and the development of artificial intelligence would help them to improve the productivity.

The third cluster (Czech Republic, Denmark, Spain, Austria, Poland, Portugal, the Netherlands, Sweden) is characterized by a weak development of job automation on the labor market. Nordic countries such as Sweden, Netherlands, Denmark are countries with high employment rates and the development of artificial intelligence would threaten the stability of this indicator. On the other hand, in Poland, Portugal, the Czech Republic and Spain the governments are skeptical about the automation of the jobs because they did not want to face the instability of the labor market and they did not support the development of these new technologies.

The fourth cluster (Bulgaria, Cyprus, Luxembourg, Slovakia) is made up of the least developed countries in Europe in terms of artificial intelligence progress. These countries have registered medium values of the indicators on productivity and unemployment and the governments have chosen not to invest in the development of large-scale workforce automation.

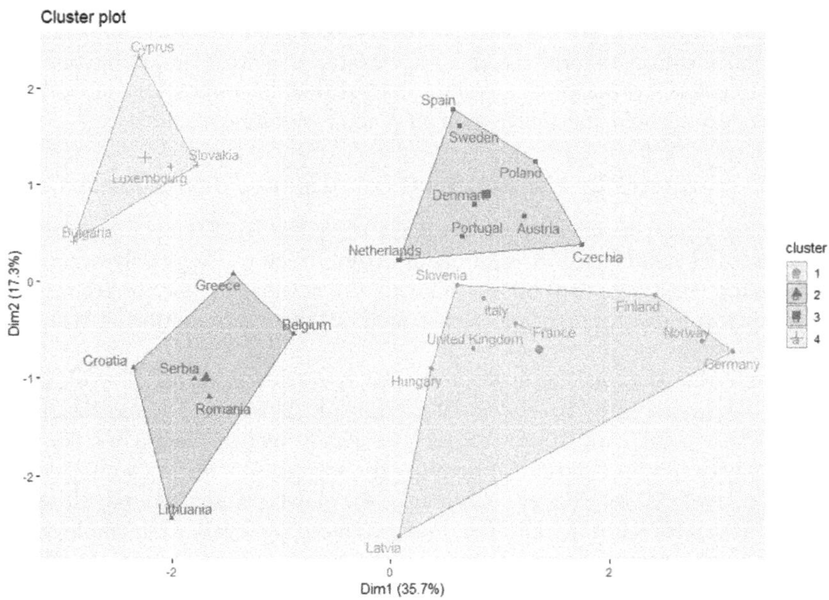

Fig. 1: EU countries by the development of artificial intelligence

Source: Cluster Analysis in R Studio, based on Eurostat data.

2.2. The impact of automation on employment rate

In the second phase we have used multiple linear regression analysis to measure the impact of the automation of each sector of activity on employment level and to prove that the development of artificial intelligence does not have a negative effect on employment market. In this analysis we have used the natural logarithm of employment rate as the dependent variable and the percentages of robots used in eight major activity sectors and the belonging to one of the four clusters defined in the previous phase as well. We have used a linear regression analysis, in which the exogenous variables included in the model were chosen by using the forward selection method. The results obtained in SAS Studio were presented in Tab. 1.

Tab. 1: Linear Regression Analysis Results

Analysis of Variance					
Source	**DF**	**Sum of Squares**	**Mean Square**	**F Value**	**Pr > F**
Model	8	147832	18479	1866.49	<.0001
Error	19	188.10807	9.90042		
Uncorrected Total	27	148021			

Parameter Estimates					
Parameter	**DF**	**Estimate**	**Standard Error**	**t Value**	**Pr > |t|**
Manufacturing Sector	-0.109215	0.062142	-1.76	0.0949	0.0879
Trade Sector	0.088994	0.042175	2.11	0.0483	0.0443
Transportation Sector	0.089912	0.036307	2.48	0.0228	0.0191
Administrative and Support Services Sector	0.107623	0.035914	3.00	0.0074	0.0063
Cluster 1	61.332356	6.403749	9.58	<.0001	<.0001
Cluster 2	64.765235	4.347056	14.90	<.0001	<.0001
Cluster 3	70.349908	5.515450	12.76	<.0001	<.0001
Cluster 4	71.204039	5.207832	13.67	<.0001	<.0001

The percentage of robots in Manufacturing Sector, Trade Sector, Transportation Sector and Administrative and Support Services Sector have a significant impact on employment rate. As we can see, the only sector in which the high automation level has a negative impact on employment rate is the Manufacturing

Sector, where the specificity of the work characterized by numerous repetitive, successive, high precision technological operations and an increased division of labor allow the robots in this sector to substantially replace the human involvement in these activities. However, this must also be seen as a generator of positive aspects, as it can be addressed through economic and social policy measures, so that – despite the high automation in this sector – the employment rate is not drastically reduced or at least to remain stable. Thus, the workforce displaced following the robotic process can be channeled to more flexible jobs, with greater creative potential, in which man – with his creative thinking – can excel and can carry out an efficient activity. At the same time, the workforce made available from highly automated workplaces, in which robots have a wide involvement, can be included in professional reconversion and training programs, in order to better respond to the new demands on the job market. In the other three sectors (Trade, Transport and Administrative and Support Services), the increasing number of robots will have a positive impact on employment rate, as the robots will not necessary replace the human involvement in the activities but will support and make their activity more efficient, increasing the labor productivity. In these sectors, the introduction and use of artificial intelligence products can create a modern framework for carrying out the activity, favoring an increased output and creating new jobs. Also, robots can replace the human workforce especially in the sectors with high pollution and maximum risk, in which human life is more exposed to danger.

The fourth cluster and the third cluster have the highest average levels of employment rates (over 70 %). Most of the countries from these clusters are highly economically developed and have already introduced the automation processes in many sectors, but not at such a high level, the employment rate not being affected.

Conclusions

Man has always been attracted to things that make his life easier, such as automated items. Acceleration of automation is a phenomenon with diverse, positive and negative implications, but many researchers consider it a challenge, trying to answer the question: does this imply a job loss or a job gain? 6 out of 10 occupations have almost a third of activities automatable. Now more than ever, the labor market is reshaping, redefining itself, so that by 2030 between 3 % and 14 % of the world labor force will change its occupational category (McKinsey Global Institute, 2017).

The present paper aims at classifying the European countries by the artificial intelligence development level, and quantifying the impact of automation process on the employment rate. In order to achieve these objectives, statistical-econometric methods of multidimensional analysis were used: nonhierarchical cluster analysis techniques (K-means method) and multiple regression analysis, applied on data provided by Eurostat, for 27 EU countries and for year 2016.

Following the application of cluster method, the European countries included in the analysis were grouped into four clusters: countries in the first cluster are characterized by a high level of workforce automation, by large differences in the level of labor productivity across countries and high employment rates. Countries which belong to the second cluster are medium-developed countries from the artificial intelligence point of view, and tend to financially invest in the development of automation process. A low development level of job automation is the main and common feature of all countries included in the third cluster. The fourth cluster consists of countries with the lowest automation level, with medium productivity and unemployment and with reduced government investments in the automation of economic activities.

In order to test and to measure the impact of automation of economic sectors on employment level, a multiple linear regression analysis has been developed, which includes the following variables: the employment rate, the percentages of robots used in eight major activity sectors and country inclusion in previously identified clusters. The results revealed that in four activity sectors the automation level significantly influences the employment rate: Manufacturing Sector, Trade Sector, Transportation Sector and Administrative and Support Services Sector. While in the Manufacturing Sector the level of artificial intelligence and that of employment are negatively (inversely) correlated, in all the other three sectors the correlations are positive (direct). The negative impact of the level of artificial intelligence on the employment in Manufacturing sector can be explained by the fact that the specificity of the work in this sector – with manual, similar, repetitive operations – allows the takeover of these operations by robots, replacing the human, leading to a decrease in employment but also to an increase in labor productivity in this sector. In order to counteract the decrease in employment, a series of corrective measures can be taken on the labor market, such as professional conversion and training of the displaced labor force, channeling it to vocational jobs, in which man can use his skills and creative potential. On the background of economic growth, the labor demand will also increase and thus the redundant workers will continue to find a place on the labor market. The positive impact of automation on employment in the other three sectors can be explained by the fact that robots do not replace man, but help him to increase the productivity of his work, in these sectors the jobs being characterized by creativity and a greater interrelation with people.

In conclusion, the widespread use of high-level technology can affect our work. The implications for employees may refer to workplace transformation, job security, skills and qualifications, or salary (McKinsey Global Institute, 2017). But, in the end, success depends on how the decision makers in the labor market manage the transition of the workforce, so that the gains outweigh the losses.

References

Eurostat, 2019a. Database on science and technology, 3D printing and robotics, available at http://appsso.eurostat.ec.europa.eu/nui/submitViewTableAction.do, accessed 17.09.2019.

Eurostat, 2019b. Database on employment and unemployment, available at https://ec.europa.eu/eurostat/web/lfs/data/database, accessed 12.09.2019.

Frey, C., Osborne, M., 2013. The future of employment: How susceptible are jobs to computerization? Oxford: Oxford Martin School.

Nedelkoska, L., Quintini, G., 2018. Automation, skills use and training, OECD Social, Employment and Migration Working Papers, No. 202, OECD Publishing, Paris, https://doi.org/10.1787/2e2f4eea-en.

McKinsey Global Institute, 2017. Jobs lost, jobs gained: Workforce transitions in a time of automation. McKinsey&Company, San Francisco.

OECD, 2018. Job creation and local economic development 2018: Prepare for the future of work, OECD Publishing, Paris, https://doi.org/10.1787/9789264305342-en, accessed 18.09.2019.

Andrei-Marius Diamescu

Information – an asset still insufficiently capitalized in the Romanian economy

Abstract The current paper emphasizes a worrying situation regarding the handling of information in the economic field in Romania: the transition to a knowledge-based economy is on a slow path and this state of facts influences our results in the research-innovation sector at the European level. Our study focused on the French model regarding the concept of "intelligence economique" introduced by Henri Marter, which determined the state to capitalize on knowledge and information for economic actors and thus to close the development gap between France and other European states in the 1990s. On the course of this contribution we present accurate data showing the negative impact of the poor handling of information and knowledge by the state in three crucial areas: innovation, research-development and computerization. Considering this impact and the fact that it leads to an even greater delay in integrating Romanian economy in the "new economy" (see the New Growth theory), we strongly suggest that the Romanian state's engagement in capitalizing on information in economic development is crucial.

Keywords: intelligence economics; knowledge; information for economic actors; innovation, research-development and computerization; new economy

General considerations

The New Growth theory, elaborated by P. Romer and R. Lucas, reveals the crucial part knowledge plays in increasing productivity and identifies, among the main development resources: accumulation of knowledge, training improvement, education and fundamental research.

A simple inductive reasoning shows that information is what stands at the basis of the majority of these "neofactors of the new economy"(Purcariu, Iacob, 2011). The informational resource is simultaneously a production factor, when we refer to innovation-research activity or the level of instruction/quality of work force (education, training), and a tool based on which strategic decisions are made.

Having noticed the fact that in the knowledge-based economy the capacity of the state to perform as an economic actor depended essentially on its capacity to manage and process the information it held, the French Henri Martre introduced in 1994 the concept of "intelligence economique" that he defined as: "the set of coordinated actions of research, processing and dissemination of useful information for economic actors."[1]

As the concept matured, the French government aimed to operationalize and maximize the benefit brought to France by this new "asset," in the face of an increasingly fierce global competition, thus managing, in a short time, to close the gap that separated it from the other developed economies of the world at the time.

The French model could be taken up by Romania, the degree of capitalizing information being extremely low in our country, an aspect revealed also by the "counter-results" that we register at the European level in areas such as innovation, research-development or computerization of economy and society.

Considering that any delay in the process of integration and capitalization of information/knowledge in the economic processes leads to the deepening of the gap between the level reached by the developed economies of the world and that of Romania, the engagement of the strategic resources of the Romanian state is not only necessary, but compulsory too.

1. The practical, economic and cultural dimension

Having reached an advanced, mainly theoretical but also practical, maturity stage, the knowledge-based economy requires more and more a holistic approach of the future world order, in which the factors of economic growth identified both by the classical theory and the neoclassical one become insufficient to a correct understanding/explaining of the mechanisms through which the contemporary economic phenomena manifest themselves.

Stimulated during the 1990s by the unprecedented development of information technology, the knowledge-based economy lead to new theories and models, the most important of them being that of endogenous growth theory, also called the new growth theory, elaborated by P. Romer and R. Lucas (Zaman, Georgescu, 2015, p. 27).

This new theory that approaches technological progress as an endogenous factor, a product of economic activity, reveals the important part that knowledge plays in productivity growth and identifies the main development resources:

- Knowledge accumulation;
- Improving formation;
- Education;
- Fundamental research;
- Infrastructure (Zaman, Georgescu, 2015, p. 33).

---

1 "L'intelligence économique peut être définie comme l'ensemble des actions coordonnées de recherche, de traitement et de distribution en vue de son exploitation, de l'information utile aux acteurs économiques", în Rapport du Groupe, Intelligence économique et stratégie des entreprises, Commissariat général du Plan, Paris, Février1994, cf. https://www.entreprises.gouv.fr/files/files/directions_services/information-strategique-sisse/rapport-martre.pdf.

Not at all surprisingly, in a time dominated by artificial intelligence considered one of the most productive engines of economic growth, the four development resources mentioned share an obvious immaterial character, intangible and hard to capitalize regarding the evaluation of an economic entity's performances and risks. Recent debate concerning the international accounting treatment of intangible assets[2] (EC, 2018) only partially solves the problem of these growth resources' capitalization, determining identification of copyrights, certificates, licenses, marketing rights and specialized know-how or trademarks and software as intangible assets. In spite of this, the dynamic of processes in the "new economics"(Suciu, 2002) outruns the conceptual framework of the accounting treatment of intangible assets, a significant part of these being nowadays impossible to classify as investments and, maybe more important, to evaluate as warrantees offered by creditors as insurance for the sums temporarily paid (Grosu, Almăşan, 2006).

Defining capitals for the contemporary economy, such as detailed and accurate knowledge of the competitive environment, "the learned lessons" in the dynamics of the state/company, knowledge organization and accessibility, the relational system of leadership or reputation are still left outside quantifiable assets, being very difficult to integrate in the contemporary management systems still dominated by accountancy and statistics.

No matter if one refers to the accounting treatment of intangible assets or the ones outside the international accounting standards, a simple inductive reasoning reveals the fact that information is what stands at the basis of the majority of these "neo factors of the new economics" (Purcariu, Iacob, 2011). In the current global economic context, information has become a strategic asset to take into account by both states and private economic actors in order to get competitive advantage or, on the contrary, to survive.

Information resource is, at the same time, production factor in relation to research-innovation activity or the work force degree of instruction/quality (education, training) and a tool for strategic action taking. From this perspective, the management of information resource becomes an essential, critical in the activity of leadership, the more complex the more one has been witnessing and accelerate process of dematerialization of information during the last decades (Gheorghe, 2008).

2 European Comision (EC), 2018, EPSAS issue paper on accounting treatment of intangible assets, EPSAS WG 17/13 rev, Luxembourg, 10th of April 2018, attests the framework of intangible assets' definition stipulated by the de International Public Sector Accounting Standards (ISPAS 31) according to the following criteria: it is identifiable and governed by legal and contractual rights; the holder (in this case the public sector – AN) has control over the asset and the capacity to limit the access of other economic entities to it; the asset has the capacity to generate future economic benefits for the holder; the cost of the asset is quantifiable.

2. Management and information

In a comparative analysis of the management of knowledge-based organizations and the traditional positivist paradigm of control and authority-based organization, Horatiu Dragomirescu outlined since 2001 the crucial part that the intangible assets played in postindustrial economy/organization (Tab. 1).

Tab. 1: Characteristics of management in the light of alternative organizational paradigms

Comparative criteria	**Paradigm**	
	Control and authority-based organization	**Knowledge-based organization**
Object of the enterprise	Classical resources, tangible assets, programmed activities	Systems and processes primarily based on intangible assets
Dominant logic	The logic of the work place and formal organizing	Logic based on organizational competences as performance sources
Orientation in time	Retrospective (control and inventory)	Prospective (engagement in projects)
Nature of the enterprise	Predominantly improving with a focus on continuity within the existent systems	Predominantly constructive with a focus on conceiving and guiding changes
Way of practicing	Routine-based, impersonal; focus on facts	Creative, customized; focus on conceptual and strategic matters
Way of concretization	Intervention to correct the deviations; reactive behaviors	Transforming intervention based on projects; proactive behaviors

Source: Dragomirescu, 2001, p. 3.

If in the past information was physically associated with the elements it referred to (raw material, supply, equipment, buildings, products etc.) thus it could be verified/evaluated, nowadays relevant information mostly targets, aspects regarding the managerial concept, the structure of the economic processes, organizational culture or the characteristics of the competitive environment. All these elements, which, generically, can be referred to as "knowledge," are dispersed, immaterial, difficult to validate and are the result of the turning of the information held by the organization's members into an efficient capacity of action.

In the knowledge-based economy, the state's or the company's capacity to perform as economic actors essentially depends on the capacity to handle and process the information they have. This fact lends a strategic valence to managerial objectives such as:

- permanent expansion of knowledge basis by stimulating organizational learning and innovation processes and by capitalizing their results;
- development of the capacity to intelligently and pertinently turn the available knowledge into successful action (Zack, 1999).

To these mainly cognitive objectives, another two strategic, practical and technology-oriented objectives can be added:

- collection of necessary data and information;
- management of relevant data and information and insuring access to it.

Noticing the crucial part knowledge, that is information, plays in the global economy, the French Henri Martre would introduce, in 1994, the concept of "Intelligence Economique" defining it as "the totality of coordinated action of research, process and dissemination of information useful for economic actors"[3] and basing it on four main anchors:

- encouragement of using "intelligence economique" in corporations;
- optimization of information exchange between public and private sector;
- creation of data bases compliant with the requests of the users;
- stimulation of education/training in this area.

The concept was not entirely new, being similar to the "competitive intelligence" used in Anglo-Saxon countries and it is based on knowledge, while information lacks relevance unless its trustworthiness and coherence are checked or it is placed in context and analyzed from the perspective of the company's/state's goals and interests so it can bring added value to founding future decisions (Marte, 2007).

Simultaneously with the ripening of the concept of "intelligence economique," the French government pursued the operationalization and maximization of benefits brought to France by this new "asset" in the context of a more and more fierce global competition. In 2003, in answer to prim-minister Jean-Pierre Raffarin's request, there was elaborated, under the supervision of deputy Bernard Carayon, a new report entitled "Intelligence économique, compétitivité et

3 "L'intelligence économique peut être définie comme l'ensemble des actions coordonnées de recherche, de traitement et de distribution en vue de son exploitation, de l'information utile aux acteurs économiques", în Rapport du Groupe "Intelligence économique et stratégie des entreprises", Commissariat général du Plan, Paris, Février1994, cf. https://www.entreprises.gouv.fr/files/files/directions_services/information-strategique-sisse/rapport-martre.pdf.

cohésion sociale" (Carayon, 2003). Along with a critical evaluation of the state's manner of implementation by of the directions of action indicated by Henri Martre, the report also contains no less than 38 suggestions for the increase of this new asset's relevance for the economic development of France, among which:

- creation, with the French central administration, of an advisory board for economic competitiveness and security;
- appointment of a minister for economic development;
- integrated approach of endeavors in the "intelligence economique" area and, last but not least, a wider regional/local implementation.

As a matter of fact, an immediate consequence of the Carayon Report was the establishment of the Strategic Workshop of Intelligence (ATELIS) within the former ESCEM School of Business and Management, aimed to elaborate studies and to offer the private sector advice/instruction in "intelligence economique" (ciworldwide.org).

3. Romania – a still uncertain course towards capitalizing on its own informational potential

What singles France out of the other economies, advanced from the point of view of capitalizing information in growing competitiveness, is the manner in which the state, the French government understood and furthered/stimulated the use of "intelligence economique." While in the majority of developed economies the specific "competitive intelligence" practices initially appeared and got developed with the private economic actors later on being integrated in the government's policies, in France the state was the advocate and the catalyst of the endeavors in this area thus being able, in a short time, to make up for the delay it had at the moment of the Martre Report.

It would be good for Romania to follow the French model as the level of capitalization of information in our country is very low, a fact made obvious especially by the results, or, better said, the "counter results," that Romania accomplished at the European level in areas concerning innovation, research-development or informatization of economy and society.

European innovation scoreboard 2019 places Romania on the last position in the European Union regarding the innovation activity while the perspectives in this area are less than encouraging, considering both the gap between Romania and the European average and the internal structure associated to this indicator.

The current situation is also a direct consequence of the very low level of public spending for research-innovation sector, an essential indicator in the transition to knowledge-based economy, set in 2018 to only 0.21 % of the GDP, under 0.30 % of the GDP – the amount spent for research-development by the private enterprises (INS, 2019) (Fig. 1).

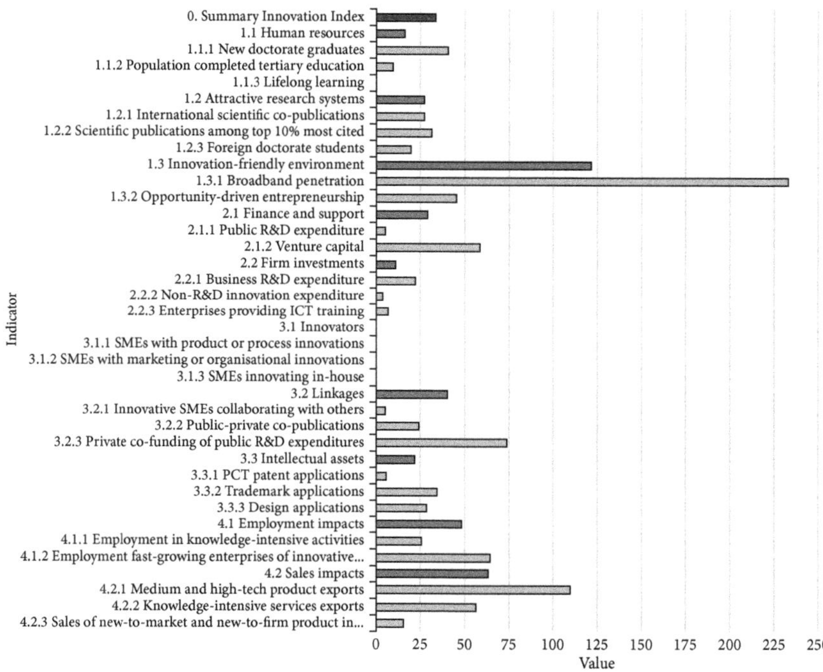

Fig. 1: The structure of the indicator "innovation activity"

Source: European Commission, European Innovation Scoreboard, 2020, https://ec.europa.eu/growth/industry/innovation/facts-figures/scoreboards.

Last but not least, the negative effects of underfunding research-development activities are worsened by the low absorption in economy of the results generated by the research-development activity, a fact revealed by the European statistics (Fig. 2).

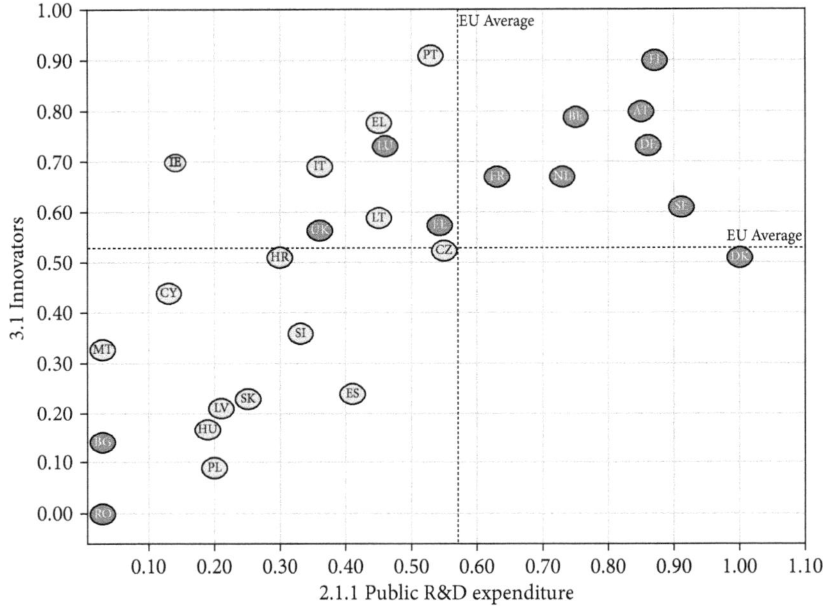

Fig. 2: The relationship between public expenses in the research-development field and the innovative enterprises

Source: European Commission, European Innovation Scoreboard, 2020, https://interactivetool.eu/EIS/EIS_2.html#.

The same worrying situation is revealed by the share of employees in the research-development field, no less than three of Romanian regions (South-West Oltenia, South-Muntenia and North-East) ranking last in the European top (Eurostat, 2019) (Fig. 3), but also by the negative trend regarding the share of employees in innovative enterprises (INS, 2018).

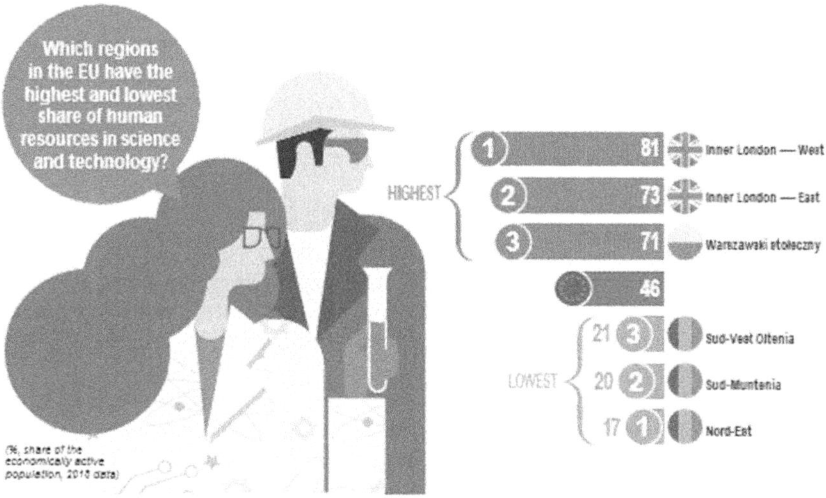

Fig. 3: Regions with highest and lowest share of human resources in science and technology
Source: Eurostat.

The data published this year by Eurostat place our country on the next to last position in the European Union also regarding Internet use of 74 % compared to the European average of 87 % (Eurostat, 2020) (Tab. 2). Regarding the computerization of public administration, there is a significant delay of our country compared to the EU average, impacting directly on the entire society, although Romania has reached the last year of implementation of the National Strategy on Digital Agenda, approved by Government Decision no. 245/7th of April, 2015.

Tab. 2: Internet use in interaction with public authorities (%of population)

	EU	Romania
Interaction with public authorities	55	12
Accessing information on the websites of public authorities	44	9
Downloading official documents	33	6
Sending filled in official documents	38	6

Source: Eurostat, 2020.

This matter of facts is caused, on the one hand by population not being used to equipment specific to information technology (last ranking position in the EU top for Romania and Bulgaria regarding this indicator, too) (Eurostat, 2019) and, on the other hand, by the lack of efficiency of public policies advanced in order to standardize the websites of various central and local public administration institutions, so they are user-friendly.

Brief conclusions

We chose these three areas of economic and social life, innovation, research-development and computerization, believing they were relevant for a correct evaluation of the degree of capitalization/use of information within the activities developed in our country.

Along with these areas many other aspects can be analyzed, such as information and knowledge management, the availability and communication of information or the use of information in decision making, all these reaching a not very satisfactory conclusion: in Romania, the passage to a knowledge-based economy is still at the very beginning, with random manifestations due to lack of a strategic option, or, in other words: "creation of knowledge-based organizations remains a must for the development of a nationwide knowledge-based economy" (Dragomirescu, 2001, p. 17).

Considering the important potential of information/knowledge within the "new economy," any delay in the process of integration and capitalization of this intangible asset in the economic processes leads to the deepening of the gap between the developed economies of the world and Romania's. Therefore, today, the scenario of the emerging development of knowledge-based economy in our country is shaking, making the engagement of the Romanian state's strategic resources not only necessary, but compulsory.

References

Carayon, Bernard, Intelligence économique, compétitivité et cohésion sociale, Paris, 2003, http://strategique.free.fr/analyses/carayon.pdf, 10.07.2019.

Dragomirescu, Horaţiu, Organizaţii bazate pe cunoaştere, in Romanian Academy prioritary project Societatea informaţională – societatea cunoaşterii, 2001, http://www.academiaromana.ro/pro_pri/doc/st_g06.doc.

Gheorghe, Ion, Informaţia şi comunicarea, componente ale proceselor manageriale, Colecţia Biblioteca economică, Seria Probleme economice, vol. 326, Centrul de informare şi documentare economică, Bucureşti, 2008.

Grosu, Corina, Almăşan, Alina, Activele imateriale, resurse importante pentru gestiunea performanta a intreprinderii, Revista AGER Economie teoretică şi aplicată, nr. 8, Bucureşti, 2006, http://store.ectap.ro/articole/140.pdf.

Martre, Henri, Pour comprendre l'information, il faut être competent, 2007, http://blogs.lesechos.fr/intelligence-economique/pour-comprendre-l-information-il-a1424.html.

Purcariu, Loredana; Iacob, Vlăduţ-Severian, Neofactorii în noua economie, 2011, https://www.finantare.ro › neofactorii-in-noua-economie.

Suciu, Marta Christina, Economics. Part I: New Economics & Knowledge Based Society, Editura ASE, Bucureşti, 2002.

Zack, Michael H., Managing Organizational Ignorance, Knowledge Directions, Volume 1, Summer, 1999, http://web.cba.neu.edu/~mzack/articles/orgig/orgig.htm.

Zaman, Gheorghe; Georgescu, George, Dezvoltarea economică endogenă la nivel regional – Cazul României, Editura Expert, Bucureşti, 2015.

Further Reading

Commissariat général du Plan, Rapport du Groupe Intelligence économique et stratégie des entreprises, Paris, Février 1994, https://www.entreprises.gouv.fr/files/files/directions_services/information-strategique-sisse/rapport-martre.pdf.

European Commission (EC), EPSAS issue paper on accounting treatment of intangible assets, EPSAS WG 17/13 rev, Luxembourg, 10 April 2018, https://circabc.europa.eu/sd/a/725ae06f-0a27-426d-a1af-880859336184/Issue%20paper%20on%20accounting%20treatment%20of% 20intangible% 20assets%20.pdf.

European Commission, European Innovation Scoreboard, 2020, https://ec.europa.eu/growth/industry/innovation/facts-figures/scoreboards https://ec.europa.eu/growth/industry/innovation/facts-figures/scoreboards/.

Eurostat, Eurostat regional yearbook 2019, 2019, https://ec.europa.eu/eurostat/en/web/products-statistical-books/-/KS-HA-19-001.

Eurostat, What do you use the internet for?, 27 January 2020, https://ec.europa.eu/eurostat/web/products-eurostat-news/-/DDN-20200127-1?inheritRedirect=true&redirect =%2Feurostat%2F.

INS, Activitatea de cercetare-dezvoltare. Anul 2018, Bucureşti, 2019, http://www.insse.ro/cms/sites/default/files/field/publicatii/activitatea_de_cercetare_dezvoltare_3.pdf.

INS, Inovaţia în întreprinderile din mediul de afaceri în perioada 2014–2016, 27 July 2018, http://www.insse.ro/cms/sites/default/files/com_presa/com_pdf/inovatie_afaceri 16 _2r.pdf.

https://ec.europa.eu/eurostat/web/products-eurostat-news/-/DDN-20200127-1?inherit Redire ct=true&redirect=%2Feurostat%2F.

http://appsso.eurostat.ec.europa.eu/nui/submitViewTableAction.do.

https://ec.europa.eu/eurostat/documents/3217494/10095393/KS-HA-19 %E2 %80 %91001-EN-N.pdf/d434affa-99cd-4ebf-a3e3-6d4a5f10bb07.

https://interactivetool.eu/EIS/EIS_2.html#.

http://s244543015.onlinehome.fr/ciworldwide/?p=949.

Valeriu Ioan-Franc, Beatrice Leuştean

Treating business ethics as an intangible asset

Abstract Reflecting on various ways business ethics is understood and implemented, also giving the vast literature that stands for the role of good governance and ethical leadership to generate not only social benefits but also economic results, the paper here provides a forgotten effect approach on the relationship among sustainability and gains. Due to the similarities between corporate social responsibility (the most common term used to define business ethics) and intangible assets, giving the nature of the studied phenomenon, that is a subjective matter, volatile, undifferentiated and, most of the times, indefinite, the paper treated ethics as inputs (or causes) in defining model's relationships. Further investigated was the evident and the non evident effects of the business ethics components treated as intangible assets and the expected results and further incentive to use a responsible leadership. The most intriguing result consisted in the almost null evident relationship between responsibility for the stakeholders, the main ingredient in defining and understanding the social role of implementing ethics in doing business, and the expectations for economic and accountable results and further incentives towards sustainability. Applying the forgotten effects method, there was detected a consistent hidden effect of the same factor, on the outputs.

Keywords: business ethics, fuzzy logic, intangible assets

Introduction

Business ethics is understood, most of the times, as corporate social responsibility. Assessing responsibility only through reporting standards is somehow limiting because of the difficulty to discern between voluntary and other activities. Standards do not always consider outcomes and impacts, at least not systematically, being two aspects of the same phenomenon and often measurement is ambiguous and limited. Approaching this issue in a different manner, there are many arguments in favor of treating business ethics as an intangible asset. Not physical in nature and used over the long term, an intellectual asset most of the times, indefinite or definable, intangible assets have a meaningful impact on generating sales. The question that arises in the matter of business ethics is if and how much of the outputs are generated by different aspects of this concept. Does this, integrated into the managerial system create measurable economical effects? There are examples of ethical success businesses and many more examples of profitable businesses that integrated various corporate social responsibility (CSR) initiatives. From this perspective, customer's perception is a good way of measuring business ethics impact on their choice. But manager's decision in deciding using responsible measures, is taken according to a mix of causes, not only estimated market share gains. This study starts with the similarities between business ethics and the goodwill. And also considers that doing ethical businesses is a leaders' decision.

This approach presents a fuzzy logic model (Kaufmann; Aluja, 1988), applied to describe the relationships between corporate responsibility and economic results, treating business ethics as an intangible asset. The scientific literature and empirical data offer the possibility to synthesize the main areas of encompassing business ethics, most of the times understood as CSR. Five ways of investigating ethical behavior were followed: a defined scope for social responsibility, accountability and transparency, respect for the stakeholders, respect for the rule of law and environmental business imprint. A defined scope for social responsibility is considered the criteria for assessing the leadership's understanding and the intentionality towards ethics. The rest are principles of social responsibility extracted from Clause 4 (ISO 26000: 2010).

In what concerns intangibles' impact valuation, as well as to iterate similarities of CSR to goodwill's, a fuzzy quantification, derived from the empirical evaluation of the relationships, is proposed. Perceived impact is defined through: expected economic results, expected accounting results, expected market share, incentive to further use business ethics and incentive to avoid using business ethics in the future. This provides, when applied according to the specific of the industry, a fine tuned business instrument (given the possibility of ranging the perceived impact on a 0 to 1 scale where 0 is no impact at all and 1 represents a total influence) in order to describe and quantify the relationship between business ethics and economic results, treating the concept as an intangible asset.

For sustaining this theoretical reasoning a pilot study, biased by the expert's opinion, was applied to a number of 98 small to medium enterprises and 3 big companies which responded to the questionnaires in a two months period. All of them were involved in various social sustainable projects or already implemented CSR in their business activity. This research might be further extended on a national and regional level, in order to find out which are the most relevant social responsibility factors that determine significant business outputs. Choosing this method is due to the nature of the studied phenomenon, that is a subjective matter, volatile, undifferentiated and, most of the times, indefinite.

1. Literature review

Several studies regarding business people's behavior and how is perceived, support this standing in favor of treating ethics as an intangible asset (Saad, 2015). Another example is the survey conducted by Deloitte in 2016 on ethics and responsibility, the results showing that 87 % of the young generation believes that "the success of a business should be measured in terms other than financial ones," and 25 % considering that ethics, trust, integrity and honesty are the basis of long-term success (Deloitte, 2016).

Business ethics research spans over various areas, from corporate governance to value based management and marketing (Sison, 2017). To find ethical entrepreneurs who often launch businesses with a virtue-driven purpose of serving a broader social good we have to look at TESLA, WIPRO, LUSH, Dean's Beans Organic Coffee Company, BCC Pacific, Beyond Meat, Patagonia and many more other examples (Manz et al., 2015). Ethics includes numerous virtues, such as compassion, integrity, and justice. These are displayed in the practices and processes of these businesses involving many stakeholders. The decisive role of leadership and strategy of implementing and conducting business ethics is what makes sustainability work. Measuring the way sustainability is performing along with measuring sustainability role in the results may be understood both as an ultimate goal and also as an intermediate goal in achieving business's success (Epstein, 2008).

Sometimes entrepreneurial culture and not the will of few malicious individuals is to blame in what concerns organizational failure in finance. The significance of this term and the relation with business ethics is often left unspecified. There are authors that discern organizational culture through a couple of perspectives: intellectualist view, the value view and the virtue view that best understands a company in terms of organizational traits (Meyer, 2016). There is also the ethic of care perspective through that the responsibility of sustaining the relationships (that means taking care of addressing the needs of others) is of utmost importance in business initiatives (Linsley, 2017). There are many applications of being ethical as managerial action in various fields, from human resources to products quality enhancement or sales. The essence here is how much of business success relies on the virtue or, else put, on how virtue shapes work (Grassl, 2015).

Edelman Trust barometer collected 34.000 data in 28 countries about the relationship between the customer confidence and profit (Edelman, 2015; 2016; 2017), the social role of the enterprise (more than 80 % of the respondents consider that it has to play a major role in solving social problems) (Edelman, 2016) and the role of the intangible assets, such as confidence, in the managerial process of the enterprise (Calvo, 2018). Digital revolution represents both an opportunity and a support for companies in the ethics and social responsibility domain. There is a major shift in data mining about businesses' economic, social and environmental impacts, interests and legitimate expectations involved, trust, reputation and affinity related to the stakeholders (Calvo, 2018). Business ethics has positive impacts upon the development of intellectual capital, as knowledge has become the most important asset of modern businesses. Business ethics is associated with the development of intangible knowledge resources-intellectual capital. In this reasoning, an ethical approach to business can encourage open communication, problem solving, knowledge sharing and creativity among employees to increase organizational capital (Su, 2014).

The role of intangible values of assets has increased for all domains of activity. And such, it changed the perspective of the measurement of intangibles and the ethical challenges implied in today's knowledge based society (Millar; Choi, 2003).

Copyrights and licenses, brands and leases, publicity and clients have become the essential wealth in nowadays economics. Their value cannot be dissociated from their physical assets support and can only be derived from the financial market's evaluation of the company's shares (Louisot, 2004) or when selling a company. Business ethics, treated as an intangible asset might be a long-time reputational standing for any organization so managing it is an essential part of the strategic role of the board of directors, who must take into account all stakeholders, whose perception of the organization will determine its reputation. There is a difficult task though given the nature of business ethics that has much in common with the more established practice of corporate brand management. There are also various strategic responsibilities, given the fact that brand reputation involves the stakeholders and this can lead to inconsistencies and even gaps in the strategy that diminishes the returns (Rankin Frost; Cooke, 1999). "Good ethics is good business" is an intuition of the possible links between ethical behavior and good business decisions (Cohen; Grace, 2014). In a similar reasoning, Robert Moment shares a quote by Louis Gagnon, social entrepreneur: "Being ethical is not a personality trait. It's not an aptitude. It's a choice. Unfortunately, too many leaders choose not to behave ethically because they can escape responsibility. I think so because the consequences of unethical behavior are often blurred, dispersed and/or invisible" (Moment, 2016).

There were also developed models of valuing intangible assets to support correct corporate value ratios (Lin; Tang, 2009) and there is a continuous process of finding the essence of value and valuing intangible assets (Christodoulides, 2010; Popovic & Bojan, 2015). Moreover, there is an inversed influence, of the social environment on branding and valuing intangible assets, as territory might become an inherent factor of corporative identity and, as such, of intangible value (Klimenko; Patlasov, 2018).

Recognition and measurement of intangible assets, especially for those that are not characterized by "identifiability" or "control" as ethical corporate responsibility is, becomes a current requirement for the social statements and integrated reporting. Their importance grew, so their inadequate disclosure, as they do not reflect the requirements of financial statements (Pucci et al., 2014). International accounting statements only recognize the controlled, identifiable, nonmonetary assets without physical substance, leaving to the goodwill all the rest of the company's ability to generate income that cannot be identified, measured or recognized in financial statements. Goodwill may be recognized only when acquired by a third party. There is a vast literature on the role, evaluation and accounting of intangible assets and on the relationship between book and market value, as a possible indicator of the magnitude of intangibles. Celemi International proposed an instrument to measure financial and intangible assets impact on returns and used this evaluation tool since 1995 to include in the annual reports the evaluation of business trends related to strategic business plans (Heisig; Runeson, 2001).

Even various methods proposed, still a need is to assess and evaluate the role of the intangible assets, especially the goodwill, in the value of a business. Moreover, it is a present issue that corporate social responsibility may be understood both as a regulatory frame and ethical behavior of a business. It depends on various factors, and is not an easy task neither to describe what is precisely means, neither its impact. Marc Epstein presents a methodology to bring social and environmental ethics into business activities through responsible leadership. This is the way he examines the structural issues and processes to be addressed to create the framework for a real not only declarative corporate responsibility implementation and reporting. Methodologies for measuring social and environmental impacts and risks, performance evaluation systems, sustainability performance metrics and mapping the actions that drive performance are explained in order to improve processes, products and projects for corporate sustainability (Epstein, 2017).

2. Forgotten effects of ethical behavior over businesses' results

When investigating causes to effects relationships, the following results were found the results from Tab. 1.

Tab. 1: The relationships among business ethics elements and outputs

Causes to Effects Matrix Evident Relationship	**Expected economic results**	**Expected accounting results**	**Expected market share**	**Incentive to further use business ethics**	**Incentive to avoid using business ethics**
A defined scope for social responsibility	0.400	0.800	0.300	0.400	0.100
Accountability and transparency	0.800	0.900	0.700	0.400	0.500
Respect for the stakeholders	0.100	0.100	0.400	0.300	0.200
Respect for the rule of law	0.900	0.900	0.300	0.600	0.600
Environmental business imprint	0.700	0.800	0.300	0.400	0.900

Source: Authors' work based on the collected data.

These figures represent averages of the quantified responses for the perception of the business ethics components on outcomes, specified in ten relevant categories. Evaluation started from 0, meaning no relationship or impact to 1, the maximum impact or a relation of identity. Scale was divided in equal 0.1 ranging possibilities.

Data above, point towards the most important evident relationships perceived by businesses in their social activity. An ethical leadership that defines goals towards social responsibility has a great impact over expected accounting results and a very small impact on the incentive to avoid using business ethics. Accountability and transparency is directly influencing, in an important manner the expected economic, accounting results and also expected market shares. It is relevant also for the incentive to avoid using business ethics. This might be explained through the opposition between efficiency and sustainability in mainstream's ideology and lack of fiscal support for sustainable initiatives. Another interesting result consists in the evident relationship between respect for the stakeholders and outcomes.

The core initiatives and sustainability by definition consists in taking into account all the parts involved in business's activity: employees, clients, community, environment, etc. This though, it is perceived as somehow influencing expected market shares and less sustaining the incentive to further use business ethics. All the other outcomes appear to be irrelevant in the decision to use business ethics, which support the opinion of those who see the CSR being only a marketing strategy. Respect for the rule of law has the most important influence on expected economic and accounting results, a moderate influence on the incentive to further use ethics and on the avoidance of it, while little influence in expected market shares. Given the environmental component of the CSR that is considered to have a major influence over the results, the hypothesis are confirmed by empirical evidence. In here, there is a major influence on the incentive to avoid using business ethics due to the estimated costs of clean production, on expected economic and accounting results. There was identified a moderate and small influence on the incentive to use business ethics and expected market shares.

Appling further the forgotten effects method, the normalized data for evident relationships, after applying the min-max choice, provide data for calculate the non evident relationship causes to effects matrix (Tab. 2):

Tab. 2: The non evident relationships among business ethics and outputs

The non evident relationships causes to effects matrix	Expected economic results	Expected accounting results	Expected market share	Incentive to further use business ethics	Incentive to avoid using business ethics
A defined scope for social responsibility	0.800	0.800	0.500	0.800	0.600
Accountability and transparency	0.800	0.900	0.800	0.900	0.600
Respect for the stakeholders	0.800	0.800	0.800	0.800	0.600
Respect for the rule of law	0.900	0.900	0.900	0.900	0.600
Environmental business imprint	0.800	0.900	0.700	0.800	0.900

Source: Authors' work based on collected data.

The final stage of the inquiry is reflecting the forgotten effects, presented in Tab. 3.

Tab. 3: The forgotten effects of business ethics over the results

The forgotten effects matrix	Expected economic results	Expected accounting results	Expected market share	Incentive to further use business ethics	Incentive to avoid using business ethics
A defined scope for social responsibility	0.4	0.0	0.2	0.4	0.5
Accountability and transparency	0.0	0.0	0.1	0.5	0.1
Respect for the stakeholders	0.7	0.7	0.4	0.5	0.4
Respect for the rule of law	0.0	0.0	0.6	0.3	0.0
Environmental business imprint	0.1	0.1	0.4	0.4	0.0

Source: Authors' work based on collected data.

From these results we extract that the respect for the stakeholders induces an important, but hidden effect over expected economic and accounting results, the evident relationship being almost indifferent. It is important to take this result into account because the stakes are high, formal inquiring giving only the possibility to evaluate visible perceptions. For example, the respect for the stakeholders hidden influence was induced through the incentive to further use business ethics (0.4), through the incentive to avoid using business ethics (0.5) and, in the end, to the expected accounting results (0.7). Other causes, such as accountability and transparency have an obvious influence on further using business ethics (0.4) and a hidden effect of 0.5, derived from the non evident relationship (0.9).

Conclusions

Role of ethics increases in the emerging global awareness paradigm and, applied to businesses' behavior, induces financial results. The last two decades, the interest for assessing sustainability increased, fact reflected in the rich scientific literature. Many authors, including this study's authors, consider there are similarities between corporate social responsibility and intangible assets, given the subjective nature of these, volatility and impossibility to differentiate or define them.

Assessing social responsibility only through reporting standards is somehow limiting and cannot differentiate between voluntary embracing ethics and other activities that only claim it for the appearances in order to, for example, gain market shares. This present study focused on a framework for treating business ethics as an intangible asset, using a fuzzy logic forgotten effects' approach.

The research has its limitations derived from the fact that, except the big national interest companies, local small and medium enterprises are not compelled by law to use any CSR assessment criteria for their reporting activity. As such, the difficulty to find data for pilot testing the proposed model, that were biased by the experts' opinion. The results sustain the hypothesis that there exists an incentive to use business ethics as a way to increase profit or market shares but also, indifferent of the reason for implementing it, there are hidden relationships that indirectly induce further incentive to apply ethics on businesses.

References

Calvo, Patrici; Osal, Cristian: Whistleblowing & Big Data: Monitoring and Compliance of Ethics and Social Responsibility. Profesional de la Information 27(1), 2018, pp. 173–184.

Christodoulides, Georges, de Chernatony, Leslie: Conceptualizarea şi măsurarea capitalurilor proprii de brand bazate pe consumator: o revizuire a literaturii. Revista internaţională de cercetare de piaţă 52(1), 2010, pp. 43.

Cohen, Stephen; Grace, Damian: Business Ethics. Oxford University Press; 5th edition, 2014.

Edelman, Berland: 2015 Edelman Trust Barometer. Global Annual Study. Edelman Berland, available at: www.edelman.com/research/2015-edelman-trust-barometer, accessed 07.05.2019.

Edelman, Berland: 2016 Edelman Trust Barometer. Global Annual Study. Edelman Berland, available at: www.edelman.com/research/2016-edelman-trust-barometer.

Edelman, Berland: 2017 Edelman Trust Barometer. Global Annual Study. Edelman Berland, available at: www.edelman.com/research/2017-edelman-trust-barometer.

Epstein, Marc J.: Making Sustainability Work: Best Practices in Managing and Measuring Corporate Social, Environmental and Economic Impacts. Berret-Koehler: San Francisco, 2008.

Epstein, Marc J.: Making Sustainability Work: Best Practices in Managing and Measuring Corporate Social, Environmental and Economic Impacts 1. Social Responsibility of Business 2. Sustainable Development Reporting. Routledge: New York, 2017.

Grassl, Wolfgang: Being and Doing: How Virtue Shapes Work. In: Sison, Aleco Jose G. (eds) Handbook of Virtue Ethics in Business and Management. Springer: Dordrecht, 2015, pp. 897–907.

Heisig, Peter; Runeson Janet: Measuring Intangible Assets for Sustainable Business Growth—Celemi AB, Medium-Sized and Fast Growing. In: Mertins K., Heisig P., Vorbeck J. (eds) Knowledge Management. Springer: Berlin, Heidelberg, 2001, pp. 157–164.

Kaufmann, Arnold; Gil Aluja, Jaime: Modelos para la investigacion de efectos olvidados. Milladoiro: Gandarina, 1988.

Klimenko, Sergey.N.; Patlasov, Oleg Yu.: Regional Authorities PR-Technologies Effectiveness and Evaluation of the Territory Brands as ITS. Science of the Person: Humanitarian Researches 3(33), 2018, pp. 203–214.

Lin, Grace T.R.; Tang, Jerry Y.H.: Appraising Intangible Assets from the Viewpoint of Value Drivers. Journal of Business Ethics 88(4), 2009, pp. 679–689.

Linsley, Philip M.: Application of an Ethic of Care to Business. In: Sison, Aleco Jose G. (eds) Handbook of Virtue Ethics in Business and Management. Springer: Dordrecht, 2017, pp. 307–319.

Louisot, Jean-Paul: Managing Intangible Asset Risks: Reputation and Strategic Redeployment Planning. Risk Management 6(3), 2004, pp. 35–50.

Manz, Karen P.; Marx, Robert D.; Manz, Charles C.; Dillon, Pamala J.: A Case Study of a Justice-Based Virtuous Organization. In: Sison, Aleco Jose G. (eds) Handbook of Virtue Ethics in Business and Management. Springer: Dordrecht, 2015, pp. 1–12.

Meyer, Marco: A Virtue Ethical Approach to Organizational Culture in Finance. In: Sison, Aleco Jose G. (eds) Handbook of Virtue Ethics in Business and Management. Springer: Dordrecht, 2016, pp. 1–11.

Millar, Carla C.J.M.; Choi, Chong Ju: Advertising and Knowledge Intermediaries: Managing the Ethical Challenges of Intangibles. Journal of Business Ethics 48(3), 2003, pp. 267–277.

Moment, Robert: Good Ethics Is Good Business, found at: http://www.millermech.com/2016/company-culture/good-ethics-good-business/.

Organizaţia Internaţională pentru Standardizare: ISO 10668: 2010 – Evaluarea mărcii: Cerinţe pentru evaluarea mărcii monetare. 2012, availabale at: http://www.iso.org/iso/catalogue_detail.htm?csnumber=46032 (12/12/2014).

Popovic, Ana; Bojan, Krstic; Milovanovic, Goran: Measuring the Financial Value of Brand as an Intangible Asset of an Enterprise. Marketing 46(1), 2015, pp. 13–25.

Pucci, Sabrina; Cenci, Marisa; Tutino, Marco; Luly, Roberta: Intangible Assets: Current Requirements, Social Statements, Integrated Reporting, and New Models. In: Russ M. (ed) Value Creation, Reporting, and Signaling for Human Capital and Human Assets. Palgrave Macmillan: New York, 2014, pp. 179–211.

Rankin Frost, Alison; Cooke, Chris: Brand v Reputation: Managing an Intangible Asset. Journal of Brand Management 7(2), 1999, pp. 81–87.

Saad, Lydia: Americans' Faith in Honesty, Ethics of Police Rebounds, Social and Policy Issues, December 21, 2015, available at: news.gallup.com/poll/187874/americans-faith-honesty-ethics-police-rebounds.aspx, accessed 07.06.2019.

Sison, Aleco Jose G.: Handbook of Virtue Ethics in Business and Management. Springer: Dordrecht, 2017.

Su, Hwan-Yann: Business Ethics and the Development of Intellectual Capital. Journal of Business Ethics 119(1), 2014, pp. 87–98.

Dr. Patricia Buckley, Dr. Peter Viechnicki, and Akrur Baruahttp, "The 2016 Deloitte Millennial Survey Winning over the next generation of leaders", https://www2.deloitte.com/content/dam/Deloitte/global/Documents/About-Deloitte/gx-millenial-survey-2016-exec-summary.pdf, accessed 05.06.2019.

Firicel Mone, Maria Vişan, Ivona Stoica

Collaborative systems and platforms in the framework of new technologies

Abstract In the framework of new technologies, more and more are increasing and very dynamic the use and development of new technologies IT&C. On behalf of the raised penetration rate of Internet users in Europe, according to Internet World Stats, the statistics show six times higher usage than Africa, but also there, IT&C technologies has known a growth regarding the investments and the usage. Wireless technology plays an extremely important role in the development of broadband technology for at least ten years from now, with most broadband users being the most passionate users of mobile telephony. Thus, increasingly alert, 5G mobile networks and technology will reach an exponential increase in demand that providers will have to meet if they want long-term upbeat and uptake, as broadband users will want more great flexibility in using m-banking, m-health applications. Information and Communication Technology will increasingly penetrate everyday life, offering a greater diversity of applications and services by using collaborative systems and platforms, taking advantage of their continuously development.

Keywords: IT&C technologies, collaborative systems, collaborative platforms, products and services

Introduction

The evolution of technology over the last 20 years can be described as a digital and informational rebirth. Communication technology and the Internet have changed the lifestyle of the individual, private organizations and governments, creating a new paradigm in how we understand inter-human interaction and the way we relate to information.

For the population, the moment that represented the turning point was the advent of World Wide Web. The Google company, founded in 1998, launched the eponymous search engine, which provided a quick way to find all the information available on the World Wide Web for all users.

Soon, Google began to be present in every home, and today, through the search engine, the Chrome browser, and from November 2007 through the Android operating system, Google, the Internet and the possibility of instant access to information have become the circumstances of an everyday reality.

Hence, collecting and processing information, in the context of the digitalization of the world economy, represent strategic management measures that not only ensure the premises of a competitive advantage, but can also make the difference between surviving in the competitive environment. The systems that provide support in the management of the organization have been classified as decision support systems (Filip, 2007).

1. Collaborative communication systems

The information society is evolving rapidly, and the pace at which information is used and consumed in interconnected work environments implies the use by managers of collaborative applications, which offers the mobility to generate decisions in real time and also to achieve efficient communication.

Internet-based Decision Support Systems (SSDs) emerged in the 2000s, as the forerunner of databases and online analytical processing (Brandaş, 2007). SSD does not have a universally valid and accepted definition, but the system is very well described by E. Turban: "Systems designed to support managerial decision-making in unstructured issues" (Ivanciu, 2019).

These systems used both by decision makers, particularly managers at all hierarchical levels, as well as assistants, in the sense of consultants, gives adapted to the future needs of the organization. However, it should be noted that the provide support for predictions, risk analyzes and the development of communication systems are based on algorithms that help the manager in identifying optimal decisions, but do not replace the manager's thinking, analysis and decision making.

"A collaborative system is one where multiple users or agents engage in a shared activity, usually from remote locations. In the larger family of distributed applications, collaborative systems are distinguished by the fact that the agents in the system are working together towards a common goal and have a critical need to interact closely with each other: sharing information, exchanging requests with each other, and checking in with each other on their status. In this chapter, we'll consider a collaborative system as one that is also distinguished by a certain level of concurrency; i.e., the agents in the system are interacting with the system and with each other at roughly the same time. So a chat session is collaborative, because all of the agents involved need to coordinate with each other to be sure that the chatters don't miss anyone else's comments. An email system isn't collaborative, because each email client simply wants to be sure that its messages get to the right server, and eventually to the intended recipient. A particular email client doesn't care about the state of any other client, and doesn't need to coordinate with any of them in order to accomplish its goal" (Farley, 1998).

The best known collaborative communications system is the FTP: File Transfer Protocol, managed by a common server of the organization. Today, there are several types of collaborative systems, adapted to the specific need of communication, depending on the field, such as collaborative systems in the field of education, banking, but also collaborative systems used in production (Mirescu, 2019).

Collaborative communication systems have the role of centralizing all the communication tools within an organization, in an integrated system, which facilitates the electronic transfer of documents and information. Depending on their characteristics and the way the communion is managed, they can be grouped as follows (Mirescu, 2019):

- network: messages circulate between users without restrictions;
- tree: messages are hierarchically targeted;
- linear: system specific to the educational field.

2. Collaborative platforms

"Collaboration platforms typically include an email client, web conferencing, social media sharing, video capabilities, document sharing capabilities, instant messaging and more. Enterprise collaboration platforms are designed to be installed on-premises or deployed via the Web as cloud-based services" (Beal, 2019).

Most organizations use these platforms and technologies. Collaboration platforms represent interconnected solutions of collaboration such as unified communication systems, which integrate several activities within the organization (Fig. 1).

Fig. 1: Unified communication systems

Source: https://www.esse-ti.it/en/press/unified-communication.

These platforms have the role of carrying out the following activities:

- simplifying communications;
- optimizing the interactions between the team members;
- accessing and sharing information in real time;
- access to information from multiple devices.

Collaboration within a team, especially if the team members do not work in the same place, is essential to be supported by a communication that records as few barriers and syncope as possible in exchange of information.

For the economic environment, there are several collaboration platforms that ensure a successful communication between the members of the organization or between different organizations. These platforms have the role of management applications for organizations and projects within, being for manager's tools for monitoring the tasks outlined.

Project management tools are critical. The most used online platforms are:

- **WebEx**

WebEx is an online platform that managers can use to conduct video conferences and webinars.

- **Trello**

Trello is a platform through which tasks can be monitored within the organization's projects, the stage of all activities can be updated and team members can communicate for assigning tasks.

- **Slack**

Slack has the advantage of instant communication and integrates communication tools that use different channels for message transmission, depending on the needs of managers.

- **Asana**

Asana offers users the opportunity to assign tasks and strategically plan the activity of the organization and projects.

- **Dapulse**

Dapulse is an online application with the role of collaboration tool, very easy to use, with an intuitive design, being oriented towards the organization's objectives.

- **ProofHub**

ProofHub offers diversified management and collaboration functions within projects.

- **Redbooth**

Redbooth offers access to a variety of functions, including the creation of Gantt charts.

- **Google Docs**

One of the most popular platforms is Google Docs. It allows editing of files at the same time, by several team members.

Conclusions

"Knowledge workers and process operators make various management and control decisions in their area of influence and responsibility; decision-making activities and styles should be adapted to the specific context of the organizations the decision unit is placed in" (Filip, 2017).

The globalization and evolution of the information society have led to major changes becoming the new economy, the business environment starting to move in the direction of process automation, digital transformation and artificial intelligence implementation.

Collaborative platforms are intelligent software solutions used more and more often in the Romanian business environment and companies have managed to assure employees the synchronous communication, sharing documents or any other work materials, meaning the information transfer is very fast and efficient in solving tasks at the workplace, whether it is from office or home (telework).

The new technologies have succeeded in coming up with new strategies and evolving both the business environment through virtual enterprises and the new types of jobs that have emerged as well as the new forms of payment by outsourcing or developing in-house computer systems with their own requirements security.

References

Beal, V., Enterprise Collaboration Platform, https://www.webopedia.com/TERM/E/enterprise-collaboration-platform.html, retrieved at 12.08.2019.

Brandaş, C., DSS Model Based on Rules and OLAP for Management by Budgets. Accounting and Management Information Systems, No. 22, 2007. Available at SSRN: https://ssrn.com/abstract=1082252.

Farley, J., Java Distributed Computing, O'Reilly & Associates, 1998, ISBN 1-56592-206-9E.

Filip, F. G., Sisteme suport pentru decizii, Ed. II Rev., Editura Tehnică, 2007.

Filip, F. G., Zamfirescu, C.-B., Ciurea, C., Computer Supported Collaborative Decision-Making, Springer, 2017, ISBN 978-3-319-47219-5.

Ivanciu, L. N., Sisteme interne de suport decizional, http://www.bel.utcluj.ro/dce/didactic/sisd/SISD_curs_2_Proces_decizional_Sisteme_de_suport_decizional.pdf, retrieved at 12.07.2019.

Mirescu, I., Sisteme de comunicaţie colaborative vs securitatea informaţională, https://rria.ici.ro/wp-content/uploads/2018/02/art-07.IuliaMIRESCU.pdf, retrieved at 22.08.2019.

Unified Communications Systems (UC), https://www.esse-ti.it/en/press/unified-communication, retrieved at 12.08.2019.

Roxana Adam, Viorel Cornescu, Andra Mărculescu

Saving and stressful decisions: an analysis of saving behavior by using the conflict theory of decision making

Abstract The novelty of the paper consist in using the conflict theory of decision making to examine the relationship between how people cope with stressful situations and the saving behavior. In this sense, a questionnaire on saving behavior was constructed by adapting to our particular purposes the Melbourne DMQ (Mann et al., 1997) and using the four factors: vigilance, hypervigilance, buck-passing, and procrastination.

The research results validated the Melbourne questionnaire as a good tool for evaluating decisions, useful to identify adaptive and maladaptive coping strategies and through the structural equations analysis causal relationships (positive and negative) have been shown between the latent variables of the conflict theory of decision making psychological factors (vigilance and hypervigilance) and saving as the belief that "saving leads to frustration" (the SEM_FRUSTRATION model); and as the belief that "saving means protecting the future" (the SEM_ PROTECTION model).

Keywords: saving, stress, decisional conflict, structural equations, vigilance, hypervigilance

Introduction

This paper is meant to be a new approach on studying savings decisions and its determinants related to stress. A recent study (Cigna, 2019) showed that from 13200 respondents to an online survey, 84 % of those surveyed said that they are stressed, while 13 % considering their stress unmanageable. Having in mind that stress seems to become one of the biggest problems in one's life, the scope of the paper was to examine if stress influences saving decisions.

The main objective of the paper was to identify if there is any relationship between how people cope with stressful situations and the decision of saving. Instead of examining the influence of different factors and the stress level of each individual, it was used the conflict theory of decision making and the Melbourne questionnaire (Mann et al., 1997) as a tool of measuring how people cope with stressful situations. On the other side, the saving decision was measured with reference to the meaning of protecting own future and, also, with reference to the frustration that may cause.

Besides the recent statistics that showed people declares itself as being stressed, the fundamental motivation of the study was the hypothesis that saving decision can be stressful for the individual when the person's budget is limited: the satisfaction of a current need vs. postponing consumption to save money so that another need shall be satisfied in the future.

To achieve the research scope, a questionnaire was created and distributed online. Based on the 345 responses two structural equation models were created in order to test the relationship between stress and saving, as above presented.

1. Literature review

A large body of research investigates stress and consumer behavior (e.g. Mathur, Moschis, and Lee, 1999; Moschis, 2007; Lou and Byun, 2018) or coping strategies and consumption (e.g. Duhachek, 2005; Karanika and Hogg, 2016; Machin et al., 2019), while just few papers are orientated toward saving behavior and stress (e.g. Asebedo et al., 2019; Yao, Xu, and Zhang, 2019) and to the best of our knowledge, no prior studies have examined the coping strategies in relation with saving behavior.

Warneryd (1999) distinguish between two important understandings of the word "saving": the residual income after deducting current consumption over a certain period of time (economic perspective) and to the process of not spending money for current period in order to be used in future (psychological perspective). At the macroeconomic level, saving has been studied with reference to the demographics (e.g. Chai and Kim, 2018), differences in income and growth rates (e.g. Attanasio, Picci, and Scorcu, 2000), taxation (e.g. Auerbach, 2015), productivity growth (Aghion et al., 2016), financial liberalization (Akinsola, 2018) and other types of variables related to income. At the individual level, saving has been studied with reference to its determinant factors, such as: demographic variables: age, gender, education or civil status (e.g. Cronqvist and Siegel, 2015); psychological factors: risk aversion, attitudes or time preferences (e.g. Guiso and Paiella, 2004); and economic factors correlated with individuals income and expenditures (e.g. Wärneryd, 1989).

Durante and Laran (2016) based on literature review sustain that a stressful event can lead to a decrease in consumption, while in the same time stress may lead to an action or to impulsive spending behaviors. According to the authors (Durante and Laran, 2016) the implication is that different perspectives offer divergent findings on whether stress leads to less or more consumption. The tentative to understand if stress influence saving behavior shouldn't be seen just from an economical or a psychological perspective, for example a representative study in the area of neuropsychobiology (Vogel, 1985) shows that biochemical, physiological and/or pathological changes in an organism do not seem to be caused by the aversive or noxious nature of the stressor (the conventional sequence of stressful event) but by the ability or inability of the organism to deal with this stressor.

Therefore, the main hypothesis of the study is that if an individual can cope successfully with the environmental challenge, little or no stress is experienced, and the level of experienced stress influences the saving behavior. In order to test the relationship between how people cope with stressful situations and the decision of saving, the conflict theory of decision making was used (Mann et al., 1997).

Mann et al. (1997) have shown that the conflict model refers to the motivational factors in decision making, in particular, to the conditions that motivate the vigilant decision regarding the (maladaptive) models. Based on the conceptual distinction between a vigilant decision-making process and major coping patterns identified in the conflict theory of decision making (Janis and Mann, 1977), a 22-item instrument, named the Melbourne DMQ, was validated for measurement of decision-coping patterns and comprising four identifiable factors: vigilance, hypervigilance, buck-passing and procrastination (Mann et al., 1997).

According to Mann et al. (1997) the buck-passing and procrastination are part of defensive avoidance and the decision maker escapes conflict by procrastinating, shifting responsibility to someone else, or constructing wishful rationalizations to bolster the least objectionable alternative. Therefore, buck-passing and procrastination are associated with incomplete and often biased evaluation of information, leading in turn to faulty decisions and overall are being associated with high stress.

The hypervigilance and vigilance are defined, according to Mann et al. (1997), as following:

- Hypervigilance. The decision maker searches frantically for a way out of dilemmas. Due to time pressure, the decision maker impulsively seizes upon hastily contrived solutions that seem to promise immediate relief. The full range of consequences of choices are overlooked because of emotional excitement, perseveration, and limited attention. In its more extreme form, hypervigilance is a "panic"-like state in which the decision maker vacillates between unpleasant alternatives. Hypervigilance is associated with severe emotional stress.
- Vigilance. The decision maker clarifies objectives to be achieved by the decision, canvasses an array of alternatives, searches painstakingly for relevant information, assimilates information in an unbiased manner, and evaluates alternatives carefully before making a choice. Vigilance is associated with a moderate level of psychological stress. According to the conflict model, vigilance is the only coping pattern that allows sound and rational decision making.

2. Research design: aim, theoretical model, instruments and procedure

The aim of this study is to analyze saving behavior with reference to: demographic factors, income and stress – as a sum of psychological factors, defined by how people cope with stressful situations.

2.1 Theoretical model

The theoretical model was design based on the literature review and the research question. The model includes: demographic variables (age, gender, urban/rural areas, level of education, marital status and employment status), economic variable at individual level (income) an psychological variables (sum of psychological factors that determinates how people cope with stressful situations): vigilance, hypervigilance, buck-passing and procrastination behavior (see Fig. 1).

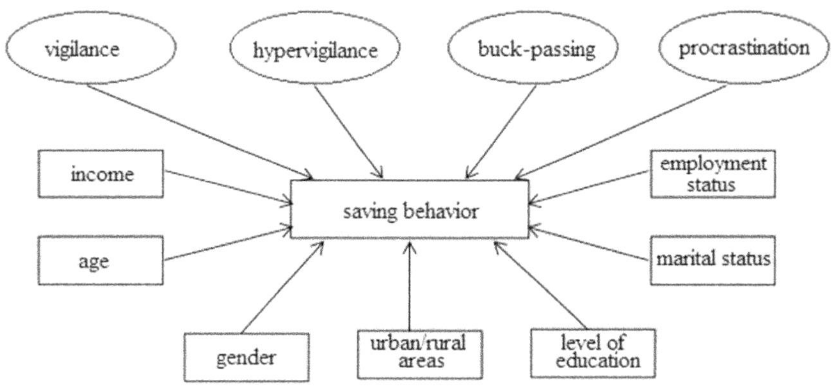

Fig. 1: General structural equations model for saving

Source: Author's conception

2.2 Instruments

A questionnaire was designed in Romanian language based on Melbourne DMQ (Mann et al., 1997) and used the 22 items of four factors: vigilance, hypervigilance, buck-passing and procrastination. The translation was checked made with the help of an authorized translator, in order to maintain the same signification as the original Melbourne DMQ.

The questionnaire consist also categorical variables for: age, gender, urban/rural areas, level of education, marital status and employment status and income, while for the saving behavior variables where design with Likert scale for the following affirmation "saving leads to frustration" and that "saving means protecting the future," (1 – strongly disagree and 5 – strongly agree).

2.3 Procedure

The exploratory research was conducted via an online platform of surveys and distributed by email to various institutions and through social media and addressed to persons residing in Romania over 18 years of age at the time of completing the questionnaire. As a result, 345 online questionnaires were validated and used for data analysis.

The 345 questionnaires were subjected to a structural equation analysis according to the theoretical model. The R software was used for statistical purpose and R package "*lavaan.*" The results are given in the next section, a descriptive analysis and two structural equation models: "saving leads to frustration" (the SEM_FRUSTRATION model) and as the belief that "saving means protecting the future" (the SEM_ PROTECTION model).

3. Structural equations models

SEM_FRUSTRATION model ("saving leads to frustration")
R software formula:

```
SEM _ FRUSTRATION <- '
vigilance =~ vig _ 1 + vig _ 2 + vig _ 3 + vig _ 4 +
vig _ 5 + vig _ 6
buck _ passing =~ buck _ pass _ 1 + buck _ pass _ 2 +
buck _ pass _ 3 + buck _ pass _ 4 + buck _ pass _ 5 +
buck _ pass _ 6
procrastination =~ proc _ 1 + proc _ 2 + proc _ 3 +
proc _ 4 + proc _ 5
hypervigilance =~ hiper _ 1 + hiper _ 2 + hiper _ 3 +
hiper _ 4 + hiper _ 5
saving _ frust ~ vigilance + buck _ passing +
procrastination + hypervigilance + agebuck _ passing ~~
procrastination + hypervigilance
procrastination ~~ hypervigilance
'
```

Hypotheses:

H1.1: As the consumer tends to be vigilant, the frustration associated with saving decreases.
H1.2: As the consumer tends to avoid responsibilities (buck-passing), the frustration associated with saving decreases.
H1.3: As the consumer tends towards procrastination, the frustration associated with saving decreases.
H1.4: As the consumer tends to be hypervigilant, the frustration associated with saving increases.
H1.5: As the consumer gets older, the frustration associated with saving increases.

SEM_ PROTECTION model ("saving means protecting the future").
R software formula:

```
SEM _ PROTECTION <- '
vigilance =~ vig _ 1 + vig _ 2 + vig _ 3 + vig _ 4 +
vig _ 5 + vig _ 6
buck _ passing =~ buck _ pass _ 1 + buck _ pass _ 2 +
buck _ pass _ 3 + buck _ pass _ 4 + buck _ pass _ 5 +
buck _ pass _ 6
procrastination =~ proc _ 1 + proc _ 2 + proc _ 3 +
proc _ 4 + proc _ 5
hypervigilance =~ hiper _ 1 + hiper _ 2 + hiper _ 3 +
hiper _ 4 + hiper _ 5
saving _ protect ~ vigilance + buck _ passing +
procrastination + hypervigilance + marital _ status
buck _ passing ~~ procrastination + hypervigilance
procrastination ~~ hypervigilance
'
```

Hypotheses:

H2.1: As the consumer tends to be vigilant, the association of saving for the protection of one's future increases.
H2.2: As the consumer tends to avoid responsibilities (buck-passing), the association of saving for the protection of one's future decreases.
H2.3: As the consumer tends towards procrastination, the association of saving for the protection of one's future decreases.
H2.4: As the consumer tends to be hypervigilant, the association of saving for the protection of one's future increases.
H2.5: The marital status different then "married," decrease the savings associated for the protection of one's future

4. Research results

The descriptive analysis shown that from 345 respondents 263 were female (76 %) and 82 male (24 %); the majority of respondents come from urban areas (93 %); 77 % of them are employees; the last level of education (or on-going) predominant is bachelor's degree (51 %) and the master's degree (27 %); the marital status of the respondents is mostly married (43 %) and unmarried (39 %) (Tab. 1).

Tab. 1: SEM_FRUSTRATION model results

SEM_FRUSTRATION							
Regressions:							
		Estimate	**Std.Err**	**z-value**	**P(>|z|)**	**Std.lv**	**Std.all**
saving_frust~							
	vigilance	-1.128	0.429	-2.628	**0.009**	-0.202	-0.185
	buck_passing	-0.042	0.352	-0.119	0.906	-0.018	-0.016
	procrastination	-0.828	0.656	-1.263	0.207	-0.335	-0.305
	hypervigilance	1.341	0.517	2.595	**0.009**	0.597	0.545
	age	0.014	0.004	3.371	**0.001**	0.014	0.172

Source: Author's conception

The structural equation model according to "saving leads to frustration" (see Tab. 1) validates just the hypotheses: H1.1, H1.4 and H1.5. Age is the only socio-demographic factor associated with the perception that saving creates frustration. An elderly person may be constrained to save due to a low income or different contextual factors.

The structural equation model according to "saving means protecting the future," the concern of saving for the protection of one's future is in significant relation with the marital status, all the other socio-demographic factors were eliminated from the model in order to improve the model fit. Significant positive causal relationships for "saving means protecting the future" were established with vigilance and hypervigilance (Tab. 2).

Tab. 2: SEM_PROTECTION model results

SEM_ PROTECTION							
Regressions:							
		Estimate	**Std.Err**	**z-value**	**P(>|z|)**	**Std.lv**	**Std.all**
saving_ protect~							
	vigilance	0.708	0.306	2.315	**0.021**	0.129	0.163
	buck_passing	-0.329	0.26	-1.264	0.206	-0.14	-0.177
	procrastination	-0.92	0.497	-1.85	0.064	-0.37	-0.468
	hypervigilance	1.192	0.396	3.012	**0.003**	0.528	0.669
	marital_status	-0.047	0.022	-2.144	**0.032**	-0.047	-0.11

Source: Author's conception

For the model fit analysis the following indices were used: Root Mean Square Error of Approximation (RMSEA), Comparative Fit Index (CFI), Tucker-Lewis Index (TLI) and Normed Fit Index (NFI). The two exploratory structural equation models above described result with a good fit (see Tab. 3).

Tab. 3: Measuring Model Fit in SEMs models

Model	**Obs.**	**DF**	**P-value (Chi-square)**	**DF**	**P-value**	**CFI**	**TLI**	**RMESA**	**SRMR**
SEM_ FRUSTRATION	345	243	0.000	276	0.000	0.928	0.918	0.047	0.059
SEM_ PROTECTION	345	243	0.000	276	0.000	0.945	0.938	0.041	0.054
threshold						**> 0.90**	**> 0.90**	**< 0.07**	**< 0.08**

The limitation of the research is related to the nature of survey sample – online voluntary self-completion questionnaires. The sample is not representative for the target population and the demographic variables aren't representative as a distribution. It is considered that this influenced the representativeness of demographic variables in the regression models due to small variabilities between the respondents.

Although the sample representativeness is a limitation of the research, we consider that the number of the respondents is enough to show a behavioral pattern for the current exploratory analysis.

Conclusions

To the best of our knowledge, no prior studies have examined the coping strategies in relation with saving behavior and the current research is a pioneer in this new approach related on stress measuring and savings.

Based on the assumption that saving decisions are not influenced by the nature of the stressor (the conventional sequence of stressful event) but by the ability or inability of the individual to deal with this stressor, the two structural models have shown causal relationships between the savings and how an individual cope with stressful situations.

It was shown positive causal relationships between the individuals that cope successfully with the environmental challenge (vigilant behavior) and saving behavior: as the belief that "saving means protecting the future," and negative with "saving leads to frustration." For the individuals with "hypervigilant behavior" the nature of the causal relationships identified are positive, but less powerful. No significant relationships were found between saving behavior and buck-passing or procrastination.

The present research shows a pattern of the relationship between conflict styles and decision saving. Future studies need to be conducted to test if the ability or inability of the individual to deal with the conventional sequence of stressful event influence the decision of savings, and results should be compared with the present study. The topic is important first of all for banks or other entities that sustains different plans of savings, but also for monetary policies. Being able to understand the characteristics of individuals and their ability to deal with the stressful events can improve the education related to personal retirement plans and saving decisions.

References

Aghion, P.; Comin, D.; Howitt, P.; Tecu, I.: "When does domestic savings matter for economic growth?" IMF Economic Review 64.3, 2016, pp. 381–407.

Akinsola,; F. A.: "Revisiting financial liberalisation and economic growth: A review of international literature." 2018.

Asebedo, S. D. et al.: "Personality and saving behavior among older adults." Journal of Consumer Affairs 53.2, 2019, pp. 488–519.

Attanasio, O. P.; Picci, L.; Scorcu, A.E.: "Saving, growth, and investment: A macroeconomic analysis using a panel of countries." The Review of Economics and Statistics, 82.2, 2000, pp. 182–211.

Auerbach, A. J.: "Taxation and saving–A retrospective." The Economic Journal 125.583, 2015, pp. 464–492.

Chai, Hua; Kim, J.I.: Demographics, Pension Systems and the Saving-Investment Balance. IMF Working Paper (WP/18/265), 2018.

Cigna: "360 well-being survey well & beyond", 2019.

Cronqvist, H.; Siegel, S.: "The origins of savings behavior." Journal of Political Economy 123.1, 2015, pp. 123–169.

Duhachek, A.: "Coping: A multidimensional, hierarchical framework of responses to stressful consumption episodes." Journal of Consumer Research, 32.1, 2005, pp. 41–53.

Duhachek, A.; Kelting, K.: "Coping repertoire: integrating a new conceptualization of coping with transactional theory." Journal of Consumer Psychology, 19.3, 2009, pp. 473–85.

Guiso, .L.; Monica, P.: "The role of risk aversion in predicting individual behaviors." Temi di discussione (Economic working papers) 546, Bank of Italy, Economic Research and International Relations Area, 2004.

Janis, L.; Mann, L.; "Decision Making: A Psychological Analysis of Conflict, Choiee and Commitment", New York: The Free Press, 1977.

Karanika, K.; Hogg, M. K.: "Being kind to ourselves: Self-compassion, coping, and consumption." Journal of Business Research 69.2, 2016, pp. 760–769.

Durante, K. M.;Laran, J.: "The effect of stress on consumer saving and pending." Journal of Marketing Research LIII, October, 2016, pp. 814–828.

Lou, Y.; Sang-Eun, B.: "Stress-driven spending: Correlates of international students' adjustment strains and compulsive online buying." Journal of International Students 8.4, 2018, pp. 1522–1548.

Machin, J.E., et al.: "The marketplace, mental well-being, and me: Exploring self-efficacy, self-esteem, and self-compassion in consumer coping." Journal of Business Research 100, 2019, pp. 410–420.

Mann, L.; Burnett, P.; Radford, M.; Ford, S.: "The Melbourne decision making questionnaire: An instrument for measuring patterns for coping with decisional conflict." Journal Behav Decis Mak 10, 1997, pp. 1–19.

Mathur, A.; Moschis, G.P.; Euehun, L.: "Stress and consumer behavior: Coping strategies of older adults." Journal of Marketing Practice: Applied Marketing Science 5.6/7/8, 1999, pp. 233–247.

Moschis, G.P.: "Stress and consumer behavior." Journal of the Academy of Marketing Science 35.3, 2007, pp. 430–444. https://doi.org/10.1007/s11747-007-0035-3

Vogel, W. H.: "Coping, stress, stressors and health consequences." Neuropsychobiology 13.3, 1985, pp. 129–135.

Warneryd, K.E.: The psychology of saving: A study on economic psychology". Cheltenham, UK: Edward Elgar, 1999.

Wärneryd, K.-E. "On the psychology of saving: An essay on economic behavior." Journal of Economic Psychology 10.4, 1989, pp. 515–541.

Yao, D.;/Yixuan, X.; Pengyuan, Z.: "How a disaster affects household saving: Evidence from China's 2008 Wenchuan earthquake." Journal of Asian Economics 64, 2019, pp. 101133.

Annex:

Annex 1: The 22 main items of the questionnaire (source: Melbourne DMQ)

a. Vigilance

I like to consider all of the alternatives.
I try to find out the disadvantages of all alternatives.
I consider how best to carry out a decision.
When making decisions I like to collect a lot of information.
I try to be clear about my objectives before choosing.
I take a lot of care before choosing.

d. Hypervigilance

Whenever I face a difficult decision I feel pessimistic about finding a good solution.
I feel as if I am under tremendous time pressure When making decisions.
The possibility that some small thing might go wrong causes me to swing abruptly in my preference.
I cannot think straight if I have to make a decision in a hurry.
After a decision is made I spend a lot of time convincing myself it was correct.

b. Buck-passing

I avoid making decisions.
I do not make decisions unless I really have to.
I prefer to leave decisions to others.
I do not like to take responsibility for making decisions.
If a decision can be made by me or another person I let the other person make it.
I prefer that people who are better informed decide for me.

c. Procrastination

I waste a lot of time on trivial matters before getting to the final decision.
Even After I have made a decision I delay acting upon it.
When I have to make a decision I wait a long time before starting to think about it.
I delay making decisions until it is too late.
I put off making decisions.

Valeriu Ioan-Franc, Andrei Marius Diamescu

Economic information and documentation, basis for building a national program to increase competitiveness of Romanian enterprises

Abstract The article approaches essential aspects of the theory and practice of scientific and technical information and documentation, a preliminary stage of research, and, simultaneously, a final stage of scientific results' communication and dissemination. The authors review the context of the field's specific literature and present the state of facts in Romania which is faced with the necessity to go through the development stages of the field at accelerated speed in order to close the gap with the developed countries.

Keywords: economic development; scientifical research; information and documentation; management; lifelong learning

1. Preliminaries

Five decades ago, the Romanian scientist Mircea Malita wrote: "Information and documentation in science, which constituted the first form and the basis of any communication and, therefore, of cooperation, make up an immense enterprise, absorbing large funds and engaging specialized staff. Far from being a simple task, it appeals to complex scientific theories such as mathematical linguistics, cybernetics, information theory, statistics and operational research, classification theory. It builds all techniques for its own use... while the material support for transmitting and processing information is in continuous transformation, culminating with computers that allow the automation of some processes of analysis and identification" (Maliţa, 1979, pp. 71–78).

Twenty years ago, between 23–24 of March, 2000, the European Council approved the document known in recent history as "Lisbon Strategy 2000" which stated in point 5: "The Union has today set itself a new strategic goal for the next decade: to become the most competitive and dynamic knowledge-based economy in the world capable of sustainable economic growth with more and better jobs and greater social cohesion" (European Council, 2000).

Ten years later, in 2010, the European Commission, faced at that time also with the need to relaunch economic growth in the aftermath of the 2008 financial crisis, presented the member states the document entitled: "Europe 2020: a strategy for smart, sustainable and inclusive growth." The proposed strategy resumes, in an updated form, the objective set in "Lisbon Strategy 2000" and develops it in accordance with the changes occurred, establishing for the decade 2010–2020 the three main priorities:

- smart growth: developing an economy based on knowledge and innovation;
- sustainable growth: promoting a more efficient economy from the point of view of resources, more ecological and more competitive;
- inclusive growth: encouraging an economy with a high degree of employment, ensuring social and territorial cohesion (European Commission, 2010, p. 3).

At the same time, for greater precision, the Strategy "Europe 2020" sets five great objectives, of which we remind those relevant for our topic:

- 3 % of the European GDP should be invested in research-development;
- at least 40 % of the young generation should have a tertiary/university degree.

We can thus easily notice that one constant preoccupation of community policies during the last two decades has been "knowledge" as a main resource of social and economic development, a fact that speaks about the rapid connection of the European leadership with the evolution of economic theories.

The majority of European countries understood the great role that research-development-innovation plays in the economic growth and took important steps in capitalizing the new "production factors" specific to knowledge-based economy. The initiative regarding the use of the "neofactors" of production came from the indigenous private economic environment or from the foreign companies, in this case being predominantly the transfer of know-how and less the technological innovation.

2. Romania – the state of affairs

Sadly, we can't say the same thing about Romania, which twenty years from the "Lisbon Strategy" and the end of the reference period "Europe 2020" strategy fill the last position in the European ranking regarding the innovation index (European Commission, 2019) as well as the number of higher education graduates and allocates for research only 0.16 % of the GDP (0.20 of the GDP cumulated with the budget allocated to the Romanian Academy) in 2020.

Our country has made little progress, noticeable mainly at microeconomic level, in areas such as information technology or automotive.

The state's involvement in promoting knowledge-based economy was minimal, specific rather to the neoclassic theory of economic growth, limited to granting tax facilities to IT and technological research companies, promoting a digital Agenda or start-up programs, without these being oriented exclusively or preferentially to entrepreneurship targeting research-development-innovation activities.

Referring to the endogenous economic growth also known as New Growth theory, elaborated by P. Romer and R. Lucas we can state that (Zaman, Georgescu,

2015, pp. 35–36) Romania's failure to achieve the objectives of "Europe 2020" strategy was caused by the "minimalism" of the state's involvement considering that "it plays an important part in ensuring the endogenous growth by making spending to stimulate investments, financing activities less productive for economic actors but necessary for society (to disseminate innovation in society), protect property rights, patents etc. This way, the social yield is superior to the private one."

In other words, the national approach regarding the area of stimulation and capitalization on innovation remained dependent on a linear cause/impulse – effect/result process, an anachronistic approach in relation to European policies, that, after going through a second generation of public policies built on the model of the system and infrastructure as support for innovation, is undergoing a full maturing process of a third generation of policies in which innovation "is not only based on research and science, technology and inventiveness, innovation [...] depends on the organizational, social, economic, marketing and other aspects of knowledge" (European Commission, 2003, p. 6).

From this perspective, the rapid reduction of the gap between national policies and European ones in the field of research-development-innovation is not only a necessity but a moral obligation of today's generation to the future ones, and in order to make this possible, in our view, there's a need for a pragmatic, applied rethink of the knowledge management at the national level as a precondition to going on an accelerated pace through the second generation of European policies we previously referred to and for the setting, in the near future, of the current European model of the knowledge-based society.

Surely, such a model is an extremely complex one, given the multitude of approaches/definitions of the knowledge management concept as well as the difficulty to extrapolate its applicability from the micro to the national macroeconomic level. Last but not least, it needs to be accepted "ab initio" that such difficulties are increased by the cultural determinations in the approach of the concept and by its multidisciplinary nature.

3. Knowledge management

Coined at the end of the 1980s, knowledge management developed initially as a field associated to intangible assets management, influenced to a great extent by the corporate culture and, from this, perspective, strongly "individualized," similar, one could say, to art, not science. In fact, according to a wide study conducted in 2001 by researchers Heisig P. and Vorbeck J., taken over by the European Guide to good practice in knowledge Management at the beginning of the 21st century, 47 % of the interviewed corporate representatives indicated corporate culture as a determining factor for the success of knowledge management implementation, while only 30 % of them pointed to structure and inner processes of the company as main factor.

However, the objectives set by the European Union in the framework of "Lisbon 2000" strategy, mainly determined by the accelerate dynamic of the economy based on research-development-innovation, led to a reconsideration of the role the knowledge management played in the maximization of the company's performance. This new perspective, a lot more pragmatic, starts from approaching knowledge as a main factor of economic growth and defines knowledge management as representing " the formalization of, and access to, experience, knowledge and expertise that create new capabilities, lead to superior performance, encourage innovation" (Chauvel, Despres, 1999, p. 8). Thus, knowledge becomes easily recognizable as the company's important competitive advantage and, by extrapolation, of the state too, a dynamizer of innovation, while knowledge management is a process meant to optimize capitalization on this important resource of economic growth.

Considering the discussed premises, we naturally ask ourselves the question: Who and in the framework of what processes can undertake the role of optimal formalization and ensuring of the access to knowledge accumulated at the national level?

The research conducted in 2006 by Akhavan P. and Jafari M. (Akhavan; Jafari, 2006, pp. 52–66) on the practices in the field existent in nine European countries (U.K., Denmark, France, Spain, Holland, Germany, Portugal, Finland and Norway) showed no less than twenty critical factors for implementation of a knowledge management system at a national level[1]: raising population/public awareness; governmental support; strategic planning; information and communication technology; attention for the public and private sector; the common reference model; publications about knowledge management; comparative analysis; academic research; leadership; attention to human resources; organizational learning; horizontal structure; investments in knowledge management; conferences and seminars about knowledge management; communities of practice; instruction/training; culture and pilot projects.

Analyzing each of these factors from the perspective of their functional relevance for each of the states studied as well as that of mutual relations/determinations, the two researchers identified two essential factors (core categories), the governmental support and culture, as well as three main factors, strategic planning, public awareness and information and communication technology, each of these playing a major part in projecting a knowledge management system at a national level.

1 The data and information analyzed were extracted from the studies regarding knowledge management carried out in the nine countries, published in various papers, reports, books, articles etc.

4. The triple helix of lifelong learning

"Orizontul fără limite al învăţării"/"The limitless horizon of learning"(Maliţa et al., 1981) (argues – as a significant theory for practice –, according to Mircea Malita, for constituting a space of consensus regarding a minimum number of universal values (Postolache, 2009), operationalizing the anticipatory and participatory learning in societal learning. In this respect, two paths are opened up for two types of learning: the maintenance learning and the innovative learning, the second one being meant to emphasize the creation of values and only preservation of some previously known and acquired. In other words, it supports the idea – later on developed by Mircea Malita, too – that learning from life (lifelong learning) is more important than learning from the past (with predominantly formative valences).

Essentially, the "Triple Helix" model proposes the transition from the predominantly separated action of the three spheres of the economic and social life to a much more integrated action of these by generating a space of mutual interaction and determination. To put it differently, the "Triple Helix" model proposes the transition from the linear demand – supply model, which places the fundamental research in the "supply" area (Nelson, Winter, 1982, pp. 14–19), to a model that approaches development in terms of network (Fig. 1).

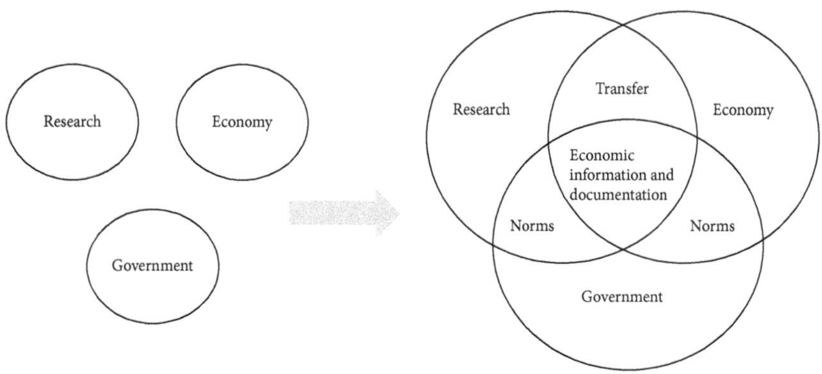

Fig. 1: Transition to the "Triple Helix" model
Source: Processed by the authors

Retrospectively deepening the analysis of the way in which the current knowledge-based economy has evolved, we can state that "the entrepreneurial universities" have, in fact, represented a pilot project of the "Triple Helix" model. Developed in the United States of America after the Second World War, in the beginning as a consequence of the scarcity of the financial resources available to the state to support education, these entrepreneurial universities have played and continue to play the role of "infusing" the economy with what we call today strategic research (Etzkowitz, 1983, pp. 198–233) or technological research.

To a great extent, the "Triple Helix" model of implementing knowledge-based economy, proposed as early as the last decade of the previous century by Henry Etzkowitz and Loet Leydesdorff (Etzkowitz; Leydesdorff, 1995, pp. 14–19), brings into a new configuration the relations between knowledge, production and regulation (governmental activity).

5. Instead of conclusions: repositioning Romania

Summarizing the facts presented, there can be identified at least three main stages in defining the concept and operationalizing the new knowledge-based economy:

- the stage of entrepreneurial universities;
- the stage of the "Triple Helix" model;
- the stage of national implementation of an integrated knowledge management system

Regarding these three stages, Romania is hard to place from the perspective of the degree of implementation of the "new economy." The Eurostat statistics place our country on the last position in Europe, with respect to research and innovation, while internal debates regarding the degree of adaption of the Romanian universities to the dynamics of the economic model and the extent to which the universities' curricula respond to the real demands of the work labor market entitle us to consider that Romania is still in the waiting room of the knowledge-based economy.

However, if we consider the hesitant governmental policies of stimulating research and innovation through the financial facilities created for the work labor involved in such activities, we could say that Romania is at the beginning of the second stage of approaching knowledge as the main source of economic growth.

No matter of the approach, it is a sure fact that, in this field too, Romania lags behind the other member states of the European Union. This is all the more worrying and requires immediate action, as we are no longer talking about a different pace of development, but a systemic gap which, if not corrected rapidly, can exponentially deepen the gap between the current economic and social development level of our country and the Western-European countries.

Being aware of the fact that the successive completion, even at an accelerated pace, of the first two stages presented (the stage of entrepreneurial universities and that of the "Triple Helix" model) is no longer enough, we believe that one solution, still possible, is the elaboration and implementation as soon as possible of national knowledge management system focused on a solid economic information and documentation that would ensure:

- unitary capitalization of internal and international economic knowledge;
- easy access to the accumulated economic knowledge;
- the capacity to transform the capitalized information into actionable information/knowledge for political decision-makers and the business environment;
- transfers of the results of research-development-innovation activity to the economic environment (with state and private capital, equally);
- regulation/facilitation of integrate cooperation between system components;
- elaboration of public policies for the stimulation of processes/mechanisms specific to knowledge-based economy.

A good exercise, that could be the subject of a case study in the field, may be the Thesaurus Project of the National Institute for Economic Research "Costin C. Kiritescu" of the Romanian Academy, developed by the Center for Economic Information and Documentation as part of the Institute. A result of a wide, European vision with real power of international breakthrough, the Thesaurus Project is currently known in the academia (and not only) as the keeper and disseminator of expertise in transition to market economy from that excessively focused on state plans, altogether with accession to the European Union (association, preparation, negotiation and actual accession in 2007) of a country such as Romania, barely out, in December 1989, from under the canons, unknown to the rest of the world, of the strictly staged economy (Chivu; Ioan-Franc, 2018, pp. 908–932).

The INCE Thesaurus currently includes, in a free format, accessible to everyone interested, through the means provided by the digitization of scientific information and documentation, the entire literature dedicated to the capitalization of academic scientific research in the dedicated institute of the Romanian Academy. The readers in the field can access a few hundred volumes totaling tens of thousands pages that plead for the conclusion: "the new Europeanization of Romania" was also an act of academic scientific research (Ioan-Franc; Pop, 2016).

Without a knowledge management system it is virtually impossible to identify new viable and necessary research themes. Lack of clear procedures for storage and dissemination of accumulated knowledge to interested institutions or even to new teams of researchers, as well as lack of collaboration protocols between research institutions with similar or complementary interests may block/delay the specific processes of knowledge-based economy. Moreover, in this case, the funds granted to research, scarce as they are, are often wasted on documentation or identification/discovery of already existent knowledge.

Such processes are all the more difficult, even impossible, one may say, in the framework accumulated knowledge by national institutions with a limited life span (work groups, laboratories) or that, for one reason or another, ceased to exist.

Knowledge discontinuities caused by such "accidents" determine a real and visible slowdown of the processes generated by new knowledge and, which may be even worse, makes it extremely difficult the transfer of the knowledge obtained between generations. This is the main reason for which, in our country, the names of the "eras" are most of the times connected to "proper names" and not economic, social, scientific processes, etc.

Currently, the responsible governments understood the importance of knowledge and the management of it, so that public policies/activities connected to these are run from the highest positions (Akhavan; Peyman, 2006, pp. 52–66). This aspect, visible mostly in the developed countries, requires an immediate reaction on the part of Romania, the set up of a national knowledge management process being already a delayed process.

References

Akhavan, Peyman; Mostafa Jafari, 2006, Critical Issues for Knowledge Management Implementation at National Level, The Journal of Information and Knowledge Management Systems, Vol. 36, No. 1, https://www.researchgate.net/publication/241701987_Critical_issues_for_knowledge_management_implementation_at_a_national_level, accessed 17.05.2019.

Chauvel, Daniele; Despres, Charles, 1999, Knowledge Management and the Management Development Function in European Business, The European Center for Knowledge Management, https://www.academia.edu/331988/Knowledge_Management_and_the_Management_Development_Function_InEuropean_Business.

Chivu, Luminiţa; Ioan-Franc, Valeriu, 2018, Cercetarea economică din România, în: Economia României după Marea Unire, Vol. II – Economia sectorială, Colecţia Civilizaţia românească (16), Editura Academiei Române.

Etzkowitz, Henry, 1983, Entrepreneurial Scientist and Entrepreneurial Universities in American Academic Science, Rev. Minerva nr. 21, https://link.springer.com/search?query=Etzkowitz%2C+Henry%2C+Entrepreneurial+Scientist+and+Entrepreneurial+Universities+in+American+Academic+Science&search-within=Journal&facet-journal-id=11024.

Etzkowitz, Henry; Leydesdorff, Loet, 1995, The Triple Helix – University-Industry-Government Relations: A Laboratory for Knowledge Based Economic Development, EASST Review 14 nr. 1, https://papers.ssrn.com/sol3/papers.cfm?abstract_id=2480085.

European Commission, Communication from the Commission. Europe 2020; A Strategy for Smart, Sustainable and Inclusive Growth, 2010, Brussels, https://eige.europa.eu/library/resource/aleph-eige000005583.

European Commission, European Innovation Scoreboard 2019, https://ec.europa.eu/growth/industry/innovation/facts-figures/scoreboard.en.

European Commission, Study Calls for a Third Generation Innovation Policy, 2003, Cordis – focus, nr. 213, Luxembourg.

European Council, Presidency Conclusions, 2000, Lisbon European Council, 23–24 March.

Eurostat, Tertiary Educational Attainment, 2020, https://ec.europa.eu/eurostat/databrowser/view/sdg_04_20/default/bar?lang=en.

Ioan-Franc, Valeriu; Pop, Napoleon, 2016, L'Europenisation de la Roumanie – un acte de recherché academique, în La Science est-elle une dimension de l'identité européenne?, Penser l'Europe 2015, Fundaţia Naţională pentru Ştiinţă şi Artă, Academia Română.

Maliţa, Mircea, 1979, Comunicarea transdisciplinară: o prioritate a informaţiei ştiinţitice, in: Viitorul social, VIII (1).

Maliţa, Mircea; Botkin, James W.; Elmandjra, Mahdi, 1981, Orizontul fără limite al învăţării, Editura Politică, Bucureşti.

Nelson, Richard; Winter, Sidney, 1995, An Evolutionary Theory of Economic Change, Belknap Press of Harvard University Press, 1982 apud Etzkowitz, Henry; Leydesdorff Loet, The Triple Helix – University-Industry-Government Relations: A Laboratory for Knowledge Based Economic Development, EASST Review 14 nr. 1.

Postolache, Tudorel, 2009, Academicieni aşa cum i-am cunoscut, Centrul Român de Economie Comparată şi Consens, Centrul de Informare şi Documentare Economică, Bucureşti.

Zaman, Gheorghe; Georgescu, George, coordonatori, 2015, Dezvoltarea economică endogenă la nivel regional – cazul României, Editura Expert, Bucureşti.

Georgeta-Mădălina Meghişan-Toma, Gheorghe Meghişan

Main sources of Big Data for the companies

Abstract The main objective of this article is to carry out a research on enterprises' sources for analyzing Big Data, such as: Enterprises analyzing Big Data from any data source; Analyze own Big Data from enterprise's smart devices or sensors; Analyze Big Data from geolocation of portable devices; Analyze Big Data generated from social media; Analyze Big Data from other sources; Big data analysis for the enterprise is done by the enterprise's own employees; Big data analysis for the enterprise is done by an external service provider. The data used in the analysis cover the European Union member states for the years 2016 and 2018. The current research can be considered a starting point in the direction of digital society through Big Data.

Keywords: marketing, strategy, Big Data, digital society

Introduction

In the current era, the companies are faced to digitalize their services and products. Thus, the enterprises, in order to transform their business strategies and innovate, can adopt Big Data. The companies should see Big Data as a marketing and management opportunity in order to generate their competitive advantage, coming from a better knowledge of the market because, "the expectations that Big Data will lead today's society to a new and captivating age of innovation are high." (Meng & Ci 2013)

The main objective of this article is to carry out a research on enterprises' sources for analyzing Big Data, such as:

- Enterprises analyzing big data from any data source;
- Analyze own big data from enterprise's smart devices or sensors;
- Analyze big data from geolocation of portable devices;
- Analyze big data generated from social media;
- Analyze big data from other sources;
- Big data analysis for the enterprise is done by the enterprise's own employees;
- Big data analysis for the enterprise is done by an external service provider;

The data used in the analysis cover the European Union member states for the years 2016 and 2018.

1. Literature review

It is very important for the companies to have the proper infrastructure to use Big Data for accessing and integrating information, in order to "identify and satisfy the existing and emerging needs of their target markets." (Urbinati et al. 2019, p. 21) An advantage of the usage of Big Data is underlined in the product strategy, because of the fact that now the services and the products of the companies can be better shaped in order to respond to the needs and wants of the customers.

Many authors focused in their research on "Big Data management." (Xiaofenf and Xiang 2013; Du et al. 2016) Thus the paradigm of management strategies changes from the perspective of their accuracy. Now the companies can design strategies, relying on digital technologies, mainly on Big Data, from different sources. (Troilo et al. 2017)

We entered in a new era of marketing decision, with the help of business intelligence systems, based on Big Data, minimizing the risks. Thus, the companies can take decisions regarding: identification of customer needs and wants; risk management and decision-making; data-driven knowledge; product and service conception; quality management; opportunity recognition and creation of innovation, but only if they have the proper technical infrastructure for Big Data analysis or if they collaborate with companies within the field of Big Data collection and interpretation. (Urbinati et al. 2019, p. 24) The techniques and methods that can be used for Big Data analysis are: machine learning (supervised learning; non-supervised learning; semi-supervised learning); data mining (deep learning; classification; association rules); statistical methods (correlation analysis; factor analysis; regression analysis; descriptive statistics; inferential statistics). (Cabrera-Sanchez and Villarejo-Ramos 2020, pp. 2) These techniques and methods are combined with the suited technologies for Big Data, such as: visual analytics software; programming languages software (e.g. Python); in-memory analytics software; software for processing big data across parallel servers; machine learning software; NLP software; social media analytics software; predictive analytics software; time series software analysis; modeling and simulation software; image processing tools. (Kamilaris et al. 2017, pp. 25; Raguseo 2018, p. 192)

2. Research methodology

Big Data sources imply: online portal content; POS data or other transactional sources; smart meter data; audio content; images; videos; other natural language text sources; social media posts; weblog posts; microblog posts; RFID system data; clickstream data; GPS data; smart devices or sensors. (Raguseo 2018, p. 191)

In the current article, the analysis is made at the level of the E.U. member states for the years 2016 and 2018. The set of variables was chosen, taking into consideration the availability of data on Eurostat data base. (Tab. 1)

Tab. 1: Variables for big data source

Variables	**Sources and approaches for measurement**
(Item 1) Enterprises analyzing big data from any data source	This variable is quantified on Eurostat
(Item 2) Analyse own big data from enterprise's smart devices or sensors	This variable is quantified on Eurostat
(Item 3) Analyse big data from geolocation of portable devices	This variable is quantified on Eurostat
(Item 4) Analyse big data generated from social media	This variable is quantified t on Eurostat
(Item 5) Analyse big data from other sources	This variable is quantified on Eurostat
(Item 6) Big data analysis for the enterprise is done by the enterprise's own employees	This variable is quantified on Eurostat
(Item 7) Big data analysis for the enterprise is done by an external service provider	This variable is quantified on Eurostat

Source: authors' own processing data

Factor analysis is used in order to establish the main sources for Big Data that the companies from the European Union consider. The value of KMO test is acceptable (0.774), with sig. 0. (Tab. 2)

Tab. 2: KMO and Bartlett's test

Kaiser-Meyer-Olkin Measure of Sampling Adequacy.		**0.774**
Bartlett's Test of Sphericity	Approx. Chi-Square	471.276
	df	21
	Sig.	0.000

Source: authors' own processing data using SPSS 21.00 software

We can see that the quality of representation is above 0.5 for all the variables (Tab. 3):

- Enterprises analyzing big data from any data source (0.921);
- Analyze own big data from enterprise's smart devices or sensors (0.793);
- Analyze big data from geolocation of portable devices (0.545);

- Analyze big data generated from social media (0.891);
- Analyze big data from other sources (0.705);
- Big data analysis for the enterprise is done by the enterprise's own employees (0.721);
- Big data analysis for the enterprise is done by an external service provider (0.665).

Tab. 3: Communalities

	Initial	**Extraction**
Enterprises analyzing big data from any data source	1.000	0,921
Analyze own big data from enterprise's smart devices or sensors	1.000	0,793
Analyze big data from geolocation of portable devices	1.000	0,545
Analyze big data generated from social media	1.000	0,891
Analyze big data from other sources	1.000	0,705
Big data analysis for the enterprise is done by the enterprise's own employees	1.000	0,721
Big data analysis for the enterprise is done by an external service provider	1.000	0,665
Extraction Method: Principal Component Analysis.		

Source: authors' own processing data using SPSS 21.00 software

The Tab. 4 presents the explained variance by one dimension that resume the information needed. The dimension allows us to explain 74,841 % of the information of the variation of the phenomenon by 7 variables. (Tab. 4)

Tab. 4: Total variance explained

Component	Initial Eigenvalues			Extraction Sums of Squared Loadings		
	Total	**% of Variance**	**Cumulative %**	**Total**	**% of Variance**	**Cumulative %**
1	5.239	74.841	74.841	5.239	74.841	74.841
2	.779	11.127	85.968			
3	.463	6.620	92.588			
4	.261	3.726	96.313			
5	.174	2.490	98.804			
6	.063	.899	99.703			
7	.021	.297	100.000			

Extraction Method: Principal Component Analysis.

Source: authors' own processing data using SPSS 21.00 software

The coefficient Cronbach's Alpha is 0.918, the scale has an acceptable viability of internal coherence. (Tab. 5)

Tab. 5: Reliability statistics

Cronbach's Alpha	N of Items
0.918	7

Source: authors' own processing data using SPSS 21.00 software

The correlation matrix reveals that all the elements are correlated, underlying the results of factor analysis, that the 7 items measure the same phenomenon. (Tab. 6)

Thus, the Big Data sources can be used in order to create adapted strategies, such as:

- Improving the existing products/services;
- Creating new products through innovation;
- Improving customer relations;
- Creating an adapted competitive advantage;
- Integrating IT within the business;
- Adapting new promotion strategies;
- Reducing communication costs.

Tab. 6: Correlations

		Item 1	Item 2	Item 3	Item 4	Item 5	Item 6	Item 7
Item 1	Pearson Correlation	1	0.857**	0.819**	0.943**	0.793**	0.710**	0.663**
	Sig. (2-tailed)		0.000	0.000	0.000	0.000	0.000	0.000
	N		56	56	56	56	56	56
Item 2	Pearson Correlation		1	0.614**	0.792**	0.724**	0.728**	0.647**
	Sig. (2-tailed)			0.000	0.000	0.000	0.000	0.000
	N			56	56	56	56	56
Item 3	Pearson Correlation			1	0.683**	0.495**	0.407**	0.478**
	Sig. (2-tailed)				0.000	0.000	0.002	0.000
	N				56	56	56	56
Item 4	Pearson Correlation				1	0.812**	0.765**	0.681**
	Sig. (2-tailed)					0.000	0.000	0.000
	N					56	56	56
Item 5	Pearson Correlation					1	0.630**	0.597**
	Sig. (2-tailed)						0.000	0.000
	N						56	56
Item 6	Pearson Correlation						1	0.880**
	Sig. (2-tailed)							0.000
	N							56
Item 7	Pearson Correlation							1
	Sig. (2-tailed)							
	N							

**. Correlation is significant at the 0.01 level (2-tailed).

Source: authors' own processing data using SPSS 21.00 software

Tab. 7: Descriptive statistics

	Minimum	Maximum	Mean	
	Statistic	Statistic	Statistic	Std. Error
Enterprises analyzing big data from any data source	3.00	24.00	11.73	.647
Analyze own big data from enterprise's smart devices or sensors	2.00	10.00	4.38	0.302
Analyze big data from geolocation of portable devices	1.00	9.00	5.3846	0.28427
Analyze big data generated from social media	1.00	15.00	5.5769	0.43797
Analyze big data from other sources	1.00	8.00	3.3922	0.26432
Big data analysis for the enterprise is done by the enterprise's own employees	2.00	21.00	9.0652	0.59823
Big data analysis for the enterprise is done by an external service provider	1.00	10.00	4.3913	0.30213

Source: authors' own processing data using SPSS 21.00 software.

3. Results

Currently, the companies interact with digital technology and the information from Bid Data is needed. According to the results of the research, the main drivers for Big Data sources across EU member states are (Tab. 7):

- Enterprises analyzing big data from any data source (with variations from 3 % to 24 % at the level of EU member states);
- Analyze own big data from enterprise's smart devices or sensors (with variations from 2 % to 10 % at the level of EU member states);
- Analyze big data from geolocation of portable devices (with variations from 1 % to 9 % at the level of EU member states);
- Analyze big data generated from social media (with variations from 1 % to 15 % at the level of EU member states);
- Analyze big data from other sources (with variations from 1 % to 8 % at the level of EU member states);
- Big data analysis for the enterprise is done by the enterprise's own employees (with variations from 2 % to 21 % at the level of EU member states);
- Big data analysis for the enterprise is done by an external service provider (with variations from 1 % to 10 % at the level of EU member states).

However, the benefits of sources of information from Big Data should be considered linked to the risks that they may encounter:

- Security issues;
- Few well trained persons within the field of Big Data;
- Reluctance of employees to implement change;
- Privacy uncertainty.

Conclusions

The purpose of this study was to analyze the sources of Big Data for the companies, across the EU member states. Depending of the economic stability of each E.U. member state, the results depend on the "relevance of business climate." (Dascălu et al. 2016, p. 138) The marketing and management strategies need to be shaped in order to be adapted to the digital society and economy, in a perfect combination for a "sustainable growth." (Andrieş et al. 2018, p. 1)

The current research can be considered a starting point in the direction of digital society through Big Data, especially focusing on the main changes the companies need to adopt in order to implement Big Data linked technology.

References

Andrieş, Alin; Marcu, Nicu; Oprea, Florin; Tofan, Mihai: Financiak infrastructure and access to finance for European SMEs, Sustainability 10(10), pp. 1–15, 2018.

Cabrera-Sanchez, Juan-Pedro; Villarejo-Ramos, Angel F.: Acceptance and use of big data techniques in services companies, Journal of Retailing and Customer Services 52, 2020.

Dascălu, Elena Doina; Marcu, Nicu; Pete, Ştefan; Ulici, Maria-Lenuţa: Dependent business climate. A network-based analysis, Romanian Journal of Economic Forecasting 19(1), 2016.;

Du, Lan; Huang, Qiuping; Yeung, Kwanho; Jian, Zhaoquan: Improving service innovation performance through the big data management closed loop competence in China mobile, International Journal of Computer Science and Applications 13(1), 2016.

Kamilaris, Andreas; Kartakoullis, Andreas; Prenafeta-Boldu, Francesc X.: A review on the practice of big data analysis in agriculture, Computers and Electronics in Agriculture 143, 2017.

Meng, Xiaofeng; Ci, Xiang: Big data management: concepts: techniques and challenges, J. Comput. Res. Dev. 79, pp. 146–169, 2013.

Raguseo, Elisabetta: Big data technologies: An empirical investigation on their adoption, benefits and risks for companies, International Journal of Information Management 38, 2018.

Trolio, G.; De Luca, L.M.; Guenzi, P: Linking data-rich environments with service innovation in incumbent firms: a conceptual framework and research propositions, Journal of Product Innovation Management 34(5), 2017.

Urbinati, Andrea; Bogers, Marcel; Chiesa, Vittorio; Frattini, Federico: Creating and capturing value from big data: A multiple-case study analysis of provider companies, Technovation 84–85, 2019.

Marta-Christina Suciu, Laura Istudor, Adrian Simion, Mircea Mitiucă, Gheorghe-Alexandru Stativa

Knowledge and innovation – engines of intelligent, sustainable and inclusive development

Abstract In the case of the emerging economies, category in which our country belongs, most companies are aware of the importance of these two engines of development at the microeconomic level. Therefore, at the microeconomic level, the economic actors often called business angels or business champions, respectively business innovators, place great emphasis on strategies dedicated to innovation and knowledge management. In this context, favorable premises are created both at the microeconomic level and, accordingly, at the mezzo and macroeconomic levels in order to ensure, in the medium and long term, a sustainable, inclusive and intelligent development having as essential engines knowledge and innovation. The paper aims to analyze the essential role of innovation and knowledge as evolutionary mechanisms meant to support increased competitiveness and to obtain, maintain and develop a long-term sustainable competitive advantage. The aim is to highlight the role of knowledge and innovation as an integrated part of the emerging economies process of catching up the developed economies.

Keywords: knowledge, innovation, sustainability

Introduction

The increasingly complex and dynamic competitive environment specific to modern industries, such as the creative, innovative and knowledge-based industries , influences the nature of the innovations and the actors operating there markets (Mitra, Edmondson, 2015). However, there is a relatively high heterogeneity both between the actors and the nature of the innovative activity. Thus, if a country spends too little on research – development – innovation, it is necessary to optimize the efficiency and effectiveness of innovation, especially in the medium and long term (Edquist, 1997). An overview of the innovator also takes into account their great diversity, one that is based on the great variety of talents that are expected to be valued on the creative-innovative side. New and improved products and processes are responses to challenges and opportunities, which vary both within the industry and in other sectors.

We propose as specific objectives the comparative analysis of the visions of intelligent development through technological advance, quantum computers, the analysis of business intelligence type and positive macroeconomic externalities of the new Fintech sector. Another specific objective is the one based on sustainable development, namely the construction of the future for our successors and what we leave them for their successors through sustainable environmental policies, sustainable consumption of resources, efficient recycling of generated waste and reducing the production of it. A third specific objective is the socioeconomic integration of the development respecting the specificities of the emerging countries, respectively the inclusion in the global functional gears and the generated streamline.

Often it is necessary that a set of key competences should be developed, which should include so-called soft skills and transversal skills respectively, in addition to engineering technical skills, specific to traditional production mechanisms. Innovation therefore requires the use of a set of complementary strategies that have multiple projections in areas that contribute to increasing competitiveness.

1. Brief literature review

Innovation is an important engine for which both internal and external factors can be identified. Internal factors that influence innovation are closely related to the size of the macroeconomic environment and the market, as well as to the knowledge and skills accumulated within the market. External factors mainly refer to technological opportunities and market forces. Two forces are at work that outline the nature of diversity – forces that are intentional and those that are not. The progress of the creation and accumulation of knowledge creation through the usual research and development activity and through alternative means, both inside and outside the company, through market conditions, changes in organizational structures and institutional development are marked by a high degree of uncertainty.

Uncertainty arises because technological change involves a trial and error process. On the one hand, it involves the type of experimentation, individual and collective learning that is emphasized in the evolutionary economy. On the other hand, it has characteristics of the type of process of cause and deterministic, rational effect, which are emphasized by neoclassical economists. The evolution of the economy shows that, as a rule, the creation and diffusion of technological change is multifaceted. Novelty takes diverse forms and innovations of different types are created and introduced by various processes from different organizations and systems. However, as in biological evolution, only some innovations survive.

This selection process results in the loss of some innovation regimes and the focus of the systems on a small set of regimes – for example, the model of innovation focused on research and development, mechanism which is started and evolves by emphasizing the knowledge society. The innovative variety appears partly due to design and partly due to chance. The variety can be found in different reasons of the economic agents, types of organizations and institutions that have developed as a result of the specific cultures of a country. These often come from random occurrences in search and learning procedures, especially in relation to scientific discoveries and, finally, unexpected changes of environmental factors (of complex interdisciplinary nature: economic, social and political).

The selection process that reduces variety by eliminating the least successful ones in favor of successful innovation processes also implies considerable uncertainty. The selection process works both at the firm and at the macroeconomical level. Firms decide what innovative ideas will be developed, what internal resources to innovate, and what complementary assets they must find within or outside their organizations. The survival of a technique by selection will depend on the volume of techniques that are chosen for the experiment and the institutional structures that exist to support certain modes of innovation (De Silva et al., 2018).

Neoclassical models try to organize the range of information into more recognized segments, while having this sometimes confusing complexity associated with evolutionary innovation models. These models argue that differences in innovation regimes may reflect not so much the random choice, but the intended responses to differences in prices and relative opportunities. Small and large enterprises face different capital costs, so it is possible to expect to choose different capital shares, both in the production process and in the innovation process. If companies can replace one type of resource with another rarer resource in their search for innovation, it would involve compromises that are well managed within the traditional neoclassical economy, while all of these elements being based on the positive externalities resulting from the accentuation of the knowledge-based society and innovation (Campbell, Carayannis, 2016).

The heterogeneity of the innovation system takes many forms, especially when it is based on knowledge extrapolated to the macroeconomic level.

First, there are distinct differences between types of innovation within industries. Each industry is made up of a complex network or system of actors, often pursuing different innovation strategies (Meadows, 2008). The technical progress in an industry takes place on several levels – in components, in the production process and in the introduction of new or improved products (type 2.0, 2.1 models, etc.). Progress is made at different moments in different parts of this process, which is coordinated by long-term market transactions and by internal knowledge transfers to organizations that can join a network of companies. In multinationals case, the latter appears as part of transactions within the same company. Sometimes, as in the case of joint ventures, they occur between separate legal entities that combine their resources to share knowledge (Nelson, Rosenberg, 1993).

Secondly, there are substantial differences between the types of products manufactured by innovative firms. A common distinction that is frequently made is between product and process innovators. Product and process innovation uses inputs, such as Research – Development – Innovation, in different volumes. This distinction is also pursued throughout this proposed study to examine differences in the development of new products and processes (Torusga, O'Donohue, 2016).

Thirdly, there is heterogeneity between size classes. The size of the company has received much attention in recent innovative studies. The relationship between enterprise size and innovation has been at the forefront of economic studies from Schumpeter's theory that associates successful innovation with firm size and monopoly power.

More recent theoretical and empirical research studies suggests that size and innovation are mutually dependent (Dasgupta, Stiglitz, 1980). Size can bring an advantage to larger firms when it comes to innovation, but successful innovators grow faster than other firms and become larger than non-innovators.

Fourthly, there are substantial differences between companies of different nationalities. In today's global economy, business ownership is becoming increasingly international and many companies are interacting across national borders. Cross-border transactions with suppliers, customers and partners offer access to information networks, other than those available to companies held in the domestic market. It is important to investigate whether foreign affiliates operating in developing countries, such as Romania, are integrated into the European innovation system. These elements are also integrated in the European standards for emphasizing the knowledge society, elements that make their presence felt slowly in Romania (Drozdiak, 2017).

Fifth, research has shown that innovation systems differ across industries, in part because technological opportunities differ from industry to industry, and the incidence and type of innovation are also closely related to the position in a product's life cycle, or an entirely new industry. The low innovation rate is found in traditional industries, such as textiles, wood products, food and cells and paper, which are favored for export to economically developed countries. Several taxonomies of industrial innovation have been constructed with industry environment differences as a basis for their classification. These studies are based on either differences in the technological opportunities of the different sectors, a concept of the product hierarchy, or the method used to diffuse innovations throughout the economy – problems related to uneven spreads and externalities. Generic knowledge is an economic good with unique characteristics.

Some new scientific discoveries and new inventions – unless they are kept secret or protected by a patent – can be used by anyone without diminishing the amount of knowledge that can be consumed by others. This fact ensures the diffusion of innovation through what economists call externalities of knowledge or information dissemination, a component within the structure of the knowledge society and which generates the efficiency of research & development, but it reduces the incentives that private companies that are aiming to maximize profit must produce – new knowledge, Innovation and knowledge creation will not be supported (Valkokari, 2015)(Valkokari, 2015). This conventional analysis of market failure has traditionally been used to provide an economic rationale for supporting the government in pursuing policies to promote research, development and innovation (Arrow, 1962).

Market imperfections arising from these issues, are addressed by the government thought the creation and application the intellectual property rights – rights that attribute the ownership of the results of ideas that lead to innovation. Although the intellectual property rights are designed to stimulate economic activity, there are not much applied research to the fact that is the case. There are two major exceptions. Research by Mansfield (1986) and Levin et al. (1987) challenged the conventional belief that rights such as patents are an effective means of protecting investments in knowledge creation.

In a related line, Von Hippel (1988) notes that adequacy problems don't affect only the amount of innovation that takes place, but also the nexus or location of the respective innovation, elements that are influenced, but also influence the knowledge and socioeconomic evolution of a nation.

Recognizing the imperfections in terms of opportunity, it identifies the stage of a vertically integrated production chain that is most likely to have inherent benefits in terms of learning the benefits of an innovation and postulates that it is the one that will drive most of the innovative activity. Companies manage to internalize externalities of all types, including those associated with knowledge creation.

In case of knowledge creation, companies often do it by adopting different strategies, others that using patents. They create their new complex product; they develop a first-degree advantage; develops partnerships with other companies and the state has the role to accelerate this process in the long term (Foray, 2004) (Foray, 2004).

Problems related to pricing an a extremely uncertain good, such as process innovation, also lead to new forms of organization to reduce the costs of transferring new technologies. The transfer of technology by a company can be done either be licensing or by exploiting its own technology through export or with production facilities located abroad. The chosen alternative will be determined by the relative efficiency in the transfer of an asset through a long-term transaction, rather than making a foreign investment or through export.

1.1. Infrastructure of Extreme Light-Nuclear Physics (ELI-NP)

ELI is a new Research Infrastructure of pan-European interest and part of the European Roadmap of the European Strategic Research Infrastructure Forum (ESFRI). The project is based on four pillars. Three of them are already in the implementation phrase: Prague (Czech Republic)-Fascicules, Szeged (Hungary)-Autoseconds and Magurele (Romania)-Nuclear physics, with an investment volume exceeding 850 million euros and this is the first research infrastructure widely built in the eastern part of the European Community. Most of the investment comes from the European Regional Development Found (ERDF).

It is a laser installation that aims to host the most intense beams in the world, the development of new interdisciplinary research opportunities with the light coming from these lasers, the secondary radiation derived from them and making them available to an international scientific community ofusers.

One of the first priority projects of the research infrastructure for Europe, ELI was brought to a organizational and scientific maturity thanks to a FP7project launched in 2007 which involved 36 months for preparation. Almost 40 research and academic institution from 13 EU member states participated in the preparation phase. After a 3-year preparatory phase of the ELI, ELI consortium was establish, and on April 11, 2013, the ELI became ELI Delivery Consortium (ELI DC AISBL).

The Association was established to promote the sustainable development of the project, establishing partnerships and collaborations with national, European and international structures and organizations. ELI-DC coordinates the transition from implementation to the operational phase, which leads to the creation of an European research infrastructure consortium: ELI-ERIC. ELI-DC supports the three pillars in the implementation phase, ensures the ELI character as a unified pan-European project, conducts negotiations towards ELI-ERIC and prepares the conditions for the establishment of the fourth pillar of ELI, planned to push the laser power borders with another order of magnitude in the sub-exawatt regime (Figs. 1 and 2).

The scientific profiles of the ELI pillars will be complementary, and the operation of the Research Infrastructure, which has started progressively from 2018, will be unified under a single legal umbrella ofELI-ER

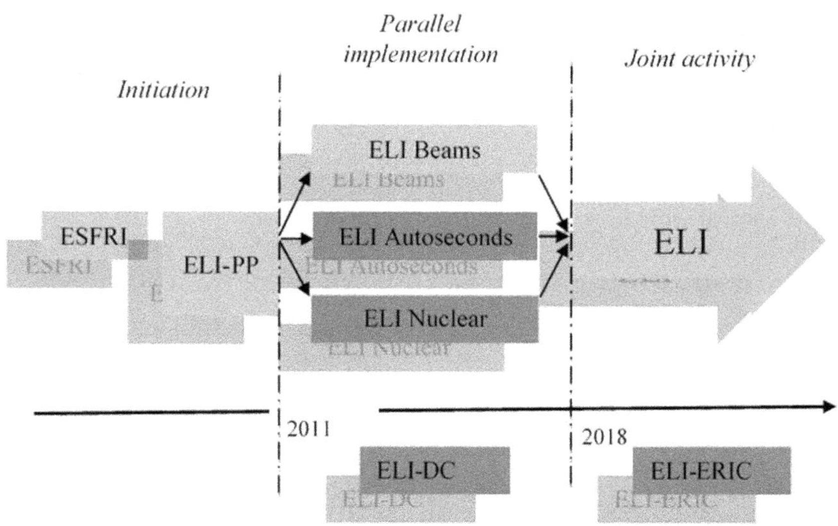

Fig. 1: Evolution of the ELI Project

Data source: ELI official website

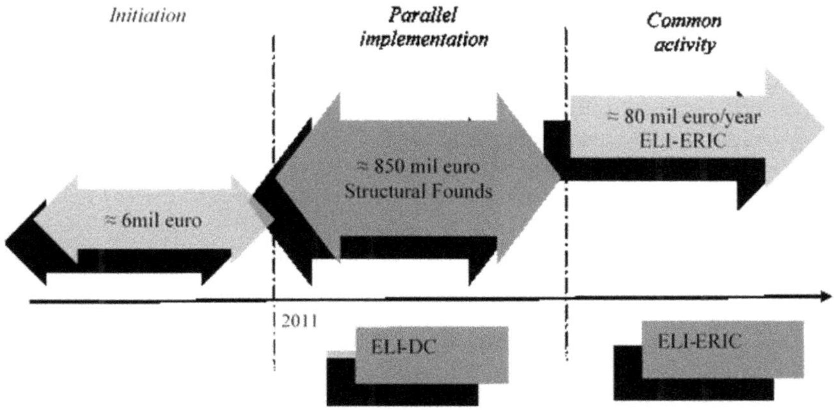

Data source: ELI official website

Fig. 2: ELI evolution and related expenses
Data source: ELI official website

The preparatory phase (PP) of the ELI project began in November 2008 and was completed in December 2010. This was funded by the European Commission with approximately 6 million euros.

The implementation phase of the first three pillars, which runs in parallel in the Czech Republic, Hungary and Romania, started in 2011 and is expected to be completed in 2017. The implementation phase has not been completed so far. It is financed by a combination of European Regional Development Funds (ERDF) and contributions from host countries, totaling about 850 million euros. It is coordinated by the International Association of the Delivery Consortium of ELI, made up of representatives of the three host countries and other countries.

The operating phase of ELI is expected to be left in the following year. The three pillars will be managed, governed and funded by a new European ERIC consortium, composed of interested members countries. ELI will function as an international laser user facility, open for access by an international user community.

1.2. ELI-NP activities

The Infrastructure of Extreme Light-Nuclear Physics (ELI-NP) is one of the three pillars of the ELI located in Măgurele and has appeared in the context of the challenges in the Romanian industry which is uninventive and disadvantaged in the global competition. The cause of this condition is the poor financial situation of large companies that impede investment in research. Only a constant support for scientific research can lead to the transfer of knowledge to the economic environment and increase its contribution to the subsequent expenses in research, development and innovation.

The massive phenomenon of "brain drain" encountered in Romania is caused by the lack of opportunities for a successful career in scientific research among researchers. This represents a challenge for the scientific competitiveness of the countries that have joined recently to the European Union. There are non-refundable EU financial assistance programs to bridge the gap between EU countries.

ELI-NP has a unique combination in the world between a high power laser system (2 × 10PW) and a very intense photon beam. This will make it possible that the research not only in fundamental physics but also applied research in the field of materials science, radioactive substance management, biophysics and medicine. ELI-NP has the potential to reach the leading position worldwide in areas that have a physical foundation. Of all the three existing ELI pillars, ELI-NP has the greatest flexibility in research due to the ability to use multiple radiation sources simultaneously and the group of potential users will therefore be highly diverse.

As a macroeconomic impact of ELI-NP we can mention the increase of local skills in the field by the participation of Romanian researchers and engineers in the development of equipment and the participation of local companies in the construction of technically advanced buildings. Also, ELI-NP will bring additional demand on the local market for different types of goods and services that until now were under exploited and will increase the competitiveness of this market. The competences acquired by participating in the successful implementation of the ELI-NP project will have a long-term effect on the Romanian economy.

Also, ELI-NP is open for collaboration. Many companies will be able to participate in the exchange of ideas and technologies, collaborate with ELI-NP in research and development projects and capitalize on the research results by putting them into practice.

The necessary premises for the realization the project were closely related to land (availability, forms of property, etc.), infrastructure (accessibility to public transport, intermodal nodes), sources of financing (European funds and state aid) and governance (the association of governance and local development agency).

The project was funded in two phases. In the first phase, the project benefited of 136.4 million euros through the Sectoral Operational Program Increasing Economic Competitiveness (POSCCE) 2007–2013 and the second phase that was co-financed by the Operational Program Competitiveness (POC) 2014–2020 with 174.5 million euros.

The first phase of the project was completed in December 2015 and has the objectives presented in Tab. 1.

Tab. 1: Expected start and end dates of ELI-NP activities

Activity	Estimate start date	Estimate end date
Real estate modernization/extension/construction activities	May 2010	December 2014
Activities for tracking the construction works	August 2012	December 2014
Purchase of CD equipment – Fascicul Gama System	August 2012	July 2015
Activities for tracking the contracts for the supply of the main CD equipment	January 2013	July 2015
Activities of technical projects (Technical Design Report – TDR) for beam transport systems	March 2013	December 2013
Activities of procurement of the components necessary for the realization of the beam transport systems	January 2014	December 2014
Activities of carrying out the beam transport systems	January 2015	July 2015
Activities of carrying out the Technical Design Report (TDR) fit the auxiliary systems	March 2013	December 2013
Acquisition of the necessary components for auxiliary systems	January 2014	December 2014
Development research activities in the field of lasers and nuclear physics	January 2013	July 2015
Activities for carrying out Technical Projects for Experiments (Technical Design Report – TDR)	January 2013	July 2015
Project management	November 2012	August 2015

Source: Official website ELI-NP.

Until December 31, 2013, 23 people were employed, including 11 researchers. According to the first phase of the project, by the end of the implementation period there would be a total of 167 employees.

In March 2016, the European Commission approved the second implementation phase of the ELI-NP Project, respectively the second phase of financing. In addition to the objectives presented in the first phase of the project, the creation of new experimental facilities, the construction of an access road to the ring road and the extension of some buildings to be used in the future were also added.

Conclusions

The research, development and innovation sector varies from one country to another in terms of investment level, but a constant pattern is maintained regarding the performance sectors and their weight in the total expenditure incurred. We can see this phenomenon both within and outside the EU member countries.

The degree of absorption of each country depends on factors such as previous experience in accessing EU funds, the qualified consultancy offered in the elaboration of projects but also the co-financing capacity of the states. One of the criteria for granting financial support is that part of the money is guaranteed by the state. One of the criteria for granting financial support is that part of the money is guaranteed by the state. Establishing more accessible criteria could improve the degree of absorption. Another determining factor is the fiscal policies that offer some advantages to companies whose main activity is scientific research. State that offer such facilities have a smaller direct contribution to the RDI, but the effects can be seen in the spending of private companies. Such a phenomenon can be observed in countries such as Slovenia, Hungary or Ireland.

Information campaigns about existing possibilities, use of more accessible language, free consultation of companies wishing to attract investment for their own projects, supporting mentoring initiatives could improve the absorption capacity of EU founds.

Between 2020–2030, the European Union will focus in promoting research, development and innovation in areas aimed at climate study, the impact of climate change on economic activities, but also ways to solve existing problems. Starting in 2020, the budget of 10 billion euros will be made available for companies that come up with innovative ideas regarding climate and nature.

In 2017, Romania allocated 0.5 % of Gross Domestic Product for RDI, being the country with the fewest investments as a share of GDP. According to the Europe 2020 Strategy, Romania aims to reach a level of investments in RDI of 2 % of GDP. Analyzing the trend of expenditure development for RDI, Romania will not be able to fulfill its obligation until the end of2020.

One of the ELI pillars located in Măgurele, represents the largest investment project in Romania's RDI. The long-term effects of ELI-NP, but also the potential of such a project can generate an incentive for economic agents to come up with new ideas that create significant addedvalue.

The expected multiplier effects of ELI-NP will be observed in the creation of new jobs both in the industries which it has a direct connection and in the sphere of services. The increase of the GDP with about 500 billions euros annually, but also the receipts to the state budget from taxes with about 120 billions can be used as reference points to predict what would be the impact of a larger number of such initiatives implemented in Romania.

References

Arrow, K. (1962) Economic welfare and the allocation of resources for invention capitol, în The Rate and Direction of Inventive Activity: Economic and Social Factors, New Jersey: Princeton University Press.

Campbell, D., Carayannis, E. (2016) The academic firm: A new design and redesign proposition for entrepreneurship in innovation-driven knowledge economy, Journal of Innovation and Entrepreneurship, no. 5, pp. 1–10.

Dasgupta, P., Stiglitz, J. (1980) Industrial structure and the nature of innovative activity, Economic Journal, nr. 358, pp. 266–293.

De Silva, M., Howells, J., Meyer, M. (2018) Innovation intermediaries and collaboration: Knowledge-based practices and internal value creation, Research Policy, vol. 47, no. 1, pp. 70–87.

Drozdiak, W. (2017) Fractured Continent: Europe's Crises and the Fate of the West, Londra: Norton & Company.

Edquist, C. (1997) Systems of Innovation: Technologies, Institutions and Organizations, New York: Routledge.

Foray, D. (2004) The Economics of Knowledge, Cambridge: MIT Press.

Levin, R., Klevorick, C., Nelson, R., Winter, S. (1987) Appropriating the returns from industrial research and development, Brookings Papers on Economic Activity, no. 3, pp. 783–831.

Mansfield, E. (1986) Patents and innovation: an empirical study, Management Science, no. 2, pp. 173–181.

Meadows, D. (2008) Thinking in Systems, White River: Chelsea Green Publishing.

Mitra, J., Edmondson, J. (2015) Entrepreneurship and Knowledge Exchange, Londra: Routledge.

Nelson, R., Rosenberg, N. (1993) National Innovation Systems: A Comparative Analysis, New York: Oxford University Press.

Torusga, N., O'Donohue, W. (2016) Progress in innovation and knowledge management research: From incremental to transformative innovation, Journal of Business Research, vol. 69, no. 5, pp. 1610–1614.

Valkokari, K. (2015) Business, innovation and knowledge ecosystems: How they differ and how to survive and thrive within them, Technology Innovation Management Review, vol. 5, no. 8, pp. 17–24.

Von Hippel, E. (1988) The Sources of Innovation, Cambridge: MIT Press.

Emil Dinga

About scientific method

Abstract The paper examines the logical and epistemological conditions in order to describe the fundamental lines of the scientific method in knowledge process. It begins with the formulation of the problem to be examined, continues with the predicates the result of research must verify, the heuristic way of the "as if," and the fundamental methodological general condition of the ceteris paribus. Regarding this concept, the paper develops a detailed analysis, putting into evidence the crucial distinctions between its use within the natural sciences and its use within the social sciences (disciplines). Based on these findings, the paper extract the set of the mandatory features the scientific method must meet.

Keywords: method, abduction, ceteris paribus

Introduction

The scientific knowledge is achieved through a specific vehicle, called the scientific method. Generally, the method ensures the conduct of the research process resulting in scientific knowledge. Through research, we understand a coherent set of actions/activities to examine a problem (in the form of questioning) in order to solve it theoretically. By theoretical solution of a problem we understand a solution with minimal context dependence (at the limit, an a-contextual solving). Research methodology is a set of philosophical principles (precepts) on the way of examining a problem theoretically formulated. There are four categories of such principles (precepts):

- principles (precepts) on the formulation of questions: the question is formulated in the margin of the problem to be solved;
- principles (precepts) on the interpretation of the "answers" given to the questions: "translation" from the code of the object-researched into the code of the subject-researcher;
- principles (precepts) regarding the formulation of the obtained results: formulation of the results means the "translation" from the subject-researcher code into the public code;
- principles (precepts) of formulating new problems as a result of the solving: generalization, particularization, association, co-lateralization, transdisciplinarization, etc.

1. Literature review

The literature concerned with the scientific method, although vast, approaches in an incredible small measure the scientific method from the logical point of view. The paper aims redirect of such a state to a new approach, based on logical, philosophical, and epistemological foundations.

2. About the scientific method in knowledge

The general way to "capture" a scientific problem to be solved could be visually expressed as in Fig. 1.

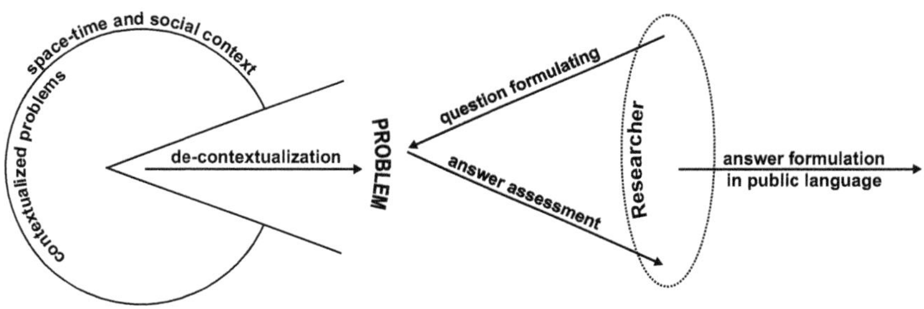

Fig. 1: General logic of the research methodology
Source: author.

Scientific research methodology is the set of philosophical principles (precepts) on the general way of obtaining a scientific solution to a given problem. By scientific solution we understand a solution that verifies the four criteria of strong scientificity: theoreticity, analyticity, replicability, testability. In its most general sense, the scientific methodology is an epistemology circumscribed to means.

An epistemology has two components: (a) an epistemology examining the possibility and conditions of knowledge in the field; (b) an epistemology examining the ways of acquiring knowledge in the field. There are two fundamental ways of scientific research: (a) the inductive path: in this case the factual generates the conceptual (there is a logical primacy of the object of knowledge); (b) the deductive path: in this case, the conceptual generates the factual (there is a logical primacy of the subject of knowledge). In fact, neither the pure inductive path nor the pure deductive path is used, but the adductive path, which is a combination of inductive and deductive, the only novelty brought from the methodological point of view is the iterativity (the iterativity is not a condition of necessity, but only one of suitability or accuracy). Fig. 2 visualizes the above considerations.

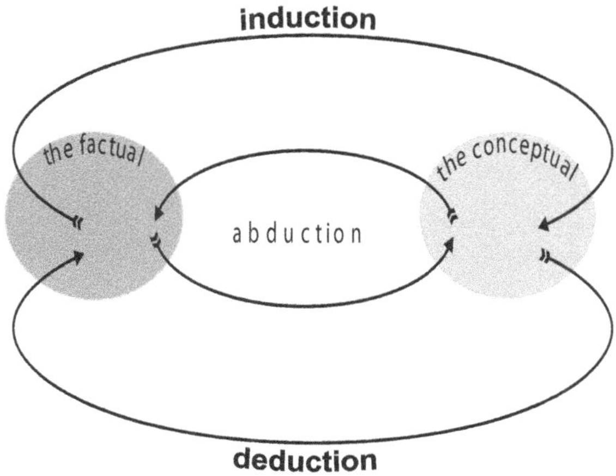

Fig. 2: Induction, deduction, and abduction in the scientific method
Source: author.

The abduction is advisable not only from a practical point of view (induction can never exhaust the particulars to extract the generality, and deduction will never be able to encompass all individuals), but also due to the necessary vulnerabilities of both induction and deduction. Thus, induction is confronted with the following problems: (a) it generates the necessary failures of knowledge (e.g. Russell`s chicken); (b) generates logical paradoxes (e.g. Hempel`s ravens); (c) poses the direct tautological risk (the theory tells us about the factual what we already know), while the deduction is confronted with the following problems: (a) the reverse tautological risk (creates the very world we aspire to know); (b) generates contingent fallibilities of knowledge (Popperian factual falsification).

From a conceptual point of view, the scientific method is the individual (particular) technique of applying the methodology. In connection with the scientific method, we would like to state the following theses:

- the method announces (prefigures) the result: the researcher always researches only what he/she already knows, in the sense that he/she pre-sees the target he/she will achieve following the application of the method;
- the method conditions the result: the result (positive or negative) is obtained or not depending on the effectiveness of the method used during the research;
- the method substantiates the result: choosing the method is based on the researcher's belief in the existence of the result; belief in the result is not one extracted from a model of rationality, but lies outside any such rationality model[1];

1 The best example here is the conjecture.

- the method validates the result: the scientific result is validated only inter-subjectively (by repeating the research by independent researchers); for this purpose, the presentation of the scientific result must be accompanied by the presentation of the scientific method by which that result has been achieved.

The main features of the scientific method are as follows:

- it is predominantly abductive: the method is relatively "blind" factually, it extracts from factuality only the indices that "illuminate" the formulation of the generalizing hypothesis;
- the generalizing assumptions are based on faith (the method is negotiable): a hypothesis is developed only in a faith-based framework (for example, in an axiomatic framework);
- it is reproducible independently (the method has public relevance): the method can be applied by at least one other researcher, independently from the first researcher who applied it;
- it transcends the phenomenon (by abduction, it refers to noumenon): any scientific method aims to describe things as they are. Although the theoretical philosophy shows (for example, Kant) that we can only know from the perspective of our theories and hypotheses, so we can only know phenomena (i.e. particular versions, intermediated by the theories and hypotheses on the thing itself, called Das Ding an Sich), the scientific method, precisely through its public and verifiable character, achieves a certain degree of objectivity, understood as an inter-subjective agreement with a certain description of the phenomenon;
- it is non-computational (cannot be algorithmized): the scientific method may have computational sub-routines, of course, but in its most subtle part it is not computational, but is based on intuition, shortcuts, happening;
- it can be of a founding nature (it does not discover something pre-existing, but invent something in-existent): in many cases, the scientific method proceeds to the creation of heuristic fictions, that is, it proceeds by invention. The invention may lead to discovery or, sometimes, to substitutes for the discovery.[2]

The necessary characteristics of the result of the application of the scientific method are:

- it is theoretically contextualized, i.e. theoretically closed (that is, it is valid only within the founding theory/hypothesis);
- it is factually non-contextualized (has spatial-temporal independence);
- it is inter-personal communicable (as a rule, verbally or propositionally);
- it addresses the intellect (it is rational, not hermeneutical nor affective).

2 For example, in the case of the scientific method applied in the social field (such as the economic field as a social species), it seems that the heuristic invention is dominant in relation to other research techniques.

Since the heuristic fiction is a very important category in the matter of the scientific method, we will make some further clarification on this concept.

By heuristic fiction we understand an operational term, associated with a distinct phenomenon (or a class of distinct phenomena), in order to establish the concept concerned in relation to that phenomenon. Heuristic fiction is defined as being the "as if" of the concept. There are two basic types of heuristic fiction:

- by role: (a) conceptual heuristic fiction (e.g. abstract work, ecosystem); (b) methodological heuristic fictions (e.g. Granger causality, probabilities);
- by way: (a) theoretical heuristic fiction (e.g. scientific theories/hypotheses); (b) empirical heuristic fictions (e.g. factual cuts –empirical sets formation).

The way the heuristic fiction operates is based on the following features:

- heuristic fiction is of the nature of invention: it involves imagination, therefore creativity, not rationality (no model of rationality can formulate heuristic fiction, the formulation of heuristic fiction cannot be computational, algorithmized, automated[3]);
- heuristic fiction involves intuition, not judgment (and so, much less reasoning), and the faith plays an important role (e.g. Kepler, Newton, homo œconomicus);
- heuristic fiction is arbitrary with respect to the phenomenon referred to (it has a referent, but it does not have meaning), i.e., it follows the logic of assigning the name (naming is non-significant in itself);
- heuristic fiction creates, cognitively, a model of the phenomenon referred to, which means that the genesis of the heuristic fiction is, predominantly, deductive (from hypothesis);
- obtaining the concept by applying the heuristic fiction follows an intensive inductive path; by extensive induction we understand generalization of the local in the same cognitive space; by intensive induction we understand "moving" the inductive conclusion into a cognitive space with more dimensions (multiple coordinates or more descriptive parameters).

One of the most used examples of heuristic fiction is the one called ceteris paribus. The semantic content of the ceteris paribus fiction is that some factors (causal, conditional) are omitted in the formulation of heuristic fiction, or, which is the same, omitted factors are considered invariants, although they are not. Ceteris paribus is of the type of methodological heuristic fiction (MEF). Methodological heuristic fiction can be classified as follows:

- based on the methodological effect: (a) MEF of reduction (MEF-R) (e.g. any reductionism), which either has the effect of reducing the de-contextualization of research or reducing the non-locality of research; (b) MEF of enlargement

3 Artificial intelligence cannot invent, but only discover through a morphological combination.

(MEF-E) (e.g. any generalization), which either results in an increase in the de-contextualization of research or in the increase of the non-locality of research;
- based on the methodological role: (a) MEF of synthesis (MEF-S) (e.g. any MEF on methodological holism), combining two or more MEFs, exclusively conjunctively; (b) MEF of analysis (MEF-A) (e.g. any MEF on methodological individualism), which decomposes an MEF in two or more MEFs, exclusively disjunctively.

Ceteris paribus is a variable MEF: it is built ad hoc depending on the purpose of the research. In fact, it is about making a methodological cutting, because by applying ceteris paribus the number of dimensions of the phenomenon studied is reduced precisely by the number of dimensions (as a rule, causal factors) omitted. This means that, by applying ceteris paribus, a projection of the original phenomenon is studied in a space with the number of dimensions equal to the number of dimensions retained from the total number of dimensions of the phenomenon in question.

There are some differences between the application of the ceteris paribus condition in the natural domain, as compared to its application in the social domain (of the economy in this case).

- the natural domain refers to areas that do not contain cultural subjects (i.e., it is not endowed with consciousness, thus free-will): these areas are dominated by necessity. Therefore, in this case, the ceteris paribus methodological fiction is reversible: after obtaining the targeted concept, the omitted conditions can be recovered without compromising the concept already achieved (e.g. friction in Physics);
- the social field (including the humanist field) refers to areas that contain cultural subjects: these areas are dominated by contingency (including, of course, the teleology). As a result, the ceteris paribus methodological fiction is irreversible: after obtaining the targeted concept, omitted conditions cannot longer be recovered without compromising the concept already achieved (e.g. law of demand or of supply). Fig. 3 visualizes such differences.

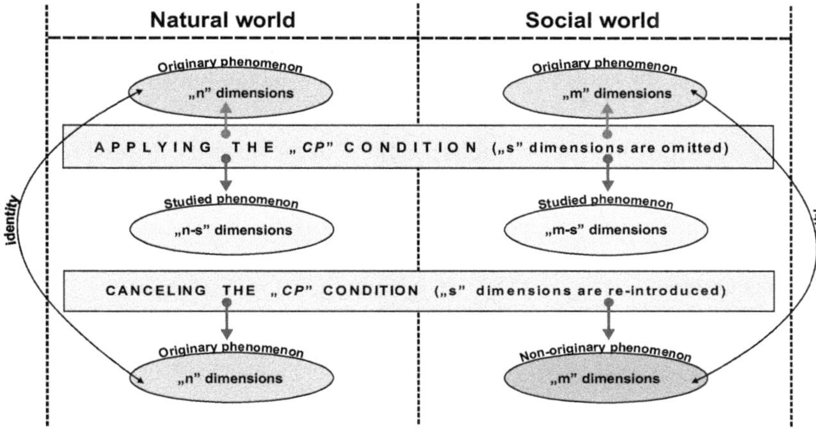

Fig. 3: The difference of the ceteris paribus condition working in the natural field, respectively in the social field

Source: author.

The genesis of the ceteris paribus condition consists in the existence (or issuance) of a hypothesis or, as the case may be, of a conjecture. By hypothesis, we understand the description of a causality that generates a known/accepted result based on a paradigm (Kuhn, 1996). By conjecture we understand a hypothesis that is reduced to the statement of a result without the description of the causality involved. It is clear that different assumptions (but on the same result) require different ceteris paribus conditions, and hence results the ad hoc character of the ceteris paribus condition. In fact, the hypothesis plays, in relation to the ceteris paribus condition, the role of a rationality model (without being a proper model of rationality itself), in the sense that the ceteris paribus condition results logically from the hypothesis.

Operating with the ceteris paribus condition implies three steps:

- step 1: the intentional establishing of the object of knowledge (cognitive object), that is: (a) nominal selection of the cognitive object (phenomenon); (b) the MEF invention that will be applied to the cognitive object[4];
- step 2: the methodological deconstruction of the cognitive object, by applying MEF and so obtaining the cognitive object response to the MEF query[5];

4 The inventory of MEFs is usually done a priori (mostly based on abduction).

5 Basically, MEF application is a way of querying the cognitive object. As we have seen above, an exhaustive query is just the content of the questioning. The questioning gives four logical decompositions (as result of deconstruction) of the cognitive object: (a) causal; (b) structural; (c) functional; (d) temporal.

- step 3: derivation (deduction) of the cognitive object concept, that is: (a) reconstruction of the cognitive object, based on the outcome of the deconstruction; (b) "choice" of the concept which can support the methodological reconstruction.

The utility of using the ceteris paribus condition in the scientific method consists in the following:

- increases the accuracy of methodological testing by eliminating (or, at least, limiting) alternative explanations that might have been "hidden" in the causal factors omitted;
- simplifies the identification ("discovery") of the concept associated with the phenomenon by proving the "basic" (dominant, leading) causality involved by the causal factors retained;
- outlines the possible modelling of the phenomenon, since the model of a phenomenon must be, by definition, simpler epistemologically than the modelled phenomenon.

However, the use of the ceteris paribus condition in the scientific method implies a number of risks:

- extends the interpretative spectrum of methodological testing: Popper's corroboration or falsification becomes more problematic (more controversial) because advocates and opponents of the hypothesis that generated the ceteris paribus condition will not agree on justifying the choice of causal factors omitted; they also do not agree on the relevance of factual testing, also on the basis of the different significance they attribute to causal factors omitted;
- "irreversibly" breaks down the causal and conditional network of the studied phenomenon. In fact, by applying the ceteris paribus condition, it simply looks for a phenomenon other than the intended one (or, at best, an irreducible version of it)[6];
- generates, contingently, a sui generis induction, which is very problematic for knowledge, because the repeated application of the ceteris paribus condition leads to "unlawful" generalizations;
- destroys the symmetry between explanation and prediction, i.e. the result obtained by applying the ceteris paribus condition is not a projectable[7] one (it can be said that the non-projectability compromises the prediction).

---

6 Here there is an interesting suggestion of entropy sui generis (we might call it methodological entropy) of the ceteris paribus condition.

7 A result is designed if it is a safe foundation for the "common sense" induction (see also Goodman's and Quine's comments on this issue of projectability – Morten White, A Philosopher's Story, Pennsylvania State University Press, 1999, and respectively, Willard van Orman Quine, Two Dogmas of Empiricism, published in The Philosophical Review 60, 1951).

A formalization of the concept of heuristic fiction of a methodological type, as is the condition ceteris paribus, can be delivered. Let be a phenomenon *F*, which is causally dependent on a number of *n* factors, f_i, with $i = \overline{1, n}$. Let be a hypothesis/conjecture about a certain state of *F* (i.e. with respect to a knowledge of *F*), noted with *H*. Let *k* number of causal factors that the hypothesis/conjecture finds constant, so they are not considered within the "basic" causality of phenomenon *F* variation. Then, the ceteris paribus condition associated with hypothesis/hypothesis is $CP = h\ (f_1, f_2, \ldots, f_{n-k})$, after a reordering of the causal factors remaining after omitting *k* factors. Let $R(H, CP(H))$ the result "predicted" by the hypothesis *H* and obtained by applying the condition $CP(H)$; obviously $R(H, CP(H)) = g\,(f_1, f_2, \ldots, f_{n-k})$. Let us assume that, after obtaining the result $R(H, CP(H))$, the causal factors omitted are recovered. Then, $R(H) = \bar{h}\,(f_1, f_2, \ldots, f_{n-(k+1)}, f_{n-k}, f_{n-(k-1)} \cdots, f_n)$ and $R(H) \equiv R(H, CP(H)) + \Delta\,(f_{n-(k-1)}, f_{n-(k-2)}, \ldots, f_n)$ in the natural domain, respectively $R(H) \not\equiv R(H, CP(H))$in the social domain.

In order to minimize the risks of using the ceteris paribus methodological condition in the social (especially economic) field, it can be made:

- limiting the "break" of the synergy of the presumptive causal factors by building the CP condition. In the natural field, synergy is always predictable, because the predictability of the synergy is given by its necessary character, while in the social field synergy is unpredictable, this unpredictability being given by contingency (i.e. by the presence of free will). In other words, contingency is the generic cause of the novelty (which is, by definition, unpredictable)
- selection of omitted factors based on their maximum approximation to the simple additivity in relation to the factors retained. In the natural sciences, the causal factors are decomposable or additively re-compassable (e.g. omission and then reintroduction of the friction force into the dynamic equations of the classical mechanics), while in social sciences causal factors are non-decomposable, respectively non-re-combinable in an additive way, but only synergic. Such a situation in the social field is generated by the fact that by the decomposition is lost more than nominal causal loss, and at the re-composition the causality gains more than the nominal yield. The marginal gain, respectively the marginal loss of causality is not symmetrical (their "measure" is not equivalent);
- preliminary linearization of the causal relationships of the studied phenomenon. In the natural field, the combination of causal factors is, generally but not always, linear (from here, the simple additivity of the effects of the reintroduction of the causal factors omitted in CP),[8] while, in the social fields (social

8 The linearity of the causal factor combination is not the same to the linear form of the dynamic or kinematic equations.

sciences plus humanities or spiritual sciences) (Gadamer, 1977), the combination of causal factors is nonlinear. As a solution, in the social fields, a preceding linearization of the causal relationships is needed, both at the level of the hypothesis generating the CP condition, and at the level of the CP itself. In the practice of the quantitative modelling in economics, linear determinations of dynamic equations (e.g. using logarithms) are used, often for purely instrumental reasons, but we have no certainty of linearization of the combination of causal factors. Therefore, it must be taken a lot of caution to "return," after obtaining the concept sought, to the original modelling (i.e. nonlinear);
- building significant-equivalent models to which the CP condition applies. In the natural domains, the respective models are functionally equivalent, while in the social domains they must be significantly equivalent. This significantly equivalence reduces from the intuitiveness (i.e. comprehensiveness) of the modelling, because it may differ both structurally and functionally from the modelled phenomenon.

There are some epistemological issues to be briefly examined here, when the CP condition is applied in the social field:

- the CP condition introduces a necessary un-determination in identifying the targeted concept.[9] The CP studies the projection of the original phenomenon on a space with a number of dimensions (coordinates, parameters) smaller than the original space.[10] Returning to the original phenomenon (i.e. identifying the concept) generates a degree of un-determination equal to the number of omitted dimensions. We have here the potential to apply the famous Poincaré conjecture (or, why not, to issue a conjecture of the same class associated with the CP condition). It is the same type of un-determination that exists in the probabilistic prediction: the prediction of the average of a population cannot be uniquely distributed to the individuals who generated the predicted average (there is a certain entropy of probabilities here);
- the application of the CP condition does not produce authentic knowledge, but only indices on knowledge. We can assert the followings: (a) no knowledge is final (the principle of fallibility) but it can be authentic; (b) a genuine knowledge (from the scientific point of view) is a knowledge factually testable; (c) the concept obtained by applying CP is not factual testable (because the un-determination (indecisiveness of assignment) mentioned above; (d) the application of the CP condition only improves the scrutiny of the concept, not to reveal it definitively; (e) applying the CP condition is of the hormesis type

9 Without breaking the principle of determinacy, so without breaking the principle of universal causality (Hodgson, 2004, especially p. 59).

10 Perhaps an inspired quantitative analysis could identify and formalize a principle of un-determination here (analogous to Heisenberg's principle) using Shannon's entropy.

(Taleb, 2008), that is, it should be iteratively continued (by recovering, one by one, the causal factors omitted) until the concept is "conquered"; (f) so, we have the justification for considering CP as a heuristic fiction species; (g) the threshold at which no further iterations are needed (the CP condition subsists only as long as at least one causal factor remains unrecorded) is an epistemologically unclarified aspect, and even less clarified from a methodological point of view.

Conclusions

The main conclusions are:

- although the statement of the hypothesis/conjecture that generates the CP condition may be theoretical, the statement of the CP condition is necessarily empirical. By theoretically statement we understand that statement (sentence) whose terms are of ideal nature, while by empirical statement we understand that statement (sentence) containing at least one factual term. The logical principle that applies to propositional statements describing the condition of CP is the principle of sufficient reason (Leibniz) while the theoretical statements "obey" the other three principles of logic (identity, non-contradiction, third excluded);
- the statement of the CP in the social field is generally a hermeneutical statement, remembering that the predicate hermeneutic applies to subject-object relationships (e.g. the economy), while the predicate theoretical applies to object-object relationships (e.g. physics);
- the statement of the CP in the social field can also be a practical statement, since the predicate practical applies to subject-subject relationships (e.g. aesthetics, politics);
- the statement of the CP condition belongs to the same discursive formation[11] as the hypothesis generating the CP condition. The concept of discursive formation (more precisely, of discursive practice) is the equivalent of the concept of Kuhn's paradigm, but from a purely phenomenological perspective;
- the concept obtained as a result of applying the CP condition (anticipated in the generating hypothesis) does not necessarily refer to truth-correspondence, but rather to a practical acceptability (NB: remember the practice refers to the subject-subject relationship). The practical acceptability is based on criteria of moral philosophy, not on the criterion of truth (that is, on practical knowledge, phronesis, not on theoretical one). Consequently, the performative act in the social field is describable in a language based on common sense, sensus

11 In the sense of Foucault, here (see Michel Foucault, The Archaeology of Knowledge: And the Discourse on Language, Vintage, 1982).

communis, or on taste (according to the practical judgment faculty – Kant) but not on theoretical, rational inferences;
- the statements made in the matter of building CP models in the social field are particular statements. They are, as an enunciate function, at the boundary between the method and the simple tact (i.e. adequacy) in the approach of the cognitive object (the phenomenon). The concept of tact in practical knowledge should be further developed in the social field and especially in the economic field (it could be "imported," for the first time, from human sciences or from the spirit ones, for example, from aesthetics).

References

Foucault, Michel (1982) The Archaeology of Knowledge: And the Discourse on Language, Vintage.

Gadamer, Hans Georg (1977), Philosophical Hermeneutics, University of California Press.

Hodgson, Geoffrey M. (2004), The Evolution of Institutional Economics, Routledge.

Kuhn, Thomas (1996), The Structure of Scientific Revolutions, University of Chicago Press.

Quine, Willard van Orman (1951), Two Dogmas of Empiricism, published in The Philosophical Review 60.

Taleb, Nicholas Nassim (2008), Black Swan, Penguin Group.

Ioan I. Gâf-Deac

The doxastic management system in the new economy

Abstract In the article are made systematizations regarding the features of the organization and management are/can be designable or selected for designability. Aspects are taken over that confirm that general management is a conceptual space, and doxastic management a compacted sub-space of the qualitative dimensions of organization and management. It is found that companies no longer remain prisoners of the act of speaking, of descriptions, but are crossed by a silent doxastic fiber, which expresses the virtual visualized conviction of the road and the objectives to be achieved. Managerial contexts thus become fields of action. The sets of rules, resources and relationships within a company have a certain degree of sustainability. It is concluded that doxastic management formulates pre-existing fields of action within organizational entities. It is appreciated that the evolution towards the knowledge-based economy is transitional, respectively one can identify the horizons that must be reached by organizing and leading without a definitive opinion of the course/advance. Achieved goals are "reasons" for organizing and leading to achieve other goals.

Keywords: doxastic management, the new economy, general management, doxastic managerial meanings

Introduction

In different practical perspectives for organization and management, some features of the managerial subject/object can be omitted, not taken into account, being classified as irrelevant. Such a derogation/disposal of redundant/insignificant "informational weight" brings the subject/object to the stage of "common thing." Reconstruction in the common sense of the subject/object can be considered an operation/process of "abstraction."

The general management can enter with the help of its doxastic sides in a projective type construction. In such a context, doxastic management could enter the world/set of projective alternatives for science in general, as the latter, in one way or another, need their own organization and leadership. It is important to remember which organizational and leadership traits are/can be designable or selected for designability. The recourse to the phenomenal world of management with the help of doxastic shows that the foundations of scientific knowledge in organization and leadership can be reversed to conventionally efficient thinking. The relations between the temporal states of the different points that mark the organization and the management are reunited in networks of managerial points.

However, the extension of contemporary management will be found in the complexity of the environment permanently subject to organization and management, but in networks of managerial nodes. Thus, on a network type network, the management becomes a persistent entity in its structure, penetrated by doxastic catalysts. Now the management suffers from nuanced knowledge, respectively the similarities of the managerial subjects/objects are confused with the equivalences. From set theory it follows that the similarity is reflexive and symmetrical. However, a calculation of managerial similarity is marked by its non-transitivity.

Doxastic in management is contributing to the formalization of a potential general norm of organization and articulated management of an entity. An original space of the set of rules springing from reflexive and symmetrical similarities would be assimilated with an epistemological continuum in the field (Gâf-Deac, 2010).

Therefore, general management is a conceptual space, and doxastic management a compacted sub-space of the qualitative dimensions of organization and leadership. Now, in ordinary management, one-dimensional modeling is at hand, structuring isomorphically a series of lines of progress through conventionally efficient organization and management. It follows, therefore, that the complex image of the relations reality-managerial thinking arises doxastically from the nuances of organization and leadership for the advance of an entity.

Doxastic management depicts reflexivity from the conceptual unreality of its own substance, which allows the avoidance of excesses of rigor in organization and leadership.

2. Research method: data collection and preparation

2.1. Managerial organization in the network of doxastic managerial meanings

The doxastic managerial theory and practice becomes an operational emblem not by virtue of the proven content of the truth, but by the utility shown for organization and leadership in the race to achieve at least a well-defined goal. However, the usefulness of managerial fiction is eliminated from the discussion.

The organization and the leadership, together, do not represent a limit object of a privileged theory/practice, this assumed status aiming at the teleological demystification in the field. On the other hand, the discovery and recognition of multiple managerial alternatives causes a certain type of discomfort in the substance of traditional management.

Through doxastic management a managerial organization as a scientific power takes place (Gâf-Deac, 2007). We found that in the contemporary world huge communication conglomerates are born and function for the organization, respectively for the leadership (Fig. 1).

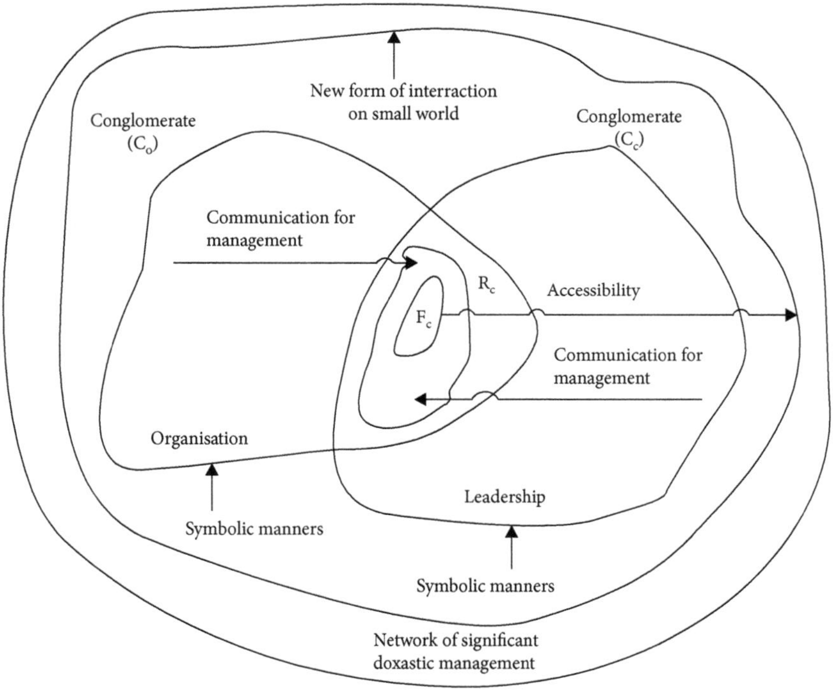

Fig. 1: The company's location in a network of doxastic managerial significance
Note: R_c = communication network; F_c = communication flow. Source: Gâf-Deac, 2013.

The development of new networks and new managerial communication flows determines the operational/organizational impact in companies. As such, new forms of entrepreneurial action are emerging in the economic and social world. In fact, new forms of interaction are emerging with the "Small Worlds" of companies, accompanied by new types open to organization and management. The company/firm as an organizational entity identifies new ways of being in contact with other entities and with itself.

The symbolic forms of interaction presuppose first of all the quasi-continuous modification of the managerial states. However, they become produced/reproduced on increasing scales, ensuring wide accessibility to operationally. The symbolic managerial exchange in the modern world supports the managerial organization, in the situation in which the contextualization of the means of organization and leadership takes place.

However, the symbolic dimensions of management are about to be circumvented, lost. There is a constant concern for the technical features of the means of organization and leadership, including communication. It is found that already in the new nascent economy is restructured the way in which organizational entities are related to each other. Companies already have the ability, capacity and willingness to create networks of managerial significance for themselves. Immediate managerial communication becomes more and more common, which is infinitesimally fixed on a lot of material, physical substances/textures, of a certain type within the company. If, in fact, managerial communication is a form of action, then it is natural to resort to the analysis of managerial action.

The companies no longer remain prisoners of the act of speaking, of the descriptions, but are crossed by a silent doxastic fiber, which expresses the virtual visualized conviction of the road and the objectives to be achieved. Managerial contexts thus become fields of action. The sets of rules, resources and relationships within a company have a certain degree of sustainability (Gâf-Deac, 2005).

Doxastic management formulates pre-existing fields of action within organizational entities. The symbolic power of the company, the coercive, economic, technological, political, etc. it conceptually and substantially outlines cultural and symbolic capital.

Moreover, the doxastic management within the symbolic capital of the company can be assimilated with the special material substrate of the set of symbolic forms/formulas of managerial action. Doxastic management favors the processes of symbolic exchange allowing a symbolic form of organization and leadership to be fixed based on the belief that it proves its expected, conventional utility. The organization and leadership "face to face" have a low degree of durability and a weak fixation, being dependent on the faculties of memory spoken, operationalized.

However, the doxastic vision becomes a more relevant fixer of the symbolic forms of organization and leadership. The mechanism of storing the managerial vision is used as a resource for exercising different ways of managerial power. The power of the manager is denser when the degree of verifying reproduction of the different states of organization and leadership is more reserved, lower. Frequent reproducibility of forms of organization and leadership induces redundancy in managerial organization.

Doxastic management allows the spatial-temporal distance of the verifiability of the organization and management. The classic management does not allow the sufficient spatial-temporal distance of the methods and techniques of organization and management, due to the imposition of the co-presence of the manager and the company. In doxastic management, the manager and the company share the same spatial-temporal reference status, when the exchanges/transformations are available to all or only those in the proximity of the manager and the company. In fact, the sedimentation of the managerial vision takes place with the help of the conceptual means advanced by the doxastic managerial system.

2.2. From transition to quasi-permanence with the help of doxastic management

Managers and companies have a changing character in their common advance on the path to becoming. However, within these entities, in their ontic essence there is something fixed, almost permanently identical. The principle of universality of management is superior to the principle of individuality of the manager or company.

In the continuous passage of time, the sensitive, concrete realities, in their individual variety, prove to be transitory. Instead, the conceptual area of the logos and managerial science, abstract and timeless, is perceived as quasi-perennial. Therefore, doxastic management has an identity with what is organized and what is conducted by analogy with the conception that there is the identity of managerial thinking with what is thought in connection with the organization and leadership in question. The principle of identity is conceptualized in the formula of the principle of the manager's existence as a state, and states that the manager can be known. Through doxastic management it is possible to leave the field of physical organization and leadership, for the ontological one. There are at least two sides of the managerial world, segmented by the paths described above (physical and ontological).

The first (physical) path marks the pragmatism of organization and leadership, based on an infinity of qualities and properties, respectively on the manager's senses. The head of the company looks at the objects and subjects subject to organization and management.

The second way highlights the fact that the manager can catch (include) objects and subjects for organization and leadership with the help of thinking. Thus, the common property of all objects and subjects for organization and management is identified, namely, that before they existed in their configurative variety, they really are (exist as such). Management appears as an essential, respectively real "predicate" of the object and subject of organization and leadership.

Doxastic management captures this transformation of visions from pragmatism to onta. Compared to the plurality of objects and subjects of organization and leadership, the management becomes one and immovable. If there is management, there may be non-management. The non-managerial path is the path of non-existence. Doxastic management is intended to extend the concern for observation equally to us or non-observation. As such, doxastic management deals in all-encompassing management and, equally, with non-management (non-management, as a mirror of the former), In any company, the managerial creation is not complete in the beginning, no matter how much the trust in the principle and its cause would be realized (Levi, 1991).

Managerial fixism in modern general management does nothing but enshrine the engagement of this science in a limited transformist theory. In management as in biology, starting from the ignorance of fixism, new articulations appear, respectively adaptations to circumstances, the distinctiveness is also manifested, the incorporation in a general fixism of principles. Managers and companies are not in front of a perfect, definitive environment.

Doxastic management is the premise contributing to the settlement of the conflict that would exist between conceptual thinking and experience in terms of organization and leadership. This new branch, doxastic management, could provide properties for a new type of chronology that organizes and synthesizes in time facts and managerial events much broader, broader than those in the programmatic area, strictly visible physically, perceived with high certainty. Doxastic managerial logic is not wrong, and managerial experience is not an illusion. Doxastic management confirms the space (the company's environment) as a continuous reality. The magnitude of this space can be divided into an infinity of segments and moments. Instead, the doxastic of organization and leadership have the merit of not evading the types of managerial movements from their total multitude. Perspectives on quantity, quality and substance offer the chance of relationships of adversity, succession and dependence (Hendricks, Pritchard, 2006).

The above reports are within the logical, epistemological and teleological content of doxastic management.

2.3. Managerial learning and organizational culture in the knowledge economy

A dynamic relationship is established between novelty/novelty and the knowledge economy, with increasing terms in absolute value. The supremacy of human capital, which is the primary source of economic values, remains. For the vast majority of workers in all spheres of activity, lifelong education and training become objective needs.

In modern management, in fact, education and training are keys to the ability to produce the manifestation of human capital, which in turn supports growth and accelerates the movement of society towards the knowledge-based economy. It is appreciated that the evolution towards the knowledge-based economy is transitional, respectively the horizons can be identified (O_1,O_2,O_3,...) which must be reached by organizing and leading without a definitive opinion of the course/advance. Achieved goals are "reasons" for organizing and leading to achieve other goals.

At the beginning of the 21st century, at least three such horizons are perceived (Fig. 2), as follows:

- the horizon (O_1), in which the preoccupation of managers is to "do better" what is good; the representative fields in which the applications are found are (a) production and trade; (b) logistics; (c) transports (d) tourism, etc..;
- the horizon (O_2), in which the focus is on innovative competitive applications, (Mathews, 2003) in new areas aimed at: (1) technologies and (2) services (respectively 2.1 – financial, 2.2 – media, 2.3 – telecommunication supported by information technologies, etc.);

- the horizon (O_3) which involves concerns for investments in new competitive applications for new fields such as: (I) research-development; (II) education; (III) emerging sectors of the future (III.1-drugs, pharmacology, III.2-biotechnology III.2-nanotechnologies, etc.). (Lessing, 2002)

The mentioned horizons successively determine short-term impact [ITS], respectively long-term impact [ITL], and in the knowledge economy low impact [ISEC], respectively high impact [IIEC].

In such a framework it is necessary to create a new managerial culture but, equally, a new type of access to the new managerial learning is needed. It is important to build a learning community with the role of focusing on factors that can accelerate the movement towards the knowledge-based economy (Williamson, 2002).

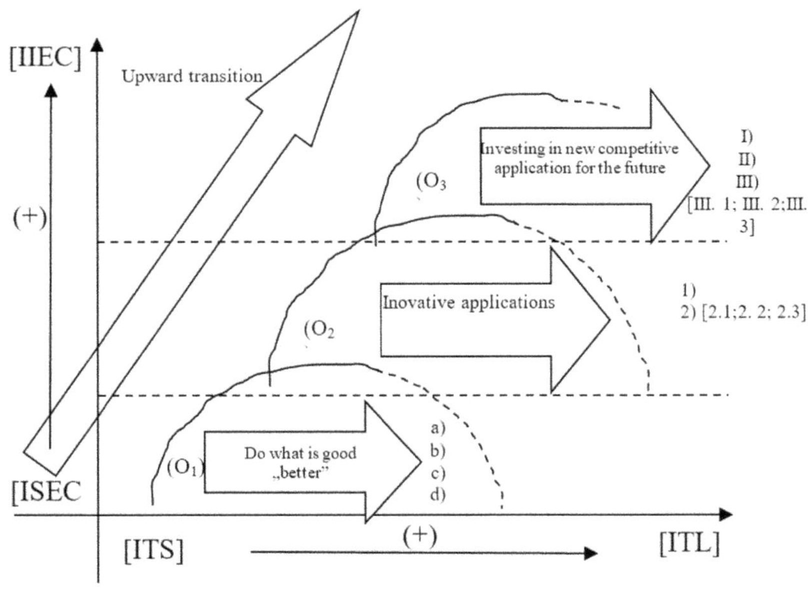

Fig. 2: Horizons (O_1; O_2; O_3) in the transition to the knowledge economy
Source: Gâf-Deac, 2013.

At the microeconomic level (at company level), points of excellence for learning and innovation can be formalized. It is deduced that the managerial activity cannot be separated from knowledge, since the substantiation of the decisions comes from the processing of the information, of the specific data of the horizons on the societal advance alignments.

Acquiring information/data means the opportunity to quantify knowledge. The process of obtaining and storing knowledge lies in learning. Managerial learning is quasi-continuous in the context in which the advance towards the knowledge-based society is continuous.

Conclusions

It is found that new forms of entrepreneurial action appear in the economic and social world. Education and training are the keys to the ability to produce the manifestation of human capital, which in turn supports growth and accelerates the movement of society towards the knowledge-based economy.

Doxastic management is the contributing premise to the settlement of the conflict that would exist between conceptual thinking and experience in terms of organization and leadership. Doxastic management could provide properties for a new type of chronology that organizes and synthesizes in time facts and managerial events much broader, broader than those in the programmatic area, strictly physically visible, perceived with high certainty.

It is necessary to create a new managerial culture but, equally, a new type of access to the new managerial learning is needed. Doxastic management has an identity with what is organized and what is conducted by analogy with the conception that there is the identity of managerial thinking with what is thought in connection with the organization and leadership in question. The principle of identity is conceptualized in the formula of the principle of the manager's existence as a state, and states that the manager can be known.

References

Gâf-Deac, I., Doxastic Management, FMP Ed., București, 2012/2013.

Gâf-Deac, I. I., Elements of the New Economy in Romania in Fields Strongly Formalized on Different Natural Resources, International Interdisciplinary Scientific Symposium Universitaria Simpro 2005, Integrare în aria europeană a cercetării, Vol. Ştiinţe Economice, Ed. Universitas, Petroşani, 2005, pp. 89–91.

Gâf-Deac, I. I., The Legal and Economic Basis of Resource Systems in the New Economy, Ed. Infomin Deva, 2007.

Gâf-Deac, I. I., The New Knowledge-Risk Economy, Ed Infomin, Deva, 2010.

Hendricks, V. F.; Pritchard, D., New Waves in Epistemology, Ashgate, Aldershot, 2006.

Lessing, L., The Future of Ideas, Vintage, New York, 2002.

Levi, I., The Fixation of Belief and Its Undoing, Cambridge University Press, Cambridge, 1991.

Mathews, J.A., Competitive Dynamics and Economic Learning: An Extended Resource-Based View, Industrial and Corporate Change, 12,1: 115–145, 2003.

Williamson, T., Knowledge and Its Limits, Oxford University Press, Oxford, 2002.

Alexandru Isaic-Maniu, Stelian Stancu, Constanţa-Nicoleta Bodea, Mihai Sabin Muscalu

IT&C sector evolution in Romania; its contribution at national level

Abstract In recent years, in the service sector, IT&C services represent the most dynamic ones. Romania is appreciated as a favorable country for the development of IT&C centers by: the tax advantages granted to the companies, the existence of a qualified and still relatively cheap workforce, the availability of a developed office infrastructure and a high speed on the Internet.

The paper discusses the size of the IT&C sector (the labor force employed, the turnover, the assets of the companies, etc.), the performance of the sector at the level of the company and the employed person, with details by size classes of companies and from the perspective of evolution over time. At the same time, the authors make a measurement of the impact of the service activity on the economy as a whole, its contribution to the national production, to the foreign trade and to the balance of payments of the country. By defining appropriate and validated regression models, authors aimed to establish the sensitivity of GDP to the modification of the different factors of influence in the IT&C sector, considered as possible levers of action to increase the value of national production.

Keywords: service sector, IT services, regression models, balance of services, trend

1. The European economic context and the position of Romania

The excessive centralized economic system, the absence of private property in the economy, the non-competitive environment, the absence of the entrepreneurial spirit, the isolation from the international markets, represent only some of the causes of the underdevelopment of the tertiary sector, as it was measured in the economy before 1990.

The process of tertiary production has triggered a series of changes in developed countries with important repercussions on the performance of these economies. In Romania, the economy is currently facing the reality of expanding service activities in the process of establishing a modern macroeconomic structure, with the effort to align ourselves with the trend of modern economies. At European level, Romania continues to recover the discrepancies registered with the other European states and with the EU average, reaching about 60 % of the EU average (compared with about 40 % in 2007) to GDP/inhabitant.

Of the increase of almost 7 % of the GDP in 2017, 6.4 % was generated by the increase in consumption, net exports had a negative impact (–0.8 %), being registered a deficit of 13 billion lei. Public investments were accounted for only 3 % of GDP, being below the average of the last 10 years and represents only 7.5 % of the total national investments. The services have the major contribution in the GDP (55.8 %), the industry having a relatively constant major share (24.2 %). In the structure of services, trade has the largest contribution (18.7 % of GDP), followed by services provided by public administration (11.4 % of GDP). The IT&C sector represented almost 6 % of GDP), constructions (6 %), and agriculture below 5 %.

2. The literature review

The review of the profile literature was carried out on two levels: the first one which deals with works that reflect the scientific concerns related to the definitions and typology of the services, and the second one on the approach of the services in the IT&C category.

First, the authors consider the Stigler's contribution (Stigler, 1956) "as being very for the consolidation of services as a distinct activity in the European economy, Stigler made a valid observation that there is no authorized consensus either on the borders or on the classification of service branches." The practical needs of international measurement and comparison have forced public statistics bodies to find pragmatic solutions for delimiting and classifying services, beyond the ongoing theoretical debates. Thus, for example, Gershuny and Miles (1983) consider that the term services can be used in different ways: service industry, service type products, occupational services, respectively function services.

Based on the conceptual clarifications which were proposed in this area, Harte and Dale (1995) define the services as "intangible outputs, rather qualitative than quantitative." Blois (1991) defines service as an activity that offers benefits, without even assuming an exchange of tangible goods. Jaakkola and Halinen (2006) highlight the organizational behavior of companies in the services field. Hill (1999) proposes a definition of services by differentiating "material"/"immaterial."

Based on a field research, Itkonen (2015), proposes to clarify both the definitions and the structure of the services. The analysis of the changes in the structure of services in Romania is performed by Isaic-Maniu, Stancu, Bodea, Muscalu (2018). Sanders and Ellman (2013) are the authors of a report analyzing the services in the US government institutions. Schmenner (1986) advocates for establishing company networks, for increasing the performance of companies and reducing the rate of their "mortality." Bell (2008) realizes a coherent theory for the IT domain, a systematization of the service activity that has a guiding character. In an interesting paper, Leung and Bockstedt (2009) point out that in the last two decades quantitative analysis has advanced, in step with the advances in the field of information technology, which use online analytical processing (OLAP). Larson (2008) offers a methodological guide of the service analysis but also develops concepts on "Service Science."

Interesting is the argument made by Schmenner (1986) in the field of strategic services management. Borangiu et al. (2016) are bringing together contributions of some national and international experts in the field of services science, and Lazea (2018) analyzes the impact of trade in services on the macroeconomic financial situation.

A method of evaluating the degree of computerization of the economy is proposed by Dóbrota et al. (2012). Alexe and Alexe (2015) propose an interesting data management-based model for the new product development processes, considering that the product lifecycle management solutions became a dominant IT trend. Sarkar (2012) presents the advantages of using informational techniques in the development of education in India. Based on the example of some African countries, Ngwenyama et al. (2017) presents the role of ICT investments in the development of poor countries. Irawan (2014) performs an applied impact analysis (ICT) on economic performance, using the I-O table. Using ICT databases for a group of 163 countries, Alderete (2017) highlights the dependence between ICT and socioeconomic evolution.

A characterization of the stage of IT development in Romania is made by Dragan and Herteliu (2018). The relationship between GDP and ICT investments is offered by Niebel (2018), using information on a sample of 59 countries.

3. The market of services for enterprises

Of the total of 224,292 service providers that activated in 2017, 86.97 % have as main beneficiary the enterprises. This sector of 195,071 enterprises employs 1,263,326 people, which represents 86.2 % of the total service providers. 92.82 % units are micro-enterprises and only 0.25 % are large enterprises (522 units), with over 250 persons. 1263326 persons are employed in the sector, of which a share of 55.5 % is in companies with more than 50 employees. Over half of the total volume of turnover (52 %) was obtained in medium and large companies. On an employee, the turnover has the highest level in small businesses (10–19 people), with 240,902 thousand lei. The turnover on a company registered the highest level in the big companies 154,779,210 thousandlei.

The gross value added at 1000 lei the turnover registered the level of 517 lei for the big companies, 400 lei for the medium ones (50–249), and very close with 399 lei for the micro enterprises. From the point of view of the profit on an employee, the best companies are placed in the group 20–49 employees with a figure of 40,282 lei, compared to 10,363 lei for large companies, respectively 20,686 average for a company in the sector. The volume of investments made in sector were 23,024.723 thousand lei, the main components being machinery (9,579.9 thousand lei) and buildings – special constructions (9,397.75 thousandlei).

One of the main effects of the service activity is found in the international trade relations of Romania. Thus, if the balance of goods registered a negative balance of –12183 million euros, up 30.9 % over the previous year (-9305), exports increasing by 9.6 %, and imports by 12.8 %, the share of the deficit of the balance of goods in GDP increased by 1 % point, up to 6.5 %, the balance of services contributed to this improvement situations. The export of goods amounted to 57187 million euros, increasing by 9.6 % compared to 2016, being favorably influenced by the positive evolution of world trade reflected in the expansion of foreign demand, especially from the European Union, both from countries belonging to the euro area, as well as from outside it. The import of goods (FOB) reached 69370 million euros, increasing by 12.8 % compared to 2016, respectively by 7892 million euros. The share of imports of goods in GDP increased by 0.8 % points, reaching 36.9 %. The balance of services recorded a surplus of 8 210 million euros (4.4 % of GDP), compared with 7723 million euros (4.5 % of GDP) in the previous year (details in Tab. 1). In 2017, the current account deficit continued to deepen: 6.464 billion euros compared to 3.499 billion euros in 2016. As a share of GDP, the current account deficit increased from 2.1 % to 3.5 %, the second largest in the EU, after the United Kingdom.

Tab. 1: Balance of services in 2017

	Indicators (mil. Euro)		**Indices(%)**	**Structure (%)**	
	2016	**2017**	**2017/2016**	**2016**	**2017**
Credit - total, of which:	**18 007**	**20 693**	**114,9**	**100,0**	**100,0**
Communications, computer and information services	3 279	3 938	120,1	18,2	19,0
Debit – total, of which:	**10 284**	**12 483**	**121,4**	**100,0**	**100,0**
Communications, computer and information services	1 364	1 872	137,2	13,3	15,0
Professional consulting	1 273	1 270	99,8	12,4	10,2
Balance – total, of which:	**7 723**	**8 210**	**106,3**		
Communications, computer and information services	**1 915**	**2 066**	**107,9**		

Source: National Institute of Statistics (INS), National Bank of Romania (BNR), Balanţa de plăţi şi poziţia investiţională internaţională a României, Raport Anual 2017, p. 19.

The services also contributed to temper the deterioration of the balance, generating a surplus of 7.963 billion euros, equivalent to 4.3 % of GDP. So, without this positive contribution, the current account deficit would have reached over 14.4 billion euros or 7.8 % of GDP. The Fig. 1 shows this dynamic, the polynomial model of degree five valid tests, the determination ratio R2 = 98 %, and the predicted values of the balance: S_{2018} = 7847,7mio.euro, S_{2019} = 7949,3 mil. euro, S_{2020} = 9124,3 mil. euro.

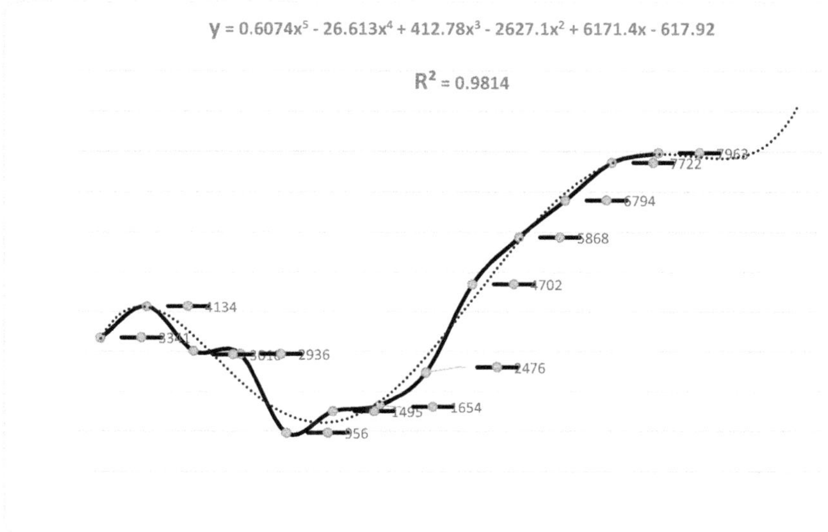

Fig. 1: The evolution of the services balance 2005–2017

Source: Rezultate si performante al intreprinderilor din comert si servicii, INS, 2007–2019.

The dynamism of this group was ensured in 2017, especially by the IT services, whose exports (+526 million euros) compared to 2016) and the positive balance (+117 million euros) increased significantly. Within the telecommunications services (-58 million euro balance) and the informational services (95 million euro balance), the increase of exports did not cover the increase of imports, which diminished the positive influence of this sector on the national balance of payments.

4. The analysis of the activity of the IT&C companies

In recent years, Romania is appreciated as a favorable country for the development of IT&C centers, through: the tax advantages granted to companies, the existence of a qualified and still relatively cheap workforce, the availability of a developed office infrastructure and a high speed on the Internet. According to SpeedTest (https://www.speedtest.net/) Romania ranks 5th in the world in broadband, with a download speed of over 91Mbps, while uploading is over 67 Mbps. On the mobile internet, Romania ranks 26th with 30Mbps and 11Mbps respectively. Also, in Romania, 4G connectivity made its debut faster compared to other European countries, and there are currently advanced preparations for switching to 5G.

The structure of the sector indicates a higher share in the turnover (50.4 %) by the information technology services (in the group of companies with over

20 employees the share is 57 %). Within the information technology services, programming services (42.3 %), information technology consulting (17.6 %) and software package development (17.8 %) together hold almost 78 % of the group's turnover. of information technology. The increase in the number of employees in this sector is among the highest in the EU, with strong competition between companies for attracting skilled workforce. This fact, together with the relative limited capacity of the education system to generate an adequate flow of specialists requested in the specific market, has generated a strong pressure on the wage increases. According to the Employers Association of the Software and Services Industry (ANIS), in Romania there are approximately 110,000 programmers employed, more than in Poland, which has a much larger population.

The market for the IT&C sector is highly competitive, with a growing number of companies and a high share of non-residents, and the main destination is export, contributing significantly to improving the country's balance of payments. Except for the period of economic crisis, the share of value added in the IT&C sector has been steadily increasing, Romania being third in the EU, after the weight of the sector in GDP (6 %).

Tab. 2: Indicators of the IT&C sector

	2008	**2009**	**2010**	**2011**	**2012**	**2013**	**2014**	**2015**	**2016**	**2017**
Share of the first 10 companies C.A. (%)	12.7	18.2	18.4	20.5	18.9	30.3	21.9	22.5	24.9	25.3
Total number of active companies (N)	7,304	7,060	6,600	6,811	7,270	7,664	8,113	8,605	9,581	10,947
Turnover (CA) total -mil. Euro	1793.9	1632.8	1810.3	1907.3	2188.9	2436.2	2842.0	3391.6	3653.7	4065.3
No. of employees (S)	51,194	35,656	36,616	41,044	47,384	52,475	57,367	68,145	75,932	84,019
CA/employee (thousands euro)	35.041	45.794	49.441	46.470	46.195	46.427	49.541	49.771	48.118	48.385
Sector assets (mil.euro) (A)	1098.6	1121.0	1359.4	1469.9	1744.7	1746.0	1851.7	2085.3	2264.6	2473.0
PIB rate (in lei)	-	0.929	0.992	1.011	1.006	1.034	1.028	1.04	1.048	1.069

Source: AEEF#62xx servicii in tehnologia informatiei, http://daeef.ase.ro/Media/Default/Studii%20-%20Cercetare/AEEF_62.pdf; Statistical Yearbooks, 2010–2018, INS.

During the analyzed period, the concentration of the sector increased, thus the first 10 companies approached and/doubled the weight in the total turnover (I = 199 %). The dynamics of the number of employees was + 64 %, well below the dynamics of turnover 227 %, which indicates an increase in labor productivity. The number of companies increased by + 49.8 %, and the turnover by 127 %. The dynamics of the turnover on a 138 % employee. All these indicators offer an image on the superior economic performances and a high profitability. Based on the data in Tab. 2, several regression models have been developed to identify the sensitivity of GDP to some influencing factors in the IT&C sector. Fig. 2 shows the regression model.

A valid model is the one that shows the GDP/inhabitant (Y) and the factorial variables: turnover (CA), number of employees (S), respectively assets of the sector (A):

$$Y_{PIB/loc} = 12.542,77 + 3,88*CA + 0,072*S + 3,166*A$$

SUMMARY OUTPUT

Regression Statistics	
Multiple R	0.990393
R Square	0.980879
Adjusted R Square	0.971318
Standard Error	1023.691
Observations	10

ANOVA

	df	*SS*	*MS*	*F*	*Significance F*
Regression	3	322545371.1	107515123.7	102.5964	0.0000151828
Residual	6	6287655.349	1047942.558		
Total	9	328833026.4			

	Coefficients	*Standard Error*	*t Stat*	*P-value*	*Lower 95%*	*Upper 95%*
Intercept	12542.77	2150.417176	5.83271686	0.001118	7280.893246	17804.65579
Turnover	3.883642	3.102250117	1.251879151	0.257205	-3.707290334	11.47457482
Number of Employees	0.072183	0.099223284	0.727478667	0.494329	-0.170607808	0.314973453
Assets	3.166176	3.311565069	0.956096682	0.375943	-4.936931441	1.26928419

Fig. 2: The regression model

The model determination is R2 = 98 %, with a correlation ratio R = 0.99. Other validated regression models, for which we do not present detailed calculations:

a) Dynamics of GDP per. place. ($_{IPIB/loc}$), depending on the turnover dynamics (I_{CA}) and the dynamics of the number of employees (I_S). Coefficient of determination R = 0.714, statistically acceptable value:

$$Y_{IPIB/loc} = 0,9063 - 0,068*I_{CA} + 0,215*I_S;\ R^2 = 51\ \%;\ R = 0,71$$

b) The value of GDP, according to the volume of turnover in the IT&C sector, the number of employees and the volume of assets:

$$Y_{PIB} = 470,32 + 0,040*CA + 0,004*S - 0,07*A;\ R^2 = 90,3\ \%;\ R = 0,95$$

c) Dynamics of the value volume of GDP:

$$Y_{IPIB} = 0,852-0,096*I_{CA} + 0,255*I_S; R_2= 71,4\ \%; R =0,845.$$

These models confirm that the results and performances of the IT&C sector significantly influence, but in different proportions, the national output, measured by GDP. is inert at the dynamics of the turnover of the sector, or at the volume of assets.

Conclusions and research

The tax advantages granted to IT&C companies have generated an energetic development of the sector, becoming among the most dynamic in the national economy. The IT&C services through the volume of the export made contributed to tempering the deterioration of the commercial balance and payments.

Most of the revenues in the sector belong to companies owned by non-residents, and sales are mainly export oriented. The IT sector is among the most dynamic with a high "birth rate"; The profitability rate of the sector is among the highest in the economy; The development of the IT&C sector has favorable effects on the growth potential of the economy, with an upward dynamics of personnel, and relatively easy investment. A growth momentum could be achieved by focusing on higher value-added IT solutions, to the detriment of implementation or outsourcing.

The IT&C sector is proving to be among the most profitable in the economy, an aspect revealed both by the indicator of the rate of operating profit and the rate of profitability; Evaluations of some specialized companies (for example PAC – Pierre Audoin Consultants 2018), indicate a weight of 12 % in the GDP, given that the sector keeps its remarkable evolution during the last 9 years; In 2015, a governmental program was adopted entitled: Digital Agenda, managed by a dedicated agency – Digital Agenda of Romania (AADR). measures to digitize the industry, cloud computing component, open data and electronic commerce, digital signature, etc.

Although most graduates in this field have higher education, their training is under the demands of employers, large companies invest in additional training; In order to increase the degree of computer readiness of the population, the M.E.C. it intends to take action through concrete measures to increase the digital skills of the new generations.

References

AEEF Trends & Analysis, AEEF# 62XX, Activitati de servicii in tehnologia informatiei, http://daeef.ase.ro/Media/Default/Studii%20-%20Cercetare/AEEF_69.pdf.

Agenda Digitala a Romaniei (A.A.D.R.), 2015, https://www.comunicatii .gov.ro/?page id=3496.

Alderete,V.M. (2017). Examining the ICT access effect on socioeconomic development: the moderating role of ICT use and skills, Journal Information Technology for Development, 23(1), pp. 42–58, https://www.tandfonline.com/doi/abs/10.1080/02681102.2016.1238807.

Alexe, C.G., Alexe, C.M. (2015). Computer solutions of management for the development process of new products, ELSEVIER Procedia Technology Journal, 19, pp. 1031–1037, 8th International Conference Interdisciplinarity in Engineering, Targu Mures, Romania, ISSN: 2212-0173, https://doi.org/10.1016/j.protcy.2015.02.147.

Bell, M. (2008). Service-Oriented Modeling: Service Analysis, Design, and Architecture, John Wiley & Sons Inc, Hoboken, New Jersey, ISBN 978-0-470-14111-3.

Blois, J.K. (1991). Product augmentation and competitive advantage, Journal of General Management, 16(3), pp. 29–43, https://doi.org/10.1177/030630709101600303.

Borangiu, Th. et al. (2016). Exploring Services Science- 7th International Conf., IESS 2016, Springer-Verlag Berlin, https://doi.org/10.1287/serv.2017.0195.

The Digital Economy and Society Index (DESI), https://ec.europa.eu/commission/index.

Dobrota, M., Jeremic, V., Markovic, A. (2012). A new perspective on the ICT development index, Journal Indexing and Metrics, June 6, https://doi.org/10.1177/0266666912446497.

Dragan, I.M., Herteliu, Cl. (2018). Comunicatii- dezvoltarea IT, in lucrarea Cunoaste Romania Centenara, cord. Iulian Vacarel, Edit.Economica, Bucuresti.

Gershuny, J., Miles, I. (1983). Serial Innovation and Division of Labor, Oxford University Press, ISBN 0-19-874130-8 https://www.tandfonline.com/doi/abs/10.1080/08109028508629012, retrived 19.09.2019.

Harte, G.H., Dale, G.B. (1995). Improving quality in professional service organizations: A review of the key issues, Managing Service Quality, 5(3), pp. 34–44. https://doi.org/10.1108/09604529510087455.

Hill, P. (1999). Tangibles, intangibles and services: A new taxonomy for the classification of output, Canadian Journal of Economics, 32(2), pp. 426–446, http://economics.ca/cgi/xms?jab=v32n2/09.pdf, retrived September, 19, 2019.

Irawan,T. (2014). ICT and economic development: Comparing ASEAN member state, International Economics and Economic Policy, Springer, 11(1–2), pp. 97–114, DOI: 10.1007/s10368-013-0248-5.

Isaic-Maniu, A., Stancu, S., Bodea, C., Muscalu, S.(2018). Structural Changes of Services Rendered to Enterprises in Romania 2008–2016, ESPERA 2018, INCE, BNR, May, 24–25.

Itkonen, M. (2015). Analyzing the Technical Structure of Service Product, Master's Thesis Industrial Engineering and Management Degree Programme in Process Engineering, University of Oulu, Finland.

Jaakkola, E., Halinen, A.(2006). Problem solving within professional services: Evidence from the medical field, International Journal of Service Industry Management, 17(5), pp. 409–429.

Larson, C.R. (2008). Service science: At the intersection of management, social, and engineering sciences, IBM Systems Journal, 47(1), pp. 41–51.

Lazea,V. (2018). Raport-Consiliul Export-Import, February 2018, www.bnr.ro, retrieved September 19, 2019.

Leung, T.Y., Bockstedt, J. (2009). Structural analysis of a business enterprise, Service Science, 1(3), pp. 169–188, https://doi.org/10.1287/serv.1.3.169.

Ngwenyama, O., Andoh-Baidoo, F.K., Bollou, F.O. (December 2017). Is there a relationship between ICT, health, education, and development? An empirical analysis of five West African countries from 1997–2003, The Electronic Journal of Information Systems in Developing Countries, 23(1), https://doi.org/10.1002/j.1681-4835.2006.tb00150.x.

Niebel, T. (April 2018). ICT and economic growth – Comparing developing, emerging and developed countries, World Development, 104, pp. 197–211, https://doi.org/10.1016/j.worlddev.2017.11.024.

Pierre Audoin Consultants (PAC), Software şi servicii IT în România - ediţia 2018, solicitat de Asociatia Patronala a Industriei de Software si Servicii – ANIS, https://www.pac-online.com/about-pierre-audoin-consultants-0, Retrieved September 19, 2019, fromhttps://www.itstudy.anis.ro/.

Sanders, G. (2013). Structure and Dynamics of the U.S. Federal Services Industrial Base, 2000–2012, Center for Strategic an International Studies-CSIS, New York, Retrieved September 19, 2019, from https://www.csis.org/analysis/structure-and-dynamics-us-federal-services-industrial-base-2000%E2%80%932012.

Schmenner, W.R. (1986). How can service businesses survive and prosper?, Sloan Management Review, 27(3), pp. 21–32, Retrieved September 19, 2019, from https://sloanreview.mit.edu/article/how-can-service-businesses-survive-and-prosper/.

Sarkar, S. (May 2012). The role of information and communication technology (ICT) in higher education for the 21st century, The Science Probe, 1(1), pp. 30–40 ISSN: 2277–9566, Retrieved September 19, 2019, from http://citeseerx.ist.psu.edu/viewdoc/download?doi=10.1.1.463.2380&rep=rep1&type=pdf.

Stigler, G.J. (1956). Frend in Employment in the Service Industries, 1956, apud, Ghibutiu Agnes, Serviciile si dezvoltarea de la prejudecati la noi orizonturi, Ed. Expert, Bucuresti, 2000.

Alexandra-Ioana Lazăr

The human resources from science and technology sector, determinant factor of economic growth

Abstract R&D activities have an essential role in the economic growth and development, a particular importance being attributed to the highly qualified personnel of the Science and Technology Sector. In order to reduce the technological and, implicitly, the economic gaps, it should be considered to promote the authentic values that constitute the core of R&D activities.

In this context, reporting us to the scientific literature and available data, we intend to analyze the connection between the share of the number of persons, with tertiary education, in the total number of the active population, aged between 15 and 74 years and/or employed in the Science and Technology Sector, in Romania, and the gross domestic product, one of the most used indicators that reflects the competitiveness of the economy, between 1999–2017, based on a VAR model (Autoregressive Vector).

The application of the EViews specific tests demonstrates the clear correlation of the two variables, highlighting the influence of the highly qualified personnel in the high technology sector on the gross domestic product.

Keywords: R&D activities, human resources, Science and Technology Sector

Introduction

Highly qualified personnel represent the link between technological progress and economic growth. Maintaining the competitive force requires a high level of qualification of the workforce whose quality is appreciated by experts as being the quintessence of the economic performance.

According to the International Standard Classification of Education (ISCED), the human resources that operates in the Science and Technology Sector correspond to 5A, 5B (short-term higher education) and 6 levels (bachelor's degree or equivalent).

Employees, with tertiary education, have a decisive role in technological innovation in all regions of the European Union.

The results of the "European Innovation Scoreboard 2019" study made by the European Commission show that, over the last eight years, innovation performance has continued to improve. The biggest increase in performance was registered in the United Kingdom, Netherlands, Malta, Lithuania, Latvia, Estonia and Greece and the biggest decrease in Slovenia and Romania, our country being placed next to Bulgaria in the category of modest innovators.

According to the "Regional Innovation Scoreboard 2019," excepting Bucharest-Ilfov region (moderately innovative region –7.9 %) all the development regions of Romania are modestly innovative: North-West (9.8 % decrease); Center (-10.8 %); Northeast (-19 %); South-East (-19.5 %); South Muntenia (-16.8 %); South-West Oltenia (-16.4 %); West (-5.7 %)

Data provided by Eurostat, shows that in 2018, the Bucharest-Ilfov Region recorded the highest percentage of people with tertiary education and/or employed in the Science and Technology Sector, respectively 50.8 % of the total active population, which suggests the concentration, in this region, of the poles of technological innovation.

The "2019 Country Report on Romania" published by the European Commission, shows that although the graduation rate of tertiary studies has doubled in the last ten years, it remains low if the EU average is taken into account (26 % in 2017, compared to the EU average of 40 %).

The personnel with tertiary education influence the performance of the economic processes, the exploitation of his knowledge determining the growth and the maintenance of the competitiveness.

The starting point in the elaboration of the present research is represented by the outline of clear assumptions:

- the personnel of the Science and Technology Sector is an essential factor of the technical progress and its stimulation programs lead to the improvement of the performances;
- personnel with tertiary education have a decisive role in the economic growth.

The objectives of the paper are to highlight the concrete role of the personnel with tertiary studies in increasing and maintaining competitiveness by applying the econometric model on stationary data and drawing the edifying conclusions regarding the aspects of interest of the approached topic.

The data sources have been provided by Eurostat, and the values refers to Romania, 1999–2017 period.

1. Literature review

OECD studies attach great importance to the structure and dynamics of human resources from the Science and Technology Sector, considering them a sine qua non condition for innovation. The Canberra Handbook (OECD 1995) defines human resources in the Science and Technology Sector as persons with high qualifications and high innovation potential, whose economic performance is based on their knowledge and ability to learn and considerable investments in research and development (Neef, Siesfeld, Cefola 2009).

In the modern economy the most important resource is knowledge and, consequently, the most important process is learning (Lundvall 2010). In this context, people with practical knowledge conditions the solution of economic problems and represents the foundation of R&D activities (Hayek 1945) which are based on an efficient system that facilitates the application of knowledge and the flow of information (Opondo 2009).

The human capital that has acquired knowledge and skills generates economic growth (Mankiw, David 1992) the impact of education on it, highlighting strong causal relationships between increasing the level of education and economic development (De La Fuente, Domenech 2006).

The increasing role of investments in education and training (Marshall 2013) provides the human factor with a higher level of qualification being associated with an expensive and performance machine (Smith 1962). Educational programs and investments in R&D have a strong impact on the evolution of the Science and Technology Sector (Martinez 2018), the knowledge acquired having a key role in the innovative processes (Steelman 1948).

An economy based on sustainable knowledge must consider a set of policies that target investments in human resources, education and training, a key role being attributed to higher education institutions and research institutions (Korres, Patsikas, Polichronopoulos 2002)

2. Methodology

In order to demonstrate to what extent the number of persons with tertiary studies and/or employed in the Science and Technology Sector influences the gross domestic product of Romania, we will build a VAR model on stationary data.

The autoregressive vector analysis is a system-type analysis in which all variables are endogenous and pursues three objectives: evaluating the effects of various shocks on the system variables (Impulse response function), decomposition of the forecast error dispersion (Forecast error variance decomposition) and identifying the relationships of causality (Granger Test). The impulse response function follows the effect of a shock that appeared at one point on the present and future values of the endogenous variables.

Decomposition of forecast error dispersion provides information on the importance of innovations regarding the effect on the dynamics of variables. The application of the *Granger Test* identifies causal relationships highlighting the utility of some variables in predicting others.

The representation of the VAR model is written as:

$$X_t = a_0 + a_1 X_{t-1} + a_2 Y_{t-1} + \varepsilon_{1t} \quad (1)$$

$$Y_t = b_0 + b_1 X_{t-1} + b_2 Y_{t-1} + \varepsilon_{2t} \quad (2)$$

in which: ε_{1t} and ε_{2t} represents the shocks (innovations) in the period t, on variables X and Y.

The purpose of the autoregressive vector analysis is to evaluate the effects of the various shocks on the variables in the system. The advantages of choosing such a model allow the analysis of the reaction to a shock, attenuates the consequences generated by the problem of accelerating the evolution of economic processes and lead to good results in the forecast.

3. The influence of the share of the number of persons with tertiary education and/or employed in the Science and Technology Sector on the gross domestic product, in the context of the VAR model

The variables used in this research are the gross domestic product and the number of persons with tertiary studies and/or employed in high technology manufacturing and knowledge intensive high technology services, period 1999–2017, according to Tab. 1.

Tab. 1: Gross domestic product and the number of persons and/or employed in the Science and Technology Sector, in Romania, 1999–2017

Year	Gross domestic product (GDP) at market prices (Current prices, million units of national currency)	Persons with tertiary education (ISCED) and/or employed in science and technology - High-technology manufacturing and knowledge-intensive high-technology services (Thousand)
1999	55126.4	65.7
2000	80873.1	63.9
2001	117391.4	70.4
2002	152271.5	78.7
2003	191917.6	71.2
2004	244688.3	66.5
2005	286861.9	74.5
2006	342762.6	89.2
2007	425691.1	88.7
2008	539834.6	94.3
2009	530894.4	101.3
2010	528247.0	103.3
2011	559244.8	104.5
2012	593742.9	116.6
2013	635459.4	121.4
2014	668590.1	121.7
2015	712587.8	153.1
2016	765135.4	150.6
2017	856726.6	172.0

Source: Eurostat, Code: tipsau10, hrst_st_nsecsex, hrst_st_nsecsex2.

Vector Autoregression Estimates
Date: 08/09/19 Time: 13:56
Sample (adjusted): 2002 2017
Included observations: 16 after adjustments
Standard errors in ( ) & t-statistics in [ ]

	GDP	D(LPERSONS_
GDP(-1)	1.208870	6.24E-07
	(0.26538)	(7.6E-07)
	[4.55532]	[0.82175]
GDP(-2)	-0.236179	-4.46E-07
	(0.26153)	(7.5E-07)
	[-0.90305]	[-0.59586]
D(LPERSONS_WITH_T...	26136.53	-0.346333
	(89044.2)	(0.25488)
	[0.29352]	[-1.35880]
D(LPERSONS_WITH_T...	209188.4	-0.516469
	(91908.3)	(0.26308)
	[2.27605]	[-1.96316]
C	36098.37	0.001394
	(21517.7)	(0.06159)
	[1.67761]	[0.02264]
R-squared	0.986138	0.353425
Adj. R-squared	0.981097	0.118307
Sum sq. resids	9.17E+09	0.075161
S.E. equation	28877.92	0.082661
F-statistic	195.6364	1.503179
Log likelihood	-184.0388	20.18271
Akaike AIC	23.62985	-1.897839
Schwarz SC	23.87128	-1.656405
Mean dependent	502166.0	0.055831
S.D. dependent	210042.1	0.088032
Determinant resid covariance (dof adj.)		4504326.
Determinant resid covariance		2128998.
Log likelihood		-161.9753
Akaike information criterion		21.49692
Schwarz criterion		21.97978
Number of coefficients		10

Fig. 1: Estimation of the autoregressive vector
Source: Author.

Based on the values presented, using EViews, we built the VAR model (Fig. 1).

Following the estimation of the VAR model we have taken from EViews the following equations:

GDP = 1.20887027378*GDP(-1) - 0.236179008436*GDP(-2) + 26136.5287292*D(LPERSONS_WITH_TERTIARY_EDUCATION(-1)) + 209188.423366*D(LPERSONS_WITH_TERTIARY_EDUCATION(-2)) + 36098.3701803

D(LPERSONS_WITH_TERTIARY_EDUCATION) = 6.24213707437e-07*GDP(-1) - 4.4607131811e-07*GDP(-2) - 0.346332598214*D(LPERSONS_WITH_TERTIARY_EDUCATION(-1)) - 0.516469380228*D(LPERSONS_WITH_TERTIARY_EDUCATION(-2)) + 0.00139427495145

According to most lag selection criteria, the optimum lag is 2 as seen in Tab. 2.

Tab. 2: The lag selection criteria for the VAR model

Lag	**LogL**	**LR**	**FPE**	**AIC**	**SC**	**HQ**
0	-201.0569	NA	3.62e+08	25.38212	25.47869	25.38706
1	-169.9298	50.58155	12291930	21.99123	22.28095	22.00606
2	-161.9753	10.93744*	7759405.*	21.49692*	21.97978*	21.52164*

in which: *LR* represents the test statistic of the maximum likelihood type modified sequentially *FPE* – the error of the final prediction, *AIC* – the informational criterion Akaike, *SC* – the informational criterion Schwarz, *HQ* – the informational criterion Hannan-Quinn.

The model fulfills the conditions of stability, the polynomial roots of the autoregressive process being inside the unit circle, according to Tab. 3.

Tab. 3: The roots of the polynomial

Root	**Modulus**
0.993429	0.993429
-0.241059–0.747607i	0.785510
-0.241059 + 0.747607i	0.785510
0.351227	0.351227

Source: Author

Causal analysis Granger shows that the change in the share of the number of persons with higher education in high technology manufacturing and knowledge intensive high technology services represents a cause for the modification of the gross domestic product to a level of significance greater than 5 % and the heteroscedasticity test indicates homoscedasticity of residues, at a level of significance greater than 5 % (Fig. 2).

VAR Residual Heteroskedasticity Tests (Levels and Squares)
Date: 08/09/19 Time: 14:04
Sample: 1999 2017
Included observations: 16

Joint test:

Chi-sq	df	Prob.
26.19302	24	0.3434

Individual components:

Dependent	R-squared	F(8,7)	Prob.	Chi-sq(8)	Prob.
res1*res1	0.559309	1.110519	0.4515	8.948947	0.3466
res2*res2	0.325480	0.422218	0.8749	5.207673	0.7352
res2*res1	0.632081	1.503242	0.3022	10.11330	0.2572

VAR Granger Causality/Block Exogeneity Wald Tests
Date: 08/09/19 Time: 14:05
Sample: 1999 2017
Included observations: 16

Dependent variable: GDP

Excluded	Chi-sq	df	Prob.
D(LPERSONS_WITH_...	5.233386	2	0.0730
All	5.233386	2	0.0730

Dependent variable: D(LPERSONS_WITH_TERTIARY_EDUCAT...

Excluded	Chi-sq	df	Prob.
GDP	3.001850	2	0.2229
All	3.001850	2	0.2229

Fig. 2: Granger causality and heteroscedasticity tests

Source: Author.

The Jarque-Bera and LM test confirms the normal distribution of errors (probability over 5 %), respectively their independence (Fig. 3).

VAR Residual Normality Tests
Orthogonalization: Cholesky (Lutkepohl)
Null Hypothesis: Residuals are multivariate normal
Date: 08/09/19 Time: 14:10
Sample: 1999 2017
Included observations: 16

Component	Skewness	Chi-sq	df	Prob.*
1	-0.802327	1.716611	1	0.1901
2	0.086083	0.019761	1	0.8882
Joint		1.736372	2	0.4197

Component	Kurtosis	Chi-sq	df	Prob.
1	2.993207	3.08E-05	1	0.9956
2	2.124878	0.510560	1	0.4749
Joint		0.510590	2	0.7747

Component	Jarque-Bera	df	Prob.
1	1.716642	2	0.4239
2	0.530320	2	0.7671
Joint	2.246962	4	0.6904

VAR Residual Serial Correlation LM Tests
Date: 08/09/19 Time: 14:15
Sample: 1999 2017
Included observations: 16

Null hypothesis: No serial correlation at lag h

Lag	LRE* stat	df	Prob.	Rao F-stat	df	Prob.
1	7.390656	4	0.1166	2.178273	(4, 16.0)	0.1179
2	3.442009	4	0.4868	0.897699	(4, 16.0)	0.4882
3	7.196910	4	0.1258	2.108260	(4, 16.0)	0.1272
4	1.767032	4	0.7785	0.438149	(4, 16.0)	0.7792
5	2.390925	4	0.6643	0.604053	(4, 16.0)	0.6653
6	4.528814	4	0.3391	1.221032	(4, 16.0)	0.3408
7	1.239777	4	0.8715	0.302613	(4, 16.0)	0.8719
8	3.599479	4	0.4629	0.943277	(4, 16.0)	0.4644
9	1.106989	4	0.8932	0.269136	(4, 16.0)	0.8935
10	1.465438	4	0.8327	0.360107	(4, 16.0)	0.8333

Fig. 3: Testing the autocorrelation of errors and the normality of their distribution
Source: Author.

It is observed that at a shock in changing the share of the number of persons with tertiary education, after a period of 2 years from the shock, the gross domestic product changes (Fig. 4).

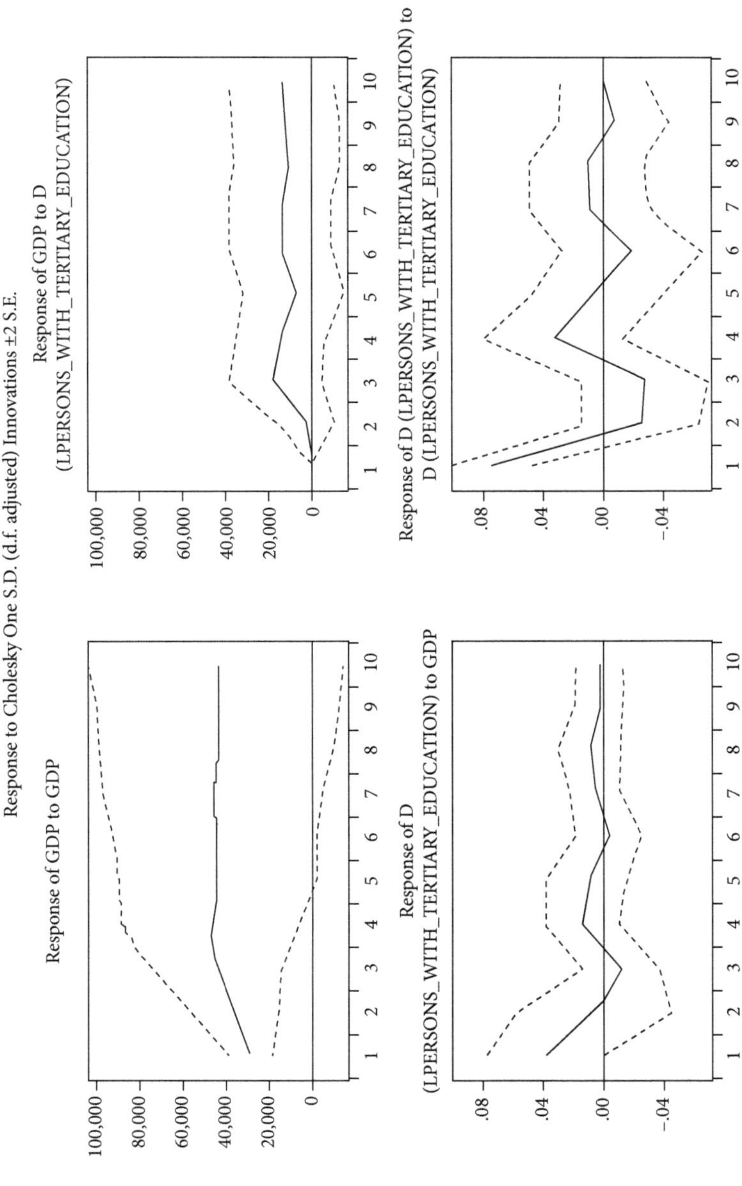

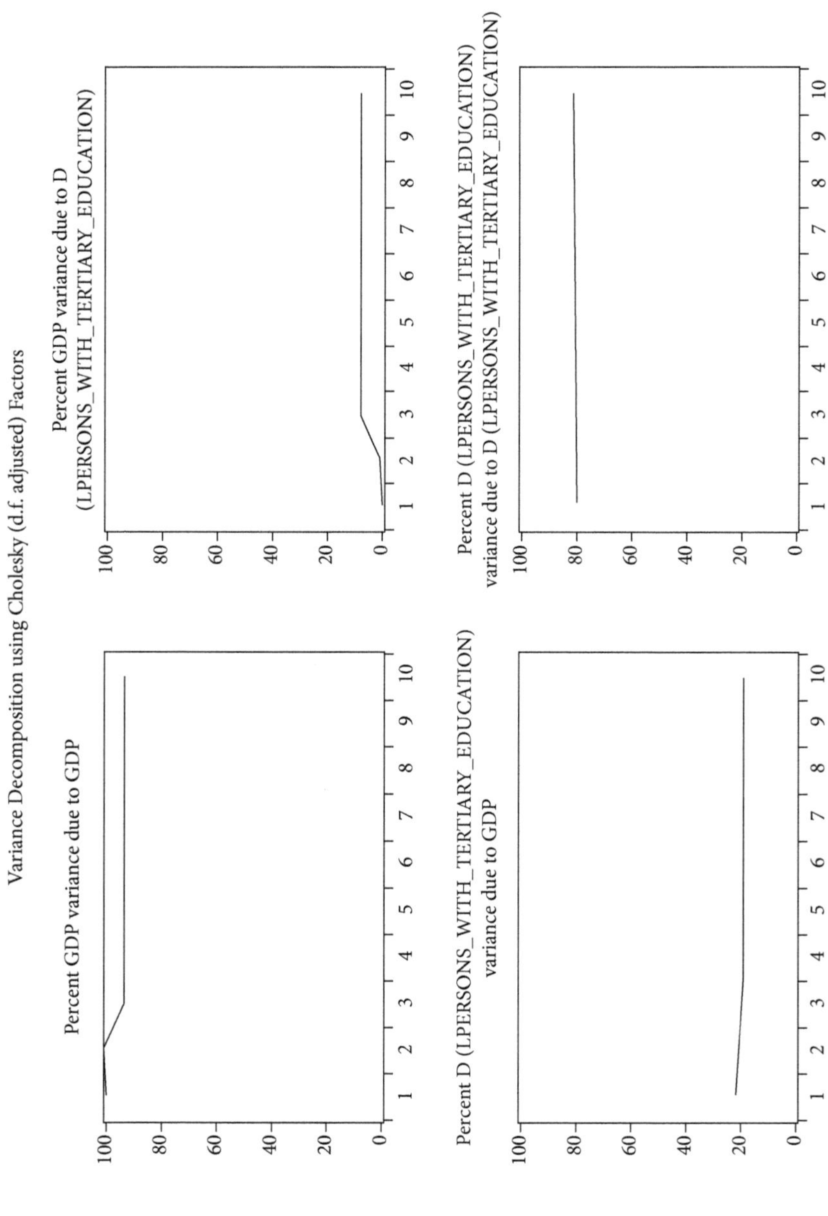

Fig. 4: The impulse response function and the decomposition of the forecast error dispersion
Source: Author.

Conclusions

The objective of the developing countries that aspire to a sustainable economic growth and which joins the world economy based on knowledge, is the development of the Science and Technology Sector, a determining factor of national competitiveness.

The sector based on knowledge and the development of technologies has generated a high demand for qualified workforce, so that the level of knowledge, the level of training of the employees with tertiary education and the efficiency with which they manage to value their professional training are assigned a decisive role in increasing the competitiveness of the economy, confirmed by the validity of the econometric model.

The application of the specific EViews tests confirms a positive influence of the share of the number of persons with higher studies from Science and Technology Sector on the gross domestic product of Romania, in the period 1999–2017.

Increasing the quality of the workforce and increasing its role in capitalizing on the technological potential are manifested on several levels, in the long term, and awareness of these aspects can contribute to a better training and use of human resources. Therefore, in our opinion, investments in CD&I, respectively, in intellectual-professional training are the key to innovation and implicitly a source of profit. Based on the ones presented, some action directions that must be considered can be outlined:

- establishing, in the long term, the sources of financing to ensure the continuous unfolding at a higher level of the R&D activities;
- introduction of norms of stimulation corresponding to the role and responsibility of the employees from Science and Technology Sector;
- the continuous diminution of the number of educational programs and their orientation towards the contribution of knowledge immediately applicable due to the pressures imposed by the demands of the market requires the increase of the competence of the employees through continuous education;
- amplifying the communication and facilitating the maintenance of permanent contacts of the Romanian specialists with those of the developed countries.

References

Chris, Opondo et al.: Applying the Innovation Systems Approach in the Field: Experiences of a Research team in Uganda. In Pascal Sanginga C. et.al. (eds): Innovation Africa. Enriching Farmers' Livelihoods, Earthscan, London and Sterling, VA, 2009, pp. 59.

Comisia Europeană: Raportul de ţară din 2019 privind România, inclusiv un bilanţ aprofundat referitor la prevenirea şi corectarea dezechilibrelor economice, Bruxelles, 2019.

De La Fuente, Angel/Rafael, Domenech: Human Capital in Growth Regressions: How Much Difference Does Data Quality Make?. Journal of the European Economics Association, 4(1): 1–36, 2006, pp. 11.

European Commission: European Innovation Scoreboard 2019, Publications Office of the European Union, Luxembourg, 2019.

Hayek, Friedrich A.: The Use of Knowledge in Society, American Economic Review, 35(4), 1945, pp. 519–530.

Korres, George M./Patsikas, Stélios/Polichronopoulos, George: A Knowledge Based Economy, the Socio-Economic Impact and the Effects on Regional Growth. Economy Informatics, (1), 2002, pp. 5–10.

Lundvall, Bengt-Åke: National Systems of Innovation. Toward a Theory of Innovation and Interactive Learning, Anthem Other Canon Economics Series, 2, Anthem Press, London, 2010.

Mankiw, Gregory N./Romer, David/Weil, David N: A Contribution to the Empirics of Economic Growth. The Quarterly Journal of Economics, 107(2), 1992, pp. 407–437.

Marshall, Alfred: Principles of Economics, Macmillan, London, 2013.

Neef, Dale/Siesfeld, Anthony G./Cefola, Jacquelyn: The Economic Impact of Knowledge, Routledge, London, 2009.

OECD/Eurostat: Measurement of Scientific and Technological Activities: Manual on the Measurement of Human Resources Devoted to S&T – Canberra Manual, OECD Publishing, Paris, 1995.

Smith, Adam: Avuţia naţiunilor. Cercetare asupra naturii şi cauzelor ei,1, Editura Academiei, 1962–1965, pp. 72–73.

Steelman, John R.: Science and Public Policy. Bulletin of the Atomic Scientists, 4(1), 1948, pp. 23–31.

Wendy, Martinez: How Science and Technology Developments Impact Employment and Education, Indiana University, Bloomington, 2018.

Bogdana Glovaţchi

The development and the usefulness of new technologies as part of the internet of things phenomenon

Abstract The Internet of Things (IoT) refers to a solution based on state-of-the-art technologies, through which anything and anyone can be connected at anytime and anywhere. Its use in practice has revolutionized the product idea as we knew it, by offering a wide range of innovative services and prospects for stable economic development. The aim of this article it to describe the Internet of Things phenomenon, analyze IoT conceptualizations and their implications. At the same time, the present paper proposes a synthesis of the development process of IoT technologies by explaining their adoption at the level of business organizations; by highlighting the main domains of implementation; and by suggesting future research directions.

Keywords: Internet of things, digital transformation, marketing

Introduction

In recent years we are witnessing an explosion of research regarding the phenomenon of the Internet of Things and its related technologies, as they significantly change the daily life of consumers and at the same time reshape the business activity of companies, in the context of their digital transformation.

Although the phenomenon itself is known and studied for over 20 years, the Internet of Things concept is constantly evolving, fact which stirs up both the interest of researchers and practitioners. In the beginning, the researchers were concerned more about understanding the phenomenon of the Internet of Things and its evolution. Nowadays, due to the digital transformation, which companies are going through, the interest of many researchers switched on the adoption, utility and use of IoT technologies in the activity of companies, in parallel with a rise in practitioners' focus on IoT implementation, as a way of ensuring stable business growth. The connection via the internet of any object or machine, leads the way for innovation to create business growth. Thus, it concerns organizations just entering the digital world, as well as those knocking on its doors.

The term "Internet-of-Things" (IoT), was first coined by Kevin Ashton in 2009 and, at that time, it described IoT as adding RFID (radio frequency identification) and other sensors to everyday objects. The term IoT has expanded its meaning over time, today is encompasses a network of entities connected by any kind of sensor, allowing these entities to be located, identified and even operated without human intervention.

By integrating IoT technologies, new business and market opportunities were identified (Miorandi, Sicari et al., 2012). Data collected through IoT sensors represents the main source of value creation. For instance, in the case of Manufacturing, these data plays a major role in increasing the operational efficiency of the machines and in reducing maintenance costs. Both the innovative hardware and the technologies involved in data transfer are the basis of the functioning of social networks, cloud computing, and smart devices, forming a vast network that supports IoT activities and data sharing in B2B marketing (Atzori et al., 2010)

The main objective of the present paper is to analyze the IoT technologies' implementation opportunities from a corporate perspective, by considering the complexity of the phenomenon, domains of technology use, as well as the problems specific to the organizations. The reason behind this research is the need to clarify the current stage of adoption and use of IoT and to reveal its future perspectives.

1. Internet of Things conceptualization and the implications

One of the most discussed current phenomena concerns digital transformation. In the age of the Internet of Things, it is obvious that the process of digital transformation through which the conversion of previously static and immobile information into dynamic information is carried out will have significant effects on the world in which we live. Through this disruptive process, unlimited possibilities, both negative and positive, will unlock and could result in a fundamental transformation of institutions and other socio-technical structures.

The expression "Internet-of-Things" (IoT) was first used by Kevin Ashton, who described the Internet of Things (IoT) as being possible to create by "[adding RFID (radio frequency identification) and other sensors to everyday objects]." The present meaning of the expression Internet of Things is currently used with reference to a network of entities connected by sensors, a situation in which these entities can be located, identified and even operated without human intervention. The entities that constitute the network, from everyday physical objects to complex machines with built-in computing devices, are interconnected via the Internet through the current technologies. The network of objects interconnected via the Internet is thus the framework in which between the component entities it is possible to carry out data transfer, at the same time they have the capacity to "think" and to "interact" thanks to the built-in computing devices, thus constituting dynamic service platforms.

From the perspective of marketing research, the Internet of Things represents a challenge, since it refers to an emerging area and involves interdisciplinary research, so in any research, at least one other discipline is needed. For clarification, we refer to the Marketing defined by the activity, the group of institutions and the processes of "creation, communication, delivery and exchange of offers that have value for customers, partners and society in general" (definition of AMA, Keefe, 2008).

Ng and Wakenshaw (2017) developed the 4 IoT conceptualizations based on theoretical ideas about: fluidization and density of information resources (Normann, 2001), digital materiality (Yoo et al., 2012), assembly systems (Hoffman, Novak, 2015) and service systems (Ng, 2010), as well as modularity and the transaction network (Baldwin, 2008). At the same time, the authors clarified the implications of the 4 conceptualizations, in order to expand the knowledge base of Marketing and to highlight the need for interdisciplinary research regarding the phenomenon of the Internet of Things. As a result, the authors have developed a comprehensive definition of the phenomenon called the Internet of Things.

Normann (2001) introduced the idea of fluidizing information resources in the sense of separating information from physical objects, thus allowing the manipulation and representation of information from various perspectives (Michel et al., 2008). The same authors explained the density as meaning "the best combination of resources to create an optimal value/cost result." In an IoT system, intelligent sensors that collect data from smart objects could provide rigorous real-time information and integrated into wireless networks will facilitate real-time monitoring and traceability of objects (Da Xu et al., 2014).

Digital materiality refers to the new functionalities that the embedded software confers on the physical object, by manipulating the digital representation (Yoo et al., 2012). As a result, objects with digital materiality will allow companies to monitor these objects, interact with them and change the behavior of these objects. The properties of these objects: senseability (context perception and context response), addressability and traceability, associability, communicability, programmability and memorability will ultimately facilitate the creation of value in different contexts, by increasing modularization and ensemble formation.

Hoffman and Novak (2015) described the assembly in IoT as a collection of interacting objects, having the ability to do things together that they would not do on their own. Ng (2014) highlighted the Internet of Things system as a human-centered smart service system.

Component objects in an IoT system can be viewed as modules of the system, having distinct capabilities, which gives the system the ability to reconfigure into contexts, allowing personalization and customization in relation to use (Ng et al., 2015). This implies that an IoT system can be augmented and can respond dynamically to changes in the environment, showing increased agility.

As a conclusion, Ng and Wakenshaw (2017) formulated a formal and integrative definition of the Internet of Things, as "a system with uniquely identifiable and connected components (called components connected to the Internet) capable of virtual representation and virtual accessibility leading to a structure similar to the Internet for locating, perceiving and operating remote in real-time of the constituents with data flows, which results in the system as a whole, which can be augmented to acquire a greater variety in results in a dynamic way, with increased agility." (Fig. 1).

In the light of these 4 conceptualizations of the Internet of Things, it is obvious that physical objects have been transformed from static products into service offerings, as Rust and Huang previously proposed (2014). Moreover, these service offerings are dynamically reconfigurable and allow customization by the users. The future of IoT will consist of socio-cyber-physical offers manifesting competencies and capabilities and will mean better service in context and on-demand, maximizing the density of resources (Lusch et al., 2010). At the same time, these flexible and adaptive services will be able to be integrated into platform thinking, in order to achieve scalability by standardizing key components and customization through a wide variety of peripheral components, as proposed Baldwin and Woodard (2011). Summarizing, in the context of the Internet of Things, physical goods are transformed into dynamic service platforms.

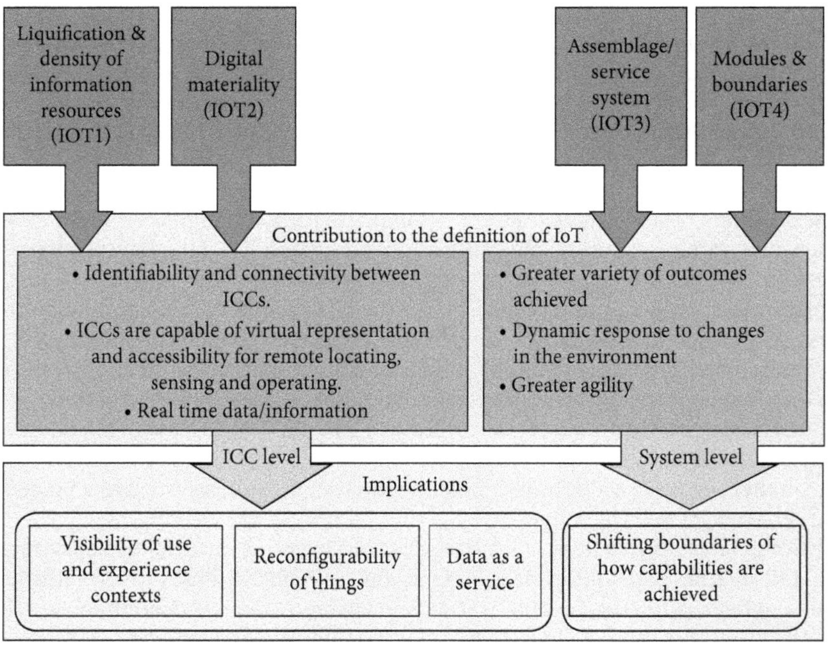

Fig. 1: Conceptualization, definition and implications ofIoT

Source: Ng & Wakenshaw, 2017, pp. 7.

In industrial contexts, IoT provides capabilities for control, coordination, and management of products, machines and infrastructure, which generates major, disruptive changes in everything that means value chains but also regarding existing business models. According to the authors of Dijkman et al., (2015), the basic elements of business model development in IoT-based ecosystems are value proposition (the source of opportunities that contribute to revenue flows), co-creation of value (all monetary benefits and nonmonetary attracting collaborators to the ecosystem) and the value network (relationship with key partners, customers and all stakeholders).

Regarding Internet of Things technologies, they did not in themselves determine their adoption on a large scale, but the markets in which they were offered and where they found their use. Therefore, it is necessary for marketing to be actively involved in clarifying and developing market mechanisms, involving interdisciplinary research to understand as clearly as possible the motivating benefits, but also the factors that inhibit the adoption of new technologies. Marketing research focused on the needs and desires of clients, involving also the co-creation of value, have the opportunity to actively contribute to the formation of new markets, through the design, configuration and location of markets (cf. Ng, 2014). An IoT era will convert physical and social spaces into hybrid socio-cyber-physical spaces, with multiple interactions, which will determine companies to create new platforms, with new possibilities for economic exchange and resources.

2. The development of the Internet of Things technologies

In the research conducted by Atzori et al. (2010), the authors stated that the term "Internet of Things" is used for those devices that have network connectivity and the ability to send or receive data and information to other connected objects. Later, Lee/Lee (2015) specified the five essential technologies of IoT involved in the realization of all IoT-based services and products: radio frequency identification (RFID), wireless sensor networks (WSN), middleware, cloud computing and software IoT applications.

Communications technologies have existed for several decades. However, the IoT era has brought very affordable chipsets and has taught customers that they can have everything connected. At the same time, equipment with communication modules embedded has already been made available on the market. In general, the adoption of technologies at the Consumer level favors their adoption in the Business area. In the case of the Wi-Fi technology, initially the companies were reluctant, invoking the security of the data, but when the Wi-Fi became ubiquitous outside the organizations, the requirement from the users who requested its implementation within the organizations was changed.

The existence of technologies, as well as the low price of chipsets, has led to the automatic implementation of IoT on all production lines. Cloud computing has developed significantly and has created new possibilities, the cloud services providing IT resources (servers, database storage) and software applications on-demand through the Internet using the "pay per use" model. In parallel, the increase in computing power and storage capacity through miniaturization of electronic components has led to a higher density of active elements, offering a greater capacity for processing and storing information.

The evolution of technologies has permanently reflected a balance between standardization and customization, as IT (Information Technology) standardization has allowed a massive reduction of prices, while customizing OT (Operational Technology) can generate valuable data that implies an economic growth relevant for business organizations. To date, a standard analytical solution does not exist, but it is an area in continuous research and development. Technologies that involve connecting machines and analytics are not a trend coming from the Consumer area, but they come from the need for business, in order to have the possibility to make predictive maintenance, centralized alarm, in order to prevent certain losses of resources, etc.

Over the last decade, IoT has developed with the help of flourish mobile technology and we can now see the rise in the number of IoT applications in the market.

Billions of IoT devices are already connected, Cisco reports say that by 2025 there would be around 75 billion. In such a scenario, it will be interesting to see the development of new performant IoT applications and their benefits to growth of the businesses. IoT is empowering the organizations to take controls to manage the operations advantageously accordingly finishing even the complex projects.

"First movers can obtain advantages through continual leadership in technology. Two basic mechanisms are considered in the literature: (1) advantages derived from the 'learning' or 'experience' curve and (2) success in patent or R&D races. In short, a company can launch a new product or service. Second, a company can adopt a new process. Finally, the company enters a new market that can claim this distinction. Considering one of the three ways achieve the above goal, most enterprises utilize IT to design a new business model in their markets or to improve process performance in their organizations. As in the argument above, we believe that the investment in IoT may also generate the same advantage for first movers in the IoT." (Tang et al., 2018)

3. Adoption and the use of the Internet of Things within organizations

The IoT indicates an extraordinary potential for changing the industrial environment and business processes and opening of new economic and market values (Santoro et al., 2018). In organizations, the value created by IoT systems and applications determines their adoption, for example in providing personalized services to their customers. (Del Giudice, 2018).

The adoption of the Internet of Things in organizations accelerates the creation of value and improves customer services, particularly from the perspective of the customer life cycle (CSLC), through the digital data flows resulting from the mass adoption of IoT devices. This real-time data flow is based on identifying, sensing, communicating and calculating the capabilities of IoT devices and represents a way to add value for organizations, involving the processing of information at every stage of the life cycle. Exploiting Internet of Things innovations at different stages, using the CSLC framework, means understanding customer requirements and preferences, improving distribution, and improving customer experience in use, tailored to current customer needs, including maintaining and completing transfer or removal needs after use. (Ives et al., 2016). Business operations can get accurate and direct feedback from the clients, bringing additional business opportunities and add-on services (Fleisch, 2010).

Before any company explores IoT opportunities, it should take a fresh look at the strategy, including the factors it considers when developing solutions. Developers of IoT solutions should focus on results, not technology, namely how a new application will improve market stability, financial performance for companies and convenience. At the same time, in addition to the technical aspects of adopting IoT technologies, companies will have to focus on coordinating activities along the value chain, as they will have to adapt their business models. It is a fact that the chances of adopting IoT technologies increase when they generate positive emotional reactions. As a result, technology developers, when developing new IoT offerings, will need to include in their offerings information on customer behavior, useful in creating products that drive strong positive feelings and accelerate adoption rates (Patel, 2017).

Most of the first IoT products were developed by the embedding of sensors or RFID tags into existing objects, thus facilitating the collection, processing, and management of information. Even if only a small number of applications and services were available, Atzori et al. (2010) stated that it is very difficult to predict the full potential impact of the IoT phenomenon, due to the ubiquitous nature and the extremely rapid evolution of the technologies that allow the realizing of a great diversity of activities, thus satisfying the diverse needs of the users.

Kim/Kim (2016) proposed an AHP (analytical hierarchy process) model to evaluate and compare the viability and perspective of a variety of IoT applications oriented to the customers, business and public-oriented. The model includes three main criteria: technological (technical functionality, technical reliability, cost efficiency, and standardization), market potential (market demand, user acceptance, business model and ecosystem building), and regulatory environment (industrial regulation, consumer protection, and government support). The market potential was classified as the most important factor, and its four sub-criteria occupied the first 4 positions in the AHP model. Also, by applying the AHP model, the researchers found that IoT logistics is the most successful IoT application, followed by the specific applications of IoT healthcare (healthcare) and the energy management in the IoT system respectively.

Tab. 1, adapted from Lu, Y. et al. (2018) summarizes IoT applications into 14 service domains, which can be categorized into four types depending on the target and the purpose of adoption. See also Fig. 2.

Tab. 1: IoT services and applications

	Application level	Service domains
1	Infrastructural level	Smart environment
2		Smart city
3		Smart energy
4		Smart tourism
5	Organizational level	Smart logistics and supply chain management
6		Smart agriculture
7		Industrial plants and manufacturing
8	Individual level	Smart home
9		Entertainment and gaming
10		Social networking
11		Smart safety
12	Public level	Smart transportation
13		Medical and healthcare
14		Education

Source: Lu, Y. et al. Technological Forecasting & Social Change 136 (2018), pp. 291

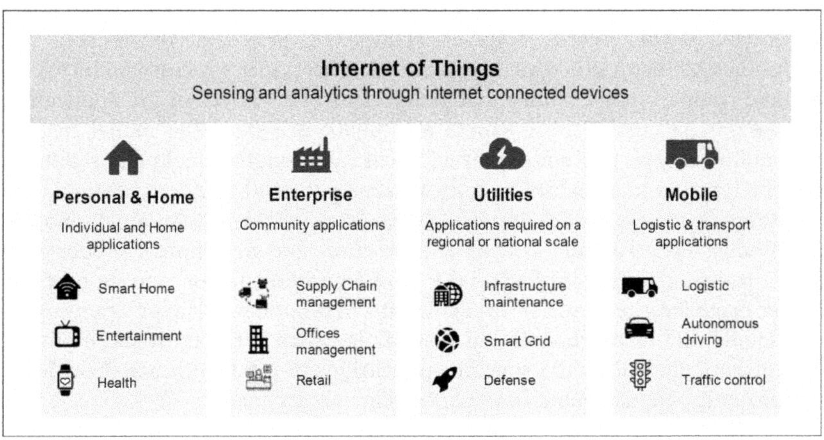

Fig. 2: Domains of IoT applications
Source: Adapted from Gubbi et al. (2013).

4. Conclusions

In this article we discussed what the IoT phenomenon is, what are the IoT conceptualizations and their implications, how the IoT technologies have evolved and their adoption in business organizations. At present, IoT is expanding at an unprecedented rate, and the data and information it communicates are becoming more accessible and more cost effective, in a very short time IoT will become highly successful in the marketplace.

The development of IoT applications for future industrial automation is an extremely promising topic in the industry and manufacture domain. Modern industrial companies are adopting IoT research to keep competitive advantages and to boost the growth of the global economy (Palattella, 2013).

Chui et al., (2018) suggest that companies still have many gaps regarding Internet of Things (IoT) capabilities: integrating IoT solutions by redesigning existing business processes, data management, identifying optimal cases and applications, analytical modeling, determining the context for the collected data, processing the data from sensors and machines. As a general feature, companies still often focus on an IoT project appropriate to a specific activity in the company. For successful integration of the IoT technologies into companies, organizations need to see the overall image of the company, including the organizational capabilities and change management programs needed to launch large-scale IoT initiatives. The fact is that in recent times more and more business leaders are beginning to understand and recognize the value of the IoT solutions and put more emphasis on building capabilities in organizations. Patel (2017) also state that reasons for optimism are also offered by recent infrastructure improvements, as well as the increased connectivity now available within the IoT. Similarly, technological advances reduce power requirements, lower costs, and promote the development of integrated IoT solutions.

IoT facilitates the development of new capabilities, from the perspective of management and control. The data generated through the IoT system gives decision-makers new ideas of potential value propositions, value creation, helping them to strengthen their relationship with customers and to adopt more effective policies and practices.

Based on IoT adoption rates, economic and demographic trends and likely technology developments over the next ten years, McKinsey Global Institute estimates that the economic impact of IoT applications could range from $ 3.9 trillion to $ 11.1 trillion. dollars per year in 2025 (Manyika et al., 2015).

Future research could explore what kind of capabilities need to be owned and developed in organizations, so that the adoption of IoT technologies can be deployed faster and easier, at the same time, the use of IoT solutions would generate a stable economic development.

References

Achrol, R.S.: "Changes in the theory of interorganizational relations in marketing toward a network paradigm", Research Article, https://doi.org/10.1177/0092070397251006, 1996

Achrol/Kotler: "Frontiers of the marketing paradigm in the third millennium", Journal of the Academic Marketing Science, 40, 2012, pp. 35–52.

Ahmed: "The role of big data analytics in Internet of Things", Computer Network, 2017, pp. 1–13.

Andal-Ancion, A. et al.: "The digital transformation of traditional businesses", MIT Sloan Management Review, 44 (4), 2003, pp. 34–41.

Ardito, Lorenzo et al.: "Mapping innovation dynamics in the Internet of Things domain: Evidence from patent analysis", Technological Forecasting & Social Change, 136, 2018, pp. 317–330.

Atzori, Luigi et al.: "The Internet of Things: A survey", Computer Networks, 54 (15), 2010, pp. 1–19.

Baldwin, C.Y.: "Where do transactions come from Modularity, transactions, and the boundaries of firms", Industrial Corporate Change, 17(1), 2008, pp.155–195.

Baldwin, C.Y./Woodard, J.C.: "The architecture of platforms: A unified view", Platforms, markets and innovation, Edward Elgar Publishing, 2011, pp.19–44.

Boyes, Hugh et al.: "The Industrial Internet of Things (IIoT): An analysis framework", Computers in Industry, 101, 2018, pp. 1–12.

Chui, M. et al.: "What it takes to get an edge in the Internet of Things", The McKinsey Quarterly, 2018.

Da Xu, L. et al.: "Internet of things in industries: A survey", Industrial Informatics, IEEE Transactions on, 10(4), 2014, pp. 2233–2243.

Del Giudice, P. et al.: "Disruptive technological change within knowledge-driven economies: The future of the Internet of Things (IoT)", Technological Forecasting and Social Change, 136, 2018, pp. 265–267.

Dijkman, Sprenkels/Peeters, Janssen: "Business models for the Internet of Things", International Journal of Information Management, 35, 2015, pp. 672–678.

Ehret, Michael/Wirtz, Jochen: "Unlocking value from machines: Business models and industrial internet of things", Journal of Marketing Management, 33, 2017, pp. 111–130.

Falkenrek/Wagner: "The Internet of Things Chance and challenge in industrial business", Industrial Marketing Management, 66, 2017, pp. 181–195.

Fleisch, E.: "What is the internet of things? An economic perspective", Economics, Management, and Financial Markets, 2010.

Gubbi, Jayavardhana et al.: "Internet of Things (IoT): A vision, architectural elements, and future directions", The University of Melbourne, 2013.

Hansen et al.: "Rapid adaptation in digital transformation a participatory process", MIS Quarterly Executive, University of Minesota, 10, 4, 2011, pp. 175–185.

Hoffman, D./Novak, T.: "Emergent experience and the connected consumer in the smart home assemblage and the internet of things", Research paper DOI:10.13140/RG.2.1.3966.1282, 2015.

Kim/Kim: "A multi-criteria approach toward discovering killer IoT application in Korea", Technological Forecasting and Social Change, 102, 2016, pp. 143–155.

Keefe, L.M.: "Marketing defined", Marketing News, 42(1), 2008, pp. 28–29.

Ives, B.: "Enhancing Customer Service through the Internet of Things and Digital Data Streams", MIS Quarterly Executive, 15 (4), 2016, pp. 279–297.

Lee, I./Lee, K.: "The Internet of Things (IoT): Applications, investments, and challenges for enterprises", Business Horizons, 2015.

Lu et al.: "Internet of Things: A systematic review of the business literature from the user and organisational perspectives", Technological Forecasting & Social Change, 136, 2018, p. 285–297.

Lusch,R. et al.: "Service, value networks and learning", Journal of the Academy of Marketing Science, 38(1), 2010, pp. 19–31.

Ly, Pham Thi et al.: "Fuzzy AHP analysis of Internet of Things (IoT) in enterprises", Technological Forecasting & Social Change, 136, 2018, pp. 1–13.

Manyika, J. et al.: "An executive's guide to the Internet of Things", McKinsey Quarterly, 2015.

Michel, S. et al.: "Reconfiguration of the conceptual landscape: A tribute to the service logic of Richard Normann", Journal of the Academy of Marketing Science, 36, 2008, pp. 152–55.

Miorandi, Daniele; Sicari, Sabrina et al.: "Internet of things: Vision, applications and research challenges", AD HOC Networks, 10, 2012, pp 1497–1516.

McKinsey: "Mapping the value belind the Hype", Executive_summary, June 2015.

Ng, I.: "The Future of Pricing and Revenue Models", Journal of Revenue and Pricing Management, 9(3), 2010, pp. 276–281.

Ng, I.: "Creating new markets in the digital economy: Value and worth", Cambridge: Cambridge University Press, 2014.

Ng, I. et al.: "Contextual variety, internet- of- things and the choice of tailoring over platform: Mass customisation strategy in supply chain management", International Journal of Production Economics, 159, 2015, pp. 76–87.

Ng, Irene/Wakenshaw, Susan: "The Internet-of-Things review and research directions", International Journal of Research in Marketing, 34, 2017, pp. 3–21.

Ngyuen et al.: "Information technology adoption in small business confirmation of a proposed framework", Journal of Small Business Management, 53(1), 2015, pp. 207–227.

Nguyen, Bang/Simkin, Lyndon: "The Internet of Things (IoT) and marketing: The state of play, future trends and the implications for marketing", Journal of Marketing Management, 33(1–2), 2017, pp. 1–6.

Normann, R: "Reframing business: When the map changes the landscape", Chichester: John Wiley, 2001.

Palattella, M.R.: "Decentralized traffic aware scheduling for multi-hop low power lossy networks in the internet of things", IEEE, 2013.

Patel, M.: "The future of connectivity: Enabling the Internet of Things", High Tech December 2017, The McKinsey Quarterly.

Rust, R. T., & Huang, M. H.: "The service revolution and the transformation of marketing science", Marketing Science, 33(2), 2014, pp. 206–221.

Santoro, G. et al.: "The Internet of Things: Building a knowledge management system for open innovation and knowledge management capacity", Technological Forecasting and Social Change, 136, 2018, pp. 347–354

Tang et al.: "The impact of Internet of things implementation on firm performance", Telematics and Informatics, 35, 2018, pp. 2038–2053.

Woodside, Arch/Sood, Suresh: "Vignettes in the two-step arrival of the internet of things and its reshaping of marketing management's service-dominant logic", Journal of Marketing Management, 33, 2016, pp. 98–110.

Yoo et al.: "The next wave of digital innovation: opportunities and challenges", A report of an NSF Research Workshop on Digital Challenges in Innovation Research, 2010.

Irina Băncescu

Household income polarization across Europe

Abstract Income inequality has risen over the past decades affecting the economy in many ways some of which being still unknown. However, income inequality is not the only one that increase, old-age dependency ratio also increased. In this paper, we discuss and analyze the connection between income inequality and old-age dependency ratio for cities, towns and rural areas of European Union. Results show that old-age dependency ratio has increased in all living area in every European Union country. Number of countries with low (in absolute value) or positive absolute income gap (meaning the mean income of over 65 years old population is greater or close to the mean income of 18 to 64 years old population) has increased during 2009–2018 period, putting a significant pressure on the pension system.

Key words: Income inequality, aging population, demography change, absolute income gap

Introduction

Last decades have been marked by rising income inequality and poverty which can potentially lead to riots, the gap between the rich and the poor being at its highest level. And it is not the only problem faced by societies in the last decades. Old-age dependency ratio also increased.

Aging population (due to an increase in longevity and decrease in fertility rates) is a major problem that needs to be addressed accordingly and fast. An aging population is associated with lower savings and higher government spending (Fougère et al. 2009, Aigner-Walder and Döring 2012). Furthermore, an increased old-age dependency ratio will reduce labor force productivity and participation (Murphy and Welch 1990).

Spatial/regional income inequality is of importance in the social and economic development of a country. Economic and social convergence is an objective of the European Union (EU). Romania has areas with low economic development and areas with high economic development (Bucharest-Ilfov and West regions, for example). For this reason, in this paper, we analyze the old-age dependency ratio and the absolute income gap between working population (aged 18 to 64 years) and retired population (over 65 years) who lives in cities, towns and suburbs, and rural areas. Analysis is performed using hierarchical clustering.

This paper is organized as follows. In Section 1, a literature review is discussed. Section 2 is dedicated to methodology, while in Section 3 we present and discuss the results. The paper ends with a conclusion.

1. Literature review

Income inequality drivers and effects have been long investigated, but yet, there is still room for more research on the matter with new insights into the complex labor market, regulations and income distributions on the bases of new income inequality measures or complex modelling (Acemoglu 2002, Piketty 2003, Piketty and Qian 2009, Militaru and Stanila 2015, Anghel 2017, Cohen and Ladaique 2018). One long debated policy for reducing income inequality is the redistribution of income in the form of an effective tax-transfer system. However, the redistributive capacity of the tax-transfer system depends on the characteristics of the system itself and also the shape of market income distribution given for most people by wages and salaries (Chivu et al. 2015a, 2015b, Herault and Azpitarte 2016).

Demographic changes and income inequality were investigated by many researchers, addressing essential issues and questions whether there is a connection, and if it is what is the magnitude of the effect and in which direction, and what can we do to properly mitigate the problem (Dahan and Tsiddan 1998, Miyazawa 2006, Rougoor and Van Marrewijk 2015, Dong et al. 2018).

Zhong (2011) has analyzed the impact of population aging on income inequality in rural areas of China and found that a significant portion of the increase of income inequality can be attributed to demographic change.

In 2019, Dolls et al. examined the effect of structural demographic changes expected by 2030 on income inequality and found that these demographic changes is anticipated to increase income inequality, Romania being one of the most affected countries along Finland, Slovakia, Denmark and Sweden.

In Baltics, Navicke (2017) showed that demographic changes has little effect on inequality.

2. Methodology

Estimators of income inequality are the absolute income and relative income gaps. In this paper, income inequality generated by population aging in cities, towns and suburbs and rural areas across European Union is investigated. This income inequality is estimated by the absolute income gap between mean income of 18 to 64 years old population and mean income of over 65 years old population. Hence, we are capturing the effect of demography changes on income inequality. Data are provided by the Eurostat database.

Absolute income gap is defined by the following formulae

Absolute income gap = mean income of population over 65 years old - mean income of 18 to 64 years old population

Old-age dependency ratio is determined for every country of EU for areas defined as cities, towns and suburbs and rural areas. Old-age dependency ratio is given by the ratio of number of population over 65 years over the number of population between 15 and 65 years old, as percentage. As the population is getting older the percentage is greater.

Based on these two indicators, a hierarchical clustering is performed. The clusters are determined using Ward's method of minimum variance which is an alternative to single-link clustering suitable for detecting outliers. Ward's algorithm, in general, constructs compact and even-sized clusters (Murtagh and Legendre 2014).

Starting with n clusters of size 1, the algorithm combines them into bigger clusters, so these new clusters have minimum variance (given by the sum of squares index). The distance between clusters is the Euclidean distance.

The Euclidean distance between two vectors $x = (x_1, x_2, ..., x_n)$ and $y = (y_1, y_2, ..., y_n)$ is defined as

$$d(x, y) = \sum_{j=1}^{n} \left((x_j - y_j)^2\right)^{\frac{1}{2}}$$

However, since the two indicators for clustering analysis are measured by different units, we need to normalize the data using min/max normalization

$$x_s = x_i - \min(x) / (\max(x) - \min(x))$$

where x_s is the normalized value of x_i.

The optimal number of clusters in determined using function NbClust() from R studio.

3. Old-age dependency ratio and income polarization across Europe

In this section, we present and discuss the clustering results for EU for 2009–2018 period.

Firstly, we observe that old-age dependency ratio for 2009–2018 period has increased for all EU countries. Based on the definition of living areas this increased can be notice also in cities, towns and suburbs, as well as rural area. Studies have shown that more and more individuals are living in urban areas than in rural areas, leaving behind an aged population having as consequence a low economic development in those areas. Therefore, spatial income inequality can increase and generate a greater polarization into societies.

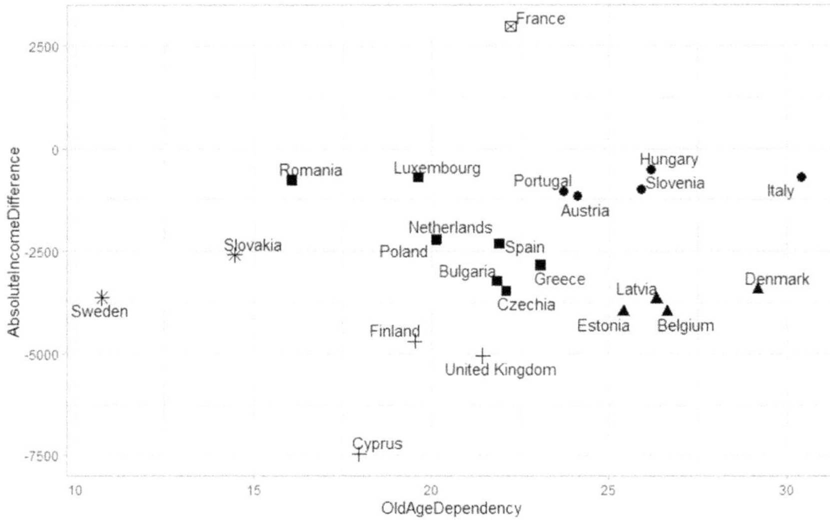

Fig. 1: Clustering results for year 2009 for EU cities. Source: Author's own calculations based on Eurostat data.

In 2009, France had the highest old-age dependency ratio among EU state members in cities, displaying also a positive absolute income gap, meaning the mean income of over 65 years old population was greater than the mean income of 18 to 64 years old population. In other words, the mean income of the collective retired individuals living in cities was greater than the mean income of the working force in France living in cities. There is significant pressure on the pension system. Unfortunately, this is not the only example of positive or low absolute income gap (Figs. 1–6).

In 2009, there were 7, 2 and 4 countries, respectively which exhibit a low (in absolute value) or positive absolute income gap in cities, towns and rural areas, respectively, which during 2009–2018 period increased, being 10, 10 and 10 countries, respectively in 2018.

Relative to other EU countries, in 2009, Romania has a low old-age dependency in cities, however its absolute income gap is low which may cause friction within the Romanian society. The lowest old-age dependency in cities, in 2009, was in Sweden.

France continued to display a low absolute income gap in cities in 2018 while its old-age dependency ratio increased. Slovenia, Portugal, Italy, Greece, Spain, Poland and Hungary were clustered together and are characterized by a high old-age dependency ratio and low absolute income gap (in absolute value).

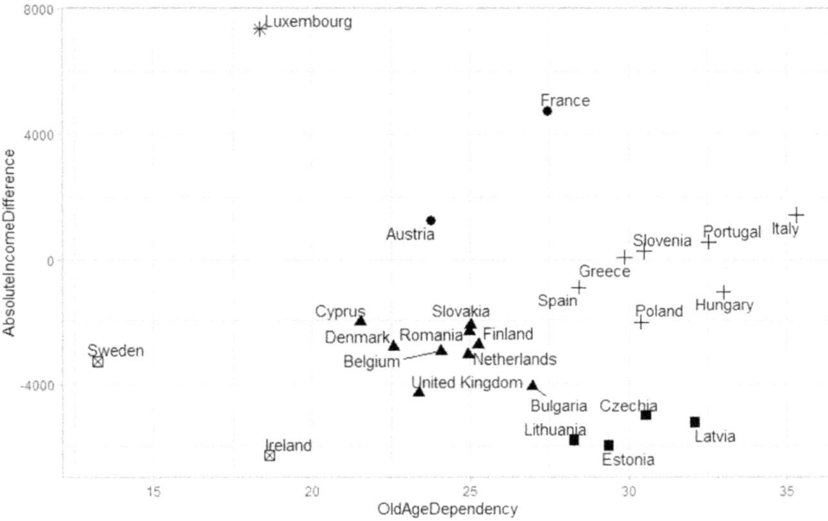

Fig. 2: Clustering results for year 2018 for EU cities. Author's own calculations based on Eurostat data.

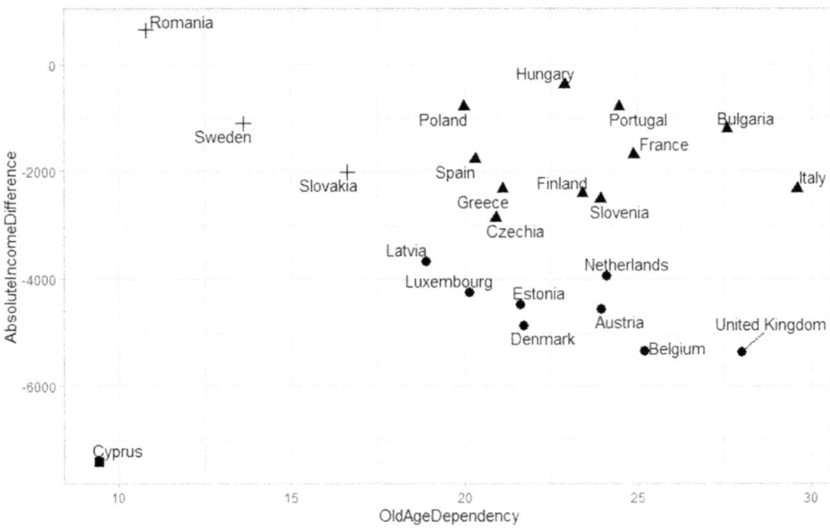

Fig. 3: Clustering results for year 2009 for EU towns and suburbs. Author's own calculations based on Eurostat data.

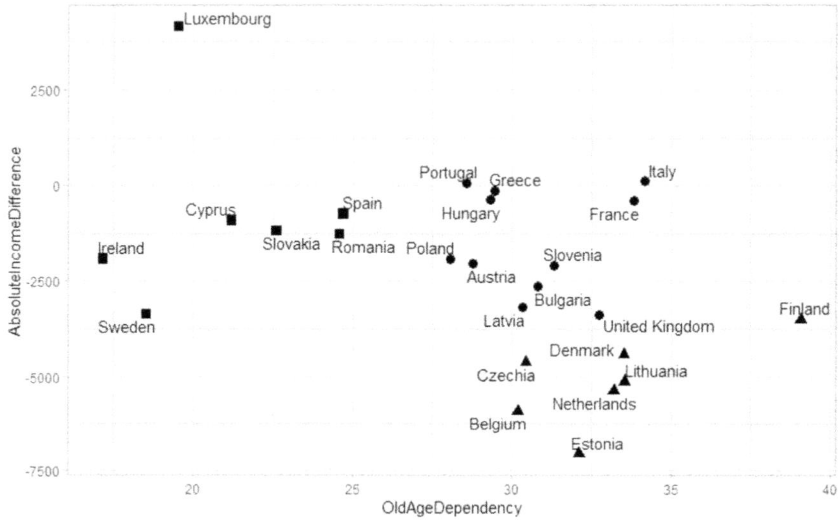

Fig. 4: Clustering results for year 2018 for EU towns and suburbs. Author's own calculations based on Eurostat data.

In towns and suburbs, the old-age dependency ratio is greater than the old-age dependency ratio in cities, in 2018, young people preferring to live in cities where there are more work opportunities. In 2009, Cyprus and Romania have the lowest age-old dependency ratio in towns, while Italy, Bulgaria and Belgium have the highest old-age dependency ratio (Figs. 3 and 4)

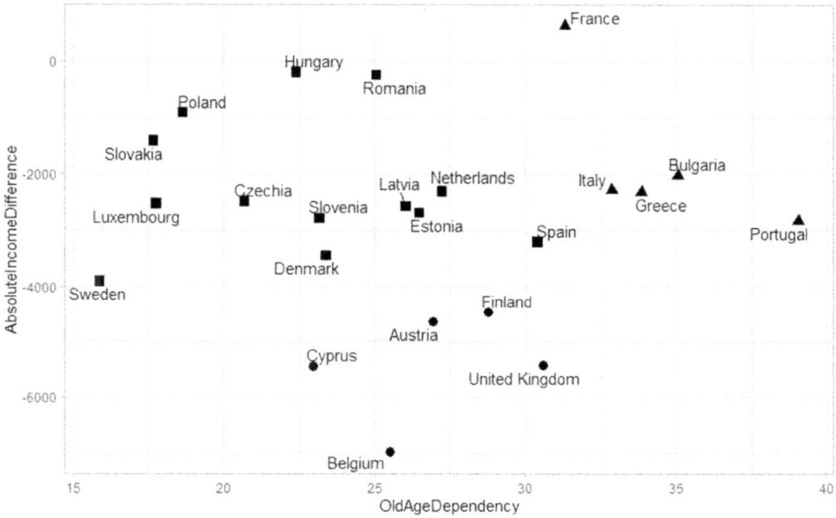

Fig. 5: Clustering results for year 2009 for EU rural areas. Author's own calculations based on Eurostat data.

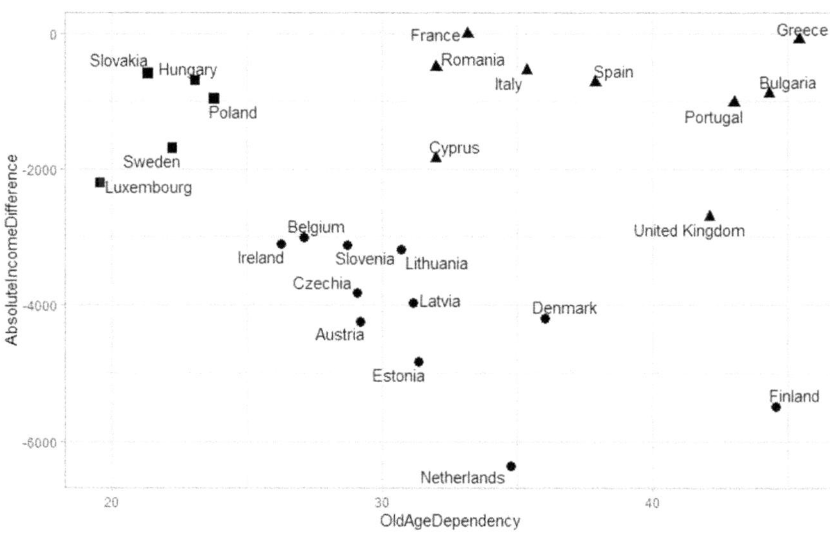

Fig. 6: Clustering results for year 2018 for EU rural areas. Author's own calculations based on Eurostat data.

France has an old-age dependency ratio of (over 30 %) in the rural areas in 2009, while having a low absolute income gap in absolute value. Romania has also a low absolute income gap in the rural areas, but a lower old-age dependency ratio. In 2018, in all rural areas the old-age dependency ratio has increased as well as the absolute income gap in absolute value.

Number of clusters from 2009 to 2018 are the same, except for towns where in 2009 the optimal number of clusters is 4, while in 2018 is 3. Furthermore, we can observe more compact (the variance within clusters has decreased) and better delimited clusters in 2018 as oppose from 2009. With proper policies some countries have managed to overcome these problems of society.

Conclusions

Old-age dependency ratio has increased in all living areas in every EU country, defined as cities, towns and suburbs, and rural areas. France has a low absolute income gap in absolute value in all living areas, in 2018, meaning the mean income of over 65 years old population is greater or close to the mean income of 18 to 64 years old population (which represent the working force of a society). There is significant pressure on the pension system. Unfortunately, this is not the only example of positive or low absolute income gap, Romania being on of them. In 2009, there were 7, 2 and 4 countries, respectively which exhibit a low (in absolute value) or positive absolute income gap in cities, towns and rural areas, respectively, which increased to 10, 10 and 10 countries, respectively in 2018.

References

Acemoglu, Daron: "Technical change, inequality, and the labor market". Journal of Economic Literature, 40(1), 2002, pp. 7–72.

Aigner-Walder, Birgit; Döring, Thomas: "The effects of population ageing on private consumption—A simulation for Austria based on household data up to 2050". Eurasian Economic Review, 2(1), 2012, pp. 63–80.

Anghel, Ionuţ-M.: "Measuring income inequality: Comparative datasets and methodological deficiencies. An overview of income inequality in Romania during postsocialism". Social Change Review, 15(1–2), 2017, pp. 55–82.

Chivu, Luminiţa; Ciutacu, Constantin; Georgescu, Laurenţiu: "Consequences of wage gaps in the EU". Procedia Economics and Finance, 22, 2015a, pp. 141–147.

Chivu, Luminiţa; Ciutacu, Constantin; Georgescu, Laurenţiu: "Household income in Romania. A challenge to economic and social cohesion". Procedia Economics and Finance, 22, 2015b, pp. 398–401.

Cohen, Guillaume; Ladaique, Maxime: "Drivers of growing income inequalities in OECD and European countries". In: Renato Miguel Carmo/Cédric Rio/Márton Medgyesi (eds.): Reducing inequalities. Palgrave Macmillan, Cham, 2018, pp. 31–43.

Dahan, Momi; Tsiddon, Daniel: "Demographic transition, income distribution, and economic growth". Journal of Economic growth, 3(1), 1998, pp. 29–52.

Dolls, Mathias; Doorley, Karina; Paulus, Alari; Schneider, Hilmar; Sommer, Eric: "Demographic change and the European income distribution". The Journal of Economic Inequality, 17(3), 2019, pp. 337–357.

Dong, Zhiqiang; Tang, Canqing; Wei, Xiahai: "Does population aging intensify income inequality? Evidence from China". Journal of the Asia Pacific Economy, 23(1), 2018, pp. 66–77.

Fougère, Maxime; Harvey, Simon; Mercenier, Jean; Mérette, Marcel: "Population ageing, time allocation and human capital: A general equilibrium analysis for Canada". Economic Modelling, 26(1), 2009, pp. 30–39.

Herault, Nicolas; Azpitarte, Francisco: "Understanding changes in the distribution and redistribution of income: A unifying decomposition framework". Review of Income and Wealth, 62(2), 2016, pp. 266–282.

Militaru, Eva; Stanila, Larisa: "Income variability in Romania: Decomposing income inequality by household characteristics". Procedia Economics and Finance, 26, 2015, pp. 227–233.

Miyazawa, Kazutoshi: "Growth and inequality: A demographic explanation". Journal of Population Economics, 19(3), 2006, pp. 559–578.

Murphy, Kevin M.; Welch, Finis: "Empirical age-earnings profiles". Journal of Labor Economics, 8(2), 1990, pp. 202–229.

Murtagh, Fionn; Legindre Pierre: "Ward's hierarchical agglomerative clustering method: which algorithms implement Ward's criterion?". Journal of classification, 31(3), 2014, pp. 274–295.

Navicke, Jekaterina: "Factors of the income inequality in the Baltics: Income, policy, demography". EUROMOD Working Paper, EM11/17, 2017.

Piketty, Thomas: "Income inequality in France, 1901–1998". Journal of Political Economy, 111(5), 2003, pp. 1004–1042.

Piketty, Thomas; Qian, Nancy: "Income inequality and progressive income taxation in China and India, 1986–2015". American Economic Journal: Applied Economics, 1(2), 2009, pp. 53–63.

Rougoor, Ward; Van Marrewijk, Charles: "Demography, growth, and global income inequality". World Development, 74, 2015, pp. 220–232.

Zhong, Hai: "The impact of population aging on income inequality in developing countries: Evidence from rural China". China Economic Review, 22(1), 2011, pp. 98–107.

Biljana Petrevska, Aleksandra Terzić, Marija Drobnjaković

Fighting with depopulation of rural areas: can tourism be a way out?

Abstract This study samples several selected villages in North Macedonia and Southeast Serbia, which have been considered particularly vulnerable to the process of depopulation caused by different factors, mainly by aging and out-migration. Deteriorated age and economic population structure indicate the shrinkage of the observed rural areas. But, should the shrinkage be ignored or can an appropriate model for slowing the depopulation down be found? The paper discusses the issue of depopulation in rural areas, and opens the question of preparedness for struggle by introducing tourism activities in villages with appropriate potential. Poor agricultural practices may be slowly and gradually shifted to new alternatives in overcoming the poor incomes and low production in order to keep the youth and working-age population, which has eroded the vitality of rural areas. Thus, rural tourism development is seen as a compatible and prospective economic activity that may encourage diversification of rural activities. The overall aim of the paper is to present a theoretical approach on the issue related to tourism-based economies within rural areas. At the same time, the authors put an accent on the possibility to cope with uncertainty like the global demographic and cultural changes. The paper offers the rural tourism as a model for boosting the local economy through the sampled rural destinations in both countries – that may serve as a good practice example. Hence, rural tourism development is considered to be a long-term solution for preventing further abandonment consequently encouraging the vitality of sparsely populated rural areas.

Keywords: rural areas, tourism, depopulation

Introduction

Today, numerous rural areas in Europe, and particularly in Southeastern Europe, are faced with many challenges and confront ever growing global changes that influence their future existence. They are usually among the less-developed within the country's region being heavily dependent on natural resources and agriculture, but also in some parts of the developed countries faced with aging. The outcome is a weak rural economy due to low production and income associated with an unemployment, aging, extreme emigration and rapid abandonment of rural areas. The population is constantly decreasing generally as a result of aging process and emigration of the young, the most active and reproductive groups, as well as females, which has eroded the vitality of the rural settlements and communities. Not only that rural-urban migration pattern occurs, the international migration is also current and very intensive trend. The process in general starts with the rural areas reflecting in the extreme levels of deprivation and poverty, outdated technologies, low educational levels, low entrepreneurship and underdeveloped infrastructure and communal services. Hence, the need for creating survival strategies is listed as the top priority for rural communities.

This paper introduced tourism activities as a way out, particular in rural areas that have tourism potential to use and enhance the existing resources, provide some economic effects, inject capital and motivate the locals. This concept may indicate more prosperous future developments, provide productive alternative and ensure certain levels of livelihood sustainability, particularly in a long-term. So, developing rural tourism becomes a global trend that is constantly growing faster than traditional mass tourism, with realistic expectations whose share in the European tourism market in the next 20 years will reach 20 % (Gašić & Ivanović, 2018; Maksimović, et al., 2015). As a complementary activity to the traditional rural ones, tourism encourages diversification of rural economic activities. Moreover, it is considered to be an additional income for the households, and as a new source of income to the agriculture and livestock.

The paper aims to present a theoretical approach on the issue of contribution of tourism-based economies within rural communities by mitigating the profound negative global demographic and cultural changes. By discussing the cases of several sampled villages in North Macedonia and South-east Serbia which are particularly vulnerable in terms of a depopulation trend, the paper argues the necessity of introducing tourism activities in rural areas with tourism potential, as a way out for saving them from disappearing from the map.

1. Literature review

There is a large body of literature that elaborates the interconnectivity between the rural areas and tourism development. Many academics argue that rural areas with their unique landscapes offer attractions to tourists to distinct the ways of life and culture, and can be seen as places for relaxation and escape from the overcrowded and stressful urban life, pure environment, finding mental peacefulness or even trying to gain a sense of balance (Dong et al., 2013; George et al., 2009; Mak et al., 2009; Urry, 2002). In past two decades, tourism is recognized as a potential and favorite one tool, but still unorganized reaction for managing and achieving a development of rural areas in this part of the Europe (Todorovic & Bjeljac, 2007; Tošić, 2011). Furthermore, Middleton and Clarke (2001), Bærenholdt et al. (2004), Popescu (2013) and Tuohino (2015) note that rural areas serve as necessary preconditions for creating a tourism product, since resource itself is not a product. Moreover, rurality is the fundamental attraction of the countryside as rural tourism destination (Crouch, 2006; Jepson & Sharpley, 2015; Lukić, 2013).

On the other hand, there are numerous authors who put an accent on the long list of factors affecting the sustainability of rural areas. The worldwide transformations in economic and social tradition structure lead mostly to global resource depletion and pollution, reduce the farmstead returns, change the traditional rural values increasing the social and cultural divergence and affecting the local values and ways of living (Theodoropoulou & Panagiotis, 2008). This resulted in high rates of unemployment, mass migrations of productive forces and demographic misbalance in rural areas (Gallent et al., 2008; Khaleel & Ngah, 2013).

2. Background material: facts and figures

North Macedonia has 2,075,301 inhabitants out of which 17.6 % live in pure rural municipalities, 99.5 % of rural economy encompasses individual rural enterprises, and 27.1 % of poor population live in rural areas. From 1,767 settlements, only 34 are urban while 1,733 are rural settlements. Serbia has 7,186,862 inhabitants (census 2011) and 59.4 % of them live in urban settlements (3,6 % of all settlements). South-east Serbia is considered to be the poorest and the most underdeveloped part of the country with 1,563,916 inhabitants of which 47.8 % live in 1,806 rural settlements. On the other hand, agricultural population share in this region is around 8 % and experiencing high decrease levels (in 2002 was 11.3 %).

Both countries have unique and well-preserved natural resources, a large number of traditional rural households and much supplementary potential, in this manner imposing great challenges for rural tourism development (Namicev et al., 2018; Terzić et al., 2019). Early 2000s are noted as years of beginnings of the rural tourism development in both countries, generally initiated by donor funded projects. From a legislative point of view, the issue of rural tourism generally is well covered by many laws and by-laws, as well as many strategic documents. Furthermore, municipalities in both countries have developed strategic documents on a local level, for example local economic development strategies, local action plans, annual programs, as well as various base-line studies and documents for developing specific tourism forms for the destinations. Many key institutions on various levels are responsible for the rural development issue in both countries, on central, regional and local level.

One of the main problems of rural areas in both countries is the mass migration towards cities which started almost parallel with urbanization and industrialization process, just after the World War II, reaching its peak by the end of 1970s. Although some were forced to return to the villages of origin due to the industrial collapse in the 1990s and the search for bare existence, the majority stayed in the big cities. Those who returned were engaged mostly in a small-scale agriculture and cattle breading, as well as in providing tourist services (accommodation, food, gastronomic products, and souvenirs). Yet, the young people are continuously leaving the small and economically drained rural areas and look for a proper employment. So, the redistribution of the population in North Macedonia and South-east Serbia is an ongoing process, with inevitable consequences for the small villages, the agricultural production and the vitality of population including the quality of living.

3. Methodology

The field research conducted between September 2018 and September 2019, was a primary source of data derived from a community-based research and evaluation (CBRE) approach. By adding the comprehensive and conceptual literature review, a rapid assessment was made on the selected rural areas. The sample consisted of 9 locations and 23 villages, out of which 5 destinations and 14 villages are in North Macedonia (Fig. 1a) and 4 destinations and 9 villages are in South-east Serbia (Fig. 1b).

Fig. 1a: Sampled villages in North Macedonia
Source: Nations Online Project.

Having its roots in the action research that entails participatory methodologies in the process of creating knowledge for growth and change, the CBRE approach enabled both, the authors as academic researchers and the local residents of the sampled rural areas as community members, jointly to discuss the community-related issues. As such, the quality and the quantity of the collected data is remarkably enhanced. The information used in the study is based on a first-hand experience of the authors, generated through observations and many informal interviews and discussions with local residents, with an aim to assess the possibility of implementing rural tourism initiatives and activities.

Fig. 1b: Sampled villages in South-east Serbia

Source: Nations Online Project.

3. Discussion and findings

The data presented in Tabs. 1 and 2 are obtained from secondary sources (official censuses) for North Macedonia and Serbia, supplemented with additional data collected from a field survey assessment upon interviews with local inhabitants during 2019, in the selected villages.

Tab. 1 presents the data on population in the sampled villages in North Macedonia. The data are obtained from the censuses carried out in 1948, 1961, 1994 and 2002 according to unified methodologies and forms for all census areas. It is noticeable that all selected villages are struggling demographically to survive. The population decline in all observed settlements is evident. In the period of 1948–2019 for some settlements the population decline is very intensive and they are struggling with a pronounced depopulation.

During the sample period of 71 years, they suffered an enormous out-migration leading to almost total depopulation. The last column of Tab. 1 presents the exponential growth rate showing how much each sampled village has lost of its population each year during the sampled period. The percentage spreads between 2–7 % per year, leading to constant depopulation over 7 decades. This means that these, and many similar small villages throughout North Macedonia, are highly depressed and depopulated and almost wiped off the map.

Tab. 1: Population in the sampled villages in North Macedonia*, 1948–2019

Destination	Villages	Population					Population
		1948[1]	1961[1]	1994[1]	2002[1]	2019[2]	decline (%) 1948–2019
1	B's	183	186	74	63	25	-2.76
	Varovište	213	192	108	87	35	-2.51
2	Konsko	111	19	0	2	2	-5.50
	Sermenin	619	502	18	18	10	-5.64
	Huma	380	44	0	2	2	-7.12
3	Velmevci	619	227	18	7	7	-6.12
	Golemo Ilino	618	412	81	52	15	-5.10
	Železnec	385	311	86	57	18	-4.22
4	Janče	375	165	155	146	50	-2.80
	Tresonče	147	184	10	8	3	-5.33
	Gari	539	454	33	10	5	-6.38
5	Nežilovo	319	333	82	63	30	-3.27
	Oreše	796	871	296	202	40	-4.12
	Papradište	612	716	4	7	15	-5.09

Note: *The censuses were carried out in: 1921, 1931, 1948, 1953, 1961, 1971, 1981, 1991, 1994 and 2002. Yet, for some censuses the definitions are different, so some census results are not presented due to their incomparability;

Source: [1]State Statistical Office of the Republic of North Macedonia (various years). Official census of population. [2]Field survey assessment.

Tab. 2 presents facts for the sampled villages in South-east Serbia, where a similar situation is detected. Over the years, almost all selected villages were faced with a high redistribution of the population leaving the rural areas highly depopulated and economically drained.

Tab. 2: Population in sampled villages in South-east Serbia*, 1948–2019

Destination	Villages	Population							Population
		1948[1]	**1961[1]**	**1981[1]**	**1991[1]**	**2002[1]**	**2011[1]**	**2019[2]**	**decline (%) 1948–2019**
1	Rogljevo	633	574	351	258	183	123	80	-2.87
	Smedovac	528	499	327	255	163	112	70	-2.81
2	Balta Berilovac	618	548	341	256	187	133	120	-2.28
	Jalovik Izvor	2,151	1,713	734	396	238	111	100	-4.23
3	Gostuša	1,308	1,050	533	269	139	70	50	-4.49
	Visočka Ržana	561	516	144	101	54	23	7	-5.99
	Slavinja	403	285	123	81	49	39	30	-3.59
4	Poganovo	1,067	763	266	133	77	31	25	-5.15
	Vlasi	710	527	188	138	71	42	30	-4.36

Note: *The censuses were carried out in: 1948, 1953, 1961, 1971, 1981, 1991, 2002 and 2011.

Source: [1]Data from official census; [2]Field survey assessment.

Based on Tabs. 1 and 2, one may conclude that some heavy impacts of negative processes of aging and rural-urban migration patterns are particularly noted during the years in both countries. Along with the expansion of the industrial production, urban centers dramatically emerged thus attracting the low educated rural population from the villages. Very slowly but gradually the mind-set of the villagers who immigrated to the cities, has transformed by adapting to the urban life style, reaching its peak by the end of 1990s. At the same time, by raising the educational levels, young people tend to leave the small communities and migrate to big cities to find proper employment. So, redistribution of the population is an ongoing process, with inevitable consequences for the small villages, the agricultural production and rural economy, the vitality of population and the quality and culture of living.

During the field survey, it was found out that some of the sampled villages already practice various activities interesting for visitors. Moreover, many other were identified as potential activities that may easily be further introduced, such as: cheese-making at a local goat/sheep farm, giving cooking classes on local traditional dishes, or doing some traditional activities like knitting, herbs and plants picking and making personal organic cosmetic products, bird watching, photo sessions in the nature, self-aromatherapy hours and weekends, traditional fishing, walk to natural waterfalls and caves, hiking and mountain climbing with a tour guide, donkey-ride, jeep safari to hunting reserves, etc. Tourism-based activities are slowly developing as a significant injection to the local entrepreneurship.

In case of practicing small scale rural tourism activities, one may expect gradually to become an important activity often promoting employment, vitality and sustainability of rural areas (Hall et al., 2003; Kneafsey, 2000). As in Brandth and Haugen (2011), it was found that sampled villages may create businesses with characteristics of repeasantization, in which products are developed incrementally from the rural resources, thus keeping strong links to the past. This was already discussed by Dimitrov and Petrevska (2012), Petrevska and Dimitrov (2013), and Petrevska et al., (2019) along with the arguments for defining and implementing measures and activities on central and local level which may raise initiatives for strengthening and enhancing the existing status of rural tourism.

It should be noted that during the summertime and holiday season, and especially when some local event is organized, the number of inhabitants in these villages grows significantly, due to the fact that most of real-estates are considered to be second-homes or holiday-homes (weekend houses). Most are inherited and used for personal tourism and recreation activities only, but few were also adapted and offered for tourists. Yet, the number of tourists is still very low in most villages, with a growing tendency.

Conclusion

The research revealed shocking facts that the evaluated villages are literally "dying," since some of them have noted a decrease in the number of inhabitants for more than 60 % over a 40-year period of time. Moreover, since 1948 the population has rapidly decreased in these village for 80–90 %. Furthermore, the study found out that the sampled rural areas in North Macedonia and South-east Serbia possess many resources that may attract tourists, like nature and landscape, the climate, culture, history, the possibility of engagement in various hobbies and activities, and accessibility.

However, upon the field survey it was detected that a modernization of the infrastructure, accommodation capacities and variability of services is inevitable, as well as minor social and cultural changes. On the other hand, as found by Sharpley (2002) and Dissart et al., (2009), the availability of tourist infrastructure does not automatically lead to development of rural areas. Among others, the diversification of rural economy from farming (productive) into tourism (service based) is considered to be a fundamental cultural change that needs to be undertaken in the selected rural areas. In addition, one must note – the rural tourism cannot be treated as a tool or a solution for structural problems that sampled villages are facing with, since the volume and seasonality of tourism in these areas are often too limited.

Finally, the research does not attempt to provide a detailed list of villages that are disappearing, but rather to suggest a model for serious consideration as an answer to the profound problem of ageing and depopulation of rural areas. Moreover, the study recommends that rural tourism may be seen as a way out for smaller rural spatial entities to stop or at least slow down the out-migration, in the first line by creating some basic conditions for a general, much higher mutual comfort of rural areas.

Besides economical, the locals might also find social and cultural motifs to continue living in family homes in areas (Vratuša & Anastasijević, 2002). The experience of the developed countries in solving the demographic problems of rural areas emphasizes the non-agricultural aspects of sustainable rural development: the manufacturing industry, indigenous crafts, trade of their own products and in particular, rural tourism (Đenadić et al., 2016).

References

Bærenholdt, J. O.; Haldrup, M.; Larsen, J.; Urry, J.: Performing Tourist Places. Aldershot, Burlington: Ashgate, 2004.

Brandt, B.; Haugen, M.: "Farm diversification into tourism – Implications for social identity?". Journal of Rural Studies, 27, 2011, pp. 35–44.

Crouch, D.: Tourism, consumption and rurality. In Cloke, P., Marsden, T., Mooney, P.H. (Eds). Handbook of Rural Studies, 2006 (pp. 355–364). London: Sage.

Đenadić, M.; Muhi, B.; Jovanović, D.: "Rural tourism – Serbia's missed chance". Economics of Agriculture, 2, 2016, pp. 515–529.

Dimitrov, N.; Petrevska, B.: "Rural tourism development zones: The case of Macedonia". Researches Review of the Department of Geography, Tourism and Hotel Management, 41, 2012, pp. 152–162.

Dissart, J. C.; Vollet, D.; Polhes O.; Mallebay, M.: The landscape: A regional development factor that spurs territory – Specific economic flows. In: Cemagref, FR, 1st International conference on Landscape Economic, Vienna, 2009.

Dong, E.; Wang, Y.; Morais, D.; Brooks, D.: "Segmenting the rural tourism market: The case of Potter Country, Pennsylvania, USA". Journal of Vacation Marketing, 19(2), 2013, pp. 181–193.

Gallent, N.; Juntti, M.; Kidd, S.; Shaw, D.: Introduction to Rural Planning. London, UK: Routledge, 2008.

Gašić, M.; Ivanović, V.: Rural tourism in Serbia and impact on economic and social development. In: Thematic proceedings "Modern management tools and economy of tourism sector in present era" (pp. 1–16). Belgrade: Association of Economists and Managers of the Balkans & Ohrid: Faculty of Tourism and Hospitality, 2018.

George, E. W.; Mair, H.; Reid, D. G. (2009). Rural Tourism Development: Localism and Cultural Change. Bristol: Channel View Publications.

Hall, D.; Roberts, L.; Mitchell, M.: New Directions in Rural Tourism. Aldershot: Ashgate, 2003.

Jepson, D.; Sharpley, R.: "More than sense of place? Exploring the emotional dimension of rural tourism experiences". Journal of Sustainable Tourism, 23(8–9), 2015, pp. 1157–1178.

Khaleel, A.; Ngah, I.: "Understanding the sustainability of rural communities within a population density context: A case study of Shaqlawa, Kurdistan, Iraq". Journal of Sustainability Science and Management, 3(2), 2013, pp. 254–267.

Kneafsey, M.: "Tourism, place identities and social relations in the European rural periphery". European Urban and Regional Studies, 7(1), 2000, pp. 35–50.

Lukić, A.: "Tourism, farm diversification and plurality of rurality: Case study of Croatia". European Countryside, 4, 2013, pp. 356–376.

Mak, A.; Wong, K. K.; Chang, R. C.: "Health or self-indulgence? The motivations and characteristics of spa-goers". International Journal of Tourism Research, 11(2), 2009, pp. 185–199.

Maksimović, M.; Urošević, S.; Damnjanović, Z.: "Theoretical concepts of rural tourism and opportunities for development in the Republic of Serbia". Economics Management Information Technology, 3, 2015, pp. 162–172.

Middleton, V. T. C.; Clarke, J.: Marketing in Travel and Tourism. Oxford: Butterworth Heinemann, 2001.

Namicev, P.; Vuksanovic-Macura, Z.; Petrevska, B.: "Vernacular architecture in Macedonia and Serbia: A comparative study". Proceedings from the International scientific conference "The Balkan Peninsula of Jovan Cvijic: Historical background and contemporary trends in human geography", Trsic, Loznica, Serbia, October 29–30, 2018, pp. 243–252.

Nations Online Project: Political Map of Macedonia 2018 & Political Map of Serbia 2018. Retrieved on 03.05.2019 from https://www.nationsonline.org.

Petrevska, B.; Dimitrov, N.: "Planning rural tourism development in Macedonia". Journal of Process Management – New Technologies, 1(3), 2013, pp. 63–68.

Petrevska, B.; Dimitrov. N.; Terzić, A.: Rural areas in Macedonia as tourism supply: Problem or a challenge?. Conference proceedings from the Fourth International conference "Geobalcanica 2019", June 15–16, 2019, Sofia, Bulgaria, pp. 513–518.

Popescu, A. C.: "Tourism development in a rural periphery. The case study: The sub-Carpathians of Oltenians". Journal of Settlements and Spatial Planning, 3, 2013, pp. 53–64.

Sharpley, R.: "Rural tourism and the challenge of tourism diversification: The case of Cyprus". Tourism Management, 23(3), 2002, pp. 233–244.

State Statistical Office of the Republic of Macedonia. Statistical Yearbook of the Republic of Macedonia, 2017, Skopje, 2018.

Terzić, A.; Dimitrov, N.; Petrevska, B.: Turistička valorizacija tradicionalnih ruralnih celina: rizici i mogućnosti u Srbiji i Makedoniji. Zbornik radova, X naučno-stručna konferencija s međunarodnim učešćem "Kulturno nasleđe-rizici i perspective", 27. maj 2019, Beograd, Srbija, pp. 199–209.

Theodoropoulou, E.; Kaldis, P.: "Changes in rural areas and regional development". Journal of Social Sciences, 4(4), 2008, pp. 275–279.

Todorović, M.,; Bjeljac, Ž. Osnove ruralnog turizma u Srbiji (The basis of the rural tourism in Serbia). Bulletin of the Geographical Serbian Society, 87(1), 2007, 135–148.

Tošić, B.: Osnove ruralnog planiranja (The Basis of the Rural Planning). Belgrade: Belgrade University, Faculty of Geography, 2011.

Tuohino, A.: "In search of the sense of Finnish Lakes. A geographical approach to Lake tourism marketing". Nordia Geographical Publications, 44, 2015, pp. 5.

Urry, J.: The Tourist Gaze. London, Thousand Oaks, New Delhi: Sage Publications, 2002.

Vratuša, V.; Anastasijević, N.: "Održivi razvoj, uređivanje prostora i seoski turizam u Srbiji na početku 21. Veka". Turizam – Časopis Departmana za geografiju, turizam i hotelijerstvo, 6, 2002, pp. 24–26.

Iuliana Țoropoc

Statistical models for assessing the socioeconomic factors impacting on infant mortality in Romania

Abstract The association of socioeconomic factors and Infant Mortality Rate (IMR) is well established. Romania is a developed country characterized by a high IMR. There are no studies to date on the relationship between socioeconomic factors and IMR with Romanian population data. An understanding of the influence of socioeconomic factors on IMR is beneficial, as the IMR is considered a valid measure of population health. A number of socioeconomic indicators are selected from the database of the National Institute of Statistics. Those found to have significant associations with IMR are introduced in a regression model with IMR as independent variable. While moderate correlations are obtained for Net Income, Number of Doctors, Marriage Rate, Age of Mother and Dropout Rate, only the Net Income is found to have an effect on IMR.

Keywords: demographics, statistical models, infant mortality rate, socioeconomic factors, fertility rate, aging population

Introduction

Together with Malta, Romania has the highest Infant Mortality Rate (IMR) within the European Union. For the year 2017, both countries had an IMR of 6.7, substantially higher than the European Union average of 3.6. For the same year, Romania had a sub-replacement fertility rate of 1.35, substantially lower than the generally accepted replacement level of 2.1, and a general population aging trend, as evidenced by the ratio of the young (those 15 and younger) to the old (those 65 and older) of 0.81. The forecasts for 2050 show a fertility rate of 1.70, IMR of 4.9 and a ratio of the young to the old of 0.38, this indicating that, in little over 30 years, Romania's population will not only decrease substantially, but will also be a predominantly old population, this having a significant impact on the country's social, economic and political structures. Therefore, a reduction in IMR is desirable for Romania's long-term demographic strategy.

The infant mortality rate is obtained by dividing the total number of deaths registered within the first year of life to 1000 live births and it is a widely used measure of population heath (Reidpath and Allotey, 2003). As such, IMR is regarded as an indicator of social and economic wellbeing. Nevertheless, it suffers from a few limitations. First, there is debate on the use of IMR as a measure for developed countries, where the majority of the infant deaths occur within the first few hours of life and are mostly attributable to biological factors (Stockwell, 1962).

Second, using IMR as a health indicator might divert funds from health policies aimed at population groups outside the area covered by this indicator (Reidpath and Allotey, 2003). To address these limitations, the disability-adjusted life expectancy (DALE) was proposed as an alternative to IMR. However, Reidpath and Allotey (2003) endorse the use of IMR as health indicator. Using data from 180 countries, they found a strong linear association between IMR and DALE. In conclusion, there is evidence that IMR is a reliable measure of population health. It follows that, the high IMR registered in Romania, raises questions about the general health state of the population and should therefore be a matter of concern for the social and health care system.

The factors that influence IMR are of socioeconomic and biological nature (Stockwell, 1962). Indeed, as early as 1910, Newsholme observed that IMR is susceptible to socioeconomic influences, while the role of biological factors was recognized in the 1960s (Stockwell, 1962). In general, the socioeconomic factors have been addressed by the social sciences and the biological factors by the medical sciences (Mosley and Chen, 1984). According to Mosley and Chen (1984), there are three groups of socioeconomic factors that are usually associated with IMR:

- Individual-level factors such as skills, typically measured by the father's level of education, health of the mother and time allocated by the mother to the standard requirements of maintaining a healthy child, e.g. breastfeeding, sickness care, household cleaning. Also included in this group are socio-cultural factors such as traditions, norms and attitudes towards children.
- Household-level factors, usually household income and household size and quality. Also included in this group are purchases of goods and services such as hygienic and sickness care.
- Community-level factors such as environmental variables, for example climate and water quality, local infrastructure including transportation and health services, health policies.

In addition to these socioeconomic variables, Mosley and Chen (1984) suggest a number of proximate factors. These are broadly grouped under maternal factors, such as age of the mother, environmental contamination, for example prevalence of chronic diseases in the population, nutrient deficiency, injury and personal illness control, as identified by immunization and antenatal care. Numerous studies have been conducted to date with the aim of understanding the impact of socioeconomic factors on IMR, with populations ranging from that of the United States (e.g. Stockwell, 1962) to that of Sub-Saharan Africa (e.g. Akoto and Tambashe, 2002). The variables considered by these studies are found in Mosley and Chen (1984). Governmental bodies, such as the CDC in the United States, regularly monitor the relationship between IMR and the associated socioeconomic factors. To our knowledge, there has been no similar published attempt with Romanian IMR data.

In summary, Romania's population is characterized by a high IMR, a low fertility rate and a general aging trend. Under these circumstances, the identification of socioeconomic factors that influence IMR may prove to be a positive first step in understanding and even tackling Romania's high IMR rate, particularly as no such effort has been identified yet. The aim of this study is to assess the relationship between a number of socioeconomic factors, as recommended by Mosley and Chen (1984) and IMR, based on Romanian population data for the year 2017.

1. Literature review

In one of the most influential studies on infant mortality, Hobcraft et al. (1984) looked at best-fit models for the death variable, based on five multi-level socioeconomic factors: education of the mother, work status of the mother, education of the father, occupation of the father and residential area. The study relied on 10-year worth of data from the World Fertility Survey, covering a total of 28 less developed and developing countries. A log linear rate model was used for the number of deaths. The education of the mother and the education and occupation of the father were the variables that appeared most often in the 28 country level models. Anomalies, i.e. an opposite direction effect to that expected, were common. For a better understanding of the impact of socioeconomic factors on infant mortality, the researchers recommended the inclusion of medical and healthcare variables.

Salarilak et al. (2009) used path analysis to assess the association between IMR and family expenditure and size, illiteracy, urbanity, employment and caesarean rates for each of the 28 provinces of Iran. The data came from national and regional surveys and official indicators. The data showed significant positive correlations for IMR, illiteracy and urbanity and negative correlations for IMR, family expenditure and cesarean. As recommended by Hobcraft et al. (1984) the study benefited from the inclusion of a healthcare variable. The researchers warned about the dangers of inferring individual correlations from ecological (population-level) data.

Stockwell (1962) investigated the relationship between the socioeconomic status of the mother and IMR within the city of Providence, Rhode Island. Correlations between IMR and measures of education, occupation, income, rent and crowding, based on census tract data, indicated that there was no association between IMR and socioeconomic status. However, when neonatal and postneonatal deaths were pursued separately, an inverse relationship was found between IMR and socioeconomic status. A cause-of death analysis revealed that 80 % of infant deaths were attributed to biological causes (birth injuries, immaturity and congenital malformations) and mostly occurred within the first days of life. Moreover, only 6 % of deaths were attributed to infectious diseases, where socioeconomic factors play a role. As a result, Stockwell (1962) questioned the role of IMR as health measure for developed countries. Nevertheless, data on socioeconomic factors, such as maternal age and marital status, is still included in the IMR reports issued by the US National Vital Statistics System (NVSS).

Dallolio et al. (2012) investigated the level of association between IMR and income inequality, household income, percentage of women with more than eight years of education and percentage of unemployed in Italy. The data was obtained from the Italian National Institute of Statistics in the form of regional indicators. Although initial univariate regressions were significant for all variables, a multiple stepwise regression identified only the unemployment rate as an influential factor, with a positive association between the two variables. The result contradicted the general belief that in high-income countries, i.e. developed countries with gross national income over $12,056, IMR is associated not with income, but with income inequality (Dallolio et al., 2012). Moreover, the result supported the economic deprivation model, according to which, the unemployed have less money and consequently poor health (Dallolio et al., 2012, Janlert, 2009). Previous evidence against this general belief was provided by Olson et al. (2010). The researchers found that both income and income inequality have an influence on IMR in the United States, a high-income country, yet with higher IMR than the EU average, this suggesting that country specifics may mediate between IMR, income and income inequality.

Akoto and Tambashe (2002) attempted to explain the difference between urban and rural IMR in Sub-Saharan Africa, where, in general, urban IMR is lower than rural IMR (Akoto and Tabutin, 1989, as cited in Akoto and Tambashe, 2002). In a meta-analysis of IMR studies conducted in the region, they identified a number of factors that mediated the relationship between the two levels of the location variable and IMR, among them: medical coverage, mother's education and mother's age.

To summarize, numerous studies to date identified associations between various socioeconomic variables and IMR. The socioeconomic factors addressed by these studies are summarized by Mosley and Chen (1984). Starting with the 1960s, the tendency has been to concentrate on less developed and developing countries/economies (see Stockwell, 1962, Hobcraft et al., 1984, Akoto and Tambashe, 2002, Salarilak et al., 2009). Nevertheless, socioeconomic factors continue to be associated with IMR in developed and high-income countries (see Olson et al., 2010, Dallolio et al., 2012, Mathews et al., 2015).

2. Methods

Data for the 42 official administrative regions of Romania were obtained from the Romanian National Institute of Statistics. Our dependent variable was IMR, while our independent variables were: Number of Immigrants, Unemployment Rate, Net Income, Number of Doctors, Marriage Rate, Age of Mother and Dropout Rate. We focused on a single year, the year 2017, as this was the closest year to present with data available for all our independent variables. We selected the independent variables, in accordance with the recommendations made by Mosley and Chen (1984).

We selected the Dropout Rate for secondary education for the previous year, 2016, as a proxy for Education. Starting with 2009, Romania has experienced an increase in the Dropout Rate, mainly due to reforms of the secondary educational system. The Dropout Rate uses the total number of students abandoning their secondary education studies during one academic year. For the year 2014/2015, Drop-out Rates of 3.7 % and 5 % were reported for secondary general education and vocational education. It is worth pointing out that, Romania has one of the highest early leavers rates within the European Union (16,7 % for 2018 in comparison to a recommended 10 %). We believe therefore the Dropout Rate to be a good proxy for educational attainment.

We used the Marriage Rate as a proxy for the socio-cultural factors, such as norms and traditions, that might influence IMR. As Romania is still a highly traditional society, with over 80 % of the population identifying themselves as Orthodox Christians in the 2011 Population Census, we suspected single, unmarried mothers to be at a disadvantage, particularly in rural areas. Indeed, the Marriage Rate is a socioeconomic factor associated with IMR in the United States, where infant mortality for those born to single mothers is 73 % higher than for those born to married mothers (Mathews et al., 2015). We included a variable for the healthcare services, as suggested by Moseley and Chen (1984), namely the number of doctors, herby referred to as Doctors. We opted for Net Income and Unemployment Rate, based on Dallolio et al. (2012), as we wanted to test the economic deprivation hypothesis on our data.

Finally, we included a novel variable in our analysis, the number of Emigrants. Since 2015, the first year with Eurostat available data, Romania reports, together with Poland, the highest number of emigrants within the European Union (Eurostat data). The impact that emigration has had on Romania's social and economic situation has been a constant source of discussion among local politicians and academics. The healthy immigrant effect (HIE) suggests that recent immigrants are healthier than their locally born counterparts (Deri, 2005). According to Jasso et al. (2004), immigration is conditioned by a health selection process in the country of origin, as healthier individuals are more likely to benefit from migration and have the skills, means and mindset to emigrate. Moreover, prospective immigrants might have above average health and financial resources when compared to their peer group in the country of origin (Kennedy et al., 2006). Their findings are indorsed by United States (Jasso et al., 2004), Canadian (Hyman, 2001), Australian (Donovan et al., 1992, as cited in Deri, 2005) and United Kingdom (Kennedy et al., 2006) data. In addition, Kennedy et al. (2006) found evidence for a positive self-selection process for European immigrants to UK, US, Canada and Australia, with age and education among the explanatory variables. Indeed, European immigrants across all sample data were healthier, more prone to healthy behavior, younger and better educated than their country of destination counterparts.

We conducted a multivariate linear regression to assess the effect of our independent variables on IMR. The independent variables for the model were selected based on initial Pearson correlations with the dependent variable. For our regression model, we conducted tests and graphical inspections for linearity, correlation and variance of the residuals, outliers, high leverage points and collinearity, as suggested by James et al. (2015). We opted for the logarithm of the dependent variable (LIMR) in order to improve the chances of the model to pass the linearity and homoscedasticity tests. Finally, we attempted a partial least squares analysis to investigate whether there are any noticeable improvements over linear regression. All statistical analysis was performed in R.

3. Results and discussion

Initial Pearson correlation tests showed significant moderate, negative relationships between Net Income, Doctors, Marriage Rate and Mother's Age and LIMR and a positive, moderate relationship between Dropout Rate and LIMR (see Fig. 1). All correlation directions were as expected. In addition, there were strong correlations among all variables, except Dropout Rate, this suggesting a potential issue with multi-collinearity. However, none of the Variance Inflation Factors were equal to or higher than 5 (see James et al., 2015), this reassuring us that our model complied with the non-collinearity requirement of linear regression.

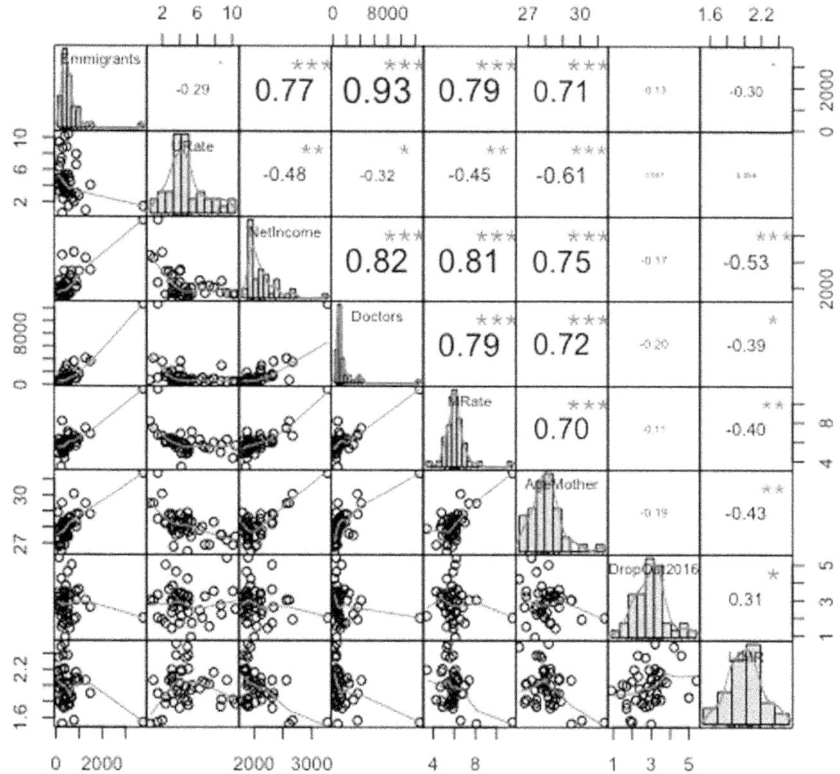

Fig. 1: Correlation data, all variables

Source: Author's own computations, using data from the Romanian National Institute of Statistics.

A multivariate regression with LIMR as independent variable and Net Income, Doctors, Marriage Rate, Mother's Age and Dropout Rate revealed a significant influence of Net Income on LIMR. According to our model, each unit increase in Net Income decreased the untransformed IMR by 0,04 %. Based on the adjusted R^2, our model explained 25.01 % of the variance in the LIMR, F-test significant. Regression diagnostics plots (see Fig. 2) indicated that our model violated the assumptions of linearity (Residuals vs. Fitted) and homoscedasticity (Scale-Location). The Breusch-Pagan test confirmed the heteroscedasticity indicated by the diagnostic plots. However, the errors were normally distributed (Q-Q plot) and there were no leverage points and outliers (Residuals vs. Leverage). Any value higher than 1 for Cook's distance was treated as a leverage point. Standardized residuals higher than 3 indicated outliers. As a final stage in our analysis, we

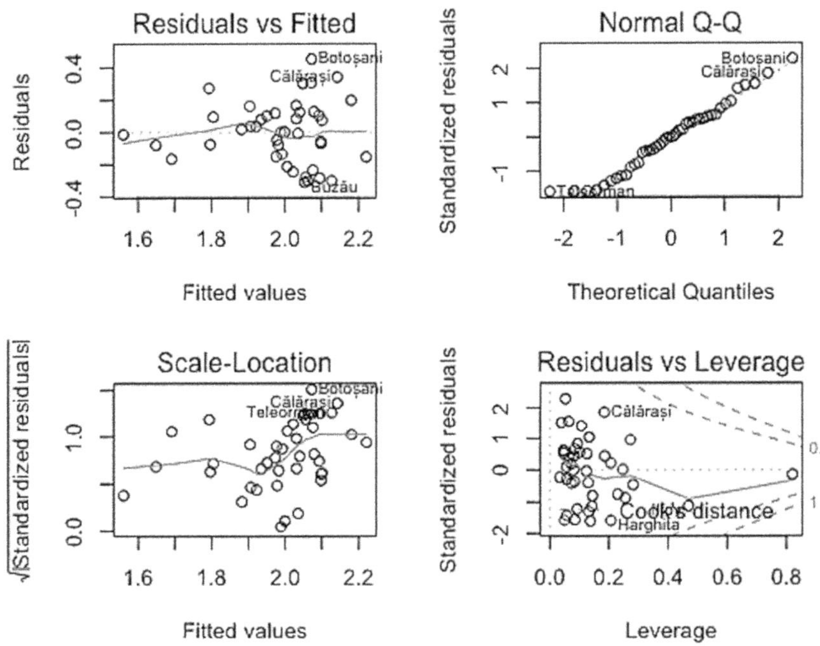

Fig. 2: Regression tests, general assumptions

Source: Author's own computations, using data from the Romanian National Institute of Statistics.

conducted a partial least squares regression to investigate whether, considering all independent variables in our initial regression model, increased the explanatory power of our model. Our analysis showed that a partial least squares regression with 3 components explained 34.15 % of the variance in LIMR.

We investigated the effect of socioeconomic variables (No of Emigrants, Unemployment Rate, Net Income, Doctors, Marriage Rate, Age of Mother, Dropout Rate) on the IMR of Romania for the year 2017. We found negative moderate associations between LIMR and Net Income, Doctors, Marriage Rate and Mother's Age and a positive moderate association between LIMR and Dropout Rate. A multiple regression with LIMR and the associated five variables indicated a negative effect of Net Income.

Regarding the relationship between IMR and Number of Immigrants, we were tempted by a potential effect of the latter on IMR. According to HIE, emigrants are generally younger than their country of origin peers and, more than likely, of childbearing age. Therefore, a high number of emigrants would have potentially lowered the fertility rates and, as a result, the IMR. Moreover, the documented migration of doctors and nurses might have had a positive effect on IMR. Indeed, annually 3000 new doctors enter the Romanian healthcare system, while 3500 exit the system via retirement, death and migration. Finally, a higher number of emigrants would have suggested a higher remittance income and better care for both mother and child. Nevertheless, this assumption was not supported by statistical evidence. Similarly, there was no statistical evidence for a relationship between Unemployment Rate and IMR, and therefore, unlike Dallolio et al. (2012), our study did not provide support for the economic deprivation model.

However, we identified negative moderate associations between IMR, Doctors, Marriage Rate and Mother's Age. The number of Doctors is a community-level variable (Mosley and Chen, 1984), recommended by Hobcraft et al. (1984) as a desirable socioeconomic factor in IMR explanatory models. Negative associations, such as those obtained by Salarilak et al. (2009) and endorsed by Akoto and Tambashe (2002) were expected. The negative association between IMR and Doctors could be regarded as a safety check for our data.

The Marriage Rate could be regarded both as an individual and a community-level variable (Mosley and Chen, 1984). Our study identified a negative relationship between Marriage Rate and IMR, this suggesting a potential influence of this variable on IMR. Indeed, in the US, IMR is higher among unmarried than among married mothers (Mathews et al., 2015). Mother's Age is an individual-level variable that has been repeatedly found to have an inverse relationship with IMR (Mosley and Chen, 1984). Studies conducted on Sub-Saharan populations indicated a high infant mortality risk for mothers younger than 20 and older than 35, with a lower risk of death for children born to mothers between 25 and 34 years of age, irrespective of area of residence (Akoto and Tambashe, 2002). Our study identified a negative relationship between Mother's Age and IMR. It is important to note at this stage that studies that include this variable use data for either the age of the mother at first birth or the average age of mother. We opted for the latter, with the youngest average age at 26.5 years and the oldest at 31.4.

Finally, our study identified a positive association between Dropout Rate and IMR. The education of the mother and that of the father are usually included as socioeconomic variables in studies of IMR. In general, the level of education, particularly for the mother, is capped at basic education, i.e. primary and lower secondary. For example, Dallolio et al. (2012) looked at women with at least 8 years of education, while Stockwell (1962) was interested in those with less than 8 years of education. Education is not only an indicator of the level of income attained by an individual, but also of the level of mothercare (Mosley and Chen, 1984). As we did not find similar data for our population of interest, we decided on the

Dropout Rate for upper secondary education and obtained a positive association between this and IMR.

Nevertheless, our study endorsed the effect of a single variable on IMR, Net Income. Studies that attempt socioeconomic explanations of IMR, take the household, not the individual income into account and usually find a negative effect of household income on IMR. Dallolio et al. (2012) identified a strong negative correlation between household income and IMR, however, their data did not endorse an effect of household income on IMR. With the exception of high-income countries, household income is generally regarded as an extremely reliable predictor of IMR (Mosley and Chen, 1984; Dallolio et al., 2012). In the US, a high-income country, an association between income and IMR is observed as early as 1925 (Woodbury, 1925, as cited by Stockwell, 1962) and as recently as 2010 (Olson et al., 2010). Working with data from developing countries, Hobcraft et al. (1984) used the occupation of the husband as a proxy for income and found, with a few exceptions, a negative effect of this variable on IMR. Our regression model indicated that 25.01 % of the variance in IMR was explained by Net Income alone. Romania has the second lowest average net income among the European Union member states (EU 27), 515 Euro, while the cost of living, rent, mortgage and public transport excluded, is comparable to that of EU 27 with an average net income at least double than the one of Romania. The ratio low income/cost of living, explains the high proportion of variance accounted by Net Income alone. However, our study did not take into account remittances and therefore might underemphasize the effects of income on IMR. World Bank data estimates for 2017, the year we selected for our study, point towards a total of 3,1 billion $ remittances in the form of private transfer and employee benefits for Romania. It is worth pointing out, that this amount is on the lower end, when compared with that of other countries in the European Union.

A partial least squares regression indicated that over 35 % of the variance in IMR was explained by a composite factor that took into account all our independent variables. However, there is still considerable variance in IMR left unexplained. An explanation for this lack of accountability is offered by Stockwell (1962). The author suggests that, for developed economies, the role of socioeconomic factors in IMR is downplayed by the medical advances that are made in battling infectious diseases (Stockwell, 1962). Moreover, our study did not separate between neonatal and postneonatal deaths, to minimize the effect of biological causes that account for the majority of the neonatal deaths (see Stockwell 1962, Hobcraft et al., 1984). In addition, unlike the majority of the studies on socioeconomic factors, our study is restricted to a one-year period. Finally, similar to Dallolio et al. (2012), our study used a number of regional socioeconomic indicators, as independent variables. In contradistinction, Stockwell (1962), Hobcraft et al. (1984) and Salarilak et al. (2009) select their data from Fertility and Household Surveys, this allowing for a more robust dataset.

Conclusions

To our knowledge, our study is the first to attempt a socioeconomic explanation of Romanian IMR. Although we did not find evidence for the effect of various socioeconomic factors on IMR, our study validated the link between income and IMR with Romanian data. This is an important finding, particularly as IMR continues to be a valid measure of population health (see Reidpath and Allotey, 2003).

References

Akoto, E.; Tambashe, B.O.: "Socioeconomic Inequalities in Infant and Child Mortality among Urban and Rural Areas in Sub-Saharan Africa". 2002.

Dallolio, L.; Di Gregori, V.; Lenzi, J.; Franchino, G.; Calugi, S.; Domenighetti, G.; Fantini, MP.: "Socio-Economic Factors Associated with Infant Mortality in Italy: An Ecological Study". International Journal for Equity in Health, 11(45), 2012, pp. 1–5.

Deri, C.: "Understanding the 'Healthy Immigrant Effect' in Canada". University of Ottawa, Department of Economics, Working Papers, 2005.

Hobcraft, J.N.; McDonald, J.W.; Rustein, S.O.: "Socio-Economic Factors in Infant and Child Mortality: A Cross-National Comparison". Population Studies 38(2), 1984, pp. 193–223.

Hyman, I.: "Immigration and Health". Health Canada Working Paper, 2001, pp. 01–05.

Janlert, U.; Hammerström, A.: "Which theory is best? Explanatory models of the relationship between unemployment and health. BMC Public Health 235(9), 2009, https://doi.org/10.1186/1471-2458-9-235.

James, G; Witten, D.; Hastie, T; Tibshirani, R: An Introduction to Statistical Learning with Applications in R, Springer, New York, 2015;

Jasso, G.; Massey, D.S.; Rosenzweig, M.R.; Smith, J.P.: "Immigrant Health-Selectivity and Acculturation". In: Anderson, Bulatao and Cohen (eds): Critical Perspectives and Racial Ethnic Differences in Health in Late Life, Committee on Population, National Research Council, Washington DC: The National Academic Press, 2004.

Kennedy, S.; McDonald, T.; Biddle, N.: "The Healthy Immigrant Effect and Immigrant Selection: Evidence from Four Countries". McMaster University, Social and Economic Dimensions of an Aging Population Research Papers, 2006.

Mathews, T.J.; MacDorman, M. F.; Thoma, M.E.: "Infant Mortality Satistics from the 2013 Period Linked Birth/Infant Death Data Set". National Vital Statistics Reports 64(9), 2015.

Mosley, H.W.; Chen, L.C.: "An Analytical Framework for the Study of Child Survival in Developing Countries". Pop Dev Rev 10(Suppl), 1984, pp. 25–45.

Olson, M.E.; Diekema, D.; Elliott, B.E.; Renier, C.M.: "Impact of Income and Income Inequality on Infant Health Outcomes in the United States". Pediatrics 126(6), 2010, pp. 1165–1173.

Reidpath, D.D.; Allotey, P.: "Infant Mortality Rate as an Indicator of Population Health". Journal of Epidemiology and Community Health, 57, 2003, pp. 344–346.

Salarilak, S.H.; Khalkhali, H.R.; Entezarmahdi, R.; Pakdel, F.G.; Faroukheslamloo, H.R.: "Association between the Socio-Economic Indicators and Infant Mortality Rate (IMR) in Iran". Iranian Journal of Public Health, 38(4), 2009, pp. 21–28.

Stockwell, E.G.: "Infant Mortality and Socio-Economic Status: A Changing Relationship". Milbank Mem Fund Q. 40,1962, pp. 101–111.

Iuliana Țoropoc

Mortality forecasting models within the context of an aging population

Abstract Longevity is a relatively new and unexpected phenomenon that has a major impact on pension schemes. Within this context, new mortality models have been developed in an effort to obtain improved mortality forecasts, particularly at high ages. Among these models, age-period-cohort (APC) models stand out as a distinct class of stochastic mortality models. In this paper we consider four APC models and evaluate their forecasting performance based on plausibility of the uncertainty of the forecasts and biological reasonableness, as recommended by Cairns et al. (2011). Our data consists of mortality rates for the Romanian female population of ages 60 to 84 for the historical period 1968–2014. We find that only one model complies with both of the two selected criteria, two models do not comply with the plausibility criterion and one with the reasonableness criterion.

Keywords: APC models, demographics, old-age mortality, aging, longevity risk, forecasting, Central-Eastern Europe

Introduction

Recognized as a worldwide demographic issue at the turn of the century, population aging has since been a major source of concern for governmental and non-governmental bodies. Population aging is particularly relevant for developed and developing economies, as it places a significant strain on resources and slows down economic growth. By 2060, the percentage of those over 65 in the EU27 will be close to 28 %, compared to 14 % for those under 15. Unprecedentedly, those over 80 will total 12 % of the population.

A number of factors are believed to be behind the aging population phenomenon, namely: falling fertility, falling mortality and increasing longevity (Harper, 2014). While low fertility rates were widely encouraged to counteract the falling mortality trend that has emerged in the 1970s, the increase in longevity is a relatively new and unexpected trend (Harper 2014, Cairns et al., 2006a). Indeed, it is only within the last decade that longevity, understood as unexpected mortality improvements at older ages, has been classified as a risk by the pensions and insurance industry. As first line of defense against longevity risk, a number of mortality models have been developed, starting with the early 2000. These models have been referred to under the umbrella term APC (age-period-cohort models), coined by Hunt and Blake, 2015. They are believed to be more efficient at forecasting mortality than the classic Gompertz-Makeham model and its extensions, particularly in the context of an aging population.

The population of Romania is experiencing a negative growth trend, with a growth rate of −0.6 % registered in January 2019, with 18.5 % of the total population being over the age of 65 and 15.6 % under the age of 15. While at present the majority of the population is aged between 15 and 64, by 2050 Romania will struggle to sustain its old age population groups (see Fig. 1). Mortality models with improved forecasting performance, particularly for the older age groups are therefore recommended for Romanian mortality.

1. Literature review

The APC models are GLM (generalized linear) models that use age, period and cohort constructs to illustrate mortality. The aim is to produce more accurate mortality rates than the standard mortality models, where age is the only factor. According to these models, mortality is not only influenced by age, but also by social and medical advances (period) and by the common mortality effects attributable to the year of birth (cohort). Cairns (2014) identifies three main classes of APC models:

a) the APC model of Hobcraft et al. (1982);
b) the nonparametric Lee Carter (1992) model and its extensions (LC);
c) the parametric Cairns-Blake-Dowd (2006) model and its extensions (CBD).

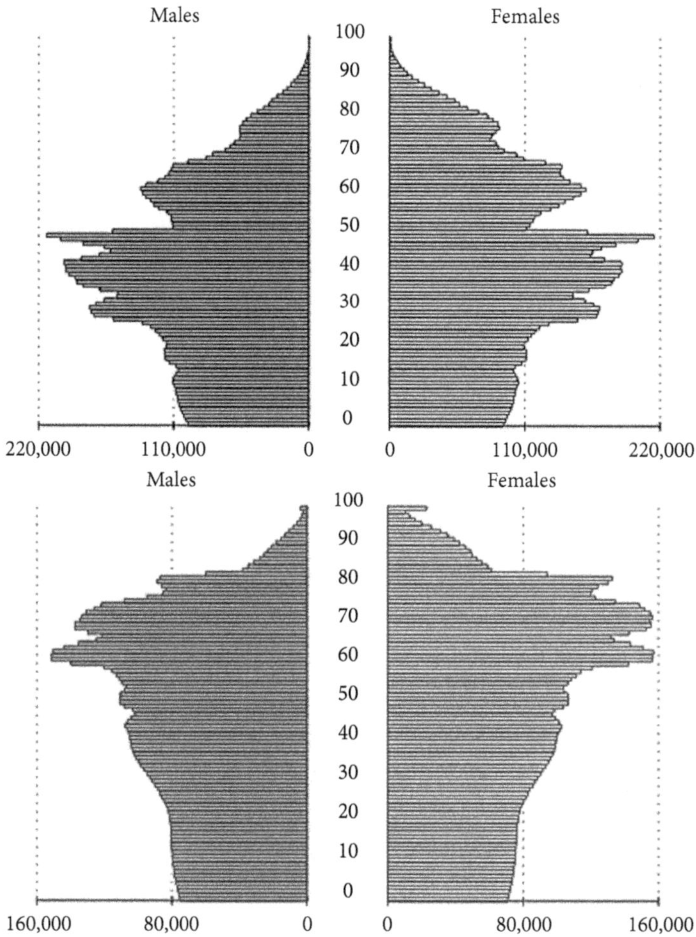

Fig. 1: Population pyramid Romania 2018 and 2050
Source: Author's own computations, using data from US Census Bureau's International Data Base.

The original and standard cohort extension forms for the LC are: $\ln(m_{x,t}) = a_x + b_x k_t$ (M1) and $\ln(m_{x,t}) = a_x + b_x^{(1)} k_t + b_x^{(2)} \gamma_{t-x}$ (M2), while those for CBD are: $\text{logit}(q_{x,t}) = b_x^{(1)} k_t^{(1)} + b_x^{(2)} k_t^{(2)}$ (M5) and $\text{logit}(q_{x,t}) = b_x^{(1)} k_t^{(1)} + b_x^{(2)} k_t^{(2)} + b_x^{(3)} \gamma_{t-x}$ (M6). The LC models work with the logarithm of the central mortality rates, the static age function,

a_x, the age/period term, $b_x k_t$ and the cohort term, $b_x \gamma_{t-x}$. Forecasts use $\hat{k}_t = k_{t-1} + \mu + Z$, where μ is the drift in k and Z is the error term and $\hat{\gamma}_c = \gamma_{c-1} + \mu_\gamma + a_\gamma + (\gamma_{c-1} - \gamma_{c-2} - \mu_\gamma) + \phi_0 Z_\gamma(c)$, where $c = t - x$, $Z_\gamma(c)$ is independent from $Z_k(t)$, ARIMA. CBD models work with the logarithm of the odds of the probability rates and two age/period terms, $b_x^{(1)} k_t^{(1)}$, with $b_x^{(1)} = 1$, and $b_x^{(2)} k_t^{(2)}$, with $b_x^{(2)} = (x - \bar{x})$ and the age/cohort term, $b_x^{(3)} \gamma_{x-t}$, with $b_x^{(3)} = 1$. Forecasts use $\hat{k}_t = k_{t-1} + \mu + CZ(t+1)$, where $k_t = \left[k_t^{(1)} + k_t^{(2)}\right]$ and C are the volatilities.

One key assumption that both models have in common is the random pattern in mortality rates for the same age at adjacent years. Although neither of the two models extends this assumption to adjacent ages for the same year, only the CBD model assumes smoothness of this relationship (Cairns et al., 2009). Model selection is informed therefore by personal beliefs about the nature of the relationship between mortality rates in the data. Another consideration at point of selection is the age range one is working with. While the LC models can be used throughout the entire age range, the CBD models are designed specifically for older ages. When used with older ages, the LC models are prone to overestimation. On the other hand, the CBD models are restricted to data where the assumption of linearity holds (Hunt and Blake, 2015). At present, the LC and CBD families of models are widely used by governmental and non-governmental bodies worldwide.

To date, the performance of these models has been evaluated in respect to various populations and age groups. In a previous paper, Toropoc (2018) attempted to evaluate the fitting performance of two age/period LC and CBD versions and concluded that LC was a better fit for the Romanian old age female population. As a good fit does not necessarily result in performant forecasts, separate evaluations are conducted for fitting and forecasting. Cairns et al. (2009) and Cairns et al. (2011) are generally considered to supply the guidelines for the evaluation of APC models. Cairns et al. (2011) focuses on the forecasting performance of the APC models and proposes a qualitative *ex ante* evaluation. The three qualitative criteria that Cairns et al. (2011) introduces are: plausibility of the forecast uncertainty levels, biological reasonableness (Cairns et al., 2006b) and robustness of forecasts relative to the historical period and age range. Plausibility of the forecast uncertainty levels requires that the uncertainty of the forecasts at different ages is consistent with the historical volatility. Biological reasonableness requires forecasts to be justified by biological, medical or environmental factors. The robustness of the forecasts relative to period and age requires that small changes made to the historical period and the age range produce only minor forecasting changes.

Cairns et al. (2011) evaluate six APC models with the help of these criteria and old age population samples from the United States (US) and England and Wales (EW). The APC models selected by Cairns et al. (2011) include the original LC and the LC cohort extension of Renshaw and Haberman (2006), the original CBD and two of the CBD cohort extensions introduced by Cairns et al. (2009). Interestingly, the simple cohort extension that we introduced further up is dropped by Cairns et al. (2011), as it is considered to be a nested, less performant, version of the following extension: $\text{logit}\,(q_{x,t}) = b_x^{(1)} k_t^{(1)} + b_x^{(2)} k_t^{(2)} + (b_x^{(2)} - \hat{\sigma}_x^2) k_t^{(3)} + \gamma_{t-x}$ (M7), where $\hat{\sigma}_x^2 = n_a^{-1} \sum_i (x - \bar{x})^2$. This extension, M7, adds a quadratic term to the age effect that is based on the curvature observed in the US data and, as a result, obtains better results than M6 (Cairns et al., 2011). Indeed, in a state residuals test performed on eight mortality models, including M1, M2, M5, M6 and M7, M7 had the smallest failure rate, being followed by M5, M6, M2 and M1 (Dowd et al., 2010). Similar to M5, M7 forecasts k_t, the period effects, as a multivariate random walk with drift. Although mean reverting alternatives are available, they are prone to increased parameter uncertainty (Cairns et al., 2011). The cohort effects, γ_c, are modelled as an ARIMA (1,0,0), $\gamma_c = \mu_\gamma + a_\gamma \left(\gamma_{c-1} - y_{c-2} - \mu_y\right) + \phi_0 Z_\gamma\,(c)$.

Cairns et al. (2011) find that M5 and M7 pass the test of plausibility, with the highest older age volatility is displayed by M7, a most likely effect of its tripartite period term. M1, M2, M5 and M7 perform reasonably well in regard with the biological reasonableness of their projected cohort effects, yet M1 and M2 do not pass the test of biological reasonableness in regard with their projected mortality rates. Both M2 and M5 show the impact of the cohort effect on the projected mortality rates. As a general observation, each model produces distinct projections, this pointing towards model risk as an important risk factor associated with the APC models (Cairns et al., 2011). From the point of view of robustness of model forecasts, the poorest performer is M2, while the best performing model is M7. Cairns et al. (2011) caution that these results are restricted to the EW and US male populations and encourage the same procedure to be repeated with different populations.

2. Methods

Our study relied on death and exposure data for the Romanian population obtained from the National Institute of Statistics. We focused on females of ages 60 to 84 and the historical period 1968–2014. We produced period and cohort effects and 50-year mortality forecasts based on models M1, M2, M5 and M7. The analysis was conducted in R with the StMoMo package. Graphs were obtained based on the recommendations of Villegas et al. (2018).

3. Results and discussion

Fig. 2 shows fan charts for mortality rates at ages 65, 75 and 84 for models M1, M2, M5 and M7. The age selection is based on the three standard key ages in APC mortality literature: young old, $x = 65$, old, $x = 75$ and $x = 84$, the closest age in our dataset to $x = 85$, oldest old. The charts are based on 50 %, 80 % and 95 %

prediction intervals. Models M1 and M2 show fans for the age 75 that are slightly wider than those produced by the same models for the ages 65 and 84. All models predict very small improvements in mortality.

Cairns et al. (2011) tested three LC models on the EW and US populations. For both populations, they obtained fans that decreased in size with the increase in age, with a marked difference between the fans for the ages 65 and 84. Unlike Cairns et al. (2011), our data show fans for the age 84 that are wider than those for the age 65. Based on the anomalous difference between the fans for the ages 65 and 84, Cairns et al. (2011) conclude that model M1 and its extensions do no comply with the criterion of plausibility of the forecast uncertainty levels. As a rule, the predicted mortality rates should mirror the trend in historical mortality rates where improvements at older ages have been lower than those at younger ages. Cairns et al. (2011) attribute this anomaly to the univariate form of k_t and, as a result, the overdependence on $b_x^{(2)}$, the age effect. As mortality improvements are generally in inverse proportion with age, $b_x^{(2)}$ is lower at older than at younger ages, this causing the fans for the older ages to be wider than those for the younger ages (Cairns et al., 2011).

An explanation as to why our results are different from those of Cairns et al. (2011) is the particular nature of mortality improvements in the Central-Eastern European (CEE) countries (Rau et al., 2018). In comparison to the Western European (WE) countries, these countries, have only recently started to show consistent improvements in mortality trends (Rau et al., 2018). Indeed, up until 1994, these countries oscillated between minor, short trend improvements and mortality increases (Kannisto et al., 1994). A quick look at our data reveals historical mortality improvements that are higher at the age 75 than at the other two ages of interest and a historical volatility that increases with age. As for the value of b_x, the largest value is associated with age 75 and the lowest with age 65. However, in our case, the fan for age 75 remains the widest and that for 65, the narrowest, indicating that the greatest uncertainty lies with the predictions for age 75. This finding invalidates M1 and M2 in regard with the plausibility of the uncertainty levels of the forecasts. The test is passed by models M5 and M7 that produce fans that are in accordance with the historical volatility. For models M2 and M7, fans for the ages 75 and 84 wobble until around 2030 and 2040 and then continue smoothly. This oscillation is explained by the dependence of the central trend on the cohort effects (Cairns et al., 2011). Indeed, our cohorts range from 1884 to 1954, this making 2029 and 2038 the last years for which the mortality rates are influenced by the cohort effect. At age 65, both models, show a smooth fan, as for this age, our forecasted period is mainly subjected to the projected cohort effect. These results are matching those of Cairns et al. (2011).

Looking at the mortality fans for the three ages of interest, we notice the following: for ages 65 and 75, the fans are wider for the cohort than for the original versions, while for age 84, the fans are wider for the CBD than for the LC versions. For all ages, the fans of M7 are the widest, this resulting from the fact that M7 has the highest number of period effects from the models that we selected. The central trends for M1 and M5 for the three ages of interest are almost identical and improvement rates gravitate around 1 %. While M5 shows a 1.1 % improvement rate for all ages, M1 shows slightly higher improvement rates for ages 75 and 84 than for age 65 (1.25 % and 1.14 % versus 1.03 %). Surprisingly, M7 shows negligible improvement rates and only for age 84. Model M2 shows the highest improvement rates (1.03 %, 1.64 % and 1.66 %). Model M7 aside, all models predict improvements that are higher for ages 75 and 84 than for age 65. Otherwise, improvements are small across all models. The degree of improvement in mortality rates can also be intuitively deducted from the shapes of the k_t parameters, as seen in Fig. 3. Fig. 3 shows k_t trends that are almost flat for M7 and slightly steeper for M2 than for M1, with the shapes of k_t for M5 pointing towards slightly smaller and more uniform improvement rates.

When judged from the point of view of biological reasonableness, the four models stand close together, all but M7 providing very small improvements that are higher at older ages. Given the particular mortality of CEE countries, it is difficult to evaluate the four models from the point of view of biological reasonableness. The fact that M1, M2 and M5 predict small improvements that are higher at older ages does not contradict the historical pattern of these countries, as exemplified by the mortality rates of Hungary and Poland (see Rau et al. 2018). One can argue that improvements only at the highest ages, as signaled by M7, are not biologically reasonable, as this contradicts the historical pattern of improvements. However, we cannot dismiss models M1, M2 and M5 for predicting improvements that are larger at ages 75 and 84 than at age 65, as this pattern of improvements is confirmed by our historical data and, in addition, by data from two other CEE countries, Hungary and Poland. Data on the Hungarian (years 1950 to 2017) and Polish (years 1958 to 2016) female populations obtained from the Human Mortality Database, show minor improvements for ages 65, 75, 84 and 85, with larger improvements at age 75 (1 % and 1.4 %) and 84 (0.68 % and 1.1 %) than at age 65 (0.66 % and 1 %)) and 85 (0.37 % and 0.95 %). Unfortunately, we do not hold data for the age 85.

Moreover, we cannot exclude any of M1, M2 and M5 based on the small improvements in mortality that are predicted for the next 50 years. Any form of predictive model works on the assumption that the future will be similar with the past. It is recognized in the literature that CEE countries have been showing smaller improvements in mortality than WE countries (see Kannisto et al., 1994, Rau et al., 2018). One of the reasons for this lagging-behind is the failure of the CEE countries to take advantage of the cardiovascular revolution of the 1970s (Rau et al., 2018). Indeed, the CEE countries have the highest cardio vascular disease (CVD) mortality among the European Union (EU) countries, with age standardized mortality rates in Romania more than twice the EU average (Movsisyan et al., 2020). While in the past this difference might have been attributed to availability of up-to date medical care, at present it is mostly attributed to differences in lifestyle, for example lack of exercise, unhealthy diets, high prevalence of smoking and alcohol drinking, stress. With various clinical interventions and preventive strategies aimed at tackling CVD already in place in the CEE countries, it is difficult to ascertain how fast these countries will manage to decrease the number of CVD deaths. It might well be that mortality (and longevity) prediction for these countries will remain an elusive exercise, at least for the foreseeable future. We therefore dismiss M7 based on biological reasonableness, but retain M1, M2 and M5 based on the same criterion.

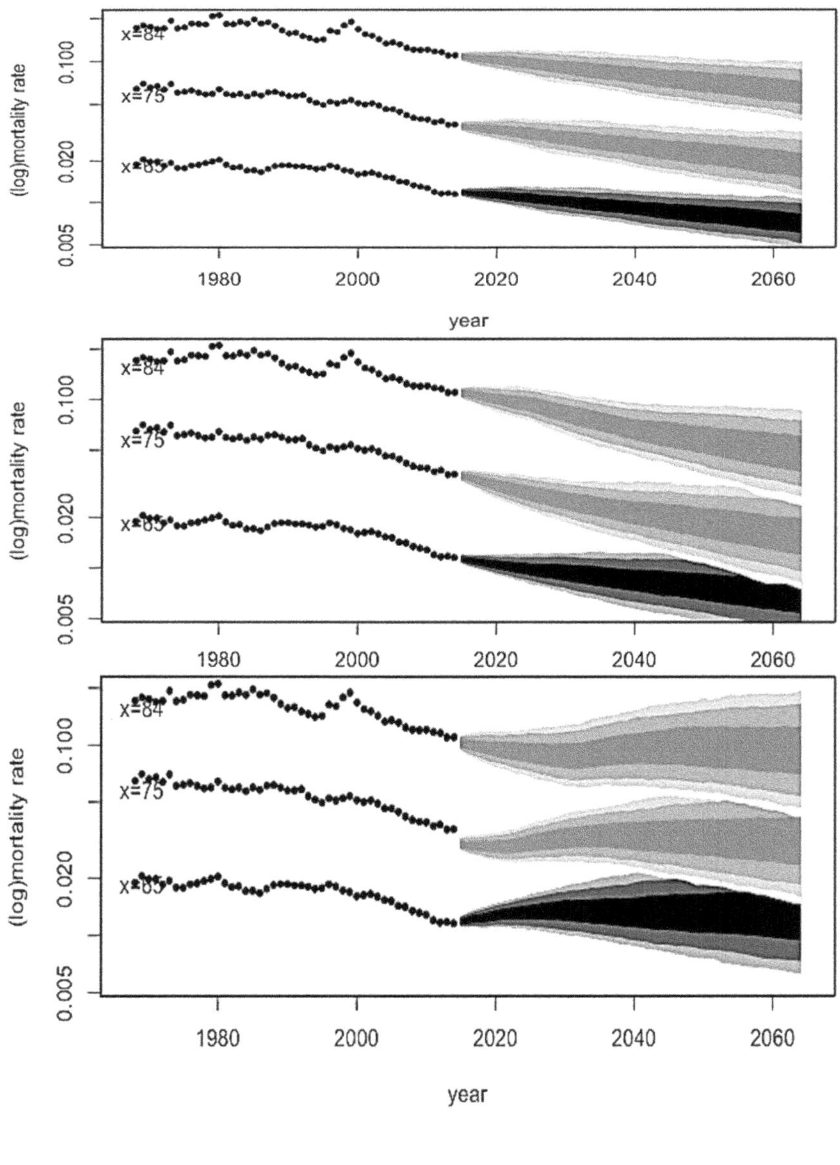

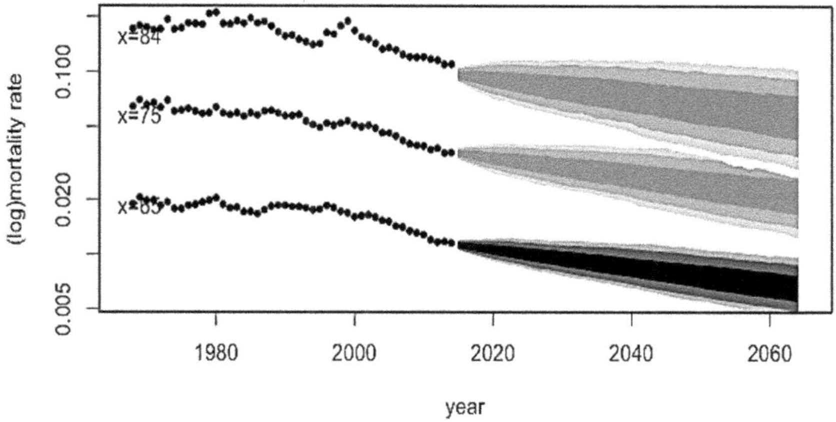

Fig. 2: Mortality forecasts for M1, M2, M5 and M7 (top to bottom order)
Source: Author's own computations, using data from data from the Romanian National Institute of Statistics.

Conclusions

In conclusion, while M1 and M2 fail to comply with the plausibility criterion, M7 fails to predict any improvement in the mortality rates for ages 65 and 75 and thus fails the biological reasonableness test. The only model that complies with both the biological reasonableness and the plausibility criteria is model M5. This is somehow surprising as, the BIC values for all four models, indicated M5 as the least performant model in regard with fit. Moreover, Toropoc (2018) found that M1 provided a better fit than M5 for the Romanian old age female population. However, we remind that a good fit is not necessarily an indicator of a good forecast.

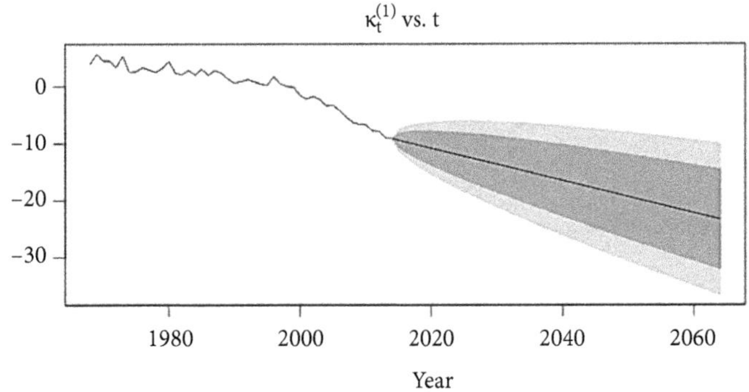

$\kappa_t^{(1)}$ vs. t
0
−10
−20
−30
1980
2000
2020
2040
2060
Year

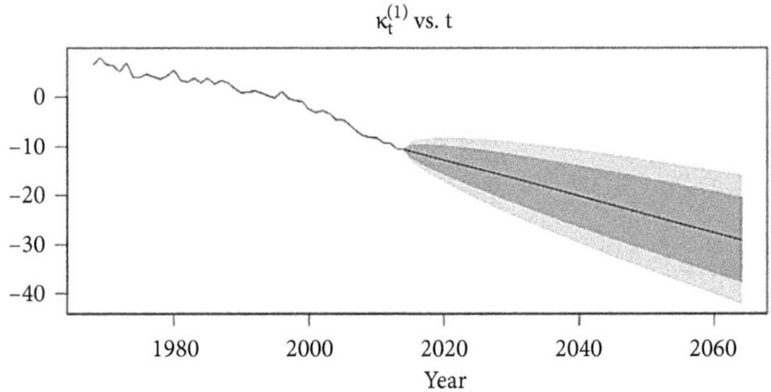

$\kappa_t^{(1)}$ vs. t
0
−10
−20
−30
−40
1980
2000
2020
2040
2060
Year

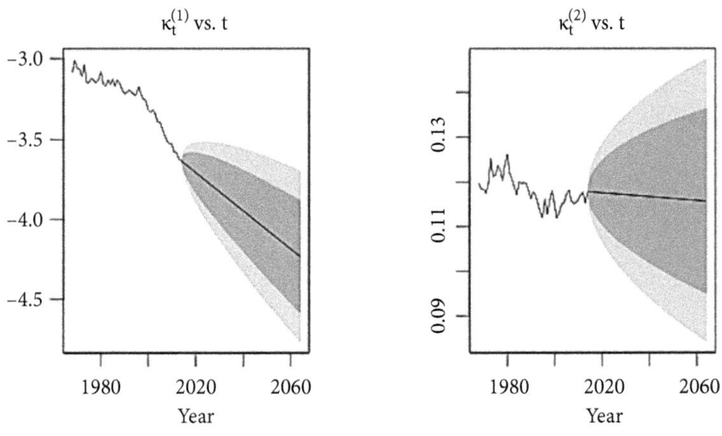

$\kappa_t^{(1)}$ vs. t
−3.0
−3.5
−4.0
−4.5
1980
2020
2060
Year
$\kappa_t^{(2)}$ vs. t
0.13
0.11
0.09
1980
2020
2060
Year

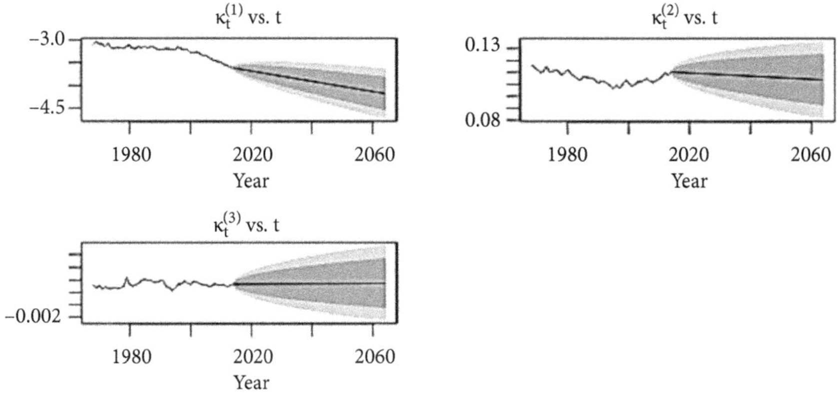

Fig. 3: $\boldsymbol{k}_t$ trends for M1, M2, M5 and M7 (top to bottom)
Source: Author's own computations, using data from the Romanian National Institute of Statistics.

Our study aimed to evaluate the forecasts obtained from four APC models based on the criteria of plausibility of the uncertainty of forecasts and biological reasonableness, as recommended by Cairns et al. (2011). To our knowledge no such attempt has been conducted yet with Romanian data. We suggest as next step the evaluation of the four models from the point of view of robustness of projections, as recommended by Cairns et al. (2011). In addition, we suggest the extrapolation of Romanian mortality data, so that it will include ages 85 to 90 (see the Human Mortality Database methodology).

References

Cairns, A.J.G.; Blake, D.; Dowd, K.: "Pricing Death: Frameworks for the Valuation and Securitization of Mortality Risk". ASTIN Bulletin 36, 2006a, pp. 79–120.

Cairns, A.J.G.; Blake, D.; Dowd, K.: "A Two-Factor Model for Stochastic Mortality with Parameter Uncertainty: Theory and Calibration". Journal of Risk and Insurance 73, 2006b, pp. 687–718.

Cairns, A.J.G.; Blake, D.; Dowd, K.; Coughlan, G.D.; Epstein, D.; Khalaf-Allah, M.: "Mortality Density Forecasts: An Analysis of Six Stochastic Mortality Models". Insurance: Mathematics and Economics 48, 2011, pp. 355–367.

Cairns, A.J.G.; Blake, D.; Dowd, K.; Coughlan, G.D.; Epstein, D.; Ong, A.; Balevich, I.: "A Quantitative Comparison of Stochastic Mortality Models

Using Data from England & Wales and the United States". North American Actuarial Journal 13, 2009, pp. 1–35.

Cairns, A. J. G.; Dowd, K.; Blake, D.; Coughlan, G. D., 2014, Longevity hedge effectiveness: a decomposition. Quantitative Finance, 14(2):217–235.

Dowd, K., Cairns, A.J.G., Blake, D., Coughlan, G.D., Epstein, D., Khalaf-Allah, M.: "Evaluating the goodness of fit of stochastic mortality models". Insurance: Mathematics and Economics 47(3), 2010, pp.255–265.

Harper, S.: "Economic and Social Implications of Aging Societies". Science 346, 2014, pp. 587–591.

Hobcraft J., Menken J., Preston S.: "Age, period, and cohort as sources of variation in demography". Population Index 48 (1), 1982, pp. 4–43.

Hunt, A.; Blake, D.: "On the Structure and Classification of Mortality Models". Pension Institute Working Paper. 2015, URL: http://www.pensions-institute.org/workingpapers/wp1506.pdf, Accessed: 10 Oct 2019.

Kannisto, V.; Lauritsen, J.; Thatcher, A.R.; Vaupel, J.W.: "Reductions in Mortality at Advanced Ages: Several Decades of Evidence from 27 Countries". Population and Development Review 20, 1994, pp. 793–810.

Lee, R. D., Carter, L. R.: "Modelling and forecasting U.S. mortality". Journal of the American Statistical Association. 87 (419), 1992, pp.659–671.

Movsisyan, N.K.; Vinciguerra, M.; Medina-Inojosa, J.R.; Lopez-Jimenez, F.: "Cardiovascular Diseases in Central and Eastern Europe: A Call for More Surveillance and Evidence-Based Health Promotion". Annals of Global Health 86(1), 21, 2020, pp. 1–10.

Rau, R.; Bohk-Ewald, C.; Muszynska, M.M.; Vaupel, J.W.: "Visualizing Mortality Dynamics in the Lexis Diagram". The Springer Series on Demographic Methods and Population Analysis 44, 2018, pp.43–68.

Renshaw, A., Haberman, S., 2006. "A cohort-based extension to the Lee-Carter model for mortality reduction factors". Insurance: Mathematics and Economics, 2006, 38 (3), pp.556–570.

Toropoc, I.: "Fitting the Lee Carter and Cairns Blake Dowd Mortality Risk Models to Gender Split Romanian Population Data". International Journal of Risk Theory 8(2), 2018, pp. 1–10.

Villegas, A.M.; Millossovich, P.; Kaishev, V.: "Package 'StMoMo' ". URL: http://github.com/amvillegas/StMoMo, 2018.

Nicolae-Marius Jula, Dorin Jula

Dynamics of regional employment structures: compositional data analysis

Abstract We analyse the changing in regional structure of employment. By developing a general methodological framework, we demonstrate that: (1) regional employment structures are compositional data; (2) for the dynamics of the structures analysis, the appropriate model is a panel data with time specific fixed effects and cross-section specific effects, weighted by the growth rate of total employment; (3) to analyse the change in structures, the appropriate model is, likewise, a panel with compositional data (a) without time specific (fixed or random) effects; (b) with cross-section specific ones, weighted by total employment; (3) the explanatory variables in the model of regional structure of employment are emigration, net regional settling of domicile, economic growth and foreign direct investment.

Keywords: regional employment structure, compositional data, panel data model

Introduction

In order to analyse the changing in regional structure of employment, we develop a methodology in two fields. First, starting from a previous analysis (Jula & Jula, 2017), we will try to set up a theoretically base for a panel data econometric model. Second, we take into account the fact that regional employment structures are compositional data and develop a methodology founded on Aitchison algebra (Aitchison, 1986). Then, by using these results, we built an econometric panel with compositional data.

1. Methodology

1.1. Theoretically base for a panel data econometric model

We start from a previous analysis (Jula & Jula, 2017) in order to set up a theoretically base for a panel data econometric model. To do this, we use the following notations:

e_i=employment in region *i;*
E=total employment;
$s_i = e_i/E$, the share of region "*I*" in total employment;
X_i=a variable which influences the dynamics of employment in region *i*;
$r^e_{i,t} = de_{i,t}/e_{i,t-1}$, growth rate of employment in the region "*I*";
$r^e_{E,t} = dE_t/E_{t-1}$, growth rate of total employment;

$r^s_{i,t}$ $= ds_{i,t}/s_{i,t-1}$, growth rate of the *i* region share in total employment;
$r^x_{i,t}$ $= dX_{it}/X_{i,t-1}$, the growth rate of variable X tied to region *i*,
$\eta_i = r^e_{i,t}/r^x_{i,t}$, regional employment elasticity with respect to *X*.

(Jula & Jula, 2017, pp. 32–33) demonstrated that growth rate of the *i* region share in total employment can be computed through the following equation:

$$r^s_{i,t} = -\frac{r^e_{E,t}}{1 + r^e_{E,t}} + \frac{1}{1 + r^e_{E,t}} \cdot \eta_i \cdot r^x_{i,t}$$

The equation asserts that: "the impact of X_i on the change in employment share of region '*I*' in total employment is positive, if $\text{sign}(\eta_i)\cdot\text{sign}\left(r^x_{i,t}\right) > 0$" and "the impact of variable X on dynamics of regional share in total employment is proportional to the regional employment elasticity with respect to X, corrected by the inverse of total employment growth index" (Jula & Jula, 2017, p. 33). Furthermore, at national level

$$\frac{1}{1 + r^e_{E,t}} \approx 1 - r^e_{E,t} \; and \; \frac{r^e_{E,t}}{1 + r^e_{E,t}} \approx r^e_{E,t},$$

so that

$$r^s_{i,t} \approx -r^e_{E,t} + \left(1 - r^e_{E,t}\right) \cdot \eta_i \cdot r^x_{i,t}$$

We develop (Jula & Jula, 2017) model so:

$$r^s_{i,t} \approx -r^e_{E,t} - r^e_{E,t}\eta_i r^x_{i,t} + \eta_i r^x_{i,t}$$

and

$$r^s_{i,t} \approx -r^e_{E,t} - r^e_{E,t} r^e_{i,t} + \eta_i \cdot r^x_{i,t}$$

given that $\eta_i = r^e_{i,t}/r^x_{i,t}$. The component $r^e_{E,t}r^e_{i,t}$ is variable both in time and cross-section. Let τ_t be the time specific effects and γ_i the cross-section specific effects. We accept the hypothesis that the time specific effects are cross-section invariant and the cross-section specific effects are time-invariant. Then, starting from the previous equation, we can build an econometric panel data model as follows:

$$r^s_{i,t} = a_0 + a_1 r^e_{E,t} + a_{2,i} r^x_{i,t} + \gamma_i + \tau_t + \varepsilon_{it}$$

where the coefficients $a_{2,i}$ correspond to η_i (regional employment elasticity with respect to *X*) and ε is the variable of idiosyncratic errors. As an alternative, we can build an econometric model in terms of dynamics, like:

$$d^s_{i,t} = a_0 + a_1 d^e_{E,t} + a_{2,i} d^x_{i,t} + \gamma_i + \tau_t + \varepsilon_{it},$$

where *d* is the difference operator.

1.2. Compositional data

Regional employment structures are compositional data (Aitchison, 1986). Most methods from multivariate statistics developed for real valued datasets are misleading or inapplicable for compositional data sets, for various reasons (Boogaart (van den) & Tolosana-Delgado, 2013):

- Independent components mixed together and closed exhibit negative correlations.
- Covariance between two components depends on which other components are reported in the dataset (this disqualifies classical covariance-based tools as objective descriptions of the dependence between just two variables).
- Variance matrices are always singular due to the constant sum constraints.
- Components cannot be normally distributed, due to the bounded range of values (the normal model is a poor one for compositions, because it is a model unable to describe bounded data).

The compositional data are widely used in spatial analysis. An historical review was presented in (Pawlowsky-Glahn & Egozcue, 2016).

Compositions were defined as vectors of positive components and constant sum. D-part *Simplex* S^D is a space of a composition data:

$$x = (x_1, \ldots, x_D)'; \; x_i > 0, \; x_1 + \ldots + x_D = 1.$$

Log ratio transformation change D-part *Simplex* S^D to real space $\Re^{D-1}$

Isometric log ratio transformation (ILR)

Let $v_1, \ldots, v_d$, $d = D-1$ be any orthonormal basis of S^D. The ILR transformation of a composition x is then defined as

$$\text{ilr}(x) = (\langle x, v_1 \rangle_S, \ldots, \langle x, v_d \rangle_S),$$

where $\langle x, y \rangle_S$ is the inner product of two compositions, defined as:

$$\langle x, y \rangle_S = \sum_{i=1}^{D} \ln \frac{x_i}{g(x)} \ln \frac{y_i}{g(y)}$$

and $g(x) = (x_1 x_2 \cdots x_D)^{1/D}$ is the geometric mean.

Distance from x to y is defined in Simplex as:

$$\Delta_S(x, y) = \sum_{i=1}^{D} \left(\ln \frac{x_i}{g(x)} - \ln \frac{y_i}{g(y)} \right)$$

The ILR retains distances: $\Delta_S(x,y) = \text{ilr}(x) - \text{ilr}(y)$

Problem: selected the orthonormal basis of S^D. We used the (Egozcue, Pawlowsky-Glahn, Mateu-Figueras, & Barceló-Vidal, 2003).

Isometric logratio (ilr) transformation

Vector $x = (x_1, x_2, \ldots, x_D)' \in S^D$ is ILR transformed to a vector

$$\mathrm{w} = (\mathrm{w}_1, \mathrm{w}_2, \ldots, \mathrm{w}_{D-1})' \in \Re^{D-1}, \text{where}$$

$$w_k = \sqrt{\frac{k}{k+1}} \ln \frac{\sqrt[k]{\prod_{j=1}^{k} x_j}}{x_{k+1}}, \quad 1 \le k \le D-1$$

The inverse of isometric logratio transformation (invilr) is given by first computing
$\mathrm{v} = (\mathrm{v}_1, \mathrm{v}_2, \ldots, \mathrm{v}_D)'$ as follows:

$$v_k = \sum_{j=k}^{D} \frac{w_j}{\sqrt{j(j+1)}} - \sqrt{\frac{k-1}{k}} w_{k-1}, \quad 1 \le k \le D-1, \; with w_0 = w_D = 0,$$

and, finally

$$x_k = \frac{\exp(v_k)}{\sum_{i=1}^{D} \exp(v_i)}$$

2. Econometric model: changes in the structure of regional employment

We built an econometric model in accordance with theoretical analysis, where the explanatory variable (regional structure of employment) is a compositional data one.

2.1. Data

We use the World Bank definition of Foreign Direct Investment: "Foreign Direct Investment is defined as investment that is made to acquire a lasting management interest (usually 10 % of voting stock) in an enterprise operating in a country other than that of the investor (defined according to residency) (...). It is the sum of equity capital, reinvestment of earnings, other long-term capital, and short-term capital as shown in the balance of payments" (World Bank, 1996, p. 182). Data concerning Foreign Direct Investment is provided by National Bank of Romania, (http://www.bnro.ro/PublicationDocuments.aspx?icid=14364). Data sources are detailed in Tab. 1.

The other data series are from National Institute of Statistics (NIS), Tempo-Online time series (http://statistici.insse.ro/shop/index.jsp?page=tempo2&lang=en&context=15)

Tab. 1: Data source

Variable	*Data source*
Employment (Civil economically active population)	NIS, Tempo-online, tables FOM103A & FOM103D
Gross Domestic Product	NIS, Tempo-online, tables CON103C & CON103I
Average number of employees	NIS, Tempo-online, table FOM104B
Permanent emigrants	NIS, Tempo-online, table POP309A
Permanent immigrants	NIS, Tempo-online, table POP310A
Net settling of domicile	NIS, Tempo-online, table POP303B
Net settling of the residence	NIS, Tempo-online, table POP306A

2.2. The panel data model

The structure of regional employment is explained by the net regional flow of external migration, by the regional economic growth, as well as by the regional foreign direct investments (Agrawal, 2015). We also consider that the inertia of the structural processes can be an explanatory variable (Albu, 2008). The panel data model is built with cross-section fixed effects and without time fixed effects. The time effects was captured by autoregressive process AR(1).

$$(w)empl_{it} = a_0 + a_1(imgr_{it} + ssd_{it} - emgr_{it})/(empl\_total_t) + a_2gdp_{it} + a_3fdi_{it} + e_{it}$$

$$e_{it} = \rho_i e_{i,t-1} + \varepsilon_{it}.$$

where

(w) – symbolise the *irl* transformation

empl – share of regional employment in total civil economically active population

imgr – permanent immigrants

emgr – permanent emigrants

ssd – net settling of domicile

gdp – growth rate of Gross Domestic Product

fdi – foreign direct investment

$a_0, \ldots a_3$ – coefficients

i – region

t – time index

The model outputs are in Tab. 2.

Tab. 2: Panel model with compositional data

Exogenous: (w)empl				
Variable	Coefficients	Std. Error	t-Statistic	Prob.
C	0.104149	0.013418	7.762167	0.0000
(imgr?+ssd?-emgr?)/(empl_total)	-0.002822	0.000684	-4.127454	0.0001
@pc(gdp?)	0.031590	0.005793	5.453196	0.0000
fdi?	0.002521	0.000620	4.066047	0.0001
BI-AR(1)	0.645676	0.070362	9.176430	0.0000
CE-AR(1)	0.806544	0.053818	14.98651	0.0000
NE-AR(1)	0.600542	0.071272	8.426059	0.0000
NV-AR(1)	0.947856	0.052979	17.89102	0.0000
SE-AR(1)	0.791564	0.062130	12.74044	0.0000
SM-AR(1)	0.836786	0.067310	12.43188	0.0000
SV-AR(1)	0.881101	0.151718	5.807488	0.0000
Fixed Effects (Cross)				
BI – C	-0.050165			
CE – C	-0.124629			
NE – C	-0.124882			
NV – C	0.148835			
SE – C	-0.123975			
SM – C	0.202143			
SV – C	0.113306			

Source: Model estimates in EViews

All the coefficients are significant at standard level. Interpretation of output is:

- Net foreign emigration coupled with net regional settling of domicile has a negative impact on regional structure of employment (the share of regional employment in total employment);
- Economic growth (measured by GDP dynamics) has a positive impact on share of regional employment in total employment;
- Net flux of foreign direct investments was positive correlated with share of regional employment in total employment;
- In the regional structure of employment there are strong inertial effects: from 64.57 % in Bucharest-Ilfov region, to 94.79 % in North-West.

There is a negative scale effect.

Conclusions

Regional employment structures are compositional data (Aitchison, 1986). For this reason, we use the Aitchison algebra for transforming the regional structures. The econometric model with compositional data has good performances of fit the empirical data concerning the regional employment structure.

Overall, Foreign Direct Investment has a significant and positive effects on changes in structure of regional employment: the growth of FDI led to an increase of that region's share in total employment. The FDI effect on productivity improvement was superior to the effect induced on employment growth for Centre, North-East and South-East Regions. For the remaining regions, the FDI effect on employment growth exceeds that on productivity.

Similarly, GDP dynamics had a positive effect: economic growth favored a differentiated increase in regional employment.

There is a significant inertial effect. In the current year, previous structures are accountant for proportions varying between 60 % (North-East Region) and 95 % (North-West Region).

References

Agrawal, G. (2015, April). Foreign Direct Investment and Economic Growth in BRICS Economies: A Panel Data Analysis. Journal of Economics, Business and Management, 3(4), 421–424.

Aitchison, J. (1986). The Statistical Analysis of Compositional Data. Monographs on Statistics and Applied Probability. New York: Chapman and Hall Ltd.

Albu, L.-L. (2008). Trends in Structural Changes and Convergence in UE. Romanian Journal of Economic Forecasting, 9(1), 91–101.

Boogaart (van den), G. K., & Tolosana-Delgado, R. (2013). Analyzing Compositional Data with R. Berlin Heidelberg: Springer-Verlag.

Egozcue, J., Pawlowsky-Glahn, V., Mateu-Figueras, M.-G., & Barceló-Vidal, C. (2003). Isometric Logratio Transformations for Compositional Data Analysis. Mathematical Geology, 35(3), 279–300. Retrieved August 14, 2019, from https://link.springer.com/article/10.1023/A:1023818214614.

Jula, D., & Jula, N.-M. (2017). Foreign Direct Investments and Employment. Structural Analysis. Romanian Journal of Economic Forecasting, XX(2), 30–45.

Pawlowsky-Glahn, V., & Egozcue, J.-J. (2016). Spatial Analysis of Compositional Data: A Historical Review. Journal of Geochemical Exploration, 164, 28–32. doi:10.1016/j.gexplo.2015.12.010

World Bank (1996), World debt tables 1996: external finance for developing countries: Analysis and summary tables (English). p. 182. World Debt Tables Washington, D.C.: World Bank Group. http://documents.worldbank.org/curated/en/405961468350191079/Analysis-and-summary-tables), accessed 15.04.2019.

Annexes

Annex 1: R code for isometric logratio transformation (ilr)

```
> library("mkin", lib.loc="~/R/win-library/3.4")
Loading required package: minpack.lm
Loading required package: rootSolve
Loading required package: inline
Loading required package: parallel
```

```
> ilr(c(0.113671  0.123400  0.155427  0.136223  0.123075  0.145361  0.105195  0.097646))
[2003]         -0.058066 -0.221927 -0.042711  0.057699 -0.104817  0.210828  0.252242
> ilr(c(0.119065  0.122270  0.152131  0.136593  0.124018  0.143598  0.103007  0.099317))
[2004]         -0.01878  -0.18925  -0.040524  0.054995 -0.088910  0.232434  0.235419
> ilr(c(0.126585  0.120149  0.150839  0.136525  0.122544  0.141697  0.102152  0.099506))
[2005]          0.036897 -0.164433 -0.029924  0.073446 -0.072596  0.241599  0.233779
> ilr(c(0.133434  0.121013  0.147143  0.136422  0.122300  0.139858  0.100716  0.099110))
[2006]          0.069092 -0.119738 -0.019150  0.082902 -0.054769  0.257673  0.238186
> ilr(c(0.138862  0.120319  0.144661  0.135974  0.121076  0.139217  0.100276  0.099611))
[2007]          0.101349 -0.091917 -0.011364  0.094991 -0.049892  0.261604  0.232777
> ilr(c(0.146530  0.119641  0.142780  0.135806  0.120910  0.137304  0.099119  0.097907))
[2008]          0.143356 -0.061599 -0.000190  0.103771 -0.031344  0.275206  0.249842
> ilr(c(0.145088  0.119110  0.143650  0.137503  0.120215  0.137907  0.099409  0.097114))
[2009]          0.139511 -0.072410 -0.013327  0.109851 -0.035639  0.272937  0.258216
> ilr(c(0.145114  0.119670  0.144206  0.137816  0.118846  0.137947  0.099482  0.096914))
[2010]          0.136316 -0.073578 -0.012771  0.122560 -0.035984  0.272228  0.260222
> ilr(c(0.146374  0.120351  0.142585  0.138270  0.117888  0.138007  0.099085  0.097435))
[2011]          0.138420 -0.058500 -0.014751  0.131205 -0.036706  0.275723  0.254487
> ilr(c(0.144580  0.121440  0.142912  0.138536  0.117975  0.137999  0.098954  0.097600))
[2012]          0.123327 -0.061724 -0.016713  0.130750 -0.036358  0.277189  0.252937
> ilr(c(0.147340  0.122007  0.141103  0.139263  0.117682  0.137012  0.097531  0.098058))
[2013]          0.133401 -0.041707 -0.018121  0.136565 -0.027328  0.291589  0.247478
> ilr(c(0.148760  0.121731  0.139971  0.140707  0.117034  0.135974  0.096516  0.099303))
[2014]          0.141789 -0.032142 -0.027265  0.143643 -0.019647  0.300723  0.233805
> ilr(c(0.152830  0.123084  0.137807  0.140997  0.116178  0.134007  0.094441  0.100652))
[2015]          0.153059 -0.00388  -0.022560  0.155694 -0.003201  0.321249  0.218634
```

Annex 2: R code for reconstructing structures

(invirl - *inverse of isometric logratio transformation*)

```
> library("mkin", lib.loc="~/R/win-library/3.4")
Loading required package: minpack.lm
Loading required package: rootSolve
Loading required package: inline
Loading required package: parallel
```

```
> invilr (c(-0.058066 -0.221926 -0.042711 0.057699 -0.104817 0.210827 0.252241))
[2003] 0.113671 0.123400 0.155427 0.136222 0.123075 0.145361 0.105195 0.097646
> invilr (c(-0.004019 -0.181760 -0.03182 0.06796 -0.08253 0.229667 0.244506))
[2004] 0.121578 0.122272 0.152325 0.136231 0.122831 0.142881 0.103399 0.098479
> invilr (c(0.040283 -0.149993 -0.026205 0.074970 -0.071731 0.239476 0.238698))
[2005] 0.127910 0.120827 0.149388 0.136229 0.122464 0.141664 0.102443 0.099071
> invilr (c(0.075455 -0.117807 -0.018554 0.087034 -0.054167 0.256158 0.241804))
[2006] 0.134321 0.120726 0.147107 0.136510 0.121878 0.139798 0.100894 0.098763
> invilr (c(0.105580 -0.094257 -0.01498 0.097293 -0.046893 0.266160 0.240517))
[2007] 0.139326 0.120001 0.145126 0.136721 0.121048 0.139015 0.099911 0.098847
> invilr (c(0.12477 -0.076167 -0.011512 0.104695 -0.033596 0.279074 0.239278))
[2008] 0.143194 0.120031 0.143920 0.137052 0.120704 0.13752 0.098660 0.098914
> invilr (c(0.118625 -0.069175 -0.018290 0.106783 -0.035900 0.279560 0.233113))
[2009] 0.142639 0.120609 0.142759 0.137799 0.1203704 0.137745 0.098561 0.099513
> invilr (c(0.12874 -0.056574 -0.016026 0.115886 -0.027201 0.286528 0.233902))
[2010] 0.145136 0.120976 0.142014 0.138135 0.1196767 0.136762 0.097898 0.099399
> invilr (c(0.136578 -0.0463327 -0.015834 0.124425 -0.024711 0.293189 0.232376))
[2011] 0.146974 0.121159 0.141235 0.138501 0.118873 0.136512 0.097239 0.099503
> invilr (c(0.141351 -0.036220 -0.016802 0.134755 -0.020235 0.296818 0.231775))
[2012] 0.148529 0.121617 0.140497 0.139075 0.117896 0.135979 0.096875 0.099529
> invilr (c(0.147976 -0.030531 -0.020353 0.139783 -0.018127 0.304248 0.230679))
[2013] 0.149731 0.121458 0.139994 0.139794 0.117479 0.135795 0.096156 0.099588
> invilr (c(0.141615 -0.024452 -0.024405 0.147267 -0.017096 0.306711 0.229327))
[2014] 0.149555 0.122411 0.139418 0.140568 0.116735 0.135687 0.095914 0.099709
> invilr (c(0.148705 -0.020082 -0.018291 0.154850 -0.015078 0.308406 0.230663))
[2015] 0.151165 0.122495 0.139466 0.140126 0.115998 0.135449 0.095747 0.099549
```

Frantz Daniel Fistung, Laurențiu David

Romanian housing market between the socialist constraints and contemporary tendencies

Abstract From the forced industrialization which supported the migration of the labor force from villages to cities, and implicitly of the national plans regarding the construction of houses, during the socialist period (1947–1989) to the current situation (1989–Present) characterized by the reverse-migration of the population, from large cities to villages, as well as the development of private housing construction on the outskirts of large cities, Romania's real estate market has suffered significant changes. Based on the "2011 Population and Housing Census" findings, the total number of dwellings relative to the total resident population, led to believe that the demand for housing did not recognize a recrudescence. In spite of this situation, while many of the existing residential areas are degraded, abandoned or placed in unattractive locations, the requests for new housing seem to remain a well-embraced option of many Romanians. The present study tries to provide the necessary answers and explanations to this paradoxical situation of Romanian housing market during the two analyzed periods, namely the pre- and post-December 1989.

Keywords: constructions, houses, building developers, housing tenants, homeowners

Introduction

Over the last seven decades, the national housing construction policy was marked by two major paradigm shifts. The imposed restrictions and requirements of the socialist system based on the command economy on one hand, and the demands of the contemporary period influenced by the requirements of the free economic market, on the other hand, have provoked contradictory tendencies, in the housing market. The Romanian communist government brought during the socialist period, in stark contrast, substantial changes with respect to the economic, demographic and architectural-urban planning policies. This aspect, per se, led to the forced-development of state-owned housing constructions.

After 1990, the policies of the successive governments of Romania have completely overturned this aspect. It is worth noting in this respect that, in a majority of cases, the tenants became the owners of the socialist-built dwellings, in which they lived. At the same time, the old state-owned construction companies disappeared, their place being taken by private contractors. While during the socialist period the urbanization policy (moving villagers to the cities) seem to dominate every aspect of housing construction sector of industry, in stark contrast, during the free market economy period, a de-urbanization started to occur (city dwellers moving in rural areas).

1. Literature review

The house has been, over the centuries, the subject of permanent debates between specialists, politicians and the general public. Whether in detail or in general, this topic was researched by many authors in the past. Some of the most representative studies that can be briefly mentioned are: "Bucharest from the past and today" (Popescu-Lumină, 2007), "Between history and present. Housing policies in Romania" (Noica, 2003), "Introduction to the economic history of Romania - Modern and contemporary era" (Axenciuc, 1999), "The construction market in Romania" (Patriche, 2003), "Capital accumulation and the organization of emerging socialist markets: real estate agents from Cluj-Napoca" (Petrovici, 2004) The majority of the studies pertaining to the style and the pace of house construction development in Romania were descriptive in nature and did not involve a comparison of any kind between different periods of times. As a result, based on the existing evidence, the present paper found imperiously necessary to fill out the existing gap in the existing research literature and produce such a study.

2. Highlights of convergence and divergence: a comparison of the real estate market in Romania between the pre and post December 1989 periods

After the end of the Second World War, Romania's house market experienced a powerful paradigm shift. The construction of houses, started to be replaced, at a fast pace, by depersonalized constructions called blocks of flats, necessary in the process of developing the envisioned socialist society.

In the classic model of socialist urbanization, it was tried to minimize the costs of urbanization, but not from the point of view of production, but by minimizing the associated social costs. The houses in the villages on the outskirts of the city were demolished in order to build the new neighborhoods of the "triumphant socialism" (Petrovici, 2005). Neighborhoods were crowded to minimize the land use, and implicitly the associated costs, without carving too much into the city's agricultural land, extensively exploited. The land transaction market was practically frozen and selling of a piece of land became a "real adventure."

The creation and development of apartments in the blocks was most strongly felt during the period of forced displacement of the rural population to the big urban centers, in order to ensure the necessary labor force, mainly, to support the forced industrialization process. The imposition of an urban model, within the residential complex (neighborhoods of blocks), as a measure of cost and production efficiency led to the creation of numerous dwellings by promoting on one hand, the typical apartments made from prefabricated panels and, on the other hand, the mechanization of the associated execution work for these apartments.

This concept of population displacement, per se, was the basis of the first divergence in the process of housing construction in Romania, carried out during the socialist and continued during the contemporary periods.

The housing crisis that existed after 1989 was inherited from the communist regime. The changes that took place after December 1989 instead of diminishing the crisis made it more acute. The reduction of activity and interest in the construction of houses, especially in large cities, can be considered the aggravating factor leading to this negative situation. Other factors such as the reduction of the construction of state-funded houses, the decrease of the purchasing power, the massive increase of the production costs of the construction materials beyond the purchasing power of the families with average incomes, contributed to the aggravation of this situation. As a result, after December 1989, in the era considered contemporary, a large migration from large cities to villages consisting of thousands of families took place. According to data gathered, the phenomenon of migration to villages intensified for the first time in 1997, when over 81 thousand Romanians moved from urban to rural, almost three times more than in 1990.The rationale for this contemporary migration process is grounded on two distinct aspects.

The first aspect can be called survival, characterized by the migration of a segment of the older population, generally, those individuals with low incomes, basically, "the victims of the forced urbanization of the country" who returned to the areas of childhood and tried to maintain a decent livable financial situation.

The second aspect can be called reorientation, and it was supported by the change in the living environment, from the super crowded and highly polluted areas, towards quieter, cleaner areas. In these circumstances, there are individuals who have chosen to live in rural areas near economically developed cities, such as Bucharest, Timişoara, Iaşi or Cluj, but whose activity was carried out in the cities close to the home, chose to commute on a daily basis. In this category could be included those who have, simply, chosen to live and work in a greener environment without commuting.

In order to better understand this phenomenon, to get the bigger picture, it is important to highlight the main landmarks of the housing market evolution in Romania, starting with the first multi-annual economic plans imposed by the communists up to the present time. The main factor that influenced the evolution of the real estate market was, as we have mentioned, the process of forced industrialization during the period of command economy. This led to a significant increase in the pace of housing construction during the 1945–1980 period (See Fig. 1).

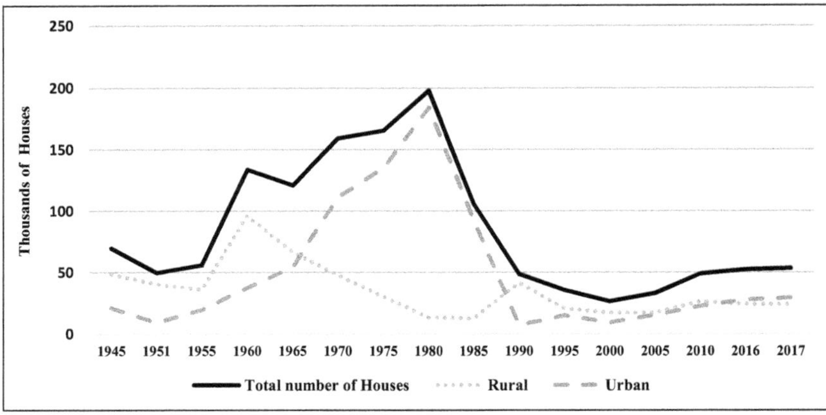

Fig. 1: Annual evolutions of the number of newly built houses in Romania, between 1945 and 2017 in both rural and urban living areas

Source: Data and processed data from: Axenciuc V., 2018 and INS, 2017.

The significant decrease of investments in the field of housing construction can be observed during the 1980–2000 period. The reason for it is multifactorial. In the first part of the analyzed interval, namely, between 1980–1989, the decrease in the number of new houses built in the urban environment, from about 200,000 to 50,000 units, was mainly caused by the involution of the national industry and the decrease of the competitiveness of the Romanian products, together with the unpleasant financial situation of possible entering in default payment as a result of accessing and using foreign loans to revitalize and modernize the main sectors of industry. Facing a huge trade deficit, Romanian government, at the time, focused it attention, with priority, on foreign currency receipts from exports while pursuing a quick and complete payment of foreign debt. This policy led to a decrease of the investments in the construction of state-funded new homes.

After 1990, the field of new housing construction continued its downward trend, due to the sudden changes at the political, economic and social levels, changes that caused a massive decrease of the public funds' investments. Under these circumstances, the economic crisis accentuated between 1991 and 1992, the rampant inflation rate of almost 250 % together with a low level of external financing, made it necessary, for the newly installed Romanian government, to apply austerity policies which, in turn, resulted in a compression of consumption. After 1992, the unjustified delay of the restructuring of the national economy negatively impacted on the country's economic recovery. The first signs pointing out at the recovery of the national economy, including in the field of constructions, appeared after year 2000. In these conditions, the year 2000 was the one in which the least newly built houses were developed (about 26,000 units) during the entire analyzed period, 1945–2017.

Analyzing Fig. 1, above, it can be observed that in stark contrast, the year 1980 (socialist era) registered the maximum number of newly built dwellings with an annual production of new housing of about 200,000 units. Interestingly, while the ratio of the number of newly built homes in the urban to rural areas fluctuated during the communist period, it was relatively constant during the 1990–2017 period. Thus, during 1945–1980, in the context of a general increase in the number of newly built dwellings, the housing stock available, in the urban area, experienced a significant growth trend, while, at the same time, in the rural area, the housing stock available recognized an important constriction. After 1980 and in the first decade of the post-December 1989 period, the activity of housing construction decreased steadily and intensely.

The second aspect, pertained to the structure and the country-wide modification of houses' ownership. Thus, the socialist period had as a main starting landmark the Decree 92/1950 issued by the communist authorities. According to Decree 92/1950 all the existing housing infrastructure was transferred "in the state property and became goods of the whole people, without any compensation and free from any real duties or rights of any kind" including the buildings of former industrialists, landlords, bankers and large traders, hotels with their entire inventory, buildings under construction, damaged or destroyed.

The old mechanisms of access to a home were replaced by the principles of communist "egalitarianism," by the "distribution" made by a state office or even by illegal occupation, often imposed by force. In this context, a large part of the homes with private status went into the state ownership, in order to be later on rented. The subsequent process of state-owned house construction, most of them in blocks of flats, encouraged the process of renting living spaces. Within this context, over the years, socialist Romania ended up having an overwhelming majority of tenants and just a small segment of homeowners. In all the industrial cities, the construction of the working-class neighborhoods began with the intended scope of accommodating the increasing number of workers as part of country's rapid forced-industrialization. These housing facilities were built essentially at the outskirts of the cities, on un-assumed lands or in suburban areas, based on the criterion of proximity to the newly built industrial units. Later, especially towards the end of the socialist era, the historical centers, of many Romanian's cities were systematized, building blocks instead of numerous houses or architectural-cultural monuments.

A novelty in the field was the idea of urbanization of rural localities. In this context, in the last decade of the command economy, it has been attempted the destruction of thousands of villages and at the same time and the almost total destruction of traditional buildings. The intent was to replace them with apartment blocks. Together with this replacement a large contingent of rural population, over 11 million people, were moved from privately-owned single-family homes, into flats as tenants. Fortunately, the plan did not succeed completely and only three villages (Buda, Vlădiceasca and Dimieni) were destroyed until 1989.

Given the increasing and relentless efforts of the socialist leaders to support the industrialization of the country, the need for dwellings intended to support the Romania's industrial development increased exponentially. This fact, in turn, determined the communist power to look for new financing alternatives. As a result, the communist government started to promote the construction of privately-funded property dwellings, creating mortgage funds guaranteed by personal incomes that allowed for the diversification of the types of housing from the collective buildings by categories of comfort. Thus, for the construction of personal property dwellings, in the urban environment, the state granted to the citizens loans for a term of 15–25 years, with an annual interest of 1.5–3 %, provided that the beneficiary puts a down-payment of 20–30 % of the value of the house, depending on the tariff salary or the gross monthly income that it realizes.

In stark contrast with the pre-December 1989, the socialist era, the post-December period allowed for an accentuation of a reverse process. According to some estimates, in January 1990, in Romania, between two and three million people were in the position of tenants, in nationalized buildings. The Decree-Law no. 61/1990, in this respect, aimed at regulating the process of privatization of state-funded residential buildings by allowing the population to buy the dwellings they actually rented if they wanted to. As a result of this legislative measure, until August 1994, about 1,825,000 homes or about 45 % of the total existing housing stock was sold to the public, at the January 1990 price (Noica, 2003).

This action prompted Romania, together with Albania, to become the countries with the highest share of private property housing out of the total existing housing fund (over 95 %) in Europe. In fact, many of the countries from the former communist bloc where the governments that came to power after 1990 promoted similar populist policies. At the opposite part of the house ownership spectrum were very well-developed countries like Germany and Switzerland where the percentage of house ownership was quite low. The explanation lies not only in the houses' acquisition high price, but also in the culture, values, norms and trends in those countries.

Subsequently, past 1990, the largest number of newly built dwellings were private property, the state financing only timid and inconsistent housing with social destinations for renting.

Thus, through the Emergency Ordinance of the Government of Romania no. 60/2009, the "First Home" program was approved, both as a measure of support for the young people on their first real estate purchase, and as a form of impetus for a real estate market which was in a deadlock at the time. The objective of the "First Home" program was, at the beginning, to facilitate the access of individuals to the purchase or construction of higher quality housing, by contracting state guaranteed loans which represented a measure of support for the internal demand of the real estate sector. The dwellings could be built by the beneficiaries who owned the land on which the house was to be built or through associations without legal personality, at least one of the associates being the owner of the land on which the houses were to be built. Subsequently, a series of changes were made to better meet the needs of customers, and each edition bore trivial chronological names such as: First House 2, First House 3, First House 4 etc.

The financial costs related to a loan, under such program, incurred by the beneficiaries, were often modified, initially with an advance of at least 5 % of the purchase price of the home, which covered the difference between the purchase price of the home resulting from the pre-sale-purchase contract and the secured financing, advance which was determined under market conditions. Bank fees were always added to it. The loan was fully guaranteed, afterwards only partially, and was granted for a maximum period of 35 years. Financially, this way of supporting the purchase of new houses was much more advantageous than the previous socialist offer. However, the low purchasing power during the contemporary period and the insecurity of jobs made this type of money lending much more risky than the one offered during the socialist era.

The phenomenon of renting houses, in the last years of the contemporary period, has begun to increase within the context of rising prices for new homes or increasing demand for specific segments (students, specialists working in areas other than official residence, tourists, etc.). Discussing about the comfort of homes relative to the total number of such newly built units it can be ascertain that from the beginning years of the socialist period until now the average of living areas within the newly built housing has had a permanent upward trend, although not with remarkable pace up to 2011 (Fig. 2).

The decrease in the number of new homes, built during 1980–2002 together with the increase of the average living area for a dwelling denotes an increase in the quality of the offer, by increasing the living space. This aspect is in contradiction with the trends from 1948–1980 and from 2002–2019.

The real estate developers, almost constantly increased, with small exceptions, the price of the square meter of housing while the financial power of the applicants often made the demand not to cover the supply. Under these circumstances, the builders adapted their supply by simultaneously decreasing the price of houses and their living areas at the cost of maintaining the upward trend of the price of square meter of housing.

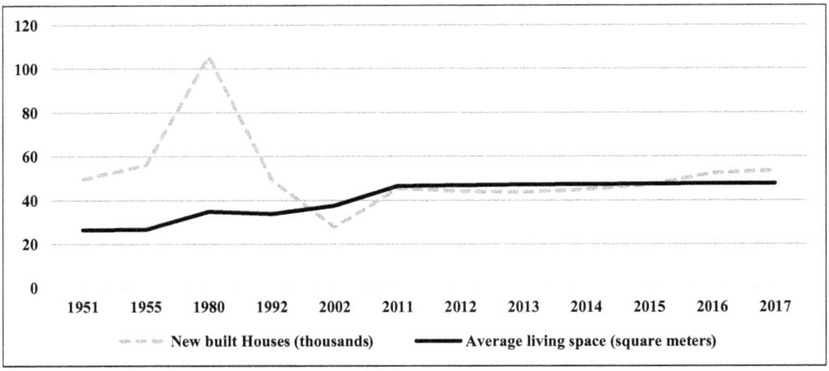

Fig. 2: Developments of indicators specific to the supply of housing, newly built, in the socialist and contemporary periods

Source: Data and processing after: Anghel I., Fistung D. and Popescu T., 2018 and INS, 2019.

Analyzing the trends during the socialist period, after 1980, it can be observed on one hand a diminishing number of houses while on the other hand an increase of the living areas fact that can be explained by the resource-based economy imposed by the communist regime (financial and material).

However, regardless of the nature of the regime, at the time, the average dwelling area per person remained low. Thus, if at the end of the socialist period the area was only 11 square meters, after two decades of free market, the level reached only 20.4 square meters in the context in which the regulations of the European Union imposed a minimum of 30 square meters.

As a result, we can say that Romanians still live in conditions of low comfort with all the changes of economic paradigm and efforts made to meet the real needs of the population. This aspect can be attributed to the lack of greater purchasing power, the high profits of construction companies, as well as the developers' indifference to the requests of potential home buyers.

3. A comparative analysis of the main characteristics of the Romanian housing market during pre- and post-December 1989 periods

During 1945–1989, the socialist policies, supported by a command economy, favored the rapid increase of the number of houses of small size and low comfort, the majority of them being built as blocks of flats for the working class. They had to satisfy more the demands regarding the relocation of the labor force from different villages across the country around big urban economic complexes. The style and the architectural imprint were rather copied according to the models established in the other Eastern European countries. In 1990, 85 % of the housing stock in Romania was built after 1945 (MDRAPFE, 2017).

The relaunch of the economic development after 1990, not only led to a dramatic decrease of the housing construction pace, but also changed the architectural concepts of the constructions. However, the total number of dwellings increased after more than two decades of democracy with just over one million. Suggestively, the characteristics of the housing market during the two analyzed periods are presented in Tab. 1, below.

Tab. 1: SWOT analysis of housing construction market during socialist and contemporary periods

Characteristics	**Period**	
	1947–1989	**1990-present**
STRENGTHS	- there was an increased level of construction - the communist government supported the construction of apartments - there was an increased demand for apartments - the state supported through its policies the renting or acquisition of apartments - the apartments constructed were reliable and safe since they were built according to the existing standards - the housing neighborhoods were created in areas with access to public utilities networks	- houses constructed were more attractive from an architectural perspective and were located in less crowded areas - the legislation encouraged the purchase of the first home - the increase a livable space close to the level of the European average
OPPORTUNITIES	- meet the demand for houses in Romania - decrease of the construction costs - increase of the level of comfort of the houses	- increase of the level of comfort of the houses - annual increase of the number of the newly built houses - construction of new residential areas in more attractive locations (economical, ecological, educational) - meet, largely, the demand for new houses

(*continued on next page*)

Tab. 1: Continued

Characteristics	**Period**	
WEAKNESSES	- the comfort for most of the houses built was low - the aging of the houses built led to degradation and decreased resistance to seismic activities - the construction of houses took place in crowded areas - the creation of residential areas was correlated to the newly developed industrial economic centers	- numerous changes in legislation - failure to comply with the construction norms favoring sometimes a poor quality work - creation of housing complexes that do not have access to public utilities (water, sewage, electricity, gas, public transport) - low annual rate of house construction
THREATS	- the degradation of the existing housing stock - the abandonment of houses created by the communist regime in those areas where the economic activities came to an end - low annual rate of house construction	-further degradation of the housing stock built during the socialist era - increase cost of houses' construction together with decreasing level of comfort - low annual rate of house construction

Source: Authors data processing

The data gathered by the 2011 Census revealed the fact that, in Romania, the average dwelling ratio is 2.3 persons/dwelling since for 20.1 million residents there were 8.7 million dwellings available (Anghel, Fistung, and Popescu, 2018). This ratio is close to that of the average size of households' membership which was 2.66. In this situation, it is assumed that, in the near future, the demand for new housing will decrease. Within this context, there is a high likeliness that the quality and comfort of the houses to-be-built in the near future will increase while their acquisition costs will recognize a downward trend.

Conclusions

The house market in Romania, during the analyzed periods, revealed many trends. The period of the command economy, with its accelerated pace of housing construction, placed a heavy imprint not only on the destination, but also on the level of comfort of these houses. The changes brought by the socialist development of the industry led to a relocation trend that took place, over the years, particularly when normal family dwellings were slowly replaced by workplace location-related dwellings. Within this context, the process of population migration from rural to urban areas recognized a significant recrudescence.

The contemporary period has greatly reduced these trends. Comparing the contemporary period to the socialist era, the pace of housing construction was more than modest, the comfort of new buildings began to increase, the new residential areas were much more attractive and the population went on a reverse migration process mode from urban to rural areas.

After 1990, the tendency of over-urbanization of the localities with important economic activities during the period of the command economy, has been superimposed on the tendency to increase the residential spaces. This aspect led to the expansion of the city limits to the bordering areas. This aspect, per se, indicates a real change of the urban concept supported by the move from the cities' epicentral agglomeration to the expansion of the urban spaces into their bordering areas. In spite of the fact that there is an increase of demand for new residential houses, it is less likely that this sector will recognize a boom trend in the near future.

References

Anghel I., Fistung D., and Popescu T.: "Public Constructions and Buildings (Romania's Economy after the Great Union", Volume II-Sectoral Economy), Romanian Civilization Collection, Vol. 16, Publishing House of the Romanian Academy, ISBN: 978-973-27-3023-2, 2018, pages 305–340.

Axenciuc V.: The Economic Progress of Romania. Secular Statistical Series 1860–2010. Vol. II, Industry and Construction, Academia Publishing House, Bucharest, 2018.

Axenciuc V.: Introduction to the Economic History of Romania. Modern and Contemporary Times, Part I, "Foundation of Tomorrow" Publishing House, Bucharest, 1999.

INS (National Institute of Statistics), Statistical Yearbook of Romania-2018, I.S.S.N.: 1220-3246; I.S.S.N.-L: 1220-3246, 2019.

Ministry of Regional Development, Public Administration and European Funds-MDRAPFE: National Housing Strategy 2017–2013, link: http://www.mmediu.ro/app/webroot/uploads/files/2017_11_09_Strategia_Nationala_a_Locuirii_2017-2030.pdf, 2017, accessed 05.02.2019.

Noica N. (coord.): Between History and Current Affairs. Housing Policies in Romania, Writing Machine Publishing House, Bucharest, 2003.

Patriche I.: Construction Market in Romania, Uranus Publishing House, Bucharest, 2003.

Petrovici N.: Capital Accumulation and the Organization of Emerging Socialist Markets: Real Estate Agents from Cluj-Napoca, Romanian Sociology Revue, II (4), Cluj Napoca, 2004.

Petrovici N.: Socio-Spatial Inequalities in Villa Neighborhoods, Babes_Bolyai University, link: http://socasis.ubbcluj.ro/seminarii/urbana/Upload/Cercetari/Norbert%20Petrovici%20-%20Noua%20urbanizare.pdf, 2005, accessed 17.05.2019.

Popescu-Lumină, N.I.: Bucharest from the Past and Today, Publishing House of the Cultural Foundation Gheorghe Marin Speteanu, ISBN: 978-973-87234-8-1, Bucharest, 2007.

Aleksandar Grubor, Nikola Milicevic, Nenad Djokic

Social marketing and physical activity of student population for increasing quality of life

Abstract In a number of researches, quality of life is considered as a benefit of physical activity. Besides, part of the researches focuses on physical activity of student population. The topic of the paper is to explore perceived obstacles for being physically active in student population. Furthermore, these obstacles were examined in the context of different socio-demographic profiles of respondents. The primary research was conducted in 2019. The convenience sample included more than 150 students from one state university in Serbia. The structural interviews by using the questionnaire were performed. The results show that in some cases the perceived obstacles can be brought in connection to certain socio-demographic characteristics. Having that in mind, within the context of social marketing, recommendations for targeting different segments in function of increasing the level of their physical activities were given.

Keywords: social marketing, physical activity, quality of life, students

Introduction

In the focus of this paper are the perceived obstacles for being physically active in student population. That question is of the special importance when having in mind that quality of life is considered as a benefit of physical activity. Furthermore, within the researches of physical activity, there is also a focus on student population.

Having all previously mentioned in mind, there are three aims of the paper. Firstly, in the part of the paper regarding literature review, the object is to explore relations between quality of life and physical activity, as well as to stress previous physical activity research of student population. Secondly, the aim is to conduct a primary research regarding the concrete topic of the paper – perceived obstacles for being physically active in student population. The primary research was conducted in 2019 on students from one state university in Serbia. The research is presented in sections Materials and methods and Results. Thirdly, the aim is to provide, within the context of social marketing, recommendations for targeting different segments of students in function of increasing the level of their physical activity. That aim is fulfilled in the part of the paper presented in Conclusions.

1. Literature review

The concept of quality of life (QoL) has been drawing the attention of many researches for decades. Following the definition of the World Health Organization (WHO) from 1947, it presents the "state of complete physical, mental and social well-being, and not merely the absence of disease and infirmity" (Post 2014, p. 168). Despite numerous disagreements concerning that definition (Post 2014), it has influenced the development of three main dimensions of quality of life (Rodríguez-Fernández, Zuazagoitia-Rey-Baltar and Ramos-Díaz 2017):

- Physical dimension – the perception of physical status and health; it may also refer to the absence of disease and its symptoms;
- Psychological dimension – state of affective and cognitive well-being; it relates to a broad range of changeable experiences, such as emotional changes, personal beliefs etc.;
- Social dimension – maintaining, developing and satisfying personal relationships, enabled by person's roles in life.

When analyzing the QoL concept, Gill et al. (2013) stated that many authors quoted the WHO definition, connecting the quality of life with positive health. They also noticed that in most models and definitions of QoL, it was presented as a multidimensional construct, consisted of physical, psychological and social domains. Bearing in mind previously mentioned, for Gill et al. (2013, p. 29), quality of life represents "a subjective, multidimensional, integrative construct that reflects optimal well-being and positive health."

Quality of life was often associated to physical activity, whereby the later was described as "an important means of increasing QoL" (Çiçek 2018, p. 1141). Positive relation between these variables was confirmed among university students from both sports and other departments (Çiçek, 2018).

Piko (2000) studied physical activity of students in the specific context of self-perceived health. Physical activity, together with psychological well-being, acute illness episodes and the frequency of psychosomatic symptoms contributed to the explanation of that variable. Although, it was not the strongest predictor (that role belonged to psychological well-being), physical activity was positively correlated to strongest predictor and was more influential among males and more active persons.

Furthermore, in a research of the students in the United Kingdom, Tyson et al. (2010) researched the relation of their psychical activity and mental health. Hereby, they segmented respondents according to the level of exercise into the low, medium and high exercise groups. Those groups differed significantly on the mental health in a manner that better results could be brought in connection to respondents who engaged in more exercise.

Physical activity can be studied in the context of socio-psychological theories, as is the Theory of Planned Behavior. Hamilton and White (2011) use different beliefs related to constructs from that theory in order to study behavioral intention and actual behavior on the example of mothers and fathers with young children. Beside obstacles i.e. Control Beliefs, which are the focus of this paper, they also use Behavioral and Normative Beliefs. Hereby, in the specific context, in relation to Behavioral Beliefs, they research whether respondents consider that physical activity would improve his/her physical health and fitness, mental wellbeing, control of the weight, and parenting practices, decrease the risk of sustaining pain/injury, provide the opportunity to socialize, or interfere with his/her other commitments. When it comes to Normative Beliefs, the authors research the influence of spouse/partner, children, other family members, friends, healthcare professionals, work colleagues, or people the person exercises with. Finally, in regard to Control Beliefs, authors consider lack of time, tiredness and fatigue, inconvenience, lack of motivation, cost, and illness and injury.

The previous topic can be considered from the aspect of six "benchmarks for identifying an approach that could be legitimately called social marketing" (Andreasen 2002, p. 7). Firstly, the focus is on the role behavior change in designing and evaluating interventions. Secondly, there is always present the research of the audience – to understand it, to pre-test elements before intervention, to get feed-back from interventions. Thirdly, target audiences are segmented. Fourthly, there must be an exchange of the value with target audiences. Fifthly, all instruments of marketing mix are used – not only marketing communications. And sixthly, competition to desired behavior is studied, as well.

2. Materials and methods

The questionnaire consisted of two parts. The first part was related to general characteristics of the respondents: gender (male, female), age (open-ended question), emotional status (in a relationship, not in a relationship), household size (open-ended question), living standard (assessed on five-point Likert scale). The second part of the questionnaire was related to perceived obstacles for being physically active. That part included measurement of Control Beliefs in accordance to Hamilton and White (2011) and included: lack of time, tiredness and fatigue, inconvenience, lack of motivation, cost, and illness and injury. All the obstacles were assessed on five-point Likert scale (from "strongly disagree" to "strongly agree").

The convenience sample was recruited from the students from the University of Novi Sad, Serbia. The research was conducted in 2019. There were 152 respondents within the sample. Their characteristics are presented in Tab. 1.

Tab. 1: Characteristics of the sample

Characteristics		**measures**	**data**
Gender	male		28.3
	female		71.7
Emotional status	not in a relationship	percent	44.7
	not in a relationship		55.3
Age		mean (	21.05 (1.61)
Household size		standard	4.27 (1.05)
Living standard		deviation)	3.72 (0.83)

Source: authors based on primary research

Data analysis was performed by using MS Office Excel and SPSS. The analysis brought in relation perceived obstacles for being physically active and socio-demographic characteristics of student population. Firstly, Independent samples t-test was used regarding gender and emotional status. Spearman correlation was used considering age, household size and living standard.

In addition, the influence of socio-demographic characteristics of respondents on each of perceived obstacles for being physically active was analyzed by multiple regression with General Linear Model. The dependent variables – perceived obstacles for being physically active – were presented by means of ratings of all respondents. Coding was performed in a manner that the value of 0 was assigned to the following levels of socio-demographic characteristics: male, younger than the average respondent, not in a relationship, with smaller household size than the average, perceiving own living standard worse than the average respondent.

3. Results

Firstly, the results regarding the average assessments (on five-point Likert scale) of perceived obstacles for being physically active will be reported. Hereby, following assessments were given: lack of time: 3.95, tiredness and fatigue: 3.45, inconvenience: 2.55, lack of motivation: 3.16, cost: 2.80, and illness and injury: 2.85.

Secondly, the relation of perceived obstacles for being physically active and socio-demographic characteristics will be explained. When it comes to different socio-demographic segments and their assessments of obstacles, the results are provided in Tab. 2.

The results of Independent samples t-test for gender are: t(df=150)= -1.669, p=0.100>0.05 for lack of time, t(df=150)= -0.944, p=0.347>0.05 for tiredness and fatigue, t(df=150)= -1.125, p=0.262>0.05 for inconvenience, t(df=150)= -0.374, p=0.709>0.05 for lack of motivation, t(df=150)= -1.092, p=0.277>0.05 for cost, t(df=150)=0.191, p=0.848>0.05 for illness and injury.

The results of Independent samples t-test for emotional status are: t(df=150)= -2.167, p=0.032<0.05 for lack of time, t(df=150)= -1.018, p=0.310>0.05 for tiredness and fatigue, t(df=150)=1.105, p=0.271>0.05 for inconvenience, t(df=150)=1.378, p=0.170>0.05 for lack of motivation, t(df=150)= -0.414, p=0.679>0.05 for cost, t(df=150)=1.073, p=0.285>0.05 for illness and injury.

The results of Spearman correlation test between age and perceived obstacles are as following: lack of time: ρ= -0.177, n=153, p<0.05, tiredness and fatigue: ρ= -0.061, n=153, p>0.05, inconvenience: ρ= -0.097, n=153, p>0.05, lack of motivation: ρ=0.015, n=153, p>0.05, cost: ρ= -0.022, n=153, p>0.05, and illness and injury: ρ= -0.142, n=153, p>0.05.

The results of Spearman correlation test between household size and perceived obstacles are as following: lack of time: ρ=0.095, n=153, p>0.05, tiredness and fatigue: ρ=0.123, n=153, p>0.05, inconvenience: ρ=0.036, n=153, p>0.05, lack of motivation: ρ= -0.029, n=153, p>0.05, cost: ρ=0.019, n=153, p>0.05, and illness and injury: ρ=0.195, n=153, p<0.05.

The results of Spearman correlation test between perceived living standard and perceived obstacles are as following: lack of time: ρ= -0.090, n=153, p>0.05, tiredness and fatigue: ρ= -0.112, n=153, p>0.05, inconvenience: ρ= -0.123, n=153, p>0.05, lack of motivation: ρ= -0.104, n=153, p>0.05, cost: ρ= -0.417, n=153, p<0.05, and illness and injury: ρ= -0.090, n=153, p>0.05.

Tab. 3 shows the values of parameters and their significance (significant marked with ** at p<0.05 and with * at p<0.10) in six regression models for each of the dependent variables.

Tab. 2: Sociodemographic segments and perceived obstacles

Segments		lack of time	tiredness and fatigue	inconvenience	lack of motivation	cost	illness and injury
Gender	male	3.70	3.30	2.37	3.09	2.60	2.88
	female	4.06	3.50	2.62	3.18	2.88	2.83
Emotional status	not in a relationship	3.74	3.34	2.68	3.32	2.75	2.99
	in a relationship	4.13	3.54	2.45	3.02	2.85	2.74

Source: authors based on primary research

Tab. 3: Results of general linear model

Independent variables	lack of time	tiredness and fatigue	inconvenience	lack of motivation	cost	illness and injury
Intercept	3.861**	3.406**	2.836**	3.512**	3.250**	3.100**
Gender	0.287	0.152	0.317	0.173	0.277	-0.038
Age	-0.573**	-0.300	-0.366*	-0.135	-0.141	-0.365
Emotional status	0.414**	0.230	-0.245	-0.326	0.101	-0.163
Household size	0.189	0.312	-0.046	-0.157	0.171	0.511**
Living standard	-0.387**	-0.363*	-0.406*	-0.328	-1.205**	-0.351

Source: authors based on primary research.

Tab. 4 presents values of dependent variables (lack of time – Ob1, tiredness and fatigue – Ob2, inconvenience – Ob3, lack of motivation – Ob4, cost – Ob5, and illness and injury – Ob6) at different combinations of levels of independent variables.

Tab. 4: Socio-demographic characteristics and perceived obstacles

Gender	Age	In a relationship	House-hold size	Living standard	Ob1	Ob2	Ob3	Ob4	Ob5	Ob6
male	younger	no	smaller	lower	3.86	3.41	2.84	3.51	3.25	3.10
female	younger	no	smaller	lower	4.15	3.56	3.15	3.68	3.53	3.06
male	older	no	smaller	lower	3.29	3.11	2.47	3.38	3.11	2.74
male	younger	yes	smaller	lower	4.28	3.64	2.59	3.38	3.35	2.94
male	younger	no	larger	lower	4.05	3.72	2.79	3.19	3.42	3.61
male	younger	no	smaller	higher	3.47	3.04	2.43	3.36	2.05	2.75
female	older	no	smaller	lower	3.58	3.26	2.79	3.55	3.39	2.70
female	younger	yes	smaller	lower	4.56	3.79	2.91	3.55	3.63	2.90
female	younger	no	larger	lower	4.34	3.87	3.11	3.36	3.70	3.57
female	younger	no	smaller	higher	3.76	3.20	2.75	3.53	2.32	2.71
male	older	yes	smaller	lower	3.70	3.34	2.22	3.24	3.21	2.57
male	older	no	larger	lower	3.48	3.42	2.42	3.05	3.28	3.25
male	older	no	smaller	higher	2.90	2.74	2.06	3.22	1.90	2.38
male	younger	yes	larger	lower	4.46	3.95	2.54	3.05	3.52	3.45
male	younger	yes	smaller	higher	3.89	3.27	2.19	3.22	2.15	2.59
male	younger	no	larger	higher	3.66	3.36	2.38	3.03	2.22	3.26
female	older	yes	smaller	lower	3.99	3.49	2.54	3.41	3.49	2.53
female	older	no	larger	lower	3.76	3.57	2.74	3.22	3.56	3.21
female	older	no	smaller	higher	3.19	2.90	2.38	3.39	2.18	2.35
female	younger	yes	larger	lower	4.75	4.10	2.86	3.22	3.80	3.41
female	younger	yes	smaller	higher	4.18	3.43	2.50	3.39	2.42	2.55
female	younger	no	larger	higher	3.95	3.51	2.70	3.20	2.49	3.22
male	older	yes	larger	lower	3.89	3.65	2.18	2.92	3.38	3.08
male	older	yes	smaller	higher	3.32	2.97	1.82	3.09	2.00	2.22
male	older	no	larger	higher	3.09	3.06	2.02	2.89	2.07	2.90
male	younger	yes	larger	higher	4.08	3.59	2.14	2.89	2.32	3.10
female	older	yes	larger	lower	4.18	3.80	2.50	3.09	3.66	3.04
female	older	yes	smaller	higher	3.60	3.13	2.14	3.26	2.28	2.18
female	older	no	larger	higher	3.38	3.21	2.34	3.07	2.35	2.86
female	younger	yes	larger	higher	4.36	3.74	2.46	3.07	2.59	3.06
male	older	yes	larger	higher	3.50	3.29	1.77	2.76	2.18	2.73
female	older	yes	larger	higher	3.79	3.44	2.09	2.93	2.45	2.69

Source: authors based on primary research

The interpretation of the obtain results will be given in the following section together with conclusions.

Conclusions

Generally, the largest perceived obstacles for being physically active by student population are lack of time (3.95) and tiredness and fatigue (3.45). Having in mind that the values are derived from five-point Likert scale, only the first largest obstacle is close to answer marked with number 4, interpreted as "agree," while even the second largest is closer to number 3 interpreted as "neither agree nor disagree." Similar conclusions can be found for all other obstacles – lack of motivation (3.16), illness and injury (2.85), cost (2.80), and inconvenience (2.55). Although the average assessments are close to neutral statement, there should be stressed that respondents do not reject those obstacles either. However, the first recommendation can be given in regard to the largest obstacle – lack of time – and the attempts should be made to try to offer possibilities for physical activities that would use the minimum of students' time (for example in the campus of the University).

When it comes to the perceived obstacle lack of time, the results of Independent samples t-test as well as of Spearman correlation test, reveal that its influence is larger for respondents that are in relationship and for younger students. The explanation can be that students in relationship have less free time in comparison to students that are single, since part of time they spend with their partners. The recommendation that can be given from the context of this result is to try to promote physical activity as one attractive way of spending time with emotional partner. The lack of time among younger students can be explained by the fact that they are getting used to students' obligations and life, that is, in most of the cases, a great change in life. Introducing physical activity as part of elective courses at least at the first or the second year at the faculties could be beneficial. Furthermore, providing students, especially of younger age, information about beneficial influence of physical activities on concentration to study and health, could also contribute to their acceptance of physical activities.

Another result, although expected, is the negative correlation between perceived living standard and cost as perceived obstacle for being physically active. However, students can be informed in details about physical activities that can be performed at no cost, and authorities should provide as much as possible infrastructure for it. Finally, the results show that as the size of a student's household rises, increases the influence of the obstacle illness and injury.

The results of General Linear Model provide deeper understanding of researched influences. Hereby, besides already expected influence of age and emotional status on lack of time, that variable is also influenced by perceived living standard. Concretely, students perceiving their standard better than the average, are also less influenced by lack of time. For the same variable are also discovered the influences of the same direction in the case of tiredness and fatigue as well as of inconvenience. In addition, inconvenience is also negatively influenced by the age. The influence of living standard on perceiving cost as obstacle and of household size on illness and injury as obstacle is as hypothesized in Spearman tests of correlation.

Generally, the main insight from the General Linear Model application is that students perceiving own standard better than the average, are less influenced by number of different obstacles. Although deeper analysis is necessary in the future, it can be supposed that part of students with lower standard might also work simultaneously with studying (what is not usually expected in the domestic context) which causes them to be prevented by the lack of time, tiredness and fatigue, inconvenience and cost to be more physically active.

The General Linear Model also provides profiles of students perceiving certain obstacles as more or less important. Hereby, by the lack of time are mostly prevented to be physically active students with following characteristics: female, younger than the average respondent, in a relationship, with larger household size than the average, perceiving own living standard worse than the average respondent (4.75). Tiredness and fatigue is perceived as the greatest obstacle for following profile of students: female, younger than the average respondent, in a relationship, with larger household size than the average, perceiving own living standard worse than the average respondent (4.10). Inconvenience presents the greatest obstacle for following profile of students: female, younger than the average respondent, not in a relationship, with smaller household size than the average, perceiving own living standard worse than the average respondent (3.15). By the lack of motivation are mostly prevented to be physically active students of the following profile: female, younger than the average respondent, not in a relationship, with smaller household size than the average, perceiving own living standard worse than the average respondent (3.68). Cost is perceived as the greatest obstacle for following profile of students: female, younger than the average respondent, in a relationship, with larger household size than the average, perceiving own living standard worse than the average respondent (3.80). By the illness and injury are mostly prevented to be physically active students with following characteristics: male, younger than the average respondent, not in a relationship, with larger household size than the average, perceiving own living standard worse than the average respondent (3.61).

Having in mind the described profiles, presented recommendations and the significance of psychical activity for quality of life, all described within this paper, each of the factors in charge of that topic regarding student populations can take appropriate actions. Future researches should try to reach more representative sample from more universities and to include additional variables, for example psychological, in explaining students' psychical activities.

References

Andreasen, Alan R.: "Marketing Social Marketing in the Social Change Marketplace." Journal of Public Policy & Marketing 21(1), 2002, pp. 3–13.

Çiçek, Güner: "Quality of Life and Physical Activity among University Students." Universal Journal of Educational Research 6(6), 2018, pp. 1141–1148.

Gill, Diane L.; Hammond, Cara C.; Reifsteck, Erin J.; Jehu, Christine M.; Williams, Rennae A.; Adams, Melanie M.; Lange, Elisabeth H.; Becofsky, Katie; Rodriguez, Enid; Shang, Ya-Ting: "Physical Activity and Quality of Life." Journal of Preventive Medicine & Public Health 46(suppl.1), 2013, pp. 28–34.

Hamilton, Kyra; White, Katherine M.: "Identifying Key Belief-Based Targets for Promoting Regular Physical Activity among Mothers and Fathers with Young Children." Journal of Science and Medicine in Sport 14(2), 2011, pp. 135–142.

Piko, Betina: "Health-Related Predictors of Self-Perceived Health in a Student Population: The Importance of Physical Activity." Journal of Community Health 25(2), 2000, pp. 125–137.

Post, Marcel W. M.: "Definitions of Quality of Life: What Has Happened and How to Move On." Topics in Spinal Cord Injury Rehabilitation 20(3), 2014, pp. 167–180.

Rodríguez-Fernández, Arantzazu; Zuazagoitia-Rey-Baltar, Ana; Ramos-Díaz, Estibaliz: "Quality of Life and Physical Activity: Their Relationship with Physical and Psychological Well-Being". In: Boas, Ana Alice Vilas (ed.): Quality of Life and Quality of Working Life. Intech: Rijeka, 2017, pp. 53–70.

Tyson, Philip; Wilson, Kelly; Crone, Diane; Brailsford, Richard; Laws, Keith: "Physical Activity and Mental Health in a Student Population." Journal of Mental Health 19(6), 2010, pp. 492–499.

Maria Livia Ştefănescu, Ştefan Ştefănescu

A longitudinal analysis of the Romanians' opinions regarding the quality of their education from 1990 to 2010

Abstract We are analyzing comparatively the population's answers regarding the quality QE of the education in Romania.

The current study was based on 13 national representative samples which have been constructed during 1990–2010 at the Research Institute for Quality of Life – Romanian Academy. The proposed statistical models analyze the behavior of categorical variables of ordinal type which are attached to the answers of the interviewed persons for question QE. In this context we have used the classical stochastic order between the variables for the comparison of the population's opinion in different years of the studied period. In order to measure some sociological phenomena of inequality or polarization we have used indicators that are specific to ordinal type variables. Using the Euclidean metrics we obtained a classification of the years 1990–2010 regarding the answers to the question QE. We remark a relative instability in time of the population's opinions regarding the quality of the received education, which recommends more coherence in the promotion of educational policies. The application of three statistical models has conducted in the end to obtaining similar results.

Keywords: education, survey, categorical ordinal variable, statistical method, classification

Aim of the paper

The development of a nation is strongly influenced by the educational level of its citizens. In such a context the population's opinion regarding the quality of the Romanian education is significantly important for the long term prosperity of Romania.

The current research is based on the Romanians 'answers regarding question QE which is present in an ample questionnaire based on the study of the quality of life in Romania. More concretely, the question QE is formulated as follows: "How do you estimate the quality of the education that your children are currently following?." The primary analysis data target the period 1990–2010 and have been taken from the data bases "Diagnosis for Quality of Life in Romania." These databases were created at the Research Institute for Quality of Life – Romanian Academy.

We intend to create a classification of the years from the period 1990–2010 from the point of view of question QE by the use of several statistical models. The statistical methods which have been applied, as well as the proposed indicators of this study are specific to the categorical variables of ordinal type (Agresti 2010).

Taking into account the restricted space allotted to the current presentation we will renounce at the presentation of results tables with numerous values. This inconvenient will be replaced by the elaboration of suggestive graphics. The programming of the used algorithms from this research for the analysis of statistical data about education was done in Excel and in Matlab programming language. We will try to summarize some of the results that have been obtained in this complex study which regards the quality of education in Romanian during 1990–2010.

1. Literature review

A higher level of education of a country's inhabitants essentially contribute to the country's development on the long term. In the educational sphere we find a large variety of problems. We can consult for this any encyclopedia which presents different important aspects regarding education (for example, see Marlow-Ferguson 2002).

Dobbins 2011 creates a comparative analysis of the evolution of the education in the countries from Central and Eastern Europe, amongst which also Romania, in order to converge towards a common educational model.

We shall mention several definite aspects for the educational field which are strongly linked with the current research. In general, the data mining on education have a hierarchical structure which contains information about pupils, classrooms, schools, localities, regions, countries (Raudenbush and Willms 1991). Taking this aspect into account, we sustain data mining in education from a multilevel analysis (Bock 1989).

Larini and Barthes (2018) analyze several problems that appear at the gathering and analysis of data. The authors synthesize a series of approaches that we have partially applied to this study. We remark among these approaches: operating with data bases, the structure of a questionnaire, graphic representation methods, univariate and bivariate mathematical indicators, confirmatory procedures in statistics, principal component and factorial correspondence analysis, prediction for quantitative variables.

The application of different statistical models and methods especially in the fields of psychology and education is largely debated in literature. We remind several reference papers, also indicating the main approached aspects: Peers 2006 (statistical inferences, rank treatment, statistical tests selection), Turner 2014 (parametric and nonparametric tests to analyze two sets of data, measuring the dependence degree between variables, the Spearman and Kendall correlations for the ranks of sequences), Leppink 2019 (sequential tests, Akaike's and Schwarz' information criterion, Bayesian estimation and hypothesis testing, treating the latent variables, factor analysis, treating missing data, correlation structure, interpreting nominal and ordinal variables, multilevel approach), Coladarci and

Cobb 2014 (methods for the representation of data, correlation and causation, regression and prediction, sampling distributions, ANOVA procedure).

In the literature are proposed different techniques of object classification. Grouping objects into classes uses different dissimilarity measures (Everitt et al. 2011). In our paper we have chosen an agglomerative hierarchical classification based on the Euclidean distance. The answers to the questions proposed by the survey are usually on an ordinal scale. In this context, the statistical models applied to the categorical variables of ordinal type have certain particularities (Agresti 2010). We have taken this into account permanently in this study when we have selected inequality and variation (polarization) indicators for ordinal variables.

2. Data

In this study we will interpret the information found in 13 nationally representative samples which characterize the period 1990–2010. More concretely, the samples E1-E13 refer to the years 1990–1999, 2003, 2006 and 2010. The volumes of these samples vary between 934 (for the year 2003) and 1479 units (for the year 1995). The databases associated to the samples E1-E13 have been created in SPSS format at the Research Institute for Quality of Life–Romanian Academy.

We will analyze the question QE: "How do you estimate the quality of the education that your children are currently following?." The respondents to this question had the option to select only one of the five possible answer variants: "very poor" (R1), "poor" (R2), "so and so" (R3), "good" (R4) and "very good" (R5). After eliminating the NR situations (non-response) and NC ("not the case") we obtain the distributions of the effective answering codes R1–R5 to the question QE, for the period 1990–2010 (Fig. 1).

A first visualization of the bar type representations for the distributions from Fig. 1 points out several aspects:

- The number of answers "good" (R4) represent in the years 1990–1992 and eventually in the year 1999 less than 50 % of the cases. The year 1991 has the smallest percentage of answers "good" (R4), approximately 40 %.
- At the same time, the year 1991 has the highest percentage of answers R2, "poor" (approximatively 15 %). Also the same year the population is undecided in the highest degree between the choice of "dissatisfaction" variants (the answering codes R1-R2) and of "satisfaction" (codes R4-R5), respectively. More concretely, the option "so and so" (R3) is selected by the population, in the year 1991, in over 35 % of the cases. So, in the year 1991 the population is dissatisfied in the highest degree with the quality of school education.

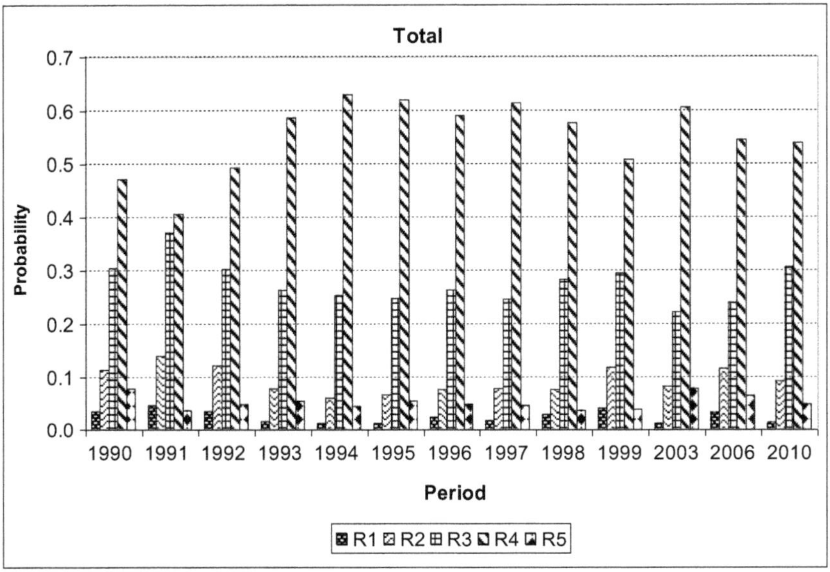

Fig. 1: The distributions of the answers R1-R5 at the question QE for the period 1990–2010

- In comparison with the previous year, 1998, in 1999 we notice the most significant degradation of the respondents' estimations regarding the subject QE. Comparing with 1999, in the year 2003 the population regards more optimistically the activity of the educational system.
- From the entire period 1990–2010, in the years 1994, 1995 and 1997 the Romanians' attitude is the most favorable regarding the received education. After the year 2000, in 2003 the population is the most satisfied with the educational system.
- The panoramic image of the distributions of answers from Fig. 1 fluctuates during 1990–2010. During this period we do not remark any increasing or decreasing trend of the positive opinions expressed by the Romanians regarding their education. This fact is a consequence of the incoherent educational policies which have been promoted by different governments which have frequently been in power during 1990–2010.

In conclusion, it is difficult to create a rigorous classification of the years 1990–2010 using directly only the dynamic image of the distributions of the ordinal categorical variable QE from Fig. 1. For a better characterization of the period 1990–2010 we will use indicators and we will propose statistical models which are adapted to categorical variables of ordinal type.

3. Stochastic order

The distributions of the ordinal variables can be compared by the use of the classical stochastic order relation "$<_{st}$" (Le Breton and Peluso 2009). We mention the fact that the order relation "$<_{st}$" is partial because two distributions cannot always be compared. More concretely, if [y1] $<_{st}$ [y2] then the opinions of the population regarding the quality of the education are more unfavorable in the year y1 comparatively with the year y2. The notations [y1] $<_{st}$ [y2] and [y2] $>_{st}$ [y1] are equivalent. By [y1] $\#_{st}$ [y2] we mention that the distributions to the question *QE* from the years y1 and y2 are not comparable. If [y1] $=_{st}$ [y2] then the distributions of the variables y1 and y2 are approximatively equal (with an error of0.01).

Following our calculations we deduce that:

- The year 1990 is the most atypical year from the period 1990–2010, because the distribution of the answers to question *QE* from that year cannot be compared with the distributions corresponding to years 1993–1998 or 2010.
- It is true the relation [1991] $<_{so}$ [y] for any year from the studied period, y different from the year 1991. So, in the year 1991, the population is most unsatisfied with the education received.
- We also have [1992] $<_{so}$ [y] for any year y from the period 1990–2010 with several exceptions: [1992] $>_{so}$ [1991], [1992] $\#_{so}$ [1998], [1992] $=_{so}$ [1999]. We remark the fact that the population's opinions from the years 1992 and 1999 are very similar.

So in the years 1991, 1992 and 1999 the population is unsatisfied in the highest degree by the education given to children in schools. Similarly we notice that in the years 1994, 1995 and 2003 the Romanians have a good opinion regarding the quality of education in schools. Some of these aspects have already been presented in the previous section. During the period 1990–2010 we remark a relative instability in time of the opinions of the population regarding the problematics *QE*.

4. Inequality and variation

In this section we will emphasize in the answers to the question QE the level of manifestation of two sociologically distinct phenomena: inequality and polarization. More concretely, the indicator IGO (Giudici and Raffinetti 2011) measures the degree of inequality present in the respondent's opinions, and POA (Apouey 2007) is an index of variation (polarization) of the distributions of the categorical variables of ordinal type which are attached to question QE. Both coefficients take values in the interval [0, 1].

In Fig. 2 is visualized the dynamics of the values of the indicators IGO and POA during 1990–2010. We notice that: $0.32 < \text{IGO} < 0.39$, $0.22 < \text{POA} < 0.36$. For each year from the analyzed period the values POA for polarization are smaller than the values IGO of the inequality. Moreover, we remark a permanent fluctuation of the level POA of polarization of the answers. This instability in time of the respondents' opinions might be generated by the lack of a continuity in the governmental promotion of the educational policies which have been proposed between 1990–2010.

Moreover, the population's dissatisfaction persists in the evaluation of the quality of education during the whole period 1990–2010. More concretely, the values IGO which measure the level of inequality perceived by the Romanians regarding the education received in schools by their children are relatively stable but take high values over the threshold of 0.32. From the point of view of both sociological phenomena, of inequality and polarization, the population is optimistic in the years 1994, 1995, 1997 and eventually 2003. Nevertheless, in the years 1990–1992 and 1999 the Romanians show the highest dissatisfaction regarding the functioning of the educational system in Romania.

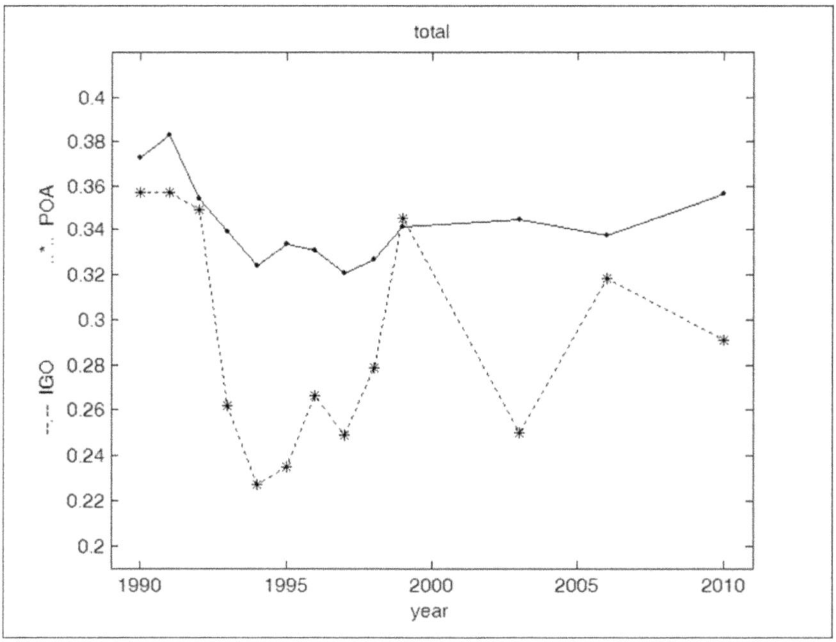

Fig. 2: The variation of the indicators IGO and POA during the period 1990–2010

5. A bidimensional representation

In Fig. 3 are represented bidimensionally the years 1990–2010 considering as Cartesian coordinates the values POA and IGO corresponding to the years. The studied years are defined in the graphical representation by their last two digits.

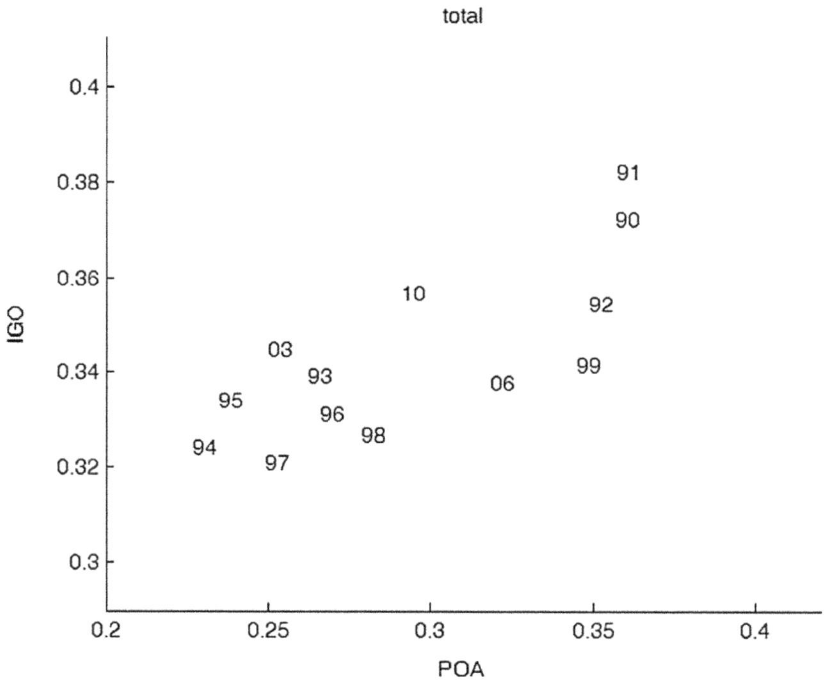

Fig. 3: Cartesian coordinates of the values POA and IGO, 1990–2010

By interpreting the image from Fig. 3 we deduce that the highest values of the indicators POA and IGO are obtained for the years belonging to class C1 = {1990, 1991, 1992, 1999}. The indicators POA and IGO take the smallest values for the years from class C2 = {1994, 1995, 1997}. So, the Romanians estimate positively the quality of education in the years C2 and are dissatisfied in the years C1. We remark the most different opinions of the Romanians in two years that are relatively close: 1991 and 1994 (Fig. 3).

The classification of the years 1990–2010 suggested by the graphic image from Fig. 3 has taken under consideration only two of the essential characteristics of the distribution of answers to question QE, that is the level of polarization and the inequality in a distribution.

6. Grouping the years

In this section we will present the grouping of the years from the period 1990–2010 after the criteria *QE*, using this time the whole information contained in the distributions of the population's answers from each year.

Everitt et al. (2011, p. 73–101), promote an agglomerative hierarchical classification algorithm based on different dissimilarity measures. At the same time several dissimilarity indexes between groups of objects are proposed. More concretely, in this research we have used the Euclidean metrics between the distributions of the analyzed categorical variables. The dissimilarity between two different groups of variables is defined as the mean of the distances between the objects of a group and the objects of the other group.

If we will divide the period 1990–2010 into just two distinct classes, then one of the classes will contain just one object, that is the year 1991 which has a special behavior.

The partitioning of the period 1990–2010 into five disjoint classes has pointed out the following groups: G1 = {1991}; G2 = {1990, 1992, 1999, 2010}; G3 = {2006}; G4 = {1994, 1995, 1997, 2003}; G5 = {1993, 1996, 1998}. In this classification we remark especially the opinions of the population from the years 1991 and 2006. The groups G1–G5 resulted from the dendrograms are in accordance with the graphical image from Fig. 3, where we have used the indicators POA and IGO. A unification of the groups G1–G5 in only two distinct classes, that is C1 = {C1, C2, C3} and C2 = {C4, C5}, has a clear significance in Fig. 3. Classes C1 and C2 partition the period 1990–2010 between the years of the class C2 in which the quality of education is evaluated as satisfactory by Romanians and the years from the class C1 for which the population is sensibly dissatisfied by the education received by their children.

The fact that we do not find in the groups G1–G5 or in the classes C1–C2 based on dendrograms a longer period of successive years suggests a lack of "continuity" in the expression of the Romanians' opinions. This fact is the consequence of complex phenomena, among which the population dissatisfaction regarding the governmental promotion of new educational policies.

Conclusions

The application of several statistical methods conducted to similar conclusions. Compare in this way the results of the analysis based on the stochastic order relation, the classification using inequality and polarization indicators (Fig. 3) or the grouping of the years from the period 1990–2010 by the use of an agglomerative hierarchical classification algorithm (Everitt et al. 2011).

The three statistical methods promoted have pointed out to years 1991 and eventually 1990 in which the population expressed the most discontent regarding the quality of received education by the students. In exchange, in the years 1994, 1995 and 1997, the Romanians have a better opinion on education.

We remark the fact that we do not have "a continuity" in consecutive years in the period 1990–2010 by the expressing in close years of similar opinions by the respondents. This aspect might be due to the constant change in the study period of the governments in power vision regarding the educational system as well as the investments allocated in this context.

In the future we intend to analyze comparatively opinions regarding education that are expressed by Romanians living in the rural or urban areas, possible gender differences, the attitude of poor families or families with more children, the eventual importance of the level of education of the respondents. We will also extend the statistical methods for the investigation (see Allen and Vignoles 2006).

In the last years the lack of consistent research funds did not allow the creation of new national samples in order to improve the proposed statistical models. Determining an educational development trend with current data will allow a much more correct prognosis of Romania's evolution in the next decade for this very important field for the country's development.

References

Agresti, Alan: Analysis of ordinal categorical data. Wiley: New York, 2010 (second edition).

Allen, Rebecca; Vignoles, Anna: "What should an index of school segregation measure?" Centre for the Economics of Education, London School of Economics and Political Science, London, Working Paper, March 2006, pp. 1–43.

Apouey, Bénédicte: "Measuring health polarization with self-assessed health data". Health Economics, 16(9), 2007, pp. 875–894.

Bock, Darrell R. (editor): Multilevel analysis of educational data. Academic Press: New York, 1989.

Coladarci, Theodore; Cobb, Casey D.: Fundamentals of statistical reasoning in education. John Wiley & Sons: New York, 2014 (fourth edition).

Dobbins, Michael: Higher education policies in central and eastern Europe – Convergence towards a common model? Palgrave Macmillan: New York, 2011.

Everitt, Brian S.; Landau, Sabine; Leese, Morven; Stahl, Daniel: Cluster analysis. John Wiley & Sons, Wiley Series in Probability and Statistics: New York, 2011 (fifth edition).

Giudici, Paolo; Raffinetti, Emanuela: "A Gini concentration quality measure for ordinal variables". Quaderni del Dipartimento di Economia, Statistica e Diritto, Università di Pavia, Serie Statistica, no. 1, April 7, 2011, pp. 1–15.

Larini, Michel; Barthes, Angela: Quantitative and statistical data in education – From data collection to data processing. ISTE – John Wiley & Sons: New York, 2018, volume 2.

Le Breton, Michel; Peluso, Eugenio: "Third-degree stochastic dominance and inequality measurement". The Journal of Economic Inequality, 7, 2009, pp. 249–268.

Leppink, Jimmie: Statistical methods for experimental research in education and psychology. Springer: New York, 2019.

Marlow-Ferguson, Rebecca (editor): World education encyclopedia – A survey of educational systems worldwide. volumes 1–3, Gale Group – Thomson Learning: New York, 2002 (second edition).

Peers, Ian S.: Statistical analysis for education and psychology researchers. The Falmer Press – Taylor & Francis Group: London, 2006 (second print).

Raudenbush, Stephen W.; Willms, Douglas J. (editors): Schools, classrooms and pupils – International studies of schooling from a multilevel perspective. Academic Press: New York, 1991.

Turner, Jean L.: Using statistics in small-scale language education research – Focus on non-parametric data. Routledge – Taylor & Francis: New York, 2014.

***** Data bases "Diagnosis for Quality of Life in Romania", Research Institute for Quality of Life, Romanian Academy (the period: 1990–2010).

Daniela Antonescu

Effects of regional policy on healthcare infrastructure in Romania: case study West region

Abstract The regional development policy pursues a series of objectives aimed to reducing territorial inequalities and a balanced process of economic growth. Through its specific instruments – the Regional Operational Program and the Structural and Cohesion Funds – the regional policy supports the balanced development by modernizing/rehabilitating/equipping the different services with local impact: social, health, transport, tourism, entrepreneurship, culture etc.

During the programming period 2007–2013, the regional policy focused on supporting and developing social infrastructure, including rehabilitation, modernization and equipping of health services infrastructure. The social domain, including the related infrastructure/specific services, is an important component of both the national/regional and the community system, supporting it by contributing to the increase of the quality of life and promoting social inclusion. This subject has been an important area of interest for the regional policy because it presents a lag behind, both in terms of investment made and development prospects.

Present article presents the ex-post impact of spending the community funds through regional policy, aimed at modernizing, rehabilitating, equipping the social healthcare infrastructure. The article present a Case study conducted in the West Region, Hunedoara County, this county having the low healthcare infrastructure and the high social problems persisting over time.

Keywords: regional development, medical infrastructure, Cohesion principle, Structural Funds

Introduction

Regional development is considered a priority for Romania, both in terms of the objectives pursued and the resources involved (human, financial, etc.). The basic elements of this process – the regional policy and the Regional Operational Program 2007–2013 (ROP) – are the pillars of the balanced development of all regions, by capitalizing on the regional and local development potential, focusing on the urban growth poles and improving the infrastructure and business environment conditions. The base of implementation of the regional policy is made up of the eight development regions (NUTS II), the institution that manages and coordinates the implementation being the Ministry of Public Works, Development and Administration (MPWDA) through the Managing Authority for the ROP and Intermediate Organisms (8 Regional Development Agencies).

The effects of regional policy and the impact of financial allocations from structural and national resources are found in particular in the creation of jobs and in the development of different infrastructure (transport, social, entrepreneurial, etc.), but they are visible and in a wider context, in areas such as: tourism (actions to promote the country brand, tourism promotion centers, etc.), urban development (integrated development plans), business sector (support of micro-enterprises), etc.

This article has the objective to highlight the outcomes of the ROP 2007–2013 in the field of medical infrastructure in the Hunedoara County.

The main sources of the data were: EU Guide for on monitoring and evaluation (EVALSED), Guide for Applicants for Major Field of Intervention 3.1 (ROP 2007–2013), data and information obtained from interviews with main applicants and beneficiary of the EU funds, Regional Development Plan of the Region West, other statistical data available in National Statistic Yearbook.

1. Theoretical approach

Evaluation is a process of "judging the value of a public intervention based on some explicit criteria and standards" (for instance, relevance, efficiency, sustainability, equity, etc.). The purpose of this process is to contribute to achieving accountable governance by feedback about efficiency, efficacity, and performances of public policies, organizations, or programmes.

At EU level, evaluation is compulsory for all programs financed by structural and cohesion funds, irrespective of the level of intervention (sectoral or territorial) (EC, 2019).

Evaluation aims a number of objectives, and is realized during various stages of the process of drafting and implementing the program.

- Strategic evaluation – pursues the analysis of the public policy evolution, as compared with national and community priorities.
- Operational evaluation (ongoing) – realized during the public policy implementation.
- Ex-ante evaluation – for optimizing allotted resources by intervention (program, project) and for improving the quality of the programming process as a whole right from its implementation start.
- Ex-post evaluation – examines the final impact of the program.

Frequently, evaluation represents a true challenge, because it does not follow just the contribution of each objective (infrastructure, environment, urban development, tourism etc.), but also the synergies between them, or the cross-sectional impact matrix.

Evaluation is affected by a series of factors, among which we mention: management of public intervention; level of involved evaluators; receptiveness of management authorities; financial resources involved. Evaluation imposes a cognitive process by which are defined the main elements and the relationships between foreseen inputs, planned activities, and expected outputs. Public interventions have as basis causality links between events occurred at various levels (inputs, activities, outputs, objectives) as shown with the aid of the following formula:

Needs →[Objectives→Inputs→Activities→Outputs→]→Outcomes→Effects

The relational system between needs, objectives, inputs/outputs, outcomes and effects substantiate the evaluation process of the program's impact. Thus, whenever the objectives determined by the program are expressed in terms of outputs, the efficiency may be measured as relationship between outputs (exits) and inputs (entries), costs and benefits, etc.

The most important element of the evaluation – *impact* – may be regarded in terms of outputs (outputs-physical results) and effects (outcomes, long-term effects on the beneficiaries). In the practice of evaluating public interventions financed by structural funds, the initial impact is known as output of implementing the program, while the long-term impact is regarded as sustainable effect in time and space. At the same time, the usefulness of the program is evaluated, along with the way in which outputs mitigate economic and social needs, and the long-term effects, etc. Depending on the impact categories taken into account, the objectives of the program can be determined as operational (outputs), specific (results), or general (outcomes) (EC, 2015).

The indicators used in public evaluations must satisfy a series of quality criteria: (1) they must overlap with the needs identified by the program; (2) they must be simple and easy understandable (number of jobs, number of kilometers of modernized public roads, number of hospitals, etc.); (3) there must be a certain balance between indicators; (4) they must present the significant implications of the decision process, and (5) they need to be found in the national or regional statistics.

The system of indicators represents the most important instrument of evaluation, and the categories of indicators can be grouped as following: specific indicators, generic and key-indicators, context and program indicators, resource indicators, output indicators, outcome, impact, relevance, efficiency, efficacy, and performance indicators. On evaluating public policy, input indicators and output indicators, together with outcome and impact indicators are taken into account predominantly.

In order to evaluate impact and progresses recorded in implementing the various public policies in the EU member-states, a number of key-indicators were set up (Regulation no. 1083/2005) that should meet the imposed quality criteria: specificity, measurability, availability, relevance and timeliness (SMART).

The quality of the evaluations is directly influenced by the quality of the existing and analyzed data and information, but also by the experience and independence of the evaluators involved in the process.

2. Analysis regarding to state of national medical infrastructure

In Romania, the health infrastructure examined by the total number of hospitals recorded an increasing tendency (except for the period 2011–2013, when the number of hospitals decreased from 503 to 464). If we investigate the situation of the medical units, by property categories, it is observed a slight decrease of the public units during the period 2007–2018, after the economic crisis, while the private units show a spectacular growth (Tab. 1).

Tab. 1: Hospitals on type of property (no. %)

	2007	**2018**	**2017 vs. 2007 (no.)**
Hospitals (total)	447	515	+68
Beds (total)	130,708	133,181	+2473
Hospitals in public property	425	368	-57
Hospitals in private propriety	22	147	+125

Source: Romanian Statistical Yearbook, 2019, NIS; Bucharest.

The medical infrastructure remains one with a high level of underdevelopment. In line with the government's commitment to strengthen the role of primary health care, the total number of hospital beds has increased. However, the number of beds has fluctuated since 2005, and in 2015 it was well above the EU average, reaching about 500 beds for acute causes per 100,000 inhabitants, compared to 396 in the EU. Hospitals are distributed evenly throughout the country, although there are some questions about accessibility in rural areas.

At national level, there are inequalities in access to health care system, with differences between socioeconomic groups (unemployed and self-employed, pensioners, agricultural workers and the Roma population) and between urban and rural areas.

In 2017, about 9.4 % of Romanians citizen reported unmet health care needs due to costs and geographical barriers or waiting lists, compared to an average of 3.2 % in the EU. This figure is slightly lower than in 2007, when 12.3 % reported unmet needs. It should be mentioned that although social health insurance is mandatory, it covers only 86 % of the population. This figure can be misleading, however, because a large number of Romanians works abroad, but they are still considered to be in Romania.

In context of regional policy, special place is presented by the support of the social sector, considered one of the lags behind, both from the point of view of the investment made and of the development perspectives. The social domain, made up of the related infrastructure and the specific services, is an important component of both the national/regional system and the community system, supporting it contributing to the increase of the quality of life and promoting social inclusion. The structural funds allocated to this sector have targeted as their final destination the rehabilitation, modernization and equipping of the health and social services infrastructure.

Along with the other priority axes of the ROP 2007–2013, Axis 3 "Improving social infrastructure" (holds 15 % of the total funds allocated) (MFEa, 2019) presents a special area dedicated to health infrastructure, namely the Major Field of Intervention 3.1. entitled "Rehabilitation/modernization/equipping of health services infrastructure" aims to produce concrete results by increasing access to health services, especially in outpatients and hospitals, but also by improving the quality of services offered and the use of high-performance equipment. The interventions (projects) financed by this field contribute, at the same time, to the diversification of health services and to the increase of their quality, by:

- achieving an increased treatment capacity (for example, rooms, beds, etc.), substantially reducing waiting time, introducing the use of technologically advanced equipment that allows advanced medical treatments, improving the operating infrastructure (renewing the utility system, modernization of rooms, access for people with disabilities, obtaining compliance with the standards in force).
- increasing in the number of patients treated – the projects that combined all the three types of interventions (rehabilitation, modernization and equipment) registered an increase in the number of users, in the period 2008–2014, compared to the projects that financed only certain types of interventions.
- increasing the satisfaction of patients, and a positive perception of the change regarding the infrastructures and the quality of services, after the implementation of the projects.

The estimated impact that the financing of this area should have had was given by the rehabilitation/modernization/equipping of 50 hospitals in the next counties: Botosani and Vaslui (North-East), Buzău, Tulcea and Vrancea (South-East), Dâmboviţa, Ialomiţa and Teleorman (South Muntenia), Gorj and Valcea (South-West), Maramures (North-West), Satu Mare, Sălaj (North-West), Covasna (Center) and Ilfov (Bucharest-Ilfov). However, this did not happen until the end of the programming period (MFE_c, 2019).

Other estimated effects were: the rehabilitation/modernization of 50 medical units, the allocated funds being of 173.58 Million euros (ERDF allotment), assuming an average spending of 3.471 million euros per medical unit. The minimum value of a medical infrastructure project was 0.2 million euros, while the maximum value is 25 million euros (Tab. 2).

Tab. 2: Allotment of Structural Funds on healthcare infrastructure (Mil. euro, %)

	Allotment (Mill. euro)	% in total allotment	Medical units (no.)	Existing (2011), (no.)	Existing (2011), (%)
North-East	28.33	16.32	8	72	14.31
South-East	23.00	13.25	7	54	10.74
South	24.7	14.22	7	64	12.72
South-West	24.32	14.01	7	43	8.55
West	17.95	10.34	6	53	10.54
North-West	20.99	12.09	6	71	14.12
Center	18.91	10.89	5	63	12.52
Bucharest-Ilfov	15.38	8.86	4	83	16.50
Total	173.58	100	50	503	100.00

Source: Data processing from the Guide of Applicant.

The hospitals modernized by the ROP represented 10 % of the total number of hospitals existing at national level (2010). Also, it is considered that the investment made in these hospitals will contribute to the 10 % increase of the access of the inhabitants to the rehabilitated/modernized/equipped medical units, at regional level.

Anyhow, the amount allotted for all Romanian hospitals is low, only 173.58 Million € in seven years. The West region where Hunedoara county is situated received only 17.95 Million € in seven years meaning 2,57 Million € per year. This low amount was appropriate only for acquiring some equipment and making some partial modernization at the existing building infrastructure. In this way the regional impact was limited.

3. Methodology

At the European Union level, a common methodology for evaluating programs and projects financed from the Structural and Cohesion Funds has been developed and formalized through Evaluation Guide – EVALSED (MFE_d, 2019) According to the Communication, the evaluation is "judgment of interventions according to their results, impacts and needs they aim to satisfy." The key notion in this definition is that it is a process that culminates in a judgment (or assessment) of an intervention. Moreover, the focus of evaluation is first and foremost on the needs, results and impacts of an intervention. The main purposes for carrying out evaluations are as follows:

- To contribute to the design of interventions, including providing input for setting political priorities.

- To assist in an efficient allocation of resources.
- To improve the quality of the intervention.
- To report on the achievements of the intervention (i.e. accountability).

According to the Evaluation Guide – EVALSED, the process of evaluation can depend on the stage at which it is performed: ex-ante, intermediate (ongoing) and ex-post.

The evaluation methodology applied in this article was performed in the ex-post phase (at the end of the implementation of the program/projects) and refers to the direct interview with the beneficiaries (public authorities and hospitals) who have accessed funds destined for the modernization of the medical infrastructure in Hunedoara County, West Region. The beneficiaries are the next municipalities and cities: Deva, Hunedoara, Petroşani, Petrila, Calan, Lupeni, Orăştie, Haţeg and Uricani. All nine cities accessed through Major Field of Intervention 3.1 needed to modernize and equip the ambulatory and medical centers, which were no longer in line with the new requirements resulting from the European Union's public health system strategy.

The Case study methodology was based on tools for collecting the information presented by the Evaluation Guide: office research, interview with representatives of local authorities and managers of medical units and on-site observation (Annex 1).

4. Impact evaluation at local/regional level: case-study Hunedoara County, West Region

4.1. Context of evaluation

Hunedoara County was strongly affected by the changes that occurred after 1989. Thus, this county, the most urbanized and the most industrialized county in Romania, was selected for the Case Study because it became the leader in the number of unemployed, as a result of the drastic restriction of the activity of mining plants and factories. The miners were left without work, this situation causing a severe stress with serious effects on the health status. In this context, Valea Jiului was declared a "disadvantaged area," benefiting for a while from a preferential economic status, which helped economic revitalization of the area, but without being able to solve all the problems. Moreover, the Jiu Valley is a region heavily polluted with environmental factors unfavorable to the health of the population and with a high incidence of occupational diseases. Also, the area is characterized by other unfavorable social indicators (alcohol consumption, family violence, high migration index, etc.), which shows an inadequate[1] state of

1 The NUTS classification (Nomenclature of territorial units for statistics) is a hierarchical system for dividing up the economic territory of the EU.

population health. Added to this was an undeveloped health infrastructure, lack of funds and modernization programs for medical units in the area.

Hunedoara County is part of the West Region NUTS-2, a region that was placed in the period 2007–2013, below the national average for many of the social indicators. Thus, the natural increase of the population registered negative values, about two times higher compared to the national average. In 2008, the birth rate was 8.5 %, mortality was 12.1 %, and the negative natural gain was – 3.6 %, well above the country average of – 1.5 %. At the same time, the average life expectancy in Romania was 71.76 years, and in Hunedoara County, it was only 70.81 years, of which 67.3 years for men and 74.46 years for women (Antonescu, 2013).

In Hunedoara County and especially in the Valea Jiului mining area, active persons have an extremely large number of days of medical leave, much higher than in the rest of the country. This extremely unfavorable situation can only be counteracted by a strong action of detection and prophylaxis.

All these negative aspects are described in the "Regional Development Plan" of the West Region, which notes that, health care institutions are relatively distributed in the region but the health infrastructure is rather poorly developed, in most cases requiring rehabilitation, modernization and replacement of outdated and outdated equipment. In these circumstances it was absolutely necessary to modernize, arrange and equip the outpatient facilities with the appropriate medical equipment for the early detection of various diseases, as well as for an effective prophylactic action.

This was a brief presentation of the general context in which the 2007–2013 Regional Operational Program, Major Field of Intervention 3.1 was applied (MFE_d, 2019). The rehabilitation/modernization/equipping of the infrastructure of the health services and which, at the same time, justifies the need for interventions in the county. The Regional Operational Program 2007–2013 supports the implementation of the National Strategy in the field of health, for the efficiency of the health services, by rehabilitating and equipping the hospital infrastructure, as well as by rehabilitating and equipping the outpatients.

Through its cities and municipalities, the county was on the first place in accessing community funds to rehabilitate, modernize and equip the integrated ambulatories and the existing medical centers within the hospitals. These municipalities and cities are: Deva, Hunedoara, Petroşani, Petrila, Calan, Lupeni, Orăştie, Haţeg and Uricani. All nine cities accessed through Major Field of Intervention 3.1 needed to modernize and equip ambulatory and medical centers, which were no longer in line with the new requirements resulting from the European Union's public health system strategy. Moreover, the nine investment projects are in line with both the objectives of the European Union's Cohesion Policy on reducing regional disparities and disparities on the level of social services in general and, in particular, on health services, and on Community policies on economic growth and the creation of new jobs promoted by the Cohesion Policy Guidelines. The main investment for which community funds were requested and accessed consisted in the rehabilitation/modernization/equipping of the health services infrastructure (Zaman et al., 2015).

The main applicants were the municipalities and towns that had the hospital building in administration, or the local and county councils. Direct beneficiaries were the inhabitants of the administrative territory of Hunedoara county; the patients consulted in the specialized outpatients (many of them settled by the Health Insurance House); the medical staff/medical staff of the integrated ambulatory; middle school staff: nurses, medical sisters and medical registrars; administrative staff; local public authorities involved in the project. Indirect, beneficiaries were the tourists who visited the area, the population in transit through Jiu Valley (MFE_e, 2019).

By making this investment in Hunedoara County, the number of beneficiaries of the rehabilitated infrastructure was increased, the early detection of diseases by modernizing and equipping the specialized Ambulatory, increasing the quality of medical services, increasing energy efficiency, reducing travel costs, etc. (MFE, 2017).

4.2. The main findings

The implementation of the projects was very important for the town halls and the local authorities, because the non-reimbursable funds were considered as a saving solution for the modernization and equipping the medical offices with high performance equipment.

- The investment through Major Field of Intervention 3.1 have produced concrete results for people living near hospitals, but also for those in remote or disadvantaged areas, by increasing access to health services, and by improving the quality of services offered and the use of high-performance equipment.
- Among the factors that have positively influenced the results obtained we can mention: very good communication between the implementation team and local authorities, the management teams, the companies that performed the rehabilitation works, the hospital managers and the doctors;
- All projects started from an adequate need assessment, by consulting stakeholders – health service partners (local authorities, medical staff) and their direct involvement in projects, but also surveys and studies on the demand and potential benefits of the intervention;
- All the projects monitored the implementation and tried to prevent any malfunctions;
- After the implementation of the projects, the capacity of the managers to attract specialized medical-sanitary personnel (also from outside the localities) has increased;
- The main relevant actors that influenced the design and implementation of Major Field of Intervention 3.1 were: the Ministry of Regional Development and Public Administration and the Intermediate Body (IB). IB influenced the

implementation of Major Field of Intervention 3.1, which led to the improvement of the quality of the healthcare services and to ensuring a balanced regional territorial distribution, in order to ensure the equal access of the population to the health services.

- From the economic point of view, the investment has led to a significant reduction of the thermal energy costs of the modernized buildings, as well as to the increase of the energy efficiency. They have also led to a reduction in the costs of moving patients to other locations to establish the diagnosis.
- Major Field of Intervention 3.1 has well influenced the competences/level of training of medical personnel, through their participation in training courses.
- The doctors were very pleased with the equipment, because the comfort in which they operate. However, long-term medical personnel need to be involved.
- Some beneficiaries considered that a greater financial allocation for the identified needs would be needed and an increased level of implementation capacity at all levels.
- Most of the activities carried out through projects were chosen according to the hierarchy of needs at the hospital/ambulatory level.

Lessons learned from evaluation and aspects that can be improved:

- Better documentation in the writing phase of the project in order to identify all the necessary authorizations, so that ineligible expenses are not declared.
- Accurate identification of expenditures that may subsequently be ineligible, because, in the case of small-town halls, these expenses are collected and they can no longer be paid.
- Decreasing the evaluation period of the projects.
- It would be useful to finance the hospitals, not just the outpatient hospitals.
- Some beneficiaries considered that the project would not have had a greater impact if it had been managed directly by the medical unit. This would have generated additional costs, both with the personnel for the implementation of the project and with the expenses related to the contribution, costs that would have made the activity of the medical unit difficult. However, the direct management by the hospital would have led to greater accountability of decision makers and greater involvement in choosing the optimal solutions.
- For small communities, the major problem remains the lack of medical staff. Doctors prefer to go to the hospital (the motivation is that they want to see the patient in bed).
- The current healthcare system is characterized by a very large movement among the medical staff. Therefore, it would be useful to reduce the evaluation periods, since many elements of the performance nature of the devices can be changed.
- In implementation, as a result of the rapid changes in the medical device market, the possibility of changing one device with another should be

allowed. The lifespan of medical equipment has decreased (they regenerate very quickly, up to 5 times). The applicant guide obliges to have a certain lifespan. Greater flexibility is required for healthcare procurement.
- The evaluation was made exclusively on the basis of the Technical Project (any changes are not take into account).
- The lack of flexibility and coordination of the needs in the field determines the possibility for the projects to change. The system is extremely rigid to change one device with another.
- Warranties to medical devices should be consistent with the life of the device (e.g., there was a problem with a colonoscopies – the image was damaged, the camera cracked due to use). The hospital paid for its repair, because the life span was 3 years and the warranty were 2 years. It has to adapt to market requirements.
- There are few hospitals that use consultants. These consultants prepare the grant application and complain that the requirements of the Guide are extremely restrictive.
- It is considered that there is too much rigidity in the Romanian medical system.
- City halls represent the development poles of the region, and the modernized outpatients attract/lead to investment with regional impact.
- High bureaucracy (some of application reached 1500 pages).
- The legal framework should be improved so that it is clearer and more predictable.
- Regarding the eligible activities – there should be greater flexibility here (there is the situation in which the family doctors were not eligible and the town hall had to pay for new equipment for them too, in order not to lose them).

Conclusions

Through the Major Field of Intervention 3.1. "The rehabilitation/modernization/equipping of the health services infrastructure" was intended to produce concrete results by increasing access to health services, especially in outpatients and hospitals, but also by improving the quality of the services offered and the use of high-performance equipment.

In the Study Case, investment in health infrastructure through regional policy were of major importance, especially for local communities, their implementation bringing significant benefits in the field of health services, an increase of confidence in medical services, modern equipment used by specialists, increased treatment capacity (more rooms, beds, etc. and substantial reduction of waiting time, improvement of operating infrastructure, renewal of utility system, modernization of rooms, access for people with disabilities, obtaining compliance with the standards in force), with visible effects on increasing the quality of health services.

Also, the investment brought a general improvement of the users' satisfaction and a positive perception of the change regarding the infrastructure and the quality of the health services, in the Hunedoara County, the West Region.

It was confirmed that the needs were very high and the amount allocated was too small in relation to local and regional needs. Expectations regarding the impact/effects of the interventions supported by Major Field of Intervention 3.1 were high, and although the call started harder, everything went well later, and the results were good.

The investment has had an important impact, because the medical units that received financing have improved the quality of the services provided to the citizens. However, they were considered more complementary investment. At regional level, the distribution of investment was balanced, with the main financing going towards the purchase of medical equipment.

It can be said that, for local communities, non-reimbursable financing from community funds through Regional Operational Programme, Major Field of Intervention 3.1, also has a long-term impact on the development process of the area, being considered as basic investment of the area (small cities).

From the perspective of the next programming period, it is considered that these categories of investment should be continued, as they are very important for the local authorities. In this context, non-reimbursable Community funds are considered a salvage solution for the modernization of the infrastructure in the health sector.

Acknowledgement

The present article summarizes the main findings results from the Final Impact Assessment Report on the Major Field of Intervention 3.1 of Regional Operational Programme 2007–2013 –"Rehabilitation/modernization/equipping of health services infrastructure," beneficiary Ministry of Regional Development and Public Administration (MDRAP).

Annex 1: Guide for semi-structured interview of beneficiaries (Local Public Authorities)

A. *Context of question: Conditions, needs and initial expectations regarding the KAI-funded intervention 3.1.*
   1. What types of funding are available for investment in health care infrastructure (hospitals and outpatient clinics only)? Did you access them? What is (approximately, value in %) the ROP funding?
   2. What were your expectations regarding the impact/effects of the interventions supported by KAI 3.1.?
   3. How did the socioeconomic conditions change during the implementation of the KAI 3.1 interventions? How did they affect the intervention and, in particular, the achievement of the expected results?

4. How have priorities in the health sector changed during the implementation of KAI 3.1 interventions? How did they affect the intervention and, in particular, the achievement of the expected results?
5. What exactly do you think should have been done differently in terms of how to implement the intervention in order to better meet initial expectations? If we were to go back in time, what should it be taken into account?

B. *Types of interventions*

6. How did you choose the type of activities (or mix of activities) carried out within the project?
7. How would you assess the efficiency/effectiveness of these interventions, compared to others, financed from the national budget or from other sources? (only if at the ATU level other investment were made, from other sources, in outpatient clinics and hospitals)

C. *Results and effects of interventions*

8. What do you consider to be the factors that influenced, positively or negatively, the results obtained?
9. Can a direct causal link be observed between the following effects and the intervention supported by KAI 3.1.? Please rate the following effects (1 to 5, with 1 being the lowest and 5 being the highest), depending on the extent to which you consider that they are directly related to the intervention supported by KAI 3.1.

Possible effects	**Note**	**Motivation**
Increasing the number of patients		
Increasing the number of services provided		
Increasing the quality of services		
Increasing the accessibility of services, from a geographical point of view		
Reducing the number of transfers to other medical units		
Increasing the accessibility of services for people with disabilities		
Improving working conditions for staff		
Improving patient opinion		
Urban development		
Other mentions		

10. What other factors (other projects/programs/private investment, events) could have led/contributed to the results?

11. If you had the power to decide on the implementation of KAI 3.1, mention three things you would change (with arguments). Under what conditions do you think better results could have been achieved?
12. How do you assess the sustainability of the interventions supported, especially in terms of equipment? (aspects related to: changes in public policy, migration of medical staff, etc. will be mentioned)
13. The intervention influenced the competencies/level of training of the medical staff in the supported medical units? How exactly?
14. What would be the main lessons learned/elements of good practice?
15. Can you identify innovative elements or activities in the implemented interventions?

D. *Project beneficiaries (Local Public Authorities/Inter-community Development Association), funding beneficiaries (medical units) and final beneficiaries (patients)*

16. To what extent do you think the intervention would have been more effective/had a greater impact if the projects had been managed directly by the medical units?
17. Is patient satisfaction with the quality of services received in hospitals/outpatients monitored?

E. *Relevant actors*

18. Which do you consider to be the main relevant actors that influenced the design and implementation of KAI 3.1 from Regional Operational Programme?
19. How did they act (direction, instruments, and funds)?

References

Antonescu Daniela, The Regional Development Policy of Romania in the Post-Accession Period, 2013, Working Papers of National Institute of Economic Research, Romanian Academy 131209, https://www.econstor.eu/handle/10419/110445.

European Commission, Guidance Document on Monitoring and Evaluation. Concepts and Recommendations, 2015.

European Commission, Regional Policy, http://ec.europa.eu/regional_policy/sources/docgener/evaluation/evalsed/guide/designing_implementing/managing_evaluations/quality_en.htm, accessed September 2019.

MFE, Final Report of Implementation of ROP 2007–2013, 2017 March version, http://www.old.inforegio.ro/ro/rapoarte-de-evaluare.html, accessed 15.04.2019.

MFE_a (Ministerul Fondurilor Europene), http://www.fonduri-ue.ro/por-2007#documente-relevante, accessed August 2019.

MFE_b, Implementation paper ROP 2007–2013, http://www.fonduri-ue.ro/por-2007#documente-relevante, accessed March 2019.

MFE_c, Ghidul Solicitantului DMI 3.1, POR 2007–2013, http://www.fonduri-ue.ro/por-2007#implementare, accessed March 2019.

MFE_d, http://www.old.inforegio.ro/ro/rapoarte-de-evaluare.html, accessed March 2019.

MFE_d, Implementation of Evaluation Plan of ROP 2007–2013 – Final Report, https://ec.europa.eu/regional_policy/en/policy/evaluations/ec/2007-2013/, accessed August 2019.

MFE_e, Indicators Specified in the Applicant's Guide MFI 3.1 (consolidated version), accessed March 2019.

Zaman Gheorghe, Georgescu George (coord.), Goschin Zizi, Antonescu Daniela, Popa Florina, Dezvoltarea economica endogena la nivel regional. Cazul României, Editura Expert, Bucureşti, 2015.

Simona Frone

Issues of efficiency in the development of water supply and sanitation infrastructure in Romania

Abstract In this paper we present in summary some research results of the project "Efficiency of investments in the development of water and wastewater infrastructure in Romania." The main objective of the research carried out in 2018 to which we will refer further, is the assessment, from a macroeconomic and historical perspective, of the size and efficiency of investments in the development of water supply and sanitation infrastructure in Romania, with some recent progress but also shortcomings or unsatisfactory trends. From a methodological point of view, there are accumulations and outcomes from the literature and our previous research, own data processing, figures and tables describing conceptual relationships, as well as adjacent calculations and static and dynamic comparative analyses of the state of development and recent evolution of the WSS sector in Romania. The conclusions and recommendations shall underline circumstances and factors of inefficiency or obstacles such as the low propensity to pay for the water utilities as well as the potential for increasing the economic and environmental efficiency of these environmental protection investments.

Keywords: sustainable development; environmental protection; efficiency; water supply and sanitation (WSS); infrastructure

Introduction

In this paper are resumed research efforts devoted to the importance and problems in development of environmental infrastructure, in this case for water and wastewater, from a macroeconomic, historical and pragmatic perspective. Thus, the main objective of the research "Efficiency of investment in the development of water and wastewater infrastructure in Romania" (2018) namely part II of the research on the Efficiency of environmental investment in Romania (1918–2018) was to conceptually and theoretically evaluate the size and efficiency of environmental investments, in the development of water and wastewater infrastructure in Romania, highlighting progress but also shortcomings or negative trends.

The methodological approach is based on accumulations and results from the literature, especially on studies developed by reputable environmental economists in Romania, theoretical and empirical researches that are reanalyzed and developed based on expertise in the field of water supply and sanitation (WSS) infrastructure.

1. Literature review

While in the first part of the research, carried out in 2017, namely Theoretical and practical foundations for environmental investments in Romania, it has been shown that, over the last century, the environmental protection policy has not been priority and pro-active in Romania, in part II, on the Efficiency of investment in the development of water and wastewater infrastructure in Romania, a consequence of this neglect of environmental infrastructure and investment is analyzed: Romania is still not sufficiently developed as regards the infrastructure providing distribution of drinking water and the collection and purification of the wastewater.

Today, especially after Romania`s accession to the EU, although investment efforts have been made for the environment, the problem of ecological and economic-social efficiency of these investments is increasingly being acknowledged. This is a chapter of environmental protection in which Romania has had and still has important lagging behind, perpetuated throughout history and never wound up, due to objective and subjective factors exposed in the work's conclusions and recommendations. The foundation and importance of environmental investments is linked to modern economic doctrines or the theory of sustainable development, and in the case of investments in water and wastewater infrastructure, the implementation of the Water Framework Directive (2000/60/EC) and related directives thus that detailed analyses have been limited to the contemporary era of Romania's economy.

There are some important and special water features as a quasi-public environmental good, which are recognized and analyzed for the identification of best practices and sustainable water management mechanisms. In addition, the water supply and sanitation utilities have fewer features of public goods (are almost private goods), because they have high degrees of exclusivity and rivalry.

It is significant that, during the command economy there have been some changes in the water sector. Water was no longer public good, but it belonged to all people, being owned by the state. This confusing formulation was one of the causes that led to the waste and degradation of water resources in Romania. Water has been regarded mainly as a production factor with priority being given to industry and agriculture (Platon, Constantinescu, 2018).

The importance of investments in environmental infrastructure (WSS) under an economic recovery programme, emerges from research dedicated to the environmental infrastructure and its management, which shows that the provision of infrastructure can influence economic activity both through demand and supply channels (Platon, 2007). Numerous research has been undertaken in the European Union's countries to determine whether the infrastructure stimulates economic growth. The evidence shows that a wider infrastructure network is typically associated with a higher economic activity (Del Bo Chiara, Florio, 2008).

Currently, in our country, with the support of European Structural and Cohesion Funds (SCF), local authorities seek to develop infrastructure so that their area still has a chance for sustainable economic growth. Development of water resources is of major importance, if directed to fighting poverty; improving water catchment quality will provide livelihoods for the poor, because usually the poorest people live in those environmentally degraded areas. Large scale investments for the development of water, such as those aimed at improving performance of utility water users' associations or inter-community development and irrigation departments will benefit the entire population involved, including the poorest (Frone, Frone, 2015).

However, it must be acknowledged that the expansion of infrastructure cannot be the main determinant of economic growth. A second reason is linked to the high cost of opportunity, so that the resources used to expand the infrastructure could have been used in other areas of public investment, such as education or health. This is why identifying and verifying the correlation between environmental infrastructure and economic development at local, regional or national level is still a conceptual methodological challenge for economic research.

Nevertheless, EU experience (Lang, 2008) shows that the structural funds, if properly targeted and managed, are the greatest opportunity for sustainable development in Europe, with mainly two large sectors where can be seen this positive impact: investments in environmental infrastructure (such as sewage, wastewater treatment stations, waste management) and in transport development.

Moreover, the costs and benefits related in Romania to the compliance with the European Union acquis in the water sector, in the present case with the WFD and the related ones, were analyzed by the study (Platon, 2004) and others (Platon et al., 2014; Frone, Frone, 2012). Analysis of the impact of the Water Framework Directive and related directives highlighted the main types of benefits:

a) Benefits for human health. The benefits of improving the quality of drinking water are applicable to residents who will connect or who are already connected to the drinking water distribution network and emerge from increasing access to the water system and improving the quality of the supplied water. The total (EU) benefits of improving the quality of drinking water are estimated at 504 million Euro/year, after total compliance with the requirements of the water directives (for Romania are estimated at 55 million €/year).
b) Specific indirect social and economic benefits for Romania. The Water Framework Directive and other related directives will protect groundwater against contamination with different pollutants, and in Romania the quality of groundwater is especially important for the rural communities, which represent about 45 % of the country's total population for which the main source of drinking water is in about 1 million wells (depths of 5–20 m).

In Romania, the total benefits of compliance with the requirements of the WFD and the other water directives were estimated at a value of 0.40–1.24 billion Euros/year; the value of benefits during the compliance period (until 2020) is between

4–12.5 Billion. On the other hand, according to recent documents, the total value of the investment estimated for compliance is approx. 13.8 billion € (about 5.8 billion € for water supply and 8.03 billion € for wastewater).

Some specific aspects of the efficiency of WSS networks and services have been analyzed in the past with important ideas and conclusions. For example, the main determinant factor of the aggregation/regionalization of water utilities is the need to improve the efficiency of the provision of services, as the WSS companies in small towns are often inefficient, too small to maximize benefits of the infrastructure. The advantage of regional WSS operators is therefore to generate economies of scale by being able to share the total production costs on a higher demand basis and thus reduce unit production costs.

A way to increase water efficiency and reduce water consumption is the of water demand management that can have several very important economic and environmental benefits in the medium and long term, such as:

- Reduce the costs of water treatment and system distribution capacity (including the infrastructure capacity for waste water collection and treatment);
- Savings in capital expenditure due to postponement or reduction in the need for new water supply and sanitation projects; Energy savings for water heating, as well as for pumping and treatment;
- Environmental benefits of lower water extraction from streams and aquifers, which leaves more water available to protect ecological resources.

Therefore, an important aspect of efficiency in the WSS sector is the price of water, i.e. the sustainable pricing of these services. Water pricing is also an economic tool aimed at achieving multiple objectives in order to: influence behavior towards the conservation and efficient use of water; support disadvantaged groups; provide incentives for proper demand management; ensure cost recovery and signal the availability of consumer willingness to pay for additional investments in water utilities (Frone, 2012).

In the case of Romania, from the research of 15 years of market economy, we were able to observe, through correlation analysis and regression based on chronological series, the important role of the tariff for water pricing in reducing excessive, unsustainable and inefficient water consumption and use, from the public water supply system, by the population. During the period of time taken into account, the variable UWPWS (the volume of water used, from the public water network), was reversed correlated with the PWATER (water unit pricing). The estimated negative parameter for the price elasticity of the demand (-0.385) means that a 1 % increase in water price leads to a quite significant decrease in water consumption, namely by 0.385 %. (Frone, Frone, 2012) During the period under review (1998–2012), the determined variable GDP/capita was inversely correlated with water consumption in the public water supply network, which may indicate that restructuring and reforms occurred in the Romanian water sector having reduced the water losses and waste in the networks, practically increasing efficiency of the water supply infrastructure nationwide.

Finally, another aspect of efficiency to be taken into account in the development of WSS networks and services is that of resource use. There is usually a direct link between economic growth and increased water consumption, as shown in (Frone, Frone, 2012, 2014). But increasing the efficiency of WSS systems can be a way of stabilizing, or even reducing water consumption with sustainable economic development.

2. Current requirements on investments in water and wastewater infrastructure and their efficiency premises

As can be seen from the figure below, at the time of EU integration, Romania's situation in terms of endowment with the WSS infrastructure was among the most critical because of large development deficits (Fig. 1).

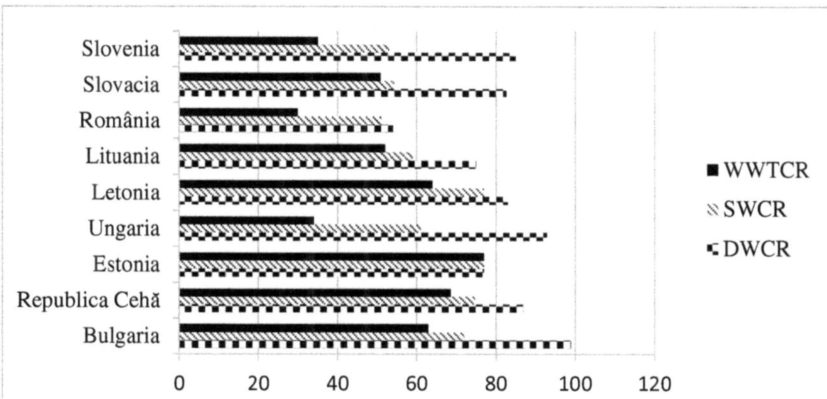

Fig. 1: Development of water/wastewater infrastructure in former socialist countries before accession to the European Union (2000)
Source: Own data processing.

Romania was, before joining the EU in 2007, at the lowest level of development of the WSS infrastructure, as expressed by some proxy indicators:

- DWCR (%population) the connection rate to the drinking water networks is the percentage of the country's total population, connected to water supply networks, 54 % in Romania;
- SWCR (%population) the connection rate to sewage networks represents the percentage of the total population of the country, connected to the sewer networks, under 50 %;

- WWTCR (%population) the connection rate for wastewater treatment systems represents the percentage of the country's total population, connected to wastewater treatment systems, only 30 % in Romania.

It can be seen that Romania had a disability in terms of the level of development of the WSS infrastructure, with imbalances which, as will further analyse, have not been mitigated very much or very quickly neither in the later or post-accession period.

Currently (Fig. 2) about two-thirds of Romania's rural population (66.5 % in 2017) is not connected to the drinking water supply and that 90 % of these inhabitants do not benefit from sewage sanitation systems is an alarm signal in terms of balanced and sustainable regional development prospects of Romania, although the situation of localities with a population of less than 2000 equivalents is not an emergency compliance with the obligations assumed by the Treaty of accession to the EU in Chapter 22 (Environment).

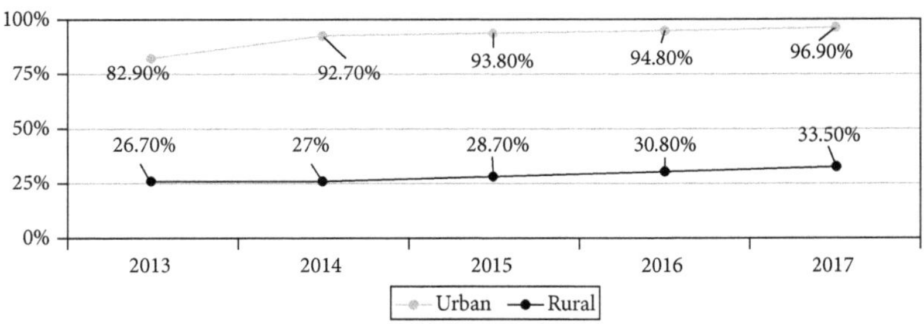

Fig. 2: Recent evolution of the Romanian urban (high) and rural (low) rate of the population with access to water supply services in centralized system (%)

Thus, as having demonstrated empirically, the function of the water demand relative to price is quite steep in Romania, so that the elasticity versus price of demand is high and so the willingness of consumers to pay for the current water is relatively low (primarily due to extreme poverty, lack of environmental and civic education and the low level of socioeconomic development in many rural areas or localities). This trend can jeopardise the prospects for sustainable development of WSS networks and services in Romania.

With regard to the environmental efficiency of the WSS infrastructure, characterized by the groundwater quality, accidental water pollution and waste water discharges, there are some recent data extracted from the National Romanian Water Agency (ANAR)-Water quality report for the year 2016. Monitoring of the quality of groundwater revealed that, about 16 % (23/141) of groundwater bodies were outside the chemical parameters prescribed. Causes of accidental pollution produced in 2016 placed in the first places: non-compliance with the technological rules on the evacuation of wastewater into natural receptors, followed by pollution with petroleum products caused by damage to the crude oil transport ducts.

In Romania, in 2016, the volume of wastewater discharged into natural receptors amounted to 1940.98 million m^3 (not including cooling waters, according to new Eurostat specification) versus 1924.66 million m^3 in 2015, reflecting a slightly increased consumption of water (approx. 0.8 %), partly explicable by the 6 times higher economic growth rate (4.8 %), which represents an important gain in terms of the efficiency of the use of the water resource.

Although the Romanian industry also contributes to pollution by wastewater, the largest and the first polluting factor is precisely the WSS sector, since, as further highlighted, there is still a large gap in Romania, between the level of development and coverage of population with water supply networks and services, and on the other hand, the level of development and coverage of the population with sewage networks and services (Fig. 3).

It may be noted from Fig. 3 below that, although after the year 2013, an average annual growth of 1 % of the population connected to the sewage network has occurred, the connecting of Romania's population to the sewage network was and is still relatively modest, too low as required for sustainable development and water quality protection.

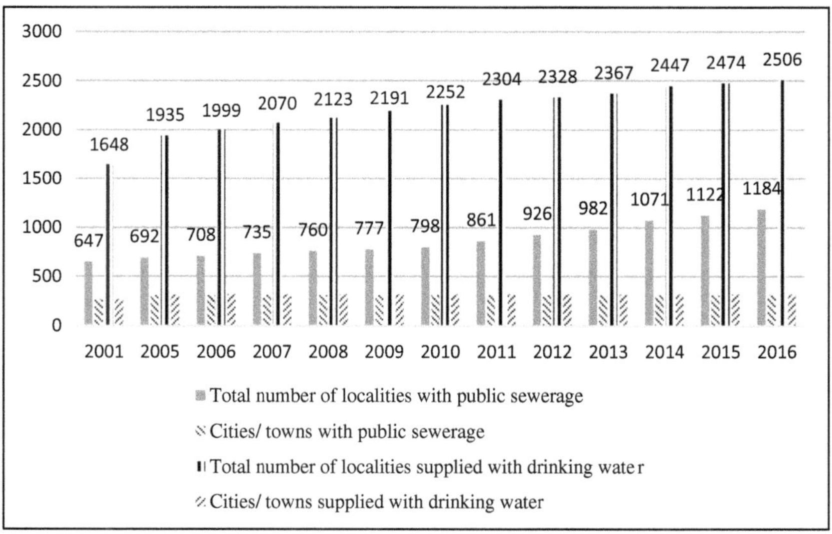

Fig. 3: Evolution of the sewage network compared to the drinking water supply network, total and urban endowment in Romania

Source: Own data processing.

The situation in towns and cities is more balanced in the sense that almost all (97 %) towns and cities supplied with drinking water, have also public sewerage, so the big gap between the two types of water services occurs especially in rural areas (Frone, Frone, 2013).

In 2017, in urban areas the population connected to sewer was 9,234,259 persons, representing 87.7 % of the urban resident population of Romania, while in rural areas only a number of 744,627 persons benefited from sewage services, representing only 8.2 % of Romania's rural population. Thus, while the total length of the drinking water distribution network had increased by more than 55 % in 2009 compared to 2001 (by 24 % in 2010 compared to year 2006), during the same period the sewage network expanded by only 26 %, so the growth rate of the sewage network was 25–50 % lower.

Moreover, this gap is reflected very clearly also in the discrepancy between the level of investment in the two main activities related to water management (Fig. 4): 36-Water abstraction and distribution; 37-Wastewater collection and treatment. In practice, an excessive priority was given to the development of water supply infrastructure, while sewage networks and sanitation plants are still undersized and fail to perform the environmental protection function at the level required by sustainable development, more specifically, by the Water Framework Directive (2000/60/EC).

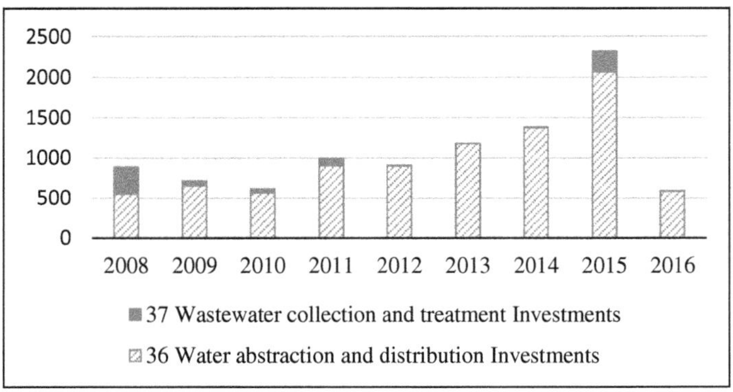

Fig. 4: Environmental investments, on the two water management activities (million lei)

Source: Data extracted and processed from TEMPO_PMI105A_28_11_2018.

However, in recent years, the expansion of sewage networks in Romania has experienced a higher rhythm dynamism, so the gap between the water supply and the sewage networks has begun to stagnate since 2013. This way, according to recent data (INS, 2018): in 2017, the simple length of the drinking water distribution network was 82090.4 km, with 3.0 % higher than in 2016; the simple length of sewage pipes was 36344.5 km, with 5.8 % higher than 2016, so an almost double growth rate that should be continued to mitigate the development gap between the WS and S network. A positive fact and real progress in terms of sustainable and integrated development of the WSS sector in Romania is also the fact that in total, in 2017, a number of 9,710,077 persons, the equivalent of 49.4 % of resident population, was connected to sewage systems equipped with sanitation plants, so virtually all the inhabitants connected receive the sewage treatment for wastewater discharged into the centralized sewage system.

An essential approach to increasing the efficiency of the WSS infrastructure in Romania was the metering of consumers, determining a drop in the consumption of water distributed to consumers. Thus, since 2014, when the degree of metering reached more than 90 % at national level, a stabilization of water consumption has begun.

Tab. 1: Drinking water distributed in centralized system, 2008–2017, national total and household level (million m^3)

	2008	**2009**	**2010**	**2011**	**2012**	**2013**	**2014**	**2015**	**2016**	**2017**	**2017/2016 (%)**
DW supplied national total quantity	1074.79	1064.85	1024.23	1022.36	1035.42	1028.36	995.49	1155.58	1030.64	1125.44	109.2
DW supplied, household level quantity	681.63	681.08	689.39	677.03	694.79	700.02	684.45	504.74	501.53	519.72	103.6

Source: Data extracted and processed from (ARA, 2018).

Although, in general, household water consumption has recently decreased (Tab. 1, Fig. 5) due to metering and to increased tariffs, and reduced its share in the total water consumption (due to increased economic activity), according to the report of the Romanian Water Association (ARA, 2018), the increase in the amount of water delivered to the households (as in 2013) was due to the increased access to services, while the amount of water consumed per person/day remained relatively constant.

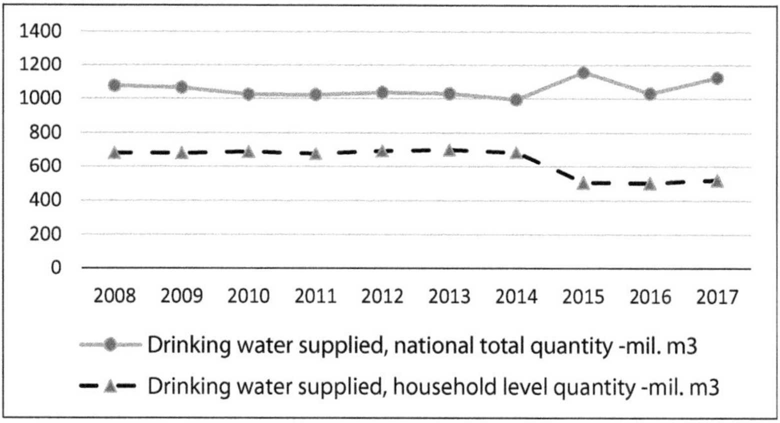

Fig. 5: Evolution of drinking water distributed in centralized system, 2008–2017, national total and household level (mil. m^3)

Actually, the household water consumption was also considerably reduced over the last about 10 years after Romania's accession to the EU and the transposition of water directives, so that in 2017, in municipalities and cities, the average daily consumption of drinking water for domestic use was 85.8 liters per inhabitant (according to the National Institute of Statistics), compared to 127.7 liters/inhabitant in 2010, so there was a 32.8 % decrease in the average daily domestic consumption of drinking water.

An issue of low efficiency concerns the evolution of invoiced water as a share in the total distributed water by regional operators. The share of non-invoiced water in total is still high, of about 45 % reported by the Romanian Water Association (ARA, 2018) due to network losses, fraudulent connection or to commercial risk of WSS utilities in Romania, i.e. the risk of non-payment of services, analyzed and explained in detail in (Platon et al., 2014).

Conclusions

Access to good quality drinking water is a quasi-public good, water consumption being absolutely necessary for life and economic activity, but also being ensured on the basis of costly and commercial-based infrastructure, by local or regional operators, such as in Romania. By estimating and quantifying the multiple benefits of connecting to the WSS infrastructure, a direct economic motivation can be formed on the investment decision for compliance measures with the EU water acquis, since there will be obtained long-term benefits in the quality of water, the environment, health and human life.

As highlighted in the cited papers, in Romania, because of the state of lagging behind in terms of access to the WSS services, necessary to comply with the Accession Treaty, the investment required in the WSS infrastructure has been and is still extremely high (over 10 billion Euro). During the period of transition to the market economy and the pre-accession period, many problems or challenges have been manifested in Romania's economy, often preventing either the proper financing of environmental investments, the application of the polluter pays principle or the effective implementation of these investment projects.

Accessing the EU's Structural and Cohesion Funds (SCF) through SOP Environment has been a great opportunity for the sustainable development of the WSS sector in Romania. The sector's development was relatively slow but undeniable: due to the latest evolution, significant progress is found, the population served with AAC services increasing from 29 % (1993) to 67.5 % (2017), while major mutations also occurred in the urban/rural population ratios. The level of equipment with centralized drinking water supply systems of the population remains still favorable to the urban environment (98.7 %, respectively 35.3 % rural, according to the national institute of statistics INS, 2018).

However, investments in the WSS infrastructure, typically achieved through major large-scale projects (amounting to more than 50 million euros), have been and are still affected by the lack of sufficient funding and of implementation capacity, low willingness to pay (WTP) of the population for connection to the WSS utilities or some of the conjuncture factors, such as the economic-financial crisis of the period 2009–2011. The causes that led to differences in the accessibility to water services of consumers, between urban and rural environments, are also valid for sanitation and sewage services. To increase economic and social efficiency, it is desirable to take the best legislative and managerial measures to ensure not only the implementation of WSS infrastructure projects and their physical installation, but also the effective growth of population connected to these utilities, despite the resistance of some of the inhabitants or their reduced availability of payment. In this regard, we consider necessary and welcome the very recent measures in law 215/2018, aiming to create a sustainable development framework for the water sector.

During the last period, at macroeconomic level, efforts are being made to coordinate investment programs financed both from government funds (PNDL,

PNADR) and from non-refundable European funds (SOP Environment, LIOP) by integrating them in the County Masterplan. Furthermore, all these investment projects must comply with the same requirements, in accordance with H.G. 677/2017 – concerning cost-benefit analysis methodology for investments in water infrastructure.

One of the great achievements of the sustainable and efficient development of the WSS sector in Romania is the regionalization process, namely the reform and institutional consolidation, on theoretical and practical foundation was conducted in some previous research. As proof of the effectiveness of this institutional model with regard to the WSS sector, international financial institutions (EC, EBRD) recommends some EU member countries (Croatia) or outside the EU (Serbia, Moldova, Albania) to analyse the regionalization model implemented in Romania as a possible solution for streamlining public water-wastewater services.

Overall, it can be said that while the development of the WSS sector in Romania has been relaunched mainly due to Romania's accession to the EU, to implement water Directives with the support of European funds, it has not been concluded since Romania has not reached in 2018 the degree of compliance assumed (AM POIM, 2018); substantial funding and measures taken at national level are still needed to support the continuation of reforms begun. However, there are efficiency gains in Romania's WSS infrastructure: the creating and operating with economies of scale of regional WSS operators; the metering of water consumers and reducing household average consumption; the increasing of water productivity as a resource, which justifies further investment efforts in the water sector.

In this context, the strategy of the Large Infrastructure Operational Program POIM for 2014–2020 aims to allocate funds for WSS investments, with the explicit condition of strengthening and expanding the regionalization process and the capacity of regional operators, necessary prerequisites to streamline the development of the WSS sector in Romania.

References

A.R.A., 2018: Raport privind starea serviciilor de alimentare cu apă şi de canalizare-epurare în anul 2017, noiembrie 2018.

AM POIM, 2018: Technical Assistance to Consolidate the Water and Wastewater Sector in Romania – Project Implementation Support Services Contract Agreed between the Ministry of European Funds and the European Bank for Reconstruction and Development, Romaqua nr. 6/2018.

ANAR, 2017: Sinteza calităţii apelor din România în anul 2016, ANAR 2017.

Del Bo, C. & Florio, M., 2008: Infrastructure and Growth in the European Union: An Empirical Analysis at the Regional Level in a Spatial Framework, IDEAS Repec, 2008.

Frone, S., Frone, D.F., 2012: Factors and Trends of Economic Efficiency in the Water/Wastewater Sector, in Procedia Economics and Finance, Volume 3, Elsevier, 2012.

Frone, S., Frone, D.F. 2013: Promoting Access to Water Supply and Sanitation: Issues and Challenges in Romania. Scientific Papers. Series Management, Economic Engineering in Agriculture and Rural Development 13(2): 165–170.

Frone, S., Frone, D.F., 2014: Challenges in Analyzing Correlation between Water Infrastructure and Economic Development. Procedia Economics and Finance 10: 197–206.

Frone, D.F., Frone, S., 2015: The Importance of Water Security for Sustainable Development in the Romanian Agri-Food Sector. Agriculture and Agricultural Science Procedia 6: 674–681.

Frone, S., 2012: Issues on the Role of Efficient Water Pricing for Sustainable Water Management. Romanian Journal of Economics nr. 1 (43)/2012.

Lang, S., 2008: Promoting Sustainable Development in Europe through Regional Funds, WWF European Policy Office, aprilie 2008.

National Institute of Statistics (INS), 2018: Distribuţia apei în anul 2017, Comunicat de presă nr. 249/28 septembrie 2018, Institutul Naţional de Statistică, România.

Platon, V., 2004: Finanţarea activităţilor de protecţie a mediului. Între teorie şi practică, Ed. Economică, 2004.

Platon, V. (coord.), 2007: Protecţia mediului şi politici de dezvoltare regională; problematica gestiunii deşeurilor la nivel regional, I.E.N., 2007.

Platon, V. et al., 2014: Financial and Economic Risks to Public Projects. Procedia Economics and Finance 8: 204–210.

Platon, V., Constantinescu, A., 2018: Water Resources in Romania during 1945–1989. Romanian Journal of Economics Vol. 47, issue 2(56), 20–33.

Ioan I. Gâf-Deac, Gheorghe Horia Chivu, Cristian Bîrdac, Anna Maria Vasile

Urban mobility: conceptual and operational challenge in Bucharest, Romania

Abstract The article shows that population mobility is the process by which people change their residential, professional or social status to another status. The authors consider that the most appropriate description and analysis of mobility is made using the cohort method (longitudinal representation), by matrix representation, through the matrix of probabilities of changing one status with another, a human condition with another state, etc. The sustainable urban mobility plan leads to the balanced development of several, more sustainable modes of transport. The proposed online application shows the parking locations on the territory of Sector 4 in Bucharest and the identification of vulcanization stations, bicycle rental, refueling points for charging electric vehicles (access hours, number of available seats, hourly rate or specific facilities).

Keywords: urban mobility, traffic management, electric vehicles market, parking model, environment, economy and sustainability

Introduction

On the territory of a large urban agglomeration, such as Bucharest/Romania, there are demographic events included, generically, in the notion of natural movement of the population. The closed type population (in the model of the stable population) is an ensemble or a community that is renewed under the effect of births and deaths.

The population is also an open system, having as variables its number and structure, at national or territorial-administrative level, with external and internal migration (migratory movement of the population). The general movement of the population has a dynamic, through the natural and the migratory movement. As such, there may be natural surplus (increase) or migratory increase, or the opposite meaning, respectively related decreases (Bell, Morse, 2008). Migration is a factor of redistribution of the population in the territory, through urban growth, social homogenization.

Population mobility is the process by which people change their residential, professional or social status to another status. There are: (1) spatial/territorial or geographical mobility; (2) professional mobility and (3) social mobility. The description and analysis of mobility is done using (1) the cohort method (longitudinal appearance); (2) by matrix representation; (3) by the matrix of probabilities of changing one status with another, a state of man with another state, etc.

So mobility is a lot of crossings, which fall under the explanatory incidence of Markov processes and chains (Camagni, Gibelli, 2002). Spatial mobility refers to the sum of the population's movements in space, over greater or shorter distances (Castillo, Pitfield, 2010).

Sector 4 is an Administrative-Territorial Unit of Bucharest, the Capital of Romania. It has an area of 34 km^2, a population of 299,414 inhabitants (density of 8,806 inhabitants/km^2) (Fig. 1a, b).

According to The National Strategy for Romania Sustainable Development – Horizons 2013–2020–2030 the negative aspects which concerns the community in Bucharest/i.e. District 4 are the following: (1) road traffic increase in Bucharest municipality and in a metropolitan area; (2) the commercial speed of urban transport is 10–14 km/h; (3) grants absorption is slow; (4) in the public transport are maintained vehicles physically and morally outdated.

a) b)

Fig. 1: Map of Bucharest, by sectors (a) and the map of Sector 4 (b)
Source: //en.wikipedia.org/wiki/Sector4.

In 2019, Sector 4 in Bucharest is a creative and dynamic "city," with beautiful and accessible housing, living neighborhoods, favorable working and shopping conditions. The diverse culture, the varied sports offers and the low crime complete the living and living environment for the inhabitants. The measures designed and implemented shall be consistent between individual and public transport. The Department of Urban Mobility (DMU) within the City Hall of Sector 4 through coordinated actions positively influences the community.

1. Literature review

"Sustainable development framework" consists in four main dimensions (economic, social, environmental, institutional) and multiple topics and subtopics related to these dimensions. EU recommended way to calculate and aggregate different indicators of this topics and subtopics is called "Dashboard Sustainability Software" (JRC, 2019).

In the literature it is shown that "current models of human activity are fundamentally stochastic from Erlang's formula used in telephony to Lévy-walk models describing human mobility and their applications in viral dynamics, queuing models capturing human communication patterns, and models capturing body balancing or panic."

However, "most important, our results indicate that when it comes to processes driven by human mobility, from epidemic modeling to urban planning and traffic engineering, the development of accurate predictive models is a scientifically grounded possibility, with potential impact on our well-being and public health. At a more fundamental level, they also indicate that, despite our deep-rooted desire for change and spontaneity, our daily mobility is, in fact, characterized by a deep-rooted regularity" (Chaoming et al., 2010).

On the other hand, "transportation and logistics is the engine for economic growth. It is crucial to move goods, people around the countries, and allow accessing employment, services, leisure activities and socialize with wider communities."

"For simulating real-time network, simulation solution will better fit due to the occurrence of state changes over time, discrete events and discontinuous equations where by using analytical solutions, the time factor is not considered as outputs functionality depends on the input" (ElBanhawy et al., 2011) The Decision Support System (DSS) is the heart and soul of the ICMS (Integrated Corridor Management System) (SwRI, 2018) The core responsibilities of the DSS are as follows: Monitor, evaluate, and respond to reoccurring congestion along the arterial network, Evaluate and respond to non-recurring congestion on I-4 within the identified network, Evaluate and respond to non-recurring congestion on arterial roadways within the identified network.

The ICMS (Integrated Corridor Management System) has some functionalities and objectives: (1) Receive live and historical data from traffic, (2) Analyze infrastructure status, (3) Analyze collected data to determine transportation performance, (4) Provide the current status of devices and performance of roadway. Real-time analysis, calibrated model retrieval, real-time simulation are functionalities and objectives in an urban mobility management program. (Lukasik, 2013).

Andreas Tschiesner et al. (2019), emphasizes that "electric vehicles (EVs) sales totaled 2.08 million vehicles globally in 2018. (...) The EV market penetration steadily increased from 0.9 percent in 2016 to about 2.5 percent of the total light-vehicle market in 2019. The fastest-growing market for EVs in 2019 is Europe."

2. Research method: data collection and preparation

2.1. Achieving the objectives of sustainable urban mobility

The Urban Mobility Plan for Sector 4 in Bucharest considers the descriptive, analytical approach and predictability for: (1) Public transport (increasing the quality, security, integration and accessibility of public transport services); (2) Non-motorized transport (increasing the attractiveness, safety and security of walking and cycling); (3) Intermodality (a good integration of different modes of movement aiming at coherence between mobility and multimodal transport); (4) Urban road safety (risk factors in urban areas); (5) Road transport (moving and stationary traffic); (6) Urban logistics (freight delivery services, related externalities, GHG emissions, air and noise pollution); (7) Mobility management (transition to sustainable mobility systems); (8) Intelligent transport systems (Dobranskyte-Niskota et al., 2016).

Achieving the objectives of sustainable urban mobility refers to: (1) integrated policy and (2) citizen-centered (Castillo, Pitfield, 2010).

Essentially, integration should be understood as "up and multilateral": vertical approach between different levels of mobility planning for an urban area which is part of a wider transport framework; territorial approach; horizontal approach in the same level, between different politics; intermodal approach, provide links between different modes of travel: public transport, private car, walking, cycling.

From the procedural perspective of mobility, urban agglomerations (including Bucharest) are subject to trends such as: expansion, the peripheries being with low population density, higher energy consumption for mobility needs; developing the motorization of families/inhabitants (Haghshenas, Vaziri, 2016); new traffic congestion density (from engines, longer travel lengths); increasing the complexity of the lifestyle (meeting new requirements).

The following are considered: new efficiency and attractiveness for urban public transport systems, and more environmentally friendly mobility practices.

The sustainable urban mobility plan leads to the balanced development of several, more sustainable modes of transport (Mendiola, 2015). The main objectives to be achieved by 2050 in the EU are: the progressive reduction (until extinction) of the use of conventional means of transport in cities; reaching 40 % use of sustainable fuels; reducing carbon emissions in the transport sector by at least 40 %; taking over about 50 % of the transport by rail and naval transport.

In fact, there is a need to formalize a type of "integrated urban mobility" that becomes a conceptual and planning support for conventional urban mobility.

According to Mobility plans, (EC, 2019), a Sustainable Urban Mobility Plan includes: long-term vision; implementation plan; the concept of participatory approach (Shiau, Liu, 2013); balanced and integrated development of travel/ transport modes; integration of horizontal and vertical mobility; performance evaluation; internal and external costs; monitoring, review, reporting; feeds, adjustments, updates.

2.2. Parking system –main features and challenges: case study

Requests for parking spaces in Sector 4 are from those who have a job in the area (medium-term parking), among those who have interests in institutions and units in the area (occasional, short-term parking). Unjustified occupation of part of the public space by illegally parked vehicles has been regulated by computerization of specific demand and supply. The "park & ride" concept seems to be a success in Sector 4 in Bucharest. Almost 1,000 new parking spaces have been set up near the largest metro stations in the sector. Areas with affected environmental landscapes were intended for the construction of parking lots. There is the possibility to place cars during the day, safe places, video surveillance, a short distance from the nearest public transport station, from where the access is direct and fast to underground and above-ground public transport, to reach the center of the Capital.

In the "park & ride" type car parks, the access of motor vehicles not exceeding the total mass of 3.5 t and/or maximum dimensions of 2.5 m width and 5.5 m length is allowed. Two more car parks are being completed. The parking lot at Piața Sudului is the first multi-storey "park & ride" construction in the Capital and also the first construction of this kind, modular, made of metal panels, built in the last 30 years in Bucharest. It has a capacity of 300 seats, arranged on three levels. Another 10,000 new parking spaces are created through works to widen the main boulevards, where 12 public paid parking lots are being arranged. (Figs. 2, 3 and 4)

Fig. 2: Parking in the Youth Park area, Sector 4, Bucharest, 2018/2019
Source: City Hall Sector 4 and Authors.

Fig. 3: Statistics of cars parked in the Parking lot in the Parcul Tineretului area, Sector 4, Bucharest, 2018/2019
Source: City Hall Sector 4 and Authors.

Fig. 4: Basic plan Parking in the Youth Park area, Sector 4, Bucharest, 2018/2019
Source: City Hall Sector 4 and Authors.

The proposed online application shows the parking locations on the territory of Sector 4 in Bucharest and the identification of vulcanization stations, bicycle rental, refueling points for charging electric vehicles (access hours, number of available seats, hourly rate or specific facilities) (Figs. 5, 6 and 7)

Fig. 5: Location of individual parking areas in the vicinity of dwellings, Sector 4, Bucharest, 2018/2019
Source: City Hall Sector 4 and Authors.

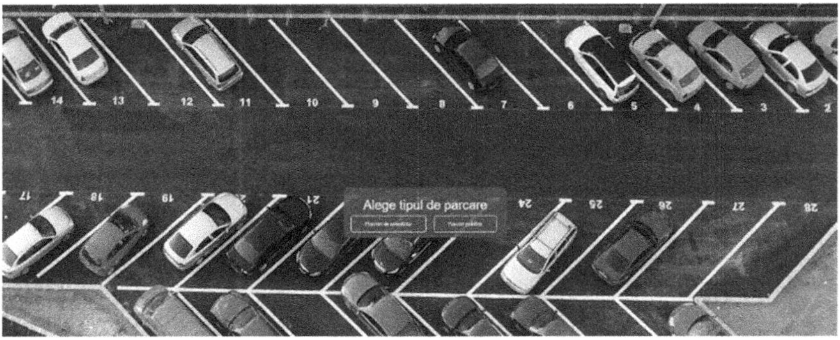

Fig. 6: Numbering for the electronic base for renting individual parking areas near homes, Sector 4, Bucharest, 2018/2019

Source: City Hall Sector 4 and Authors.

Fig. 7: Map with the database for the electronic/online model for renting individual parking areas near homes, Sector 4, Bucharest, 2018/2019

Source: City Hall Sector 4 and Authors.

The computerized model of dynamic allocation of parking spaces in the vicinity of homes in Sector 4 was designed at the Directorate of Urban Mobility, and is original, unique in the modern, efficient parking system in Romania.

2.3. Model control and testing

The ability of the DMU to correctly model daily urban activities for traffic control, energy consumption and urban planning has positive critical effects on the quality of people's lives and the day-to-day operation of Sector 4. Contributions for such models are based on surveys, collecting information on the quality of DMU services, socioeconomic, demographic, traffic, pollution, etc. data. We found that the mode of large-scale urban mobility, well established in Sector 4, depends on detailed travel surveys, on the calibration of solutions (Fig. 8).

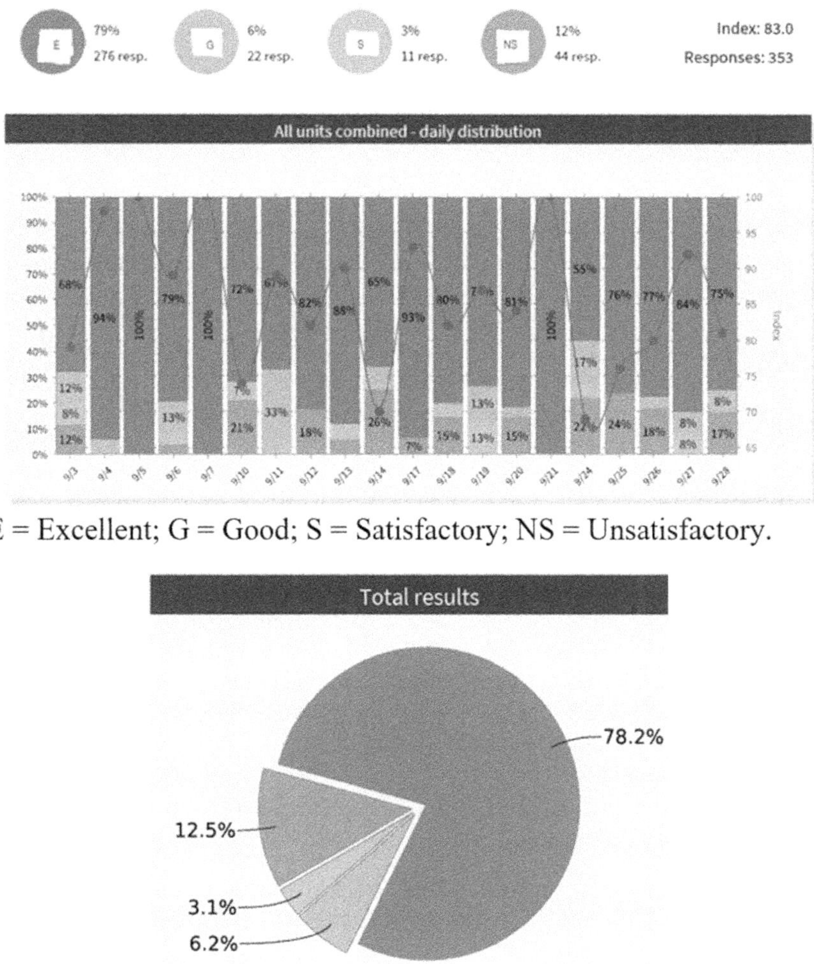

Fig. 8: Management Report, Urban Mobility Directorate Sector 4 (2 units) Sector 4, Bucharest, 2018/2019

Source: City Hall Sector 4 and Authors.

In the policy of important projects, it is planned to extend the metro line with another 1–2 stations and manage the traffic demand during major events or to prepare for emergencies, through reliable urban travel demand models. These high-resolution models simulate individual mobility and are tested by surveys.

2.4. Traffic management solutions

Within Sector 4, Bucharest, the following are envisaged: (1) simulation software for traffic modeling with suggested response plans; (2) mesoscopic traffic model used by traffic modeling simulation software; (3) quality analysis system and integration analysis of intelligent traffic systems; (4) software that probes traffic signal systems for recommended active signal plans; (5) the decision support system (intelligent decisions from the engine of expertise rules, predictive engine and evaluation engine with modeling the results of the selected answers).

We appreciate that traffic forecasting solutions based on simulations, offer/can provide answers to incidents or traffic management strategies/tactics. (Tanguay et al., 2016). Instead, it is important to use real-time inputs from different sources of information (from field traffic controllers, detectors, incident reports, and live data streams from key intersections) (Burggraf, 2014).

The basic goal must always be to recover the calibrated model. Dynamic simulation (mesoscopic or microscopic) provides, in fact, real-time traffic scenarios, forecasts of traffic conditions for at least the next 30–60 minutes.

In the period 2018–2019, from a topological point of view, in Sector 4 in Bucharest it was necessary to quantify the degree of integration of the sector network in the structure of the general municipal network, by calculations regarding the properties of graphs corresponding to the infrastructure networks. The types of network integrations were: (1) the hyperintegrated graph (when an arc of the sector network overlapped over an arc of the municipal network, (2) the hypointegrated graph (when the Sector 4 network is connected in a peripheral node to the municipal network) and (3) rationally integrated graph (when the transport network of Sector 4 and the municipal network proved to be tangent). In this context, practically, all 3 variants of graph were met, but mainly it turned out to be the type of hyperintegrated graph.

2.5. The green cadaster, the bicycle infrastructure and the pedestrian movements

The green cadaster is a computer system for registration and evidence of green spaces, located on the urban territory of Sector 4, for active monitoring (inventory and prevention of deforestation).

Reducing carbon emissions in urban areas through investments targets types of projects such as:

- improvement of urban public transport: electric rolling stock, green vehicles (EEV); extension of public electric transport routes; rehabilitation of depots;

exclusive lines for public transport vehicles; rehabilitation of public transport stations and construction of new intermodal stations and terminals; e-ticketing systems for travelers; bicycle tracks; rehabilitation of transport corridors) (Camagni, 1996);
- increase of electric and non-motorized transport (filling stations for electric cars); routes for cyclists; areas and pedestrian routes, reducing car traffic in certain areas);
- reduction of CO2 emissions (video monitoring of traffic management; park and ride systems; forest curtains).

The challenges related to urban mobility in Bucharest are found in the alignments: (1) without transport congestion, (2) greener locality, (3) smarter urban transport, (4) more accessible and (5) safe.

Cycling has become a growing mode of transport, both at the city level (short-term rental systems), there has been local infrastructure (bike paths), and leisure activities in nature, in the mountains, on a river or at big (Amekudzi et al., 2011; Scăieşteanu, 2018). Walking is the fundamental form of mobility: on pedestrian facilities: (interrupted/pedestrian crossings and uninterrupted/alleys).

Conclusions

Traffic forecasting solutions based on simulations, provide/can provide answers to incidents or traffic management strategies/tactics. The case study presented reveals that using IT tools the DMU has the ability to correctly model daily urban activities for traffic control, energy consumption and urban planning has positive critical effects on the quality of people's lives and the daily functioning of Sector 4. The computerized model of dynamic allocation of parking spaces in the vicinity of dwellings in Sector 4 was designed by the Urban Mobility Directorate, and is original, unique in the modern, efficient parking system in Romania.

The "park & ride" concept is a success in Sector 4, in Bucharest. Almost 1,000 new parking spaces have been set up near the largest metro stations in the sector. Areas with affected environmental landscapes were intended for the construction of parking lots. It can be a good practice that can be transposed in other sectors and cities.

As externalities, diverse culture, varied sports offers and low crime complete the living and living environment for the inhabitants. These are additional arguments to conclude that the solutions designed and implemented shall be consistent between individual and public transport.

References

Amekudzi, A., Meyer, M., Ross, C., Barrella, E., Transportation planning for sustainability guidebook. Prepared for US DOT Federal Highway Administration, 2011.

Bell, S., Morse, S., Sustainability Indicators: Measuring the Immeasurable? 2nd Ed. London: Earthscan.

Böhringer, C., Jochem, P.E.P., Measuring the immeasurable – A survey of sustainability indices. Ecological Economics, 63(1), 1–8, 2008.

Burggraf, K., Why is monitoring and evaluation a challenge in sustainable Urban mobility planning? Report of CH4LLENGE Programme: Addressing Key Challenges of Sustainable Urban Mobility Planning, 2014.

Camagni, R., Principes et modèles de l'économie urbaine, Paris, Economica, 1996.

Camagni, R., Gibelli, M.C., Urban mobility and urban form: The social and environmental costs of different patterns of urban expansion. Ecological Economics, 40, 199–216, 2002.

Castillo, H., Pitfield, D.E., ELASTIC – A methodological framework for identifying and selecting sustainable transport indicators. Transportation Research Part D: Transport and Environment, 15(4), 179–188, 2010.

Chaoming, S. et al., Limits of predictability in human mobility, Science, 327, 1018, 2010.

Dobranskyte-Niskota, A., Perujo, A., Pregl, M., Indicators to assess sustainability of transport activities, Part 1: Review of the existing transport sustainability indicators initiatives and development of an indicator set to assess transport sustainability performance. European Commission, Joint Research Centre. Emisia S.A., 2016. Available at: www.emisia.com (accessed 8 September 2018).

ElBanhawy, E.Y., et al., Real-Time Electric Mobility Simulation in Metropolitan Areas, School of the Built and Natural Environment, Northumbria University, UK, 2011.

European Commission, www.mobilityplans.eu, 2019.

Gilbert, R., Tanguay, H., Sustainable Transportation Performance Indicators Project, Phase 2 Report. GIS Portal of the Municipality of Thessaloniki, 2016. Available at: gis.thessaloniki.gr (accessed 11 November 2018).

Haghshenas, H., Vaziri, M., Urban sustainable transportation indicators for global comparison. Ecological Indicators, 15(1), 115–121. Hellenic Statistical Authority, 2016. Available at: www.statistics.gr (accessed 8 April 2018).

Lukasik, A.D., Integrated Corridor Management on I-15 in San Diego, Traffic Technology Today, March 2013.

Mendiola L., González P., Cebollada A. (2015). The relationship between urban development and the environmental impact mobility: A local case study. Land Use Policy 43, 119–128.

Scăieșteanu, D., Proiect pilot mobilitate urbană, www.bikex.ro, București, 2018.

Shiau, T.A., Liu, J.S., Developing an indicator system for local governments to evaluate transport sustainability strategies. Ecological Indicators, 34, 361–371, 2013.

Tanguay, G.A., Rajaonson, J., Lefebvre, J.F., Lanoie, P., Measuring the sustainability of cities: An analysis of the use of local indicators. Ecological Indicators, 10(2), 407–418, 2010.

Tschiesner et al., The road ahead for e-mobility, How OEMs can win consumers and achieve mass-market EV adoption, McKinsey Center for Future Mobility, Draft, 2019.

Southwest Research Institute (SwRI), Central Florida Regional Integrated Corridor Management System, Project owner Florida Department of Transportation (FDOT), Aimsun – A Siemens Company, Period March 2018 – March 2023.

The Joint Research Centre (JRC) European Commission (EC), International Institute for Sustainable Development (IISD), Sustainability dashboard – non-commercial software, 2019.

Mariana Stanciu

A decade of social and economic development for Romania in European Union

Abstract The accession to the European Union in 2007 facilitated a series of important changes for Romania, opening new opportunities for the economy and new opportunities for social development. The present paper tries to formulate some answers to questions like this – how profound are the changes that Romania has registered after 10 years since joining the EU? What did she win? What did she lose? Where are they heading in the future? GDP and GDP per capita increased significantly in 2017 compared to 2006, but what does this mean if we compare our country with other EU countries in this regard? About two or three million Romanians work abroad and send 2–3 billion euros annually to the country, but what will be over a decade with the generations of children who grew up without parents? In the following I will try to select some of the most outstanding achievements of our country after a decade of development in the EU, but also some social costs or missed social opportunities. The Romanian realities will be presented from a European perspective.

Keywords: economic indicators, standard of living, competition

Introduction

The first decade of Romania`s development within the European Union (EU), 2007–2017, come after another two decades of underdevelopment and explosion of poverty, as a result of the change of the political regime from December 1989. A wider balance of Romania's achievements in its first decade of integration into the EU would bring more clarity in Romania's projects for the next decade.

In the present communication, however, we will only refer to some strengths/ weak issues of the period 2007–2017, to the extent that the available statistical indicators will allow us to do so. Such an approach is all the more useful since, some recent events in the EU, such as the strong anti-community views of some states, the consequences of Brexit and so on, require the adoption of a more adapted behavior from Romania, regarding its strategy as a member country of the community bloc.

1. The amount of European funds attracted in Romania between 2007–2017

This communication uses data and information published in the last decade by Romanian and foreign social analysts, but also by some international institutions

(European Commission, World Bank, International Monetary Fund, etc.) and data published by Romanian or foreign statistical institutes (Eurostat, National Institute of Statistics (NIS) and others).

A decade have passed, on January 1, 2017, since Romania's accession to the European Union. From January 2007 to November 30, 2016, Romania received from the EU over 40.5 billion euros as European non-reimbursable funds, and contributed to the EU budget with approximately 13.6 billion euros. The net positive flow for Romania was 26.9 billion euros in almost 10 years (without a month). (CEPU, 2017). These European funds were allocated in two programming periods: 2007–2013 and 2014–2020.

The absorption rate of European funds in the first financing period of Romania, in the budgetary exercise of the European Union 2007–2013, was over 90 % – this is considered a relatively good result for a first budgetary year (Deacu, 2017). Between 2007 and 2013, Romania received from the EU over 37 billion euros. Post-accession funds, more consistent went to:

- rural development: 7.73 billion euros – absorption rate over 90 %;
- direct payments per hectare: over 7.65 billion euros;
- structural and cohesion funds for road and rail infrastructure, greening garbage pits, urban and rural sewage, social projects, investments of private companies, research, development projects, etc.): 17.25 billion euros. Absorption degree 89.13 %.

Between 2007–2013, East European EU member states performed better than Romania in attracting EU funds and therefore in their own development (Tab. 1).

Tab. 1: Performance in attracting EU funds, between 2007–2013 (billion euros)

Romania	**Hungary**	**Czech Rep.**	**Poland**
19.7	25.3	26.7	67.3

Source: EU Romania, 2008.

In the period 2014–2020 Romania received 3.48 billion euros, during 2014 to 30 November 2016, of which: structural and cohesion funds: 1.35 billion euros – advances paid by the European Union to start projects; funds for rural development and fisheries – over 600 million euros; direct payments per hectare in agriculture: 1.18 billion euros.

2. Significant social evolutions of the period 2007–2017

Population evolution and number of households: According to the NIS, between 2007–2017, the resident population of Romania decreased from 20,882,980 to 19,639,600 persons. (Government of Romania, 2019; NIS, 2018). The number of households (as well as their demographic structures) has undergone significant changes, decreasing from 7,315,891 (NIS, CPH 2002) to 7,086,394 (NIS, CPH 2011) mainly as a result of the phenomenon of emigration increase.

The phenomenon of emigration and the problems of children left at home: About three million Romanian residents left the country after 2007, which produced social effects of strong destabilization of the social structures and of the domestic economy. On a social level, the number of children abandoned by one or both parents, the children left unattended at home, the number of divorces, etc. had a special impact. In 2016, in Romania there were about three million children, of which 57,279 in the special child protection system. According to data from the Directorates-General for Social Assistance and Child Protection, in 2016, 95,308 children had at least one parent left for work abroad, 18,646 children being left at home alone, and 17,553 children being cared for by relatives up to the fourth grade, but lacking social protection. And at that moment, Romania was in the last place in the EU regarding the financing of children's allowances (Postelnicu, 2017). Over the last decade, about 2.5 million Romanians have emigrated (Mihai, 2016).

The persistence of poverty and underdevelopment in rural areas: The rural population in Romania had and still has the highest degree of poverty among the persons employed, from the European Union. For about 20 % of the rural Romanians who had a job in 2014, the incomes obtained were not enough to remove them from poverty. This is when 55 % of the rural residents were exposed to the risk of poverty or social exclusion (compared to 31 % in small towns and suburbs or 28 % in large cities), in 2014 (EU, 2016). Also in 2014, only 27 % of the rural population was connected to the public water supply system (92.7 % in urban areas) and only 5.3 % was connected to the sewage system (82.8 % in urban areas). According to the same source, only 34 % of the rural households had a toilet inside the house, in 2014, this being the case, however, the percentage of households with a toilet in the house doubled in the first 8 years after the country joined the EU (EU, 2016).

Employee payment on the labor market represented on average 47.5 % of EU.28 GDP, at market prices, in 2016. At that time, Ireland had the lowest proportion in terms of employee payment from the EU.28 states – (31.3 %), followed by Greece (33.4 %) and Romania (34.2 %), proportions of over 50.0 % being registered in Germany, France and Denmark. Between 2007–2017, as a rule, if the ratio between the share of GDP regarding the payment of the employees and the profit was, in the western countries, of respectively, 60 % to 40 %, in Romania, this ratio was reversed over the whole interval [Eurostat, 2018].

Trends in population incomes: The weights of the Romanian population that transited upwards of more than one decile of income, during three years prior to the reference year mentioned in Tab. 2, between 2011–2016, were lower than those related to the EU average.28. They formed a downward trend (similar to the EU.28 average) from 14.3 % in 2011 to 11.0 % in 2014. The downward transition of more than one decile of income (% of the total population) formed, by also, a more pronounced downward trend in Romania (from 14.2 % in 2011, to 6.2 % in 2015, which means a progressive decrease in the number of people whose incomes have registered a decrease (Di Meglio, 2018) (Tab. 2).

Tab. 2: Weight of the population that has transited more than one decile of income, during three years, before the mentioned year, between 2011–2016

	Upward transition of more than one decile of income (% of total population)						**Downward transition of more than one decile of income (% of total population)**					
	2011	2012	2013	2014	2015	2016	2011	2012	2013	2014	2015	2016
EU28	17.8	17.1	16.6	16.7	15.9	15.2	17.2	16.7	16.4	16.1	15.4	14.6
Bulgaria	22.5	20.8	19.4	20.2	18.3	17.0	20.3	20.3	18.3	17.8	17.5	19.0
Czech Rep.	21.7	16.4	18.6	18.5	18.9	17.0	20.4	18.7	18.4	18.3	18.0	15.6
Hungary	19.2	19.0	19.2	18.6	17.8	19.6	20.2	17.6	17.8	18.7	18.9	18.3
Poland	21.5	19.4	18.4	19.2	19.8	19.9	20.5	19.1	18.0	17.4	17.2	19.1
Romania	14.3	11.9	11.8	11.0	11.3	…	14.2	11.3	9.6	7.7	6.7	…
Slovakia	19.0	20.3	18.6	19.8	19.3	…	19.2	17.4	18.3	19.1	21.1	…

Source: Di Meglio Emilio (ed), 2018.

The nominal purchasing power per person in Romania in 2017 increased by only 2 % points compared to 2007, representing still less than half of the average of the EU28 countries (Tab. 3).

Tab. 3: Consumer price index. 2007, 2017 EU28, average = 100

	2007	**2014**	**2015**	**2016**	**2017**
Czech Rep.	71	58	58	61	64
Lithuania	66	57	56	58	60
Hungary	61	53	53	55	58
Poland	57	53	51	51	53
Romania	46	48	47	48	48
Bulgaria	40	43	42	43	44

Sources: $Eurostat_c$, 2018; Eurostat 2008.

The consumption expenditures of the Romanian households represent the highest weights in the country's GDP, being higher than the EU.28 averages in both 2006 and 2016. However, their tendency was to decrease from 67.2 to 60.8 % (Tab. 4).

Tab. 4: Household consumption expenditures, 2006, 2011, 2015 and2016

	Share in GDP at current market prices (%)			**Per capita (PPS)**	**Per capita (euro): average annual growth rate (% per year)**	
	2006	2011	2016	2015	2006–2011	2011–2016
EU28	55.6	55.4	54.6	15,800	0.1	0.4
Czech Rep.	46.5	48.4	46.3	11,700	1.1	1.2
Slovenia	50.6	55.1	50.9	12,200	1.7	-0.4
Hungary	51.7	51.0	48.6	9,400	-1.6	2.0
Slovakia	55.3	56.2	53.8	12,100	2.5	0.9
Poland	61.1	60.5	57.9	11,400	4.1	2.2
Bulgaria	66.3	61.9	60.2	8,400	3.5	2.4
Romania	67.2	61.5	60.8	10,000	3.3	4.6

Source: Eurostat, 2018.

This happened, however, when, in 2015, only Hungary and Bulgaria recorded per capita consumption expenditures (PPS) slightly lower than those of Romanians. The largest increase in consumer spending was recorded in 2011–2016.

3. Evolutions of economic indicators after Romania's integration into the EU28

Global Economic Competitiveness Index (ICG) (WEF, 2007), in the report for 2005/2006, placed Romania 68th out of 125 countries, with an ICG of 4.02. The Global Competitiveness Report 2016–2017 (WEF, 2018), ranks Romania 52 out of 140 states, with an ICG of 4.30. Global Competitiveness Index 4.0 measures national competitiveness, defined as the set of institutions, policies and factors that determine the level of productivity (Tab. 5).

Tab. 5: Romania – Selected indicators – Social and economic performance 2006–2017

Indicators	2006	2007	2016	2017
Global competitiveness index	4.02			4.30
GDP per capita US$ PPS	13,923	15,366	22,369	24,508
10-year average annual GDP growth %				2.4
5-year average FDI inward flow % GDP				2.1
Income Gini 0 (equality) -100 (inequality)	33,0			35.9
Household consumption (%) in GDP	77.9	75.3		70,0
Agriculture contribution to GDP, %		(2009)7.0	3.9	4,4
Minimum wage per economy (euro)		114		275
Unemployment rate %	4.1	6,4	5.9	4.9
Public debt (% of GDP)	10.9		37.4	35.0
External debt (% of GDP)		27.14	54.7	49.8
Inflation rate (CPI, annual change, %)	6.6	4.8	0.5	3.3
Exchange rate (vs. euro)	3.52	3.33	4.54	4.66
International reserves (billion euros)	20.0		34.2	33.5
Average labor productivity (industry), % in EU.28	(2005)86.2		131.8	137.4

Sources: INS, 2018, Comunicat de Presă no. 84/05.04.2018; INS, 2007…2018, Anuarul Statistic al României, 2006…2017; WEF, 2018, The Global Competitiveness Report, 2016–2017

In the decade 2006–2017 indeed, Romania registered a real economic growth, but not as fast as expected (Tab. 6).

Tab. 6: GDP per capita (PPS) (EU28 = 100)

	2007	2008	2009	2010	2011	2012	2013	2014	2015	2016	2017
EU28	100	100	100	100	100	100	100	100	100	100	100
Romania	43	51	52	51	52	54	54	55	56	59	63

Source: $Eurostat_b$, 2019

If Romania's gross domestic product (GDP) increased 1.92 times, from 97.7 billion euros in 2006 to 187.9 billion euros in 2017, GDP per capita (PPS) increased more slowly, by 1.46 times.

Between 2007–2013, there were large differences between performances in attracting foreign investments by EU Member States. For example, for Bulgaria and the Czech Republic this indicator was 9 %, for Hungary and Slovakia 6–7 %, and for Latvia, Lithuania, Poland and Romania it was 4–5 % (UE, 2008). The European trend showed a slight decrease in the share of investments, between 2005 and 2015, in all three sectors – public, business and households. Their highest share was in business, and the smallest – in public investment (Tab. 7).

Tab. 7: Investments at market prices, in 2005, 2010 and 2015, % of GDP

	Total investments			**Public investments**			**Investments in businesses**			**Investments of households**		
	2005	2010	2015	2005	2010	2015	2005	2010	2015	2005	2010	2015
EU28	21.1	20.4	19.9	3.2	3.5	2.9	12.2	11.3	12.0	6.5	5.6	5.0
Bulgaria	25.9	22.2	21.0	3.7	4.6	6.6	20.9	16.4	13.7	1.3	1.3	0.8
Czech Rep.	28.3	27.0	26.3	4.9	4.7	5.1	18.2	16.4	16.5	5.1	5.8	4.7
Hungary	23.9	20.4	21.7	4.2	3.7	6.6	14.2	12.7	12.3	5.5	4.0	2.8
Poland	18.9	20.3	20.1	3.4	5.6	4.4	10.3	9.7	10.9	5.3	5.0	4.8
Romania	22.9	24.9	24.8	2.9	5.8	5.2	19.1	13.3	14.7	1.0	5.8	4.9
Slovakia	27.4	22.1	23.0	3.4	3.6	6.3	18.4	13.6	12.3	5.5	4.8	4.4

Source: Eurostat$_a$, 2018.

In Romania, between 2005 and 2015, the total investments were slightly higher – in relative values – than those of the EU28 average, an important role in this respect having the investments of the companies (downward trend from 19.1 % in 2005, at 13.3 % in 2010 and 14.7 % in 2015) (Tab. 7). In Romania, after the entry into the EU, the trend of public investments has slightly increased from 2.9 % (2005) to 5.8 % (2010), respectively 5.2 % (2015) of GDP (Tab. 8).

Tab. 8: Evolution of the gross value added at the basic prices, in Romania and the EU.28 average, in 2006 and 2016, (% of the total gross value added

	Agriculture, forestry, fishing		**Industry**		**Construction**		**Trade, transport, accommodation, food services**		**Communications and information**	
	2006	2016	2006	2016	2006	2016	2006	2016	2006	2016
EU28	1.6	1.5	20.2	19.3	6.3	5.3	19.0	19.1	5.0	5.0
Romania	8.7	4.3	28.0	25.7	8.9	6.7	21.5	20.2	4.6	6.1
	Financial and insurance services		Real estate activities		Administrative and professional support services		Public administration, defense, education, health, social assistance		Leisure and other services	
	2006	2016	2006	2016	2006	2016	2006	2016	2006	2016
EU28	5.4	5.1	10.8	11.2	10.0	11.0	18.2	19.0	3.4	3.5
Romania	2.0	4.1	7.9	9.1	4.1	8.3	11.6	11.7	2.7	3.6

Source: Eurostat, 2018.

In Romania, the largest contributions of gross value added (GVA) to GDP came from the industry, although the share of the respective contribution decreased, between 2006 and 2016, from 28.0 to 25.7 %. On the second place were the commercial, hotel, food and transport services – and they decreased from 21.5 to 20.2 %. The contribution of agriculture decreased significantly, from 9.8 to 4.3 %, and that of constructions, from 8.9 to 6.7 %. The public administration services as well as the other public services (education, health, social assistance etc.) maintained their contributions at the level of 11.6–11.7 %. The basic branches of the national economy – industry, agriculture, constructions – suffered a categorical decline between 2006–2016 in terms of GVA. At EU28 level, the trend of the average GVA had a similar meaning, but the decreases of GVA of the mentioned branches were less consistent than in Romania.

The transport infrastructure is very poorly developed, with Romania ranking 128th out of 138 countries for the quality of road infrastructure in the Global Competitiveness Report 2017 (FEM, 2017) also, the rail system, old and slow, occupies a place near the tail of the ranking – 79, provided that the highways do not exceed 750 km.

The average employment rate in the EU-28 for ages 20–64, in 2016 was 71.1 %, representing the highest annual average employment rate recorded for the EU ($Eurostat_b$, 2017). However, Romania was part of the group of countries with rates of 60 % along with Poland, Slovakia and Bulgaria.

Labor productivity per worker calculated on adjusted data for price changes, in order to eliminate the influence of inflation, has increased, in real terms, between 2006 and 2016 in almost all EU Member States. And Romania has made a progress with a slightly more consistent jump between 2011–2016, yet recording the lowest labor productivity in the EU, after Bulgaria (Tab. 9).

Tab. 9: Actual labor productivity, 2006, 2011 and 2016

	Thousands of euros per employee			Euro per hour worked		
	2006	2011	2016	2006	2011	2016
EU28	50.5	51.8	53.2	30.1	31.4	32.7
Romania	11.2	12.5	15.7	6.0	6.6	8.7

Source: Eurostat, 2018.

In Romania's agriculture is widely practiced subsistence production and family work, unpaid (Tab. 10).

Tab. 10: Employment in agriculture by employment status (total employment = 100.0)

	Family work force	Permanent employees	Temporary employees
Bulgaria	86.22	10.01	3.77
Greece	94.07	1.94	3.98
Poland	96.38	2.17	1.44
Czech Rep.	36.30	60.75	2.95
Romania	97.15	1.34	1.51
Slovakia	47.92	50.16	1.92
Hungary	88.02	8.90	3.08

Source: Eurostat, 2017.

In most EU countries most of the agricultural labor force comes from farmers' families. (Eurostat$_b$, 2017). At this chapter highlights Romania, Poland and Greece.

Conclusions

1. The development gaps persist. In the present scientific communication, we have considered only a few aspects of the quality of life, where the presence of European funds, has produced consequences, in the sense of modernizing society and reducing the phenomenon of poverty. However, there are also areas where integration has certainly had adverse consequences. Integration in the EU has brought about major changes in the economic and social field, but Romania has not, however, overcome the development gaps that have separated

it for centuries from the West. Starting from the strictly financial criterion, however – how much money Romania gave and how much Romania received from the EU – Romania seems to have gained from this process, several tens of billions of euros.

However, a much more attentive analysis, of the actual inflows and exits of wealth in/from Romania, after 2007, but also in the pre-accession period, is still a necessary but unrealized objective of the Romanian specialists. Such an approach would involve a huge amount of data and information, which far exceeds the economic and social sphere.

2. The social field. The population of Romania has accentuated the exodus to the West Europe after accession to EU, which has had negative effects on the national economy, or in the field of raising and educating children, those who left the country but especially those who left without parents in the country. The responsible factors are also at EU level, because they forced the maintenance of a few inadequate policies in the field of remuneration in Romania, for reasons related to their direct economic interests. The social impulse generated by remittances from abroad, in the last three decades, has not generated a widely distributed social development (social polarization has increased – Gini coefficient 30.2 in 2007–37.4 in 2015, 35.1 in 2018) ($Eurostat_a$, 2019), because the implemented social policies belonged to a minimalist social state, including in the field of social protection.

3. Economic development. The structure of the branches of the national economy has changed markedly, the resisting industries have adapted to the economic relations and the niche demand in the EU states. The share of agriculture in the realization of the GDP has decreased noticeably, but the small peasantry seems quite inadequate to the new economic realities. The Romanian rural communities in very large weights are still struggling with the phenomenon of monetary poverty, the Romanian agricultural production mode being quite weakly marketed. Overall, the WEF assessment using the Global Competitiveness Index shows that the Romanian economy has exceeded the first stage of competitiveness based on production factors (cheap labor, natural resources), promoting to a stage where the main focus is on strengthening economic efficiency. In the latter stage, however, most European states are already many steps ahead of Romania, and competition is fierce.

4. Difficulties in using European funds. Internally, although it is not widely recognized, we have many difficulties in using European funds, due to the low availability of accountability (too many examples of failed practice or corruption in this area) and because of the reduced capacity and lack of real transparency of national authorities with responsibilities in this regard, to propose and support the implementation of national development projects from European funds. In addition, there is a tendency of fuzzy pressure and suspicion of guilt on those with initiative in this area, by some representatives of the judicial system, called to clarify certain cases of use of European money.

References

Camera de Comerţ şi Industrie a României, 2018, Analiză privind evoluţia economiei României în 2017.

CEPU, 2017, 10 ani de UE: Cate miliarde de euro au intrat in Romania, Centrul de Elaborare Proiecte Unionale.

Deacu, Elena, 2017, Dezastru la absorbţia fondurilor Europene. România nu a atras deloc bani europeni, după trei ani din noul exerciţiu financiar, 16 martie, Adevărul.

Di Meglio Emilio (ed), Living conditions in Europe – 2018 edition, Statistical Books, Eurostat.

European Anti-Fraud Office, 2017, The OLAF report 2017.

Eurostat, 2008, Statistics in focus, 112, Economy and finance, GDP per capita, consumption per capita and comparative price levels in Europe.

Eurostata, 2017, Labor force categories: number of persons and farm work (AWU) by sex of worker, legal status of holding and agricultural size of farm (UAA).

Eurostata, 2018, Conturile naţionale şi PIB-ul, Statistics explained.

Eurostata, 2019, Gini coefficient of equivalised disposable income – EU-SILC survey, http://appsso.eurostat.ec.europa.eu/nui/show.do?dataset=ilc_di12&.

Eurostatb, 2017, Statistici privind ocuparea forţei de muncă.

Eurostatb, 2018, Distribution of income at current market prices, 2016 (% share of GDP) YB17.png, Conturile naţionale şi PIB-ul, Statistics explained.

Eurostatb, 2019, GDP per capita in PPS, Index EU.28 = 100, https://ec.europa.eu/eurostat/databrowser/view/tec00114/default/table?lang=en.

Eurostatc, 2018, GDP per capita, consumption per capita and price level indices.

Guvernul României, 2019, Populaţia rezidentă a României pe judeţe la 1 iulie în anii 2002–2002, 2003, de vârstă, de vârstă, 2004, 2005, 2006, 2007, 2008, 2009, 2010, data.gov.ro › download › populatia-romaniei-grupa-de-varsta-mediu.

INS, 2003, Recensământul Populaţiei şi Locuinţelor, 2002.

INS, 2007–2018, Anuarul Statistic al României, 2006...2017.

INS, 2012, Recensământul Populaţiei şi Locuinţelor, 2011.

INS, 2018a, Comunicat de Presă nr. 84/05.aprilie 2018.

INS, 2018b, Populaţia Rezidentă la 1 ianuarie 2018 şi migraţia internaţională.

Mihai, Adelina, 2016, ZF 10 ani de la aderarea la UE. Trei milioane de români au plecat din ţară în ultimul deceniu, devenind cei mai mari investitori străini din România, ZF Profesii, 18 noiembrie.

Postelnicu, Valentina, 2017, Avem trei milioane de copii în România. 57.000 sunt în sistemul de protecție socială și aproape un milion au părinții plecați în diaspora Libertatea, 28 mai.

UE, 2016, Raportul de țară pentru România, 9 martie.

UE România, 2008, In slujba regiunilor, Politica regională a UE 2007–2013.

WEF, 2007, The Global Competitiveness Report 2005–2006.

WEF, 2017, The Global Competitiveness Report 2015–2016.

WEF, 2018, The Global Competitiveness Report, 2016–2017.

Alina Bratiloveanu

The national internal control frameworks for public entities

Abstract National internal control frameworks are sets of norms containing internal control requirements imposed to Romanian public entities by various normative acts.

We propose an analysis that pursues three main objectives: (a) to determine the foreign internal control frameworks that have influenced the national frameworks; (b) to establish an evolution of those frameworks that reflects: (b1) the contexts in which they have been developed, (b2) the aspects in which they have influenced each other and (b3) the nature of their influences over the national frameworks;(c) to make a parallel regarding the main aspects of internal control within the analyzed frameworks (definition, scope and components) in order to reflect the origin of these components in the national frameworks.

The study ends with concluding remarks that sum up the various findings and try to determine possible evolutions in the future for the current national internal control framework.

Keywords: internal control; internal control framework; system of internal managerial control; Internal Managerial Control Code; public entities, COSO

Introduction

A “framework” is a standardized set of concepts, practices and criteria to apply to a particular type of problem, which serves as a reference to propose and solve problems with similar connotations. In our case, an internal control framework includes a set of rules or recommendations necessary for the implementation of an effective internal control system.

The object of our study is represented by the national (i.e. Romanian) frameworks regarding the internal control imposed on public entities and adopted by different normative acts (government ordinances, orders of the minister of public finance, orders of the secretary general of the government). The notion of “public entity” is defined in these normative acts and includes, in general, public institutions and authorities, autonomous authorities, national companies and state-owned companies.

1. Correlations and influences between foreign and national internal control frameworks

1.1 Definitions of the "internal control" concept

The definitions existing in the analyzed control frameworks (Tab. 1) are not unitary but they are not contradictory either. They complement each other in an attempt to present in a particular way new facets of the concept. The lack of unity regarding the definition of internal control also characterizes the Romanian legal framework. Thus, there are three Romanian normative acts that offered definitions and all of them are different. However, over time, there have been some attempts to standardize.

The first normative act that offered a definition of the notion of "internal control," and which practically introduced it in the Romanian legislation, was GO no. 119/1999 (GR, 1999). The normative act makes no reference to its source. Law no. 672/2002 regarding public internal audit (in its original form) (PR, 2002) presented a different definition of the concept, but we do not have information about its origin. The republished version of the GO no. 119/1999 (GR, 2003), issued in 2003, took the definition from Law no. 672/2002.

The first framework dedicated to internal control, approved by OMPF no. 946/2005 (MPF, 2005a) took the definition adopted at European level, as mentioned by the normative act itself: "For an adequate understanding of the concept of internal control, viewed through the general principles of good practice accepted internationally and in the European Union, the definition adopted by the European Commission is reproduced below."

In 2011, both OMPF no. 946/2005 and Law no. 672/2002 were republished. OMPF no. 946/2005 republished in July 2011 (MPF, 2011) maintained the definition from the initial form of the order (MPF, 2005a). Instead, the new version of Law no. 672/2002 (PR, 2011) republished in November 2011, introduced a new definition, much more similar to the one existing at European level. It did, however, present a number of minor differences from that of OMPF no. 946/2005.

The new control frameworks developed by the specialized structure within the General Secretariat of the Government, approved by the OSGG nos. 400/2015 (GSG, 2015) and 600/2018 (GSG, 2018), have taken the definition in GO no. 119/1999 republished which, as mentioned above, had taken it from the initial version of Law no. 672/2002.

The definitions were constructed on the basis of four elements (Tab. 1): the nature of internal control, the components of internal control, the persons responsible for internal control; and the scope of the internal control.

Tab. 1: Definitions of "internal control"

Framework	**Definition**
INTOSAI Guidelines for IC Standards [a]	Internal control structures are defined as the plans of an organization, including management's attitude, methods, procedures, and measures that provide reasonable assurance that the objectives are being achieved.
COSO Internal Control Framework [b]	Internal control is broadly defined as a process, effected by an entity's board of directors, management and other personnel, designed to provide reasonable assurance regarding the achievement of objectives in the following categories: Effectiveness and efficiency of operations; Reliability of financial reporting; Compliance with applicable laws and regulations.
GO no. 119/1999 [c]	The set of measures taken at the level of a public institution regarding the organizational structures, methods, procedures and control and evaluation systems, set up for the purpose: to perform the tasks at an appropriate quality level and to perform regularly, economically, effectively and efficiently, adopted policies; respecting the legality and the provisions of the management; the protection of assets and resources; making and maintaining correct and complete accounting records; timely provision of accurate and complete information to substantiate management decisions.
COM (2000) 200 final/2 [d]	The whole policies and procedures conceived and put in place by an organization's management to ensure the economic, efficient and effective achievement of its objectives; the adherence to external rules and to management policies and regulations; the safeguarding of assets and information; the prevention and detection of fraud and error, and the quality of accounting records and the timely production of reliable financial and management information.
SEC(2001) 2037/4 [e]	[*Quotes the definition from COM(2000) 200 final/2* (EC, 2000)]
Law no. 672/2002 [f]	Ensemble of forms of control exercised at the level of public entities, including internal audit, established by management in accordance with its objectives and legal regulations in order to ensure public funds administration in an economical, efficient and effective manner; it also includes organizational structures, methods and procedures.
GO no. 119/1999 republished [g]	[*Quotes the definition from Law no. 672/2002* (PR, 2002)]

(continued on next page)

Tab. 1: Continued

Framework	**Definition**
INTOSAI Revised Guidelines [h]	Internal control is an integral process, effected by an entity's management and personnel and is designed to address risks and to provide reasonable assurance that in pursuit of the entity's mission, the following general objectives are being achieved: executing orderly, ethical, economical, efficient and effective operations; fulfilling accountability obligations; complying with applicable laws and regulations; safeguarding resources against loss, misuse and damage.
OMPF no. 946/2005 [i]	Internal control represents the set of policies and procedures designed and implemented by the management and staff of the public entity, in order to provide reasonable assurance for: achieving the objectives of the public entity in an economical, efficient and effective way; compliance with external rules and management policies and rules; protection of goods and information; the prevention and detection of frauds and mistakes; quality of accounting documents and timely production of reliable financial and management information.
SEC(2007) 1341 [j]	[*Quotes the definition from SEC(2001)2037/4*].
OMPF no. 946/2005 republished [k]	[*Same definition as in the initial form of the order*].
Law no. 672/2002, republished [l]	Ensemble of policies and procedures elaborated and implemented by the management of the public entity to ensure: achieving the entity's objectives in an economical, efficient and effective way; respecting the rules specific to the field, the policies and the decisions of the management; protection of goods and information, prevention and detection of frauds and errors; the quality of the accounting documents, as well as the timely provision of reliable information for management.
COSO Revised Internal Control Framework [m]	Internal control is a process, effected by an entity's board of directors, management, and other personnel, designed to provide reasonable assurance regarding the achievement of objectives relating to operations, reporting and compliance.
OSGG no. 400/2015 [n]	[*Quotes the definition from GO no. 119/1999 republished*]

Tab. 1: Continued

Framework	**Definition**
C(2017) 2373 final [o]	Internal control applies to all activities, irrespective of whether they are financial or non-financial. It is a process that helps an organization to achieve its objectives and sustain operational and financial performance, respecting rules and regulations. It supports sound decision making, taking into account risks to the achievement of objectives and reducing them to acceptable levels through cost-effective controls.
OSGGno. 600/2018 [p]	[*Quotes the definition from GO no. 119/1999 republished*].

Source: author's own work.

Note: [a] INTOSAI (1992: par. 7); [b] COSO (1992: 13); [c] GR (1999), art. 2(i); [d] EC (2000: 37); [e] EC (2001:5); [f] PR (2002), art. 2(b); [g] GR (2003), art. 2(d); [h] INTOSAI GOV 9100 (2004:6); [i] MPF (2005a) – Annex 1 'Code of Internal Control comprising internal/management control standards for public entities' Sec. 1 'A new approach to internal control' – Definition; [j] EC (2007: 4); [k] MPF (2011) – Annex 1 'Code of Internal/Managerial Control comprising internal/management control standards for public entities' Sec. 1 'A new approach to internal/managerial control' – Definition; [l] PR (2011), art. 2(g); [m] COSO (2013: par. 14); [n] GSG (2015) – Annex 1 'Code of Internal/Managerial Control comprising internal/management control standards for public entities' Sec. III 'Glossary'; [o] EC (2017: 2); [p] GSG (2018) – Annex 1 'Code of Internal Managerial Control of public entities' Sec. I 'Glossary'.

Tab. 2: Elements of the definitions of "internal control"

	Framework	Nature of IC	Elements of IC	Persons responsible for IC	Scope of IC
1.	INTOSAI Guidelines (INTOSAI, 1992)		x		x
2.	COSO Internal Control Framework (COSO, 1992)	x		x	x
3.	GO no. 119/1999 (GR, 1999)		x		x
4.	COM (2000) 200 final/2 (EC, 2000)		x	x	x
5.	SEC(2001)2037/4 (EC, 2001)		x	x	x
6.	Law no. 672/2002 (PR, 2002)		x	x	x
7.	GO no. 119/1999 republished (GR, 2003)		x	x	x
8.	INTOSAI Revised Guidelines (INTOSAI GOV 9100, 2004)	x		x	x
9.	OMPF no. 946/2005 (MPF, 2005a)		x	x	x
10.	SEC(2007) 1341 (EC, 2007)		x	x	x
11.	OMPF no. 946/2005 republished (MPF, 2011)		x	x	x
12.	Law no. 672/2002 republished (PR, 2011)		x	x	x
13.	COSO Revised Internal Control Framework (COSO, 2013)	x		x	x
14.	OSGG no. 400/2015 (GSG, 2015)		x	x	x
15.	C(2017) 2373 final (EC, 2017)	x			x
16.	OSGG no. 600/2018 (GSG, 2018)		x	x	x
	Total (%)	4 (25 %)	12 (75 %)	13 (81,25 %)	16 (100 %)

Source: author's own work.

Only 4 definitions, representing 25 % of those analyzed, referred to the nature of internal control. All of them showed that it is a process.

12 of the 16 analyzed definitions (75 %) include information regarding the elements of the internal control. Regarding the elements of internal control, the following were exemplified: procedures (8 cases – 50 %), policies (6–37,50 %), forms of control (5–31,25 %), methods (2–12,5 %), measures (2–12,5 %) plans of an organization, management attitude, organizational structure and control and evaluation systems (one case each – 6,25 %).

13 of the definitions (81,25 %) indicate the persons responsible for the implementation of the internal control. The persons presented as having responsibilities regarding the implementation of internal control were management (14 cases – 87,50 %), board of directors (2 cases – 12,50 %) and other personnel (5 cases – 31,25 %).

All definitions specified that the purpose of internal control is to support the fulfillment of the entity's objectives and provided an enumeration/classification of these objectives. The objectives of internal control, depicted in Tab. 3, will be analyzed in the next subsection.

1.2 Scope of internal control

As reflected in Tab. 3, the analyzed frameworks mentioned 3 to 5 internal control objectives. Although their number is different and at first sight they seem different, a closer look reveals that their content is very similar.

Let's consider the case of COSO (2013) and INTOSAI GOV 9100 (2004) frameworks. The first classify the objectives in three categories (Operations; Reporting; and Compliance), while the latter comprises the four categories (Operations; Accountability; Safeguarding of assets; and Compliance). The COSO (2013) framework regarded the aspect of safeguarding of assets but did not considered that this should be a separate objective. It included it in the "Operations" objective and specified that it is up to every entity, depending on its specificity, if this aspect should be treated as a standalone objective.

Similarly, INTOSAI GOV 9100 (2004) included a category of objectives named "Accountability" and specified that "This will be realized by developing, maintaining and making available reliable and relevant financial and non-financial information and by means of a fair disclosure of that information in timely reports to internal as well as external stakeholders" (INTOSAI GOV 9100, 2004: 10). Consequently, the reporting objectives can be seen as a part of the larger category of "Accountability."

Tab. 3: Objectives of "internal control"

INTOSAI (1992) [a]	COSO (1992)[b]	SEC(2001) 2037/4 [e]	INTOSAI GOV 9100 (2004) [f]
1. Promoting orderly, economical, efficient, and effective operations and quality products and services consistent with the organization's mission;	1. Operations	1. Ensure the economic, efficient and effective achievement of the entity's objectives	1. Executing orderly, ethical, economical, efficient and effective operations.
2. Safeguarding resources against loss due to waste, abuse, mismanagement, errors, and fraud and irregularities;		2. Safeguarding of assets and information 3. Prevention and detection of fraud and error	2. Safeguarding resources against loss, misuse and damage due to waste, abuse, mismanagement, errors, fraud and irregularities.
			3. Fulfilling accountability obligations.
3. Developing and maintaining reliable financial and management data and fairly disclosing that data in timely reports.	2. Financial Reporting	4. The quality of accounting records and the timely production of reliable financial and management information	
4. Adhering to laws, regulations, and management directives;	3. Com-pliance	5. Adherence to external rules and to management policies and regulations	4. Complying with laws and regulations.

Note: [a] INTOSAI (1992: par. 7); [b] COSO (1992: 15–16); [c] GR (1999), art. 3; [d] GR (2003), art. 3; [e] EC (2001: 5); [f] INTOSAI GOV 9100 (2004:9–11).

OMPF 946/2005 initial [g] & rep [h]	SEC(2007) 1341 [i]	COSO (2013) [j]	OSGG no. 400/2015 [k] & OSGG no. 600/2018 l	C(2017) 2373 final [m]
1. Effectiveness and efficiency of the operation.	1. Ensure the economic, efficient and effective achievement of the entity's objectives	1. Operations objectives	1. Effectiveness and efficiency of the operation.	1. Effectiveness, efficiency and economy of operations.
	2. Safeguarding of assets and information			2. Safeguarding of assets and information.
	3. Prevention and detection of fraud and error			3. Prevention, detection, correction and follow-up of fraud and irregularities.
				4. Adequate management of the risks relating to the legality and regularity of the underlying transactions, taking into account the multiannual character of programmes as well as the nature of the payments concerned
2. Reliability of internal and external information.	4. The quality of accounting records and the timely production of reliable financial and management information	2. Repor-ting objectives	2. Reliability of internal and external information.	5. Reliability of reporting.
3. Compliance with laws, regulations and internal policies.	5. Adherence to external rules and to management policies and regulations	3. Com-pliance obj.	3. Compliance with laws, regulations and internal policies.	

Source: Author's own work.

Note: [g] MPF (2005a) – Annex 1 'Code of Internal Control comprising internal/management control standards for public entities' Sec. 1 'A new approach to internal control' – Nature of objectives; [h] MPF (2011) – Annex 1 'Code of Internal/Managerial Control comprising internal/management control standards for public entities' Sec. 1 'A new approach to internal/managerial control' – Nature of objectives; [i] EC (2007: 4); [j] COSO (2013: par. 19, 45–57); [k] GSG (2015) – Annex 1 'Code of Internal/Managerial Control comprising internal/management control standards for public entities' Sec. I 'General considerations' – 1. The concept of internal/management control; [l] GSG (2018) – Annex 1 'Code of Internal Managerial Control of public entities' Sec. II 'General considerations regarding the concept of internal managerial control', pt. 6; [m] EC (2017: 2)

The objectives of the internal control contained in GO no. 119/1999 (GR, 1999; 2003) are similar to those of the Guidelines on Internal Control Standards elaborated by INTOSAI in 1992. Both those in OMPF no. 946/2005 (initially and republished) as well as those of OSGG nos. 400/2015 and 600/2018 are similar to those of COSO (1992). We note that although they were elaborated after the revision of the COSO framework in 2013, the two Romanian frameworks from 2015 (GSG, 2015) and 2018 (GSG, 2018) kept the names of the objectives from the initial version of COSO, the one from 1992.

1.3 Components of internal control

Most of the internal control frameworks analyzed proposed internal control models comprising five components, except that approved by SEC (2007) 1341 (EC, 2007), which contains 6 components. Moreover, this framework was intended to be an innovative one, with a new approach to the components of internal control.

As shown in Tab. 4, the five components proposed by the COSO Framework (1992) influenced all the frameworks that followed. Three of its components were taken by the other frameworks (e.g. the "Control Environment," "Control Activities" and "Information and Communication" components), except EC (2007), and the other two were adapted. For example, the second component of the COSO model, respectively "Risk Assessment," was named "Performance and risk management" in the European frameworks of 2000, 2001 and 2017. In the initial version of the COSO framework (COSO, 1992), the last component was named "Monitoring," name taken in COM (2000) 200 final/2 (EC, 2000) and in the Guidelines developed by INTOSAI GOV 9100 (2004). In the model approved by SEC (2001) 2037/4 (EC, 2001) this component was called "Audit and evaluation," a name taken by the models approved by the two forms of OMPF no. 946/2005 (initial and republished). In its revised version, COSO (2013) changed the component name in "Monitoring Activities," a name taken in the latest version of the EC control framework (EC, 2017).

Considering the correlations identified above, it can be concluded that the components of the model approved by OMPF no. 946/2005 were based on those of the model SEC (2001) 2037/4 (EC, 2001), which in turn were influenced by those of the COSO (1992) model. Models approved by OSGG nos. 400/2015 (GSG, 2015) and 600/2018 (GSG, 2018) comprise the same components of internal control. They are also based on those of SEC (2001) 2037/4 (EC, 2001), with the exception of the fifth, which was taken from the model contained in SEC (2007) 1347 (EC, 2007).

In order to better illustrate the correlations between the components of the current internal control framework, approved by OSGG no. 600/2018 (GSG, 2018), we can compare them with the ones used in the previous frameworks and describe the degree of correlation by using the following scores: 1 – if the components have the same name; 0,5 – if the components have similar names, hence they are similar in essence; an 0 – if there is no connection between the names of the components. Results are shown in Tab. 5.

Tab. 4: Components of "internal control"

	Component	COSO (1992) [a]	COM (2000) 200 final/2 [b]	SEC(2001) 2037/4 [c]	INTOSAI GOV 9100 (2004) [d]	OMPF 946/2005 [e]	SEC(2007) 1341 f	OMPF 946/2005 rep. [g]	COSO (2013) [h]	OSGG 400/2015 [i]	C(2017) 2373 final [j]	OSGG 600/2018 [k]
I.	Control Environment	x	x	x	x	x		x	x	x	x	x
	Mission and Values						x					
II.	Risk Assessment	x	x		x				x		x	
	Performance and risk management			x		x		x		x		x
	Planning and Risk Management Processes						x					
III.	Control Activities	x	x	x	x	x		x	x	x	x	x
	Operations and Control Activities						x					
IV.	Information and Communication	x	x	x	x	x		x	x	x	x	x
	Information and Financial Reporting						x					
V.	Monitoring	x	x		x							
	Audit and evaluation			x		x		x				
	Evaluation and Audit						x			x		x
	Monitoring Activities								x		x	
VI.	Human Resources						x					

Source: author's own work.

Note: [a] COSO (1992: 16–18); [b] EC (2000: 37); [c] EC (2001: 5–6); [d] INTOSAI GOV 9100 (2004: 13); [e] MPF (2005a) – Annex 1 'Code of Internal Control comprising internal/management control standards for public entities' Sec. 2 'Purpose and definition of internal control standards'; [f] EC (2007: 6); [g] MPF (2011) – Annex 1 'Code of Internal/Managerial Control comprising internal/management control standards for public entities' Sec. 2 'Purpose and definition of internal/management control standards'; [h] COSO (2013: par. 34); [i] GSG (2015) – Annex 1 'Code of Internal/Managerial Control comprising internal/management control standards for public entities' Sec. I 'General considerations' – 2. Purpose and definition of internal/management control standards; [j] EC (2017: 2); [k] GSG (2018) – Annex 1 'Code of Internal Managerial Control of public entities' Sec. III 'Purpose and definition of internal managerial standards', pt. 4.
INTOSAI (1992) and GO no. 119/1999 (initial & republished) are not represented in the table as they do not contain references about the structure (i.e. components) of the internal control system.

Tab. 5: Influences regarding the components of "internal control" in the current national internal control framework

	Internal control components in the framework approved by OSGG no. 600/2018	**COSO (1992)**	**COM (2000) 200 final/2**	**SEC(2001) 2037/4**	**INTOSAI GOV 9100 (2004)**	**OMPF 946/2005**	**SEC(2007) 1341**	**OMPF 946/2005 republished**	**COSO (2013)**	**OSGG 400/2015**	**C(2017) 2373 final**
I.	Control Environment	1	1	1	1	1	0	1	1	1	1
II.	Performance and risk management	0,5	0	1	0,5	1	0,5	1	0,5	1	0,5
III.	Control Activities	1	1	1	1	1	0,5	1	1	1	1
IV.	Information and Communication	1	1	1	1	1	0,5	1	1	1	1
V.	Evaluation and Audit	0	0	0,5	0	0,5	1	0,5	0	1	0
	Total	3,5	3	4,5	3,5	4,5	2,5	4,5	3,5	5	3,5

Source: author's own work.

According to the data in Tab. 5, the current national framework shares the best correlation with the framework adopted by the European Commission in 2001 by SEC (2001) 2037/4 (EC, 2001), with a score of 4,5. They share the same names in the case of components I to IV and have similar names in case of the fifth component, only the topic being reversed ("Audit and Evaluation" compared to "Evaluation and Audit"). The name of the fifth component has been taken from the following framework of the European Commission, adopted in 2007 by SEC(2007) 1341 (EC, 2007). In fact, this is the only perfect correlation with this framework.

There are three approaches to describing the components of internal control (Tab. 6). In the initial version, COSO (1992) opted for a narrative description of the components. The revised version of the INTOSAI GOV 9100 (2004) guidelines has adopted this vision and it is still maintaining it. Instead, the European Commission opted for a standards-based approach, considering that there must be concrete criteria against which the degree of implementation of internal control can be evaluated. This approach was also maintained in the control framework from 2007, with the mention that its number of standards was reduced from 24 to 16. In 2013, COSO revised its control framework opting for a principle-based approach. In this regard, the COSO model proposed 17 principles detailed by 87 focus points. As a consequence, the latest control framework adopted by the European Commission, embraced this approach, by adapting the COSO principles to its control environment.

Tab. 6: Description of the components of "internal control"

Type of description	COSO (1992) [a]	SEC(2001) 2037/4 [b]	INTOSAI GOV 9100 (2004) [c]	OMPF 946/2005 [d]	SEC(2007) 1341 [e]	OMPF 946/2005 republished [f]	COSO (2013) [g]	OSGG 400/2015 [h]	C(2017) 2373 final [i]	OSGG 600/2018 [j]
Narrative description of each component	x		x							
Standards (No. of IC standards)		x (24)		x (25)	x (16)	x (24)		x (16)		x (16)
Principles (No. of principles)							x (17)		x (17)	

Source: author's own work.

Note: [a] COSO (1992: 23–78); [b] EC (2001: 7–24); [c] INTOSAI GOV 9100 (2004: 17–42); [d] MPF (2005a) – Annex 1 'Code of Internal Control comprising internal/management control standards at public entities' Sec. 2 'Purpose and definition of internal control standards'; [e] EC (2007), Appendix 1 'The Revised Internal Control Standards for effective management'; [f] MPF (2011) – Annex 1 'Code of Internal/Managerial Control comprising internal/management control standards for public entities' Sec. 2 'Purpose and definition of internal/management control standards'; [g] Principles: COSO (2013: par. 69–79). Focus points: COSO (2013: par. 111–114); [h] GSG (2015) – Annex 1 'Code of Internal/Managerial Control comprising internal/management control standards for public entities' Sec. II 'List of internal/management control standards for public entities'; [i] EC (2017: 2); [j] GSG (2018) – Annex 1 'Code of Internal Managerial Control of public entities' Sec. IV 'List of internal managerial control standards for public entities'.

1. Normative acts and regulations that do not contain references about the structure (i.e. components) of the internal control system and, implicitly, do not contain descriptions of those components were not represented in the tab. 2. INTOSAI (1992) contains 5 general standards and 6 detailed standards. Even though, it has not been included in the table since they are not attached to components. 3. COM(2000) 200 final/2 (EC, 2000) only mentions the components of internal control without detailing them.

The Romanian frameworks were built taking into account the standards-based approach of the European frameworks, the links between them being obvious (Tab. 7): the framework approved by OMPF no. 946/2005 (MPF, 2005a) contains 25 standards based on the 24 standards of the European framework SEC(2001) 2037/4 (EC, 2001). The decrease of the number of standards within the SEC(2007) 1341 (EC, 2007), from 24 to 16, was reflected in the Romanian frameworks approved by OSGG nos. 400/2015 (GSG, 2015) and 600/2018 (GSG, 2018).

Tab. 7: Correlations between the internal control standards within European and Romanian frameworks

SEC(2001)2037/4	OMPF no. 946/2005	SEC(2007)1341	OSGG nos. 400/2015 & 600/2018
S_1. Ethics and integrity	S_1. Ethics, integrity	S_1. Mission	S_2. Responsibilities, functions, tasks
S_2. Mission, role and tasks	S_2. Responsibilities, functions, tasks	S_2. Ethical and Organizational Values	S_1. Ethics, integrity
S_3. Staff competence	S_3. Competence, performance	S_3. Staff Allocation and Mobility	S_3. Competence, performance
S_4. Staff performance	---	S_4. Staff Evaluation and Development	
S_5. Sensitive functions	S_4. Sensitive functions	S_5. Objectives and Performance Indicators	S_5. Objectives
S_6. Delegation	S_5. Delegation		S_6. Planning
S_7. Objective setting	S_7. Objectives		S_7. Performance monitoring
S_8. Multiannual programming	---	S_6. Risk Management Process	S_8. Risk management
S_9. Annual management plan	S_8. Planning	S_7. Operational Structure	S_4. Organizational structure
S_{10}. Monitoring performance against objectives and indicators	S_{10}. Performance monitoring	S_8. Processes and Procedures	S_9. Procedures
S_{11}. Risk analysis and management	S_{11}. Risk management	S_9. Management Supervision	S_{10}. Supervision
S_{12}. Adequate management information	S_{12}. Information	S_{10}. Business Continuity	S_{11}. Continuity of activity
S_{13}. Mail registration and filling systems	S_{14}. Correspondence and archiving	S_{11}. Document Management	S_{13}. Document management

S_{14}. Reporting improprieties	S_{16}. Reporting improprieties	S_{12}. Information and Communication	S_{12}. Information and communication
S_{15}. Documentation of procedures	S_{17}. Procedures	S_{13}. Accounting and Financial Reporting	S_{14}. Record-keeping and financial reporting
S_{16}. Segregation of duties	S_{18}. Segregation of duties	S_{14}. Evaluation of Activities	---
S_{17}. Supervision	S_{19}. Supervision	S_{15}. Assessment of Internal Control Systems	S_{15}. Evaluation of the internal managerial control system
S_{18}. Recording exceptions	S_{20}. Exceptions management	S_{16}. Internal Audit Capability	S_{16}. Internal audit
S_{19}. Continuity of operations	S_{21}. Continuity of activity		
S_{20}. Recording and correction of internal control weaknesses	S_{24}. Review and evaluation of the control		
S_{21}. Audit reports	S_{25}. Internal audit		
S_{22}. Internal audit capability			
S_{23}. Evaluation	S_{24}. Review and evaluation of the control		
S_{24}. Annual review of internal control			
	S_{6}. Organizational structure		
	S_{9}. Coordination		
	S_{13}. Communication		
	S_{15}. Hypotheses, revaluations		
	S_{22}. Control strategies		
	S_{23}. Access to resources		

Source: author's own work

Furthermore, the framework approved by OMPF no. 946/2005 (MPF, 2005a) adapted the way of describing the standards from SEC(2001) 2037/4 (EC, 2001), including the following sections: description of the standard, general requirements and main references. This structure was passed on to the frameworks that followed it and is still used today.

Conclusions

By following the evolution of the frameworks developed at European level, we find that they were in close relation with those developed by COSO. For instance, the frameworks approved by SEC(2001)2037/4 (EC, 2001) and SEC (2007) 1341 (EC, 2007) started from the philosophy of the initial model included in COSO (1992) and took its elements and customized them according to their own vision. For example, they made some changes in the names of the components, but maintained their essence, and chose to describe them through a system based on control standards and not through narrative descriptions, as was the case in COSO (1992). The change of approach regarding the way of explaining the components of internal control in the revised framework published by COSO in 2013 was embraced by the most recent framework developed in 2017 at the level of the European Commission, contained in the Communication C(2017) 2373 final (EC, 2017).

The same phenomenon of mimicry, which leads to a uniformization of the control frameworks, has also manifested itself between the Romanian and European frameworks. Although in the documents drawn up by the regulatory authorities in the field of internal control, the COSO framework is repeatedly cited as the source of the internal control frameworks adopted at national level, applicable to public entities, by analyzing the structure of the components of internal control, how they were defined, respectively, through a system of control standards, and the way these standards were built, we can see that their general philosophy and the models they proposed were influenced primarily by the existing European frameworks. These, in turn, were built on the basis of the COSO frameworks from 1992 (those developed in 2001 and 2007), respectively from 2013 (the one approved in 2017). Therefore, we can consider that the COSO model proposed through the 1992 framework had a rather indirect impact on the national frameworks, manifested through the European ones, and the revised one from 2013 did not exert any influence.

The first national internal control frameworks, respectively those approved by OMPF no. 946/2005 (MPF, 2005) and OSGG no. 400/2015 (GSG, 2015) were built on the basis of those existing at European level and, with a certain lag, reflected the modifications made within them. In contrast, the current Romanian framework (approved by OSGG no. 600/2018) was largely built on the backbone of the previous one without taking into account the changes that intervened within the most recent European framework, the one included in C(2017) 2373 final (EC, 2017).

Therefore, it is interesting to see if in the future a new variant of the Romanian framework currently in force (approved by a republished version of the current order or by a new order) will propose a modification of the structure of the components and will proceed to their description based on principles (possibly detailed through focus points), out of a desire to align with foreign frameworks, or will maintain its current approach.

References

COSO (1992), Internal Control Integrated Framework; September 1992; Committee of Sponsoring Organizations of the Treadway Commission.

COSO (2013), Internal Control – Integrated Framework; 2013; Committee of Sponsoring Organizations of the Treadway Commission.

EC (2000), Reforming the Commission: A White Paper – Volume I; COM (2000) 200 final/2; Commission of the European Communities; Brussels, 05.04.2000; URL: http://aei.pitt.edu/1189/1/reform_commission_pt_1_COM_2000_200.pdf [accessed: 01.10.2019].

EC (2001), Une base pour la mise en oeuvre des standards de controle interne pour les services de la Commission au 31 Decembre 2001 – Communication de Mme Schreyer, en accord avec M. Kinnock: Memorandum to the Commission of Mrs. Schreyer, in agreement with Mr. Kinnock, on the baseline for implementation of the Internal Control Standards by the Commission's service on 31 December 2001; SEC(2001)2037/4; Commission Europeene; Bruxelles, 19 dec. 2001; URL: http://ec.europa.eu/transparency/regdoc/rep/2/2001/EN/2-2001-2037-EN-4-0.Pdf [accessed: 01.10.2019].

EC (2007), Communication to the Commission: Revision of the Internal Control Standards and Underlying Framework – Strengthening Control Effectiveness; SEC(2007)1341; Commission of the European Communities; Brussels, 16 October 2007; URL: http://ec.europa.eu/budget/library/biblio/documents/control/sec_ 2007_1341_en.pdf [accessed: 01.10.2019].

EC (2017), Communication to the Commission from Commissioner Oettinger: Revision of the Internal Control Framework; C(2017) 2373 final; European Commission; Brussels, 19.04.2017; URL: http://ec.europa.eu/budget/library/biblio/documents/control/C_2017_2373_Revision_ICF_en.pdf [accessed: 01.10.2019].

GR (1999), Government Ordinance no. 119/1999 regarding internal audit and preventive financial control, modified and completed; The Government of Romania; Official Gazette no. 430/31.08.1999.

GR (2003), Government Ordinance no. 119/1999 regarding internal control and preventive financial control, republished; The Government of Romania; Official Gazette no. 799/12.11.2003.

GSG (2015), Order of the Secretary General of the Government no. 400/2015 for the approval of the Code of internal/managerial control of public entities; Official Gazette no. 444/22.06.2015. Repealed by OSGG no. 600/2018.

GSG (2018), Order of the Secretary General of the Government no. 600/2018 Regarding the Approval of the Code of Internal Managerial Control of Public Entities; Official Gazette no. 387/07.05.2018.

GSG & MFP (2018), Strategy for Developing Internal Public Financial Control in Romania for the Period 2017–2020, revised; The General Secretariat of the Government & The Ministry of Public Finance (Bucharest); February 2018; URL: http://sgg.gov.ro/new/wp-content/uploads/2016/04/SKM_C22718030611571.pdf [accessed: 02.06.2018].

INTOSAI (1992), Guidelines for Internal Control Standards; International Organization of Supreme Audit Institutions (INTOSAI) – Internal Control Standards Committee; June 1992; URL: http://www1.worldbank.org/publicsector/pe/befa05/internalcontrolstandards.pdf [accessed: 01.10.2019].

INTOSAI GOV 9100 (2004), Guidelines for Internal Control Standards for the Public Sector; International Organization of Supreme Audit Institutions (INTOSAI) – Internal Control Standards Committee; URL: http://www.issai.org/en_us/site-issai/issai-framework/intosai-gov.htm [accessed: 01.10.2019].

MPF (2005a), Order of the Minister of Public Finance no. 946/2005 for the Approval of the Code of Internal Control, Comprising the Standards of Management/Internal Control at Public Entities and for the Development of Management Control Systems; Official Gazette no. 675/28.07.2005. Repealed by OMPF no. 808/2015.

MPF (2005b), Strategy for Developing Internal Public Financial Control in Romania; The Ministry of Public Finance – Central Unit for the Harmonization of Public Internal Audit (Bucharest); September 2005; URL: http://discutii. mfinante.ro/static/10/Mfp/audit/Policy_Paper_sept2005.pdf [accessed: 21.01.2018].

MPF (2010), Strategy for Developing Internal Public Financial Control in Romania for the Period 2010–2013; The Ministry of Public Finance – Central Unit for the Harmonization of Public Internal Audit & Central Unit for the Harmonization of Financial Management and Control Systems (Bucharest); August 2010; URL: http://discutii.mfinante.ro/static/10/Mfp/audit/StrategiaCFPI2010.pdf [accessed: 21.01.2018].

MPF (2011), Order of the Minister of Public Finance no. 946/2005 for the Approval of the Code of Internal/Managerial Control, Including the Standards of Internal/Managerial Control at Public Entities and for the Development of Internal Control/Management Systems, Republished; Official Gazette no. 465/05.07.2011.

MPF (2012), Report on Internal Control for the Year 2011; The Ministry of Public Finance – Central Unit for the Harmonization of Financial Management and

Control Systems (Bucharest); URL: http://discutii.mfinante.ro/static/10/Mfp/control_prev/raport_2011_ controlintern.pdf [accessed: 20.01.2018].

MPF (2014a), Strategy for Developing Internal Public Financial Control in Romania for the Period 2014–2016; The Ministry of Public Finance – Central Unit for the Harmonization of Public Internal Audit & Central Unit for the Harmonization of Financial Management and Control Systems (Bucharest); January 2014; URL: http://discutii.mfinante.ro/static/10/Mfp/audit/Strategie20142016.pdf [accessed: 21.01.2018].

MPF (2014b), Report on Internal Control for the Year 2013; The Ministry of Public Finance – Central Unit for the Harmonization of Financial Management and Control Systems (Bucharest); URL: http://discutii.mfinante.ro/static/10/Mfp/control_prev/RAPORT_UCASMFC_2013_LG_FINAL.pdf [acc: 20.01.2018].

MPF (2015), Report on Internal Control for the Year 2014; The Ministry of Public Finance – Central Unit for the Harmonization of Financial Management and Control Systems (Bucharest); URL: http://discutii.mfinante.ro/static/10/Mfp/control_prev/RAPORT_UCASMFC_2014_MFP.pdf [accessed: 20.01.2018].

PR (2002), Law no. 672/2002 Regarding Public Internal Audit; The Parliament of Romania; Official Gazette no. 953/24.12.2002.

PR (2011), Law no. 672/2002 Regarding Public Internal Audit, Republished; The Parliament of Romania; Official Gazette no. 780/03.11.2011.

Vasile Dogaru

Steps towards a Romanian model of decoupling of resources

Abstract Modeling the decoupling of resources starts, as an analytical concern, to pull ahead of the calculation of the assigned metrics to similar fundamental concepts resulting from the worldwide environmental analytical research (sustainability, climate change). For the below middle income countries, the integrated analysis of the two main sides of this fundamental paradigm, the consumption of resources and the value added, has some specific requirements, related to the different normative targets of spatial economic evolution. The present research argues the necessity of differentiated modeling of these corridor targets for the next decades, 2021–2050, with a more detailed analysis in the case of Romania. Ensuring the intergenerational equity simultaneously in the resource consumption and in creating and distributing by sectors the value added are another two complementary objectives pursued by the research, which mark the economic process in below-middle income countries worldwide. In summary, the analyzed case shows that the countries where the income level in some human collectivities is below the minimum living standard are on the opposite direction of the value evolution for resources decoupling. The modeled corridors for decoupling in Romania suggest through the synthetic indicator (value added/resources used) an approximation of the average European level in the next three decades for some intra-regions. The research points to the need of supporting the global normative-real cooperation for the resources decoupling through the exchange of resources-goods and technological know-how. The modeling of the new paradigm of resources decoupling ensures the continuity of the analytical research by transferring knowledge from some existing fundamental concepts.

Introduction

The need for the decoupling of resources was anticipated from a procedural point of view before the onset of the resource crisis (Georgescu-Roegen, 1971) and subsequently was analyzed in a model and a matrix rigorously constructed analytically (Georgescu-Roegen, 1979). The move to systematic evaluation of the first five developed countries came after two decades (Mattheus et al., 2000). For Romania and other below middle income countries, the analysis of the two main sides of this fundamental paradigm for current (applicative) science from the perspective of the economic evolution targets has some specific requirements. The concept of economic (and social) evolution has been analyzed under multiple aspects while evaluating the consumption of resources (Georgescu-Roegen, 1979). The existence of an important part of the population (over 15–30 %) below the minimum living standard, which is not found in this case in real processes of economic evolution, requires a different direction for these countries, which is somewhat reversed. Modeling the decoupling targets for the next decades for the value added creation and leaking channel inside and outside the country can be done in detail by sectors for these countries.

The present article aims (within the given editorial limits) to analyze the framework for substantiating the decoupling of resources for countries with below middle income. There were modeled the evolution corridors for Romania with their vertical integration for the consumption of resources and for the creation of nominal added value. This value is different from the real value of a (modern) barter exchange process and can be analytically reduced to the latter, for easier decoding (Dogaru, 2006).

1. Literature review

The paradigm of resource decoupling begins to advance and analytically integrate the results of the research of some fundamental concepts to be found in the present analysis such as sustainability, environmental pollution, circular economy and climate change. The decoupling of resources involves, in a synthesis, the simultaneous analysis of a consumption of resources and a volume of value added, both metrics supposed to be decreasing (according to a typical graph, which can be found in the scientific literature). These two targets are normative levels in economic science. The synthetic indicator proposed and accepted worldwide is resource productivity (Eurostat, 2019; OECD, 2019, UNEP, 2019). The analysis of synthetic targets and indicators is not usually detailed for some regions or population segments.

Other research directions are on a somewhat different path/path of analysis. Some authors have argued analytically almost half a century ago the need to separate the modeling of the consumption of resources from the nominal value economic evaluation (Georgescu-Roegen, 1979). These directions and the two sides of the decoupling overlap. The integrated modeling of resource decoupling worldwide is made by means of intensity indicators of the creation of the added value for resources extracted or processed as synthetic indicators (OECD, 2019, UNEP, 2019). Essentially the paradigm of resource decoupling does not have explicit criticism regarding the separation of resource evaluation and value analysis.

Decoupling, as an arithmomorphic concept (Georgescu-Roegen, 1972; Burkard, 2018, note 72, p. 101), is tacitly linked (in a weak sense) to other fundamental dialectical concepts. One question remains: whether economic science, which manages the value metric (at least) for resource decoupling, is a science (Rupert, 2007). Samuelson Paul was also asked this question by mathematician Stanislav Ulam after the establishment of the Nobel Prize, and the answer came after a few years. (Samuelson, 1969; WTO, 2019).

The concept of circular economy aims to be linked to economic prosperity, while social (intergenerational) equity is barely mentioned (Kirchherr et al., 2017). The concept is little explained by metrics to show the technological and economic limits of recirculation (Georgescu-Roegen, 1979) of an observed analytical process. Although it comes later, the concept is little related to that of sustainability (sustainable development) (Kirchherr et al., 2017).

Climate change focuses on modeling the results, in particular the increase of temperature, the appearance of islands or heat waves, the increase of ocean levels or other complementary phenomena (William, 2009). Some large cities in Romania have considered these effects at the street nano-spatial level (RNAEP, 2017) for their future development modeled by Building Codes (PMT, 2016). Some research has supported this direction (RNAEP, 2016; Dogaru, 2019a, 2019b). The concept of pollution is also measured as an effect, being less related to the limitation to the direct cause, the increasing consumption of resources, now integrated in the decoupling paradigm.

The analysis of decoupling requires the simultaneous detailed knowledge of the stock of resources, the total volume of materials handled and the consumption of resources. The need for hierarchical classification-enumeration as total resources, available, technologically viable and economically efficient (Georgescu-Roegen, 1976, 1983) is beginning to be used (van Oers et al., 2020). In Romania, modeling the dynamics of resource exploitation over the last 50 years, by types of resources and by economic sectors is somewhat at the beginning. The different figures in different databases for the same indicator, the internal exploitation of resources for examples, confirms this fact (Fig. 1, below).

The value side of decoupling

The second side of decoupling, the creation of value added (VA), has grown during the last century simultaneously with the consumption of resources (Krausmann et al., 2009). A simultaneous similar increase of the increment for the two sides can be modeled for periods of 10 years (Dogaru, 2016b). After 1990 more and more studies in international trade focused on value added transfer (Dietzenbacher et al., 2013). A justification for the interest appears to be the recoupling of regional chains of value added transfer, previously segmented by the existence of the separate block of control of planned (communist) economies. Analytically, the transfer of value added to the individual (Ricardo, 1817/1951) and collective level (Manoilescu, 1929, 1940), in its maximum extent is supported by the international forums through non-contradictory mathematics – a theoretical level of science as Georgescu-Roegen (1971) puts it – under the umbrella of the law of comparative advantage. This principle-law is considered the most substantial acquisition in (normative) economic science (Samuelson, 1971). Paradoxically, at that time, Samuelson argued in a literal text the existence of rigorous theoretical metrics (in Georgescu-Roegen's sense) of this principle (although in an 1939 article he referred to Manoilescu's work). The concept of collective comparative advantage (CA) was rejected in literal form in particular (Murphy, 2013) until 1990.

The basic concept of comparative advantage supports the exchange based on cooperation and specialization and is related to the creation of added value. The concept has been relatively altered or diluted in some cases. In the first case, the concept of smart specialization proposed the change in the meaning of CA, and thus slowed down the modeling of comparative advantage between the European

NUTS2 regions (Dogaru, 2006; Foray et al., 2012). In the second case, it was analytically invalidated in space exchanges of foreign direct investments (FDI), as there is no accurate assessment of the transfer of (indirect) consumption of resources and of value added. In this case, the metrics of spatial decoupling of resources may be undermined.

For the part of generation, distribution and dissipation of value added between the countries-sectors the research has advanced (Dietzenbacher et al., 2013). Currently, modeling regarding the distribution of value-added at product level is being conducted. The distribution of value added at the sector-product level is becoming more detailed. For example, two cases of sub-sector products of cars and telephones are analyzed (Timmer et al., 2015; Xing, 2011).

Efforts to manage the decoupling of resources are currently focused on integrating resource consumption or disaggregated by resource types and by economic sectors or type products (PRODCOM level) (EU, 2019).

The metrics for the chain of value added between two parties-partners is already detailed at economic sector level. This in-depth analysis is not performed in detail simultaneously on the two sides of the decoupling. Additionally, the research of the consumption of resources is conducted with the continuous change (in different studies and cases) of the temporal and spatial boundaries of the analytical economic processes, from processes-firms, the aggregate ones according to the economic sector code, up to timeless borders ones of the "from cradle to grave" kind or similar. Or, the establishment of spatial and temporal boundaries is a problem of "finesse" (Georgescu-Roegen, 1971).

Adding up to these problems, there is the (unitary) definition of the dialectical concept of economic evolution. An analytical solution proposed almost five decades ago seems to lead us towards solving the problem. The concept of economic (and social) evolution is argued at the level of the individual. The solution for the economic evolution is that each nano-process (individual or household), but also the joint nano-processes to be above the analytical point of minimum required consumption (Georgescu-Roegen, 1979).

2. Method and calculation

The present research uses the Roegenian flow-funds model. The model and its two phases, metric modeling and complementary literal explanations was clarified (see Dogaru, 2008). Modeling through the simultaneous explicit use of the two phases was validated in some researches (Giampietro et al. 2009). The possible corridors in the economic evolution, under the umbrella of the decoupling of resources will be further modeled. Decoupling resources is a paradigm under which people act under a norm (Burkard, 2018, according to Naess, p. 75).

The consumption of resources in an economy is modeled from the internal extraction of resources (IE). It is modeled in corridors for the next three decades, with limits between the maximum consumption of 2000 and the minimum level of 50 % of this level (Tab. 1).

Tab. 1: Structural level of domestic extraction (DE), Romania, 2000–2010 and 2030–2050

Structural level of domestic extraction (DE)	**MU**	**Corridor level**	**2000**	**2010**	**2030**	**2050=2000**	**2050 = 50 % * 2000**
Abiotic (min) extraction used	[Mt] [10^6]		111.8	209.5	*232.0*	*111.8*	*55.9*
Abiotic extraction unused	[Mt]		104.9	164.7	*182.2*	*104.9*	*52.4*
MOR	[Mt]	average	148.8	201.8	*146.1*	*148.8*	*74.4*
MOR	[Mt]	min	132.3	173.6	*112.5*	*132.3*	*66.2*
MOR	[Mt]	max	165.4	230.1	*177.7*	*165.4*	*82.7*
Total abiotic +MOR	[Mt]	average	365.5	576.0	*560.4*	*365.5*	*182.7*
Total abiotic +MOR	[Mt]	min	348.9	547.8	*526.8*	*348.9*	*174.5*
Total abiotic +MOR	[Mt]	max	382.0	604.3	*591.9*	*382.0*	*191.0*
Biotic used	[Mt]		54.8	60.9	*53.0*	*54.8*	*27.4*
Biotic unused	[Mt]		13.8	15.9	*13.8*	*13.8*	*6.9*
Sum biotic	[Gt]		68.6	76.9	*66.8*	*68.6*	*34.3*
Sum used min+bio	[Mt]		166.6	270.4	*285.0*	*166.6*	*83.3*
Sum total min+bio+ MOR	[Mt]	average	434.1	652.9	*627.1*	*434.1*	*217.0*
Sum total min+bio+ MOR	[Mt]	min	417.5	624.6	*593.6*	*417.5*	*208.8*
Sum total min+bio+ MOR	[Mt]	max	450.6	681.2	*658.7*	*450.6*	*225.3*

Note. Our calculus; sources EU, 2019; OECD, 2019; UNEP, 2019; Bringezu, 2015; For a Vision 2050, using literal description, see STFG (2011). MU- Measurement Unit. MOR- movement of other resources.

The structural level of the extraction of resources for Romania increased significantly for the period 2000–2010. The level modeled for the period 2030–2050 follows the same modeling direction as the zero neutral pollution level, with the reference level 1995 (Tillie et al., 2009; Dogaru et al., 2019a). Consumption modeling was done on all levels of resources involved the level of minerals, the biotic one, on three levels: the used resource, unused resource and the movement of other resources (MAR) to access the main resource. For modeling, there were used the worldwide unitary extraction figures, while the level of extraction and consumption in Romania from 1970–2017 was used for validation.

The lack of unique data integrated into international databases renders some comparative measurements necessary. Thus, the ratio between the DE figures of the OECD and UNEP for Romania for the period 1970–2017 was calculated for the total and for 5 subcategories (Fig. 1).

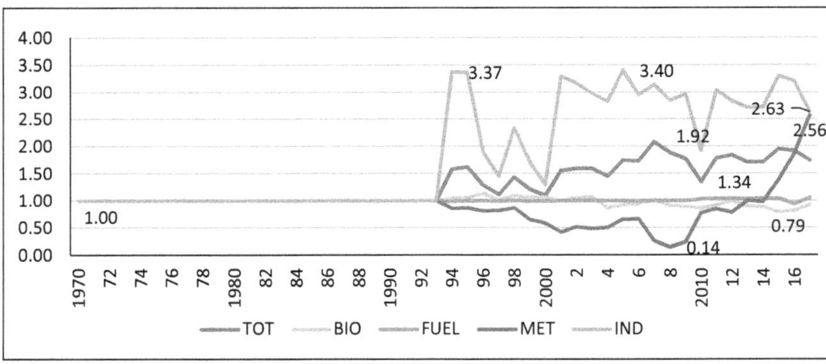

Fig. 1: Ratio for DE figures for OECD and UNEP, Romania, 1970–2017, total and 5 subcategories

The significant differences between the figures in the 2 databases are located after 1992 on the total resources extracted (TOT) with significant report values of 1.34 in 2010 and 1.74 in 2017 and on three categories: extracted metals (MET) with significant report values of 0.14 in 2008 and 2.56 in 2017 and non-ferrous materials extracted (IND) of 3.40 in 2005 and 2.63 in 2017.

Next, the calculation of the ratio (reversed from Fig. 1) between the DE figures of UNEP and OECD for Romania for the period 1970–2017 on the total, non-ferrous and the report of domestically consumed material and the material footprint (DMC/MF)

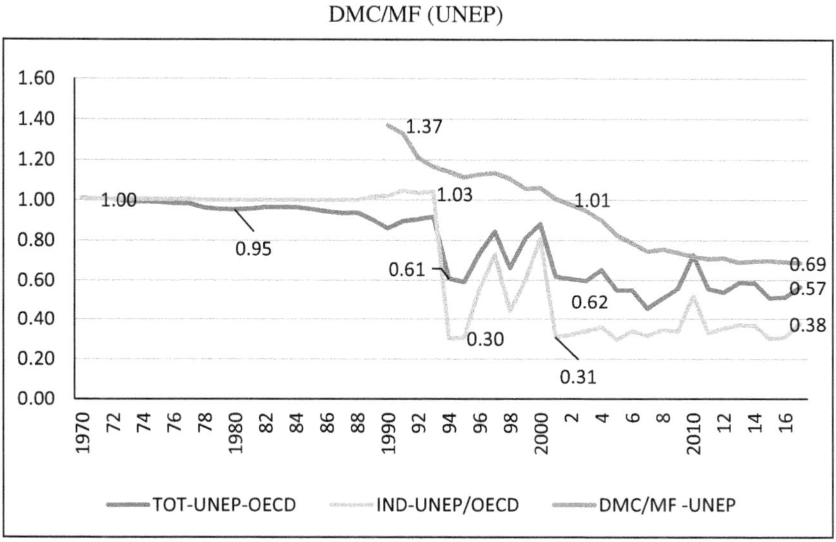

Fig. 2: Ratio of DE figures for UNEP şi OECD, Romania, 1970–2017, total, non-ferrous and DMC/MF (UNEP)

The ratio between DMC and MF is steadily decreasing as a general trend from 1.37 to 0.69. Essentially the products contain less (included) material compared to the equivalent weight of the products (Fig. 2). The ratios for DE are reversed (UNEP/OECD figures) compared to those in graph 1 – to fit the unit scale of graph 2 – for total extracted (TOT) and non-ferrous (IND) materials.

Modeling in the EU28 of the VA for the CANE sectors in Romania (3 digits) was done for productivity (VA/worker), number of workers and salary fund, average salary and salary/gross VA ratio for 2008 and 2015. There were modeled the hierarchy of all sectors for the 28 countries taking into account that there were over 2000 country-sectors for each year from 2008–2016. The positions of sectors without data and the years that reported little data by EU 28 countries were removed. Finally, there were chosen 2 years, 2008 and 2015, for establishing the hierarchy and for calculating the indicators attached to the level of labor productivity.

The first and last 5 positions for Romania were extracted from the modeled database (Tabs. 2 and 3).

The highest level of VA generation per employee, the growth rate in 7 years between 0.76–1.42 shows us an overview of the VA capture in Romania, located in the EU in the middle level area (Tab. 2). The small number of employees, below 2000 out of the total number of employees in these sectors, gives us a sense of the peak of labor productivity for the sectors in Romania. Modeling the decoupling for the value added part is necessary to increase the number of employees in the sectors with productivity above this level.

Tab. 2: Classification of NACE sectors, labor productivity (LP) and other related figures, ranking Romania's first five positions out of 68 sector-countries, 2008–2015

Nace_r2 sector	Range (from 1864 Sectors-country)	LP 2015	LP Index 2015/2008	Employed persons (EP) 2015	EP Index 2015/2008	Fund of salaries (FS) 2015	FS Index 2015/2008	Average salary 2015	% salary/ VAB
N77	691	54.6	1.42	7337	1.19	56	1.70	7.56	0.14
D35	849	45.2	1.40	72333	0.81	1029	0.86	14.23	0.31
J61	967	38.1	0.76	44249	0.86	606	0.86	13.70	0.36
J60	1077	32.9	1.21	9713	0.77	138	0.89	14.20	0.43
L68	1106	31.9	0.86	44976	0.91	250	0.99	5.57	0.17

The first five sectors and average levels of labor productivity in 2015 are: B06 (391), C19 (204), C12 (177), D35 (176) and J61 (160).

The low level of VA generation per employee, the 7-year growth rate between 1.1–1.21 and the existence of about 10 % of the total number of employees in Romania in these sectors provide a clear picture for the decoupling modeling for the value added part (Tab. 3).

Tab. 3: Classification of sectors NACE, labor productivity (LP) and other related figures, ranking Romania's last five positions out of 68 sector-countries, 2008–2015

Nace_r2 sector	Range (from 1864 Sectors-country)	LP 2015	LP Index 2015/2008	Employed persons (EP) 2015	EP Index 2015/2008	Fund of salaries (FS) 2015	FS Index 2015/2008	Average salary 2015	% salary/ VAB
N80	1856	4.6	1.10	122964	1.09	528	1.41	4.30	0.93
I56	1851	5.3	1.10	118177	1.21	452	1.55	3.82	0.72
C14	1841	6.1	1.15	157296	0.75	781	0.99	4.96	0.81
N81	1840	6.1	1.13	40114	1.24	158	1.53	3.95	0.65
C15	1835	6.4	1.21	58448	0.80	309	1.07	5.29	0.83

The last five sectors and the average levels of labor productivity in 2015 are: I56 (20), C14 (20), N81 (21), N80 (24) and G47 (27).

Labor productivity fluctuates on a relative scale from 1 to 12. In 2015, the sectors that remained in modeling cover around 80 % of the number of employees in Romania. The weighted labor productivity was calculated separately and it equaled 13.37 thousand euro per employee in 2015. The labor productivity (unweighted) increased by 1.06 on average during 2008–2015 (Tab. 4).

Tab. 4: Some statistics for labor productivity and related figures, Romania, 2008 and 2015

	LP 2015	**LP Index 2015/2008**	**Employed persons (EP) 2015**	**EP Index 2015/2008**	**Fund of salaries (FS) 2015**	**FS Index 2015/2008**	**Average salary 2015**	**% salary/ VAB**
MIN	4.60	0.34	553	0.57	3.30	0.29	3.82	0.14
MAX	54.60	2.27	472557	2.00	2486.30	3.27	24.90	2.17
AVERAGE	16.23	1.11	60720	0.97	438.36	1.25	8.67	0.61
GEOMEAN	14.07	1.06	30660	0.93	243.44	1.16	7.94	0.56
STDEV	9.62	0.34	80199	0.32	504.21	0.54	3.97	0.26
COUNT	62	62	62	62	62	62	62	62
SUM			3764659		27178			

An optimal situation for Romania would be the positioning of the analyzed average indicators at the maximum level found in the table for the same sector and at least doubling the existing maximum level in the next decade. It is necessary to reduce the standard deviation to decrease the number of low level income households. These requirements accomplished, the evolutionary development and a real coupling of the VA with a necessary level of resource consumption (Tab. 1) can be achieved for Romania.

The metrics modeled so far allow for a start of vertically integrated calculation on the Timisoara-European Union axis (EU28) for both sides of resource decoupling and for the 2 years at both ends of the time scale (2018 and 2050) (Tab. 5).

Tab. 5: Corridors for the decoupling of resources on the spatial chain Timisoara-UE-28 for period 2018–2050

	Year	**Production**	**DMC**	**PIB**	**PIB/loc**	**Resource productivity**
Region		billions Euros	billions tone	billions Euros, 2018 prices	thousands Euros/ inhabitant	euro/kilo DMC
UE28	2018	35336	7093	15901	31.03	2.24
	2050	80094	7567	36042	68.82	4.76
Romania	2018	455	421	205	10.48	0.49
	2050	1555	173	700	41.83	4.05
Region NUTS 2 West	2018	44.7	40.3	20.1	11.32	0.50
	2050	165.4	15.6	74.4	46.53	4.78
Region NUTS 3 424 Timis	2018	20.6	17.0	9.3	13.26	0.55
	2050	121.5	9.1	54.7	84.09	6.00
Timisoara	2018	12.0	9.2	5.4	16.16	0.58
	2050	73.4	5.0	33.0	98.84	6.58

Note. Our calculation; Sources, EU, 2019; The first metrics for 2050 were done for CJT (2015).

The average corridor modeled for 2050 for the amount of materials-energy consumed by 173 million tons has as its reference point the quantity of 166.6 million tons for the quantity of materials-energy extracted from nature. The difference of 6.4 million tons is the balance for the raw materials equivalent of the import-export balance for products and services.

3. Discussions

The modeling of resources decoupling is relatively different depending on the trends of worldwide production projection through specialized reports (PwC, 2015). At the global and regional level, the new paradigm of decoupling is still the only integrated solution for the material consumption-value added pair and further, for the high pollution-climate change one. The paradigm of resources decoupling opens a new chapter in the area of strategic decisions.

The concept of evolutionary development points to us some gaps in the decisions related to national economic processes. They can be simultaneously identified in the vision, the modeled normative decoupling corridors. The decoupling can perhaps be an effective indicator of alert-warning for below-middle income countries. In the analysis of decoupling, started worldwide, this case of evolution is not explicitly included as distinctive stage. The evolutionary development is also specific to the developed countries until the transition to the actual decoupling stage. The (relative) high increase of the VA is more pronounced for below-middle income states. In addition, for these states, there is a necessary increase in the generation and capture of structural VA, by economic sectors (products and services), on the interregional transfer chain. At the same time, a diminishing consumption of resources ensures the gradual transition towards the actual decoupling. Integrating the value added growth with the evolution of resource consumption in absolute decline may be a chance for these countries. The nominal value added currently measured in the simple exchange of products and services is different and dual-contrary to the value achieved in a barter (modern) exchange of goods. The value added amount of a barter (modern) exchange is decreasing, a fact proven by the lower prices (both) of the products negotiated and selected by each of the two partners in the exchange based on AC (Dogaru, 2016a). In time, there is the possibility of this becoming a basic solution for decoupling resources. Some economic blocks (BRICS) are testing such solutions. In the case of a simple exchange, the solution is only casual.

The integration of over 102 national strategies in Romania, which may inherently contain contradictory elements regarding the overall economic development and/or evolution, appears to be the first objective of the government. Their gathering in a single strategy to integrate the positive parts selected and argued by neutral scientific expertise, can be done under the umbrella of a Vision 2050–2100, starting with the NUTS2 tested level (CJT, 2015). The ongoing classification and unitary integration of the legal norms in force, related to the evolutionary development, provides fundamental support in the decisions related to the coupling of the economic sectors (products) in Romania to this new paradigm. It is necessary that the directions of programming established based on the governmental decisions, in line with the EU ones, ensure the innovative and simultaneous integration of the tasks for decoupling the resources, the ones regarding the climate change, but also a channel for the generation of viable value added of the majority of the economic sectors, classified on three levels: security and natural-social/health disasters; minimum required consumption and export of products over the national required consumption. Some NUTS 3 regions in Romania validated the three levels (CJT, 2015).

The improvement of (intergenerational) equity between firms-people and countries-regions can be done by distributing an increasing value added on sectors. The process was systematically analyzed by Manoilescu (1929, 1940) using data from international trade. Manoilescu's solution ensures simultaneously profit for companies and a higher VA for the process-region where the analyzed companies run their activities. Up to 1990 the solution was explicitly or tacitly challenged (but only partially), sometimes in some literal texts (Murphy, 2013). As a rule, the analysis of the VA transfer is done outside the CA chain, therefore outside the spatial (smart) specialization based on EU cooperation. In this case it is possible that we do not have the necessary VA needed for the target of the decoupling of resources, in order to ensure the economic evolution at least for below-middle income countries. So, the measurement of value added is currently becoming increasingly systematic through public databases (Dietzenbacher et al., 2013; EU, 2019; OECD, 2019), but without separate metrics for the specialization in the CA base.

Complementary to the CA principle is the principle of absolute advantage, which tacitly supports the development of an area without exchange and without analytical spatial boundaries between the two processes analyzed comparatively in the exchange of goods. Modeling the absolute advantage is usually done within the framework of exchange based on cooperation under the CA umbrella. Considering an asymmetric (relatively unequal) exchange in the transfer of goods, technology-processes and know-how can ensure identifying an actual case. Globalism, although it has now taken a step back, seems to tacitly support interregional transfers of foreign investment funds (FDI) while following its march towards its objective, globalization (Burkard, 2018, according to Ankie Hoogvelt). Globalism includes the ideological characteristics in a unique thinking (Burkard, 2018, according to Ignacio Ramonet).

This investment transfer process is actually included under the umbrella of the absolute advantage concept and implies a new spatial relocation of a technology within the partner's processes, without exchange and specialization in an exchange process based on CA (Dogaru, 2006, 2016a), therefore in other analytical borders not rigorously analyzed or changed for both partners. Thus, the CA analysis for the observed processes is invalidated by the simultaneous change (during the game/analysis) of the borders of the processes (countries or regions) that make the exchanges. In other cases, for example in the EU, the definition of

CA has been modified in the current programming period (2013–2020), so that the measure of the exchange of VA for specialization is made by an altered instrument (it is not explicitly overlapped with CA), unknown and unrecognized by researchers.

Georgescu-Roegen's two solutions – the starting point of the economic evolution and the separate (or limited) quantitative analysis of resources and value analysis – appear necessary to integrate the previous results of analysis, also related to the existing fundamental concepts in the new paradigm of decoupling. A temporary intermediary concept of evolutionary development can be a solution to model the transition stage to the new paradigm. In this case, the connection and transfer of metrics and literal explanations between the existing fundamental concepts and the new world paradigm can be explicitly ensured.

The lack of simultaneous ranking of the efficiency of the economic sectors on the European market in all NUTS2 countries and regions becomes an unaccomplished step in establishing NUTS2 smart specialization within the EU. In other circumstances, the strategic decisions based on the metrics modeling for the decoupling of resources, in relation to the needs of evolution in parallel of regions on the time axis (not necessarily with two speeds), are blocked. However, the EU has specialization itself as an aim, which can be done in plenary, through resource savings by measuring CA (Dogaru, 2016a). It is necessary that the goal of smart specialization is maintained, reformulated and rigorously pursued in the next 2021–2027 programming period by the EU-27, without United Kingdom. Discussions on European reindustrialization are becoming more and more consistent. These discussions are important (Karl Falkenberg, October 2016, European Resource Forum, Berlin) and are linked, inside the EU, to the evolutionary development supported by the transfer of resources and strategic know-how between EU regions.

The differentiated growth per chain of VA per inhabitant on the aggregate axis Timişoara-EU is between 2–7 times in three decades and 3–10 times higher for VA per worker. This modeled corridor needs to be supported simultaneously through real intra-European cooperation and evolutionary development for all local communities. Otherwise, in the absence of cooperation on Single Market, the targets will be achieved through the allocation of own investment funds by each country. The solution of competition in accessing European funds in the event of decoupling must be replaced by the allocation of necessary funds based on the normative levels of decoupling established at a disaggregated and differentiated level according to nano-processes (cities or parts of urban-rural processes).

The analysis of resource consumption in the last two centuries has been focused on the last half of the period (Krausmann et al., 2009). The main databases contain relatively different numbers (see Figs. 1 and 2). Some differences come from including excavation (extraction of pure tailings from the vicinity of the deposit) or unused (unusable) resources after the extraction of the deposit (Bringezu, 2015;). Others may come from the modeling of different figures (extracts, total tailings).

The modeled corridors of evolution are normative and they are to ensure Romania's integration into the Single Market, over four decades after accession. After the shock of the first two programming periods (2007–2020), due to the lack of anticipation of the consequences generated by the pre-requisite condition for accession, to deal with the competitive market forces and the European policies, the new European conditions for evaluating the national and regional economy through normative levels of resource consumption and correlated to pollution level can generate a new shock. The lack of initial expertise, found in the neutral reports attached to the oscillating decision in the ever-changing policies also contributed to the annihilation of the past experience of state factors.

In the last three decades, in Romania, a considerable volume of resources (over 60–80 % of their consumption) out of the Single Market common stock have been wasted. The transfer of know-how for the industrial sectors with higher average performance existing in the 1990s – as it happened in the other Eastern and Central European states– was hardly accomplished. Under the umbrella of two objectives of the Single Market for regional cooperation and smart specialization, it was added the unjustified use of high-skilled labor in elementary processes, due to the migration process.

The classification of sectors according to three levels (low, medium and high) of resource processing, does not provide sufficient information on value added (EU, 2019). For countries with below middle incomes and/or with a significant population volume (over 10–15 %) below the minimum standard of living, a systematic analysis of the value added chain is needed.

The central and local budgets of a country cannot guarantee a secondary redistribution of the value added for large segments of the population for a long time (2–5 decades). The issue of reports for the decision makers for identifying variants that simultaneously ensure the decoupling of resources and the creation of value added appears as necessary. Supporting the penetration of foreign direct investments in these economies is necessary, but not sufficient. In addition, it can mitigate the positive effects of explicit and simultaneous smart specialization among all over 1300 regions NUTS2 in the EU-28, in relation to decoupling process of the resources.

Conclusions

The increase of VA per inhabitant and worker is normatively differentiated on the aggregate axis Timişoara-EU for the next three decades, and the decrease of the consumption of resources for the year 2050 is considered in reference to the year 2000. The differentiated increase of VA per inhabitant on the chain is 2–3 times lower compared to labor productivity. The concept of evolutionary development, together with a certain vision and normative decoupling corridors, can be an effective warning signal for below-middle income countries. For these countries a structural procedural development is required, at the same time with the decoupling of the consumption of resources. The analysis of the recessive relation between development (progress) and evolution, as Florian (1982) puts it, may offer a variant of decoupling analysis for these countries.

It is necessary to support through strategic decisions the management of technology transfer, with priority within the European Union, as well as to establish minimum key sectors of development for each region-country. In case of extreme events such as large uncontrollable movements of the population (another type of modern migration), pandemics or similar processes, conflicts explicitly or not explicitly based on strategic resources, these sectors provide a viable solution for the regional human communities.

The modeling of the corridors within limits (maximum-minimum) for the next decades followed the specific development and evolution needs in Romania. Depletion of resources and, simultaneously, low productivity in each economic sector and lack of a certain vision become the main research objectives in Romania and, at the same time, basic challenges for state decision-makers. The political factors are to integrate the scientific results and the evolution variants proposed by the professional structures of the nation state. The way to guarantee intergenerational equity both regarding the consumption of resources and the creation and distribution of added value is up to the economic evolution in its essence in below-middle income countries.

References

Bringezu, Stefan, 2015. Possible Target Corridor for Sustainable Use of Global Material Resources, Resources, 4(1), 25–54, 54.

Burkard, Michael, 2018. Conflicting Philosophies and International Trade Law: Worldviews and the WTO, Palgrave Macmillan, Frankfurt.

Consiliul Judetean Timis (CJT) (County Council Timis), 2015. Strategy for Social and Economic Development (in Romanian), 2015–2020, http://www.cjtimis.ro/servicii-online/hotarari-ale-consiliului-judetean.html?a=s&p_3659=HOT%C4%82R%C3%82REA%20nr.%20216/16.12.2015, accessed on 15 May 2019.

Dietzenbacher, Erik, Los, Bart, Stehrer, Robert, Timmer, Marcel, de Vries, Gaaitzen J., 2013. The Construction of World Input-Output Tables in the WIOD Project, Economic Systems Research, 25:1, 71–98. DOI: 10.1080/09535314.2012.761180

Dogaru, Vasile, 2006. Manoilescu Generalized Scheme Regarding the International Goods Exchange – A General Presentation, Probleme economice (Economic Issues), no. 226–227 The National Economic Research Institute, Romanian Academy, CIDE, 2006.

Dogaru, Vasile, 2008. Roegenian Method and Comprehension of the Economic Processes, in Proceedings of the 5th International Seminar on Quality Management in Higher Education, June 2008, Iasi, Performantica, pp. 189–194.

Dogaru, Vasile, 2016a. The Expanding of Constructal Law in Economics – A Justification for Crossed Flows of Similar Macro Goods, International Journal of Heat and Technology, 34(1), s. 59–74, January 2016, DOI: 10.18280/ijht.34S108.

Dogaru, Vasile, 2016b. The Consumption of Materials and Energy – A Georgescu-Roegen Perspective for Decoupling (Extended Abstract), in Eco-Energy. Join the Green Revolution (Brochure), Conference 22–24 June 2016, West University of Timisoara Publishing House, p. 29–32.

Dogaru, Vasile, Brandas Claudiu; Cristescu Marian, 2019a. An Urban System Optimization Model Based on CO2 Sequestration Index: A Big Data Analytics Approach, Sustainability, 11, 4821, 1–14.

Dogaru, Vasile, 2019b. In-Process Measurement of Urban Energy-Oxygen-Pollution for the Main Residential Building Areas in Timisoara, Clima 2019 Congress, 26–29 May 2019 Bucharest, E2S Web Conf. 111 06078 (2019), S.I Tanabe, H. Zhang, J. Kurnitski, M.C. Gameiro da Silva, I. Nastase, P. Wargocki, G. Cao, L. Mazzarela and C. Inard (eds.).

European Union (EU), Eurostat Database, https://ec.europa.eu/eurostat/, accessed on 15 December 2019.

Eurostat, 2016. EW-MFA Manual 2016, Draft Version on DPO, Annex to EW-MFA Manual 2015.

Eurostat, 2013. Economy-Wide Material Flow Accounting (EW-MFA) – Compilation Guide 2013.

Eurostat, 2018, Circular Material Use Rate. Calculation Method, European Union, Luxembourg.

Florian, Mircea, 1982. Recesivitatea ca structură a lumii, 1982, Editura Eminescu, vol. II.

Foray Dominique et al. (John Goddard, Xabier Goenaga Beldarrain, Mikel Landabaso, Philip McCann, Kevin Morgan, Claire Nauwelaers, Raquel Ortega-Argilés), 2012. Guide to Research and Innovation Strategies for Smart Specialisation (RIS 3), May 2012, https://s3platform.jrc.ec.europa.eu/documents/20182/84453/RIS3+Guide.pdf/fceb8c58-73a9-4863-8107-752aef77e7b4, accessed 17.04.2019.

Georgescu-Roegen, Nicholas, 1971. The Entropy Law and the Economic Process, Harvard University Press, Cambridge, MA.

Georgescu-Roegen, Nicholas, 1972. "Analysis versus Dialectics in Economics", in Mircea Buescu, ed., Ensaios Economicos, Homagem a Octavio Gouvea de Bulhoes, Rio de Janeiro: APED, pp. 251–278.

Georgescu-Roegen, Nicholas, 1976. Energy and Economic Myths: Institutional and Analytical Economic Essays, Pergamon Press, New York, 1976.

Georgescu-Roegen, Nicholas, 1979. Energy Analysis and Economic Valuation, Southern Economic Journal, XLIV, 1023–1058.

Georgescu-Roegen, Nicholas, 1983. The Promethean Condition of Viable Technologies, Materials and Society , 7, 425–435.

Giampietro, Mario, Mayumi Kozo, 2009. The Biofuel Delusion: The Fallacy of Large Scale Agro-Biofuel Production, Earthscan.

Kirchherr, Julian, Reike Denise, Hekkert Marko, 2017, Conceptualizing the Circular Economy: An Analysis of 114 Definitions, Resources, Conservation & Recycling, 127, 221–232.

Krausmann, Fridolin, Simone Gingrich, Nina Eisenmenger, Karl-Heinz Erb, Helmut Haberl, Marina Fischer-Kowalski, 2009. Growth in Global Materials Use, GDP and Population during the 20th Century. Ecological Economics, 68(10), 2696–2705, doi:10.1016/j.ecolecon.2009.05.007.

Manoilescu (Manoilesco), Mihail, 1929. La théorie du protectionnisme et de l'échange international, Giard, Paris, 1929. (English version, The Theory of Protection and International Trade. London: P. S. King & Son, Ltd., 1931).

Manoilescu, Mihail, 1940. Die teoretische Problematik des Aussenhandels, Synthese-Beweisfuhrung-Polemik, Weltwirtschafliches Archiv (Review of World Economics, in English), January 1940.

Mattheus, Emily et al., 2000. The Weight of Nations, http://pdf.wri.org/weight_of_nations.pdf, accessed 14.03.2019.

Murphy, Eithne, (2013). The Evolution of Trade Theory: An Exercise in the Construction of Surrogate or Substitute Worlds? PhD Thesis, SOAS, University of London.

OECD, OECD Database, http://stats.oecd.org/Index.aspx, accessed on 15 December 2019.

Primaria Municipiului (City Hall) Timisoara (PMT), 2016, New General Urbanistic Plan, 2010–2016, https://www.primariatm.ro/index.php?meniuld=2&lg=ro&viewCat=3257, accessed on 14th May, 2019.

PwC, 2015, The World in 2050. Will the Shift in Global Economic Power Continue? https://www.pwc.com/gx/en/issues/the-economy/assets/world-in-2050-february-2015.pdf, accessed on 10 December 2019.

Ricardo, D., "On the Principles of Political Economy and Taxation," 1817, in P. Sraffa (ed.), The Works and Correspondence of David Ricardo, vol. I, Cambridge University Press, Cambridge, 1951.

Romanian National Agency for Environment Protection (RNAEP), 2016, Report no. 2932/29 November 2016 of West University of Timisoara, 2016.

Romanian National Agency for Environment Protection (RNAEP), 2017, Local Environment Permit no. 1/2017 for New General Urban Plan of Timisoara. Timisoara.

Rupert Read, 2007. Economics Is Philosophy, Economics Is not Science, International Journal of Green Economics, 1(3/4).

Samuelson, Paul Alan, 1969. "The Way of an Economist", in P.A. Samuelson (ed.), International Economic Relations: Proceedings of the Third Congress of the International Economic Association, Macmillan: London, pp. 1–11.

Staff Department of the Flemish Government (STFG), 2011. Flemish Strategy for Sustainable Development, Pushing Back Frontiers Together – Vision 2050, https://www.sd-network.eu/pdf/country_profiles/BE_Vision%202050%20 Sustainable%20Development%20Strategy%20Flanders.pdf, accessed on 14 December 2019.

Tillie, Nico, Dobbelsteen Andy Van Den, Doepel Duzan, Joubert Marc, De Jager Wim, Mayenburg Dave, 2009. Towards CO2 Neutral Urban Planning: Presenting the Rotterdam Energy Approach and Planning (REAP), Journal of Green Building, 4(3), Summer 2009, pp. 103–112, https://doi.org/10.3992/jgb.4.3.103.

Timmer, MarcelP., Dietzenbacher, Erik, Los, Bart, Stehrer, Robert and de Vries, GaaitzenJ., 2015. An Illustrated User Guide to the World Input–Output Database: The Case of Global Automotive Production, Review of International Economics, 2015. DOI: 10.1111/roie.12178

United Nations Environment Programme (UNEP), UNEP Database, https://www.resourcepanel.org/global-material-flows-database, accessed on 15 December 2019.

UN et al., 2012. SEEA Accounting 2012 – Central Framework, 2014, https://unstats.un.org/unsd/envaccounting/seeaRev/SEEA_CF_Final_en.pdf, accessed on 15.03.2019.

van Oers, L., Guinée, J.B., Heijungs, R., 2020. The International Journal of Life Cycle Assessment, 25, 294. https://doi.org/10.1007/s11367-019-01683-x.

Williams, Paul D., 2009. Rapid Climate Change: An Overview for Economists, International Journal of Green Economics, 3(1), 63–76.

World Trade Organization (WTO), WTO Database, https://www.wto.org/english/res_e/reser_e/cadv_e.htm, accessed on 14.12.2019.

Xing, Yuqing, How the iPhone Widens the US Trade Deficit with China, https://voxeu.org/article/how-iphone-widens-us-trade-deficit-china, 10 April 2011, accessed on 14.12.2019.

Vasilii Erokhin

U.S.-China trade tensions and their possible effects on stability of global food markets

Abstract Tensions between China and the USA keep escalating, as a new round of tariffs on both countries' exports came into effect in September 2019. Agricultural sector appears to become one of the most vulnerable in this trade war, since by raising import tariffs on food and agricultural products in response to protectionist policies, the countries may face a situation of rising prices for consumers, limited market access for producers, and increasing pressures on food security. Apart from the two countries, major trade partners of both the USA and China, which are the EU, Canada, Mexico, Brazil, and Russia, among others, may suffer from tariff vulnerability and increasing unpredictability of global agricultural markets. In the light of a new pack of tariff measures, many food companies worldwide are forced to modify their production, distribution, and commercial activities. In this paper, the author explores possible effects of higher protectionist barriers on US-China trade in food and agricultural products, as well as on the stability of global markets and food security.

Keywords: agricultural products, China, food security, protectionism, tariff, trade, USA

Introduction

Trade tensions between China and the USA keep escalating, as a new round of tariffs on both countries' exports came into effect in September 2019. The war has actually started around the trade deficit in US-China trade. US imports $3.1 trillion, exports $2.5 trillion which results in $600 billion deficit. Out of this $3.1 trillion that comes in, $539.5 billion is import from China, which is 17.3 %. But out of $2.5 trillion that goes out, U.S. export from China is only $120.3 billion, which is 4.8 %. It follows that China's share in the U.S. total trade deficit is 67 %.

The U.S. motivation for imposing higher tariffs on China's imports thus seems explainable. It appears that the U.S. is doing that to reduce its trade deficit with China, keep manufacturing jobs in the country, get the U.S. out of debt (which major holder is again China with over $1.1 trillion), and ultimately – choke off China's 2025 strategy and keep the U.S. as dominant economic power in the global market.

U.S. is good and ideas and innovations, technologies, and free-market competition regime. China, on the other end, has got cheaper labor and developed manufacturing sector. So, who does the trade war hurt the most? Surprisingly, not only the U.S. or China but other countries and the global economy in large. Major trade partners of both the U.S. and China, which are the EU, Canada,

Mexico, Brazil, and Russia, among others, are suffering from tariff vulnerability, increasing unpredictability of trade and financial markets, and expected slowdown in the two belligerent global powers. Trade tension is also hurting the small business owners and farmers in the USA. A lot of U.S. small businesses rely on buying products from China on a certain price and go into the red when the price increased due to the tariff. Although President Trump often says the tariffs are paid by China, they are not, because consumers and businesses that import goods actually pay the cost.

In US-China trade tensions, agricultural sector appears to be one of the most vulnerable. In the USA, farmers' income fell by over $12 billion in the first half of 2019 on the rise of the trade tension even before the new round of tariff escalation in September 2019. Farmers in Illinois, Indiana, and Wisconsin have the highest rate of bankruptcies level in the last decade. In China, emerging trade tension endanger food security since the USA has been and still is one of the major suppliers of food and agricultural products to the country, particularly, soybeans – a critically important crop for supporting security of Chinese domestic food market. According to Ghosh and Ghoshal (2017), increased access to a wide range of affordable and nutritious food, structural changes in global food market have put in place concerns and challenges related to food prices, stability of food supply, and trade-economic aspects of food accessibility and affordability. That is why it is crucial to track changes in trade policies and interpret them in terms of food production and trade in agricultural commodities, so both agricultural producers and exporters may fit well with the changing requirements of domestic resources and global market (Erokhin, 2020). As both the U.S. and China's agricultural sectors are the integral elements of globalized food market, trade relations between the two countries affect stability of food markets globally bringing about price volatility and food security concerns. This paper overviews China-US trade in agricultural commodities and food and assesses possible effects of rising protectionism on global trade in food, stability of global food markets, and food security.

1. Literature review

Agricultural trade has been emerging as one of the major topics in global agenda in the previous decades. Most of the countries in the world has been increasingly focusing on the implementation of various tools and practices to support domestic farmers and improve the structure of agricultural exports. The majority of global agricultural trade is captured by the countries with a competitive advantage in the processed agricultural products (Liapis, 2011), while those which specialize in primary and raw agricultural commodities make do with a low share of the global market. It is true even for the world's biggest agricultural producers, for example, China which must ensure food security of its population and thus poses scarce abilities to expand agricultural exports.

Before the economic reforms of 1980s, China's foreign trade had been restricted down to exporting surplus raw materials and simple manufactured goods to cover payments for imported goods (Sun & Heshmati, 2010). Since the start of trade liberalization, the country has been deeply integrated into the global trade system, experienced unprecedented economic growth, and skyrocketed to become one of the major exporters and importers worldwide. Dohmen (1976), Wu (2006), and Liberthal (2004) provided in-depth analysis of foreign trade policy of China in general. Lardy (2002), Panitchpakdi and Clifford (2002), and Anderson et al. (2010) studied the implications of China's membership in the World Trade Organization (WTO) on both China's internal policies and foreign trade.

In agriculture, where production is affected by many variables, including natural factors, changes in trade policy do not go smooth. Trade liberalization can affect the availability of certain foods by removal of barriers to imports, but also to foreign investments in the development of domestic production. Thow and Hawkes (2009) found that availability of processed food has risen in developing countries after foreign direct investment by multinational food companies. Thus, changes in trade policies have facilitated the rising availability and consumption of foods. Dorosh (2004) found the positive contribution of trade liberalization to food security and stabilization of supply and food market. Protection policies, including administrative restrictions of food imports with a view to the increase of food self-sufficiency of the country, on the contrary, may cause unnecessary social costs and place food self-sufficiency into conflict with the goals of food security and poverty reduction. Warr (2011) studied the effects of an import ban on rice introduced in Indonesia and concluded that it let to achieve the required level of food self-sufficiency, but at the expense of reducing food security.

2. China's demand for food: retrospective and projection

By now China has achieved self-sufficiency on major kinds of food and agricultural products on the level of about 91–97 % of domestic consumption. However, taking into account scarce land resources coupled with the world's biggest population, China remains heavily dependent on agricultural imports. Zhou (2010) records growth of consumption of food products of higher quality, nutrient value and price in China (meat and meat products, milk and dairy products, and seafood) – to the prejudice of cheaper and fewer nutrient crops. According to Nath et al. (2015), by 2030, China will need to increase agricultural lands under crops by 21 % to be able to meet the growing internal demand for food. According to Gao (2018), China's demand for cereals will rise up to 700 million tons in 2020, including imports of 100 million tons. By 2022, China will double import of feed grain, beef, and pork, as well as increase purchases of soybeans by 40 % (Fig. 1). Huang et al. (2017) predict China's overall food self-sufficiency to reduce to 91 % by 2025.

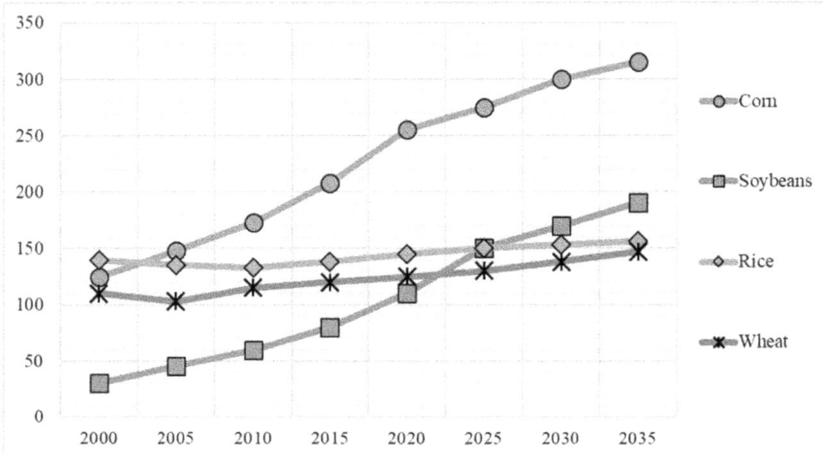

Fig. 1: China's projected demand in major crops, million tons per year
Source: Author's development based on Gro Intelligence (2018).

In view of expected rise in consumption of food, Zhu (2016) and Yu et al. (2015) consider high dependence of China on imports as a potential threat to food security. Zhang and Cheng (2016) show that China's grain imports have continued to grow in spite of increased domestic grain production in the 2010s. In 2004–2014, grain imports nearly tripled, and imports of rice, wheat, and corn increased eightfold. Zhang (2016) points out that large-scale agricultural imports, particularly, soybeans from the USA, has almost destroyed domestic soybean production sector causing China to lose control of its supply chain to foreign producers and suppliers. In a situation of expanding trade tensions between the USA and China and, potentially, between China and other countries, such over-reliance on foreign food supply equips China's counterparts with a power to influence on China's trade policies by pressing its food market and threatening food security of its population.

3. China-US trade in food and agricultural products

China's import of many kinds of food and agricultural products, particularly, such value-added food products as soybeans and meat, is focused on the USA. In the situation of trade tensions and tariff escalations between the USA and China, the agricultural sector is one of the most vulnerable. The U.S. economy is external-oriented, but to a lesser degree compared to that of China. In the USA, export-GDP ratio is 11.9 %, while that in China is 19.2 %. Such trade position of China in relation to the USA limits the response resources in trade tensions. By raising import tariffs on food and agricultural products in response to recent U.S. protectionist policies, China may face a situation of food insecurity.

According to Zhang (2016), the USA supplied 36 % of total China's oilseeds imports, 42 % of cereals imports, 30 % of cotton imports, and 25 % of meat imports. Gale et al. (2015) report that the USA is also one of China's top three destinations for agricultural exports. Bilateral agricultural trade has experienced phenomenal growth from 2001, the year of China's accession to the WTO. U.S. imports of agricultural products from China increased from less than $0.9 billion in 2000 to over $8.0 billion in 2018; whereas its agricultural exports to China skyrocketed from about $2.1 billion in 2000 to almost $24.0 billion in 2018 (Fig. 2).

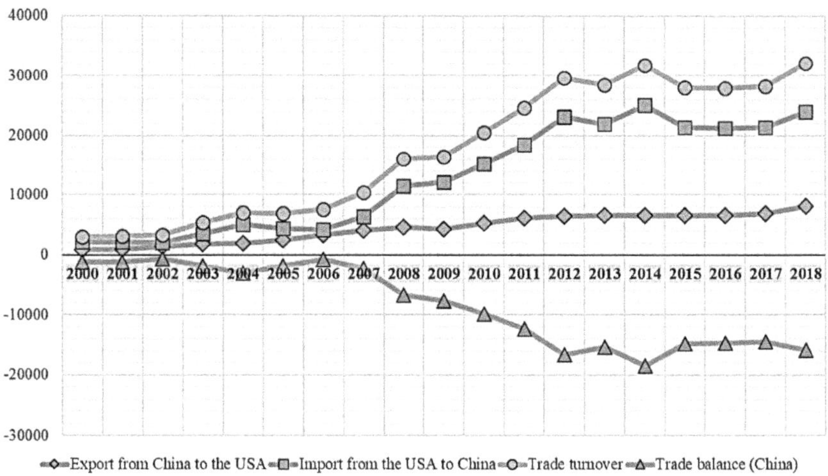

Fig. 2: China-USA agricultural trade in 2000–2018, $ million
Source: Author's development based on UNCTAD (2019).

In 2018, China was the USA's fourth-largest supplier of agricultural imports. Particularly, China is a large supplier of aquatic invertebrates, mollusks crustaceans, fish, fruit and vegetables, roots and tubers, and edible products and preparations to the USA (Fig. 3).

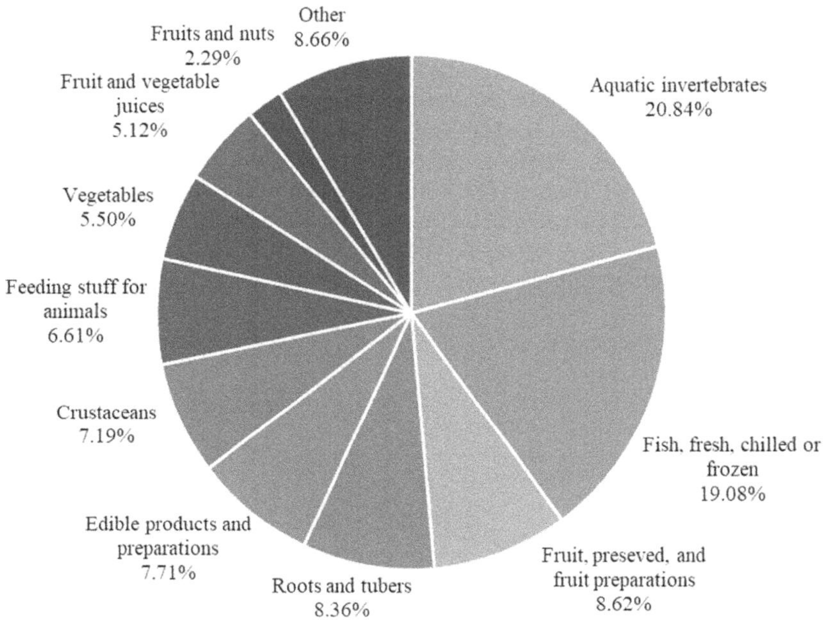

Fig. 3: China's agricultural export to the USA in 2018, percentage of total agricultural export

Source: Author's development based on UNCTAD (2019).

China is a major agricultural export market for the USA that has grown tremendously over the past two decades. In fact, China was the second-largest export market for the USA in 2017 behind Canada, accounting for 14 % of the U.S. agricultural exports (Bakst & Beaumont-Smith, 2018). In terms of value, the largest China's agricultural import from the USA is oilseeds (mainly soybeans) and oleaginous fruits totaling over $15.1 billion in 2018. The USA is a large suppliers of feeding stuff for animals, cereals, meat and edible meat offal, edible products and preparations, and milk and dairy products to China (Fig. 4).

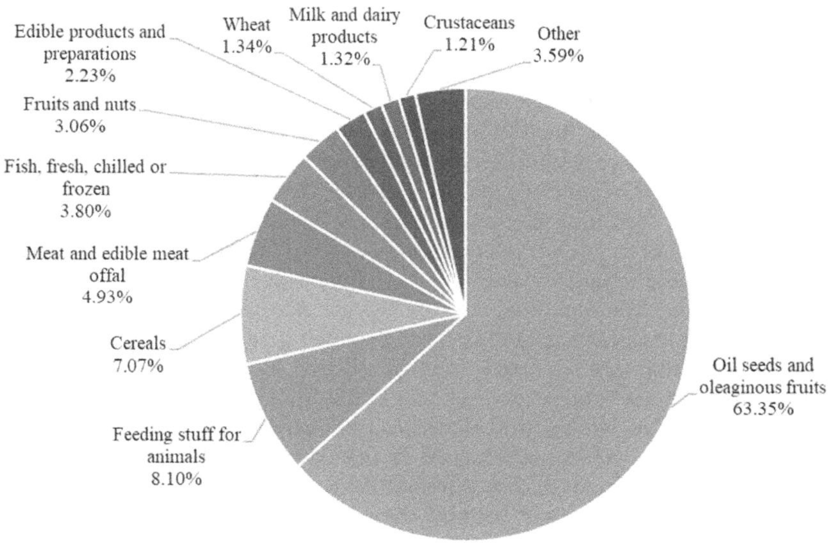

Fig. 4: China's agricultural import from the USA in 2018, percentage of total agricultural import

Source: Author's development based on UNCTAD (2019).

China has threatened to impose a 25 % tariff on 128 products, including agricultural commodities and food products, in response to a U.S. proposal to impose a 25 % tariff on imported products from China (Taheripour & Tyner, 2018). In April 2018, China began imposing tariffs on U.S. goods including soybeans, dairy, and pork, and more tariffs were added in July 2018 (Filloon, 2018). The problem with a trade tension is that it may easily emerge into an economic war between the global superpowers and in such a way pressure to change global supply chains. In the light of a new pack of tariff measures, many companies in China, USA, and worldwide are forced to modify their production, distribution, and commercial activities. Taken together, China and the USA are the world's biggest producers, suppliers, consumers, and value generators. An aggravation of trade tensions between them will, in the short-run, create turmoil in global food markets, while in the long run, decelerate economic growth in agriculture and lead business in both countries to decline. In China, in addition, trade tension may aggravate food insecurity problem. In any economic tensions like that, there are no winners, only losers.

Conclusions

Being the country with the world's biggest population, China has still achieved self-sufficiency on major kinds of staple foods, primarily, crops. Despite that,

China is the world's biggest consumer of agricultural products and increasingly – of high-nutrient and high value-added foods, such as meat and edible products, milk and dairy products, and soybeans. Many of such products (most of the soybeans strategically important for food security of China) are now imported by China from the USA. Amid the escalation of trade tensions between the two countries, agricultural sector becomes at risk of a disruption of supply and value chains, economic and market losses for the U.S. farmers, and food insecurity problems for China. Both countries and wider – the entire global food market must adapt to those transformations, diversify food supply chains, intensify domestic production, and develop alternative export and import channels.

In this paper, the author analyzed the current state of China-US agricultural trade on major kinds of commodities and demonstrated that import volumes to China grew as domestic demand was restructured in favor of qualitative food products of high nutrient value. The study shows that potential negative impact of trade tensions on agricultural trade must be investigated further. Threats of trade tensions on agricultural trade shook the agricultural production globally, that is why a deeper analysis is required in the sphere of the trade policy impact on not only agricultural trade, but also changes in agricultural production, producer prices, and welfare.

Acknowledgment

This study has been conducted in the framework of the research projects supported by Fundamental Research Funds for the Central Universities (grant no. HEUCFJ170901 and 3072019CFP0902).

References

Anderson, Kym; Martin, Will; van der Mensbrugghe, Dominique: "China, the WTO and the Doha Agenda". In: Greenaway David, Milner Chris and Yao Shujie (eds.): China and the World Economy. London: Palgrave Macmillan. 2010, pp. 1–20.

Bakst, Daren; Beaumont-Smith, Gabriela: "Agricultural Trade with China: What's at Stake for American Farmers, Ranchers, and Families". Retrieved December 2, 2019, from https://www.heritage.org/agriculture/report/agricultural-trade-china-whats-stake-american-farmers-ranchers-and-families, 2018.

Dohmen, Holger: China's Foreign Trade Policy. Intereconomics 11(7), 1976, pp. 197–201.

Dorosh, Paul: Trade, Food Aid and Food Security: Evolving Rice and Wheat Markets. Economic and Political Weekly 36(39), 2004, pp. 4033–4042.

Erokhin, Vasilii: "Transformation of China's Agricultural Trade in Response to Emerging Tensions on the Global Market". In: Coskun Ozer Ahu (ed.): International Trade Policies in the Era of Globalization. Hershey, PA: IGI Global. 2020, pp. 1–28.

Filloon, Whitney: These Are All the Foods Being Affected by Trump's Trade War. Retrieved December 5, 2019, from https://www.eater.com/2018/7/18/17527968/food-tariffs-trump-canada-china-mexico-eu, 2018.

Gale, Fred; Hansen, James; Jewison, Michael: China's Growing Demand for Agricultural Imports. Washington. DC: Department of Agriculture, Economic Research Service. 2015.

Gao, Tianming: "Food Security and Rural Development on Emerging Markets of Northeast Asia: Cases of Chinese North and Russian Far East". In: Erokhin Vasilii (ed.): Establishing Food Security and Alternatives to International Trade in Emerging Economies. Hershey, PA: IGI Global. 2018, pp. 155–176.

Ghosh, Ishita; Ghoshal, Ishita: "Implications of Trade Liberalization for Food Security under the ASEAN-India Strategic Partnership: A Gravity Model Approach". In: Erokhin Vasilii (ed.): Establishing Food Security and Alternatives to International Trade in Emerging Economies. Hershey, PA: IGI Global. 2017, pp. 98–118.

Gro Intelligence: China's Road Map to Food Security. Retrieved November 30, 2019, from https://gro-intelligence.com/insights/chinas-roadmap-to-food-security, 2018.

Huang, Ji-Kun; Wei, Wei; Cui, Qi; Xie, Wei: The Prospects for China's Food Security and Imports: Will China Starve the World via Imports? Journal of Integrative Agriculture 16(12), 2017, pp. 2933–2944.

Lardy, Nicholas: Integrating China into the World Economy. Washington, DC: Brookings Institution Press. 2002.

Liapis, Peter: Changing Patterns of Trade in Processed Agricultural Products. Paris: OECD Publishing. 2011.

Liberthal, Kenneth: Governing China: From Revolution Through Reform. New York, NY: W. W. Norton. 2004.

Nath, Reshmita; Luan, Yibo; Yang, Wangming; Yang, Chen; Chen, Wen; Li, Qian; Cui, Xuefeng: Changes in Arable Land Demand for Food in India and China: A Potential Threat to Food Security. Sustainability 7(5), 2015, pp. 5371–5397.

Panitchpakdi, Supachai; Clifford, Mark: China and the WTO: Changing China, Changing World Trade. Singapore: J. Wiley & Sons. 2002.

Sun, Peng; Heshmati, Almas: International Trade and Its Effects on Economic Growth in China. Bonn: Institute for the Study of Labor. 2010.

Taheripour, Farzad; Tyner, Wallace: Impacts of Possible Chinese 25% Tariff on U.S. Soybeans and Other Agricultural Commodities. Choices 33(2), 2018, pp. 1–7.

Thow, Anne Marie; Hawkes, Corinna: The Implications of Trade Liberalization for Diet and Health: A Case Study from Central America. Global Health 28, 2009, p. 5.

United Nations Conference on Trade and Development: Statistics Database. Retrieved December 2, 2019, from http://unctad.org/en/Pages/Statistics.aspx, 2019.

Warr, Peter: Food Security vs. Food Self-Sufficiency: The Indonesian Case. Canberra: The Australian National University. 2011.

Wu, Yanrui: Economic Growth, Transition and Globalization in China. Cheltenham: Edward Elgar Publishing Limited. 2006.

Yu, Wusheng; Elleby, Christian; Zobbe, Henrik: Food Security Policies in India and China: Implications for National and Global Food Security. Food Security 7(2), 2015, pp. 405–414.

Zhang, Hongzhou: "Food in Sino-U.S. Relations. From Blessing to Curse?" In: Wu Fengshi and Zhang Hongzhou (eds.): China's Global Quest for Resources. Energy, Food and Water. Routledge: London. 2016, pp. 100–118.

Zhang, Hongzhou; Cheng, Guoqiang: "China's Food Security Strategy Reform: An Emerging Global Agricultural Policy". In: Wu Fengshi and Zhang Hongzhou (eds.): China's Global Quest for Resources. Energy, Food and Water. London: Routledge. 2016, pp. 23–41.

Zhou, Zhangyue: Achieving Food Security in China: Past Three Decades and Beyond. China Agricultural Economic Review 2(3), 2010, pp. 251–275.

Zhu, Yu: International Trade and Food Security: Conceptual Discussion, WTO and the Case of China. China Agricultural Economic Review 8(3), 2016, pp. 399–411.

Elena Otilia Manta

The competitiveness of the Romanian companies in the context of the current challenges of globalization, as well as of the current integration in the euro area

Abstract We are currently part of the process of defining strategic priorities and scenarios for increasing competitiveness at the level of the Romanian and European companies, which can contribute actively to the economic convergence at national and European level through the support programs of the European Union for the programming period 2021–2027. Starting from this objective we consider that in addition to presenting the relevant general information regarding the competitive context of Romania, respectively the macroeconomic framework at national level, economic sectors with competitive potential in the current context of economic convergence, the territorial dimension of competitiveness at national level, as well as the establishment of a set of economic-financial indicators reflecting the state of the real economy at present and supporting a new indicator, respectively the competitive index at company level. Moreover, we consider that starting from the general principles regarding the role of competitiveness in achieving the objectives of economic development, as well as the monitoring and evaluation of the competitiveness of the companies at national level, but especially the current place of Romania according to the Global Competitiveness Index and the factors of interest. To increase competitiveness, they can lead us to determine the economic convergence.

The determination of the impact on the economic convergence is given by the comparative analysis of the companies at the level of the EU branches and at the level of the economic branches in Romania, models of economic convergence testing, as well as the competitiveness at European level in the current global context, oriented directly to the detail of the indicators and indices. Of competitiveness relevant to the economic convergence of the business environment at national level in the European context. Further to analyze the competitiveness of the real economy, we consider that a set of indicators calculated at the level of the branches of the real economy based on the accounting balances of 490,000 active economic agents at national level, can give a clear picture on the competitiveness of the real economy at national level.

Keywords: competitiveness, economic convergence, sustainability

Introduction

The competitiveness at the level of the Romanian companies is supported by the strategic document supporting the National Strategy for Competitiveness (RG, 2013; OECD, 2017), but more is given by the current context of the existing technologies at global level (including the 4.0 and 5.0 technology) with direct impact on the competitiveness of the companies at the national level, European and global, including from the perspective of the territorial dimension and rural development, labor market development and the adaptation of the human factor to these technologies.

The National Strategy for Competitiveness (GR_a, 2013; OECD, 2017)arises from the desire to build on a strategic basis and according to the current challenges of a better future for the Romanian economy and for the citizens in general. At global, regional and local level we have in the specialized literature defined regarding competitiveness indices, respectively at global level we have the global competitiveness index calculated based on the 12 pillars of competitiveness at the global level; at European level we have calculated the regional competitiveness index, and at the company level to identify the competitiveness of the company we have not identified the existence of a competitiveness index (GR_b, 2013; EC, 2020).

Starting from these aspects and in conjunction with the real state of the economy based on economic-financial indicators, in our paper the competitive index at the firm level represents the novelty element of our research.

Research methodology

In order to base the research methodology on the project, we used classical observation and examination instruments, research methods based on the basic principles of scientific research. We used procedures based on factual analysis, intensive documentation at the level of internal and international literature, using the databases and the scientific material existing in the endowment of libraries of specific institutes in Romania and internationally.

The methodology of the paper has as direct instruments the collection of data and information from the literature and from the existing practice in public and private institutions, but especially scientific articles published on specialized research networks (Research Gate, Academia.edu, etc.), articles published in various journals, relevant books in the field of reference, legislation, analyses and studies, official documents of various tax bodies, tax documents and interactive database of the National Bank of Romania, other relevant sources identified in the libraries: Romanian Academy, National Institute for Economic Research "Costin C. Kiriţescu" (NIER), National Library, etc. Moreover, we analyzed the documents using the comparative, analytical, descriptive method, the no participative and participatory observation, and the use of a set of informational sources, the collection of financial data in the established databases. The work is also based on annual reports, publications, consolidated statistical data provided by the National

Bank of Romania, the European Central Bank (ECB), the International Settlement Bank (BRI), the European Commission, OECD, published annually, data that have been processed for can provide a general and analytical picture of the most important changes taking place in the financial markets in the European Union as a whole but also globally – considered to be representative of the understanding of the phenomena studied, and especially in Romania (Manta, 2019).

The information support of the research was provided by the monographs, books, scientific articles, materials of the scientific conferences, the balance sheets of SMEs during 2008–2017 from Ministry of Public Finance, as well as other materials, which are presented in the scientific papers and publications displayed on the official pages of the national and international research institutes, international financial institutions (research centers), etc.

The economic-financial indicators were calculated based on a calculation methodology. Moreover, the new indicator, the competitive index at the firm level, defines it as a composite index calculated by aggregating derived indicators (such as turnover per employee (CA; S), value of exports per employee (Exp; S) and of a composite indicator (the technological development index of the company, calculated as the total value of investments in technology and innovation per employee). Moreover, at the level of the branches of the real economy and by development regions, we consider for the internal analysis of the competitiveness of the real economy the following relevance indicators to be calculated and detailed within the paper, respectively: Evolution of the economic rate of return of the asset in the period 2007–2017 for the branches of the real economy (%) and by regions, Evolution of the turnover rate of the assets during the period 2007–2017 for the branches of the economy real (%) and by regions, Evolution of labor productivity in 2007–2017 for the branches of the real economy (lei; sal.) And by regions, Evolution of the immediate solvency, in the period 2007–2017 for the branches of the real economy (%) and by regions, The evolution of the average gross value added per employee in the period 2007–2017 for the branches of the economy real (lei; sal.) and regions.

1. Literature review

Competitiveness at the level of companies should not be considered limited at the level of the respective entity, but must be adapted to the economic context in which it operates (Bodea, Mihuț, 2013). To be competitive and create value added at product; service level, companies must meet international standards and implement technological innovations and at the same time attract and train employees to meet the new demands imposed by the evolution of digital technologies at national and global levels. In order to face the competition based on the competitiveness, the economic agents have to resort to the implementation of technological innovations (being one of the biggest current challenges) (Apergis et al., 2012), and in parallel they must attract a well-prepared workforce to face this new scientific challenge and technological. For example, starting from industry 4.0. with its digitization component of activity at the level of companies Rüßmann et al. (2015) “there will be an increase in productivity in the manufacturing industry, the economy will change, industrial production will increase and the profile of the labor force will change - ultimately changing the competitiveness of companies and regions" (Rüßmann et al., 2015, p. 6). More Parviainen et al. (2017) believes that "digitalization has been identified as one of the major trends that change society and business in the near future and in the long term the impact of digitalization will be important; it has been compared to the industrial revolution by several authors" (p. 64). E. Stolterman and AC Fors (2004), Parviainen et al (2017) state that the term digitization refers to "the action or process of digitization; conversion of analogue data (images, video and text) into digital form," while digitization (Rachinger et al 2018) is refers to "can be understood as the changes that digital technology causes or influences in all aspects of human life" (Parviainen et al., 2017; Stolterman, Fors, 2004, p. 689). Moreover, Kagermann (2015) mentions that digitization is "the continuous convergence of the real and virtual world and can be regarded as the main engine of innovation and change in all sectors of our economy." Brennen and Kreiss (2014), define that digitization refers to "the adoption or growth of the use of digital technology or computers by an organization, industry, country, etc." At the same time innovation-driven technologies and the surrounding ecosystem of applications have shifted the political and regulatory status quo into forms of indirect national and EU-level interventions (including the Connecting Europe Facility proposed by the European Commission and several national Broadband Plans backed with support schemes) to supplement the cases where the market players will simply not invest (Gruber, Hätönen and Koutroumpis, 2014), and this will be have direct impact for the competitiveness environment.

All these concepts and theories determine us to re-evaluate the competitive sectors both through the analysis of the data at the level reported by the companies (Becker et al., 2010), but especially through the adaptation and adoption by them of the new (digital) instruments that have a direct impact on their business model. According to the source I-scoop.eu, digitization could be defined as "the transformation from analogue to digital or digital of a physical element in order to digitize and automate processes or workflows" (Clerck, 2019; Manta, 2019)

2. Research results

The macroeconomic framework at national level

The existence of a stable macroeconomic and financial framework is a precondition for creating a favorable ground for affirming the competitive potential of the business environment.

According to the National Commission for Strategy and Forecast (CNSP) for Romania, an economic growth for 2019 is estimated with 5.5 % of the Gross Domestic Product (GDP) as against 3.6 % as it was in November 2018. However, we can mention that at the level of the evolution of the gross domestic product by branches in Romania, in 2018 the Commission carried out the projection of the indicators as follows in the table below (Tab. 1).

Tab. 1: Evolution of Gross Domestic Product (GDP) by branches in Romania

- percentage changes from the previous year, % -	2016	2017	2018	2019	2020	2021
Gross Domestic Product	4.8	6.9	6.1	5.7	5.7	5.0
Industry						
Output	1.8	8.5	5.4	5.2	4.5	4.3
Gross value added	5.3	8.0	5.7	5.4	4.6	4.3
Agriculture, forestry, fishing						
Output Gross value added	4.6	15.7	2.0	2.0	1.1	1.0
	4.7	18.3	1.9	1.9	0.9	1.1
Constructions						
Production	5.8	-2.6	8.0	7.0	7.4	7.0
Gross value added	12.7	-0.6	8.2	7.2	7.7	7.1
Total services						
Production	4.3	7.7	6.9	6.3	6.6	5.7
Gross value added	4.0	6.5	6.7	6.2	6.4	5.6
Total economy						
Production	3.6	7.5	6.2	5.8	5.7	5.1
Gross value added	5.0	7.0	6.3	5.8	5.8	5.1
Net taxes on the product	3.6	6.9	4.5	4.3	4.4	3.8

Source: author based on Projection of the main macroeconomic indicators 2018–2021, National Commission for Strategy and Forecast, 2018

Forecasts indicate a moderate dynamics of GDP, above the EU average, against the backdrop of uncertainties related to external economic developments. The highest annual growth rates for real GDP in 2017 were recorded in Ireland (7.2 %), Romania (6.9 %), Malta (6.4 %) and Slovenia (5.0 %), while the lowest rates of variation were recorded in Belgium and the United Kingdom (both 1.7 %), Italy (1.5 %) and Greece (1.4 %) (IMD, 2006; OECD, 2016) (Tab. 2).

Tab. 2: Romania's economy in the EU and in the world

	2008	2018
The share of Romania's GDP in world GDP	0.33	0.25
The share of Romania's GDP in EU GDP	1.1	1.1
The share of Romanian exports in world exports	0.31	0.35
The share of the Romanian population in the EU population	4.2	3.9
The share of Romanian agriculture in EU exports	0.8	1.0
The share of Romanian agriculture in European agriculture	4.8	4.1
The share of the Romanian industry in the European industry	1.5	1.9

Source: author based on UNCTAD, Eurostat, 2019

The share of Romania's GDP in EU GDP was in 2013 the same as in 2008, respectively 1.1 %. The share in world GDP has decreased from 0.33 % in 2008 to 0.28 % in 2009 to 0.25 % in 2012 and 2013, which means that the rest of the countries of the world have grown much faster than us. Regarding the Romanian exports, their share in the global exports increased from 0.31 % in 2008 to 0.33 % in 2009, 0.32 % in 2012 and then increases again, reaching 0.35 % in 2013, according to the latest WTO data (MPF, 2019). At the European Union level, there is progress: Romanian exports represent 1 % of total European exports in 2013 compared to 0.8 % in 2008. According to the NBR, the trade balance deficit decreased by 975 million euros, and the surplus recorded by the balance of services was 721 million euros, compared to a deficit of 130 million euros in the same period of 2012. Regarding the balance of payments, between December 2012 and December 2013, the current account of the balance of payments registered a deficit of 955 million euros, compared with 5,331 million euros in the same period of 2012, against the background of reducing the trade balance deficit (by 3,519 million euros), the increase of the surplus recorded by the balance of services (by 1,434 million euros) and by the balance of current transfers (by 292 million euros). According to the Inflation Report, the annual rate of CPI inflation reached the minimum of the last 24 years at the end of the IV quarter 2013, lowering to the lower limit of the ± 1 % point variation interval associated with the 2.5 % stationary target.

Regarding the European funds, respectively their impact on the increase of the competitiveness of the Romanian companies, the situation of the European funds is presented on May 31, 2019 according to the reports presented by the Ministry of European Funds, as follows (Ministry of European Funds, 2019) (Figs. 1 and 2):

- 8.8 billion euro European money entered in Romania through Cohesion Policy and Agricultural Policy. To these amounts are added another 6.7 billion euros direct payments to farmers;
- approx. 25 billion euros – the total value of the open financing lines, representing over 91 % of the total allocation of Romania;
- 43 billion euro the value of the projects submitted for these financing lines;
- approx. 22.5 billion euros the total value of the financing contracts signed. The contracting rate has increased more than 15 times, from 5 % in 2016 to approx. 79 % of the allocation at present. The absorption rate of Romania is approx. 29 % compared to the EU average, which is 31 %.

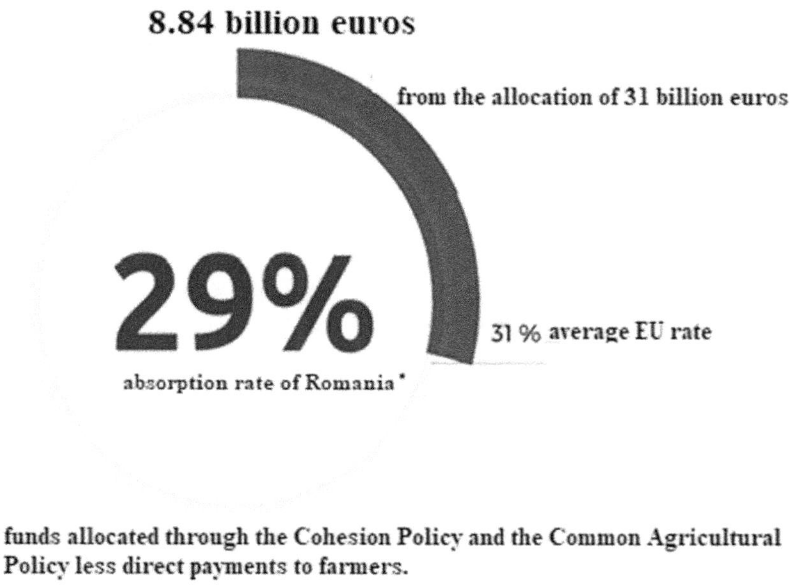

Fig. 1: The amounts reimbursed by the EU to Romania until May 31, 2019

Source: author based on http://mfe.gov.ro/wp-content/uploads/2019/06/ff18ea6dbdf45aa1f620e63 1d02a74a8.png.

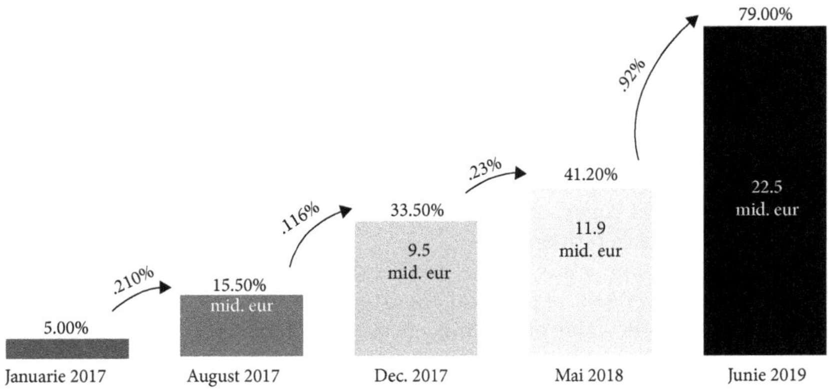

Fig. 2: Evolution of the contracting rate of European funds between January 2017 and June 2019

Source: author based on http://mfe.gov.ro/wp-content/uploads/2019/06/fd7a3947b875347b2a3031ed3dd00f96.png.

Economic sectors with competitive potential in the current context of economic convergence

The analyzes carried out led to the identification of 10 economic sectors with competitive potential that correlate with the areas of intelligent specialization identified in the National Strategy for Research, Development and Innovation 2014–2020. At European level, the territorial approach is becoming increasingly important in strategic planning. Although traditionally seen as an integral part of Cohesion Policy, space development has received increasing recognition in other EU policies in recent years. In view of the trends at European level of analyzing the territorial component of competitiveness, the European Commission proposed in 2011 the calculation of a Regional Competitiveness Index (ICR) (EC, 2013; Eurostat, 2013; IMD, 2013). The calculation methodology starts from the premise that in a spatial context the economic competitiveness is determined by a complex system of factors, which concentrates, among others: the creative and innovative exploitation of the regional potential, the creation of connections at territorial level by stimulating the appearance and strengthening of the intra and inter-industry on value chains, capitalization of natural and cultural heritage, use of research-innovation potential and improving connectivity and accessibility.

ICR is composed of 11 pillars that describe the different aspects of competitiveness. Through these pillars, the index assesses the strengths and weaknesses of a region. The pillars are classified into 3 groups: elementary, efficiency and innovation. The elementary group comprises 5 pillars: institutions; macroeconomic stability; infrastructure; the health; basic education. These pillars are the essential elementary drivers of all types of economy. As a regional economy develops and progresses, in terms of its competitiveness, factors related to a skilled labor force and a more efficient labor market can come into play. These factors are part of the efficiency group. It comprises 3 pillars: higher education, vocational training and lifelong learning; labor market efficiency; the size of the market. In the most advanced stage of development of a regional economy, the drivers of improvement are part of the innovation group, which consists of 3 pillars: technological maturity; sophistication of the business environment; innovation.

Based on the ICR, whose calculation formula closely follows the Global Competitiveness Index, the map of regional competitiveness at European Union level has been elaborated. Between the countries of the European Union, the development regions of Romania are in the last places, both in terms of ICR and in almost all the rankings of the indicators that compose this composite index. The region of the capital has the highest values in terms of competitiveness, but the positive effects on the neighboring regions are limited.

Under these conditions, in the case of Romania, cohesion policy must contribute not only to reducing regional disparities, but also to achieving Romania's competitiveness objectives. The results offered by the Competitive Potential Index (CPI) at NUTS 3 territorial level (county) help us to outline some economic aspects related to the diagnosis and the measurement of the economic performance of a territory. The analysis of the distribution of these values leads to at least two findings:

- an axis of the counties with high values of the Competitive Potential Index, which runs almost diagonally across the country and overlaps the most complete infrastructure in Romania (European, national roads, railways, airports).
- a mosaic aspect of the distribution of this index that overlaps the western, central and southern slopes. The east of the country is characterized by a homogeneous distribution of values, which translates into the landscape of economic performance through an inability to properly value natural and anthropic capital (low technology transfer, low capital, limitations in the area of polarization of Moldovan cities).

At the local economy level, according to the hierarchy of the CPI values, Arges county is located on the first place, with an index value of 0.78, compared to a country average of 0.31, which reflects a large volume of total exports (the second by country), the highest ratio between exports and the employed population (10,925 euros; employee) and the highest share of medium-high technology exports (20.3 % of the total in the country and 24 % of the total in the county). On the second place, with an index value of 0.68, is located the city of Bucharest, having the highest values of the export, but also the largest occupied population. Timis County ranks 3rd, with the largest high-tech exports. No county in the NE region ranks among the top 20 in the ranking, as a competitive potential.

The current place of Romania according to the Global Competitiveness Index and the factors of interest for increasing the competitiveness.

WEF assessments from the 2018 report (MPF, 2019), published in 2019, place Romania 52nd out of 140 countries in 2017, gaining 10 places compared to 2006, although the value of the index has improved (from 4.02, in 2006 to 6.35 in 2017). This tells us that in absolute terms there has been an improvement in competitiveness compared to other countries; the finding clearly shows the meaning of the evaluations regarding the evolution of competitiveness – that of the place where one country is placed in relation to the others. Or, from this point of view, the greater improvement of the competitiveness of the others has led to the loss, for Romania, of another place in the hierarchy.

Regarding the stages of the evolution of the contribution of the competitiveness factors, the evaluation made by WEF using the global competitiveness index shows, for the first time, that Romania came out of the first stage – that of the competitiveness based on production factors (cheap labor force, natural resources)., stage in which the basic conditions for productivity were created: institutions (legal framework), infrastructure, macroeconomic stability, basic level of education and health – and is in the second stage, where the main orientation is strengthening of efficiency. The important factors at this stage are the High level of education (RO: position 50, with a score of 4.34 as against a maximum of 5.66 – US); Market efficiency – RO 76th place, with a score of 4.03 out of max. of 5.69 – Hong Kong; Technological training – RO position 49, with a score of 3.59, compared to max. 6.01 – Sweden).

According to these assessments, in order to increase competitiveness, the priority for Romania is represented by the technological endowment and the use of the existing technologies (the development of own technologies, but also technological transfers, by the known modalities – FDI, technological imports) and the extension of the scope of the labor force education at the level of university education., to prepare the ground for innovation. Romania must also focus on the proper functioning of the markets – the labor market, the capital market, to create conditions for competition, in order to result in a good allocation of resources, a judicious use of public money.

Economic convergence of the business environment at national level in the European context.

"It is clear that the potential for economic convergence in Europe exists, and it is the role of imaginative political leaders and creative economic policy specialists from transition economies to find the key to success" (EC, 2020).

Economic convergence – conceptual aspects

There are different concepts of the concept of convergence. First, a distinction is made between nominal convergence and real convergence. The nominal convergence aims at a gradual fulfillment of the criteria of the Treaty of Maastricht, in order to participate in the third stage of the European Monetary Union; it is practically a convergence of nominal variables that reflect a certain degree of macroeconomic stability and is a mandatory criterion for EMU.

Broadly speaking, we talk about convergence when there are similarities in the performance patterns of national economies in the long term, or a certain synchronicity of their business cycles. In a narrow sense, real convergence means a reduction of the existing gaps in development and the level of incomes of different countries. For the latter, there are several types of real convergence, namely long-term real convergence, the poorer economies grow faster than the richer economies, thus reaching a certain alignment of the macroeconomic variables. In this sense of the conceptual definition and according to the Country Report 2018 on Romania drafted by the European Commission, we present below the economic situation of Romania in the current context and with direct impact on the sustainable convergence (Tabs. 3 and 4).

Tab. 3: Values of the nominal economic convergence indicators of Romania with the European Union, between 2007–2018

Year	Indicators				
	Annual average inflation (HICP) (%)	**Average annual nominal long-term interest rate (%)**	**Annual nominal average exchange rate, change from previous year (%)**	**General consolidated budget balance (%of GDP)**	**The share of total gross public debt in GDP (%)**
2007	4.9	7.1	-5.4	-2.7	11.9
2008	7.9	7.7	10.4	-5.4	12.4
2009	5.6	9.7	15.1	-9.1	22.1
2010	6.1	7.3	-0.7	-6.9	29.7
2011	5.8	7.3	0.6	-5.4	34.0
2012	3.4	6.7	5.2	-3.7	36.9
2013	3.2	5.4	-0.9	-2.2	37.6
2014	1.4	4.5	0.6	-1.3	39.2
2015	-0.4	3.5	0.0	-0.7	37.8
2016	-1.1	3.3	1.0	-2.9	37.3
2017	1.1	4.0	1.7	-2.9	35.1
2018	4.1	4.7	1.9	-3.3	35.1

Source: author based on calculations based on Eurostat data, update (March 22, 2019). For the data regarding the budget deficit and the public debt for 2018, Ameco data (forecasts) were used.

Tab. 4: Evolution of the reference values for nominal economic convergence, according to Maastricht criteria, between 2006–2017

Year	**Indicators**				
	Annual average inflation (HICP) (%)	**Average annual nominal long-term interest rate (%)**	**Exchange rate variation band**	**Limit of the balance of the general consolidated budget (%of GDP)**	**Limit of the share of total gross public debt in GDP (%)**
2007	2.8	6.4	±15 %	-3.0	60.0
2008	4.1	6.2	±15 %	-3.0	60.0
2009	1.5	5.9	±15 %	-3.0	60.0
2010	2.4	5.2	±15 %	-3.0	60.0
2011	3.1	7.7	±15 %	-3.0	60.0
2012	3.2	5.1	±15 %	-3.0	60.0
2013	1.8	6.3	±15 %	-3.0	60.0
2014	1.6	5.4	±15 %	-3.0	60.0
2015	1.5	3.6	±15 %	-3.0	60.0
2016	1.5	2.3	±15 %	-3.0	60.0
2017	2.1	3.3	±15 %	-3.0	60.0
2018	2.2	3.2	±15 %	-3.0	60.0

Source: author based on Inflation and long-term interest rate calculations are performed based on Eurostat data (update, March 22, 2019).

Overall, the fulfillment of the five criteria of nominal economic convergence is varied, in the sense that there is not a certain stability (to meet the criteria) and not even a tendency of the indicators to converge to the reference values (for the inflation rate criteria) and the interest rate, or to fall lightly within the limits imposed (for the criterion regarding the budget deficit). An exception is the criterion regarding the total gross public debt, which is easily fulfilled during the whole period analyzed (2007–2018). And even though the values of this indicator have gradually increased until 2014, they not only remain well below the 60 % of GDP threshold, but are on a downward slope in the last four years. The criterion regarding inflation and the budget deficit remain the main vulnerable elements for Romania, from the perspective of nominal economic convergence.

In order to reflect the competitiveness of the real economy at branch level and by region, the following reference indicators were calculated, respectively: The evolution of the economic rate of return of the asset in the period 2007–2017 for the branches of the real economy (%) and by regions, the evolution of the turnover rate. of assets in the period 2007–2017 for the branches of the real economy (%) and by regions, Evolution of labor productivity in the period 2007–2017 for the branches of the real economy (lei; sal.) and by regions, Evolution of the immediate solvency, between 2007 and 2017 for the branches real economy (%) and by regions, Evolution of the average gross value added per employee in the period 2007–2017 for the branches of the real economy (lei; sal.) and regions (Tabs. 5 and 6).

Tab. 5: Evolution of the rate of economic return of the asset between 2007 and 2017 for the branches of the real economy (%)

No.	Branches of the national economy	2007	2008	2009	2010	2011	2012	2013	2014	2015	2016	2017
1	Agriculture, forestry and fishing	3.31	2.70	3.04	2.68	2.72	1.74	2.86	3.84	4.10	5.69	6.97
2	Extractive industry	2.81	1.19	0.34	0.26	0.21	0.09	0.52	1.28	2.55	1.64	2.12
3	Manufacturing industry	2.60	1.54	1.07	1.38	0.72	0.70	1.68	2.67	4.52	4.98	5.27
4	Production and supply of electricity and heat, gas, hot water and air conditioning	1.38	0.43	0.66	0.47	0.09	0.06	0.05	0.00	0.03	0.01	-0.05
5	Water distribution, sanitation, waste management, decontamination activities	4.43	4.49	2.51	4.62	2.98	1.47	2.43	4.20	5.00	7.14	9.82
6	Constructions	11.73	5.26	2.26	1.86	1.35	1.24	3.21	5.16	9.09	9.82	11.60
7	Wholesale and retail trade, repair of motor vehicles and motorcycles	1.91	1.05	-0.18	0.06	-0.15	-0.13	0.12	1.25	4.20	5.47	5.72
8	Transport and storage	2.57	0.52	-1.74	-0.77	0.07	0.18	3.35	4.71	8.78	9.63	11.13
9	Hotels and restaurants	0.63	-0.11	-3.94	-4.78	-4.47	-6.28	-3.91	-0.86	5.63	7.03	7.87
10	Information and telecommunications	11.20	6.82	5.10	4.78	4.33	8.10	7.72	9.70	11.06	23.74	26.11
11	Real estate transactions, leasing and service activities mainly provided by companies	3.55	1.26	0.84	0.51	0.48	0.71	1.77	2.07	4.43	6.79	8.06

(*continued on next page*)

Tab. 5: Continued

No.	**Branches of the national economy**	**2007**	**2008**	**2009**	**2010**	**2011**	**2012**	**2013**	**2014**	**2015**	**2016**	**2017**
12	Professional, scientific and technical activities	15.54	13.37	9.24	7.37	7.60	6.74	10.67	12.90	16.59	22.65	25.50
13	Administrative service activities and support service activities	12.45	5.46	4.81	4.64	4.41	4.11	8.25	9.76	13.16	16.55	19.04
14	Education	4.71	2.11	-1.16	0.36	1.62	2.89	8.06	10.10	16.43	22.22	18.72
15	Health and social assistance	11.00	9.11	6.67	7.51	5.61	5.37	9.39	12.35	17.05	28.48	30.29
16	Entertainment, culture and recreational activities	5.52	6.81	5.37	5.27	5.49	0.08	9.48	11.65	15.62	15.19	18.86
17	Other activities of the national economy	-1.28	-5.97	-15.28	-13.05	-13.75	-3.16	-14.15	-7.64	1.16	7.11	7.28

Source: calculated based on data provided by the Ministry of Public Finance (annual financial statements of companies active in the real economy of Romania)

For the calculation of the Indicator The rate of economic return of the asset was used the formula:

$$R_e = \frac{Pbt}{At} * 100$$

Pbt= gross profit;
At= total assets.

Tab. 6: Evolution of the economic rate of return of the asset for the period 2007–2017 for the development regions in Romania (%)

No.	Development regions	2007	2008	2009	2010	2011	2012	2013	2014	2015	2016	2017
1	NORTH-WEST	3.52	1.75	0.95	1.36	0.74	0.88	2.41	3.88	6.92	8.89	10.23
2	NORTH – EAST	2.66	1.60	1.56	1.66	0.76	0.92	2.11	3.39	6.19	8.17	9.37
3	SOUTH – WEST	3.29	2.48	1.52	1.96	1.04	1.03	2.12	4.11	7.33	9.25	10.54
4	SOUTH – EAST	3.45	2.12	0.56	1.15	0.76	0.62	2.16	3.69	7.70	9.20	10.05
5	SOUTH	4.11	2.82	1.81	2.07	1.07	1.02	2.32	3.54	6.69	8.64	9.23
6	CENTRE	3.60	2.08	1.23	1.52	1.13	1.11	2.88	4.41	7.80	9.71	11.01
7	WEST	2.97	1.68	0.39	0.90	0.66	0.57	1.87	3.68	7.12	9.14	9.76
8	BUCHAREST – ILFOV	9.17	5.60	1.90	1.18	0.78	0.48	2.46	4.11	8.43	12.48	14.81

Source: calculated based on data provided by the Ministry of Public Finance (annual financial statements of companies active in the real economy of Romania)

At the level of the real economy, during the period 2007–2017 there were significant increases in the value of the rate of economic profitability in the following branches of activity respectively: Agriculture, forestry and fisheries; Water distribution, sanitation, waste management, decontamination activities; construction; Professional, scientific and technical activities; Education and Health and social assistance (an increase of the rate of return from the real economy by approximately 3 times as of December 31, 2017 compared to December 31, 2007). Moreover, at the regional level the breakdown by branches, for the period 2007–2017, is presented in the table above, respectively the Bucharest-Ilfov region an increase from 9.17 % in 2007 to 14.81 % in 2017 (Tabs. 7 and 8).

Tab. 7: Evolution of the turnover rate of the assets for the period 2007–2017 for branches of the real economy (%)

No.	Branches of the national economy	2007	2008	2009	2010	2011	2012	2013	2014	2015	2016	2017
1	Agriculture, forestry and fishing	107.39	107.28	95.03	88.61	99.33	92.55	93.02	87.41	91.11	92.01	92.48
2	Extractive industry	97.55	89.93	67.94	68.84	66.86	70.10	60.12	66.96	77.54	73.84	67.09
3	Manufacturing industry	134.71	139.62	115.72	113.03	121.51	123.54	122.59	125.08	126.36	133.91	129.23
4	Production and supply of electricity and heat, gas, hot water and air conditioning	138.09	129.32	62.20	71.84	51.21	63.28	38.54	38.24	38.01	31.05	25.51
5	Water distribution, sanitation, waste management, decontamination activities	183.25	172.94	156.76	169.77	177.33	189.87	172.65	177.26	149.19	158.10	145.53
6	Constructions	152.72	150.25	122.82	112.72	127.14	130.66	125.16	126.02	126.99	129.85	124.49
7	Wholesale and retail trade, repair of motor vehicles and motorcycles	199.97	195.39	175.22	164.32	165.71	169.41	153.11	157.87	173.59	186.02	184.81
8	Transport and storage	121.72	123.28	115.67	138.54	172.83	186.88	187.87	189.59	185.09	185.58	176.62
9	Hotels and restaurants	223.86	187.84	191.81	180.00	194.66	214.37	205.93	219.35	253.57	280.12	273.11

10	Information and telecommunications	178.44	156.42	143.56	132.91	133.08	141.80	128.69	126.66	118.88	139.80	132.85
11	Real estate transactions, leasing and service activities mainly provided by companies	92.85	74.34	54.93	47.35	42.99	46.41	45.05	39.79	47.48	56.67	61.72
12	Professional, scientific and technical activities	151.37	144.54	136.53	124.91	130.98	132.69	127.34	121.67	113.71	133.97	131.42
13	Administrative service activities and support service activities	169.41	177.56	170.60	157.21	158.38	158.61	156.09	152.46	147.20	150.48	146.43
14	Education	201.47	183.94	190.14	250.31	313.77	347.26	326.99	322.83	303.61	333.32	331.78
15	Health and social assistance	156.49	153.60	157.58	154.47	168.11	180.11	180.72	179.87	189.93	206.12	204.87
16	Entertainment, culture and recreational activities	168.26	160.39	154.25	144.00	151.06	166.03	145.22	142.10	139.99	192.00	189.46
17	Other activities of the national economy	209.96	201.51	210.97	211.75	248.05	242.49	261.83	289.88	333.42	295.08	302.98

Source: calculated based on data provided by the Ministry of Public Finance (annual financial statements of companies active in the real economy of Romania)

Tab. 8: Evolution of the turnover rate of the assets during the period 2007–2017 for the development regions in Romania (%)

No.	**Development regions**	**2007**	**2008**	**2009**	**2010**	**2011**	**2012**	**2013**	**2014**	**2015**	**2016**	**2017**
1		158.31	151.89	140.00	133.94	141.68	150.58	143.56	146.19	150.82	162.02	156.41
2	NORTH-WEST	155.74	149.19	138.04	130.60	135.36	144.83	137.68	141.04	150.10	161.47	162.30
3	NORTH – EAST	176.54	157.80	150.72	141.59	147.95	152.42	141.43	146.54	152.97	167.20	165.05
4	SOUTH – WEST	190.41	172.70	162.42	159.34	167.91	176.78	167.14	170.54	178.26	186.34	181.44
5	SOUTH – EAST	180.01	167.99	157.80	148.28	153.16	160.96	152.28	153.28	160.53	171.69	170.43
6	SOUTH	166.14	163.52	144.95	140.54	148.24	155.31	149.12	151.20	155.83	171.41	169.83
7	CENTRE	172.71	161.22	152.20	145.21	146.97	155.75	151.14	154.42	160.60	170.73	169.02
8	WEST	149.01	153.31	131.14	128.30	135.28	139.74	135.19	133.26	138.88	149.94	147.26

Source: calculated based on data provided by the Ministry of Public Finance (annual financial statements of companies active in the real economy of Romania)

The turnover rate of the total assets is calculated according to the formula below, respectively:

$$V_{rot} = \frac{Vt}{At} * 100$$

where,
Vt = Total income;
At = Total assets.

With regard to the turnover rate of assets in the branches of the real economy, during the period 2007–2017 there were significant increases in the turnover rate of assets in the following branches of activity: Education and Health and social assistance (an increase in the rate profitability of the real economy of 130.31 pp at 31 December 2017 compared to 31 December 2007 in the education branch). Moreover, at the regional level the breakdown by branches, for the period 2007–2017, is presented in the table above, respectively the region North-East and Center, with modest growth as shown in the table above, in the rest of the regions one can observe decrease (Tabs. 9 and 10).

Tab. 9: Evolution of labor productivity in the period 2007–2017 for branches of the real economy (lei; sal.)

No.	Branches of the national economy	2007	2008	2009	2010	2011	2012	2013	2014	2015	2016	2017
1	Agriculture, forestry and fishing	6442650	6625400	8926050	9642000	11952500	15035850	12796050	14090250	13858350	17755850	17909400
2	Extractive industry	7823560	10133783	9527525	9561450	10345100	11160100	10139625	12532000	16308450	14976500	12923400
3	Manufacturing industry	4647900	6317550	6365700	5232375	5918500	5893675	5588725	7924800	8372900	8344433	8100633
4	Production and supply of electricity and heat, gas, hot water and air conditioning	10346256	23070010	11465850	10429550	10866550	16372650	28499900	57242800	79740200	91812500	53147700
5	Water distribution, sanitation, waste management, decontamination activities	9439200	14871333	16455550	12522967	9578250	11093467	9548933	10076533	9270267	10498533	12037567
6	Constructions	3808033	4690867	5227750	5922450	4700967	7401100	6954700	7529050	8822150	8739400	8946950
7	Wholesale and retail trade, repair of motor vehicles and motorcycles	5787700	9100000	12277600	6331750	6701050	6739150	6173350	13424300	15940700	17336100	18300800
8	Transport and storage	5505150	6849700	5722750	6633400	7407750	7494800	7521500	7887200	8526950	8549650	17217500
9	Hotels and restaurants	4477350	6102250	4618850	4437250	4816050	4826350	4585750	5119550	6654800	7470000	8381450

10	Information and telecommunications	7269500	11333800	8735600	8957800	9612000	10499000	9735400	9876300	10014100	11603800	11877600
11	Real estate transactions, leasing and service activities mainly provided by companies	7592800	10277300	8719500	8858100	9668300	9180100	9176700	10030400	9898600	11000000	11572300
12	Professional, scientific and technical activities	7329100	9583300	7788100	7597800	8563800	8691100	8570500	8985400	9507000	9739400	10255000
13	Administrative service activities and support service activities	6342800	4543150	3730750	4264350	4824750	5433750	5013000	10672800	11344300	12716700	12957000
14	Education	3458550	2750667	3001500	3775000	4067500	4025000	3871450	8154700	9163400	9450500	9047300
15	Health and social assistance	2586700	3805050	3451250	3559500	4094350	4421250	4520450	5070850	5843150	6102800	13509900
16	Entertainment, culture and recreational activities	6288400	9531300	7406100	7528600	8707500	6035800	9211100	9834000	9949900	6997700	7154300
17	Other activities of the national economy	1757700	2281600	1935750	1945850	2157200	2433100	1953100	2131050	2533800	5850000	6059400

Source: calculated based on data provided by the Ministry of Public Finance (annual financial statements of companies active in the real economy of Romania)

Tab. 10: Evolution of labor productivity in the period 2007–2017 for development regions in Romania (lei; sal.)

No.	Development regions	2007	2008	2009	2010	2011	2012	2013	2014	2015	2016	2017
1	NORTH-WEST	4949450	6652100	5087250	5432750	5876300	6202100	5941100	6381550	7187500	7341950	15048500
2	NORTH – EAST	4892300	6444000	5226650	5448900	5814150	6124200	5793950	6327800	7235000	7425100	15339900
3	SOUTH – WEST	4368700	6568350	9344600	4716300	5047450	5004000	9228900	10199400	11927900	12729700	13440100
4	SOUTH – EAST	4831050	6499150	4994850	5120700	5540050	5544600	5305300	5713350	13205900	13571600	14135700
5	SOUTH	5141900	7196400	5378100	5589150	5905900	6126500	5860000	6313950	7100000	7440200	15373200
6	CENTRE	5280000	7233350	5511300	5848150	6449400	6731250	6449700	7043500	7952000	8065700	16927100
7	WEST	4950350	6678250	5061950	5403200	5825750	6033750	5951400	6520500	7348050	7705400	15976500
8	BUCHAREST – ILFOV	6324700	9253950	12923300	6681750	7217150	7226150	13851200	14389900	15676800	16187000	16811500

Source: calculated based on data provided by the Ministry of Public Finance (annual financial statements of companies active in the real economy of Romania)

The labor productivity indicator (in financial expression) is calculated according to the formula below, respectively:

$$W_f = \frac{Ca}{Ns}$$

where:
Ca= Fiscal value;
Ns= Number of employees.

Another relevant indicator regarding the competitiveness at the branches of the real economy is the labor productivity, during the period 2007–2017 there were important increases of the labor productivity in the following branches of activity respectively: Agriculture, forestry and fisheries, Extractive industry, Service activities administrative and support service activities Education and Health and social assistance (for example, labor productivity in the Administrative service activities and support service activities 48.95 %). Moreover, at the regional level the breakdown by branches, for the period 2007–2017, there is an increase of labor productivity in each development region (see in the table above), but the largest increase is observed from the data presented in Bucharest-Ilfov region (Tabs. 11 and 12).

Tab. 11: The evolution of the immediate solvency, between 2007 and 2017 for the branches of the real economy (%)

No.	Branches of the national economy	2007	2008	2009	2010	2011	2012	2013	2014	2015	2016	2017
1	Agriculture, forestry and fishing	99.28	88.18	92.89	94.20	95.92	93.52	98.02	102.90	106.71	107.29	118.09
2	Extractive industry	92.55	74.71	81.78	76.56	79.76	90.40	98.73	91.59	102.33	90.86	95.94
3	Manufacturing industry	89.94	83.94	84.83	83.17	85.44	86.96	94.65	102.69	116.52	109.84	122.20
4	Production and supply of electricity and heat, gas, hot water and air conditioning	106.62	106.14	126.55	134.21	120.70	88.36	86.65	79.44	78.44	65.04	62.14
5	Water distribution, sanitation, waste management, decontamination activities	111.39	98.74	113.38	119.76	117.22	115.85	116.25	136.90	148.34	143.51	178.58
6	Constructions	160.70	139.04	130.97	116.31	118.85	121.88	137.30	157.61	185.74	202.52	237.92
7	Wholesale and retail trade, repair of motor vehicles and motorcycles	56.58	54.32	51.33	48.46	50.37	51.13	54.87	59.67	68.39	71.24	79.17
8	Transport and storage	78.00	57.00	60.22	67.42	73.77	74.78	85.69	97.14	113.39	124.17	143.80
9	Hotels and restaurants	43.73	47.81	44.10	42.26	42.76	37.10	48.36	52.11	68.34	69.47	80.48

10	Information and telecommunications	154.81	160.35	162.62	156.45	181.45	217.55	214.97	239.95	291.23	371.29	467.26
11	Real estate transactions, leasing and service activities mainly provided by companies	109.00	104.95	114.23	102.03	115.20	133.18	145.94	157.25	218.48	204.03	243.63
12	Professional, scientific and technical activities	188.05	187.31	205.02	187.94	208.86	224.09	266.14	313.24	386.65	344.30	420.29
13	Administrative service activities and support service activities	177.55	123.87	134.81	128.63	153.76	140.29	189.99	220.19	270.75	236.32	276.63
14	Education	65.76	61.27	60.50	50.19	62.74	66.14	98.73	117.54	159.65	189.75	189.06
15	Health and social assistance	100.87	105.04	102.67	104.89	113.22	118.17	152.78	179.96	231.72	279.96	366.03
16	Entertainment, culture and recreational activities	112.38	141.28	151.73	138.11	157.84	79.98	220.69	257.03	316.33	202.10	280.92
17	Other activities of the national economy	47.70	43.87	38.05	37.17	37.01	55.59	40.12	40.88	48.67	82.01	92.82

Source: calculated based on data provided by the Ministry of Public Finance (annual financial statements of companies active in the real economy of Romania)

Tab. 12: The evolution of the immediate solvency in the period 2007–2017 for development regions in Romania (%)

No.	Development regions	2007	2008	2009	2010	2011	2012	2013	2014	2015	2016	2017
1	NORTH-WEST	103.41	96.57	96.70	90.57	94.78	99.19	110.73	123.08	143.35	148.39	173.71
2	NORTH – EAST	91.40	88.40	89.24	84.90	92.12	98.12	113.03	127.27	152.24	162.53	190.17
3	SOUTH – WEST	74.56	75.00	71.41	69.25	74.15	78.16	87.63	98.16	121.54	125.72	150.61
4	SOUTH – EAST	84.33	84.81	79.37	74.36	79.52	82.25	92.51	102.53	124.23	130.91	152.17
5	SOUTH	91.65	89.21	83.61	78.98	82.73	86.54	96.08	107.72	124.42	131.56	148.33
6	CENTRE	94.01	91.52	95.86	88.92	97.73	103.11	117.46	133.36	157.67	156.89	178.56
7	WEST	93.25	87.87	84.94	80.56	87.26	90.76	103.00	113.28	129.76	133.64	154.80
8	BUCHAREST – ILFOV	117.44	111.83	111.43	99.25	102.91	104.55	113.35	122.10	142.12	147.64	175.57

Source: calculated based on data provided by the Ministry of Public Finance (annual financial statements of companies active in the real economy of Romania)

The Immediate Solvency indicator is calculated as follows:

$$S_i = \frac{Ac - St}{Dt} * 100$$

where:
Ac= Current assets;
St= Stocks;
Dt= Total debts.

Immediate solvency is another relevant indicator for competitiveness in the branches of the real economy, during the period 2007–2017 there were significant increases of the immediate solvency in all branches of activity except branch Production and supply of electricity and heat, gas, water heat and air conditioning which decreased from 106.62 pp at 62.14 p.p. Moreover, at the regional level the breakdown by branches, for the period 2007–2017, there is an increase of the immediate solvency in each development region (see in the table above), but the largest increase is observed from the data presented in North-East region (Tabs. 13 and 14).

Tab. 13: Evolution of the average gross value added per employee in the period 2007–2017 for the branches of the real economy (lei; sal.)

No.	Branches of the national economy	2007	2008	2009	2010	2011	2012	2013	2014	2015	2016	2017
1	Agriculture, forestry and fishing	943500	1017233	1480150	1500700	1834250	2243650	1991100	2223950	2321750	2889500	3008100
2	Extractive industry	1478740	1730150	1905150	1845525	1985250	2339875	2292775	2124050	2900075	3254925	3283720
3	Manufacturing industry	846225	1260775	1471233	1085025	1267700	1261825	1208400	1688600	1872400	2091067	2238967
4	Production and supply of electricity and heat, gas, hot water and air conditioning	1666089	3504910	2315950	1363950	1423800	2055450	2032200	4010600	12147100	18652400	20841100
5	Water distribution, sanitation, waste management, decontamination activities	737500	1566867	1795600	1223233	1176400	1398400	1216533	1456567	1669500	1990867	2441733
6	Constructions	606033	884000	1170450	1093900	874467	1224450	1131900	1223800	1389050	1635100	1824500
7	Wholesale and retail trade, repair of motor vehicles and motorcycles	535300	938150	1447000	701900	820800	809950	788100	1619500	1825300	2252400	2660100
8	Transport and storage	928900	1341700	1348850	1290050	1259300	1168650	1094900	1116050	1246800	1434800	3246700

9	Hotels and restaurants	708750	1089500	934000	893400	1084650	1099500	1066950	1151800	1348350	1701200	2014150
10	Information and telecommunications	899000	1567100	1346200	1295500	1305000	1274600	1264000	1128700	1219700	1273600	1378900
11	Real estate transactions, leasing and service activities mainly provided by companies	1059500	2034400	1629800	1635600	1644200	1443900	1206500	1072500	1110400	1242100	1428800
12	Professional, scientific and technical activities	941300	1413700	1263100	1270900	1301500	1276900	1098800	1039500	1111100	1440300	1644600
13	Administrative service activities and support service activities	764800	878200	774900	835000	867400	866800	858250	1754000	1878400	2146800	2360100
14	Education	861050	813533	1040350	1200800	1131550	993800	885250	1758100	1747400	1795900	1741400
15	Health and social assistance	711250	1045850	1112150	1160000	1263100	1352700	1298000	1361950	1430300	1338650	2839700
16	Entertainment, culture and recreational activities	791500	1368900	1196000	1217000	1227100	1049400	1088700	1029900	970100	917200	882000
17	Other activities of the national economy	633700	873400	808400	789500	950550	767400	884700	928700	1022250	1857000	2120800

Source: calculated based on data provided by the Ministry of Public Finance (annual financial statements of companies active in the real economy of Romania)

Tab. 14: Evolution of the average gross value added per employee in the period 2007–2017 for the development regions in Romania (lei; sal.)

No.	Development regions	2007	2008	2009	2010	2011	2012	2013	2014	2015	2016	2017
1	NORTH-WEST	654900	1077900	935600	949600	1066750	1032650	982150	1012750	1126050	1282750	2818800
2	NORTH – EAST	636400	1001300	881600	850700	1008800	1017950	971400	1004050	1127250	1321900	2867500
3	SOUTH – WEST	483000	933950	1303900	630150	734600	730300	1426200	1514000	1807000	2174000	2475200
4	SOUTH – EAST	585400	969250	809550	771300	879700	871650	836000	884750	1987800	2320900	2618800
5	SOUTH	586900	983850	827500	802050	959900	953500	920050	960200	1067700	1261900	2777500
6	CENTRE	784000	1239200	1081350	1055150	1187250	1160050	1085850	1130500	1250700	1423900	3166400
7	WEST	745650	1140350	933200	920950	1055950	1056800	1000600	1043500	1151700	1329950	2936900

Source: calculated based on data provided by the Ministry of Public Finance (annual financial statements of companies active in the real economy of Romania)

The VAB; employee indicator is calculated according to the formula:

$$Vab/s = \frac{Csa + Am + Pbt}{Ns}$$

where:
Csa = staff costs;
Am = expenses related to the depreciation of tangible assets;
Pbt = gross profit (profit-loss balance);
Ns = Number of employees.

From our point of view the most relevant indicator is GVA; employee and reflects the competitiveness at the branches of the real economy, in the period 2007–2017. Among the branches with the largest growth and which have an impact on the real economy are Agriculture, Forestry and Fisheries, Education and Health. Moreover, at the regional level the breakdown by branches, for the period 2007–2017, is observed an increasing evolution of the average gross value added per employee in the period 2007–2017 for the development regions in Romania (lei; sal.) (See in table above), but the largest increase is observed from the data presented in the Center region.

External competitiveness Romania's net international investment position (PIIN) has continued to improve. PIIN reached -49.9 % of GDP in 2016, almost 5 % points above the level of 2015 (chart 3). This decrease occurred despite the deepening of the current account deficit and is mainly due to a strong GDP growth. Foreign direct investment (FDI) remained generally stable as a share of GDP, while the share of other external liabilities decreased as Romania repaid its external debt, a trend that is expected to continue (Fig. 3).

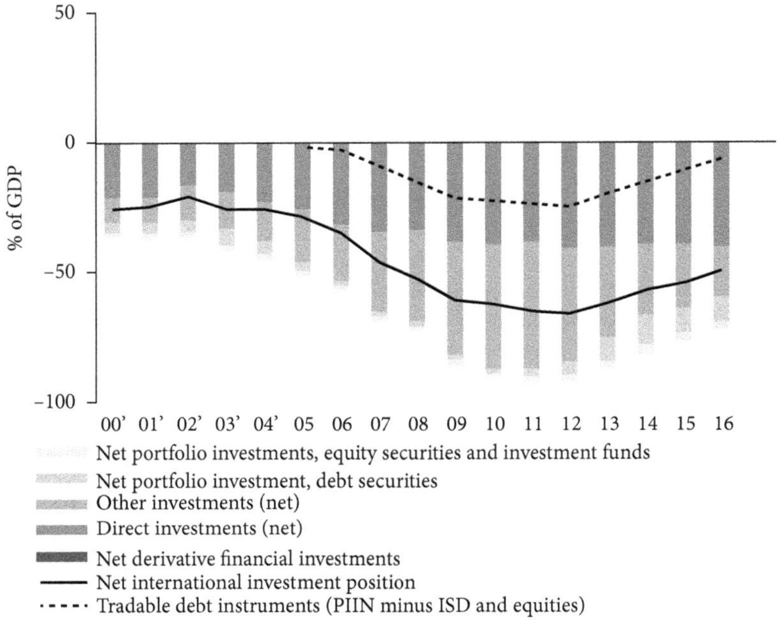

Fig. 3: Net international investment position
(1) Data corroborated BPM5; BPM6-ESA 2010.Source: European Commission, 2018.

Conclusions

Following the harmonization of the interests of the new Member States in order to align with the general standards imposed by the European Union, the structure of the Romanian economy has undergone transformations both as a structure, but especially in terms of its competitiveness and dynamics, with a direct impact on internal economic convergence and external. Moreover, periods of recession and economic decline, although generating imbalances, in some extremely serious cases, can be perceived in certain situations, as generating progress. This fact is argued by the adaptive capacity that involves developing new policies and strategies to be able to evolve (see the evolution of the IT sector in the economy). The combination of efforts focused on finding new solutions to restore balance and, going further, to register increased levels of performance ultimately leads to economic growth. The process of globalization affecting today's economies everywhere, considered as the most complex form of internationalization of economic activity (Afonso, Furceri, 2007), implies absolutely reaching a high level of convergence between economies. Being a result of progress, economic competitiveness and human innovation and being based in particular on trade and financial flows, economic growth implies the continuous integration of economies, which can be noticed especially at EU level. In order for this integration process to take place in the optimal parameters, it is necessary to have a system of supranational supervision and regulation that coordinates the activity of each state in order to establish general policies to be followed in order to meet common objectives based on performance indicators and of competitiveness.

Over time, the impact of integration on the process of growth and convergence has been a much debated issue. In Iain Begg's (2006) sense of effects generated can be grouped into three main categories:

- changes in the macroeconomic structure at national level;
- transformations of the labor market (the phenomenon of labor migration) with a direct impact on the competitiveness of industries at national and European level;
- effects induced on the structure of the economy.

The recent accession stages are only a step towards intensifying the convergence at the level of the new EU Member States with the existing community structures. The next natural step is the adoption of the common currency, an issue so far certified by five new Member States (Slovenia, Slovakia, Malta, Cyprus and Estonia). Seven other states, among the new states that joined the European Union, including Romania, are making intense efforts to fulfill all the commitments that this important process implies. On this subject, the Maastricht convergence criteria, known as the formal criteria that an aspiring member of the euro area membership must meet, serve as a reference point. Recently, the representatives of the European Central Bank at the NBR conference of May 24, 2019 stated "... in addition to the convergence criteria from Maastricht, institutional convergence will also be introduced ...," which determines us to specify that in addition to the clear and good criteria known, there will be other criteria that will depend on the institutional capacity of each Member State.

The convergence criteria established by the Maastricht (Apergis et al., 2010; Begg, 2006), treaty have aroused over time a series of controversies due to both theoretical approaches and empirical analysis. Thus, a series of questions were raised regarding their role in ensuring macroeconomic stability as well as the connection that is established between these criteria and the economic growth of a country. The main idea was that a monetary union can exist only between states that have reached a certain level of nominal convergence that can be translated into achieving a high degree of harmonization of macroeconomic policies. But are these criteria sufficient to assess the ability of an economy to give up its own currency in favor of a common one?

Certainly, in addition to these criteria, more attention should be paid to a particular category of indicators whose GDP; capita, implicit to the real economy, is important. This indicator is an integral part of what is known as real convergence. Although these criteria do not have a foundation established by treaties, such as the one in Maastricht, the officials of the European Central Bank have supported the introduction of these criteria, in addition to those on nominal convergence for Central and Eastern European countries that joined the EU in. 2004 and 2007. Hans Reckers, an official of the Bundesbank's management committee, suggested in a statement in the Financial Times in September 2000 that the accession of new states to EMU should be conditional on the recording of an average GDP; capita at the level of these Member States 70 % of the EU average.

Convergence, both from a nominal and a real point of view, together with a number of other complementary factors, constitutes one of the impetuous premises necessary for the efficient functioning of any monetary union and even more so than that existing at the level of the European Union (Backe, Thimann, 2004). A harmonious interweaving of the functioning mechanisms existing at the level of the euro area is proving to be extremely important for both its member states and those outside the euro area or in the process of adopting the common currency due to the high degree of interconnectedness of these economies. The existence of a vast specialized literature in this field has allowed us to outline some reference frameworks regarding the different methodologies for assessing the degree of convergence between economies as well as the determining factors of this process in conjunction with the one of economic growth. The focal point of this scientific endeavor was to provide answers to a series of questions that continue to arouse the interest of economists, politicians, businessmen or simply citizens of the European Union, namely: What is the current state of convergence at European Union level? Is convergence a stimulating factor of economic growth? What is the optimal mix of policies that ensure a sustainable degree of convergence? Does the convergence directly influence national and European competitiveness? During the present paper one of the central objectives was to evaluate the degree of convergence of the national economy in the current context of economic convergence at the level of European economies, based on the analysis of the macroeconomic framework at national level, on the analysis of the economic sectors with competitive potential, on the territorial dimension of competitiveness at national level, on monitoring and evaluating the competitiveness of companies at national level, on analyzing Romania's place according to the global competitiveness index, etc.

The most relevant indicator that shows whether the economy of the states converges towards each other at European level is given by the growth rate of GDP; capita. In order to validate this assertion, models of convergence testing were used, respectively Sigma convergence testing using the coefficient of variation and Beta convergence using econometric modeling using software.

Focusing on the development of these sectors should be a basic objective of the national authorities at the level of these economies if the convergence and sustainable economic growth are pursued. Long-term sustainability is also extremely important because finding compromise solutions that will only produce results over short periods of time is not a successful strategy and, moreover, it can trigger a negative effects gear that could be felt by states after a certain period of time and which can cause massive economic imbalances (Anghelache et al., 2006). Despite the fact that the results of the statistical methods confirm the hypothesis of convergence at the level of the new Member States, the extremely large gap that exists between these economies and the average of the European Union or the euro area must be taken into account, an aspect surprised in the analysis undertaken by us by estimating the number of years needed to achieve convergence. Future strategies must be geared towards reducing these differences in particular so that the convergence process is truly a perfect one.

The impact of the economic-financial crises on the economies of Central and Eastern Europe has led to a reconfiguration of the models of economic growth, of the processes of convergence as well as of the economic policies engaged for this purpose. Considering these aspects as well as those mentioned above we can conclude the following:

a) the quality and sustainability of the convergence process is an essential indicator of the economic growth of each economy;
b) achieving a sustainable convergence requires a long period of time;
c) the new EU Member States are showing convergence trends among themselves, but in relation to the EU average, many actions still need to be taken.

These considerations must be taken into account by the national authorities when developing either the strategies for adopting the common currency, or for economic growth or competitiveness at national level. Moreover, the analysis of the real economy based on the accounting balances of the companies active in the economy, we consider that should be one of the basic tools for the elaboration of policies and strategies, especially in the economic field (fiscal and financial). By extrapolating this analysis to the European states, we could identify more clearly the economic branches that are strategic for one state or another, and in this sense, the financing programs within the multiannual financial framework could be oriented.

The ability of the new Member States to adapt to macroeconomic changes has been proven by the level of convergence that exists between these competitive economies. Under current conditions, this ability will prove to be vital and will be a representative indicator of the economic progress of the European Union member countries.

References

Afonso, A., Furceri, D., (2007), "Business Cycle Synchronization and Insurance Mechanisms in the EU", Working Papers 2007/26, Department of Economics at the School of Economics and Management (ISEG), Technical University of Lisbon.

Anghelache, C., Isaic-Maniu, A., Mitruț, C., Voineagu, V., (2006), "The System of Indicators Used to Measure Poverty", available at: https://www.researchgate.net/publication/4982435_Indicators_System_for_Poverty_Measurement, accesed 12.03.2019.

Apergis, N., Gabrielsen A., Payne J., (2012), "Testing for Convergence in the European Insurance Sector: A Non-Linear Factor Approach", Asian Journal of Finance & Accounting, Vol. 4, no. 2, 493–545.

Apergis, N., Panapoulou, E., Tsoumas, C., (2010), "Old Wine in a New Bottle: Growth Convergence Dynamics in the EU", Atlantic Economic Journal, Vol. 38, 169–181.

Backe, P., Thimann, C., (2004), "The Acceding Countries Strategies towards ERM II and the Adoption of the Euro: An Analytical Review", European Central Bank Occasional paper no. 10.

Becker et al., (2010), "Whiter Growth in Central and Eastern Europe? Policy Lessons for an Integrated Europe", Bruegal and WIIW, Vol. 11, 131–147.

Begg, Iain, (2006), "Is Full Participation in the EMU Likely to Favor or Slow Real Convergence", published in Living standards and the Wealth of Nations-Successes and failures in real convergence, MIT Press, Cambridge, London.

Bodea, G., Mihuț, I. S., (2013), About Feed-Back-Change in the Context of Financial Crisis Management, International Management Conference, Managerial Challenges of the Contemporary Society, Cluj-Napoca, Romania.

Brennen, S.; Kreiss, D., (2014). Digitalization and Digitization. Worship. Digit., p. 8.

Clerck, J.-P.D. Digitization, Digitalization and Digital Transformation: The Differences Available online: https://www.i-scoop.eu/digitization-digitalization-digital-transformation-disruption/ (accessed on Feb 11, 363 2019).

European Commission (EC) (2013), Commission Services Working Paper: Evaluation of the 2013 National Reform Program and Romania's Convergence Program, Brussels, 29.5.3013, SWD (2013) final.

European Commission (EC), Research & Innovation, Horizon 2020. Available at: http://ec.europa.eu/research/horizon2020/index_en.cfm.

Eurostat pocketbook (2013), Science, Technology and Innovation in Europe, 2013 Edition World Bank – Europe and Central Asia Region (2013), Functional Analysis of the RDI System in Romania, 2012. Available at: http://www.sgg.ro/docs/File/UPP/doc/rapoarte-finale-bm/etapa-II/Cercetare_RO_Romania%20RD&I%20Functional%20Review%20-%20Final%20Report-RO.pdf.

Global Competitiveness Report (2018), World Economic Forum (Geneva).

Government of Romania (GR_a), (2013a), National Strategy for Research, Development and Innovation 2014–2020.

Government of Romania (2013b), Convergence Program 2013–2016, Bucharest, April 2013, p. 24.

Gruber, Hätönen and Koutroumpis, (2014). Broadband Access in the EU: An Assessment of Future Economic Benefits, Telecommunications Policy, Vol. 38 (11), pp. 1046–1058.

IMD, World Competitiveness Factors (2006), available at http://www01.imd.ch/wcc/factors.

IMD, World Competitiveness Yearbook, May 2013, by IMD – World Competitiveness Center (Lausanne).

Kagermann, H., (2015). Change through Digitization — Value Creation in the Age of Industry 4.0. In Management of Permanent Change; Springer, Switzerland, 2015; pp. 23–45.

Manta, O., (2019). The Role of Competitiveness on the Sustainability of the National Real Economy, ISSN 2537-4222, The Journal Contemporary Economy, Vol. 4 (1), pp. 138–146.

Ministry of Foreign Affairs (2013), Main Commitments for the National Reform Program 2013, Annex no. 2, Romania, April 2013.

Ministry of Public Finance (MPF), Romania http://discutii.mfinante.ro/static/10/Mfp/Prezentarebuget2019.pdf, 2019, accessed on 23.07.2019.

National Bank of Romania (NBR), Financial Stability Report 2013, p. 93, available at www.bnro.ro/files/d/Pubs_en/RSF/RSF2013.pdf.

National Strategy for Competitiveness 2015–2020 and European Strategy for Research and Innovation 2021–2027.

NBR, Report on Financial Stability 2014, 2015, 2016, 2017, 2018.www.bnro.ro.

OECD (2016), OECD Competition Assessment Reviews: Romania, OECD Publishing, Paris, document available at: http://dx.doi.org/10.1787/9789264257450-en.

OECD (2017), Reviews of Evaluation and Assessment in Education, Kitchen, H., et al., Romania 2017, http://dx.doi.org/10.1787/9789264274051-en.

Parviainen, P.; Tihinen, M.; Kääriäinen, J.; Teppola, S., (2017). Tackling the Digitalization Challenge: How to Benefit from Digitalization in Practice. International Journal of Information Systems and Project Management, Vol. 5, 63–77.

Rachinger, M.; Rauter, R.; Müller, C.; Vorraber, W.; Schirgi, E., (2018). Digitalization and Its Influence on Business Model Innovation. Journal of Manufacturing Technology Management, Vol. 30, no. 8, pp. 1143–1160.

Rüßmann, M.; Lorenz, M.; Gerbert, P.; Waldner, M.; Justus, J.; Engel, P.; Harnisch, M., (2015), Industry 4.0: The Future of Productivity and Growth in Manufacturing Industries. Boston Consult. Group 2015, 9, 54–89. 352.

Stolterman, E.; Fors, A.C., (2004). Information Technology and the Good Life. In Information Systems Research; Springer; Boston, pp. 687–692.

Technopolis Group, GEA Strategy & Consulting, FMM Consultancy, "Mid-Term Evaluation of the National Strategy and of the National RD&I Plan 2007–13", Final Report, 23 January 2012, Bucharest, pp. 6–12.

World Bank (2013), "Competitive Cities. Remodeling the Economic Geography of Romania". Available at: http://www-wds.worldbank.org.

World Economic Forum (2017), Global Competitiveness Report 2017–2018, document available at: http://www3.weforum.org/docs/GCR2017-2018/05FullReport/TheGlobalCompetitivenessReport2017%E2%80%932018.pdf.

The World Bank (2011) "Romania Functional Review. Research, Development, and Innovation Sector", Final Report, 31 May, p. 21.

Rossitsa Rangelova, Valentin Bilyanski

Foreign trade and economic growth of Bulgaria and Romania in the years of EU membership

Abstract Bulgaria and Romania share similar political, social and economic development in the EU accession process and beyond. However, since 2007, economic data show many differences, which indicate that the two economies do not benefit equally from their EU membership and adapt to it differently. In most cases, Romania achieves better results. The key convergence indicator, such as GDP per capita in purchasing power standard (PPS), demonstrates the significant progress that Romania has made compared to Bulgaria in just 10 years. The report examines the dynamics and structural changes of foreign trade in a comparative plan between Bulgaria and Romania, as well as the dynamics of economic growth, with an attempt to establish a link between them. The period covers the years of EU membership of the two countries – from 2007 to 2018.

Keywords: foreign trade, economic growth, structural changes, Bulgaria, Romania, EU

Introduction

During the period of transition to a market economy and preparation for EU accession, Bulgaria and Romania faced similar problems. The deterioration of the production structure and the inability of most enterprises to adapt and compete at the markets of the developed countries have led to an equally significant problem for the two economies, namely the low value added of their output. Another problem was the loss of the foreign markets within the former COMECON, and especially in the former Soviet Union, which was more relevant to Bulgaria.

Both countries endured sharp deterioration of the economic environment, as in the period of initial capital accumulation, any inappropriate solution in the privatization process was justified by the need for rapid privatization. The absence of a transition strategy in Bulgaria, the way reforms were implemented, and the lack of care to preserve what was achieved in industrial development, the postponed and shock privatization, and then the lack of post-privatization control had a decisive impact on the dynamics of the production and the efficiency of the industry (Rangelova and Sariiski, 2019, 23–37). Different programs for alternative employment and alternative production have been developed to mitigate the adverse effects. Strategies for attracting foreign direct investment and for restructuring production activities have been implemented, the main effect of which has been the gradual reorientation of local producers to subcontracting and component production, mainly for large companies in Western Europe.

Bulgaria and Romania have undertaken significant efforts to build functioning market economies and to meet other conditions for EU accession (From Uneven Growth to Inclusive Development, 2018). They have achieved economic progress. The two countries have become full members of the EU at 1 January 2007. As economic data show, the two economies do not benefit equally from EU membership, they adapt to it differently.

The report examines the specifics of the relationship between foreign trade and economic growth in Bulgaria and Romania. The analysis covers the period 2007–2018, including the years of membership of both countries in the EU so far. In addition, it provides a benchmark against developments before their accession to the EU and provides an opportunity to take into account the state of foreign trade and GDP before the onset of the last global financial crisis, crisis and post-crisis development. In fact, the period under consideration completes more or less the adaptation of the production structure to the conditions of the EU single market and participation in integration policies.

1. Dynamics of the Bulgarian and Romanian GDP

At the beginning of the transition to market economy Bulgaria and Romania had relatively close economic performance (Rangelova and Sariiski, 2017, 19–30). In 2006, the difference between them in GDP per capita based on PPS (EU average = 100 %) was only 2 % points (p.p.), respectively 37 % for Bulgaria and 39 % for Romania. By 2017, Bulgaria managed to increase the indicator by only 12 p.p. and reached 49.2 %, while Romania managed to improve the ratio to 63.5 %, thus showing faster convergence with other EU countries.

With the onset of the global financial crisis, Romania's GDP contracted by 5.5 % in 2009 against -3.6 % for Bulgaria. This forces the government to seek international assistance from the IMF, the EU and other financial institutions. Since 2011, the country has again registered growth, mainly generated by stable exports and, in the last few years, by household final consumption expenditures (growing at about 2 times higher rates than those in Bulgaria). After the crisis, economic growth in Romania is invariably higher than in Bulgaria.

In 2018, Bulgaria was among the New Member States (NMS) with the lowest economic growth. The growth was 3.1 % against 5.1 % in Poland, 4.9 % in Hungary, 4.8 % in Latvia, 4.5 % in Slovenia, 4.1 % in Romania and Slovakia. Such economic growth cannot have a noticeable impact on poverty reduction, overcome economic and social inequalities, and fulfil the role of inclusive catch-up development. On the contrary, with the post-crisis pace of economic growth, Bulgaria is increasingly establishing itself as the least developed economy in the EU.

The dynamics of the individual components of GDP for 2018 compared to 2006 show that in none of them Bulgaria has achieved better results than Romania (Fig. 1). An increase in household final consumption expenditure is a manifestation of the faster improving purchasing power and, to a certain extent, of the standard of living of Romanian citizens – in 2018 compared to 2006, it was 58.1 % in Romania and 42.7 % in Bulgaria.

The dynamics of investment in both countries follow a similar trend – a sharp increase over the pre-accession period to the EU and over the first years of the membership, which coincide with the time before the global financial and economic crisis and a sharp decline during and after it. Romania has seen some recovery after reaching the bottom in 2010. In Bulgaria, there is no sign of recovery of pre-crisis levels, and even more there is stagnation in investment activity. A significant weakness of the Bulgarian economy is the insufficient domestic investment, which coincides with the declining inflow of foreign direct investment and the deterioration of their structure.

The exports, regarded as the engine of the Bulgarian economy, also has significantly lower performance than that of Romanian. Romania's exports of goods in real terms over the membership period have increased more than 4 times, while Bulgaria's exports – 2.7 times. Over the same period, exports of services from Romania increased by 63.1 %, while those of Bulgaria decreased by 18.9 %. Due to the slowdown in export growth in Bulgaria and also due to stronger domestic demand (incl. for consumer goods) affecting the volumes of imports, net exports, which until recently were a major driver of growth, have already made a negative contribution to overall growth (Bobeva and Zlatinov, 2019, 103–137).

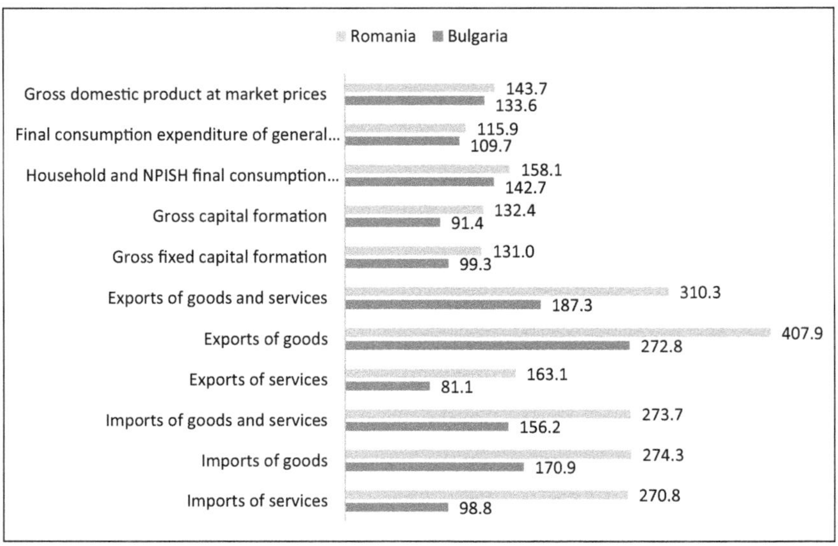

Fig. 1: GDP and its components in 2018, 2006 = 100 %

Source: Eurostat, Economy and Finance, National Accounts.

Different rates of change in GDP components also lead to changes in its structure (Tab. 1). In both economies, the share of final consumption expenditure of general government remains almost at the same level in 2018 compared to 2007. The most significant changes are observed in the share of investments, with share in Romania was higher than the share in Bulgaria at the beginning of the period, but also the decrease is higher – by 14.1 p.p. to 21.2 %, in Bulgaria the reduction is 9.3 p.p. – up to 19 %. The share of household final consumption expenditure also decreases to a lesser extent. These components of GDP are losing ground at the expense of exports, which directly demonstrates its growing role in the economic development of the two countries during a period under consideration. The share of imports in GDP is moving in opposite directions in the two countries – an increase for Romania and a decrease for Bulgaria, but Bulgaria remains a much more import-dependent country.

Tab. 1: GDP structure of Bulgaria and Romania, and correlation between the rate of change in GDP and that of its individual components

	GDP structure, %				**Correlation between the rate of change of GDP and that of its components, 2006–2018**	
	BG		RO		BG	RO
	2007	2018	2007	2018		
GDP	100.0	100.0	100.0	100.0		
Final consumption expenditure of general government	16.7	16.5	15.4	16.6	0.56	0.62
Household and NPISH final consumption expenditure	68.5	61.9	67.4	62.5	0.85	0.92
Gross capital formation, incl.:	33.6	20.7	31.3	24.2	0.80	0.76
Gross fixed capital formation	28.3	19.0	35.3	21.2	0.75	0.70
Exports of goods and services, incl.:	52.4	64.5	24.7	41.6	0.63	0.47
Exports of goods	36.5	49.0	17.2	30.5	0.57	0.26
Exports of services	15.9	15.5	7.5	11.2	0.19	0.53
Imports of goods and services, incl.:	71.2	63.6	38.8	44.9	0.81	0.62
Imports of goods	60.0	53.7	33.7	37.8	0.78	0.52
Imports of services	11.2	9.9	5.1	7.1	0.29	0.79
Foreign trade balance of goods and services, incl.:	-18.8	0.9	-14.1	-3.3		
Foreign trade balance of goods	-23.5	-4.7	-16.5	-7.3		
Foreign trade balance of services	4.7	5.6	2.4	4.1		
Trade Openness	123.6	128.1	63.5	86.5		

Source: Author's calculations based on data from Eurostat, Economy and Finance, National Accounts.

The correlation coefficient in Bulgaria between the rates of change in exports of goods and services and GDP for the period 2007–2018 is 0.63, and the one between imports of goods and services and GDP is 0.81, which shows a greater dependence of GDP on imports than of exports of goods and services (Tab. 1). The corresponding coefficients in Romania are significantly lower, 0.47 and 0.62. This indicates that the performance and development of the Bulgarian economy, as a more open economy, is more influenced by the international economic situation. On the other hand, the correlation of imports and exports of services and GDP in Romania is significantly higher than that of imports and exports of goods only, which indicates a more intense foreign trade activity of this country in the services sector.

2. Dynamics of the Bulgarian and Romanian foreign trade flows

2.1. Trade openness and the role of exports and imports for economic the growth

Practice shows that as a result of integration into a common market such as the EU, there is an increase in the volume and share of intra-community trade in the total foreign trade flows of the participating countries. Both in Bulgaria and Romania, there has been an increase in trade openness (ratio of exports plus imports to GDP) to EU countries over the period under consideration. As a rule, integration processes stimulate foreign trade, especially within the community, but at the same time create conditions for amplifying the negative effects for the participating economies in times of economic crisis (Marinov, E., 2019, 63–82).

A comparative analysis of the trade openness of the two economies shows that the relative share of exports and imports as a percentage of GDP for Bulgaria is significantly higher than for Romania. However, the rise of the indicator is much higher for Romania – from 65.3 % to 86.5 %, i.e. by 21.2 p.p., while for Bulgaria it is from 123.6 % to 128.1 %, i.e. only by 4.5 p.p. The slower increase in the trade openness of the Bulgarian economy can be explained by the much higher starting values (the share of foreign trade is well above 100 % of GDP), which is hard to increase significantly. Moreover, the slight increase is due both to the relatively slower growth of exports of goods and services and to the relative decline in imports of goods and services to GDP in Bulgaria. The role of foreign trade in economic growth can be analyzed through the contribution of exports and imports to the GDP rate of change (Zlatinov, D., 2018, 211–226).

During the period under consideration, the relationship between the two indicators in Bulgaria and Romania underwent similar changes (Fig. 2). From the beginning of EU membership to 2011, the rate of change of GDP and the contribution of foreign trade moved in the opposite direction – GDP growth was accompanied by an increase in the negative contribution of foreign trade to its rate of change. This is an expression of the high trade openness of both economies, the underdeveloped industry and the high dependence on imports of consumer and investment goods. In other words, the increasing purchasing power and investment activity during the economic expansion is largely satisfied by imported products. On the contrary, the sharp contraction of the economy during the global financial and economic crisis has led to a much stronger contraction in imports relative to exports, thus foreign trade was playing a role in limiting GDP decline. After 2012, the nature of the relationship is gradually changing – the direction of GDP change and the contribution of foreign trade are both starting to move in the same direction, reflecting the greater role that foreign trade and exports particularly play in economic activity.

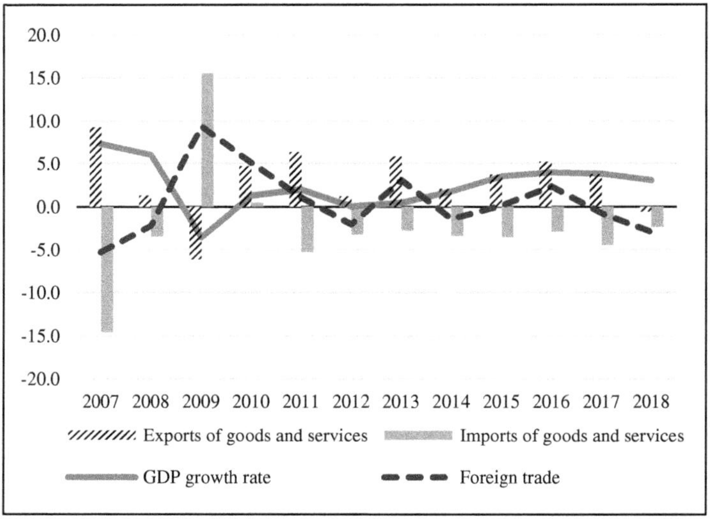

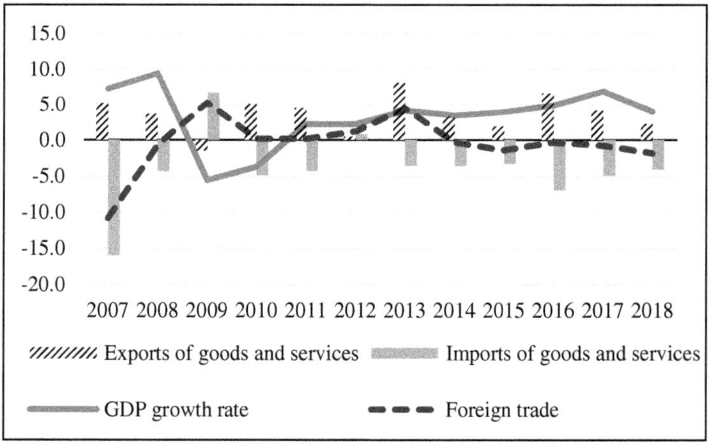

Fig. 2: Role of exports, imports and foreign trade in GDP change (percentage points) and GDP change rate (%) – Bulgaria (left chart) and Romania (right chart)

Source: Author's calculations based on data from Eurostat, Economy and Finance, National Accounts.

3. Dynamics of foreign trade flows

The dynamics of exports of goods and services follow similar trends in the two countries, with Romania's exports characterized by greater fluctuations and usually higher growth rates. Encouraged by the accession to the EU single market, exports of both countries increased by more than 20 % in 2007, with the pace of growth slowing down since the beginning of the 2008 global financial and economic crisis. In 2009, there was a decrease, two times bigger for Bulgaria than for Romania. However, the declines in exports were significantly less than that of imports, which reflected in a drastic contraction of the countries' trade deficit, Bulgaria even reached a trade surplus in 2011. Thus, foreign trade acted as a kind of automatic stabilizer for the economies of both countries. After the global financial and economic crisis, Bulgaria has not been able to recover and even moves closer to its pre-crisis export growth rates, while weak import growth rates are helping maintain a trade surplus in some years. It should be noted that this surplus is due to trade in services, which manages to cover the deficit in trade in goods.

Unlike Bulgaria, Romania has managed to reach or approach pre-crisis export growth rates in some years, with rates twice as high as those in Bulgaria. Romania also has a trade surplus in services, but is unable to cover the deficit in goods.

During the period under consideration, exports and imports of Bulgaria and Romania predominantly follow the general trend of EU foreign trade flows, but the pace of change is higher – both in growth and in times of decline. In 2018, however, Bulgaria was the only EU country to report a decline in exports of goods and services. This was entirely due to the drop in exports of goods, which can be explained by the economic problems of neighboring countries and major trading partners – Turkey and Greece, as well as a decline in exports to other neighboring countries – Serbia and North Macedonia, Russian economic sanctions imposed to the EU, which hinder exports, etc.

In both countries, intra-community exports are characterized by a much lower degree of variation than exports to third countries. This applies to total exports to the EU or to group of third countries, but also to the individual countries into the two groups, i.e. it cannot be said that fluctuations in exports outside the EU are due to the greater number of trading partners and the presence of those with which smaller and occasional transactions are carried out. A reasonable assumption can be made that companies from Bulgaria and Romania are better integrated into the supply chain with EU partners, which is at the heart of a long-lasting and sustainable relationship. This cannot be said to be true with non-EU counterparties. It should also be noted that intra-community trade is more resilient in times of crisis.

4. Changes in the product structure of exports

In the years of EU membership, the exports of both countries have undergone similar changes, but they are different in strength and intensity. Both Bulgaria and Romania registered a decline in the share of exports of primary commodities. In

2006, primary commodities accounted for 44.7 % of Bulgarian exports (peaking at just over 50 % in 2012 and 2013), dropping to 38.8 % in 2018.[1] In nominal terms, however, exports of raw materials for the years during the period under consideration doubled from EUR 5.3 billion to EUR 10.9 billion. Share of primary commodities in exports to third countries decreased (from 58.6 % to 48.1 %), while exports to other EU Member States remained almost unchanged – a slight decrease from 36.3 % to 35.4 % (the share did not variate significantly over the years). The share of primary commodities in the total value of exports follows and is largely determined by the price dynamics of these products on international markets.

In Romania, where the share of primary commodities in total exports is generally much lower than in Bulgaria, it fell from 20.8 % to 17.3 %, with a decrease only in trade with third countries. The share of primary commodities in intra-community trade (13.6 %) is significantly lower, more than twice that in extra-EU trade (29.6 %). In contrast, the share of exports of finished products (machinery and transport equipment) from Romania is much higher than that of Bulgarian one – more than twice both to EU countries and to third countries. Romania is attracting investment in companies producing finished goods and managing to achieve it at significantly higher corporate tax rate. For example, the automotive industry is traditionally one of the leading industries of the Romanian economy. Romania is a leading car manufacturer in the region of Eastern Europe.[2] The share of car exports to international markets is also significant (over 20 %). Romania's geographical location defines it as a distribution center in the region with easy access to the relatively large markets of Russia, Turkey, Ukraine and Poland. Exports of automotive components also increased significantly (by 30 % in 2010). The manufactured components include electrical and electronic systems, tires, cables, steering wheels, gearboxes, safety systems, seats, and more.

Bulgaria has a relatively more active position compared to Romania regarding manufactured goods classified chiefly by material. The group is with diverse composition (includes leather, textile, rubber, paper, iron and steel, non-ferrous metals) and in most cases the products are not highly processed and with high value added. Non-ferrous metals, iron, and steel are the main products that participate in the Bulgarian exports of this group, and for most of the period under consideration they form between 60 % and 70 % of it.

It can be noted for Bulgaria that it retains predominantly commodity exporter. The country is emerging as an exporter of mainly low value added goods. Consumer imports continue to increase significantly (Nestorov, 2019, 54–58). Typical

1 The dynamics of the raw materials share is largely determined by fossil fuels. Without them, the primary commodities form from 28.2 % to 35.9 % of the total exports, and there are no particularly large fluctuations in values of this exports.

2 The country is the successor to two automotive plants - the Dacia (Renault division) and the Ford (Ford Motor Company). Dacia Duster is the bestselling model car made in Romania.

of Bulgaria's exports is that its value added is significantly lower than other EU economies, while it is much higher in imports. This shows the high dependence of the country on imports for realization of its foreign economic activity and significant presence in the global value chains (Panushev, 2017, p. 219).

5. Export structure according to its technological level

Along with the increase in the exports of industrial production, the structure of this exports by the quality of the used labor is changing in a favorable direction. The share of labor-intensive and resource-intensive products decreased significantly – by 13.3 p.p. to 22.3 % in Bulgaria and by 12.8 p.p. to 17.6 % in Romania for the period under consideration. The proportion of goods requiring low-skilled labor is also decreasing, with the decrease being more pronounced in Romania.

At the same time, in both countries the share of production requiring medium and high-level qualification workforce is increasing. Romania is far better represented both as a baseline and at the end of the period considered, and in 2018 it reached 58.4 % compared to 37.7 % for Bulgaria. There is also a slight increase in the share of production requiring highly skilled workforce – it is larger in Bulgaria – 5.0 p.p. to 25.2 % and less in Romania – 2.5 p.p. to 13.5 %. In both countries, especially in Bulgaria, the share of this type of products is higher in exports to third countries than in the intra-community exports. The processes described however are more intensive in trade with the EU than with third countries.

At the start of EU membership, the two countries had an equal share of high-tech exports in the total exports (3.5 %), which is among the lowest in the union. For Bulgaria it remained at this level until 2014, and afterward increased to 5.9 %. For Romania, this share is growing faster, reaching 8.4 % in 2018. Despite the increase, this share remains among the lowest in the EU-28, with the EU average at 16.1 % in 2007 and 17.9 % in 2018.

Conclusion

The export sector, considered to be the engine of economic growth in Bulgaria, also has significantly weaker positions than those of Romania. In the years of EU membership, Romania's exports of goods have increased significantly more than Bulgaria's, and the exports of services from Romania increased while those of Bulgaria decreased (in real terms). Bulgaria has a much more open economy than Romania. As a result of integration with EU countries, an increase in the volume and share of intra-community trade in the overall trade flows of these countries has been registered, with Romania being more pronounced.

The position of the least developed economies among the EU-28 countries remains for both countries, despite the reforms resulting from the accession process. However, the Romanian government's long-term strategy, aimed at providing a better environment for investors by creating an adequate institutional framework is proving favorable. In a relatively short time period, the country manages to achieve a significant improvement in its export structure (in terms of its value added) and higher growth rates.

For Bulgaria it is necessary to develop perspective industries and activities leading to production of higher value added products. Adequate management mechanisms could develop competitive national productions of higher value-added goods and services that can be traded both within and outside the EU.

References

Bobeva, Daniela; Zlatinov, Dimitar: Structural Imbalances and Risks for the Economy. In: Economic Development and Policies in Bulgaria: Estimates and Expectations. 2019 Annual Report Part Two. Topic of Focus: Structural Imbalances and Risks for the Economy. Economic Research Institute, BAS, ed. Gorex Press, Sofia, pp. 103–137. ISSN 1314–8893. [in Bulgarian]

Marinov, Eduard: Post-Crisis Development of Bulgarian International Trade Relations. Economic Thought Journal, (6), 2019. pp. 63–82. ISSN 0013-2993. [in Bulgarian]

Nestorov, Nedyalko: Foreign Trade. In: Economic Development and Policies in Bulgaria: Estimates and Expectations. 2019 Annual Report Part One. Economic Development and Medium-Term Expectations. Economic Research Institute, BAS, ed. Gorex Press, Sofia, 54–58. ISSN 1314-8893. [in Bulgarian]

Panushev, Emil: Bulgaria's Foreign Economic Orientation. In: The Bulgarian Economy: 10 Years in the European Union. 2017. pp. 213–220. FastPrintBooks. [in Bulgarian]

Rangelova, Rossitsa; Sariiski, Grigor: Bulgaria and Romania in EU: Economic Progress in Comparative Perspective. In: "Bulgaria and Romania & Country Members of the EU, Part of the Global Economy". International Scientific Conference Proceedings. ERI-BAS, Sofia, 2017. pp. 19–30. ISBN 978-854-9313-06-6.

Rangelova, Rossitsa; Sariiski, Grigor: Comparing Progress in Bulgaria and Romania. In: International Economics Department at BAS. 2019. International Scientific Conference Proceedings "Bulgaria and Romania: Country Members of the EU, Part of the Global Economy" – 2018. Sofia: ERI-BAS. pp. 23–37. ISBN: 978-954-9313-14-7. Available at: https://inecoconference.wordpress.com/2018-2/2018-papers/, retrieved on 15.06.2019.

World Bank Group: From Uneven Growth to Inclusive Development. Romania's Path to Shared Prosperity. Systematic Country Diagnostics (2018). IBRD/the World Bank. ISBN: 978-1-4648-1317-7, DOI: 10.1596/978-1-4648-1317-7.

Zlatinov, Dimitar: "The Validity of the Export-Oriented Economic Growth Hypothesis in Bulgaria. In: Is the Time of New Protectionism Coming?. Publishing House" St. Gregory Theologian, Sofia, 2018. pp. 211–226. [in Bulgarian]

Ioan I. Gâf-Deac, Sorin Mihai Radu, Ioan Petru Scutelnicu, Otilia Teodora Rachieru, Alina Roşca Ţurcanu, Viorel Streza

Linear governance: the new economy versus old production

Abstract In the article, the authors find that knowledge flows are nonlinear and this feature is crucial in the participation and influence of the generation of economic novelty, born of nonlinearity. The transition from linear to nonlinear also emphasizes meta-knowledge as a premise for the new economy. Nonlinear knowledge, as a result of meta-knowledge, is related to the human action capacity that has the predisposition of linear knowledge in economics. At the same time, we are witnessing the transition from the classical linear economy to the new nonlinear economy, based on knowledge and risk. The visibility of the nonlinear economy becomes mediated by the course of the real economy, through conceptual expressions related to the theory of value. The authors identify formulas for the qualitative transition from one set of economic conditions to another. New goods and services represent the "substance" of economic growth in the new continuous economy. It is observed that a network is not a hybrid form but rather a composition of forms, among which profitability is established as the formal closure; approach; articulation of the components is manifested, through which a compensatory transfer is achieved, attenuating conventional positivity accepted of the productive-economic processes. As such, the network in the system becomes a means of decision ("unit" of decision) for coherent behavioral adaptations of any productive-economic entity to the state of the environment and to disturbances.

Keywords: new economy, meta-knowledge, nonlinear economy, network transaction costs, variable economic geometry, linear governance

Introduction

Knowledge and technologies become incorporated in the function of neoclassical production, but also in that of modern and post-modern production.

Mainly, the new theories of growth prove their purpose in explaining the role of knowledge and technology in economic growth.

Evolutionary economic theories refer, through similarities, to the applicative side of systems theory. Technological and organizational changes through articulation offer an innovative perception of the trajectories of production processes.

As such, it is necessary to identify the essential elements that will induce economic growth trajectories, in segments; time intervals as long as possible. However, evolutionary theories do not foresee the visible inclusion; comprehension of knowledge in the neoclassical economic equilibrium, associated with the production function.

We find that knowledge flows are nonlinear and this feature is crucial in the participation and influence of the generation of economic novelty, born of nonlinearity. In this way static balances are obtained.

The uncertainties associated with investments in knowledge can be overcome with the help of well-defined organizational levels, namely those in the operational flow of macro-systems when the need is felt, in the short and medium term, for static balances.

Economic theories of social perspectives, starting from the linear managerial commitment to the nonlinear one in a network of knowledge flows, assume that there are social elements that mark the growth perspectives, such as: general societal characteristics; "Social effects" of knowledge in economic growth; the effects in society of the knowledge processes, as the differentiated use of the effective knowledge.

The transition from linear to nonlinear also emphasizes meta-knowledge as a premise for the new economy.

Metaknowledge is the knowledge about knowledge. In this context, it signifies a systemic problem in association with a dependent flow of knowledge in the real economy, characterized by the independence of knowledge from the future economy (Gâf-Deac, 2010).

A first level of meta-knowledge systemically involves modeling, learning and planning methods (Ciutacu, 2001).

The effectiveness of meta-knowledge has repercussions on intelligent entities made up of people, organizations, the economy, society as a whole.

Nonlinear knowledge, as a result of meta-knowledge, is related to the human action capacity that has the predisposition of linear knowledge in economics.

At the same time, we are witnessing the transition from the classical linear economy to the new nonlinear economy, based on knowledge and risk (Ciutacu, 1997).

The visibility of the nonlinear economy becomes mediated by the course of the real economy, through conceptual expressions related to the theory of value.

1. Literature review

Levy A. and Murname, A., (2006), systematize human capabilities, in an economic context, from the procedural perspective of knowledge, categories such as:

- The expert director. (It refers to solving problems in the economy for which solutions are not usually formulated. Information technologies assist human action by processing information that can be accessed and understood more operationally).
- The complex communicator. (It aims at the interaction between people in the economy, being realized the managerial persuasion).

- The applicant of the cognitive routine. (Intentions for linear economic action are mentally pre-formulated, and operationally is in routine economic processes).
- The applicant of the assembly routine. (Operations, considered linear, are repetitive in productive flows in which labor is predominantly physical, material, in tangible assets).
- The non-routine operations applicant. Actions begin to become nonlinear, distanced from liberalized regulatory knowledge, quasi-nonlinear in economic processing).

The new economy based on organization and nonlinearity must grow significantly by appealing to the expert director and the complex communicator.

The value, respectively the added value, are found explained in the general economic epistemology, but the trajectory of the evolutions of the effective, real economy towards the New Nonlinear Economy is characterized by stages and phases that refer to (Gâf-Deac, 2010):

- Classical political economy (William Petty; 1623–1687; founder of English political economy); French physiocrats. (F. Quesnay), further Adam Smith; 1723–1790; with The Wealth of Nations, 1776, and David Ricardo; 1772–1823, respectively, which express the differences between labor itself and labor power, John Stuart Mill; 1806–1873 with his paper Principles of Political
- Economy emphasizing economic commensurability, based on an objective or the cost of production.
- Marginalism (William Stanley Jevons; 1835–1882; expounding in The Theory of Political Economy/1871, the theory of the marginal utility of value; Leon Walras; 1839–1910; who advanced the idea of generalizing the intensive use of mathematical analysis in the study of general economic equilibrium; Alfred Marshall; 1842–1924 shows that price comes from aspects of marginal utility and Vilfredo Pareto; 1848–1923; supports the introduction of mathematical applications in economic analysis (Mind and Society, 1916).
- The economic model of the neoclassical economy (consolidated the use of the notion of utility in economic models based on: independent individual economic entity, achieving a state of market equilibrium, as the economy began to be perceived as a dynamic system, with operationality partial equilibria, which solved the deviations from the path of economic advance, as a whole of time.
- Economics based on structuralism (Emile Durkheim; 1858–1917/, showing that economics is a form of construction, with reflections in social construction; Ferdinand de Saussure; 1857–1913; who developed the methodology of operationalizing structuralism, aiming at economic functionalism, respectively pragmatism; John Maynard Keynes; 1883–1946; is the founder of the post-depression economy, advancing the thesis of state action (intervention) in market regulation and control; Milton Friedman (1992) is the architect of the post-1968 period, aiming at the conceptual departure from Keynesianism,

being accepted marginal substitution "between goods, and monetarism supports market force."
- Microeconomics and economic rationalism (refers to the thesis of the reform of return to "microeconomics" and the added value becomes the basic notion of economic theory and reference period.
- Post-structuralist economy (marks the actional, concrete delimitation between the schemes of economic management related to the so-called stabilized macro-economy and the visible beginning of the reform towards micro-economy).
- Economics of complexity (Since the 1980s there have been adaptations for the theory of general economic equilibrium, – Peter Albin, Duncan Foley, Brian Arthur and others for the "absolute rationality of behavioral presumption" of economic agents, "finite memory of behavior generating information; equivalent intelligence," "the speculative; speculative role of producers," economic artificial intelligence, – Kurt Gödel and Alan Turing, the problem of optimization, the complexity of language structure, becomes a precursor of formalizing hierarchy problems in the complexity of economic activities, – Naom Chomsky). Complex economic behavior emphasizes the unpredictable movement of economic activities towards different equilibrium states, or towards periodized behaviors, including chaotic ones. It is found that economic systems dominated by complexity are indefinitely sensitive to the initial and formally unpredictable conditions. Highly formalized economic models have complex general behavior. In this context, "border rationality" is the one that offers the most convenient ways to advance the "economic realism" of the New Economy.
- Economic complexity and development (as extremely simplified, essentialized expressions of the world). Simplification formalizes an immense complexity of the New Economy, as the speed of information movement in the flow of general knowledge increases. The modern economy is found in the network of relative partial equilibria, which ensures the faster and faster reproduction of production and business cycles, against the background of a continuous vacuum in the operationalized economic system.
- The "green" theory of value in the New Economy. (Essentially, the current GDP would become a notion that expresses "underestimation" and the new GDP would represent "evaluation." For the future, it might be useful to formulate and familiarize a new concept, regarding "over-evaluation"). This "green" interval (between undervaluation and evaluation) must be awarded by the New Economy.

The future of economic value (The environment of change becomes for value the location of productive exchange of forces, of real frictions and of exchange for changes).

The variables of entry into the New Economy determine the formalization of new metaphysical entities, which are the basis of the "mechanical structure" of the New Economy, as it is formalized more and more visibly in the real (world) environment. The analysis of the behavior of complex systems represents the multitude of opportunities to generate economic influences, as "variable" type reflections in the beginning of the New Economy based on knowledge and risk.

The emergence and recognition of the functioning of the New Economy is reflected in the theoretical and practical situation of the sciences, as a supporter of the new content, of the new procedural and behavioral configuration in the economy.

Horkheimer, M., (1972) formulated appreciations by which the Critical Theory of sciences is distinct in relation to the Traditional Theory of sciences and philosophy, attacking the abstraction, which in their opinion, has a role mainly in creating boundaries (delimitations) between disciplines.

The mentioned authors show that economics as a science plays a constitutive role in all social processes. In such a conceptual context, it is considered impossible to discuss "politics" in a concrete way without discussing "economics," just as one cannot assess the economy itself without taking into account the role that politics plays. and culture in the formation of effective economic science and practice.

In other words, the boundaries between disciplines are criticized, being at hand the promotion of the theory of interconnections, which can also be called the mediation between sciences.

Kellner, D. (1989), starting from "fatal strategies" (Baudrillard, 1983) points out that the New French Theory and the Critical Theory of Science prove to be disruptive of the boundaries between disciplines. It is considered that the division of labor is the one that motivated the separations between the academic disciplines on the one hand and (1) economics, (2) political sciences, (3) philosophy, (4) sociology, etc. on the other hand.

At the beginning of the 21st century, it is appreciated that the action of reconceptualizing the appreciations about sciences is necessary, as a new type of division of labor and a new economy, more and more visibly based on knowledge, are manifested. In essence, it is necessary to approach (1) epistemological and (2) metaphysical the problems that should aim at abstracting the interconnections between the phenomena of the surrounding world (including economic) and their experiences as practical expressions. An interdisciplinary transgression is needed, a situation in which new disciplines, new theories and new discourses can be created, more appropriate to the new economy, characterized by a new division of labor.

In the 1930s, the Critical Theory of Science issued the view that philosophy could be considered a collective over-discipline of syntheses, avoiding the interdisciplinary cataloging.

At present, the New French Theory of Science is in line with the support of the radical socio-political transformations suffered by the world economic system after 1989, insofar as the disciplines can no longer be isolated, separated, autarkic, which corresponds to the incipient phase of a new theories of social criticism.

The economy is unleashed by ideologies (critique of ideologies) that legitimized the superiority of one social system over another. In fact, economic postmodernism is the one that creates borders only between the historical, evolutionary stages, with the role of recording outputs and not so much with the diachronic role of marking the stages of development.

Baudrillard, J., (1989) points out that the production and proliferation of signs (knowledge) – values determine a certain Radical Semiurgy, which leads to the creation of the Society of Simulation, governed by Implosion and Hyperreality.

Conceptually similarity with those who proclaim the "end of history" (Fukuyama, 1992) or the "end of democracy" is also found in this type of primordialist thinking: it is possible to issue theses such as: the end of political economy and the closure of Marxist problems by the "end of labor," "end of production," etc. The linear economic discourse closes. (Gâf-Deac, 2005) The above conceptual elements would advance towards restriction, concentration, so towards relative disappearance.

What is important in the new economy is summed up in the status that every share and every "shareholder" should acquire, by becoming "a network terminal," fulfilled functionally and concretely, palpable in constant outputs.

In essence, it is an "ultimate economic determination" that can characterize the knowledge economy as well as the knowledge and risk-based economy.

2. Research method: data collection and preparation

2.1. The new continuous economy based on supradisciplinary knowledge

An economy is in a continuous transition. It is essential to identify formulas for the qualitative transition from one set of economic conditions to another. New goods and services represent the "substance" of economic growth in the new continuous economy (Gâf-Deac, 2010). Science-based representations foreshadow the "possible future," marked by the "competitive advantage" (Gâf-Deac, 2007).

The orientation of the economy towards the future is reflective. Therefore, through the knowledge-based economy, meta-stabilizations of stabilized historical systems are obtained. When stabilization and destabilization in the economy are perceived as historical processes, the potential for meta-stabilization becomes a factor in changing the dynamics of the system related to the new economy (Gâf-Deac, 2002).

The meta-stabilizations of the knowledge-based system reflect, under some conditions, globalization. The new economy proves its quasi-continuity through knowledge.

2.2. Models of the new economy

It is appreciated that the new economy, in the spirit of objectifying its description, is necessary to be found in the family of economic models, as a self-inclusive conceptual alternative in the traditional typology, or as a new alternative, added to the general classification of activities related to human communities.

In essence, it is necessary to identify the proportion of analogous behavior of the new economy in the real economy.

In this context, the thesis is launched that a contemporary macroeconomic model cannot evade the informational substance of the new economy that appeared in the real economy.

As such, in the conventionally accepted cybernetic vision ("inputs-processing-outputs") it is found that the increasingly "dematerialized" knowledge-based flows are strengthening.

The incipient modeling infrastructure can be formalized equationally in the following way (Gâf-Deac, 2010):

$$\begin{cases} \{K\} \underset{\Delta(F_{vn} * F_{pt})}{\overset{\approx}{\rightarrow}} \{Q_{MS}\} \\ (K)\rangle\,(MAT) \rightarrow (P_k)\rangle P\,(MAT) \\ (\mathit{II})\rangle\,(IM) \rightarrow optim(Q_{MS}) \end{cases} \tag{1}$$

It is suggested that for the behavioral explanation of the new economy, macroeconomic modeling must be seen conceptually as a "process," or as an approach to "communication processing." The generic substance in circulation on the equational channels of the model ("non-controllable values – processing; transformations – controllable values") is composed of: a) material quantities (MAT) and b) informational quantities (K).

This modeling co-substantivity causes the conceptual change of the modeling approach.

If until now, the central preoccupation of the modelers is found in (1) the formulation of the model and (2) the materialization of its functioning (experimentation) based on material; physical quantities; qualities, in the new vision, the conceptual and action preponderance is focused, in order on: (1) identification of communication processes; (2) identification of the quantitative; qualitative proportions of the circulating co-substantivity in the model and (3) the physical and meta-physical formulation of the model (Gâf-Deac, 2007).

This new conception presents the post-formalizing opportunity of approaching the research of the analogical behavior of the new economy in the real economy.

2.3. The new economy and the new enterprise

The pyramidal structural vision of the enterprise in the new economy is kept in the usual conceptual plan.

Level I (innovation) causes the manifestation of economic intelligence (information) and knowledge management.

Level II (integration) aims at accommodating internal and external relations.

The paradigms of the traditional enterprise (mechanic, function analysis, property; owner logic) are transformed into the paradigm of the learning enterprise (systemic, process analysis, service logic).

The main objectives of the traditional enterprise (efficiency, effectiveness) reach the enterprise of the new economy to be represented by flexibility and transversely.

In this context, we are witnessing the transition from classical Taylorist management to process management.

Level III targets the company's virtual decisions. In fact, there is an "internetization" of the productive; reproductive units and of the distribution; consumption ones.

The new business models in the new economy, synthetically refer to: the company dependent on market locations; "aggregator" type company; the company in alliance; network company; the company in new value chains (Drucker, 1993).

It follows that networking becomes; is more efficient than hierarchical work.

2.4. Networks for the new economy

The network is a mechanism that outsources the transactional consequences between actors (firms), eliminating the relational discretization of the economic processes of production; reproduction and distribution; consumption.

In the new economy, the singular mobilization (self-mobilization) of companies for economic operation is proving more and more difficult; restrictive.

Networking is a phenomenon through which companies find themselves reunited in families; classes based on partnerships, which have the role of generating the following three common contextual situations: (1) "transactions" become "a transaction" (singular, osmotic); (2) the initial transactions, considered distinct, visible by their articulation in a "transactional singularity" become invisible, and (3) the network meeting offers the opportunity to carry out the singular transaction, invisible, at an instantaneous time; moment (Gâf-Deac, 2005). For Romania, we appreciate that, in fact, the most important requirement in the networking context of the new economy is the identification of ways to conceptualize; formalize the network; networks.

Burt, R.S. (1992) show that "the whole; all structural" refers to the "separation between non-redundant contacts" in the network. In this context, the component companies, even if they are not able to transpose in "regular conditions" (of action normality), they still function normally thanks to the non-redundant (non-redundant) "structural whole" in terms of contacts; tangents.

It is observed that a network is not a hybrid form but rather a composition of forms, among which profitability is established as the formal closure; approach; articulation of the components is manifested, through which a compensatory transfer is achieved, attenuating conventional positivity. accepted of the productive-economic processes.

Coase, R. (2002) emphasizes that the action of collective solution of companies' problems in the network of the new economy does not refer only to the aspects aiming at the interrelationships in markets and hierarchies, but also to correct applications in the theory of transactional costs. transaction, by improving the functions of: (1) coordination, (2) information and (3) control through; with the help of network structures.

There are differences in favorability between the transaction; regular transaction costs and those related to the network, the positive predominance being found in the network (Fig. 1).

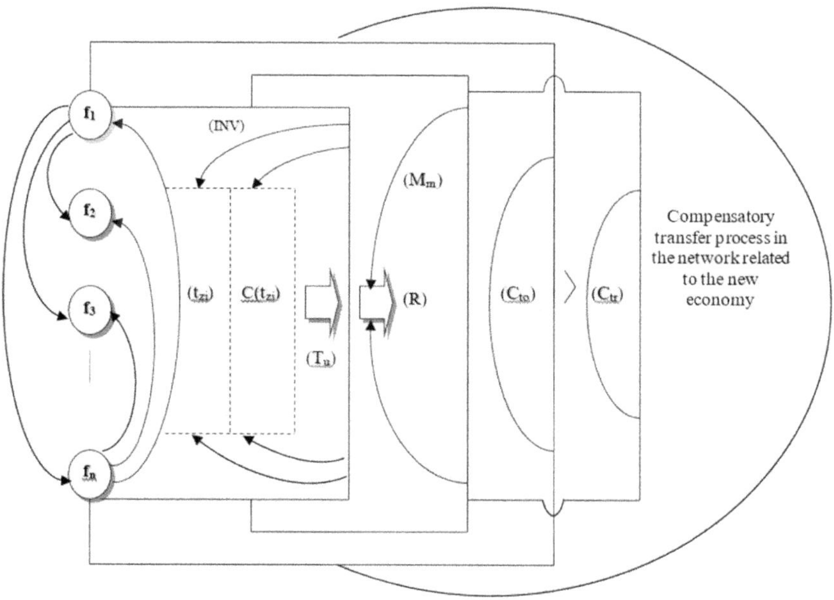

Fig. 1: Manifestation of the process of compensatory transfer of favorability in the network of the new economy

f1, f2, f3, ...fn = firms; (Mm) = mediating mechanism; (Ctr) = network transaction costs; (R) = network;

C(tzi) = transaction; transaction costs; (Tu) = single; singular compound transaction; (tzi) = transactions;

(Cto) = ordinary transaction costs; (INV) = invisibility of initial transactions.

Source: Gâf-Deac I.I., 2010.

It is estimated that the competitive advantage has more favorable chances of emergence and manifestation in the new economy, insofar as the productive-economic networking is carried out with a high degree of consolidation and functionality.

Conclusions

Any attempt at autarky is harmful as long as the "whole" is subjected to clustering, networking, and systemic construction. The productive; reproductive and distribution; consumption effects are quasi-anticipated, given that the formal boundaries of firms remain, but their survival actions are found between the strategic boundaries of clusters and the network. In other words, the network in the system becomes a means of decision ("unit" of decision) for coherent behavioral adaptations of any productive-economic entity to the state of the environment and to disturbances.

The problematization of organizational borders is a premise for identifying (shaping) the boundaries of the functional relations of the company; firms in the new economy (Allee, 2000).

However, a new power of flows is expected to be born. It is considered that, in this context, the formalization of an ontology specific to the modern society, which hosts the new economy, dominated by the realized economy, is foreseen. In fact, jumps, dislocations, relocations, adjustments, restructurings, etc. can take place. between contexts and entrepreneurial situations.

It is a "variable economic geometry" (this original expression being launched for the first time) based on the multiplicity of final economic effects, conventionally accepted. In a network, each company is "a center" and "its own center," as long as the new economy is technologically centered through the duality of infrastructure-connections with the complex world. The essential managerial aspect in the new vision is reduced to the way in which the mentioned "centers" can be controlled, how it is possible to disseminate the role and functionality of each "center" in the network.

It is observable that the network, in itself, through formalization produces limiting, restrictive effects, and even leads to the "melting" of the delimiting structures and intended to enter under the incidence of organization and management according to established methods and techniques. Such a trend is natural, as the traditional company is "hierarchical," while the company in the new economy is "horizontal," "lateral," "networked."

In the modern company of the new economy, managers have wider spaces for action, but they encounter a wider field of uncertainties and risks, even systemic ones (Malhotra, 2001). In the knowledge economy, top managers have the role of creating spaces that are opportune for the circulation of capital flows, technologies and human resources, contributing to the satisfaction of the "network interest."

In such a sense, networking in the new economy is not a problem of fragmentation or non-fragmentation, but a problem of assembling interactions.

References

Allee, V.: The Value Evolution: Addressing Larger Implications of an Intellectual Capital and Intangibles Perspective, Journal of Intellectual Capital 1, no. 1, 2000.

Baudrillard, J.: Les Strategies Fatales, Bernard Grasset, Paris, 1983.

Burt, R.S.: Structural Holes: The Social Structure of Competition, Harvard University Press, Massachusetts, 1992.

Ciutacu, C. (col.).: Problems of the Transition to the Market Economy in Romania, Editura FRM, Bucureşti, 1997.

Ciutacu, C.: Reform and Metareform, Editura Expert, Bucureşti, 2001.

Coase, R.: The New Institutional Economics, E. Brausseau & J-M Glachant, 2002.

Drucker, P.: Innovation and the Entrepreneurial System, Ed. Enciclopedică, Bucureşti, 1993.

Friedman, M.: Capitalism and Freedom, Ed. Enciclopedică, Bucureşti, 1992.

Fukuyama, F.: The End of History and the Last Man, Penguin, New York, 1992.

Gâf-Deac, I.I.: Centralization and Decentralization of Authority,- Revista Management şi Marketing Contemporan, Bucureşti, nr. 3/2002.

Gâf-Deac, I.I.: Elements of the "New Economy" Based on the Valorization of Natural Resources,- Second Edition of International Conference «Economic Growth in Conditions of Internalization», Academia de Ştiinţe a Moldovei, M. Economiei şi Comerţului al RM, Institute of Economy, Finance and Statistics, International Institute of Management, Chişinau, September 6–7, 2007.

Gâf-Deac, I.I.: The Integrated Sense of Social-Economic Transformation on Primary Phase of Glogalization in Romania,- Sesiunea Internaţională de Comunicări Ştiinţifice cu tema "Provocări ale securităţii şi strategiei la începutul secolului XXI", Ministerul Apărării Naţionale, Universitatea Naţională de Apărare, Geopolitică şi Geostrategie, Bucureşti, 14–15 aprilie 2005.

Gâf-Deac, I.I.: The Legal and Economic Bases of Resource Systems in the New Economy, Ed. Infomin, Deva, 2007.

Gâf-Deac, I.I.: Model of Growth of the Performance Cluster Area in Comparable Competitive Terms in the Romanian Economy, Lucrările Ştiinţifice International Interdisciplinary Scientific Symposium Universitaria SIMPRO 2005, Integrare în aria europeană a cercetării,Vol. Ştiinţe Economice, Ed. Universitas, Petroşani, 2005.

Gâf-Deac, I.I.: Noua economie între cunoaştere şi risc, Ed. Infomin, Deva, 2010.

Horkheimer, M.: Traditional and Critical Theory, Critical Theory, Seabury, New York, 1972.

Kellner, D.: Jean Baudrillard: From Marxism to Postmodernism and Beyond Cambridge, Policy Press, Stanford, 1989.

Levy, A.; Murname, A.: How Computerized Work and Globalization Shape Human Skill Demands, MIT IPC Working Papers, IPC-05-006, Cambridge, 2006.

Malhotra, Y.: From Information Management to Knowledge Management: Beyond the 'Hi-Tech Hidebound' Systems, in Srikantaiah, K. & Keonig, M.E.D. (Eds.); Knowledge Management for the Information Professional. Medfort, NJ: Information Today Inc., 2001.

Adriana Grigorescu, Amalia-Elena Ion

Comparison of American vs. European SMEs public policies

Abstract Research has provided with considerable information on American and European public policy especially that related to the SMEs, a growing global sector both in size and in economic impact, but only from separated perspectives. Of the various methods of understanding qualitative data, content analysis has proved its potential and value. As a result, the aim of this paper is to bring together in a comparative review the content analyses results of the Small Business Act of the USA versus the Small Business Act for Europe. Further, this paper reports interesting and important findings, identifying similarities and contrasts in the analyzed official documents. The comparison suggests that, regardless of the European version of the SBA being inspired from the American counterpart, there are two very different approaches to the regulatory and legal frameworks of the SME sectors in the two studied federal systems. While the US SBA focuses on the role of the administration on providing guidance to the small and medium-sized enterprises, the European SME industry is being translated into the SBA based on intensive market research and a persistent business approach.

Keywords: SME public policy; qualitative data; EU SBA; US SBA; comparison analysis

Introduction

There are several points of view regarding the impact of the SME sector, and their capability of facing the economic challenges of the globalization. Each prominent economy has diverted its attention to caring for this sector of the industry by regulating and creating legal frameworks for the SMEs, with the ultimate scope of providing a nurturing environment for the latter, supporting SMEs in the pursuit of finding the market positioning and comparative advantage in contrast to the large enterprises, and financially aid the SMEs, especially in the first three to five years of activity.

Considering two federal systems, the United States of America and the European Union, each with its own particularities and similarities, the research has challenged the legal frameworks developed by each administration under the name of Small Business Act. The legal documents were created from the need of regulating the SME industry, by providing with better regional stability, a more opportunistic environment for this business sector, and a clearly defined manner of bringing together resources, information and expansion possibilities to any SME.

By observing the way in which public policies influence the economic context of the world, including the SME sector, in a comparative analysis of the

SBAs, similarities and differences of the two approaches will be underlined, as an advantage to the researchers and policy-makers for getting out the best from each perspective. The paper will therefore identify both similarities and differences within the two SBAs with regard to the following indicators of the SME sector: information and resources access; public assistance in developing business related activities and in the pursuit of internationalization; legal and regulatory frameworks for SMEs.

1. Literature review – EU public policy vs. American public policy

The sense of the end of an era is closing in on the European Union, with internal challenges such as the new populist and nationalist political direction, the failed trade agreements between the big economic forces of the world scene, the considerable gap between the poor and the rich that continues to gain momentum, all sorts of political and economic storms, including the Brexit, and the continuously increase of the communication rifts produced internally within the European Parliament and the Commission, especially now when the new leaders of the EU are lining up to start working on their proposals and strategies. The EU must pertain to the consolidation of the Union more than ever, and to find suitable measures to institute peace and pace in the regional economy. On the "other side of the pond," the US government "(…) has grown from a small, simple 'night watchman state' providing defense, police protection, tax collection and some education into an immense network of organizations and institutions affecting the daily lives of the citizens in countless ways" (Peters, 2019, p. 3); and, today, the American economy under the Trump rule seems to be of maverick proportions and power, at least in the official statements and released declarations. More or less, the same political "dystrophies" appear to endanger the stability of the area, and the rippling effects are visible worldwide.

Public policy has always managed to be a step ahead in finding the best solution for long-lasting stability and economic growth. Or at least this has been its purpose. Both economies discussed within this paper have made important steps into developing legal frameworks for all sorts of situations and for all the sectors of the industry. Of considerable importance, especially for the European economic system, has been the SME sector; nevertheless, a still significant industry in the US is represented by the business created within the small and medium-sized territory, with particular importance given the down falling large enterprises industry on the American continent. The United States of America have a system of public policy that embraces strict principles; it is very important that particular elements are well understood, such as the decisions made by the government, alongside the bureaucrats and public authorities that affect the citizens, the outputs or the actionable policy choices, and the effect those two elements have on the citizens.

Critical economic periods of time have chiseled into the European Union, as the founding members have worked towards creating programmes with the aim of supporting Member States in both less fortunate and growth-trending periods (Zahariadis, Buonanno, 2017). The resulted public polices have guarded the stability and prosperity of the region, with the Single European Act of 1986, completed in 1992, by which the qualified majority voting (QMV) was instituted in cooperation with the European Parliament. Alongside, the Court of First Instance was created with the aim of assisting in legislative and juridical cases of competition and unfair trade. The next step of the European integration was solidified by the introduction, in 2002, of the single currency – EURO. Twelve Member States have adhered to the new currency, and the attention has been drawn towards the decision-making status of the Member States in the European policies.

The liberalization of trade of services occupied a focal point in the legal agenda of the EU, considerably since the services account for 90 % of the jobs in the European Union. By 2009, the EU-28 has instituted the Services Directive, and started the fight against discrimination, non-democratic practices, administrative or licensing rules that would inquire significantly higher costs for the SME industry compared to that of the large enterprises. The European Union also ensured that the enterprises selling products and services on the single market follow common regulations; and so the Action Plan for European Standardization stipulated the exact requirements for goods/services that are subject to trade on the European market, with bodies of regulation such as ESO and CEN to closely watch over more than 18 industrial sectors.

Compared to the US corporations, the EU enterprises are smaller in size, and do not benefit from a common language and a homogenous domestic market. As a result, the EC has adopted measures against protectionist strategies, by forcing national government to prosecute acts of non-competitiveness and unfair competition strategies, with fines as high as 10 % of the enterprise's turnover.

The European Union has revised its merger regulation, adopted in 1989, in 2004, exactly with the idea in mind that the economic concentration will be facilitated, and the national authorities' involvement will be diminished in accord to the neoliberalism practices. Moreover, the EU made necessary steps towards expanding the business competitiveness and cooperation internationally, and it had worked towards fostering good partnerships for the SME industry with emerging countries (e.g. Brazil, China, India).

In the same time, the Washington government, in its vastness, with revenues of one dollar in three of the total national production, with one in six citizens employed by it, has also tackled important public policy issues, with the involvement of the subnational governments of its federal system. Contrary to the EU system, in the United States some of the government policies are being implemented by private organization and/or by individual citizens.

Since its beginnings, the central government of the United States has worked in close cooperation with the federal state governments, and the political power has been dispersed across the central and federal governments with the scope of diminishing any non-democratic tendencies. This resulted in a highly fragmented American political system. On one hand, this system provides with different and numerous decision-makers, helping reduce the risks, and providing the citizens with the opportunity of being involved in the policy-making process as much as possible. On the other hand, the significant lack of policy coherence and coordination has left a mark on the regulatory and legal frameworks, with the example of the "gridlock" situations that kept on showing up within the American system from the 1980s to the 2010s.

As a general principle, the United States of America use a number of elements as instruments for public policy: the law, the services, money, and taxes. The United States of America have a taxation system by which they either encourage or discourage a certain type of activity and/or behavior. The taxes can be useful in the implementation of public policy decisions.

One of the most evident divisions in the US system, legally binding by the 9th and 10th Amendments, is represented by the allocation, in the Constitution, of the government powers as a dually powered institution. This situation has been somehow aided by the fact that experts in different fields of interest to the public policy-making are involved in the political power, so that the federalism is equally divided between the political and administrative perspectives. Furthermore, the American government showcases its division one more time through the particular case of "veto points," which all must be met before any public policy begins its journey towards implementation. The US Constitution designated the President and the Congress to both agree on any public policy before translating it into law. The Presidential institution and the American Congress can only make amends and changes with considerable difficulty; the bureaucracy in the USA acts as a machine that requires some repairs, and the whole policy-making system seems quite conservative and deeply rooted into the past.

2. Methodology

The paper has analyzed, in a comparative manner, the results of the content analyses of official documents under the title of Small Business Act for Europe (2008 and 2011 review), and Small Business Act of 1953 of the United States of America. The content analyses have been drawn from the Grigorescu A., Ion A.E. 2019 on the European and American SBAs. The format of the content analyses has been a simple one, and the information from the documents has been grouped in the categories, and has been coded, so that the frequency of units of analysis to be performed. The content analyses were constructed as depicted in the frequency analyses in the Grigorescu A., Ion A.E. 2019.

Based on the results of the content analyses, a comparison of the two SME public policies approaches was performed, pointing out the similarities and particularities of the American versus European contexts for SMEs.

Discussion and conclusion – general comparison on SME public policy strategy in the USA and the EU

The research paper was constructed around the content analyses of the Small Business Act (Public Law 85–536, as amended) of the United States of America, and the Small Business Act for Europe (2008 and 2011 review), in a comparative review, focusing on three major areas of interest – information and resources access for SMEs, public assistance in developing business related activities and in the pursuit of internationalization, and legal and regulatory frameworks for SMEs (also related to social, gender, or minority public policies).

In terms of access to information and other types of resources, the SBAs have proved to have a set of similarities when it comes to the access to finance, and a few particularities regarding their measures and action programmes, as well as their initiatives and overall focus of the public policy for SMEs.

In the EU, SMEs have a significant impact on the overall economy of the region, whereas in the States, SMEs are not necessarily reaching the same importance. Moreover, the EU is focused on increasing the skills of SMEs and that through innovation, and R&D programmes that are based on environmental management systems. In the same time, the European SBA created an eGovernment Action Plan with the scope of reducing the waiting time for SMEs, by developing Points of Single Contact. The EC has been actively pushing the public policy towards improving the environment for industry and businesses, with the SMEs at the core of the innovation and research policy. Given the stage of integration between the Member states of the EU, the public policy has underlined the need for eliminating any barriers and restrictions on tariffs and raw materials, by opening up services and procurement markets, and making the SME sector resource-efficient.

On the other side, the American SBA mentions all other sorts of resources needed by the SME sector, such as the access to business analysts, to translation services, to online database services, to information specialists and part-time professional specialists, to technology transfer, to laboratories, and academic communities, to automated flexible manufacturing systems, to the possibility of developing shared production facilities, to develop and reorient the marketing and production strategies, to technical assistance especially for rural businesses. Moreover, the American government has written the public policy with the scope of enhancing the ability of SMEs to compete against imports, but also in the idea of strengthening the technological competitiveness of small business concerns in the States.

Similarly, both SBAs mention the fact that the public policy is to facilitate SMEs' access to finance. The US SBA has developed the public policy of SMEs access to financial resources, by providing with details on the modalities of gaining financial resources – through increased awareness of credit practices and requirements, assisting SMEs in obtaining financial aid for exporting activities, and Export Bank financing programmes for start-ups or for expanding the business especially in tourism. Moreover, it is reminded the financial assistance for non-profit organizations, runned by women, as well as outreach, financial support, and technical assistance to technology based small business concerns.

Based on the EU SBA information report on SMEs, the European small enterprises have lower productivity and grow slower than their American counterparts. Moreover, the US SMEs increase their employment by 60 % in their 6th year of existence, compared to 10–20 % employment gains among the EU SMEs. The considerable difference in employment capabilities is perhaps a result of the financial problems European SMEs face, as 21 % of them indicate having difficulties in accessing finance, for an instant.

Both economies have developed their public policy for SMEs towards encouraging the industry to benefit from the growth potential of international markets, and to promote exporting as a business development opportunity for small business concerns.

When it comes to public assistance in developing business-related activities and in the pursuit of internationalization, both the American and the European versions of the SBA mention the necessity of supporting SMEs throughout their life cycle with information, public assistance, and even incentives. The Washington government has designed a programme based on business development centers meant to provide assistance and know-how to SMEs from within and from outside the States. Within the business development centers, SMEs can work with individuals that specialize in business planning, financial applications, contract proposals, and compliance and regulatory requirements.

Although the basic idea of supporting SMEs can be spotted in both official regulating frameworks, there are particularities to each approach. For example, the European SBA was designed so that the SMEs profit from the Single Market and the Single Market policy, through possibilities offered by the Community State Aid, such as friendlier standards for SMEs, their interests are better represented, and their access to patents and trademarks is facilitated. In the same time, SMEs benefit from market-specific business training and other forms of support, such as the "Erasmus for Young Entrepreneurs" programme, which fosters the cooperation of the young entrepreneurs to experienced ones. Other programmes started by the EU are "An Agenda for New skills and jobs" or the "Youth on the Move." The first focuses on the future skills needed in micro enterprises and in craft-type businesses, and the latter comprises of trainings for the young to acquire the right skills to start and manage an SME. Another measure for allowing SMEs to benefit from simpler arrangements within the Single Market policy is represented by the Single Euro Payments Area (SEPA). The latter provides also with a development platform for the Pan-European electronic invoicing.

Also, the internationalization, export and expansion opportunities for SMEs are provided within both SBAs, with the public policies offering different solutions and ideas for internationalization, export, and expansion abroad. The EC has opened in 2010 an SME Centre in China, where small enterprises are being offered information, advice, training, so that they are better prepared for exporting and/or investing on the Asian market. On the other hand, the American government created the HUBZONE programme, which is meant to provide with qualified assistance. The business development centers in the US are also involved in assisting small enterprises in exporting, as they collaborate with the Department of Commerce, the State Office of International Trade and other relevant Federal agencies through which linkages between US SMEs and foreign enterprises and buyers can be developed. They also provide assistance in helping SMEs to participate in international trade shows, and to establish online connections through the Export Assistance Centre programme. Moreover, the federal government of the US developed a State Trade Expansion Programme, which assists eligible small businesses with participation in foreign trade missions, by offering a subscription to services provided by the Department of Commerce, including the payment of website fees, the design of marketing media, a trade show exhibition, participation in training workshops, or any other initiative considered appropriate by the Associate Administrator.

The European SBA has managed to provide with some statistics and concrete data regarding the progress of the public policy effects on the SME industry. For instance, the Member States are making huge steps towards creating a cheaper and faster start up process of a company. In 2010, on average, the time and cost to start a private limited enterprise was of about 7 days and 399 EUR. Moreover, the SBA for Europe mentions the fact that the EU has had a far better public policy for internationalization and expansion for businesses then their counterpart in the USA and Japan, accounting for results such as the following: 25 % of the EU SMEs have exported (on the Single Market and internationally) from 2009–2011. The EU also points out the great opportunities for the SME industry to expand their ventures into the BRIC countries, where the markets are served by only 10 % of the exporting EU SMEs.

The SBAs have another common element, that of collaboration clusters and networks of businesses from different regions or countries, with the purpose of stimulating a coherent and coordinated strategy towards achieving a common goal without hindering the independence of the SMEs involved.

At the same time, the US SBA mentions that any small enterprise will benefit of assistance with concerns on foreign trade missions, on translating documents, interpreting conversations, and providing referral lists for translation services, with that enhancing the exporting capability of SMEs and their overall effectiveness and efficiency in competing on foreign markets.

Although pursuing basically the same idea, the legal and regulatory frameworks of the public policies for SMEs listed in both SBAs could not be more different.

The American SBA has given considerable attention to the means of financing the SMEs, as numerous public authorities, such as the Congress, the Federal Government, the Administration of the Small Business Administration, the Associate Administrator for the International Trade, the Department of Commerce etc., have been involved in the pursuit of aiding and assisting the SME sector to access long term capital for investments and development. In case of changes in the market, due to poor economic conditions, US small businesses can receive a maximum loan of 200,000 USD. The Microloan programme was set in place to assist veterans, women, minority entrepreneurs, and any other business owners that operate an SME successfully, and is based on a fixed rate, maximum loan of 50,000 USD. Comparatively, the EU SBA mentions that any business with a turnover of less than 2,000,000 EUR has the opportunity of benefiting from an optional cash accounting scheme, which delays the accounting for VAT until the businesses receive their payments from the customers. Moreover, the EC has increased the number of financial instruments within the Competitiveness and Innovation Framework Programme and the Progress Microfinance Facility initiative, in order to facilitate VC investments and provide improved and more efficient loan guarantee schemes to SMEs.

The American version of the SBA focuses for a significant length of the paper on the business development centers as entities of the US government which closely collaborate with other American public institutions and administration, with the scope of delivering information and support related services to small enterprises. They are to serve the business community of the SMEs by informing the latter regarding trade promotions, finance, data collection etc. The business development centers are also required to assist small businesses in their pursuit of understanding the export and international trade programmes, and are to encourage the financial institutions from the area to develop financial support programmes for those businesses ready to engage in export initiatives.

The declared policy of the Congress stipulates that the American government should protect, aid, counsel, and assist any small business in order for the market to remain free and competitive, especially when it comes to the government contracting private enterprises. Therefore, "a fair proportion" of the contracts and subcontracts for the government have to be placed with small business enterprises. As a result, the overall economy of the US is, apparently, maintained and strengthened. Similarly, the EU SBA comprises of measures to protect the SMEs against harmful and unfair contractual terms. Also, the EU SBA regulated the market so that SMEs do not get harmed by anti-competitive practices, such as cartels or abuse of dominant positions, and the EC has launched a public consultation on the European collective redress.

The Congress also made sure that all the administrative institutions involved in the international trade and commerce should support small enterprises to compete on international markets, should facilitate the technology transfer, should improve the accessibility of export promotion programmes, as well as providing small businesses with complete information on exports and international trade. The US SBA also mentions State Trade Expansion Programmes, or mentoring networks, alongside Mentor-Protégé programmes, or women and veteran trainings and programmes. The overall idea of those initiatives is for the SMEs to be covered a series of services, starting with having the necessary information, and ending with the financing opportunities for this type of business.

For instance, the State Trade Expansion Programme was created for enterprises that have been in business for more than one year, and it has the scope of making sure that the enterprise has access to enough resources to cover a range of costs associated with the export and international trade initiatives of the latter.

A recurring theme is the importance both SBAs have reflected in their public policies and public assistance for gender, minority-related, or rural small and medium-sized businesses. The EC has created in 2009 the European Network of Female Entrepreneurship Ambassadors, comprising now of almost 250 members, with the purpose of inspiring more women to become entrepreneurs; the EC has also developed cohesion programmes as part of the European Agricultural Fund for Rural Development strategy to encourage different regions of the EU innovate based on the "smart specialization strategies."

Apart from the general strategic direction both SBAs have followed, with regard to the fiscal consolidation, pro-active policies to drive growth, programmes for female entrepreneurs and other minorities, improving the access of SMEs to different resources especially financial support, etc., the EU SBA showed interest in assisting SMEs that follow different business models, such as non-profit associations, foundations, and any other society within the social economy. Moreover, the European approach has some specific elements to the overall SBA strategy, with its public policies related to fostering entrepreneurship initiatives especially in young people, with the specific policies related to the procedures of bankruptcy for SMEs, with the "Think Small First" principle and the simplification of all regulatory and administrative procedures for SMEs, with the application of "fitness checks" to both the legislation and to the SMEs (the so-called SME test that assesses the impact of the legislation), and with the integration of mechanisms for monitoring and coordinating the SME industry in relation to the legislation.

As a conclusion, both official documents comprising of considerable relevant legislation to the SME industry have more or less the same general legislation approach, both are meant to contribute to the achieving of all the ambitious initiatives related to the sector, but it is clear that the interpretation of the overall strategy for SMEs has been set out under the form of particular actions and frameworks contributing to the specificity of the economic character of the region.

References

Communication from the Commission to the Council, The European Parliament, The European Economic and Social Committee and the Committee of the Regions "Think Small First" A "Small Business Act" for Europe, Brussels, 25.6.2008 COM (2008) 394 final [Web log post]. Retrieved June 2, 2019, https://eur-lex.europa.eu/legal-content/EN/TXT/PDF/?uri=CELEX:52008DC0394&from=EN.

Communication from the Commission to the European Parliament, the Council, Economic and Social Committee and the Committee of the Regions Review of the "Small Business Act" for Europe, Brussels, 23.2.2011 COM (2011) 78 final [Web log post]. Retrieved June 2, 2019, https://eur-lex.europa.eu/legal-content/EN/TXT/PDF/?uri=CELEX:52011DC0078&from=EN.

Consolidated version of the Treaty on the Functioning of the European Union [Web log post]. Retrieved June 2, 2019, https://eur-lex.europa.eu/legal-content/EN/TXT/PDF/?uri=CELEX:12012E/TXT&from=EN.

Grigorescu A., Ion A.E. (2019). A Content Analysis on the SMEs in the United States of America, Business Systems Research Journal, Volume X, No. X, 39–52.

Grigorescu A., Ion A.E. (2019). An Empirical Review of Public Policies in the Sector of SMEs in the European Union, Organizacija, Volume X, No. 1, 1–22.

Peters, G. B. (2019). American Public Policy: Promise and Performance, Thousand Oaks, CA: SAGE Publications.

SMALL BUSINESS ACT (Public Law 85–536, as amended) of the United States of America, including PL 114–125, enacted 2/24/16 [Web log post]. Retrieved June 2, 2019, https://www.sba.gov/sites/default/files/2019-03/Small_Business_Act.pdf.

Zahariadis, N., Buonanno, L. (2017). The Routledge Handbook of European Public Policy, Abigdon: Routeledge.

www.ingramcontent.com/pod-product-compliance
Ingram Content Group UK Ltd.
Pitfield, Milton Keynes, MK11 3LW, UK
UKHW020833290926
15470UKWH00004B/1319

9 783631 838259